MINOAN ZOOMORPHIC CULTURE

Since the earliest era of archaeological discovery on Crete, vivid renderings of animals have been celebrated as defining elements of Minoan culture. Animals were crafted in a rich range of substances and media in the broad Minoan world, from tiny seal stones to life-size frescoes. In this study, Emily Anderson fundamentally rethinks the status of these zoomorphic objects. Setting aside their traditional classification as "representations" or signs, she recognizes them as distinctively real embodiments of animals in the world. These fabricated animals – engaged with in quiet tombs, bustling harbors and monumental palatial halls – contributed in unique ways to Bronze Age Aegean sociocultural life and affected the status of animals within people's lived experience. Some gave new substance and contour to familiar biological species, while many exotic and fantastical beasts gained physical reality only in these fabricated embodiments. As real presences, the creatures that the Minoans crafted artfully toyed with expectation and realized new dimensions within and between animalian identities.

Emily S. K. Anderson teaches in the Department of Classics at Johns Hopkins University, where her work focuses on the visual and material cultures of the Aegean Bronze Age and the ongoing lives of ancient forms and materials. She is the author of *Seals, Craft, and Community in Bronze Age Crete* (2016).

MINOAN ZOOMORPHIC CULTURE

BETWEEN BODIES AND THINGS

EMILY S. K. ANDERSON

The Johns Hopkins University

Shaftesbury Road, Cambridge CB2 8EA, United Kingdom

One Liberty Plaza, 20th Floor, New York, NY 10006, USA

477 Williamstown Road, Port Melbourne, VIC 3207, Australia

314–321, 3rd Floor, Plot 3, Splendor Forum, Jasola District Centre, New Delhi – 110025, India

103 Penang Road, #05–06/07, Visioncrest Commercial, Singapore 238467

Cambridge University Press is part of Cambridge University Press & Assessment, a department of the University of Cambridge.

We share the University's mission to contribute to society through the pursuit of education, learning and research at the highest international levels of excellence.

www.cambridge.org
Information on this title: www.cambridge.org/9781009452038

DOI: 10.1017/9781009452045

© Emily S. K. Anderson 2024

This publication is in copyright. Subject to statutory exception and to the provisions of relevant collective licensing agreements, no reproduction of any part may take place without the written permission of Cambridge University Press & Assessment.

First published 2024

Printed in the United Kingdom by TJ Books Limited, Padstow Cornwall

A catalogue record for this publication is available from the British Library

A Cataloging-in-Publication data record for this book is available from the Library of Congress

ISBN 978-1-009-45203-8 Hardback

Cambridge University Press & Assessment has no responsibility for the persistence or accuracy of URLs for external or third-party internet websites referred to in this publication and does not guarantee that any content on such websites is, or will remain, accurate or appropriate.

Funding received from Office of the Dean, Krieger School of Arts & Sciences, Johns Hopkins University.

for Elías and Camilo,
and their happy hum

CONTENTS

Acknowledgments		*page* viii
Chronology		xi
1	LIFE AMONG THE ANIMALIAN IN BRONZE AGE CRETE AND THE SOUTHERN AEGEAN	I
2	CRAFTINESS AND PRODUCTIVITY IN BODILY THINGS: THE CHANGING CONTEXTS OF CRETAN ZOOMORPHIC VESSELS	38
3	STONE POETS: BETWEEN LION AND PERSON IN GLYPTIC AND ORAL CULTURE OF BRONZE AGE CRETE AND THE AEGEAN	102
4	LIKENESS AND INTEGRATION AMONG EXTRAORDINARY CREATURES: RETHINKING MINOAN "COMPOSITE" BEASTS	159
5	SINGULAR, SERIATED, SIMILAR: HELMETS, SHIELDS AND IKRIA AS INTUITIVE ANIMALIAN THINGS	246
6	MOVING TOWARD LIFE: PAINTED WALLS AND NOVEL ANIMALIAN PRESENCES IN AEGEAN SPACES	310
	CONCLUDING THOUGHTS: RESTLESS BODIES IN THE MINOAN WORLD	372
References		380
Index		408

ACKNOWLEDGMENTS

Much of this book was written during the difficult times of the Covid-19 pandemic. Work on the manuscript, and engagement with the rich and stimulating ideas of a robust community of scholars (past and present), was an uplifting force both during that challenging moment and as we have collectively emerged from it. In this context, the support of the many friends and colleagues who have contributed to this book, in a variety of ways, has been especially heartening. I give my deep gratitude to Christos Doumas, Andreas Vlachopoulos, Peter Warren, Jane Hickman, Ute Günkel-Maschek, Yannis Galanakis, Efi Sapouna-Sakellarakis, Olga Krzyszkowska, Metaxia Tsipopoúlou, Maria and Joseph Shaw, André Wiese, David Reese, Amalia Kakissis, Klaus Robin, Jan Shearer, Javier Barrio de Pedro, Christoph Uehlinger, and Stella Chrysoulaki at the Herakleion Museum for their remarkable generosity with material. I thank Diamantis Panagiotopoulos, who hosted my stay at the Corpus der minoischen und mykenischen Siegel (CMS) in Heidelberg during fall 2019, for conversation while there and for sharing the incredible resource of the CMS imagery with me for the book. Many others have shared discussion and support with me. While I cannot name here everyone whose involvement I have valued dearly, I especially thank Thomas Brogan, Cynthia Colburn, Sylviane Déderix, Emily Egan, Sarah Finlayson, Karen Foster, Vesa-Pekka Herva, Carl Knappett, Robert Laffineur, Stephanie Langin-Hooper, Agnete Lassen, Tom Palaima, Nikos Papadimitriou, Holly Pittman, Lauren Ristvet, Sarah Scott, Alan Shapiro, Georgios Spyropoulos and Nancy Thomas. I have felt particularly encouraged along the way by a fellow traveler on this path, Andrew Shapland, whose excellent book came out with Cambridge University Press while I was submitting my own manuscript. Working alongside a scholar as gifted and kind as Andrew has been a wonderful experience, and it is a joy to think of our ideas sitting on the bookshelf together.

I have benefited greatly from sharing ideas contained in this book in numerous talks. Early and partial versions of some chapters were workshopped in these contexts and have, in some cases, appeared in publications. This process has been hugely helpful as I refined the work, and I thank those involved immensely, in particular Kathryn Morgan (who organized a stellar conference at the Oriental Institute in 2019 where I gained rich feedback on my discussion of the zoomorphic vessels), Thomas Tartaron and the group at the University of Pennsylvania, for discussion surrounding the ideas in the lions chapter in spring 2019, and both Jane Carter and Elma Sanders at the *American Journal of Archaeology*. The *Zoia* conference organized by Tom Palaima and Robert Laffineur sadly could not happen because of the pandemic, but working on my contribution to the volume was highly productive (and the other papers gathered in that volume embody exciting further steps forward). At Hopkins, I am very fortunate to be surrounded by a group of stimulating peers who are also truly encouraging colleagues. I give special thanks to Karen ní Mheallaigh, Matt Roller, Jen Stager, Sanchita Balachandran, Kate Gallagher, Betsy Bryan, Glenn Schwartz, Mike Harrower, Chris Cannon, Silvia Montiglio, Josh Smith, Nandini Pandey, Richard Jasnow, Paul Delnero, Jake Lauinger and Alice Mandell. Both Shane Butler and Marian Feldman have been steadfast mentors and deeply valued interlocutors who have had huge impacts on my thinking. I sincerely thank the Dean's Office at Hopkins for a subvention to support color imagery throughout the book. My students at Hopkins have been a rich source of stimulating discussion, weaving in new perspectives that challenge how I look at familiar things. At Cambridge University Press, I truly valued feedback on the manuscript from two anonymous reviewers. Edgar Mendez has been a remarkably supportive resource through every twist and turn. Throughout production, Reshma Xavier's and Preethika Ramalingam's guidance has been vital. I have been deeply thankful for the exceptional talent that hawk-eyed Kathleen Fearn has brought to the text – I couldn't have wished for a more thoughtful and thorough reader. Beatrice Rehl has proven to be a dedicated captain and advocate for this work from its earliest stages, whose wisdom, insights and interest have been absolutely crucial to its coming to happy fruition.

There is a special pleasure, and comfort, to be found in friends who also know the joys and challenges of this line of work. I thank Maria Anastasiadou for the meals, laughs and conversations that have traversed Aegean glyptic and so much more, especially during my time in Heidelberg. Hallie Franks' friendship continues to be a source of support and inspiration that unwaveringly crosses years and miles. My family has been the nourishment for this undertaking, and all others. As a child, I was surrounded by animals, in body, thing and story. My father shared his love of birds with me as far back as I can remember, and an appreciation of their peculiar wonder has driven many areas of my research for this book. My mother grew up on a working farm, and her stories of a world in which animals were part of daily life and livelihood, in all its practical and emotional depth, were baked into my upbringing and outlook. I have drawn on her knowledge, on situations ranging from escaped bulls to dealing with feral pigs, on countless occasions while writing. My uncle, Mack

Keller, shared insights concerning cattle that have been crucial in rethinking the realities of engaging with the impressive beasts. Many of my formative experiences with animals were shared with my big brother, Elisha, who was my coconspirator in all sorts of adventures involving creatures great and small as we ranged through our childhood domains, including the fields, woods and pasture streams of my grandparents' farm each summer. Subtending all else, I am grateful beyond measure to the three centers of my life, Elías, Camilo and Leo. As I write this, I cross the happy mark of having spent half of my life (and growing!) with Leo, who is a more wonderful partner than one could ever hope for. He not only keeps the boat afloat but makes the voyage through the unchartered waters of daily being a joyful source of discovery. Elías and Camilo are my greatest, most cherished and most humbling teachers. Their wholly loving presence, creative perspectives and insatiable questioning open the world anew, from rooster's crow to moonrise (and in-between). Theirs is a precious space in which renderings of animals carry keen wonder, seriousness and levity; being here with them brings the reality of fabricated creatures into vivid light and tangible contour and reminds me that open-endedness is a virtue.

★

Certain discussions in the present book appeared in earlier form in other contexts:

Chapter 2: "The Reinvented Social Somatics of Ritual Performance on Early Crete: Engagements of Humans with Zoomorphic Vessels," In K. Morgan, ed., *Pomp, Circumstance, and the Performance of Politics: Acting Politically Correct in the Ancient World*. Oriental Institute Seminars. Chicago: Oriental Institute of the University of Chicago; *in-press 2024*.

Chapter 3: "The Poetics of the Cretan Lion: Glyptic and Oral Culture in the Bronze Age Aegean," *American Journal of Archaeology* 124 (3); July 2020: 345-379.

Parts of Chapter 5 and 6: "Intuitive Things: Helmets, Shields, Ikria and the Uniqueness of Aegean Composites," In T. Palaima and R. Laffineur, eds., *ZOIA: Animal Connections in the Aegean Middle and Late Bronze Age*. Leuven: Peeters, 2021:149-160.

CHRONOLOGY

Dates BCE	Period	Crete	Cretan period	Cyclades	Mainland	Mainland period
3100–2700	EBA	EM I	Prepalatial	EC I	EH I	
2700–2400		EM IIA		EC II	EH IIA	
2400–2200		EM IIB		EC II	EH IIB	
2200–2000		EM III		EC III	EH III	
2000–1900	MBA	MM IA	Protopalatial	MC I	MH I	
1900–1800		MM IB		MC II	MH II	
1800–1700		MM II				
1700–1600		MM III	Neopalatial	MC III	MH III	Early Mycenaean
1600–1525	LBA	LM IA		LC I	LH I	
1525–1450		LM IB		LC II	LH IIA	
1450–1400		LM II	Final Palatial		LH IIB	
1400–1300		LM IIIA(1-2)		LC III	LH IIIA(1-2)	Palatial
1300–1200		LM IIIB	Postpalatial		LH IIIB	
1200–1070		LM IIIC			LH III C	Postpalatial

Chronological table adapted from Shelmerdine 2008: 4 fig. 1.1, and Knappett 2020: xv.

Abbreviations EBA: Early Bronze Age; MBA: Middle Bronze Age; LBA: Late Bronze Age. *Aegean Chronology* EM: Early Minoan; MM: Middle Minoan; LM: Late Minoan; EC: Early Cycladic; MC: Middle Cycladic; EH: Early Helladic; MH: Middle Helladic; LH: Late Helladic. *Egyptian Chronology* OK: Old Kingdom (2700–2136); FIP: First Intermediate Period (2136–2023); MK: Middle Kingdom (2116–1795); SIP: Second Intermediate Period (1795–1540); NK: New Kingdom (1540–1070).

ONE

LIFE AMONG THE ANIMALIAN
IN BRONZE AGE CRETE
AND THE SOUTHERN AEGEAN

INTRODUCTION

The sociocultural spaces of the "Minoan" Aegean were teeming with animal bodies. These bodies – the tiny and the massive, the watchful and the hunted, the engaging and the aloof, the human and the nonhuman – invigorated Aegean contexts in complex and particular ways. Many of these animals were alive, but many were not – and never had been. It is the latter that are our focus here. These fabricated Aegean animals have traditionally been described as "representations" and have long been celebrated in this capacity, but their relationship to living beings was not limited to a role as imitative depictions. Through remarkably dynamic renderings, realized across a range of media, such as zoomorphic vessels, wall paintings, engraved seal stones and amulets, animals' bodies took on a rich diversity of material and spatial qualities that could afford distinctive interactive experiences; worn objects prominently fashioned of animals' teeth and skins further blurred the distinction between the biological and the artificial, and the human and nonhuman. By recognizing both biological and fabricated entities as *real* embodiments of animals, which could coexist and interact in Aegean spaces, the nature of our discussion changes. We see that the dynamics of representation were caught up in a much wider field of relationships that involved these bodies and characterized their engagements with people. Doing so moves us beyond questions of signification and intentional design, and toward a fuller recognition of people's actual experiences of animalian bodies. Looking closely at a variety of venues, ranging from palatial courts to a modest bench in the corner of a house, our focus thus can turn to how the world of *animalian things* was a crucial part of social life in Bronze Age Cretan and Aegean spaces, and how direct interactions with these other animal bodies were a central, yet often overlooked and minimized, component of human relations with nonhuman beasts. These fabricated creatures brought a wealth of new character to the identities of species in Crete and the southern Aegean – and to the active place of animals in Aegean social experience.

Beyond a "Brilliant Naturalism"

Vibrant renderings of animals have long been hailed as a defining element of Minoan creative culture, distinguishing its identity amid its contemporaries within the eastern Mediterranean. The handling of animals' bodies, and especially the conveyance of movement and feeling, have been considered integral to the broader "brilliant naturalism"[1] of Minoan visual and material cultures, which also involves striking engagements with other elements of the natural world, from plants and water to stone. Each of these entities of the natural environment – animalian, floral and geological alike – can be rendered in vivid detail, texture and color, both as subjects of individual studies and as elements of complex compositions and scenes; this is especially apparent in the extant evidence of the Middle and Late Bronze Ages. Animals and the natural world are also extensively represented in the traditions of other Bronze Age societies within the greater eastern Mediterranean and the Near East, and the evidence of exchange and cultural sharing is strong. Contemplations of this sharing played an important part in the modern establishment of Minoan archaeology, when the identity of the ancient Aegean culture was, in some senses, first construed.[2] Arthur Evans made extensive arguments for seeing substantive relations with the art of these neighboring societies, while also specifically asserting that naturalism and certain types of technical prowess distinguished Minoan works. Regarding Egypt, for example, despite detailing many aspects of Crete's "indebtedness" to the grand culture to its south,[3] Evans posed its influence as ultimately running counter to and potentially stifling Crete's unique artistic sophistication, writing that "too direct reproduction of Egyptian models had a deadening effect on Minoan Art. It may, indeed, be truly said that the epochs in which that Art showed its purest naturalism and freedom were coincident with periods when the connexions with Egyptian civilization were at their weakest."[4] Hence, we can see that the notion of a Minoan naturalism is coeval with the modern discipline of Minoan archaeology itself in the early twentieth century CE. And because its visual and material cultures have been a principal means through which scholars have differentiated Minoan culture from its contemporaries in the Near East and Egypt, representations of animals, as frequent foci of its celebrated naturalism, have been central elements – even icons – of the identity articulated for Minoan Crete as a distinct (and by some arguments, distinctly European) ancient cultural entity.[5]

Such characterizations of Minoan naturalism, including the appropriateness of the terms "Minoan" and "naturalism" themselves, have been variably challenged, embraced, plainly rejected, further developed and reconceived over the years.[6] Likewise, Evans' ambivalence toward cultural connections with societies beyond Crete, especially those to its east and south (an ambivalence surely steeped, in part, in the sociopolitical context of Evans' day, as he explicitly posed Minoan Crete as the "cradle of European civilization"),[7] have continued to charge scholarship of the Bronze Age Aegean, both on the surface and below. While we have for the most part moved away from ascribing "genius" to a sociocultural formation, or discussing differences in style as matters of "ability,"[8] we remain fascinated with the strikingly animate renderings of nature, including animals, that were crafted and experienced in Crete and the southern Aegean during the centuries of the late third through mid-second millennia BCE. Further discoveries have both enhanced our interest in Aegean renderings of the natural world and forced us to rethink its identity. From the beginning, objects diverse in both scale and medium have been drawn on to demonstrate the distinctiveness of Minoan handling of natural forms, but of particular early importance were discoveries of wall paintings from Knossos and other "palatial" sites on Crete that embody animals and plants in lively color and seemingly in the midst of movement, their forms relating a keen sense of animation and dynamism.[9] In the 1960s to 1970s, excavations at the site of Akrotiri on the island of Santorini (Thera), some 100 km north of Crete, revealed a host of wall frescoes preserved by ash from a major volcanic eruption in Late Bronze I, which included numerous remarkable renderings of animals.[10] Deposits at Akrotiri also contained a wealth of other animalian objects, such as zoomorphic rhyta and seals. This material, as well as rich finds from other Cycladic sites, made clear that the vibrancy of Minoan renderings of the natural world did not originate in Crete alone; indeed, they have forced us to fluidly expand the contours of the modern notion of "Minoan" to include a plurality of sociocultural spaces.[11] Meanwhile, strong affinities between the animal imagery of objects from the early Mycenaean mainland and ones from Crete and the islands brought further complexity to the picture. With this, consideration of Aegean engagements with representational traditions across the eastern Mediterranean during the first half of the second millennium BCE has coexisted with scrutiny of the Aegean itself as a dynamic field of sharing and innovation.

Decades of further discovery and investigation in the Aegean, including important developments in the methods of scholarly analysis, have brought more depth and scope to our characterization of the representation of the animalian world during the Bronze Age. Certain trends can be seen as running through studies that have dealt with material from a range of sites. One has considered the symbolic roles of renderings of animals in Aegean visual and material cultures. In this light, animals have often been discussed as religious icons or conventional means of metaphoric illustration. Species both "real" and "fantastic" have been approached in this way – ranging from bulls, to birds, to griffins and so on – and interpreted as signifying a host of cultural and religious content. Scholarship has varied both in the formality with which it posits codified roles for animals and in the theoretical approaches employed. On one end are studies that treat animal imagery as something of an iconographic subsystem in itself, such as Marinatos' argument that there existed in Minoan symbolic culture a formal hierarchy of beasts, each occupying a distinct level of relation toward the divine.[12] Meanwhile, other scholars have investigated the significations of representations of particular animals embedded within contexts of ritual activities, such as Rehak's valuable examination of frescoes depicting monkeys at Akrotiri.[13] In yet more cases, the treatment of animals as symbolic entities does not constitute the principal focus of the study but explicitly or implicitly forms a crucial part of the analysis.[14]

A related approach, also frequent in analyses of Minoan animal representation, can be described as taxonomic. I include here both efforts to associate depicted animals with regional biological species evidenced through faunal data, as well as discussions tracing the origins and distribution of particular iconographic types. Concerning the former, much attention has been paid to the abilities or desires of Cretan artists to depict the idiosyncratic attributes of specific animals, a matter scholars often relate to the sophistication of the Minoan naturalistic style. In terms of iconographic taxonomy, generations of scholars have been concerned with the speciation of distinct formal attributes in the repertoire of animal representations throughout the broader Bronze Age eastern Mediterranean, seeking to chart geneses, trajectories, mutations and amalgamations in the particular renderings of a beast over time and space. Often these efforts are part of larger projects that assess systems of sociocultural interaction and networking. Discussions of the griffin, for example, have closely parsed the characterization of wings, beaks and pose in an effort to establish the origins of the beast within the broad eastern Mediterranean and the specific trajectory of its evolution between cultures therein; these considerations of the creature's iconography and bodily composition are laced with implications of sociocultural sway between social formations.[15]

Each of these lines of analysis has borne important fruit for the field and contributed to our consideration of how renderings of animals were part of sociocultural life in the Aegean. At the same time, each can involve a necessary abstraction from the specific example of an animal representation for the sake of the appraisal of a broad cultural phenomenon, with the risk that the individual instance ultimately becomes but an iteration of a type or phase. The present project tackles this loss directly by fundamentally realigning the means and focus of inquiry. Drawing together recent work in the areas of material culture and animal studies, I problematize first and foremost the actual object-manifestations of animals. I recognize each as being a true physical embodiment of an animal and, with this, as tangibly contributing to the species' identity within its lived sociocultural context. I also consider a group of unique Aegean objects that are distinctly animalian in aspects of their substance and character, although they do not take the overall form of a creature's body.

My analysis works through a series of case studies that draw out distinctive dynamics at work in Aegean fabricated embodiments of animals from the late third to mid-second millennium BCE, with a primary emphasis on the socio-cultural spaces of Crete and their interconnections on and beyond the islands; evidence from Akrotiri on Thera provides another principal focus of my discussion of the later Middle Bronze Age (MBA) to Late Bronze I (LB I). These case studies follow chronological waves through and across the chapters, beginning with clay vessels of the Cretan Prepalatial era and ending with wall paintings of the Neopalatial and early Third Palatial periods. The subjects of the case studies have been selected in order to explore a variety of species,[16] media, materials and settings. With this, my focus encompasses the particular relations and spatialities that these things contributed to as parts of different lived contexts and, through this, how they may also show, on certain levels, areas of overlap or persistence in the dynamics of Aegean animalian things, both within and over time. Thus, the aim of my study is not to be exhaustive – the sheer plethora of animals within the material and visual cultures of these periods would make that an overwhelming and unwise task. Instead, my intention is to draw out specific indications of how fabricated animals could bring novel dynamisms to the identities of nonhuman creatures and to people's experiences of them. As such, these object-embodiments invested distinctive animal pres-ences in the thick of Aegean sociocultural life.

Embodiments of Relation

Fundamental to my approach to Aegean fabricated animals is an appreciation that their status as objects is not extraneous to their identity as embodiments of animals: both the animalian and the thingly are essential and coterminous aspects of these entities. This brings an integrative character to the core of their statuses, which can be further developed in a wealth of specific ways. The case studies indicate that these Aegean animalian things could be especially extraordinary in their realization of relations between species and between bodies. With this I have in mind the cosenses of "realize," both to apprehend and to actualize; that is to say, these things were, at the same time, responsive and generative in their embodiment of relations. I draw out how, in one aspect of this, the objects could cultivate similarity between the forms of different animals, or between those of an animal and a nonanimalian entity. I refer to this as *formal assonance*. We see such, for example, in vessels that bring together the swelling bodily contours characteristic of an upright bird, a woman and a jug; or in a painting that juxtaposes an animal and a plant in a frieze and describes each with the same outlines and textural details, both rendered in the same manner. Such formal assonance lays the ground for comparisons that could wed a host of associations surrounding each of the related entities, thus imbuing the animalian body with dynamic cultural and formal novelty. In some cases, it was not form, but position and role that asserted comparability. This occurs, for example, between lions and humans. Over centuries in the Aegean, lions were consistently experienced as bodies set side by side with persons, as seal stones engraved with the feline beasts were worn strapped against the skin of human seal owners; in much of the Bronze Age Aegean, especially Crete and the islands, this was essentially the only way in which lions were met in physical embodiments. Through close examination of such relations, interspecific and intercorporeal dynamics emerge as distinguishing facets of the Aegean animalian objects, realized in potently particular manners.

Connected to the relational complexity of these Aegean animalian things was their distinctive affordance of space. Space was created in a variety of ways by these object bodies and arose from their involvement with other entities and contextual circumstances, including the sociocultural and environmental. We will see how such matters as their size relative to human bodies, dimensionality, texture, layering, stance and implication of depth made for powerful and often tense spatialities. This also carried temporal weight. Such is at play, for example, in an anthropomorphic vessel's ability to sit and hold liquid on its own while gazing into the room of a house, creating an indefinitely ongoing aura of pregnant bodily presence, as part of the place.

In the chapters ahead, we will radically rethink, from the objects up, a range of entrenched categorizations that often structure discussion of renderings of animals in the Bronze Age Aegean. These include classifications that pertain to the traditional partitioning of the human from the nonhuman, the real from the fantastical and the animate from the inanimate; as well as those concerning the nature of composite or hybrid creatures, and the otherness of exotic beasts. Much of this rethinking arises from consistently bringing new focus to people's experiences of animalian things as opposed to concentrating on matters of intention and signification, which tend to consume analyses of "representations." It is not that intentional design is not relevant in our consideration of these objects, but it is but a strand of how they were actually engaged with by people in the social spaces of the early Aegean. By ultimately stepping away from aspects of conventional classification, we will freshly recognize a host of other dimensions that were at work in people's interactions with these embodiments of animals. This permits us to newly recognize the unique ways in which these animals were present and active in the practical and emotional fiber of sociocultural life – from the daily movements of hand-to-hand exchanges to the creative weaving of oral culture, from the vigor of overseas travel to the pains of battle and in both heightened moments of public ceremony and the intimate motions of familial death.

Drawing these aspects of my approach together, I propose that our examination proceed on the basis of four fundamental and interrelated reconceptions concerning how to approach the Aegean animalian things:

1. They are real embodiments of the animal and, as such, their qualities and capacities would have been part of what the animal or species was within a lived Aegean context, contributing along with biological embodiments.

2. We need to approach the work of these bodily things beyond the confines of representation, to take in the far greater diversity of affordances, contributions and relations that they brought to the table and through which they enriched the identity of animals in Aegean culture.

3. These embodiments of animals were creative in their essence. This creativity concerns not only their design and manufacture, but also how each of the objects stood as a distinct realization of physical coincidence between the characters of animals and of things and, furthermore, how they engendered suggestive relations between different species and bodies.

4. In diverse ways, the animalian things had dynamic potentials that enhanced and complicated their spatial and temporal presences. With this, they sometimes challenged the boundaries of their media and uniquely contributed to the unfolding of broader sociocultural contexts and moments.

THE CASE STUDIES

My analysis works through five case studies, each of which focuses on a particular type of animalian object from the early Aegean and examines its distinguishing character, relations and involvement in people's experiences as part of Cretan and other Aegean social spaces. The case studies arise from different time periods between the late third and mid-second millennia BCE and consider a diversity of species, media and contexts. In each instance, the objects are my starting point. These embodiments of animals reveal themselves to be highly dynamic and engaging, each in very specific ways that would emerge through their distinctive qualities and interactions. Because of the engaging characters of these things, my discussion necessarily integrates close consideration of recent research concerning the social and cultural ecologies of Bronze Age Crete and the southern Aegean – including the nature of interactions occurring both within and between Aegean communities, over land and sea, and farther afield, through involvement with people and material across the broader eastern Mediterranean.[17] By approaching such contexts of interaction primarily through people's experiences involving the animalian objects, we are able to move beyond traditional assumptions concerning influence and motivations, to think innovatively about how engagements with these creative embodiments of nonhuman creatures provide new perspectives on the actual, lived nature of sociocultural interconnections, extending near and far, during the Bronze Age.

In Chapter 2, I begin with a group of extraordinary body-form vessels from Prepalatial Crete (ca. 2300–1900 BCE). While these have typically been described as anthropomorphic, I argue that we do better to appreciate their unique identities as surpassing this category. These corporeal vessels are distinctly animalian, yet they decidedly do not conform to a particular species, and their affordances as objects that can hold and pour liquid are equally integral to what they are and how they were experienced. By taking these aspects together, focus can turn to how these peculiar vessel bodies are distinguished by a marked autonomy: not only do they defy the grip of simple classification, each can sit attentively on its own, with liquid held in its clay belly, and, even as each can itself be described as a vase, the role of living humans in producing liquid by manipulating the objects is concealed through particular physical qualities. Instead of highlighting the agency of the biological person, the bringing forth of liquid seems to occur in the hands of the small clay bodies themselves, in some cases through their pierced breasts, and in others through a miniature jug held by the figure, which communicated with the main vessel's hollow body through a hidden opening in its interior. With this, I argue that the clay figures could have been experienced as possessing their own productive agency.

The autonomous disposition of these unique animalian objects made them remarkable fabricated bodies. They could engage and perform – in their own right – as elements of early Cretan social contexts that also involved other bodies. Careful consideration of the clay figures' depositional circumstances allows us to investigate how their distinct bodily presences would have contributed to situations of social experience in Prepalatial Crete. I examine the complex spatialities of the clay bodies, which may have participated in creating community social space as they were moved between tomb and settlement. In this dynamic position, the body vessels could have been part of a range of collective actions involving living and dead humans who were in their company. I consider the evidence in light of recent problematizations of Prepalatial social structure, including arguments that early Crete was characterized by "house societies."[18] Recognizing the clay figures as members in-corporate of their communities, experienced as productive bodies, allows us to freshly interrogate their involvement in microcontexts of Prepalatial social life.

The second half of the chapter looks forward, through the subsequent Protopalatial and Neopalatial periods, to consider how animalian vessels continued to be part of social venues in the island, while subtle changes to *how* they embodied animals implied shifts in their community presence. We will see that across these periods, vessels embodying cows had notable prominence, but that from the late Protopalatial period, a novel relation developed between the vessel bodies and living humans' bodies. At this time, we begin to see rhyta rendered in the form of a bodiless animal head; the majority are bovine. Typically, the secondary opening of these rhyta was positioned in the mouth. Unlike the earlier vessels, the head rhyta could not hold fluids over time on their own – without active human intervention, the liquid would simply run out of the lower mouth hole. Indeed these animalian things would have seemed remarkably dependent on humans. Resting on their own, they would have appeared keenly lifeless and inanimate, as if decapitated heads; yet raised and filled by visible human hands, the heads would have momentarily been dramatically reanimated, as fluid was held in by carefully placed fingers and then permitted to flow out through the animalian mouth. Given the mechanics of the rhyta, these performances would have required considerable skill on behalf of the dexterous humans handling the heads; it was their impressive agency that would have been experienced as causing the liquid's emergence, even though it issued from the bovine's mouth. By shifting to a diachronic view on zoomorphic vessels, it thus becomes possible to appreciate a profound divergence in bodily emphasis in how these animalian things would have been experienced – from the remarkable impression of independent agentive production embodied in the Prepalatial vessels to the dramatic manipulation of a body fragment in human hands in the later head rhyta.

A primary interest of Chapter 2 concerns how movable renderings of animals contributed to developments in sociopolitical experience in Crete during certain moments of the Bronze Age. At the close of the chapter, discussion turns to how apparent changes in interregional dynamics during the Neopalatial period, likely spurred by specific social and climatic matters, may have involved novel claims on contexts of engagement with nonhuman animals, notably cattle, as elements of power grabs on the island. While economic and ritual interactions with cows have typically been separated in scholarly discussions, working in line with Shapland's consideration of "animal practices," I explore how activities involved in the raising and processing of cattle would have naturally crossed such categories and sketch out what a more holistic experience of "cattle culture" on the island may have involved. This approach entails examination of both the distinctive behavioral and environmental aspects of herd maintenance, as well as Cretan renderings of bovine bodies. Across these phenomena, I focus on aspects of bodily engagement between persons and cows and argue that we may see a distinguishing cultural emphasis on craftiness and quickness surrounding a host of activities and material, including in the unique affordances of certain bovine things. Prepalatial-era renderings of humans grappling cattle indicate that displays of crafty skill around the beasts were a long-standing component of rural agricultural life. During the Neopalatial period, palatial interest in cattle seems to have peaked, given the wealth of elite representations of the beasts, especially at Knossos. Increased environmental pressure on raising cows may have been part of this, with Knossos flexing control over a prominent and valuable crop. But we can also consider that if cattle culture had a somewhat-transgressive characterization in Crete, attempts by the palace to absorb and recontextualize the culture may have been part of a more dynamic sociopolitical interest in the beast during a turbulent moment.

The next chapter (Chapter 3) takes us to the tiny bodies of lions engraved in Aegean seals. Here, I again work from the Cretan Prepalatial period forward, tracing developments in the objects and their Aegean contexts, from their earliest instances in the late third millennium BCE through the LB II. Although the Cretan embodiments of lions were themselves tiny, the emergence of the beast within the material and visual cultures of the island necessitates a partial recalibration in the scale of our analysis, to also consider interactions extending overseas, because biological lions were not a species that lived on Crete – hence, experiences with the living beast were not the basis of its recurrent rendering in the seals. I examine how this situation also has profound implications for the fundamental characterization of the lion in Crete. For centuries, the beast's embodiments in seals and clay impressions were the primary means through which people actually engaged with lions as a physical reality on the island. This fact puts tremendous emphasis on these small, stony and clay-ey Cretan lions, and what they uniquely afforded. The objects' scale, material and formal nature, as well as their spatial dynamics, practical capacities, involvements within sociocultural processes and distinct relationships with other entities, all directly informed what the lion was in Crete, by characterizing how it was experienced. In this context, the bodily juxtaposition of lion and human becomes a crucial matter to consider. Seals engraved with lions were worn strapped against the bodies of their human owners, and the impressions stamped with the seals, which also embodied the lion, worked as distinct, moving objects that nevertheless had a powerful relationship of shared identity with the human seal owner. This meant that from their earliest known appearance in Crete, and for hundreds of years thereafter, lions were known by and large as bodies that physically – and figuratively – paralleled humans.

This intimate juxtaposition, perpetuated over many generations, inevitably would have impacted the lion's dynamic identity in Crete; it also would have coincided with the other creative form through which the beast was surely known by people of the island – oral culture. My examination of how the lion reached Crete from abroad takes in both of these types of creative culture, the material and the spoken. I consider the human dimensions through which such sharing with cultures of southwest Asia and Egypt would have occurred, and how the beast seems to have rapidly taken on a distinct identity in the Aegean. Through close analysis of changes to the rendering of the lion evident in Cretan glyptic of the MBA, I explore how the particular characterization of the beast fluidly developed even as its overarching juxtaposition with humans strongly persisted.

My discussion culminates in another consideration of sociocultural engagement overseas, in this case concerning Crete's extensive interaction with other areas of the Aegean during the early LBA, including with Thera and the early Mycenaean mainland. Material evidence clearly indicates that seals engraved with lions were part of this significant period of intra-Aegean interaction, during which objects, people, technical knowledge and the practice of writing were shared and developed. After the lion's absence from earlier phases of visual culture in the mainland, during this moment, when connections to Crete intensified, the lion becomes one of the most popular subjects of early Mycenaean seal imagery. This moment also saw a blossoming of other material media in which the lion is embodied (e.g., wall painting, metal weapons, cups), and scenes involving the beast more often pair it with a human. My discussion looks at this material culture in tandem with evidence for the contemporaneous development of the Aegean epic tradition, which includes a wealth of similes that parallel lions and heroes – as do the seals. This multimedia approach allows me to freshly consider how the poetic juxtaposition of lion and human may have continued to develop between material and oral cultures at this time, drawing in new dimensions in the context of Aegean interactions. With this, animalian objects are newly recognized as productive contributors to cultural interconnections during this crucial moment in Aegean prehistory. This perspective moves us away from discussions of sociocultural dominance and aggression that vex consideration of intra-Aegean relations in the LBA, instead drawing attention to the things, stories and people that gave daily body to cultural sharing – the likes of sailors and seal stones, singers and scribes, fabricated heroes and lions.

The third case study, in Chapter 4, fundamentally rethinks the identity of "composite" or "hybrid" creatures as they were embodied and experienced in Crete and the southern Cyclades from the late third to mid-second millennium BCE. I begin with an iconic creature of the Aegean Bronze Age, the griffin. Through close consideration of its early embodiments in Cretan objects,

I question whether, as is commonly presumed, the griffin was actually experienced in Crete as a set coupling of corporeal features stemming from other particular species. By letting go of assumptions, and focusing on the objects and their contexts, we can appreciate that people may have encountered the early Cretan griffins quite differently – not as additive derivatives, but as exotic creatures with wide similarities across species. The deposit of hundreds of stamped-clay seal motifs at Phaistos from which our earliest Cretan griffins stem provides a contemporaneous view upon renderings of other animals, in the same medium, that were active within the same social space as the griffins. Set in this context, we see that the bodily features characterizing the griffins occur across a range of other animals as well. With this, there is little ground for asserting that their presence in the bodies we identify as griffins would have been thought of as a matter of borrowing and reassembling parts from a fixed combination of two species. Instead, the evidence suggests that the griffins had a bodily nature and capacities (e.g., winged flight; but also sphragistic signification, as the engraved marks of a seal) that would have been experienced as comparable to a variety of other creatures. Looking from the objects up, it thus appears more likely that the griffins were experienced not as "counterintuitive" agglutinative combinations, but as distinctive wholes that could be likened, in various respects, to other beasts known in the flesh and through objects. In this light, embodiments of griffins may have been approached in a manner broadly comparable to renderings of occurrent foreign species (such as lions or hippopotami) that the vast majority of Cretans never encountered in biological form, as well as those of other beasts that we today define as fantastical.

Discussion in this chapter proceeds in two sections. In each, close examination of the griffin becomes a starting point for reconsidering other "composite" creatures rendered in the early Aegean, and, in this fresh light, for rethinking a range of animals that have not traditionally been included in this category. Each section is based on an investigation of one of two notable bodily features shared by the earliest extant Cretan renderings of the griffin: head appendages and chest embellishments. Consideration of these two attributes opens into recognition of a wider clutch of distinctive corporeal features embodied by a host of extraordinary animalian entities encountered in Cretan and southern Aegean material culture from this period. With this, I argue that griffins were among a group of creatures that initially would have been met in imported small-scale objects and then became dynamically incorporated into Cretan ecologies of animals that involved both biological and fabricated embodiments. This perspective requires casting the net more broadly, both in terms of the foreign and the local Aegean animals we consider.

By investigating a wider array of creatures rendered in the types of material culture that were being imported to Crete during the first half of the second millennium BCE, we can appreciate with greater subtlety how certain qualities occurring across these beasts may have become related to local animals and animalian culture on the island, as a given quality was potentially viewed as being shared with, or similar to, that of a known animal. This perspective recognizes how the generation and development of animalian forms could occur through intercultural relationships that creatively drew together likeness, versus joining dissimilar parts. It also permits us to see how these generative relationships took in creatures that are not described as composites. For example, we can see how, in Crete, sphinxes rendered *en face* in imported objects may have been experienced in light of local views on the unique potency of a direct forward gaze[19] and, therewith, likened to familiar animals on the island who keenly embodied it, such as the owl. Through this likening of creatures, properties connected to imported objects imaging the sphinx, such as amuletic seals or personal items, may have become associated with renderings of the owl and its gaze – an animal that appears in Cretan-made seals. This interspecific relation seems to be evidenced in Cretan renderings of owls with peculiar curving head appendages that resemble those of sphinxes in material culture from overseas, including Syrian cylinder seals.

In such objects, we see a creative relating of animals – including species foreign and local, fabricated and living, "fantastic" and biologically attested – that was being actively realized in novel thingly embodiments. These object-bodies appear to give the lie to such strict binaries and indicate how the identities and affordances of the implicated species could grow through people's experiences with dynamic animalian things, given the distinct qualities and associations they brought to the table. From this perspective, we can, in part, appreciate these Cretan embodiments of creatures as materialized venues of intercultural and formal relation. Hence, these crafted animalian bodies both stood primarily, in their own right, as unique and *present* bases for direct intercorporeal encounter with humans and, simultaneously, creatively manifest fertile ground for realizing associations between animals, and between animals and other phenomena.

The productive relational work manifest in these things did not happen in the hands of craftspersons alone, but also through engagements between the animalian objects and a wider group of people after their manufacture. Based on these experiences, including people's perception of similarities between the embodiments of animals at-hand and their experiences with other creatures or entities, connections would have been recognized around the animals, con-tributing to the identity of the rendered creature and others deemed compar-able. These connections would have arisen from a range of matters, including perceived similarities in form, disposition, affect, capacities or contexts of encounter; some of these naturally are more accessible to us than others. I trace out numerous potential lines of such relation and identify a host of Aegean creatures that seem to have been caught up in this type of creative integration. This discussion ultimately brings us back to the griffin and its Aegean associations. Here, I reexamine the well-noted rendering of a longer vulture-like beak in Minoan embodiments of the beast, along with other distinctive bodily features, by considering characteristics of biological species of vulture indigenous to Crete with which people on the island may have been relating the griffin, especially the Bearded Vulture (*Gypaetus barbatus*). My aim is neither to assert the Aegean's cultural weight in originating a feature of the griffin's iconography, nor to assess the technical skill of Aegean artists in replicating elements of a biological type (simple imitation of a living species is not apparent). Instead, I am drawing out how creativity realized in the identity of creatures could emerge from engagements occurring within distinctive ecologies of fabricated *and* living animals. Through this examination, we see that connections made with impressive biological animals, encountered in the flesh, may have brought the griffin distinctive power in the Aegean that rivalled the drama of qualities we had deemed the stuff of fantasy.

The status of composite creatures in the early Aegean is fundamentally revised through this discussion. I argue that, when pondered closely and in their contexts, many of the creatures to which we apply this term would have been experienced not as counterintuitive mergings of parts but, instead, both through and *as* realizations of similarity. These lines of similitude could concern matters of form as well as other aspects of the creatures' natures (e.g., color, efficacies). With this, the traditional category of the "composite" being is set aside as a larger swath of interconnected creatures comes into view. These *whole* creatures share amongst them the quality of having apparent connections both beyond the Aegean, with thingly embodiments of beasts from overseas, and more locally, with other Aegean fabricated and biological animals. I argue that this dynamic of interculturalism, likely involving a certain degree of strangeness, would have been a more prominent aspect of how many of these creatures were experienced than was a status as compounds, with the latter characterization perhaps not even being appropriate to a thick description of many of the beasts typically described as composites in the Aegean cultural sphere. In order to demonstrate this point, I highlight a markedly unique case of renderings of animals, from a deposit of preserved sealings in east Crete, in which a compounding logic *does* seem to have been in play. Comparison of these clearly fused figures to other contemporaneous Minoan creatures traditionally described as "composite" makes clear how differently they would have been experienced.[20]

Following upon our discussion, in Chapter 4, concerning the apparent discrepancy between the relational creative dynamics evident in Aegean fabricated creatures and the "counterintuitive" combining of derivative parts traditionally understood to define "composite" creatures, I turn in Chapter 5 to examining a clear alternative. Here, I somewhat provocatively suggest that we can appreciate in three particular entities crystallizations of a distinctly Aegean manner of animalian compositeness that is highly *intuitive* in its integration of animals and objects. These three characteristically Aegean entities – the boar's tusk helmet, oxhide shield and *ikrion* (ship cabin) – embody this dynamic in a potently arrant fashion, since, while each is distinctly animalian and bodily, they do not take the shapes of animal physiques themselves. Each very prominently incorporates recognizable fragments of animals' bodies into their form and substance, and each holds intimate relationships with the human body that are simultaneously formal, practical and significant. Direct engagements between humans and living biological animals, what Shapland describes as "animal practices,"[21] were prominent in the extended formation processes of these objects, as tusks and hides were procured in potentially significant events. Such interactions with biological animals and their contexts were part of the objects' biographies and would have informed the connections that could be made between the objects and other phenomena (e.g., between a shield, a cowhide and the quick-wittedness of a bull-trapper or warrior; or between ikria, a herd of cows and a fleet of ships); hence, these interactions were elements of the specific animalian character these entities embodied. The helmets, shields and ikria also brought novel, conventional forms to animalian presences in the Aegean. By *not* standing as animals themselves, these three entities draw out with great starkness and effectiveness the deep relational dynamics that could be realized *between* creatures (e.g., humans and boars), and between creatures and things, which here come together in entirely distinct types of entity often encountered on their own. With an initial focus on the boar's tusk helmet, I closely examine how these three entities seem to have held extraordinary places in Aegean sociocultural experience while also standing as robust condensations of many of the dynamics also seen more broadly in the ecology of fabricated Aegean animalian things.

As Chapter 5 continues, my interest turns to the added dimensions of complexity brought to the statuses of boar's tusk helmets, oxhide shields and ikria as they were reembodied in movable representational media such as glyptic and painted ceramics. My discussion closely considers a characteristic way of handling these three entities that distinguishes their renderings within the surfaces of numerous seals and painted pots: articulation in series of repeated or juxtaposed elements. While, in studies of Aegean art, the occurrence of an entity in a series is often read as simplifying its status to something merely ornamental, I argue that, quite to the contrary, the frequent rendering of these three entities in series imbued them with a peculiar dynamism that throbbed with ambivalent and apparently contradictory implications. Within friezes of elements set side by side, these entities could be singled out for repetition or juxtaposed with other entities in a manner that keenly afforded comparison. The rendering of shields, helmets and ikria as repeated elements in a series seems to extract them from action, leaving them without grounding in any represented context; but it could also be taken to directly relate to the manner in which they were experienced as objects in-the-round in scenarios of collective action (e.g., as repeated elements seen across a file of soldiers or adorning each ship of a fleet). In certain cases, such a series could even create the impression of a line of objects hanging upon a wall, thus flirting with emplacement. The bare-bones style of the seriated friezes gave an illusion of straightforwardness but also left matters such as these unresolved. This irresolution contributed to the potency of the three entities in their poetic, sociocultural and physical dimensions.

This chapter depends on close considerations of renderings of shields, helmets and ikria within the tiny surfaces of seals and seal impressions, and across the curved walls of painted ceramics. The particular circumstances and qualities of these movable media powerfully impacted the relational, spatial and poetic dimensions through which people knew the three animalian entities. We see that instances of formal assonance were cultivated in both media, in distinct ways. The scale of seals, and the nature of their engraving, contributed to a potential likening of certain forms, for example, a helmet and a bundle of "sacral cloth" rendered nearly identically.[22] In ceramics, we see similar instances of assonance developed in other ways, for example, upon a rhyton where what appears to be a front-facing (dying?) swine's head was painted alongside a squill rendered in a form highly comparable to a boar's tusk helmet. Such situations indicate how juxtaposition and substitution could act in tandem with relationships of formal assonance to create compelling connections between phenomena. In some cases, at least, we can speculate that cultural links may have also been active between the phenomena that were rendered as assonant (e.g., squills, like helmets, may have held protective value); these relationships of cultivated assonance, substitution and parataxis possess rich poetic potential. Meanwhile, we will see that in both glyptic and painted ceramics, the handling of shields and helmets at times generated keen ambivalence in the spatial status of the entities. Focusing closely on embodiments within these two movable media allows us to appreciate both the unique impacts each would have had on how people experienced helmets, shields and ikria, as well as areas of overlap in their effect that indicate particular dynamisms in the entities' cultural identities.

In Chapter 6, we turn to examining the boundary-breaking spatial and social dynamism of animalian entities embodied within polychrome wall painting of the Neopalatial and Late Minoan (LM) II periods. In these frescoes, the entities innovatively engaged with both their painted and lived contexts in ways that brought the animalian new manners of presence in certain Aegean sociocultural spaces; in some cases, the paintings generated fundamentally new aspects of creaturely identity and relation. My discussion of murals begins with consideration of the three entities closely considered in Chapter 5: boar's tusk helmets, oxhide shields and ikria. Considering a number of frescoes from Crete and Akrotiri, we see how renderings of these animalian entities challenged long-standing parameters concerning two-dimensional representation of bodies – in some respects building upon the creativity evident in later MBA painted ceramics. The large wall paintings, however, had fresh dynamics as immovable contributors to the vital fabric of particular places. In this context, my discussion broadens beyond helmets, shields and ikria to consider how the embodiment of animals in polychrome wall paintings realized powerful new dimensions of nonhuman animalian involvement in Aegean sociocultural experience, by novelly unsettling the built spaces in which the beasts were manifest. Innovations in color and scale and the generation of taut spatial depth in the frescoes all contributed to shaping new engagements with animals that in some ways approached how bodies were experienced in life in-the-round. Yet, simultaneously, details of the frescoes kept the creatures, and the spaces they occupied, tenaciously embroiled in the fabricated order of the painted wall. We see this vividly embodied, for example, in fragments of a wall painting at Knossos involving tethered griffins, where the creatures' bodies were innovatively built up in relief with stucco. These bodies were caught in limbo between the flat wall in which they were caught and the extending space of the room, into which their rounded bodies swelled. Through a variety of qualities, a characteristic tension thus took form across animalian bodies in Neopalatial and LM II wall painting – between the engaging dimensions of as-in-life experience that they afforded and their concurrent identity as embodiments of remarkable artifice. This tension, essentially between different varieties of presence, would have peculiarly charged the social spaces of which the frescoed animals were part during distinct moments of social recalibration in both the Neopalatial and LM II periods.

Chapter 6 closes with a focused study concerning how polychrome wall paintings could foster a radical newness in the identities of animals, in essence giving rise to new species. My focus is on how simians in wall paintings from Crete and Akrotiri were consistently rendered as blue-bodied. I argue that this blueness, whether or not originally intended as an approximation of biological simian hues, would have contributed to establishing a distinct sociocultural status for the animal within the Aegean. I consider the blueness of these Aegean creatures in the context of the markedly human-like activities in which they typically engage in the paintings, activities which, in multiple instances, overlap with undertakings and contexts associated with women and young persons. These two aspects of the Aegean painted monkeys – their vivid blueness and actions that make them like (small) people – come together with new dynamism in light of the fact that blueness also distinguished the bodies of youthful humans in the wall paintings. In the frescoes preserved at Akrotiri, where we have a unique wealth of paintings of young persons, these figures are characteristically rendered with their heads shaved, either over much of the scalp or in select parts; the shaved areas are conventionally colored a vibrant blue. The sideburn emerges as a zone of the head that consistently indicates this youthful shaving across different specific styling patterns, as a vibrant blue flash in front of the ear. People would have been able to relate the characteristic blueness shared between the bodies of simians and young humans, which were sometimes copresent in buildings or rooms. This blueness was based in a common corpus of colorants used for both animalian subjects, bringing yet further substance to their sharedness. Whatever their "origin," the blue simians of Aegean walls existed as a species with remarkable, substantive closeness to human young.

The case studies in Chapters 2 through 6 provide a robust examination of the peculiarly dynamic involvement of animalian things in the sociocultural life of Bronze Age Crete and areas of the southern Aegean. My aim with these is not to offer an exhaustive overview of Minoan representations of animals, but, instead, through close parsing and contextualization, to newly recognize the profound and highly distinctive ways in which fabricated animals actively contributed to social space and experience, through keenly dynamic potentials. The subjects of the case studies have been selected to take in a range of key topics that can productively overlap, including the unique animacies and spatiotemporal dynamics of objects; the cultivation of similarity and relation between species, including humans and nonhumans; the distinct experiential factors surrounding exotic species; and the ways in which people's experiences with animalian things could extend a species' character and identity into unprecedented and unexpected ground. These matters involve close consideration of the total ecology of animals in Crete and the Aegean, including people's engagements with both biological and crafted embodiments and the involvement of representational and nonrepresentational animalian things, as well as experiences with contemporaneous nonmaterial renderings of beasts, within oral culture. These issues force us to reckon anew with certain traditional binaries that have structured earlier analyses. Yet more fundamentally, they ask us to take seriously how the existence of creatures as fabricated things enriched the identity of species in the early Aegean, by creatively realizing novel dynamics of reality and relation in animalian presence.

THINGS AS ANIMALS: A GROUNDWORK

Representations and (Re)embodiments

While much of the material culture I consider in this study can be described as *representational*, reliance on this notion, while comfortable, can obscure some of the very dynamics at work in the objects that are my main interest. The issue is in large part a matter of emphasis. Basically put, working through the notion of representation focuses us on the degree of formal closeness that an embodiment has with, or can effect in relation to, a model.[23] In studies of material culture, the term representation generally refers to an object created with the (presumed) intent of sharing a primary aspect of its identity with another entity or model, based either on elements of formal similarity with the model or what can be conventionally taken as a conveyance of its formal nature.[24] The model entity need not be a specific concrete thing but is taken as a guide in leading the formation of the representation. Hence, a figurine embodying a bull could share its general species identification with a biological bull because their bodily forms would be recognized as comparable in prominent respects. If a bull is embodied in a wall painting, its flatter body does not share the three-dimensional aspects of form with that of a biological bull in the round as would a sculptural bull, but it can, through a variety of possible means, be experienced as conveying the form of the three-dimensional body. However, working in another light, we can of course see that a crucial part of the generative dynamism of representational things – or what we can alternatively describe as things that *newly embody* an entity – is that, even as they share key aspects of identity with other embodiments of a common subject (potentially with both nonrepresentational and representational embodiments, including what traditionally would be described as a model), they simultaneously differ from them, whether subtly or tremendously. Consequently, I do not limit the notion of "zoomorphism" to objects that render an animalian body in the round. Each rendering of an animalian form is a new embodiment of it – distance and closeness to another embodiment (including a hypothetical model) can be realized through a rich diversity of relationships, not limited to shared physical contours alone. This distance between embodiments is, in many senses, the space within which my analysis of Aegean animalian things works. With this, the degree of formal closeness recedes in importance, as does the relationship of deference to a model or models, since, instead, we are recognizing *a plurality of embodiments in the field together*.

By recognizing both biological and fabricated embodiments as *real* and coexistent animalian presences within the lived physical and sociocultural world, I am able to foreground problematization of people's direct experiences with the diverse embodiments over matters of verisimilitude. This shift in focus also allows our consideration to substantively extend to a wider range of human engagements with the animalian objects, without implicitly privileging the maker's intentions in their design. With this, representational embodiments can be approached not as secondary and reflective manifestations, but as true bodies, in the mix of lived experience along with other bodies – some fabricated, some not. Accordingly, since use of the term representation can carry such implications of secondary or mediated status in relation to biological embodiments of animals, I limit my use of it. However, even if not my focus, in most cases I assume a basic premise of intent to reproduce elements of an animal's form as underlying the manufacture of the animalian things that take a corporeal shape, and, in this basic respect, the term representation is not inappropriate and can indeed be efficient. But this is but one aspect of my interest in the animalian things and their relationship to other bodies and entities. Yet more crucial to my analysis are a host of other matters: the distinctive contributions that fabricated animals have within lived contexts of sociocultural action, their qualities beyond form that impact humans' experience, and their dynamics of similarity with other entities that can involve form but also arise from further dimensions of comparability and nearness.

There are other reasons why a primary focus on the representational dynamics of these animalian objects would be problematic. We cannot claim to grasp specific metaphysical concepts of representation and mimesis active in the Aegean Bronze Age, nor can we assume that overarching conceptions on these matters, as such, were in circulation. Questions such as whether, or how, phenomena that we would describe as representational were, in their essence, thought to hold distinct ontological status or moral weight must be left open-ended. Likewise, a diversity of phenomena that we classify together unproblematically as being representational may not have been experienced as having a common nature. These are matters that can vary profoundly between and within cultures and moments and are exceedingly difficult to get ahold of concerning the distant past, even with the aid of textual sources, which we lack for these periods. Examinations of Plato's writings concerning *mimesis*, for example, suggest that notions of imitative representation that we attach to the term likely were not its primary associations in his day or before, when the term instead, at least in the works of some thinkers, involved more "dynamic" meaning, arising around drama, with a sense more like "enactment," which Plato extended to characterize the visual arts, potentially as a metaphoric means of critiquing another creative form, poetry.[25] I am surely not proposing that Plato's ideas concerning *mimesis*, or the particular enactment-oriented notions with which Plato was creatively engaging, would have been active in the Aegean Bronze Age sociocultural formations that are our focus here – or even that, if such conceptions were in circulation, they would have been considered relevant to the range of material culture we will be discussing. My point is instead that, even for situations in which we are in a far better position to consider the characterization of concepts of representation, reproduction and *mimesis* that were in play, it is deeply challenging to appreciate how these were part of lived experience, not least because their connection to things engaged with in the world could have been fluid and variable.[26] I instead aim to stay close to the particularities of the objects and their contexts of engagement, and to avoid treating them through a generic or presumptuous lens of representation. This means, fundamentally, taking seriously the distinctive capacities and relations that could be realized through their involvement in action, and examining how such qualities of the things would have been taken together with their animalian identities – as unified aspects of their presences in lived experience.

Hence, it was not simply imitative representation, but generative new embodiment of the animalian that distinguished these fabricated creatures. The power of the bees in the Protopalatial pendant from Malia,[27] for example, arises not merely from their brilliant imitation of a living bee's golden hue, but from their embodiment *as gold*. They are distinguished by the bold symmetry of bodies that answer each other with eternally poised precision, and by artful formal echoing that resonates across their corporeal union: in the central orb of granulated honeycomb, the two round eyes, the three pendant circular charms, the perfectly suspended drop of metallic honey, and the encaged ball that tops the insects' heads. These bees' bodies shimmered with their own vigor – not the vital hum and flutter of living bees, but one that shone with both nearness to the alive and a distinctly thingly artifice.[28] As a pendant worn in life and ultimately deposited in a tomb, these bees could rest upon human skin without inspiring fear of a sting and would not disappear when summer ended.

Such things stand out because *their thingliness was realized as beastliness, and vice versa*. We will see that Aegean zoomorphic objects could be highly dynamic, in a diversity of particular ways. This was realized through peculiar material properties, temporalities, physical involvements in lived social actions, and distinguishing affordances. Moreover, in many of the cases we consider, the objects were renderings of corporeal forms, meaning that their unique dynamism was incorporated into a creature's bodily copresence with a human, as two animalian bodies in a space together. In this light, we can appreciate that these objects were far from simply imitational; they were, in their essence, creative. Fully recognizing the animalian and corporeal nature of these things brings us much deeper in our consideration of their distinctive involvements in sociocultural experiences, simply by dealing with their unique capacities to participate in the contexts of action and relation in which they were immersed.

Beastly Things

My particular aim, to problematize Aegean animalian things beyond their traditional treatment as representational objects, can be placed in the context of a broader and diverse field of scholarship that rethinks how material culture is part of human experience. Alfred Gell's work has become a bastion and signpost in efforts to breach the divide between artifact and artwork, by drawing together anthropological and art historical thinking about objects. Many of his ideas have become standard parlance in examinations of ancient material culture, subtending a host of studies that have developed since *Art and Agency* was published in 1998.[29] I engage with some of Gell's ideas in this book, especially concerning an object's potential to confound a person engaging with it (see Chapter 2). Working from a different disciplinary perspective, Brown's 2001 "thing theory" has likewise done much to stimulate studies across a range of fields toward freshly recognizing the realities of people's engagements with entities in the lived world. As Brown notes, the term "things" possesses an "audacious ambiguity," as it "denotes a massive generality as well as particularities."[30] Brown considers the persistent intellectual fascination with the idea of the thing, through the works of Heidegger, Mauss, Lacan and others, and how approaching something as a thing has been taken as a means of challenging and getting below or beyond classifications that can bind our considerations. In archaeological work, the term has been favored by persons working in a range of theoretical directions.[31] Recently, advocates of a symmetrical archaeology have argued for a focus on things as a means of working beyond the privileging of only particular aspects of an entity – for example, to escape bias in analyses that implicitly favor a certain contextualization over others and can lead to artificially partitioning or disregarding moments in the thing's existence. While attracted by some of the same potential qualities of the term, my usage does not follow any particular theorization of it. I am drawn by how the nonspecificity of the term thing leaves our initial classification of something open-ended and, I believe, brings the matter of its immediate at-hand presence into a stronger and less preconstrained light. With the initial open-endedness the term affords, greater emphasis in the particularization of a thing can come to considering how it would actually be experienced, given its specific character. In this way, the nonspecificity of the term can help us to appreciate the specificity with which people engage with things in everyday life; Heidegger's notion of a thing's *Jediesheit,* or quality of "being-this-one," is relevant here, as is his discussion of how time and place are elements of the particularity inherent in a thing.[32] This refocus also provides for simultaneously recognizing different aspects of a thing's nature, arising from its various particular qualities, instead of one categorization taking precedent over the other from the get-go. Moreover, the open-endedness of the term facilitates a wider potential for comparison between things, instead of only within a particular category of objects. For the sake of structure and coherence in my discussion, I have not, however, followed this to the extreme. For example, I do discuss types of thing (e.g., vessels or seals) as one way of organizing consideration of relations that could have been realized between pieces of material culture embodying animals, based on people's engagements with them and the comparisons that would involve. Moreover, while one approach could have been to use the term thing to pertain widely to all material phenomena, whether crafted, biological, inanimate or animate, that is not the path I took.[33] This is mainly because I feel that acknowledging my primary focus on fabricated animals is important, and further because – while I treat both fabricated and biological animals as real and in the experiential field together – appreciating their differences is also crucial to my discussion. Hence, I use the phrase "animalian thing" to refer to material culture for which a principal aspect of its identity is connected to animals. In many cases, this animalian identity arises from the thing's embodiment of an animal's corporeal form, but in the case of boar's tusk helmets, oxhide shields and ikria, it is the prominent incorporation of a part of an animal's body that I have in mind (an incorporation that is also emphasized in renderings of these entities). From a slightly different perspective, I am also attracted by how "thing" nudges the object down off its lofty perch (at least to begin with) and immerses it in the stream where other subjects hold sway along with it, while also reorienting us toward the rich if messy engagements in which its specific character is realized in its relational complexity. A thing is decidedly in the mix. It is this potency of the term thing – which essentially demands looking around itself while also being resolute in its own grounded presence – that I am interested in, and which underlies my discussion of *animalian things*.

It is worth noting that Shapland's use of the term "animal thing" in his excellent recent study of human–animal relations in Bronze Age Crete (2022) differs conceptually from my understanding of "animalian thing." The basis of my consideration of embodiments of animals in material culture is distinct from Shapland's, which fundamentally poses them as "traces" that signify back to instances of direct engagement with biological nonhuman animals (i.e., "animal practices"). While I do share Shapland's identification of some material as "traces," including elements of biological animals' bodies that have been recontextualized by people (e.g., a large animal tooth that was saved after a hunt or cut to be used as an engraved seal stone), I believe that viewing renderings of animals primarily as referents to past encounters with biological animals is not enough by itself; we also must fully recognize the authentic immediacy such renderings possess as embodiments of animals. Hence, while Shapland's analyses of the objects ultimately return to a fundamental focus on human engagements with biological animals, my primary emphasis is on human engagements with the fabricated embodiments of animals themselves. I believe these two emphases – which coincide in some areas – complement each other in many ways; set in dialogue with one another, they draw out key dynamisms in the material.

The Engaging Lives of Things

A range of recent studies across various disciplines have focused on problematizing the dynamic existences of things within lived environments and the nature of their engagements with people. The impact on archaeology has been substantive and valuable. The work of Shanks, Küchler, Gosden, Miller, Tilley, Ingold and Knappett, among others, have helped to establish a new region of inquiry in archaeological theory, concerned primarily with the ways in which objects and materials actively contribute to human experience and how this often supersedes, or is indifferent to, matters of human intention or prediction.[34] This work has assumed various theoretical points of departure and reached into divergent areas of interpretative practice. Phenomenological and ecological approaches have been prominent, arising from foundational works by authors such as Merleau-Ponty, Husserl, Heidegger and Gibson; in some cases, these studies have focused specifically on the lenses of sensual bodily experience and materiality.[35] The topics of object and material agency, and object biography, have reoriented attention on material culture by thinking of things through notions often reserved for humans, sometimes with provocative effects.[36] Some of these discussions have engaged with actor-network theory, which has become a significant force in shaping archaeological approaches to material culture, in part because its ideas provide a productive means of recognizing nonhuman animals and things, along with humans, as each potentially contributing within contexts of action and meaning.[37] Meanwhile Shanks, Witmore, Olsen, Webmoor and others have advocated for archaeological work informed by the principles of "symmetry" in order to get beyond some of the dualisms that have structured and inhibited interrogation of material culture.[38] Over the past three decades, cognitive and mind–body approaches have become an established element in studies of ancient objects, with many important contributions.[39] Malafouris' work is notable here, including his radical rethinking of objects' relationships with humans' bodies, especially through theories of extended self.[40] With a more specific focus, Wengrow's analysis of the cognitive, material and social aspects of the development of "modular" phenomena in contexts of emergent urbanism in the Bronze Age Near East and eastern Mediterranean, including "composite" creatures represented in the material culture, is impressive; his study forms a crucial interlocutor in my discussion of fantastical beasts identified as composites in the Bronze Age Aegean material record (Chapter 4). In his analyses of Aegean objects, Knappett's work engages with various of these approaches, including especially "pragmatological" and "praxeological" ideas, as developed in the work of Witmore, Holbraad, Hutchins, Lemonnier and Warnier.[41]

Creativity in the Mix

Knappett's scholarship has done much to infuse the field of Aegean prehistory with innovative, substantive theoretical perspectives. In his 2020 study of Aegean Bronze Age art, he describes one of his aims as being to "prompt a creative outlook on the real."[42] His discussion is keenly effective in its problematization of what Aegean objects could do as active, generative elements of sociocultural experience, and, in the present study of animalian objects, I very deeply share the view that objects can be fundamentally creative in their nature. Knappett opens objects, including those deemed representational, as nodes of interaction. Recognizing the pioneering work of Poursat in Aegean art history,[43] Knappett looks through a diversity of objects in his discussion, stressing the need to work above traditional classificatory divides. In this, he draws out a host of relational potentials that distinguish the complexity of Aegean objects, including combining, imprinting and containing, which are also key matters in our discussion of animalian things. Elements of Knappett's analysis of Aegean art build on his important earlier work drawing Gibson's notion of "affordances" into archaeological discussions.[44] Affordances are capacities of entities that arise when their particular qualities are interacted with by another entity or multiple entities, including humans, within specific contexts. Affordances can vary dramatically in their nature and contexts. They can involve both manufactured and naturally occurring phenomena, and both human and nonhuman beings. We can see this across examples such as a large, smooth, slanted stone at a river's edge that affords gleeful sliding to a troupe of children on a hot day, or in a basin that usefully collects rainwater under a downspout while also affording a robin a cool bath. Affordances clearly have physical and mechanical dimensions, but also sensorial and emotional ones, from warm relief, to rigid surprise, to comfortable reassurance.[45] Meanwhile the disposition of entities relative to one another can afford experientially and socioculturally rich dynamics, such as comparison, familiarity, similarity, difference and nearness. Discussion of affordances turns attention to the instance of interaction and hence can support reaching beyond matters of intention alone – a move which is central to my analysis.[46] In the case of an artifact, while it is not denied that the intentions of the craftsperson in forming an object can be understood to persist and inform how it is subsequently interacted with by others, such matters of design are recognized as being but part of what potentially contributes to the experiences of the thing that take form, and hence to its identity. Moreover, for our discussion, concentrating on what comes of moments of active engagement and perception provides us with footing for considering how interactions with other phenomena – such as substances, forces and other nonhuman entities – were also part of the situated existences of the Aegean animalian things. Hence, while my focus is ultimately on engagements between the things and people, the discussion of affordances can fruitfully lead into consideration of posthumanist matters that enrich our recognition of fuller relational contexts. In this, a range of other works, including Bennett's *Vibrant Matter* and Harman's development of "object-oriented ontologies," are relevant for their focuses beyond human determination of material and sociocultural worlds. Across these matters, the notion of affordances can aid us in recognizing how relations realize the fundamental character of the thing within a context.

Other recent work has also characterized relation within environments as being fundamentally creative, but is based in distinct thinking and has a different emphasis on the action of a perceiver. Noë argues that perceptual experience is "enactive," taking form over time and space through an animal's (including a human's) back-and-forth interaction with the environment, and that it entails both the perceiver and the environment: "Experience isn't something that happens in us. It is something we do; it is temporally extended process of skillful probing. The world makes itself available to our reach. The experiences comprise mind and world. Experience has content only thanks to the established dynamics of interaction between perceiver and world."[47] Noë's emphasis on skillful action is important. He describes that we bring "sensorimotor" "knowledge" or "skills" "to bear" when engaging with entities in our environment, and with this, we work to find out "how things are from an exploration of how they appear."[48] It is this skillful process that enables us to move from "innocent"[49] retinal images to a comprehension of something's complex formal nature – for example, to figure out that a plate viewed sitting on a nearby table, which creates an elliptical retinal image, instead has a perfectly circular circumference as a three-dimensional thing, or that what our eye encounters as a group of meeting line segments and angles of different degrees, sizes and colors, all set within a larger rectangle, is "in fact" a cluster of rooftops, glimpsed through a window, as they recede in space before us. As some occurrent qualities or "details" of a thing are encountered as present by a perceiving person, others are sensed as potentialities and, as the relation between the person and the thing develops, for example, through changes in vantage point or altered conditions, further details come into view as others recede.[50]

Noë likens the process of perceptual experience to the act of painting, an analogy which highlights its creative nature:

> Seeing, on the enactive view, is like painting ... When a painter works from life he or she makes continuous and ongoing reference to the world. The painter looks to the world, then back to the canvas, then back to the world, then back to the canvas. Eye, hand, canvas, paint, world are brought into play in the process of constructing the picture. Seeing, like painting, involves the temporally extended process of reaching out and probing the scene. Seeing, on this approach, would depend on brain, body, and world.[51]

With this, perception is appreciated as a matter of generative skillful activity, through which variable outcomes or impressions can arise. In other words, as we engage with a thing, our perception of it arises as a matter of variable interaction with and access to its qualities, which contribute to shaping that thing's very status in our experience and understanding. According to Noë, this process of forming an impression of a thing should not be divorced from the life of concepts; perceptual experience and conceptualization can act together as someone dynamically forms an understanding of what they see and encounter:

> To have a perceptual experience is precisely to direct one's powers of thought to what one experiences; the experience, and the conceptualizing, are *one and the same* activity. Neither is logically or conceptually prior. As Kant held, concepts without intuitions are empty, intuitions without concepts are blind. ... Mere sensory stimulation does not add up to experience. We don't *apply* sensorimotor skill *to* experience. ... Perceptual experience *just is* a mode of skillful exploration of the world. The necessary skills are sensorimotor and conceptual.[52]

Noë's work powerfully argues for approaching human perceptual experiences of entities in the world as, in essence, processes of engagement and formation. In this, he is broadly considering engagements with entities that constitute the environment, but part of his discussion also involves some provocative rethinking of representations specifically. In consideration of pictorial representations, he steps away from approaching likeness between a representation and a "real" represented entity as arising primarily from the former's ability to successfully recreate the retinal image projected by the latter in the human mind.[53] He instead shifts emphasis to the active engagement a person has with both entities, and the shared means of discovery and understanding that each calls into use, wherewith relatable experiences of the entities take form: "What a picture and the depicted scene have in common is that they prompt us to draw on a common class of sensorimotor skills."[54] This view thus recognizes an autonomy to the representation, while also problematizing its correspondence to the represented entity (with which it can be taken to "depict" it) as being a matter of sharedness between how a perceiver actively engages with each. This move away from a basic characterization of representation as replicative formal depiction, and toward one of "commonality" realized between two entities, is crucial, as is seeing active engagement with the qualities of both as being the source of their perceived likeness. There is clearly also difference between the qualities of the representational entity and the represented entity, and between how one engages with each. Since Noë's enactive view considers perceptual experience as a matter of accessing an entity's qualities through ongoing skillful action, his approach provides for experiencing particularity and difference as being copresent with likeness, as a person accesses and senses various qualities of a thing.

In what follows, I examine the dynamics of likeness and difference that Aegean animalian things could realize. Most fundamentally, this tension took form across their beastly and thingly statuses. These things were themselves embodiments of relation and coalescence between animals and objects; moreover, they were, at once, relatable to biological and fabricated things, to animate and inanimate elements of the lived world. The connections they afforded extended into a diversity of entities and contexts. In order to appreciate the dynamic presences these things could have in Aegean sociocultural spaces, we must first take them seriously as true embodiments of animals, with unique characters.

A Diversity of Bodies and the Peculiarity of Animals

That we should accept representational objects as legitimate, dynamic embodiments of animals might seem far-fetched, but the notion should be considered further. The underlying point is that people actually encounter and relate to nonhuman creatures in a rich multiplicity of bodily forms – in other words, people's direct experiences of animal bodies potentially (and often) involve bodies that are not those of biological beings. Moreover, the distinctive qualities, animacies and interactions of these (other) bodies contribute in their own peculiar ways to humans' experience of nonhuman animals and, in turn, to animals' positions in sociocultural spaces. Recognition and examination of this fact have come from various disciplinary perspectives. In their study of human experience of nonhuman animals in late modernity, Beardsworth and Bryman articulate four primary "modes of engagement" through which people interact with wild animals; these include encounter, representation, presentation and quasification.[55] *Encounter* involves direct, unmediated copresence of the human and "the unrestrained animal in its own environment, so that it can be perceived via one or more of the senses." *Representation* refers to the "figurative representation of wild animals," potentially in media as diverse as painting, sculpture, drawing and, in contemporary culture, video. *Presentation* involves engagement with live captive wild animals "presented" to viewers and hence "subjected to a level of human scrutiny which it might otherwise avoid." Venues of presentation would be menageries, circuses, zoos or staged hunts in game parks or arenas, such as the Assyrian *ambassu*.[56] *Quasification*, which hovers between presentation and representation, recreates the wild animal, often making use of materials such as skins gleaned from living creatures. Here, it is not that the beholder is fooled into believing they are encountering a living animal – the lifeless nature of the animal is also to be noted. Beardsworth and Bryman refer to natural history museums as a typical modern space where people engage with quasified wild animals. In the ancient past, pelts could act in a similar position, something that is simultaneously experienced as being both authentically of a wild animal and certainly not a living beast.[57] How likeness and sameness were conceived is difficult to assert and may have been fluid. For example, it may be that rendered embodiments of animals in innovative Aegean Bronze Age media – ones, for example, that rose up to the scale of biological animals (e.g., in large-scale polychrome murals) or brought creatures' bodies out in relief and modelling (e.g., ceramic vessels with zoomorphic relief appliques, including ones crafted through molding of biological animals, such as sea shells) – were experienced as possessing, in their own right, some of the same attributes as biological embodiments, even while also introducing their own highly distinct character to the animal (see Chapters 5 and 6). In her consideration of humans' diverse types of interaction with the natural world, including interactions with animals, Corbett elucidates similar variabilities as those articulated by Beardsworth and Bryman.[58] What clearly arises from these studies is recognition that human engagements with other animals are complex in nature – varying in medium, venue and interactive potential – and that binary divisions between "real" and "false"/"imaginary" embodiments alone do not capture the multiplicity of ways in which humans can experience other animals as physical, material, embedded realities.

Different ways of engaging with nonhuman animals are of course just that – different – and we would be wrong to equate or inadvertently elide them. Each should be appreciated for its particular attributes and context-specific dimensions. Hence, to state the obvious, a human's direct interaction with a living beast in its natural environment[59] would be remarkably distinct from an engagement with an object embodying an animal in a built social locale. Fundamentally, the object does not share the status of living, thinking, sentient being, nor the ineffable unpredictability with which such a being throbs. But at the same time, we should also recognize that there would be a dramatic distinction between a person's unexpected encounter with a lion upon a mountainside and the same person's interaction with a living lion in an orchestrated ritual context such as a staged sport or "hunt"; Berger's discussion of sharing a wild animal's gaze in the wild versus (not being able to) in a zoo aptly gets at the profundity of the experiential difference that comes with such recontextualizations.[60] Shapland engages with Berger's views and probes how "sameness and difference" between animals and representations of them would have been felt by persons in the Bronze Age, taking into account differences in cultural worldview (see pp. 62–63).[61] Without question, there are intensely meaningful distinctions between people's interactions with other living beings versus those they have with nonliving entities. But the boggling diversity of living animals, and of the character of their interactions with one another, is a reminder that engagements of humans and nonhumans can and do vary in the deepest of senses.[62] A distinction between living and nonliving bodies is not the only meaningful one, and indeed we stand to gain from thinking (also) about how bodies of many varieties, crossing this divide, could dynamically engage. These engagements, motley and fluid, constitute the substance of people's experience of other beasts.

Recent discussions in the fields of posthumanism and animal studies provide further means for problematizing the interaction of humans and nonhumans and the complex position of nonliving animal bodies therein. Heise has probed the presence of artificial animals in contemporary Western culture and their involvement in humans' lived experience and imagination.[63] Surely the historical issues and contexts at stake are distinct, but some of Heise's observations and questions are instructive for our examination of the Aegean animals, indicating more nuanced ways of interrogating nonhuman things for their embeddedness in sociocultural experience. A basis of Heise's discussion of artificial animals is the way in which "technology" "mediates" people's experience of the natural world.[64] In contemporary spaces, this technology already involves and frequently imagines yet further instances of nonliving animals that, in one way or another, perform something understood as lifelike (be that movement, self-replication, responsiveness and so on). The technology through which many of these artificial beings take form has arisen from developments of recent centuries, both realized and hypothetical (e.g., motorized circumlocution, electronic power, robotics, engineered genetic mutation, organ regrowth and manufacture, digital evolution). It would seem, then, that the role of technology in human–animal relations and the relevance of these artificial organisms is incredibly far removed from the Aegean Bronze Age. Yet "technology" is a fluid category, and its involvement in people's experience of animals, including manufactured animal bodies, extends to many sociocultural contexts beyond our present. The term pushes us to probe the fabrication of something, or its status *as fabricated*, and what this implies in its particular moment. Just as available materials and techniques would have been different in the past, so, too, would people's senses of interest, relation and wonder with things created. This could extend to how people experienced a thing to be dynamic, vibrant, even animate. With a remarkably different landscape of materials, discoveries and practices, people of the Bronze Age Aegean may have marveled at life(-likeness) in forms, places and substances quite different from where we identify such. Herva eloquently explores aspects of this in his outline of an "ecological" approach to Minoan visual culture, where he questions whether archaeological evidence indicates that even certain "inanimate" elements of the environment, including stone, in fact may have been experienced as vitalistic.[65] Meanwhile Shapland, following the work of Descola, argues specifically that human relations with nonhumans in Bronze Age Cretan culture were led by a primary "mode of identification" describable as "analogism," in which a division of "the whole collection of existent beings" according to "a multiplicity of essences, forms and substances" is active, yet can be "resolved" through "a dense network of analogies that link together intrinsic properties of the entities that are distinguished in it."[66] For Shapland, like Descola, representational objects, as "depictions of" animals, will shed light on the relations of humans and nonhumans generated by such an ontology. In this situation, given that from the perspective of an analogist mode of identification "all the entities in the world are distinct," "the function of images is to help order them in some way." Hence, images of animals are significant as they serve as *means of connection* between (what are being judged as *more* real) entities.[67]

These are provocative and significant ideas, and, in some respects, they are compatible with the considerations I offer in the chapters ahead. I do feel that we need to leave open our understanding of the specific framework of ontological judgments that would have shaped people's perspectives on animals and animal relations in Bronze Age Crete and the Aegean, and the position of crafted embodiments therein. Hand in hand with this, I advocate, instead, for stepping back to recognize a more fundamental aspect of human–animal engagement that, I believe, is often implicitly overlooked: that people would have directly encountered animals not only as fleshy corpora but also as crafted embodiments. This certainly does not assume that people identified life in fabricated animals or accorded them the same ontological status as biological things. Nor does it claim that people saw renderings of animals in certain specific signifying positions relevant to biological creatures (although surely such significations were active); these matters we cannot ascertain surely, even if considering the possibilities has real merit. In what follows, I at times explore such ideas concerning further possible dimensions of fabricated animalian entities, but these are hypothetical and are announced as such. As a basis underlying such possibilities, we can, however, appreciate that people knew animals in a range of embodiments and, in recognizing this, we can take seriously the work of following through the implications. These fabricated embodiments were met directly, as real, physical figures in engagements with people. Impressions of a species were inevitably informed through these encounters. The impressions formed through engagements with fabricated bodies, like those made when engaging with biological embodiments (if such were known and/or existed), would have contributed to one's broader sense of the species and its similarities and associations with other animals and phenomena. In this respect, the fabricated embodiment, like the biological one, should be recognized itself in a *primary* position in human–animal relations, and not essentially as a referent or connector between other (absent) entities. That is, however else they may have varied in their status, constitution and roles from biological creatures, they were, fundamentally, real animalian presences that were met and contended with as entities in their own right, and which, therewith, directly participated in characterizing specific animals and the animalian ecology more broadly.

For the people engaging with them, certainly these fabricated animals could indicate, or more correctly *realize*, connections with other beasts and phenomena. But we can likewise imagine how an interaction with a biological animal could give rise to such impressions of similarity. Of course, when the embodiment is fabricated, there is the potential for those links to be (perhaps consciously) created and cultivated, as in instances of *formal assonance*, when likeness in form is realized and potentially developed. Morgan has discussed the dynamic of likeness in Aegean visual/material culture from various angles. In a particularly brilliant examination of glyptic objects, she considers how the formal, spatial and relational aspects of an image can be powerfully enriched by open-endedness or "ambiguity"; renderings of animals are prominent in her discussion.[68] Recognition of this quality – of a form being in a sense open to and generative of relations and relational dynamics – underlies my identification of formal assonance and various other types of formal dynamism evident in (and between) Aegean renderings of animals in various media. Morgan's examination is also admirable for cutting straight through the question of intended design to also consider, as equally important, the potentially variable perceptive experiences that people could have with the images. Skeuomorphism, closely considered by Knappett, stands as another crafted relationship through which connections could be dynamically materialized in Aegean material culture. Such rich potentials for realizing connections would have arisen through the primary existence of the fabricated animals as real, present embodiments. This is a basic power of the fabricated beast: to be present as an animal and to shape what the presence of an animal is.

There may be much that we cannot assert confidently about meaning associated with animals in the Bronze Age Aegean. However, there is yet much that we can carefully draw out concerning the specific dynamisms of fabricated embodiments of animals, and how such would have contributed to the particular ways in which animals were experienced as distinctive participants in sociocultural spaces. Such embodied dynamics are not trivial – they realized specific character within the animal's perceived presence that would have been crucial to what and how the animal actually *was*.[69] Character, in this respect, draws together material, social, mechanical and potentially affective aspects of the animalian embodiments: how could they act, engage, condition and potentially excite? Did they afford containment, shelter, surprise, comparison, dependence or agitation? Did they persist in place across sociocultural moments, and how would their affordances have altered across different momentary contexts?

Working from the qualities of material culture outward, Knappett offers a nuanced consideration of the potential efficacies or agencies of objects as they actively participate in human experience, thereby challenging the binary animate/inanimate. His discussion takes in things as varied as cyborgs and Minoan skeuomorphic ceramics, stressing how the potential agency of a thing subtly arises within its momentary relational and environmental contexts – a topic in which consideration of affordances is of course highly relevant and helpful.[70] The efficacy of a thing is experienced in the midst of contexts that are always particular, in interactions that have their own sensorial, emotional and practical character. Objects' contributions can be established or unexpected, can go unremarked upon or might instead invoke wonder and imagination. One is reminded of the lifelike inhabitants of Hephaistos' workshop in *Iliad* 18, not only the pensive golden handmaids, but also the bellows that blow forth air on command and the golden-wheeled tripods that can move of their own accord (*Iliad* 18.373–377, 416–420, 469–473).[71] How might these figures indicate broader experiences of objects as having remarkable active potential, even in quieter, more familiar things? What of the rapid and exacting drive of a stone carver's bow lathe, or a leather flask that swells and contracts as liquid enters and exits its supple belly? In such things, we again see how people's engagements with their world and its diverse inhabitants may not correspond to the binaries we expect and project (animate/inanimate, organic/inorganic, real/artificial, animal/object); or, just as importantly, they can supersede and draw connections across them in fascinating ways. When dynamic things are also embodiments of animals – such as a rhyton in the form of a bull's head that issues liquid through its muzzle, or a seal engraved with a lion that sinks into clay to form impressions – its potential animacy becomes animalian.

Problematizing the dynamic experiences of both likeness and incongruity that representational entities entail becomes distinctly important in the context of renderings of animals. This complication arises, in part, from the unique human experience of engaging with a living nonhuman. Payne examines how a person's relation to other animals involves, even necessitates imagination. It is through imagination, he explains, that one does more than acknowledge and describe the living status of an animal. One instead contemplates its existence as a "life" and, through this, senses its relation to humans.[72] In his now classic discussion, Berger also gets at the em-/sympathetic relation of humans to nonhuman animals when he describes the uncanny recognition people can feel in the presence of another beast, a recognition that is intense and potentially disquieting, emotional and physical.[73] While Berger sees this dynamic between humans and nonhumans as being especially active in the preindustrial world, he also offers vivid recollections of how his own experiences sharing the gaze of a beast pulsated with such jarring intensity. One is reminded here of Derrida's description of the great discomfort he experienced being naked under his cat's watchful eye.[74] There are ways in which this sensation can be compared to the uncanniness felt when a nonliving thing is experienced by a human as lifelike, something that extends toward the alienation of the hyperreal.[75] This experience is sometimes measured and analyzed in its replicative dimensions with notions such as the Uncanny Valley and Turing Test; phenomena such as Reborn Dolls manipulate along these lines, sometimes to highly emotional ends.[76] At its core, the experience does not necessarily arise from a straightforward instance of replication. Indeed, the sense of simultaneous sameness and insoluble incongruity experienced between humans and other living animals echoes the tension inherent in representation that we discussed above – not representation in an imitational sense, but as a matter of multiple kinds of embodiment potentially holding parity with one another while also being substantively distinct. Between such multiple embodiments of an entity (whether representational or nonrepresentational), as between humans and nonhuman animals, this relation is one of identity between this and that, here and there, what is and what is non-. When the representation is also an embodiment of an animal, these echoing experiences coincide in a distinctly moving way, since the human, as an(other) animal, is always implicated. The "nonhuman" status of both objects and animals is one in these entities, in part through the ways that both can be experienced as being, also, human-like.

That a fabricated embodiment of an animal will always be inescapably different from a biological one, despite their potentially moving similarity, is not a shortcoming in representational capacity, but a distinction in character. In substance, persistence, affect and affordance, the fabricated creature differs, arising from practices and interests that lace this animalian body with human relation from the inside out. From its moment of generation onward, the fabricated animal will also have unique relations with other phenomena, beyond its engagements with humans, and these will be as crucial to its existence (e.g., relations with moisture, sediment, the sun, materials that surround and penetrate it, plants, other organisms, things and so on).[77] This universe of relations contributes to the thing's reality over time, a reality that involves human input but also exceeds it. Artificial animals are always bodies where imagination and realization are one, where even the most straightforward rendering is inherently the offspring of a present that integrates human creativity, accident and a momentary environment replete with myriad interactors. Hence, its ongoing relational potential is unique, as a thing and as a body.

NOTES

1. Evans 1921: 28. See extensive discussion of "naturalism" in Shapland 2022: 212–220.
2. See, for example, Hitchcock and Koudounaris 2002; Papadopoulos 2005; Hamilakis and Momigliano 2006; Eller 2012; Shapland 2022.
3. For example, Evans 1928: 362, and his characterization of the iconography of the griffin as a back and forth of influence between Egypt and the Aegean (1921: 709–714; discussed in Chapter 4).

4. Evans 1928.1: 361.

5. See stimulating discussions of Minoan Crete's modern lives in Hamilakis and Momigliano 2006.

6. See valuable recent discussion in Shapland 2022.

7. Evans 1921: 24–25.

8. For example, in discussion of the presumed Cretan origin of the "flying gallop" pose, Evans asserts: "their [the Cretans'] Egyptian contemporaries proved themselves wholly unable to depict any rapid form of animal movement" (1921: 714).

9. For example, as powerfully discussed by Groenewegen-Frankfort 1951.

10. See Doumas 1992 for overview of site history and presentation of the frescoes.

11. On the history and problems of the modern concept of "Minoan" society, see, for example, Hamilakis 2002, and now Shapland 2022. My use here of the term "Minoan" acknowledges that we are working under the burden and limitations of such modern classifications. I use "Minoan" to recognize strong elements of sharedness between material–cultural evidence from numerous locales in Crete and the southern Aegean between ca. 2500 and 1400 BCE, but *not* to indicate (or assume) that these areas were part of a single social formation – or that cultural life between these spaces was the selfsame. I consider indications of both similarity and difference between contexts.

12. Marinatos 1993.

13. Rehak 1999.

14. For example, Chapin 2004; Vlachopoulos 2008; Morgan 1995b.

15. For example, Kantor 1947. Kantor's pioneering study laid the groundwork for many later considerations.

16. Unless otherwise indicated, I use "species" here to refer to a distinguishable class or kind of animal; this does not necessarily align with modern zoological classificatory notions (see Shapland 2022: 40 concerning such in relation to the Bronze Age Aegean). Consequently, the parameters of a species would depend on the perspectives of the group or person encountering the animals. Our focus should be on indications of consistent features across crafted embodiments, recognizing the input of the medium. In the context of discussions of particular material, I consider how the contours of a given species may have arisen, varied and changed.

17. Within the present study, my reference to the "broad eastern Mediterranean" includes the sociocultural formations of the Aegean, Egypt and western southwest Asia. At times I will also include (as indicated) cultures focused farther inland. It is understood that sociocultural boundaries were not hard and fast, and that a broader ambit of cultures could become incorporated in the eastern Mediterranean sphere through interaction.

18. See references in Chapter 2.

19. See Morgan 1995a.

20. This concerns glyptic from Neopalatial Kato Zakros in eastern Crete. See Anastasiadou 2016a; Weingarten 1983, 1985; and discussion in Chapter 4.

21. Shapland 2022.

22. Morgan (1989) discusses such ambiguity with great astuteness and McGowan's recent (2011, 2018) writing on ambiguity in Minoan glyptic provides important problematization of these subjects (see Chapter 5 for discussion).

23. For discussion of the interpretive aspects of representation in art and archaeology, see Tilley, Hamilton, and Bender 2000.

24. The scholarly literature on the matter of representation is of course massive. Important studies include, among many others, Ruskin 1971 [1857]; Auerbach 1953; Korzybski 1958; Gombrich 1960; Noë 2004 (with which I engage below).

25. On these ideas, see esp. Keuls 1978, who also engages with further important sources.

26. Recent work on the history of the term and notion of "reproduction" demonstrates similar variability; see Hopwood 2018.

27. The insects could also be wasps. Demargne 1930, pl. 19.

28. In their superb characterization of the sensory complexity of this ornament, Simandiraki-Grimshaw and Stevens (2012: 600–601) instead stress the successful imitation of living insects it performs, writing that it "closely imitates the behavior of actual buzzing, hovering, bobbing and mating of these animals"; they suggest that its sound may have inspired a sense of danger to the wearer.

29. For recent discussion of Gell's impact, see chapters in Küchler and Carroll 2020.

30. Brown 2001: 4.

31. For example, Miller 2008, 2010, the latter of which takes the turn to consider "stuff"; Malafouris 2013, 2020; Henare, Holbraad, and Wastell 2007; Gosden and Larson 2007; Webmoor and Witmore 2008; Wylie 2002.

32. Heidegger 1967, especially 15–16, as part of a broader consideration of things, which also examines the complexity of things as being *vorhanden* or "present-at-hand." The rendering of the German *Jediesheit* as "being-this-one" and of *vorhanden* as "present-at-hand" or "existing" are from this 1967 translation of Heidegger's essay by Barton and Deutsch.

33. See also, for example, Webmoor and Witmore 2008.

34. The contributions of these scholars cannot be elided. Their ideas have been pivotal in establishing approaches that are frequently in dialogue with one another and, as such, help form the basis of this region of archaeological problematization. A debate in the 2007 issue of *Archaeological Dialogues* (14.1) between Ingold, Tilley and Knappett, concerning approaches to materials and materiality, highlights such productive engagement between differing perspectives. For meaty surveys of trends in materials and material culture studies, see Tilley, Kuechler-Fogden; and Keane 2006; Knappett 2010; Hodder 2012. See also Ingold 2000; Tilley 2004; Gosden 2005; Drazin and Küchler 2015.

35. See, for example, Hamilakis 2014; Tilley 2004; Knappett 2004; Thomas 2006; Ingold 2000; Herva 2006; Ihde and Malafouris 2019.

36. Discussions of object biography and agency have been embedded in many studies and have also formed a primary focus; see, for example, works by Latour (e.g., 1990, 1993, 2013); Gell 1998; Kopytoff 1986; Knappett 2002; Gosden 2005; Knappett and Malafouris 2008; Joy 2009; and debate in *Archaeological Dialogues* issues 22–26 between Lindstrøm, Ribeiro and Sørensen.

37. On this, see, for example, Latour 1990 (esp. 7–8), 2007.

38. For lucid discussions of what this approach advocates, including connections to Bloor's (1976) notion of symmetry, see contributions by Witmore, Webmoor, Olsen and Shanks in *World Archaeology* 39.4.

39. For example, Renfrew and Zubrow 1994; DeMarrais, Gosden, and Renfrew 2004; Renfrew, Frith, and Malafouris 2009; Abramiuk 2012; Henley, Rossano, and Kardas 2019; Currie and Killin 2019; Barona 2021.

40. See, for example, Malafouris 2008, 2010, 2013, 2020.

41. For example, Hutchins 2005; Warnier 2006; Witmore 2012; Lemonnier 2016, also Henare, Holbraad, and Wastell 2007.

42. Knappett 2020: 98.

43. See especially Poursat 2008, 2014.

44. For example, Knappett 2004, 2020.

45. For example, Miller 2008 on the potential comfort of things.

46. Knappett's development of Gibson's thoughts on affordances, especially concerning "transparency"(2004: 46), could give ground for thinking fruitfully beyond intent.

47. Noë 2004: 216.

48. Noë 2004: 165.

49. Noë (2004: 175–176) refers to (and critiques) Ruskin's characterization of painting as involving "what may be called the *innocence of the eye*; that is to say, a sort of childish perception of these flat stains of color, merely as such, without consciousness of what they signify – as a blind man would see them if suddenly gifted with sight [1856] [*sic*] 1971: 27)."

50. These ideas are developed throughout Noë 2004; chapters 2 and 5 are especially relevant.

51. Noë 2004: 222–223.
52. Noë 2004: 193–194; also 187.
53. Noë 2004: 177–178, engaging with the ideas of Pinker (1997) and Hayes and Ross (1995).
54. Noë 2004: 178.
55. Beardsworth and Bryman 2001.
56. Alden 2005: 340–342; cf. Berger 1980.
57. Beardsworth and Bryman 2001: 86–87.
58. Corbett 2006.
59. Defining an animal's "natural environment" can be challenging, since the encounter indicates at least some level of human interference in the context.
60. Berger 1980: 4–5, 23–28.
61. Shapland 2022: 62–63.
62. Derrida, Mallet, and Wills 2008.
63. Heise 2003, 2009.
64. Heise 2003, 75.
65. Herva 2006.
66. Shapland 2022: 39, quoting Descola 2013: 201.
67. Shapland 2022: 46, 62.
68. Morgan 1989; see also, for example, Morgan 1995b on parallelism.
69. Following Noë's characterization of perception.
70. Knappett 2002.
71. See Morris 1995.
72. Payne 2010: esp. 13–22.
73. Berger 1980.
74. Derrida and Wills 2002, and discussion in Payne 2010.
75. Baudrillard 1981.
76. Reborn Dolls are created by artists who assemble and paint premanufactured doll body parts to resemble lifelike human infants; see www.reborns.com.
77. See Harman 2018, Ingold's work (e.g., 2000).

TWO

CRAFTINESS AND PRODUCTIVITY IN BODILY THINGS

The Changing Contexts of Cretan Zoomorphic Vessels

BODIES POLITIC

That bodies are political entities is an uncontroversial assertion, even if how bodies participate in political action is a complex and knotty matter. Human bodies, as community members, are the basis of political practice in a fundamental sense, yet the particular nature of the relationship between the body and the collective political realm can vary profoundly. This concerns matters of inclusion and exclusion, but also how certain bodies are recognized, invested with specific power, given freedoms, made to conform or produce. They can resist or facilitate, cooperate or act alone. In some cases, the individual body, as such, can be understood to have a very particular relationship to sociopolitical institutions – as a vessel, as a metaphor, as an analogue and so on. From the ancient world to the present day, this relationship has been embodied, contemplated, debated and analyzed through a diversity of means.[1]

Attempts to locate individual persons' bodies and their sociopolitical lives in the prehistoric archaeological record are often thwarted by a lack of resolution at this scale.[2] In this respect, Prepalatial Crete (ca. 3000–1900 BCE) is something of an exception. Much of our archaeological data from Prepalatial Crete stem from funerary contexts, which have been used to approach various aspects of sociopolitical life. Given the readiness with which funerary contexts can seem to speak of individual humans, the bodies of Cretan community members have been, in certain senses, more present in interpretations of social experience during this period than in those concerning later moments in the prehistory of the island for which we actually have more settlement data.[3] How the body has been approached has varied considerably. Once scholars moved beyond the penchant for romantic reconstructions of individual figures that earlier archaeological studies sometimes tendered, considerations of the body became more evidence-based and self-conscious.[4] In terms of data from funerary contexts in early Crete, recent studies have approached the sociopolitical body through close analysis of extant human remains, as well as through indicators of microenvironmental conditions with which a person's experience in a specific community setting can be problematized; recent work at a number of cemeteries demonstrates the potential fruits of such approaches.[5] Spatial dimensions of people's bodily movements within and between arenas of social action have also been examined.[6] In other cases, studies have focused on extant material culture that seems to imply the individual person, physically and/or socioculturally, and its scale of action and participation in community life – objects of adornment and identification, such as seals and jewelry, have been prominent in these approaches.[7] Hamilakis' exploration of the peculiar sensorial dimensions of biological human presence (both living and dead) within Prepalatial tholos tombs, and how such would have been part of potent community experiences, was path-breaking. His work examines the unity of bodily and sociopolitical experience during this period in new light.[8] Beyond tomb contexts alone, numerous studies have interrogated crafted renderings of human bodies for indications of living humans' corporeal experiences; studies of figurines have been especially notable.[9] My discussion shares aims with many of these approaches, especially concerning the experiential dynamics that took form between biological and crafted bodies, and the cultural and microsociopolitical implications of such. Yet my focus shifts more to problematizing the *non*human nature of particular bodily things. The open-endedness of the term "nonhuman" is important here. I intend it to embrace both artificial bodies that present in some ways as human-like and the bodies (biological and artificial) of animals beyond the human species. I am interested in how these categories coincide in certain objects, and the unique effect of that coincidence. More broadly, I am concerned with how certain renderings of creaturely bodies as things, including objects that have been identified with both human and nonhuman species, bring distinctive dynamisms to animals' presence in community worlds.

My discussion begins with a group of Prepalatial Cretan objects that are most frequently described as anthropomorphic vessels. I investigate their particular physical, material, mechanical and interactive characters, with a focus on their potential for distinctive "body techniques" that could variously engage or deemphasize living humans who interacted with the vessel bodies. Thus the fact that these things were experienced *as bodies* becomes extremely important for understanding their entangled practical and social dimensions. Problematizing them, in part, through certain notions developed around and often reserved for biological humans can help us to freshly consider the performance of these object-bodies, and how that performance both coincided with and profoundly diverged from that of living people in their company. Of equal focus are the objects' contexts, both material and sociopolitical. Working with their depositional settings as well as current discussions of social organization and community life in Bronze Age Crete, I investigate the participation of these other bodies in venues of collective action. By foregrounding the corporeal status of the objects and, with this, their rich *inter*corporeal dynamics, new matters of relation arise. I suggest that to really appreciate the particularity of what these partially human-form vessels afforded as participants in social contexts, we in fact need to view them more broadly as *zoomorphic*, opening the door for new comparisons and insights across species.[10]

Working in the broader light of zoomorphic objects, my discussion turns next to examining developments in the physical character of animal-form vessels and related media as Crete progressed from the Prepalatial to palatial phases. I closely consider a growing prevalence during the Neopalatial period of vessels that embody only part of an animal, the head; cattle heads are especially numerous. I argue that such changes in the bodily character of animalian things would have poignantly contributed to sociopolitical reformulations on the island by altering the corporeal dynamics of key ritual actions. I further consider these objects within the particular lived environments of their time – social and natural. Given the prevalence of bovine objects, I examine the holistic dynamics of "cattle culture" during this moment, taking in interactions with biological and thingly bodies alike, and consider how the notable *craftiness* involved with both would have contributed to the identity of cattle and their recontextualization in palatial Crete.

OF KIN GROUPS, CLAY AND FLESH

In the early twentieth century CE, Cretan society was in a period of labored redefinition. The island's modern population was enduring a tumultuous transition from Ottoman rule to a tense marriage with the Great Powers, and eventually to union with the young nation state of Greece. The prehistoric past of the island was caught up in these political and cultural throes, as another nascent sociopolitical entity. While informal and smaller-scale archaeological investigations had taken place on Crete previously, by local and foreign figures, the first decades of the new century brought both intensified motivations to formulate the island's past and altered social circumstances in which the undertaking would be facilitated.[11] In this context, Stephanos Xanthoudidēs, a scholar born in Crete and educated there and in Athens, undertook a series of excavations throughout the southern Mesara Plain of Crete. The excavations explored multiple monumental stone tombs constructed and used throughout the Prepalatial period, from the EBA to the early MBA. These "tholos" tombs, characterized by a distinctive vaulted form, were collective and multigenerational, their use sometimes spanning centuries. They, and further tombs throughout south-central Crete and other regions of the island, have become vital to our understanding of the Prepalatial phase and the objects and spaces that characterized it. Xanthoudidēs' work remains a crucial resource for anyone working in this period.

Within the material culture Xanthoudidēs recovered in his early excavations of the tholos tombs at Koumasa, published in 1924, were several extraordinary clay objects. Xanthoudidēs described these as anthropomorphic vases. The best preserved, HM 4137, was found in the area between three tholos tombs at the site (Figure 2.1).[12] It stands 16 cm high. In outline, the body is trapezoidal, with broad, rather sharply angled shoulders that gently taper downward and inward to the base. The region through the shoulders is narrow in profile but widens toward a flat base that has an ovoid footprint. The overall form of the body is that of a hollow, narrow bell, closed at the bottom. A solid spade-shaped protrusion upward from the line of the shoulders forms a head. The front of the head has been drawn out into a T-shaped ridge suggesting the brow and rhinal crest; three inclined triangular planes meet along the sides and top of this ridge. Two of these planes constitute the sides of the face and contain indentations forming eyes. The third and upper plane widens back from the brow ridge into a slightly curved triangle that forms the top of the head; it has been painted red. A conical projection emerges from the left shoulder of the body, widening upward. It is open and takes the shape of a small jug or vessel; its bottom is fused into the body of the figure who seems to hold it. The interior of this miniature jug communicates with the hollow interior of the whole vessel body – this is, in fact, the only opening in the entire object.

Two thin ropes of clay, painted with fine red dashes, have been added to the object. One originates at the neck, outlines the top edge of the right shoulder and then angles downward across the side of the torso. The other rope roughly parallels the placement of the first, beginning behind the miniature jug that is positioned at the figure's left shoulder, wrapping around it and downward across the left side of the torso. The identity of these rope features is rather unclear, at least to modern eyes. They are suggestive of thin arms, one of which would hold the jar at the left shoulder, but they also appear serpentine; both interpretations have been proffered.[13] In the upper center of the front of the body, two small pellets have been affixed, presumably constituting nipples or simple breasts. A pair of delicate clay bands ring the front of the neck and may be taken as necklaces. The object-body is a light buff color, and red paint has

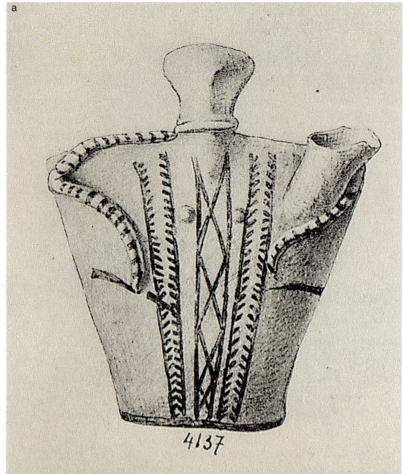

2.1. Body-form vessels from Prepalatial Koumasa. a. Drawing of Vessel 4137. b. Photograph of Vessels 4139, 4137, 4138 and 4993. From Xanthoudidēs 1924, pls. II and XIX. Herakleion Museum. Objects © Hellenic Ministry of Culture and Sports

been added in linear and geometric patterns on the front and back. On the front, along the central vertical axis of the body and running between the breasts, a narrow panel of bounded X-motifs extends from neck to base. It is flanked by double-lined panels, each line of which is fringed with short projections directed inward. On the back of the figure, red painted lines swoop from the base of the neck to the sides of the body, creating arcs. A simple vertical handle has been placed precisely in the middle of the back; it is not visible when facing the object from the front.[14]

In addition to HM 4137, Xanthoudidēs found three highly comparable yet less well-preserved corporeal vessels at Koumasa (HM 4138, 4139, 4993; Figure 2.1).[15] These range in size, two being smaller (HM 4139, HM 4993) and one larger (HM 4138) than HM 4137. The head is missing on two of these (HM 4193 and HM 4138). Along with strong similarity in their overall body form, certain finer details preserved on these vessels also closely recall those of HM 4137. These include an added striped rope element that drapes across the shoulders of HM 4139, and linear motifs painted on the front of 4138. All except HM 4138 have an aperture set in the shoulder, like HM 4137 (Warren is likely correct in asserting that the aperture of HM 4138 would have been in the figure's head).[16] Like HM 4137, the figure of HM 4993 has a smaller cylindrical vessel-like form integrated at its left shoulder, which, here too, provides the sole opening into the whole object. An applied ridge in the body of HM 4993 wraps around and below this small secondary vessel, as if it is an arm supporting it. The ridge originates on the back of the figure, behind the small vessel set at the shoulder, and runs around its left side toward the lower chest area; this is the same location in which one of the striped rope features is located on HM 4137, where a supporting arm also seems suggested.[17]

Since Xanthoudidēs' discovery of these vessels, five further Prepalatial objects, each very similar to the Koumasa jug-holders, have been found at sites around Crete, including Trapeza Cave, Ayios Myron, Yiofyrakia, and Archanes-Phourni (Figure 2.2).[18] In addition, three other vessels have come to light, each clearly akin to this group but differing in certain interesting ways (Branigan and Warren established this wider corpus of vessels, which has since been discussed and developed by others).[19] In 1969, Warren's team at the Early Minoan (EM) II site of Myrtos Fournou Korifi uncovered a distinctive corporeal vessel in a settlement context (ANM 7719; Figure 2.3).[20] It sits just over 21 cm high. Its body has a bell shape like the Koumasa vessels, but here it is much more inflated, almost globular. A remarkably long cylindrical neck extends narrowly upward from the rounded shoulders, ending in a petite head with clear eyes, pronounced ears and a beak-like nose – Cadogan describes this small head as "virtually a pinhead in relation to the rest of the figure."[21] A long, slender right arm crosses the body to meet the other arm at the articulated handle of a well-formed tiny jug, clutched to the figure's left shoulder; as noted by others, this miniature jug appears nearly identical to full-size EM II ceramic vessels from Myrtos Fournou Korifi and the broader region.[22] As with the other anthropomorphic vessels, this miniature jug communicates with the interior of the entire hollow object and provides its only

2.2. a. Photograph of Prepalatial body-form vessel found at Trapeza Cave (Agios Nikolaos Museum, 9399). Photograph from Warren 1973: pl XXI.3. Courtesy of Peter Warren. b. Body-form vessel from Area of the Rocks, Archanes Phourni (Herakleion Museum, ΗΜΠ 25770). Photograph from Sakellarakis, Yannis and Efi Sapouna-Sakellaraki, *Archanes: Minoan Crete in a New Light* (Athens: Ammos Publications, 1997), 540 fig. 538. Courtesy of Efi Sapouna-Sakellaraki. Objects © Hellenic Ministry of Culture and Sports

opening. A number of geometric hatched panels have been painted in red on the figure's body, perhaps indicating textiles or anatomy; painted single lines with herringbone-like projections run up the sides. These red-on-buff linear markings are broadly similar to what we see on the vessels from Koumasa. There is no handle on the Myrtos figure.

From Mochlos and Malia, we have two vessels much like the others described, except that these do not clutch jugs but instead have pierced breasts (HM 3499, from Mochlos, Figure 2.5; HM 8665, from Malia, Figure 2.4).[23] The vessel from Mochlos is, as Warren states, "the most anthropomorphic" of the bunch.[24] Notable is the smooth band that encircles the head, punctuated only by a single bulb. The band could be some sort of hair garment, cap or, in Warren's view, a snake.[25] It appears somewhat similar to the formation of the top of the head area on HM 4993, from Koumasa, where a ring-like character is also apparent. The Mochlos figure cups her breasts with her hands, each of which is carefully articulated with delicate fingers. Intricate linear motifs painted in white cover the dark reddish ground of the vessel body. These take the form of a band around the neck and horizontal lines across the upper chest, while paneled motifs, hatched and with s-spirals, are visible on the lower body; the painted elaboration is comparable to that of the Koumasa and Myrtos corporeal vessels, although the colors are inverted. The face of the Mochlos figure

2.3. Body-form vessel from Prepalatial Myrtos Fournou Korifi (Agios Nikolaos Museum, 7719). a. Photo by Zde (CC BY-SA 4.0). b. and c. From Warren 1972: pl. 69. Photos courtesy of Peter Warren. Objects © Hellenic Ministry of Culture and Sports

has been subtly formed, with a gentle brow ridge, slight concavities in the eye areas, a small mouth protuberance and a finely modeled nose.

While the visage of the Mochlos body vessel seems human, the one from Malia appears only somewhat humanoid. A dramatic contrast is effected on the body between bold white linear designs and the gray ground of the object. These painted designs run in curving strips and panels of hatching, zigzags and rectilinear components, filling the surface. The area of white painting extends around the figure's back, shoulders and arms to then almost meet – or part, as if opening – on the front of the torso, between the breasts. Four painted bands are positioned at the neck of the figure, suggestive of draping textile or necklaces. A strip of hatched rectangles extends along the base, as if trim on a garment (this area of the vessel is fragmentary). The face is striking in its simplicity. The eyes,

2.4. Prepalatial body-form vessel from Malia (Herakleion Museum 8665). Photo by Olaf Tausch (CC BY 3.0). Object © Hellenic Ministry of Culture and Sports

2.5. Prepalatial body-form vessel from Mochlos (Herakleion Museum 5499). Photo by Olaf Tausch (CC BY 3.0). Object © Hellenic Ministry of Culture and Sports

heavily ringed in white, are large and pronounced, filling the concave sides of the face. These concavities meet in a sharply projecting rhinal ridge that dominates the center of the face. A small painted strip connects the eyes across the top of the rhinal ridge; no other facial features are present. The top of the head is formed as a wreathlike ring with incised striations, perhaps representing a cap or hair, which broadly parallels the characterization of the head of the Mochlos vessel and HM 4993 from Koumasa. The limbs of the Malia figure are not articulated as arms but instead rise in wing-like draped masses from the sides of the vessel. This object, like the one from Mochlos and the majority of the others, has a vertical handle on its back.

IN WHOSE HANDS?

I wish to draw out several distinctive and interrelated features of these peculiar object-bodies that would have dynamically impacted their performative character. First is that, in each case, the objects can stand on their own, without the aid of human hands, a quality that sets them apart in the broader sphere of anthropomorphic objects from Prepalatial Crete. It is their peculiar, flaring body shapes that afford this independent deportment, with their rotund frames extending unimpeded downward to the surface upon which they sit – indeed there is only one example where feet have been added (Archanes 1; Figure 2.2b).[26] Related to this ability to sit – or stand – on their own is the fact that each of these clay bodies could hold a liquid. This might seem unremarkable, but it is a corporeal affordance that, quite significantly, is not shared by other contemporaneous representations of humans, notably figurines (a distinction also noted by Simandiraki-Grimshaw).[27] This capacity also distinguishes our objects from animal-form rhyta with upper and lower orifices, which could momentarily shape the flow of liquid, but could not hold it over time. Having the ability to hold liquids thus impacted both the basic nature and the *temporality* of our clay figures, extending their performative capacity indefinitely, between the moments of being filled and emptied. In the interim these were bodies – like our own – with liquid in their bellies. In this vein, Simandiraki-Grimshaw argues that some of the Cretan "anthropomorphic" vessels "provided metaphors for the biological body" and that the liquid contents could have been considered "an integral part" of the vessels.[28] However, we can also consider how the presence of fluid naturally would have had notably distinct effects within the clay bodies, and that these effects would have been highly significant to the bodies' character. The *changeable* (and hence nonintegral) presence of the liquid in the clay bodies was part of what crucially distinguished their particular corporeal dynamism – as animalian entities that could be similar to biological bodies but were also characterized by remarkably different qualities that crossed statuses and occupied unique ground. With each of these bodies, fluids held inside would have markedly affected the quality and distribution of its weight, lightening the figure and bringing it a responsive variability that would react to each movement, angle and rhythm that engaged it – responses that distinguished these thingly bodies from the biological beings to which they were related. More fundamentally, receiving and holding liquid charged their participation in a social context with a powerful and unique potential energy that could be drawn out toward their performative climax. The ability to fully empty of liquid (and then to fill, hold and empty again) arose from the peculiar existence of these figures, as both objects *and* bodies, and surely was elemental to their particular identity and presence. It did not weaken their capacity for metaphor, but instead strengthened their status as bodies that were both relatable and distinct.

In the kinetic moment of decanting, these figures would strikingly take responsibility for the stream of liquids. This is because, in each example, the current of liquid would actually be seen to originate out of something handled by the figure: in ten instances, the figure uses a jug; in two, its breasts. These are the means through which the liquid would emerge, appearing as the immediate yield of the clay figure's effort instead of a fleshy living human's. Indeed, while the whole clay body is also a thing that we could refer to as a vase, there seems to be an attempt to distance this aspect of its identity from its performances. A vase is something that an animate agent can manipulate to bring forth a liquid. Here, that productive manipulative agency is literally put in the hands of the clay figures. The ability of these object-bodies to hold a liquid over time would have afforded further potency to their autonomy as producers: if a living human's act of filling the clay vessel was concealed – removed in time and perhaps space from the performative context in which it brought forth liquid – the clay bodies would, in that later moment, appear to generate the liquid of their own accord as they decanted. In some cases, the filling may in fact have been a separate moment of performance, in which the clay body was seen to actively receive liquid, for example, if added into the miniature jugs held by several of the figures.[29] In each instance of subsequent decanting, there would be a clear emphasis on the figure's independence as a productive body, as liquids appeared through its own corporeal undertakings.

Specific formal details of the objects support this impression of independence. In most of the examples where the body holds a miniature jug, that small vessel provides the only opening in the whole object, through which all liquid would have to enter or exit. With this, the entry into the larger clay body is effectively hidden. The lack of a pronounced vessel mouth or spout, as such, effectively erased the status of receptacle/pouring device from the clay body's persistent physical form. With this, there was no formal contradiction to the clay figure's bringing-forth on its own and no suggestion that the diminutive vessel held by the figure is but a secondary ornamental novelty. This establishes the integrity of the miniature vessel and dramatically legitimates the figure itself. In other words, the *miniature* jug is made the primary vessel and the clay body the principal agent.

In the two cases where liquid is instead produced through pierced breasts, there is in fact another opening in the object, presumably for filling, but it is discreetly located on the back of the head, behind the raised ridge of the cap or hair, such that it would not be readily visible to those who faced the clay being. The fact that most of the objects have handles is also relevant. In each of these cases, the handle extends from the back of the figure, opposite to the direction in which the clay figure faces. With this, the living human hand that would grasp the handle to tip the vessel bodies, enabling them to decant, would in a sense be removed from the action, discreetly kept behind the scenes instead of visibly gripping around and manipulating the small body. The handles are situated in this way, inconspicuously behind the figure, even if that position does not correspond to the axis along which the objects would be inclined to pour – this suggests that the issue of concealing the handle's (and the hand's) visibility from a person facing the figure was foremost. Hence, various features of these objects could cleverly obscure the living human's role in providing the liquid or in motivating its reappearance. Instead, the uncanny clay body would be experienced as unusually, movingly animate and independent – not as a device employed, but as an active and productive participant.

The erasure or concealment of the living human's role in conjunction with these small bodies could have been motivated by a variety of interests or beliefs concerning the status of the clay bodies, their makers or the people who engaged with the objects. I do not want to venture into readings of the specific meaning that their independence carried in Crete. It is however worth noting that in other contemporaneous cultural traditions within the broader region, we have evidence of fabricated bodies being actively distanced, even divorced from the work of human hands. In late third- to early second-millennium Mesopotamia, certain anthropomorphic cult statues of deities were accorded great autonomy, effected through remarkable means. The statues were considered true embodiments of the divine. The hands of the craftspersons who manufactured the statues were to be cut off, severing human agency from the divine bodies by extinguishing the mortal flesh that had fashioned the forms. The treatment of the statues – from "mouth opening" ceremonies to their daily feedings of perishable food offerings – were ritually prescribed and recognized the crafted bodies as vital beings in their own right.[30] We certainly cannot assume that such status surrounded the Cretan body vessels. Their corporeal autonomy and apparent agency were realized in distinctive ways, and they were embedded within different cultural contexts. Yet it is important to keep in mind the richness of sociocultural traditions that potentially surrounded people's interactions with these unique crafted bodies, realizing their extraordinary affordances.

Simandiraki-Grimshaw has undertaken investigations of the ergonomics of the Cretan body vessels.[31] Her work crucially reminds us of the potential variability in human engagements with such things – indeed, there was not one way to hold them, but multiple, afforded by the peculiarities of the object-bodies and their contextualized relations with different human hands. The presence and dexterity[32] of larger, fleshy hands, and their role in the movements of the smaller, clay bodies, could be more or less remarkable, the performative effect of the vessels being altered and intonated therewith. The clay figures, like the humans who held them, varied in size and character. It could be that particular ways of filling, holding and decanting were learned as traditional skills surrounding these peculiar things (this certainly would not preclude improvisation in the realization of such actions). In this light, it is especially important to consider how these objects *were* and how they acted *across* moments – as bodies expressively standing on their own and as bodies engaging with different bodies, in variable environments. What was it that they themselves brought to the table (and to the hand)?

TECHNIQUES OF PECULIAR BODIES

That objects and materials have the potential to dynamically engage and inform human experience, in unpredictable as well as intended ways, is a matter that has received a great deal of attention in recent years, notably through questions of "object agency" and material ontologies.[33] While it is important to recognize and problematize such active potential in material culture broadly, it is of course always actually experienced in particular contours, textures, contexts and interactions. It is in this particularity that the dynamic character of an object is realized. Hence, it is incredibly significant that our clay vessels, their abilities and affordances, were articulated in corporeal form, including in bodily attributes that are distinctively human-like: these were *bodies* that were animated – bodies that in parts were familiar to the humans who engaged with them. At the same time, they were always also fundamentally unlike the human bodies that surrounded them. I will return to this tension in the next section but wish now to closely consider how the clay bodies' capacities for distinctive animations would have been experienced.

The impression that these little bodies could autonomously produce liquid may have been quite moving, even wondrous, to living persons who shared a social context with them. Wonder can be found in a wide diversity of traits and circumstances. It can be felt when confronting something unexpected, unprecedented. But that probably was not the case here. If these clay bodies could inspire wonder in their performative autonomy, it was through movements and abilities that likely were expected, traditional and established – even if acutely extraordinary. A person in the presence of one of the vessels would be able to predict the animation to come. Even in the case of someone who was seeing one of the vessels for the first time, the open jugs the figures carry, or their pierced breasts, may have been gazed upon with anticipation of fluid's imminent appearance. These features were familiar sociophysical phenomena, known from people's daily lived experience to have certain affordances. This familiarity with the secondary attributes (jars, breasts) would have contributed to the power invested in the whole clay bodies: people's engagements with them were charged with expectant energy. Beyond the anticipation that such attributes elicited, these clay bodies may have been established presences in their communities, who were seen in action time and again. Moreover, the fact that we already have numerous contemporaneous Cretan clay vessels that share these distinctive corporeal characteristics indicates that people between Cretan communities (even between the sociocultural spaces of different regions) may have approached these objects with a knowledge of what they were and what they could do. In other words, these not only were bodies in possession of iconic cues that conjured familiar experiences involving liquid; they themselves likely were also established (if remarkable) material forms, associated with certain characteristic and hence foreseeable capabilities. Thus, it was not *what* they were doing that was extraordinary, but *their doing*.

Mauss' foundational notion of "body techniques" provides an unexpectedly powerful means for thinking about the actions of these object-bodies. Mauss develops the idea of body techniques to get at the cultural specificity of the movements, "attitudes," "habits" and "mechanical" processes undertaken by bodies. He stresses the external derivation of these techniques, arguing that even bodily actions as basic as sleeping and walking are in fact carried out through particular movements that do not emerge "naturally" in the individual body but are, somehow and variably, "transmitted" to it from its social and material world.[34] As such, these techniques are in some sense learned and hence repeated, their iterability being at the core of their very nature. At the same time, these movements can be specific to certain bodies or groups of bodies within a society (Mauss gives examples that are differentiated by age, gender and occupation)[35] and can involve the engagement of multiple bodies with one another;[36] they entail and solicit specific social engagements. They are thus familiar, predictable and traditional, but also keenly compelling and efficacious. They are a realization of a body's social existence in a lived world, and they contribute to realizing its identity therein.

Mauss' discussion embraces the potential involvement of nonhuman entities – including other animalian beings and material culture – in the body techniques of people but also opens the door for stepping in a further, reciprocal direction. That nonhuman animals can impact our culturally specific and regularly experienced movements can be comfortably recognized. One obvious example would be instances where horse riding is a principal means of transportation or farming, and the beast is central to the human's bodily practices involved therein. Likewise, we are increasingly appreciative of how objects can be active elements of the particular movements, attitudes and dispositions of the human body, and its felt sociocultural experience, in myriad ways.[37] Mauss discusses, for example, how shoes "transform the position of feet," impacting our gait, our ambulatory habits and character – something also discussed more recently by Ingold.[38] Think also of how a chair or hammer impacts the basic nature of sitting or making (clearly relevant here is the work of Heidegger and Sennett).[39] Working with Gibson's notion of affordances, as well as the work of Latour and Bourdieu, among others, Knappett has provided stimulating discussions of how things, even "inanimate" ones, in fact should be recognized for their generative roles within actions that emerge through ever-particular relations between humans and environments.[40] Working on a related but distinct path, Malafouris has investigated the idea that some things can become effective extensions of a human's active body, in "prosthetic" cognitive and physical relationships.[41]

The value of Mauss' work has persisted across the decades, within this context of further rich theorization, in part because of its razor-sharp focus on the embodied physical and practical aspects of sociocultural action, or, to put it another way, because of his unwavering assertion that *bodily* work, in its bare and subtle dimensions, is the basic stuff of sociocultural life. He problematizes body techniques as being repeated but also distinct in their realization – varying within and between cultures, given the bodies involved and their relations with each other and their environments. It is here that we can see the contributions of object-bodies and living bodies playfully coincide, and, in some ways, Mauss' ideas are especially useful for contemplating such coincidence. If one's primary focus were on the living human's body, theories that have developed in part on the shoulders of Mauss' work might better get at the inevitable cognitive and emotional dimensions of bodily action and experience. But for the present discussion, it is absolutely crucial to recognize the unique dynamics at play when the *things* humans are interacting with are understood *as bodies* – as complexly nonhuman (but uneasily *sort of* human) bodies that had their own distinct potentials, ones that were dynamic, social and keenly engaging.[42] In other words, these things were part of humans' body techniques but also were experienced as having body techniques of their own, which engaged humans.

Understanding the performance of our Cretan vessels through Mauss' notion of body techniques thus brings them into the fold of animated social bodies; it takes seriously how the actions carried out by their clay bodies could also have contributed to the social habits, relations and experiences that characterized social formations in early Crete.[43] It is important to make clear what I do not mean by this. The corporeal techniques of the clay bodies certainly would not have been the same as those of living humans – they instead would have been highly specific to the physical and social existences of these objects, a specificity that characterizes all body techniques. I also do not conflate the conscious, organic vigor of living bodies with the peculiar potential animacy of these objects. What I instead mean is that, within the social spaces of early Crete, these uncanny clay things would have been experienced as dynamic bodies, characterized by their own culturally established repertoire of bodily techniques, dispositions and anticipated relational engagements, as were living human actions. Hence, it is the fundamental iterative, social nature of their bodily praxes that we can understand these particular object-bodies as having held in common with living actors, with the techniques of *both* types of bodies being constitutive elements of the social spaces they shared.

The iterative nature of the vessels' body techniques merits closer consideration. Replication likely would have been inherent to people's experiences of the clay figures in two respects. Part of this arises from the likelihood that the different anthropomorphic vessels would have been in some senses linked to one another – considered comparable and capable of comparable actions. In this respect, each may have been understood as a manifestation of a special type of body, thus being conceived as part of a common kind (even if in some ways they were quite singular). But we should also recognize an iterability pertaining to each of these objects on its own, over time: each one of these bodies would have been expected to perform, or to be able to perform, certain techniques time and again. These techniques were culturally articulated and surely had specific significances, even if we cannot access them. But they were also material in nature – they arose with and characterized a body and hence were potentially present in each context in which that body dwelt with humans who recognized its particular affordances.[44] The "transparency" of these affordances to human community members would have meant that the clay bodies' techniques could be realized between contexts, providing for their traditional involvement in sociocultural action. This does not preclude other affordances – and body techniques – taking form with the objects. It means instead that there could be powerful persistence in the clay bodies' involvement in social actions, even as those actions were also characterized by aspects of innovation and unpredictability.[45]

The reiteration of the techniques of these relatively stable social bodies linked the various contexts between which they could move as portable things. But each instance of repetition was of course always in fact also something new, materially and socially. People will bring different emotions and responses to the room. Within a given context, someone watching the small clay body seem to produce liquid through its breasts may have been comforted by its display of renewed provision – or perhaps an unexpected gurgling sound afforded a transgressive chuckle to a child watching in hushed company. Meanwhile, the vessel bodies themselves could provide variation between different momentary contexts. These objects also age, if in their own ways and with distinct temporal rhythms. They wear and chip; some may have been intentionally damaged.[46] The clay bodies may have decanted different liquids or stood on different surfaces. They may have streamed their liquids upon different things, bodies – living or dead, human or nonhuman – each with different characters. Thus, in a powerful way it was not so much the vessels that were consistent but their perceived bodily potential, something that certainly involved their ongoing materiality but was as crucially social, relational. If social space is constituted by active relations, by their character and realization over time (as discussed by, e.g., Lefebvre and Soja), then these clay bodies can be understood as generating a distinctive space, potentially in different places.[47]

ABJECT AND DOMESTICATED

The clay bodies would not have acted alone, and the relations they were part of fundamentally involved other bodies, movements and matters. There are, however, reasons to expect that these diminutive bodies were especially prominent and efficacious within social contexts. Some of this concerns the nature of community organization at the time, a topic I will consider shortly. But it also has to do with the objects' unusual bodily nature. From an interpretive perspective, these things are hard to categorize. They are vessels – clay containers – but they are also sculptural, representational figures, robust, vibrant and potentially active bodies. Simandiraki-Grimshaw describes them as "not matter of fact" and, working with the notion of containment, considers how they could act as both "artefactual" and "biological bodies."[48] Such complicated identity, frustrating to the modern scholar in search of efficient terminology, was almost certainly part of the objects' unique efficacy within their Bronze Age contexts. These things seem designed to challenge clear ontological classification and – more relevant to our discussion – experiences with them would have *realized* a blurring of the animate and inanimate.[49] Their affordances arise from their various aspects, thingly and bodily, not as a combination of distinct capacities but as relational corporeal potentials realized as both: the ways they attentively sit, produce, receive and engage cannot be reduced to one facet of their identities or the other. Their statuses are complex in other senses as well. Usually described simply as anthropomorphic, their characters are more restless than this neat term acknowledges. Their distinctive bell-like body shapes, the curious formation of the faces, and in some cases even their appendages, eschew straightforward human identity; the prominent markings added in paint and relief bring yet further complexity.[50] The figures are sometimes described as fully robed, or as nude, as female, or male, as decked in a full-length garment or, in one view, as just a torso. These interpretations are hard to reconcile.

The closest contemporaneous parallels we have for the distinctive body shapes of these objects occur in nonhuman zoomorphic vessels, especially ones identified by Koehl as "hybrid birds," which have avian-like body forms and heads characterized by features associated with other animals.[51] Frankly, the heads of our "anthropomorphic" figures are themselves quite problematic. Warren, who excavated the Myrtos vessel, states of it that "although clearly female, the representation is far from literal and clearly not intended to be literal. The long, stalk-like neck suggests it is not intended to represent a human figure."[52] In several of our vessels, the pronounced central ridge of the face appears more like a beak than a nose, an impression that is strengthened by the proportionally very large eyes, set low in concave spaces flanking the rhinal protrusion. The pronounced rhinal ridge would have been readily formed by pinching the clay as a figure was shaped, an affordance of the moist substance interacting with human fingers. Whether the potter had intended the resultant feature to be bird-like, human-like or something else we will never be able to certainly know, but the beaked outcome brought dramatic definition to the figures' visages. In this way, it is the agency of the resultant animalian objects, and not their human makers, that is felt: as these clay vessel bodies interacted with living people over the years of their use, their beaked faces creatively suggested a nonhuman character, complicating their identities. The face of the Malia figure exemplifies this ambiguity especially dramatically. Its body form also strongly suggests the avian, with "arms" that are equally wing-like as they gently rise away from the sides of the body as soft and lightly perforated triangular sails, and with sweeping painted designs that contribute to the effect.[53] That the protrusions from the sides of the body could be read as cloaked arms or wings, and the face as avian or human (but neither clearly, fully), keeps the figure in a powerful limbo. Is it a bird, a human, a human costumed as/transitioning into a bird? Such tense open-endedness is also embodied in many of our other clay figures, who likewise have an uneasy fit with human identity. Simandiraki-Grimshaw describes Aegean animal–human hybrids as embodying a "thirdspace" "detached from full animality or full humanity."[54] Such detachment finds a moving place in these vessels, as they stand as human-like nonhuman bodies whose presences, as animals *and* clay things, are robustly autonomous even as their species statuses are in flux.

It is important to consider the broader context in which people may have recognized bird-like character in the Malia body vessel, and perhaps

2.6. Terracotta beak-spouted jar, EM II, from Vasiliki. Metropolitan Museum, NY, 07.232.14 (CC0 1.0); www.metmuseum.org

also in several of the other vessels with prominently beaked faces. Avian vessels were widespread in Prepalatial Crete. These ranged from clearly zoomorphic objects that were overtly bodily figures to jugs that subtly but certainly gave the impression of birds through their upturned beaked spouts and the frequent addition of pellet eyes (Figure 2.6). As the MBA progressed, the form of these beaked jugs was further developed on the island and in the Cyclades, to the north of Crete. The Cycladic developments elaborated the bodily character of the vessels, clearly drawing gender into their distinctive corporealities. So-called "nippled ewers" of the late Middle Cycladic (MC) and early Late Cycladic (LC) I were given simple breasts, unmistakably insinuating the human female into the bodies. Woman, bird, vase: each aspect is powerfully present, but no single one dominates the form, as the articulation of each remains engagingly elusive (Figure 2.7). A remarkable Late Minoan (LM) IA White Coated Theran jar perpetuates and further complicates the nippled ewer's dynamism, as it itself becomes a painted motif: imaged upon the jar are upright nippled ewers set within a plant-filled landscape; on each, protruding breasts, an upturned beak/spout, wing, handle and base-turned-feet are readily apparent.[55] These, then, are bird-woman-vases, standing in an animal's natural environment, painted upon a vessel. All of these ceramics differ from our Prepalatial corporeal vessels in their more open engagement with the form of a jug that would be handled by a human: the conventional form of a spout is not altered or concealed but recognized for its similarity with the shape of a bird's beak. The handles likewise proudly rise in full view, announcing the object's identity as a vessel as strongly as its identity as an animalian body.

2.7. LC I nippled ewer from Akrotiri (National Archaeological Museum, Athens, 877). Courtesy of the Akrotiri excavations. © Hellenic Ministry of Culture and Sports

In some respects, the merging of womanly and avian identities, which is especially developed in the Cycladic nippled ewers, is also evident in LBA Crete, where we have ample evidence of woman-bird creatures embodied in material culture, especially in glyptic (see also Figure 4.24b, p. 236).[56] Simandiraki-Grimshaw considers such "bird ladies" to be "homosomatic hybrids" of woman and bird.[57] Wolf (referring to Anastasiadou) has commented on the marked ambiguity that can exist in these glyptic motifs between avian tails and women's wide skirts. She describes this as a case of "ambiguous fusion" in glyptic imagery; we could also relate this ambiguity to the broader phenomenon of formal assonance.[58] McGowan provides a valuable rethinking of these figures, considering how their forms may have been opened into distinct associations with other entities altogether, for example, the arced wings that some possess, in combination with breasts, may have been likened to renderings of bucrania also in glyptic – in this, she refers to Weingarten's related observation.[59] Perhaps our Prepalatial body vessels, in their own way, materialized what would be a long-standing if fluid cultural association of women and birds in the southern Aegean. What is very clear is that these were extraordinary bodies that hovered across identities – spanning different species of animal and thing.

The bodily unconventionality of the vessels would have brought them a distinct poignancy as physical social presences. Even with their small stature, they would have been conspicuous members of a social gathering – standing out among people and things alike, attracting attention in part because of their vibrant nonconformity. In this sense, these can be understood as "abject bodies," a notion Butler develops building on the ideas of Kristeva. Kristeva discusses abjection as arising from breaches or transgressions of boundaries – in bodies, identities, laws and expectations – that are marked by a sociocultural regime.[60] The release of liquids from bodies, and the productive maternal body, are two aspects of Kristeva's discussion that clearly resonate with the distinctive character of the Prepalatial clay bodies.[61] Butler's work further develops the notion of abject bodies as those that deviate from and in a sense supersede the discursive norms through which a society knows and regulates human bodies.[62] Natalie Wilson argues that within Butler's work, which primarily characterizes bodies as discursively constituted, abject bodies are uniquely problematized for their substantive, material reality.[63] That their immediate and undeniable material manifestation "fails to fit normative criteria" brings them a unique status. Such bodies can become distinctly effective in sociopolitical life, Wilson argues, precisely because their material realities fall beyond the catchment of subsumable bodily norms.

This is a compelling lens through which to consider our clay bodies and the social effect of their irreducible character. It can be compared to Simandiraki-Grimshaw's powerful assertion that Minoan animal–human hybrids exert a "mastery" over their "audiences" that could be socially "transformative."[64] In art historical conversations, Butler's abject materiality finds interesting echoes in Gell's notion of an object's ability to "captivate" and "enchant."[65] Gell describes captivation as occurring when a fabricated object "embodies agency which is essentially undecipherable."[66] While Gell focuses on the potential mystification experienced by a beholder unable to fix how an object came into being, he discusses how captivation – and the perceived agency that is at its root – can also stem from other aspects of the object. If one were to approach the Prepalatial body vessels through this notion, it might be helpful to think beyond the matter of a vessel's origination, and toward the agency at play in its own performative origination of liquids. Gell's discussion on the matter of captivation might also be especially relevant if we wished to isolate a person's initial engagement with one of our vessels. But I think to get at the power of these objects more fundamentally we need to appreciate them specifically *as bodies* – and as bodies who likely were engaged with recurrently by members of a social group. The familiarity that they likely came to hold in a community (and in a broader cultural group, as a type of body) likely would have diminished their inconceivability yet would have enriched their distinctively complex social identity and efficacy as a part of the collective fabric.

Did our clay vessels' abnormal "human" bodies, their potently irascible statuses, bring them a unique social efficacy? This seems highly probable, especially when we consider that they were embedded in crucial contexts of community action. At the same time, we need to recognize that these particular social bodies were fabricated things, selected for participation in community contexts. They certainly are remarkable objects,[67] and some examples are deeply idiosyncratic, but it seems that as bodily outsiders and confounders, they did find company in one another, constituting a distinctive type. As such, while powerfully extra-ordinary, these bodies and their bodily potential were at the same time actively incorporated into the shape of community experience. Thus, they were simultaneously abject and domesticated – a paradox, to be sure, but so were many other dimensions of these peculiar things.

MAKING SPACE BETWEEN PLACES: THE WORK OF UNIQUE COMMUNITY BODIES

If these corporeal vessels were social bodies, what were the social contexts in which they participated? To get at this, we need to wade into ongoing discussions of social organization in Prepalatial Crete. Several of the vessels were found in the area of communal-built tombs, including stone-domed tholoi of south-central Crete. From such contexts, it has been assumed that the vessels had funerary roles – but how funerary were the tombs?[68] Clearly multigenerational, it has been argued by numerous scholars that the tombs were connected with relatively small social groups, perhaps based on kinship ties. Recent work has complicated this idea. Concerning the tholoi, Whitelaw argues that depositional data indicate that multiple social groups may have used a given tomb over time as they settled in its area, with the tomb's incontrovertible position in the landscape potentially imparting territorial legitimacy and time-depth to a group's presence.[69] Meanwhile, Legarra Herrero posits that the scale of social groups associated with the tombs varied, and that in some cases a tomb may have served a more dispersed community.[70] Likewise, Murphy and others have considered not only the social scale of the tombs' relevance, but also the nature of their involvement in Prepalatial community actions. Déderix has investigated their position within local and regional interactive landscapes of the period, crucially recognizing the significance of movement *between* places in examination of the tombs' social contributions.[71]

Working in a different but complementary direction, Driessen has rattled traditional views concerning the role of the tombs within the living fabric of communities by rethinking the fundamental funerary identity of these places.[72] Through careful consideration of the skeletal remains found both within Prepalatial tombs and without, he has argued that in fact the tombs often were not final resting places for dead individuals, but instead "temporary repositories, places of transition, structures that served the decomposition of the bodies, before specific parts were selected to be stored elsewhere."[73] Thus, Driessen postulates that the remains of many, even most, individuals would have had only an ephemeral position in the tombs, while mortuary processes occurred. After that, he argues that the remains seem to have been "interfered with," as certain elements of the skeleton, especially craniums, cranial fragments and long bones, were removed and placed in new locations. These new locations could actually be "elsewhere" within the tombs, typically in heaps along with bones from many bodies, or in separate places – other structures or locales near or away from the tombs, sometimes in settlements.[74]

Driessen contends that at this point of removal, the bones were deindividualized and generically identified with a collective ancestry. With this, he describes the secondary practices involving skeletal material as "having in fact little to do with death."[75] In other words, the bodily remains became mobilized and, therewith, were part of nonfunerary social rituals. This is how Driessen reads a cranial fragment found within the settlement at Myrtos Fournou Korifi, next door to the room where the body vessel was uncovered. He submits that the cranial fragment was curated as a focus of ancestral veneration, having been extracted from a tomb. He then suggests a parallel tomb-to-settlement trajectory for the body vessel itself, given that similar vessels have been found in funerary settings. Thus, Driessen's suggestion is that the body vessel from Myrtos was originally placed in a tomb associated with the community, presumably as an element of "funerary paraphernalia" and, like the cranial fragment, was later selectively withdrawn from that context and repositioned within the domestic area of the village of Myrtos.[76]

Driessen's reevaluation of the Myrtos body vessel in light of the nearby cranial material is astute, and the link between the tomb and the settlement indeed seems highly significant, even if I see the path of the clay figure in a somewhat different light. Posing the Myrtos vessel as *displaced* from a funerary context may miss some of the complexity of its unique mobility, as an object that was not of one place and then secondarily another, but instead potentially of numerous places, the potentiality being key. This is not to say that these clay bodies were placeless, but that they may be better understood as generative of spatial relations that linked their situatedness in different locales.

The Myrtos figure was found fallen off of a low, fixed stone structure or "stand" in Room 92 at Myrtos Fournou Korifi. Warren identified the room as a community "shrine" and the structure associated with the vessel as an "altar." This identification was largely based on the presence of the vessel itself, which he saw as divine, dubbing it the "Myrtos Goddess."[77] While I am not comfortable identifying this as a representation or embodiment of a divine being (it could be such, but that is not a question which is especially relevant to my discussion), I am interested in the relationship of this small body and its sociospatial context. Whitelaw's careful reassessment of the architecture and material culture at Myrtos suggests that Room 92 and the three surrounding rooms (89, 90, 91) formed a regular domestic household unit that had parallels in both form and content[78] elsewhere within the conglomerate architectural zone of the settlement; his reading has been generally accepted.[79] The stone structure/platform associated with the vessel was low, probably no more than 30 cm high. The platform had a preserved height of 0.13 m when excavated, but Warren notes that another "loose slab" had been removed from it earlier in excavation, which could have, in his opinion, "at least" doubled the height.[80] Even at 0.26 m, it still would have been a low platform. Gerald Cadogan, who excavated the object, describes the piece of furniture and the deposition of the clay figure:

> This stand (two flat-topped stones with a clayey filling set on the floor) was only 13 cm high as found. At any rate, the figure had not fallen far, since it was unbroken (until hit by the little pick in excavating). It was in a clayey fill (presumably decayed mud brick) above the floor which was about 15 cm further down: this could suggest that it did not fall at the time of the EM IIB destruction by fire ... but later, perhaps decades or even centuries later, as collapse(s) continued. ... There is no evidence that anything else had occupied the stone structure.[81]

We can imagine the clay figure there, independently standing upright, attentively looking outward. In this still position, it could be engaged with as people would see and perhaps touch it. At the same time, it certainly would have moved. Its filling may have happened while it stood there, but also could have taken place elsewhere, perhaps in the storage space just next door. The object would have moved in people's hands during filling, its altering weight and variable contours being directly perceived.[82] Cadogan points out that if the vessel were immersed to fill, it would have made a "glug-glugging" sound as air escaped through its small opening, extending its sensorial impact into the auditory; the same can be said of its decanting, as Simandiraki-Grimshaw notes.[83]

Given how low its supporting platform was, it is likely that some people interacting with the Myrtos vessel would have been sitting in front of it in the room. There is about a meter of space between the front edge of the platform and a pier in the middle of the room. To the north of this pier, there was a more open space, but the presence of the pier would have partially defined an intimate area around the figure. For decanting, a person could have stood or kneeled beside the small platform and inclined the vessel. They also may have stood with it, in which case people seated would have been positioned below, and the figure's lowered face may have come into view as it leaned to the side and poured from the miniature jug in its hands. This close interior area was potentially a charged sociopolitical space, defined not only by the architectural constraints but also by the bodies of both living humans and the clay nonhuman, engaged in close proximity.

The dynamics of hands and handles are quite complex with the Myrtos body vessel. This vessel stands out amongst the other Prepalatial body vessels for not (itself) having a handle. With this, the presence of a living human's grasping hand would have been more pronounced during the act of pouring. At the same time, as Simandiraki-Grimshaw notes based on her ergonomic experimentations, the Myrtos figure's face is gazing in a direction "almost the opposite" of that in which liquid would flow from the small jug it clutches in its dramatically attenuated arms, since this jug is essentially aimed backward.[84] Such positioning might seem odd, but in fact it foregrounds the clay figure's careful grip upon the little jug. Hence, the reversed directionality of the miniature jug, with *its* handle projecting forward along with its clay bearer's steady gaze, allowed living people facing the figure to appreciate its grip upon the source of liquid. With this, the agency of the clay jug bearer would be center stage as it stands at the ready, perhaps for a prolonged period, charged with potential social energy leading toward the moment of pouring.

The dynamism of the Myrtos figure and the other Prepalatial body vessels may have extended into other dimensions of their physical presence as well. In addition to their potent performance potential within one place, there are reasons to suppose that the body vessels may have moved back and forth between local contexts. This point returns us to the question of tombs and settlements, and social movement between them during the Prepalatial period. In the Mesara, most tholos tombs are positioned less than an eighth of a mile from a settlement – a distance that would have been no impediment to the regular passage of things and people. Some of the body vessels have been found within tomb chambers themselves, where they may have performed in funerary rites by decanting liquids on a dead or living body. But they likely also were part of nonmortuary activities in the chambers, perhaps those involving the masses of ancestral bones often located therein. The vessels have been found outside of tomb chambers as well, yet still within the zone of built tombs – areas that are increasingly recognized as venues for nonfunerary community action.[85] These spaces sometimes have paved courts and have produced evidence of repeated consumption activities. Courts also were located within settlements. Whitelaw has identified two paved courts within the Myrtos settlement that he postulates were used for community actions. It is possible that, underlying certain significant variations, court spaces positioned in different community locales held common associations and were seen to afford similar experiences.[86] Such common associations may have related actions taking place in the areas of tombs with ones held in residential zones, something that is suggested by comparable material culture recovered in both. Murphy has stressed that within the small-scale communities characterizing the Mesara during the Prepalatial period, evidence indicates that many places were multifunctional, eschewing single distinct identities – for example, as being "domestic" or "religious."[87] She discusses the discovery of similar types of objects (some traditionally associated with ritual action)[88] between different places, such as tombs and houses, as well as the diversity of material found within each. This indicates not only that each of these places may have been home to an assortment of practices, but also that common varieties of action, involving the same or similar distinctive things, occurred across places. Focusing on anthropomorphic vessels, Simandiraki-Grimshaw highlights the common "liminality" that characterizes the different spaces in which the vessels have been found; this status could subtend actions in both (and between) tombs and residential courts, as well as other places.[89] The vessel found at Trapeza Cave incorporates yet another type of place into the performative field of these bodies, one in a mountainous setting, characterized by stalagmites, stalactites, rocky niches and a dramatically enclosed air. The recent discovery at Charalambos Cave of a remarkable platform, formed of human long bones and topped with skulls, indicates how these unique natural loci could be charged social contexts. These caves did not easily align with a simple mortuary identity and may indeed have held distinct (suprafunerary) social status.[90]

Bodies, Places and Time

In recent years, research concerning further dimensions of sociocultural life in Bronze Age Crete has emphasized similar matters of place, past and interconnections *between* places and generational moments. Driessen and Letesson, among others, have worked with Lévi-Strauss' notion of House Societies to reconsider the social structures of Bronze Age Crete, arguing that such microsocial formations were active on the island. Following the work of other archaeologists, they explicitly do not adhere to Lévi-Strauss' definition of a *House Society* lock, stock and barrel but instead outline their understanding of the nature of a distinctly "Minoan House," emphasizing the centrality of "locus-boundedness" and "intergenerationality."[91] As Driessen and Letesson write concerning the Cretan Prepalatial period specifically:

> the foundation of the ideological basis that tied the House members together was a shared sense of belonging to the same place, in the past, now and in the future. The "locus-boundedness" is inherently spatial and implies the proximity of House members at a specific location. It also entailed a close connection between the living and the dead.[92]

In a study of structures at Prepalatial Phaistos, Todaro argues that a complex House-based social formation may be evident. She suggests that although residences of many House members would have been dispersed beyond the site, through collective building and rebuilding, *in situ*, of buildings on the hilltop, as well as through commensal gatherings there, corporate bonds were maintained. It was through such active place-based engagements that the Houses existed, as such, and were perpetuated.[93] Todaro's discussion highlights how the movement of bodies between places could be inherent in the life of Prepalatial Houses (in this case, most notably between residences and the central places on the hilltop). The House bonds she describes would in a sense justify such movement, or, looked at another way, the House bonds would depend upon it.

Papadatos takes a variable view on how, or whether, evidence of social structure from different regions of Prepalatial Crete aligns with the notion of House groups. He argues that remains from the north and east of the island are more indicative of House societies than those from the Mesara, where, by the later Prepalatial, the impression of corporate social relations indicated in the tholos tombs may have been an ideological construct emulating earlier phases of social structure in the region, rather than a reflection of current organization.[94] Papadatos' consideration of the built structures that in some sense would have served as the "material representation" or core loci of Houses is important, as well, for indicating how it is not merely the type of place that is significant, but its active position as a long-standing shared social locus – this certainly involves physical platial presence and investment therein, but not a single consistent kind of structure. Concerning the Mesara, he asserts that the monumental collective tholoi fit more with the character of an essential built space of a House group than do residential houses in the surrounding area.[95] Thus, while domestic structures are at the center of discussions of House societies, we can see from these studies that characterizations of Minoan Houses, as social entities, potentially involve varieties and networks of places – including tombs, prominent shared loci and sometimes multiple settlements.[96] These arguments are compelling and resonate with ample evidence that Cretan social organizations did not fit neatly, or solely, within traditional analytical units such as villages or nuclear families but instead fluidly hovered across and around these.[97] The Cretan House emerges from these studies as something that was crucially *emplaced* but greater than a particular materialization of place itself.

My interest here does not lie in establishing whether Prepalatial social structure is best characterized through the model of the House; such a project is beyond the scope of my analysis of the body vessels. Yet discussions of Minoan Houses are useful to consider because they foreground various dimensions of sociocultural experience in Prepalatial Crete that are deeply relevant to problematization of the body vessels' contexts, specific capacities and contributions as part of community spaces. Here, it is important to heed

MAKING SPACE BETWEEN PLACES

Papadatos' emphasis on recognizing variation between contexts, as comparing the proveniences of the different body vessels draws out notable distinctions while also allowing us to appreciate certain shared implications between their situations. The case of Koumasa is interesting. Four body vessels were discovered at the site, all within the general area of the tholos tombs. Yet upon closer inspection, their positioning provides further insights. Three of these vessels, numbers 4138, 4139 and 4993, were associated with the same tomb, Tholos B: vessels 4138 and 4139 were found within the tholos, while 4339 was sitting outside of its doorway. These findspots suggest movement of the vessels between distinct activity areas at the cemeteries – a picture further supported by the other body vessel from the site, 4137, which was uncovered in an area between tombs (Area Delta). Hence, placements within and outside of the tombs were equally represented at Koumasa. With this, we see that the vessels may have been present within social experiences both as part of the dark, enclosed "heterotopic" space of a tholos' interior[98] and in areas outside and beyond the tomb chambers. Given that the Prepalatial "cemeteries" are increasingly being recognized as dynamic spaces of collective actions, also of nonfunerary character, the distinction between the locations of the vessels is significant. The findspots of the vessels suggest not only that they could move between these distinct spaces, to have relevance in both, but also that their movement and presence may have connected these different spheres of social experience.

At the same time, body vessels 4138, 4139 and 4993 from Koumasa also indicate that more than one of these peculiar things could be associated with the same tholos. This brings complexity to how we consider a body vessel's relationship to a social group – and potentially how we understand a social group's relationship to a tholos. While all of the vessels belong to the Prepalatial period, the precise dating of both the objects and their depositional contexts at Koumasa is unclear (dating between scholars ranges from EM II to MM IA).[99] Generally speaking, the dating of the Mesara tholoi is complex, and objects associated with them, which may have been kept in circulation across periods (or temporarily removed from circulation and later returned to active use), present further chronological challenges. Meanwhile, research in the region demonstrates variability in how tholoi were associated with nearby sites, indicating both fluctuation in the social groups using tholoi across time (as Whitelaw has argued)[100] and that the number of kin/social groups utilizing a tomb at a given time may have varied.[101] Moreover, following Papadatos' discussion, we have seen that the nature of association between social groups may have altered, and that relationships asserted between smaller kin groups through use of a common tomb may not have carried over into social affiliations between the living communities. If the body vessels at Koumasa were in use contemporaneously, would two different kin groups have been using two separate but similar body vessels within Tholos B? Were the two vessels found inside the tomb both associated with the same kin group, or with a larger corporate group (a House?) of which two kin groups were members? And how do the two body vessels found outside the tombs relate? Were they associated with the same social group(s)? Just as importantly, given the possible divergence between social bonds expressed in the treatment of the dead in the collective tombs versus associations pertaining to the broader experience of their living communities, would the body vessels located beyond the burial chambers of the tombs have been embedded in other (potentially nonfunerary) varieties of community action, where different intergroup relations were pertinent? If so, did the body vessels in some sense connect these spaces and the social relationships active within each? We will not be able to sort out the particulars of these matters on current evidence, but my point in posing such questions is twofold. On one level, we see that even when considering the evidence of these body vessels from a single site, we need to leave space open for considerable variation in interpretation. At the same time, within this openness, we can appreciate how these clay bodies draw out important dynamics concerning social experience and relation, in part because of the peculiar standing they could have had within and between social spaces.

The other extant Prepalatial body vessels were discovered in regions beyond the Mesara, and in contexts that are distinguished in other ways. That most of these vessels stem from northern and eastern Crete may allow them to be more comfortably associated with the model of House societies, especially during the later Prepalatial, as Papadatos considers.[102] Information concerning their find-spots is rather limited, but helpful nevertheless. Between locations that at first glance appear predominantly funerary, there is in fact considerable variation across the vessels' contexts. These include a cave (Trapeza), an ossuary (Malia, Ossuary II), a house tomb (Mochlos Tomb XIII), the Area of the Rocks at Phourni (two vessels, from distinct zones, one a burial stratum) and a bench in a residential house (Myrtos). These spaces are distinct from one another in terms of their physical character and the sensorial experiences they could afford. They also vary concerning the number of people that potentially could be copresent within them and in some of the particular types of social activities they likely saw – which may have ranged from mortuary undertakings to ancestral rites, and from actions directly engaging with the natural environment to those within a built residential space. This variation is significant. It lends further support to the idea that the portable clay bodies could be part of a host of actions, between places, in addition to the likely variation of actions that could occur within each context. Within and across these places, the vessel bodies were distinguished by their own type of material and temporal persistence. Their contexts were, in each case, settings where the generational depth of the community (real or imagined) was potentially a focal interest, although each locale could have afforded different experiences of this depth, through distinct circumstances and practices. In this light, we should avoid an urge to ascribe generic labels to these body vessels that would too closely determine their significance (e.g., as being funerary objects, or signifiers of fertility). By leaving such particular associations open-ended, the identity of the vessels becomes less fixable, but their distinctive interplatial character comes into clearer view. With this, the clay bodies, smaller yet also greater (socially, temporally) than a living human's, could have been powerfully resonant with, or even constitutive of, the ongoing relations of the community, as social entities that were perpetuated through times and places. If we follow Peatfield's argument that water, and its manipulation, were a central component of Minoan ritual culture,[103] then the provision of liquid performed by these clay bodies may have been one particular way in which they, as individuals, were involved in legitimating or maintaining social space.

It is quite possible that the body vessels were experienced as tangible symbols of social groups. As such, each could have been a "miniaturized, animated proxy of the humanity of its community," as Simandiraki-Grimshaw suggests,[104] or even a conventional emblem of such collectives, such as an "ancestral figurine" of the type discussed by González-Ruibal and Ruiz-Gálvez concerning House societies (although this, of course, would be very difficult for us to ascertain). Yet if they acted in these roles on some level, they were also always, and more fundamentally, something else. These were bodies among other bodies within communities, and we miss the power of this point if we instead characterize them principally as referents or substitutes. They were in the thick of things *along with* human community members, as fellow contributors – and not merely as imperfect imitations of human forms. Surely it would have been striking when aspects of their bodily character seemed to overlap with those of biological people (e.g., in their water-filled bellies),[105] but these extraordinary, indefinable clay bodies brought unique affordances and dynamics of copresence to social spaces. While they could engage living humans in various ways, they also engaged other elements of their contexts, from materials to things (liquids, associated bones, benches and so on). Hence, it was not just their aspects of likeness with living people that was relevant, but also their peculiar nonhumanness and bodily independence, which brought them distinction as active producers in Prepalatial community actions.

PRESENCE AND (DE)EMPHASIS: CHANGES OVER TIME

Each of the Prepalatial body vessels that we have considered placed remarkable emphasis on itself. Their physical nature and mechanical affordances contributed to this. Each creatively gave shape to an animalian body that was human-like, but not identifiable as fully anthropomorphic. Each was a body that could sit on its own and hold liquid over time; thus, each could act as an unflinching participant in social contexts, even when not being touched by a human. When the vessels were being filled or decanted, the living human was still potentially marginalized: the clay body clearly could hold its own, either as an active receiver of a liquid provision, or as the foregrounded, direct producer of fluids that appeared through the jar or breasts that it manipulated. What I want to draw out is that the performances of these uncanny objects, likely occurring within charged sociocultural environments, deemphasized the individual living human actor by instead placing the focus on themselves. When they are considered as figures that could move *between* contexts – tomb chambers, community gathering places, houses – we can appreciate that they likewise could carry the emphasis with them, as bodies that crossed time and space differently than living bodies, and could persist with distinct somatic stability through changing events, places and generations, as independent bodies.

If we now take a longer view, into the subsequent palatial periods of the later Middle and early Late Bronze Age, we find that vessels rendered in bodily forms enjoyed a marked continuity on the island. That said, most of these later vessels do not integrate human attributes into their animalian bodies; they instead assume various nonhuman zoomorphic forms, ranging from birds to bulls. Bovine vessels had a particular prominence on the island and, through their specific physical attributes, in many cases seem to have brought a distinctive emphasis on craftiness and cunning ability to their human manipulators – something that I examine in terms of both the living biological people who would have handled the bovine objects and, in certain instances, the humans who were rendered interacting with the bodies of cattle as part of the objects themselves. This craftiness is evident in a variety of bovine objects from the Bronze Age (beyond vessels alone), but we find especially potent embodiments in a type of zoomorphic vessel that appears at the transition to the Neopalatial period, which takes the form of a bodiless animal's head. These distinctive bovine-form vessels are explored, along with other types of contemporaneous bovine object, as contributors to a significant recontextualization of "cattle culture" on the island during the late MBA and early LBA – a moment of likely social and environmental upheaval that would have recalibrated relations that involved human–cattle engagements.

Zoomorphic Vessels in Palatial Moments

Representation of human forms in the round certainly continued after the Prepalatial period, but primarily as figurines, which lack the fundamental animating affordances that characterized the Prepalatial body vessels. There are, at present, three exceptional anthropomorphic objects known from the Protopalatial period that were vessels. All are from the site of Phaistos, but notably not from the palace itself.[106] In each case, these vessels had secondary openings positioned such that they could not hold liquid on their own over time; instead, they would only mediate its active flow. One of these vessels is highly anthropomorphic: a standing skirted woman whose form closely parallels that of contemporaneous figurines (e.g., a clay figurine from Protopalatial Chamezi, who also makes a nearly identical gesture).[107] The two other vessels, however, are remarkably peculiar bodies. Simandiraki-Grimshaw describes them as "monkey-like," and indeed both – with crouching, heavily curved postures, bodies sunk between high-swung knees, and low, neckless heads – appear quite simian. These "anthropomorphic" vessels may in some respects embody a continuity in abject corporeality from what we saw in the Prepalatial objects, again integrating the human and nonhuman in a vessel form. However, the nonhuman species involved are different, and, on current evidence, their occurrence is limited to a single site.

Moving into the Neopalatial period, our evidence of anthropomorphic or humanoid vessels essentially ceases. Simandiraki-Grimshaw identifies just one vessel, which could also be Postpalatial in date. It is an imported Egyptian alabaster cylindrical jar with "plastically rendered features"; a hole drilled in its side effectively turned the jar into a rhyton.[108] There are, however, a host of Neopalatial vessels, as well as ones from the Protopalatial period, which, although falling outside the category of the "anthropomorphic," nevertheless can be compared to the Prepalatial body vessels for similar characteristics. I believe this point should spur us to more deeply recognize the nonhuman context of our Prepalatial vessel bodies and to consider diachronic developments in a broader *zoomorphic* light.

Zoomorphic vessels were there from the beginning, found at the same Prepalatial sites as our more anthropomorphic body vessels, sometimes in the very same contexts. Bird forms were especially prevalent and, in some cases, had similar bodily affordances. Some were rendered quite extraordinarily, with highly exaggerated or unrealistic features (e.g., a quadruped bird from Koumasa [HM 4121] and a three-legged one from the Chania area [Chania Π345], the latter with an exceptionally elongated neck). We also have some possible "hybrids" combining corporeal features of birds with those of other beasts; such combination may have brought these avian bodies a wondrous nonconformity that resonated with that of the contemporaneous abject human-like vessels.[109] In some cases, distinctive features may have brought useful affordances to the object-bodies (e.g., a steadying "extra" leg), enriching the novelty that they realized in animalian bodies while heightening their thingly creaturely tension. Meanwhile the MBA and LB I vessels discussed

2.8. Prepalatial vessel in form of bull with humans, from Koumasa (Herakleion Museum 4126). Photo by Olaf Tausch (CC BY 3.0). Object © Hellenic Ministry of Culture and Sports

above, which maintain the recognizable form of a pitcher but realize avian features therein, push the formal boundaries separating animal and thing (e.g., Figure 2.7). That some of these have explicitly female human anatomy (notably breasts) further stresses a relatedness to the more anthropomorphic vessels.

Beyond vessels in bird form, bovine vessels are evidenced through all phases of the Cretan Bronze Age, and cattle in fact become the most common zoomorphic subject for rhyta in the palatial periods.[110] Underlying this continuity, we find significant fluctuations in the forms and contexts of the bovine vessels. During the Prepalatial period, bovine vessels typically took the form of an entire beast's body. These vessels could stand on their own and hold liquid, most having a primary opening on the top of the neck or back-end, and a secondary one through the muzzle; some stand on articulated legs. A few bovine vessels create *events* that also involve human actors (Figure 2.8). Full-bodied bovine vessels have been found in the areas of Prepalatial tombs and settlements. Four stem from the peak sanctuary of Kofinas, located in south-central Crete, in the same region as numerous tholoi and their nearby settlements. One example was found in the settlement at Myrtos Fournou Korifi, in a small "vestibule" space along the south entrance path leading through the architectural zone, just before one of the two courtyards that Whitelaw proposed as a venue for community activities, and not far from the room where the "Myrtos Goddess" body vessel was discovered.[111] In other cases, too, bull vessels have been found in the same Prepalatial sites as the more anthropomorphic vessels we have considered, sometimes within in the same specific areas (e.g., in Area Delta at Koumasa).

The occurrence of full-bodied bovine vessels drops off considerably in Crete after the Prepalatial period, paralleling the situation with anthropomorphic vessels.[112] Phaistos has produced the few examples known from the Protopalatial and transitional Neopalatial period. Three were discovered in what has been identified as a foundation or "completion" deposit for the MBA palace, and one was found outside the palace, in the town, within a room likely associated with ritual.[113] Given the "virtual explosion by MM IIB" of rhyta that were nonfigural,[114] it is possible that these relatively rare full-bodied bovine vessels at Phaistos may have been intentionally archaizing – indeed, their type was well represented in the same region of the island during the Prepalatial period. Use of the old-fashioned vessels in a foundation ritual, in particular, may have been part of an effort to assert time depth in the regional identity associated with the newly constructed palace. During the Neopalatial period, full-bodied bull rhyta continue to be very limited in distribution. On the island, they are known from LM IB Pseira, where they were found individually in houses, an exceptional context for rhyta in this phase.[115] Fine examples are also known from LC I Akrotiri, on Thera.[116]

Bodily, in Part

During the Protopalatial period another type of zoomorphic vessel became prevalent, examples of which are evidenced in both palatial and nonpalatial contexts. These were rhyta that took the form of an animal's head alone, typically from the neck up; bovines were the most common (Figure 2.9).[117] As rhyta, these vessels have two apertures, upper and lower, allowing liquid to flow through. Currently there are three published early examples of these animal-head rhyta. All are bovine, and all are from late Protopalatial contexts in south-central Crete: two from Phaistos and one from Kommos.[118] These three rhyta have a wide primary aperture, formed by leaving the back of the neck shaft open (Koehl's Type III). Koehl sees these earlier animal-head rhyta as being derived from MBA Anatolian head-shaped cups, to which the affordances of rhyta were innovatively integrated through secondary openings; Shapland has questioned this view.[119] Rhyta in the form of animal heads became much more popular during the Neopalatial period. Beyond two "nearly identical moldmade faience" bovine-head rhyta (probably calf heads) known from Zakros, there are few examples from this phase that have wide primary apertures.[120] Instead, a smaller primary aperture seems to have been preferred and was usually positioned along the top of the head/neck (Koehl's Type II).[121] Koehl's study describes that, beginning in the early Neopalatial period, most of the animal-head rhyta are found in "cultic" storage areas along with many other objects apparently linked to ritual, both within the palaces and beyond.[122]

The animal-head rhyta constitute a dramatic, substantive shift in what we can broadly call Cretan zoomorphic vessels – taking in renderings of both human and nonhuman bodies. The mechanics of the animal-head vessels are quite distinct from those of the full-bodied ones, altering the nature of the

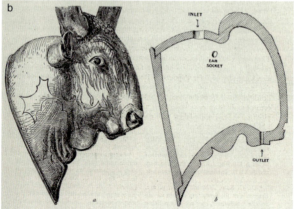

2.9. Neopalatial stone bull's-head rhyton from the Little Palace at Knossos (Herakleion Museum HM-Λ1368). a. Photo by Zde (CC BY-SA 4.0). b. Cross-section drawing from Evans 1928: fig. 332. Object © Hellenic Ministry of Culture and Sports

objects' participation in social contexts. Given the positioning of the two apertures (one high and the other low on each vessel), these isolated heads were unable to independently retain liquid. Consequently their entire performance took place in a moment, and more passively in human hands. With two openings to manage, a living human would need to carefully manipulate the vessel in order to control the liquid's movement. In the case of the examples with wide primary openings (the three Protopalatial vessels and the faience pair from Zakros), a hand could have held the small secondary aperture in the muzzle closed while another filled the rhyton through the open neck. A coordinated person may have accomplished this alone – especially if some sort of filter had been placed in the interior (Koehl discusses a piece of wool), slowing flow, or if an immediate fast flow was acceptable – yet having two people involved would ease the process.[123] Koehl believes that the Neopalatial animal-head rhyta with small primary apertures likely were filled by being partially immersed in liquid (e.g., Figure 2.9). If a hand was placed over the upper/primary opening before the vessel was lifted out of the liquid, a vacuum would form, trapping the liquid inside as the rhyton was pulled out.[124] With the vessel held aloft, the hand could be removed from the primary opening and the liquid would flow outward. Supporting the vessel while also operating the orifices would have required knowledge, skill and dexterity, especially with the larger stone rhyta, which Younger estimates could weigh 6 kg when full.[125] Given these mechanical demands, emphasis thus fell on the performance of the living human or humans who manipulated the fabricated animal head. Unlike with the Prepalatial body vessels, the holding and passing of liquid were markedly fleeting with these rhyta; the process was bound to the impressive adeptness of living people in the moment, without agency being apparent on the side of the animalian vessels themselves. Beyond the moment when a person was actively handling it, the head would have laid lifelessly, resting prone on its flat back plate, or perhaps on its side or face.[126]

The fact that the majority of these rhyta have been found in storage contexts underscores how, as mere animal parts, they likely were only engaged contributors to social experience for spurts of time – these were potentially intense, stirring events, but strikingly short-lived. Moreover, by being isolated heads, these rhyta were conspicuously incomplete bodies. It was only while being held up in the hands of a living human that they gained corporeal completion, in a sense acquiring human bodies from the neck down, while also receiving temporary vigor from the person's remarkable manipulations. This fleeting effect would correspond to what Simandiraki-Grimshaw describes as a "heterosomatic hybrid," in which part of animal's body is taken on by another, such as a human wearing a hide or helmet.[127] The considerable size of some of the rhyta would have augmented the sense of their being heads divorced from bodies. With their entire size dedicated just to the head, these vessels pushed into a novel representational scale compared to most other contemporaneous renderings of animal bodies. Many render the length of the beast's head in the range of an average human face or head; a fragment of a stone vessel from Juktas is thought to be from a life-size rendering of a bovine's head as a rhyton.[128] These sizes would connect the three-dimensional head vessels to people's experience of living animals, making the separation of the head from a body highly pronounced and suggestive of death.[129] Morgan argues that in Minoan art, an animal's full-frontal gaze indicates death or dying.[130] Perhaps some of these bovine heads, issuing forth liquid while momentarily staring straight ahead, were experienced as being in the throes of death in human hands – or its bloody aftermath.[131] It might also have enhanced the effect of the head taking on a lower body when it was held up in human hands, but this would depend on other factors as well.[132]

Performances with these palatial-era objects thus had remarkably different somatic, social and potentially political emphases compared to those involving the Prepalatial body vessels. Now, it was the body of a living human figure that was given the performative power, as the nonhuman was rendered a vividly partial body, whose invigoration – which may, paradoxically, have been connected to the moment of a beast's *loss* of life, through ritual killing[133] – was prominently dependent on the human's hands. The radically reformulated performances involving these head rhyta took place in novel social places as well. The Neopalatial evidence suggests a formalization to ritual experience, involving rotating, perhaps event-specific paraphernalia and more dedicated cultic places, some of which were located within the palace complexes. The Cretan palaces were core venues in regional-scale social formations that were significant to multitudes of smaller communities. Within these broader "networks of relevance,"[134] people likely developed new social interests, related to emergent scales of social comparison that played out in newly established cultural contexts – or in old venues, such as peak sanctuaries, that now had novel associations.[135] Gatherings at palatial sites likely drew together people who did not all share the same degree or type of affiliation that had been a basis for comparison and common experience within the locations where the Prepalatial corporeal vessels performed (e.g., within a local cemetery). Driessen and Letesson argue that during the Neopalatial era, both "communal sharing" and "authority ranking" were active within House groups but also became pronounced *between* them, as marked elements of their external relation. With this:

> the beginning of the Late Bronze Age seems to have witnessed the emergence of Houses that became so large and so wealthy – probably by integrating lesser Houses or smaller social units – that they considered themselves above others. Such major Houses developed a privileged

relation with the "palace," with better access, use and control of its collective resources. One could even hypothesize that they "became" the "palace" to which they were linked.[136]

The novel bodily and performative dynamics of the animal-head rhyta, which emerged at this time, find an interesting contextualization in such ideas. The palaces likely were venues of activities that realized more clearly ranked statuses, yet these practices may have drawn upon earlier sociocultural forms. With this, the continued use of zoomorphic vessels in collective rituals may have been experienced as a potent perpetuation of a traditional social practice, recreated to contribute in the context of a new scale and nature of community.[137] The structure of performances involving the head rhyta, which placed agentive emphasis on the impressive actions of a human (instead of within the body of the vessel itself), echoes these more pronounced scalar relations of the Neopalatial contexts. I am not implying that it was necessarily the leader of a powerful House (or other sociopolitical authority) who held a head-form rhyton during events, but rather that performances involving the head rhyta would have inherently marked out the notable efficacy of a living human figure, thus also enacting an aggrandizing social dynamic. That is, the structure of a ritual performance may have resonated with and contributed to active structures of emergent sociopolitical relation.

Certainly, the sociopolitical contexts in which the zoomorphic vessels were involved would have been complicated in a multitude of particular ways, in both the Prepalatial and later Neopalatial cases. Smaller-scale local communities would have seen antagonisms, including assertions of authority, just as there surely would have been interests in asserting similarity and sharedness in the larger regional social formations engaged by palaces. Yet changes in social structure and the sociospatial dynamics of political relation are clearly evident between these periods. In this context, these animalian things could have keenly contributed to a recharacterization of arenas of social action on the island, from the immediate loci of their peculiar bodies outward.

THE CRAFTINESS OF PEOPLE'S ENGAGEMENTS WITH CATTLE: IN FLESH AND THING

Among the broader category of bovine vessels found in Prepalatial Cretan contexts, three stand out for depicting a beast engaging with humans. The first, HM 4126, dates to EM II–III and was discovered in Area Delta at Koumasa, the same area where body vessel 4137 was found (Figure 2.8).[138] The bovine vessel has a light ground with broad dark-red stripes painted vertically across its body. A tubular handle, painted red, arcs from the back of the vessel, atop the beast's hips, forward to the upper neck. The beast stands on three legs (two in front and one in the rear). The primary aperture is located on the animal's hips (just beside the base of the handle) and the secondary one is through the pierced muzzle. The bovine has dramatic horns projecting outward from the sides of its head (the tip of one is lost); a small round ear appears below each. On each horn we find a single human figure suspended, their heads held upward (one is restored). The arms of each figure extend across the top of the horn to which they cling with articulated fingers; the legs wrap about the horns from below, nearly reaching around to the hands. A third human appears splayed spread-eagle across the face and forehead of the bovine, with its head (restored) directed upward toward the handle; its legs separate across the tubular muzzle. Koehl describes each of the human figures as being naked save for a belt and identifies them as male.[139]

A second vessel, found within the tholos tomb at Porti, is quite similar, if more fragmentary. It is dated to MM IA.[140] The white-slipped, boxy bovine body stands upon four short legs. The primary opening emerges from the upper back, behind the neck; the secondary opening is through the muzzle. A hatched pattern in red paint covers the beast's back; this has been read as a net, perhaps for catching.[141] Painted red lines descend across the front of the head and face. Only one of the two horns is extant. Here, we find a human figure hanging, with one arm curving over and the other under the horn; its fingers are indicated. The side of the human's torso and its parted legs are attached to the bovine's neck. While the second horn is missing, it is possible that another human figure was suspended on the other side of the beast, echoing the first.

The third object is but a fragment (HMp 2192), which I include because of its apparent similarity to the first two. Found at Juktas and dated to MM I–II, it takes the form of a bull's head with, as Foster describes, "part of a human figure clutching its right horn."[142] We cannot be certain that this was a vessel, but its ceramic materialization in the round of human and bovine bodies together, their tight contact focused on the horn, embodies an interaction remarkably comparable to that manifest in the other two Prepalatial things.

These objects clearly relate to the wider tradition of full-bodied bovine vessels that we have discussed, which is weighted in the Prepalatial period. Like the others, these clay cattle stand on their own and hold and produce liquid. But these bovine things also embody moments of relation between species – each is a thingly realization of intercorporeal engagement. The small human figures clinging to the beasts' horns create an interactive event. But what type of event? A more fundamental question is *how* they embody this interaction and how it would have contributed to people's broader experience of the relationship between humans and cattle. On both Prepalatial vessels, the human bodies are clearly distinguished from the comparatively massive body of the bovine, yet their hold on the creature engrosses the entirety of their smaller bodies, as they wrap and drape across the bovine's head, maximizing contact between their forms and its. Younger has read both of these objects as representations of novices engaging with a beast, "probably trying to drag the bull down by force."[143] This might be the case. But I would also like to recognize how the material and practical aspects of these clay things are contributing very substantively to the particular articulation of interspecific relations that they embody, in ways that potentially depart from the maker's representational aims. Let us consider the more complete vessel from Koumasa. The full bodily contact and close entwining grip of the humans upon the bovine do give a sense of concentrated, heavy grappling. But this is not simply a matter of representational design and intent. This type of bodily engagement also practically allowed the small figures to be securely attached to the vessel body, making use of the protrusions of the horns and muzzle: in other words, for a fired clay object in the round to successfully materialize the interaction of four animalian bodies, true close contact between them was necessary. The craftsperson who made the vessel instead may have had in mind a scene of a human leaper nimbly passing *over* the center of a bull's head, through the air between its horns, while other persons assisted from the sides – we see such compositions in later representations, for example, in the Taureador fresco from Knossos (Figure 2.10). But, despite such possible intentions, what *came into being* was a bull held within the firm, simultaneous embrace of a group of humans who do not seem to be letting go any time soon. Their efforts, and mass, concentrate on the bull's horned head. This lays emphasis not only on the most feared element of the beast's aggressive body, but also on the vessel's crucial locus of animating action – where a liquid would flow outward from the creature's pierced muzzle, passing directly between the gripping legs of one of the humans.

2.10. The Taureador fresco from Knossos. Herakleion Museum. Photograph in public domain (CC0 1.0). Object © Hellenic Ministry of Culture and Sports

2.11. "Bronze group of a bull and acrobat" (British Museum, 1966,0328.1), LM I. Shaw Fund. © The Trustees of the British Museum

The Prepalatial "bull-grappler" vessels from Koumasa and Porti (and perhaps the fragment from Juktas) stand out amidst the broader group of full-bodied bovine vessels of their period. Their embodiment of an interactive, cross-species event can be compared in some ways to two later renderings in the round of humans engaging with bovines. The first is a Neopalatial copper-alloy figure purchased in Rethymno which, Shapland notes, may have been found at an open-air sanctuary near the Preveli Gorge (Figure 2.11).[144] It embodies a large bull with a man springing over its head and back. The man faces upward, his back arched. The object was cast as a single piece, and what is either an extension of the man's long locks, or a projection connecting to them, provides the point of contact between the human and nonhuman components. While the man's legs are discontinuous after the thighs, the pair of human feet situated on the upper hips of the bull indicate that when cast, the two bodies were meant to have a second point of contact here.

Again, in this object we have a realization of a moment of bodily engagement between human and bovine – another instance of "bull sports" – but the dynamics have changed. Shapland notes that physical contact "is part of the interaction between bull and leaper" afforded here.[145] Yet we can see that the touch between the human and bovine in this copper-alloy object is light and focused, quite different from the full entwining of human bodies upon the bull in the Prepalatial vessels. In the Neopalatial copper-alloy group, we seem to find the lithe human figure in the midst of a calculated movement, caught in what could only be a fleeting moment of touch. The insubstantial substance of falling hair, here frozen in an unbending column, connects the two figures. The casting drew out the fluid metal into the arc of the human's body, midmaneuver, in a way that clay could not. But the use of metal also involved its own risks, and we seem to see those realized. The British Museum indicates that the truncated arms and discontinuous legs of the human figure may have been the result of casting faults, with the metal failing to flow completely through the mold in the areas of the limbs.[146] If this is indeed the shape in which the object was experienced by persons within LBA Cretan sociocultural contexts, these "faults" were part of the interspecific relation that the metal object actually materialized, contributing to its particular character. The discontinuity of the legs further lightens the touch between the two animals, leaving but one moment of contact while suggesting another, as the brief extension of the human's legs to the bull's back is both present and not.

Within a "closet" in the area of the Domestic Quarter at Knossos, Evans' team discovered several fragmentary ivory human figures rendered in-the-round (Figure 2.12). Careful depiction of musculature and even veining is apparent on the finely worked things.[147] The elongated, seemingly horizontal posture of the most complete figure strongly suggests that it, and perhaps the others, were part of a group representing bull-leaping. The lithe body extends in a rhythmically undulating course, from the pointed toes, across the rises of the hips and head, through an outstretched hand. Hair made of "gold-plated bronze wire" was found with the ivory figures and is believed to have attached to them through extant "holes for attachment" on their heads;[148] the flow of long hair seems crucial to these bodies-in-movement, as it was on the copper-alloy leaper reportedly from the Preveli Gorge.[149] The waist area of the best preserved of the ivory figures is missing, but Evans was confident that the

2.12. Neopalatial ivory "bull-leaper" figure from Knossos (Herakleion Museum, HM-O-E3). Photo DEA/ G.DAGLI ORTI/Contributor. Object © Hellenic Ministry of Culture and Sports

leaper's midsection had been covered by a "metal girdle" (although no evidence of such remained). If this figure is indeed a leaper, with his posture indicating that he is midsoar, how was he suspended above a bull? According to Evans, "not certainly by [his] taper feet or delicate fingers," which show no signs of a means of fixation. Evans hypothesized that the missing midsection held the answer, and that the figure was likely "suspended in a downward slanting position from the girdle by means of fine gold wire or chains."[150] The waist does seem the most probable area in which the figure was somehow held, and the use of wire – already evidenced on these ivory bodies for their hair – is a possibility. Whether held by wire or another means, it is apparent that this leaping figure (and perhaps his companions) would not have been rendered in bodily contact with a bull – but instead, by some exceptional means, was likely held aloft. Hence, in this apparent encounter of human and nonhuman, of person and bovine, the bodies would have been dynamically distanced. We can only imagine the full scene that this group created, which may have been a dazzlingly three-dimensional multimedia display of bodies in coordinated, suspended motion – if wires did suspend the ivory humans, there may have been some active swaying movement as well. This group would have brought the intercorporeal event of bull-leaping new wonder, realized through the fabricated beings in their splendid materials and forms, poised in relation to one another.

Each of these objects embodying bovine and human animals together was distinctly crafty. They endowed the relationship of cattle and people with particular character through exceptional means and were surely interesting not only in what they represented, but in what they themselves did with the animalian bodies. Each outwitted the typical boundaries of their medium to embody dynamic interaction between figures. As Evans wrote concerning the ivory leapers, this dynamism, "is hard to reconcile with the fixity of position inherent in statuary in the round."[151]

The bovine body was also embodied in other remarkably clever things during these periods. In the late Prepalatial period, the terracotta body of a piebald cow (now in Chania) was fitted with "pierced protuberances in place of legs,"[152] seemingly in order to receive wheeled axles, allowing the small bovine to run. During the Neopalatial period, the exquisitely crafted bull-head rhyta brought their own impressive artifice to the table. Koehl's reconstruction of the mechanics of using the bovine head rhyta[153] involves what amounts to a magic trick (even if solemnly enacted), as the human handler would momentarily deny the flow of liquids through the orifice in the muzzle by covering the upper aperture to create a vacuum; only when the person chose to release their hand would the fluids dramatically flow. This momentary suspension of the fluid's passage would have toyed with expectation.[154] Rehak's argument that the stone bull-head rhyta may have been ritually "killed" underscores the potential power (risk?) of these objects, which were vessels of animating artifice in skilled hands.[155]

The guile of these bovine things should be considered in the context of how cattle were experienced in other contemporaneous situations on the island, including as living beasts. Shapland has powerfully argued for the importance of considering engagements of humans with biological nonhumans as we approach representations of animals from the Bronze Age Aegean – including those representations traditionally related to realms of ritual and religious symbolism. Especially relevant here is his crucial relating of Neopalatial depictions of bovines and human-bovine performances to an expansion of "palatial collectives" (notably Knossos) over further animal practices involving cattle.[156] Working in this light, we should note that various activities involving living cattle – especially bulls – require notable shrewdness. Certainly, this is the case for the types of undertakings we describe as bull sports or games (e.g., fighting, leaping, grappling, catching), but it also can be true of less formalized interactions. Activities involved in regularly occurring farming practices can require similar sure-footedness and quick wits and could provide the experiential basis of more performative activities.

We cannot easily grasp how Minoan renderings of bovines relate to lived experiences with biological cattle. Shapland has observed that there are very few representations of cattle involved in "domestic" activities.[157] Instead, interpretations of bovine imagery have often been connected to ritual actions, ranging from sacrifice to events in which people engaged in risky feats involving the massive beasts. Beyond those objects in the round that we have been considering, many Minoan renderings of bovines engaging with humans stem from the Neopalatial and Final Palatial periods, especially from the site of Knossos. In fresco, we have the famed "Taureador" scenes, in which people are seen leaping over bulls, holding onto the beasts' horns or standing around them with raised arms (Figure 2.10).[158] Some scenes involving bulls place the events in a built context, for example, in the fresco imaging a front-facing bull amidst architecture from the Room of the Ivory Deposit at Knossos,[159] on the Boxer Rhyton from Ayia Triada or in glyptic.[160] Others are clearly set outdoors, as in the large-scale stucco relief painting involving a bull and an olive tree from the North Entrance Passage at Knossos. Evans connected this to scenes of bull capture on two gold cups discovered in a LH I tholos tomb context in Vapheio (see Figure 5.18, p. 299).[161] One of these cups shows a bull trampling and goring humans, along with the use of a net to catch a raging beast, while the other cup seems to depict quite a different method for ensnaring the massive animal: introducing a distracting female cow while a rope is tied about the unsuspecting bull's leg.[162]

These representations of human–bovine interaction suggest a range of activities. Younger has cataloged such scenes in a series of articles and provides consideration of possible lived practices being depicted, which he describes as bull games and sports.[163] He suggests that the depicted actions could have varied considerably in character and may have involved people from different elements of society. Although he sees most of the interactions as elements of festivities held at central places,[164] he proposes that the Prepalatial vessels from Koumasa (Figure 2.8) and Porti represent amateurs engaging in "impromptu" events, exhibiting "adolescent bravura"; he also raises the possibility that they were a sort of opening act for more skilled performers in "controlled sport," such as clowns preceding serious competitors in rodeos. Meanwhile, in the scene on the more violent of the two Vapheio cups, and in imagery from a later ivory pyxis from Katsambas, he sees evidence of youths engaging in bull chases in fields, in some cases prodding the beasts toward nets.

That engagements with cattle would occur in different types of place, involving different people, should not be at all controversial if we think through the realities of these animals' presence in humans' lives. As with "sports" involving cattle, agricultural practices with the beasts require not only strength, agility and quick-wittedness, but also close knowledge of the species and individual animals – what bullfighters/rodeo clowns in the USA describe as "cow sense."[165] Many Spanish bullfighters describe their first fights as being childhood encounters they had with bulls on farms, where the aura of performance coincided with the rural economic base.[166] Indeed, the spectacular and the utilitarian, the thrilling and the laborious, the painful and the amusing dimensions of human interaction with cattle cannot be neatly separated from one another.[167] They can characterize the very same practices. For example, Bill Pickett, the famed originator of the "bulldogging" rodeo act, first undertook and developed the trademark maneuver as a means of subduing calves while they were being branded; yet he went on to perform it for thousands.[168] A handful of Neopalatial depictions of humans grappling with horned caprids, in scenes that closely parallel imagery of bull sports (Figure 2.13),[169] suggest that such activities may have been part of a broader rural tradition involving animals with which people regularly engaged for their livelihood; the far more frequent rendering of such interactions with cattle could reflect a bias of representation and elite interest.

Theft of livestock may have also been part of human–bovine relations in Bronze Age Crete–an idea that Shapland also raises.[170] This activity would have drawn together the economic, sociopolitical and dramatic aspects of engaging with the living beasts. Livestock raiding is a recurrent subject in post–Bronze Age ancient Aegean literary culture and may have roots in earlier oral traditions.[171] The practice is well evidenced in the modern Aegean. Herzfeld has documented and analyzed the practice of raiding flocks in modern Crete, emphasizing its role in establishing (or rupturing) social bonds between members of different village communities, as well as powerfully contributing to individual identity.[172] Campbell's ethnographic work with the Sarakatsani in northern Greece also examined a complex context of livestock theft and its

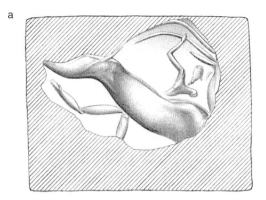

2.13. Neopalatial renderings of goat grappling. a. Drawing of the motif of a sealing from Knossos, CMS II.8.235. Courtesy CMS, Heidelberg. b. Fragment of a stone relief vessel from Knossos. From B. Kaiser. *Untersuchungen zum minoischen Relief*. Habelts Dissertationsdrucke, Klassische Archälogie 7 (Bonn, Habelt-Verlag 1976), courtesy Habelt-Verlag. Objects © Hellenic Ministry of Culture and Sports

sociopolitical roles.[173] In both of these cases, sheep and goats formed the animal populations that were raided, and the communities involved were small-scale pastoralists and farmers. The intellectual dimensions of raiding – the stealth, adeptness at reading and handling the beasts and slyness during and around the actual moment of the theft – are crucial aspects of both scholars' characterizations of the undertakings. While each cultural context is distinct in important ways, the politics of deceit surrounding these acts within both social formations are weighty and involve a complex array of potential gains and risks. In a situation where the animals involved were cattle instead of caprids, the stakes would be altered and heightened in certain respects. The areas of the landscape involved could differ (with more visible pastures in lower areas being preferable for cattle farming). Likewise, in cattle raiding, the massive animals pose far more of a bodily challenge and threat to thieves trying to abscond with them – and they also would embody a greater prize, in terms of wealth and potentially esteem.

We can appreciate that interactions with cattle that took on the status of social rituals and spectacles may have been based on the lives of farming communities and their relations. Recognizing such a rural basis would not deny the possibility that the activities also became embroiled in other social contexts, including eventually being formalized in more elite settings. The specific environment of Crete during the late MBA and early LBA would have brought particular significance to cattle and to humans' engagements with them. Besides the direct challenge of their massive size and potentially aggressive nature, bovines are a demanding crop in other respects.[174] Their bodies require ample nutrition and water.[175] Open, soil-rich bottomland, with multiple water sources within a relatively close distance of one another, provides an ideal setting for the creatures but is not available in many areas of Crete.[176] Isaakidou notes the restriction on grazable land in Crete as one factor that complicates the notion that there were feral or wild cattle populations on the island during the Bronze Age (even if that possibility cannot be ruled out, especially in the case of evidence of very large individual beasts, as seen at LM III Chania).[177] Higher elevations, including mountains and "upland plateaux," would have been problematic due to winter snow cover.[178] The Mesara Plain in south-central Crete, where numerous bovine-form objects have been discovered (see above, p. 69–78), stands as one of the stronger contexts for raising cattle on the island, given its opportunities for grazable land. Yet even in such a relatively favorable context, and during a moment less arid than the present day in the region, the southern Mediterranean climate would have posed distinct challenges, especially through long dry seasons and increased aridity as the Bronze Age advanced.[179] While cattle can adapt quite well to various climates, they need water, vegetation and shade. Cattle do not weather drought conditions well. Drought not only limits available vegetation to forage and water to drink, it also can drive cattle to eat toxic plants typically avoided. Moreover, as body health is impacted, breeding potential and milk production are both disrupted.[180]

Beyond the range of typical variations, we have reason to believe that the Cretan climate – both natural and sociocultural – may have been impacted by the LM IA eruption of the Theran volcano.[181] While the timing of this event and its particular effects are still debated, it is important to take into account Driessen and MacDonald's discussion of possible contamination of water sources in Crete. This, and other potential changes in agricultural circumstances connected to the eruption and related seismic activity, could have made raising cattle an even more restricted and contested undertaking on the island during part of the Neopalatial period. In Driessen and MacDonald's pioneering study, and in a host of subsequent research concerning this moment of potential unrest, environmental matters are taken in tandem with social ones; this integration is also relevant regarding our discussion of cattle. If social power on the island became more fragmented around this time, and Knossos' grip on its own and other regions was rattled, could this have affected the status of rituals involving cattle? I do not believe we are going to find clear answers to these questions in the material culture embodying bovine animals, not least because the dating of these objects is not sufficiently refined, and some of the objects may have stayed in circulation long enough to effectively become part of multiple sociopolitical moments. We can, however, highlight several important contextual factors.

In the faunal remains from Bronze Age Knossos, Isaakidou has observed that some cattle exhibit remarkably large size. She suggests that one possible reason for this could be intentional raising of large individuals for prestige purposes.[182] Sizable individuals may also have been raised for plow teams.[183] Raising large cattle is especially difficult in contexts of drought or resource depletion,[184] but the animals represented in the Knossos faunal remains appear to have had consistent nutrition.[185] Knossos' relationship with south-central Crete, including Phaistos and its pasturelands, becomes relevant here. This relationship potentially was variable during the Neopalatial period, when we have a wealth of representations of cattle and human–bovine interactions from Knossos.[186] In terms of faunal remains, Isaakidou stresses that what we have from Knossos are the "remains from the public/elite core of the site" that "should be strictly regarded as representing very selective consumption of animals bred in a wider geographical area, and acquired for elite consumption."[187] She further points to the urban character of Knossos during the later palatial eras (citing a population estimate of up to 18,000 during the Neopalatial period) as limiting the potential for pasturing and farming in the immediate area of the site.[188] Meanwhile, working with the Linear B archives of the Final Palatial period from Knossos and from Mycenaean Pylos, Halstead has indicated the possible utility of keeping "breeding flocks" in "peripheral regions,"[189] and he, as well as others, refers to the suggestions of Palaima and Killen that animals destined for sacrifice at palatial centers were brought in from distant pastures and fattened up at the central site.[190] Palaima, considering tablets from Pylos, argues that living cattle were moved over significant distances from "cattle grazing districts" to central locations for ritual sacrifice; his discussion of such long-distance movement of beasts draws in cross-cultural comparanda.[191] Killen extends his argument for this practice, based on Linear B documentation from Thebes, to include Knossos.[192]

The Mesara stands as the home of the largest flocks recorded in the Linear B documents from Final Palatial Knossos, indicating the feasibility of animals administered by and/or destined for Knossos being raised in the superior grazing areas of the south-central plain. I do not assume that the same palace-based economic practices existed between the Neopalatial and Final Palatial periods. My point is solely that there is ample reason to believe that, as in the subsequent period, Neopalatial Knossian interests in livestock, including cattle and their tending, could have involved sociopolitical relations with agriculturally rich south-central Crete, whence cows themselves and perhaps social rituals involving them may have moved. In essence, this would be an integration of aspects of Mesaran cattle culture into the Knossian "palatial collective."[193] Driessen has suggested that Knossos may have had a degree of control over the Mesara during LM IA (perhaps via Ayia Triada, which exhibits "Knossian" architectural features), but that rebuilding at Phaistos in LM IB could signal a resurgence of more independence in the region and a retraction of Knossos' reach at this time, related in part to the disruptions of the Theran eruption and associated seismic activity.[194] Within this context, Knossos' access to pastures and livestock in the Mesara may have been altered. This situation likely would have impacted the status of cattle at Knossos and the culture surrounding them, including engagements with and attitudes toward both living beasts and representational embodiments of them; indeed, it is quite difficult to believe that there would be no impact.

The exceptional wealth of bovine imagery at Neopalatial Knossos, including multiple representations of bull sports, has been discussed by many scholars; it has even been described as a form of Knossian "propaganda."[195] Blakolmer's study has elucidated the dramatic prominence of bovine imagery in glyptic during the Neopalatial period, especially at Knossos.[196] In his careful context-ualization of Knossian Neopalatial bovine imagery, Shapland asserts that "bull-leaping became the animal practice that defined the palatial collective at Knossos."[197] In this light, upsets to the status of cattle may have contributed to changes in the palace's political culture, potentially altering the role of existing cultural forms or catalyzing the creation of new ones. Meanwhile, multiple scholars note calibrations in architecture and material and visual cultures between various locations on the island during the Neopalatial period and argue that this relates to new levels and types of influence on the part of the palaces, especially Knossos. Peatfield has compellingly argued that during the Neopalatial period, activity at rural ritual places, including the so-called peak sanctuaries, became restricted as palaces asserted claims on specific sites, and others went out of use; Devolder's recent work expands on this observation and sees it as part of a politically driven development in religious ideology on behalf of the elite.[198] Could rural social rituals involving cattle, and the display of cunning skills associated with them, have undergone a similar type of appropriation at this time, or at least have gained an elevated place in Cretan culture, which related in part to the (yet more) restricted status of bovines as a resource? It is interesting to note that both Campbell and Herzfeld discussed cattle raiding as an action that served to ease social pressures. Campbell described theft as mitigating the risks of hostility by placing it within an established competitive framework.[199] In this light, it is tempting to recognize in much of the elite Neopalatial material culture representing bull sports evidence of an emergent recontextualization for these activities with their inherent guile, as well as what might be described as a formalization of their sociopolitical affordances, as the acts, in Shapland's words, 'became performances.'

Shapland has connected the profusion of representations of bull sports from Neopalatial Knossos with the "turbulence" of violent territorial disputes between palatial collectives at this time, during which claims on cattle were made. He also sees cattle raiding as likely, but in the context of "warfare" connected to this territorial competition, and the killing of rivals animals.[200] I do not think we can necessarily connect the renderings of bull sports to warring specifically. They seem more readily and fundamentally associated with rural practices that took on new associations and significance within a landscape struggling with environmental changes resulting from the Theran volcanic events – changes which would have had real, direct bearing on cattle culture. But Shapland's relation of the objects to a broader changing social context involving cattle is highly compelling and I feel my reading largely agrees with his while bringing further weight and new ecological and cultural emphases to the situation of Knossian expansion that he also describes.

Interest in Heads and Horns

Before leaving the matter of Neopalatial renderings of bovine bodies and their social contexts, I would like to return to the bovine-head rhyta (e.g., Figure 2.9). We have seen that these impressive objects perform differently from their full-bodied cousins – dramatically so. These rhyta also begin to appear at the same time that other distinctive renderings of bovine bodies or bodily elements become more frequent. I am thinking here of representations of horns, oxhide and bodiless bovine heads in glyptic and painted ceramics – a matter that Shapland considers as well.[201] These bovine forms may be connected to one another not only symbolically, but also through a recontextualization of certain practices involving the biological beasts. There is no question that resources as basic as cattle hides and horns had long been procured by Crete's human inhabitants and used to make a variety of fabricated goods, ranging from tools, to garments, to means of protection, such as shields. During the later Middle and early Late Bronze Ages, however, we can detect an increase in representations of horned bovine heads and oxhide. Some of this surely has to do with changes in representational techniques and media – for example, developments in figural painting, in both ceramics and fresco, where these motifs often appear – but this fact in no way diminishes the phenomenon. Real developments in the identities of these animalian entities occurred with such new materializations. For example, in the case of oxhide, we can appreciate

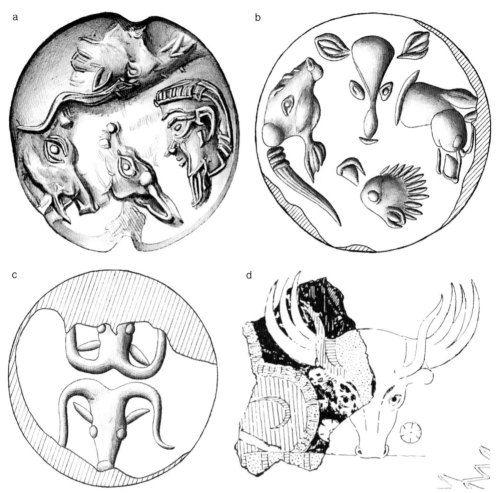

2.14. Neopalatial renderings of isolated bovine heads. a. Seal CMS II.3.196; b. Impression CMS II.6.92; c. Impression CMS II.6.55; d. Detail of fresco fragment from Northwest Fresco Heap at Knossos (Evans 1930: 41 fig. 25a). Glyptic images courtesy of CMS Heidelberg. Objects © Hellenic Ministry of Culture and Sports

that representation in polychrome wall painting brought the substance new vibrant character and contextualizations, including as a prominent element of built spaces (see Chapter 6). Within media such as painting and glyptic, bodiless cattle heads could be rendered in a fixed *en face* perspective, and may have taken on apotropaic qualities associated with a frontal gaze (Figure 2.14).[202] More generally, these heads appear in distinct contexts from renderings of full-bodied bovines – for example, in repetitive friezes, as part of groupings with bodiless heads of other species, or as symmetrical attachments to vessels.[203] With this, a head can become a distinct entity in itself, even while its isolation can also afford being experienced as a fragment, isolated or recombinable.[204] And while we should understand "horns of consecration" as most likely being connected to Egyptian and Near Eastern symbols for the horizon or mountain, and potentially carrying similar meaning in the Aegean,[205] it is possible that a visual assonance was recognized between their form and representations of disembodied bull's horns.

Along with developments in the representation of bovine heads, horns and hides, there also may have been changes occurring in the circumstances of people's interactions with biological cattle that focused on these elements of the animal's body. Shapland observes that isolated animal heads occur as pictographic signs, which he argues could indicate the head's "association with consumption events."[206] Whittaker has argued that the double axe, long taken as an implement and symbol of sacrifice,[207] which became associated with the bull's head in iconography of the Neopalatial period, may instead (or additionally) have been used in a process of horn-shaping on certain living cattle.[208] Such shaping, which fixates on the physical form of the horns, may have distinguished particular beasts at a stage in their biographies; the undertaking itself, involving close human–animal engagement, may have had specific sociocultural implications. Cattle horns separated from a beast's body were also valued. Isaakidou discusses that during the palatial periods, craft activity with bovine horn seems to have been of a restricted, elite character, associated with the palaces.[209] She takes sawn horncores, sectioned relatively high up, at heights above the base, as byproducts of horn-working (versus removal of horns simply connected to food preparation, which would likely involve a basal cut).[210] Evidence of such horn-working is rare, but clear; Isaakidou documents multiple examples from Protopalatial and Neopalatial Knossos alone.[211] Her discussion also draws in Final Palatial textual evidence, which supports seeing horn-working as a restricted "luxury" craft in which the later palaces had direct interest. In a text she cites from Knossos, *Ra*(2), horn is named as a material combined with ivory in objects.[212] In tablet Un 142 from Pylos, Killen reads a reference to a "horn worker" and proposes that the document records the sending of objects to the craftsperson for finishing, probably in a centrally located palace workshop.[213] Killen also refers to Melena's observation that horn appears in Linear B texts as a material used in prestigious items, including reins and swords, as a less expensive substitute for ivory.[214] Meanwhile Shapland convincingly suggests that Neopalatial tortoiseshell-ripple Vapheio-form ceramic cups may have been skeuomorphs of objects made of horn, further indicating appreciation of the substance.[215] Material evidence of sawn cattle horn is known from LB III sites in Crete and the mainland.[216] The restricted nature of horn-working and its association with the palaces appear to have begun during the Protopalatial period and continued through the Final Palatial.

The apparently elite status of bovine horn-working during the palatial periods broadly echoes what we have considered above concerning recontextualizations of other activities involving cattle during the later Middle Minoan and early Late Minoan periods. It is possible that an increase in renderings of bovine heads – in the round, as rhyta or in the flatter surfaces of other media, such as glyptic and painted objects – was related to new associations made with practices in which this area of the body was manipulated. While the horns of cattle can be removed (cut off) when the beast is alive in order to prevent injury, this is a harrowing process for cow and human alike, and potentially quite risky. Disbudding, the removal of the horn bud from calves before it has attached to the skull, tends to be vastly preferable. After the horn bud has attached to a young cow's skull, the hollow horn core communicates directly with the sinuses. Consequently the physical challenge of removing an established horn, and the heightened pain involved for the animal, is accompanied by a considerable risk of infection and injury.[217] Removal of fully grown horns from a bovine's head instead is often undertaken after the animal's death, as part of the processing of the carcass, when the body below the head would also be of interest, for meat, hides and more. The head is typically removed to ease handling of the body, with horn removal occurring from the severed head.[218] This would not preclude other actions involving the separated head taking place before the removal of the horns. In his contextualization of renderings of bovine heads, Shapland contends that, during the Cretan palatial periods, decapitated cows' heads, with flesh still on, acted as "trophies" of commensal eating following the killing of the animals and could have been displayed by being hung up.[219] Younger has highlighted the possible representation of a suspended horned bovine head in an unprovenanced hematite amygdaloid seal dated stylistically to LM I (CMS VIII.10a) and also on Mycenaean painted ceramics.[220] Working on this model, he sees the bull-head rhyta as perhaps acting as stand-ins for biological bull's heads, or counterparts to them, used within contexts of elite palatial feasting. Shapland importantly contributes to this idea, suggesting that the head rhyta, as powerful, nonperishable "substitutes" for severed biological heads, may have been exclusive indexes not only of acts of sacrifice (a traditional focus in the scholarship), but also of butchering and commensal eating – both also socially significant acts.[221] We should appreciate, however, that the bovine-head rhyta, even if acting as substitutes or representations in some sense, unquestionably brought new affordances to the form of the bovine head, as objects with their own capacities, material character and mechanical nature. Here, Shapland's discussion of their fine crafting is important.

There are of course other potential fates for the head of a slaughtered or sacrificed bovine. Elements of a bovine's head can be consumed (e.g., tongue, cheek). The skulls, with or without horns attached, can be intentionally preserved.[222] The cleaning of the skull for preservation might follow another preliminary phase involving the decapitated head (e.g., ritual action, display, horn removal) or could be undertaken directly after death. A skull can be cleaned by exposure and/or manual removal of soft tissue; the process can be extended over a period of time. A separated cow head could form part of a curated deposit, along with other objects. The discovery of cattle bones and horn cores together with multiple bovine-head rhyta within an ashy deposit under the later Temple of Zeus Diktaios at Neopalatial Palaikastro indicates that both biological and representational embodiments of bovine heads contributed in tandem to contexts of social experience in this significant urban venue.[223] At Knossos, cattle heads, perhaps as cleaned skulls, were deposited in the so-called House of the Sacrificed Oxen. This deposit has recently been redated by Mathoudaki to MM IIIA.[224] Here, the horned skulls of cattle were found along with painted tripod tables. Evans describes this deposit, with characteristic flourish, as evidence of a ritual following destruction in the area by earthquake.[225] Different depositional scenarios can be (and have been) reconstructed for this context.[226] For the sake of our present discussion, it is a more basic aspect of the deposit that is notable: its clear indication of another physical form in which the bodiless heads of cattle were contributing to the articulation of social spaces at the palatial site.

Through such evidence, we can appreciate that a range of different circumstances for interaction with the heads and horns of cattle existed at central Neopalatial sites, with Knossos prominent among them. Certainly, we should not assume that these sites were the only locations for such activities. Moreover, other bovine-related practices were surely being carried out elsewhere contemporaneously, in quite different contexts that may have been rural, agricultural or domestic. These settings also would have contributed to the beast's identity during this period, as part of a wider context of relations. What does emerge here, however, is that during the MBA and LBA, and especially from the later MBA onward, prominent central sites were involved in cultivating distinctive aspects of cattle culture on the island.

A More Holistic View on Cattle Culture and Its Recontextualization

Shapland's study challenges us to recognize how renderings of animals, even exclusive objects, potentially were related to interests in biological animals and activities involving them, including consumption and resource extraction. Meanwhile Simandiraki-Grimshaw has questioned whether Minoan renderings of animal parts (especially those that could be combined with a human, as "homosomatic hybrids") could relate to the animal's edibility and the sustenance it provided.[227] Stepping back slightly, we can place our observations concerning activities focused on the head and horns of cattle within this broader light. Impressive events involving cattle – such as round-ups, grappling, leaping-over and netting – were likely related, in part, to moments surrounding procurement of substances from the beasts (even if these showy events also may have occurred at other times). Such is assumed in scholarly reconstructions that see religious sacrifice following bull sports,[228] but of course the procurement of meat, hides, horn, tissue for adhesives[229] and so on all stand as instances of potentially more mundane resource extraction that also could have followed dramatic engagements with cattle; unfortunately, these often become falsely isolated from one another in our analyses. Extractions of such substances from a bovine's body often happen as part of the same extended moment of processing the carcass, when the animal's body is "open," and progress through conventional sequencing[230] (subsequent processing of the derived materials could be carried out later by persons with distinct skillsets, perhaps acting within separate spaces).[231] Hence, interactions with the living beast would flow into a series of practices involving different elements of its dying and newly deceased body, in a connected chain or network of substances and experiences.[232] Given this integrative context, qualities related to engagements with living cattle may have become fluidly associated with materials derived from their bodies and with related material culture. In particular, the quick-wittedness demonstrated in various aspects of dealing with the beasts, or the social relationships in which the animals were involved (e.g., territorial or wealth-based relationships), may have become connected to extracted bovine resources (e.g., hides, horns) and representational things; this view agrees with and builds on Shapland's consideration of such materials as "indexes" and traces of animal practices.[233] Broadly speaking, this type of integrative experience surrounding cattle and cattle-things was surely long-standing in Cretan communities. It was likely at play behind the Prepalatial vessels from south-central Crete that rendered bovine and human bodies together. We should further note that the craftiness of these representational embodiments, in turn, could have contributed to the status of biological cattle and interactions with them. In this light, it is especially significant that we can observe new emphases taking form in the contributions of bovine material culture during the Neopalatial period.

While numerous scholars have discussed the wealth of (especially exclusive) bovine imagery that appears in the Neopalatial period, particularly at Knossos, Shapland importantly considers this in terms of the broader (changing) social context of people's relationships with animals. Here, I find it especially significant that some of the new contextualizations of human–bovine engagement may have been occurring within a moment of social and *environmental* stress in Crete. Such circumstances could have placed marked pressure on cattle resources and on palatial control, in light of heightened competition (perhaps between multiple factions or House groups). This possibility brings new depth to our consideration of representations of nonhuman bodies and activities involving them. We have seen that certain celebrated elements of human interaction with bovines in Bronze Age Crete were characterized not only by physical strength, but seemingly also by exceptional guile and agility – an impression to which the physical peculiarities of the material culture contribute. Might palatial interest in cattle culture have arisen, in part, from a desire to disarm a threatening cultural current by trying to absorb it and its trappings? Or was there an attempt to lay claim to the perceived strength of this culture, in practice or as a "symbolic exploitation,"[234] as a means of increasing the palace's mediation of ritual life? On this we can only speculate, but my primary point in posing these questions is to notice that the novel contextualizations of cattle culture evident during the palatial periods, especially during the later MBA and early LBA, should be approached, as Shapland does, as being part of a highly dynamic sociopolitical landscape. Given the strong evidence we have that during the Neopalatial period the palaces were interfering in domains of rural ritual, by taking over certain peak sanctuaries and limiting access to such spaces and the actions that took place in them,[235] the developments in the realm of human–bovine activities likely should be understood as related to larger changes and possible appropriations, by "palatial collectives."[236] Furthermore, representations of cattle and of people engaging with cattle in restricted material culture do not merely reflect or signify this new contextualization, they are active participants in it. To put this another way, it is not enough to say that these contexts and interests in cattle culture become visible at this time through representational objects. We instead should realize that these material embodiments are integral elements of the recontextualization of cattle culture – they are instances of its enactment and hence provide direct evidence of its occurrence. This recontextualization emphasized the impressive ability of humans in relation to the imposing nonhuman beasts. This occurred not only through the represented actions involving cattle and people (such as leaping), but also through the particular character of their embodiments in objects, which fragmented the bovine body and placed it in human hands, celebrated human craftiness in exclusive things and substances and placed the bull's strength within the stately walls of the palace. The remarkable power of the living human is very apparent in these restricted palatial-era bovine things – far more so than in the Prepalatial "anthropomorphic" vessels.

NOTES

1. Such a relationship is embodied, for example, in the Neo-Assyrian "mural-crown" that has the shape of city fortifications; when worn by the queen, it effectively merged the sociopolitical realm with her human form (Gansell 2018). In Minoan material culture, we find the powerful bodies of individual persons in similarly provocative associations with urbanscapes – for example, in the Master Impression, from Chania (KH 1563), and the Mountain Mother impression, from Knossos (CMS II.8). Within the preserved works of the classical Aegean, Plato (after Socrates), Aristotle (after Plato) and Pindar, among others, discussed the relation of the biological body and the collective social entity – the "body politic." In the Middle Ages, this was further explored (e.g., in the *Policraticus* of John of Salisbury, state society is envisioned as a human body, with its constituent parts [Sherman 1995, esp. III:18]). In the modern era, the relationship of the human body and

sociopolitical life has been problematized from various angles, for example, in Freud's work (see *Civilization and Its Discontents*, which foregrounds struggles with the sexuality body) and Foucault's corpus (notably 1975).

2. For example, Meskell 2000; Crown 2007; Knapp and Van Dommelen 2008.

3. On the absence of persons, as such, in studies of the subsequent Protopalatial period, see, for example, Nikolaidou 2002. Historically, imagery of humans in Neopalatial visual cultures (especially wall paintings) has been embraced more readily for studies concerning people's action and lives. Some of these studies have been remarkably innovative, for example, Alberti 2002; Simandiraki-Grimshaw 2010a; Soar 2014.

4. For example, valuable discussions in Mina, Triantaphyllou, and Papadatos 2016.

5. Fortunately, there are a host of recent studies of cemeteries and funerary material from Prepalatial Crete that offer sophisticated analyses of evidence regarding dimensions of identity, bodily and sociocultural experience and demographics; see, for example, Betancourt and Davaras 2003; Vasilakis, Branigan, Campbell-Green et al. 2010; Boness and Goren 2017; Branigan 1998; Galli 2014; Girella 2018; Girella and Todaro 2016; Legarra Herrero 2014; Murphy 2001, 2011; Nafplioti 2018; Nafplioti, Driessen, Schmitt and Crevecoeur 2021; Panagiotopoulos 2020 (and earlier reports); Papadatos 2005; Schoep 2018; Schoep, Crevecoeur, Schmitt, and Tomkins 2017; Soles 1992; Todaro 2004; Triantaphyllou 2016; Tsipopoúlou 2017, Tsipopoúlou and Rupp 2019 (and further research at the Petras cemetery); Vavouranakis 2014.

6. See, for example, Branigan 1993; Murphy 1998; Déderix 2015; Paliou and Bevan 2016; Déderix and Sarris 2019; Relaki 2004; Hamilakis 2002.

7. Such studies work from various perspectives, for example: Sbonias 1995; Pini 1999; Schoep 2006; Colburn 2008, 2011; Hickman 2008; Malafouris 2008; Relaki 2009; Anastasiadou 2016b; Flouda 2013; Anderson 2016, 2019; Finlayson, Bogacz, Mara, and Panagiotopoulos 2021; Crowley 2012.

8. For example, Hamilakis 2002, 2014; Hamilakis and Sherratt 2012.

9. See Morris and Peatfield's meticulous studies of figurines from the peak sanctuary at Atsipadhes and possible connections to bodily actions of living humans at the site (e.g., Morris and Peatfield 2002, 2013); also, for example, Mina 2008; Soar 2015; Zeman-Wisniewska 2015; various works by Simandiraki-Grimshaw, for example, 2010a, 2013; and Günkel-Maschek's project, Gesten und Gebärden in den Bildwerken der minoischen Kultur.

10. For a valuable foundational study of Minoan zoomorphic vessels, including characteristically insightful problematization, see Miller 1984. On the case of rhyta specifically, see Koehl's important 2006 study.

11. See McEnroe 2002, Papadopoulos 2005; Momigliano and Farnoux 2017.

12. Xanthoudidēs describes this as Region Delta, between Tholoi A, E and Γ (1924: 33, 39).

13. See, for example, Xanthoudidēs 1924; Warren 1973; Cadogan 2010.

14. Xanthoudidēs 1924: 13, 33, 39. See also Warren 1973: 138, tav. XVIII 1–2; Simandiraki-Grimshaw 2013: 50.

15. Xanthoudidēs 1924, pp. 12–13, XIX. See also Warren 1973: 138, tav. XVIII 3–4 (HM 4993); Simandiraki-Grimshaw 2013: 50–51.

16. Warren 1973: 138.

17. Warren 1973: 138, Cadogan 2010: 44.

18. From Trapeza Cave (HM 9339; EM I–MM, EM IIB or EM III); Ayios Myron (Alexiou 1969: pl. 273α; EM III–MM IA or EM II–III); Yiofyrakia (Marinatos 1933–35: 50 fig. 2 no. 8, 3; EM III or EM III/MM IA); two from Archanes Phourni, Area of the Rocks (HMΠ 25770 (EM III or MM IA) and unknown museum number (EM III); Sakellarakis and Sapouna-Sakellaraki 1997, vol. 2, figs. 538 and 539). Simandiraki-Grimshaw (2013: 46–52) provides dating and further bibliography.

19. Warren 1973; Cadogan 2010, and Simandiraki-Grimshaw 2013, who positions these vessels within a multiperiod catalog and provides a sophisticated problematization.

THE CRAFTINESS OF PEOPLE'S ENGAGEMENTS WITH CATTLE 95

20. Warren 1972: 208–210, fig. 92, and lengthy discussion in Warren 1973, esp. 139, 140–141, tav. xx–xxi; also Simandiraki-Grimshaw 2013: 46.

21. Cadogan 2010: 42.

22. Warren 1972: 210.

23. From Malia, Ossuary II (HM 8665; dated EM III–MMIA or MM IA, although its context contains some LM material; Demargne 1945: 14, pl. 31 (1–2); Warren 1973: 138, tav. xix 1–2; Simandiraki-Grimshaw 2013: 48); Mochlos Tomb XIII (HM 3499, EM III or EM III–MM IA; Seager 1912: 64 figs. 32, 34 no. XIIIg; Warren 1973: 138–139; Simandiraki-Grimshaw 2013: 47).

24. Warren 1973: 138.

25. Warren 1973: 138.

26. Sakellarakis and Sapouna-Sakellaraki 1997, vol. 2: fig. 539; also Simandiraki-Grimshaw 2013, catalog no. MAV 006 with image and further bibliography.

27. Simandiraki-Grimshaw (2013: 33–34), who works with the notion of "containment."

28. Simandiraki-Grimshaw 2013: 27, 33.

29. See Warren 1973; Cadogan 2010.

30. Hurowitz 2003, with review of literature and further references.

31. Simandiraki-Grimshaw 2013.

32. See Mauss 1979: 108–9.

33. See Chapter 1.

34. Mauss 1979: 108; also Bourdieu's notion of "habitus" (1977) and Csordas (1993) regarding "somatic modes of attention."

35. Mauss 1979.

36. Mauss (1979: 111) discusses, for example, a toddler's responsive perching on a mother's hip.

37. See Chapter 1.

38. Mauss 1979: 102; Ingold 2004; also Anderson 2015 and forthcoming concerning how the presence or absence of footgear would impact the bodily sociocultural experience of pilgrimage.

39. Notably, Heidegger 2006 and Sennett 2008.

40. For example, Knappett 2002, 2004, 2010, 2011; Gibson 1986. Cf. Heidegger 2006 on "readiness-to-hand."

41. For example, Malafouris 2008, 2013, concerning "extended self."

42. Knappett's discussion of marionettes is relevant here, given their bodily, and often specifically human-like, nature (2002: 113–114).

43. Mauss' discussion is not without its shortcomings, yet his explicit focus on the significance of the *particular* actions and dynamisms of bodies, and on their social nature, undermines a notion of universal or natural (human) corporeality, replacing it with a focus on what bodies do and how they do it, thus leaving space for a real diversity in the character of the bodies themselves. This allows us to appreciate points of commonality and distinction with bodies that otherwise were implicitly treated as incomparable.

44. Compare Simandiraki-Grimshaw 2013.

45. Knappett 2004: 46–47 discusses the "transparency" of affordances, including critique of Gibson's (1979, esp. ch. 8) notion of "direct perception." Knappett stresses that the transparency of a thing's affordances may vary between contexts and interactors.

46. See Simandiraki-Grimshaw 2013: 34–35.

47. For example, Lefebvre 1991, Soja 1996, 2008.

48. Simandiraki-Grimshaw 2013: 25–29, 33–34. Concerning gender in and through Minoan objects, including these, see Goodison 2009.

49. See also Simandiraki-Grimshaw 2013: 35; also Knappett 2002 on complicating the division of animate/inanimate.

50. Compare Simandiraki-Grimshaw 2013: 22.

51. See Koehl 2006: 17–18.

52. Warren 1972: 210.
53. Simandaraki-Grimshaw raises the possibility that another material was fitted onto this vessel's limbs at the perforations, and that some of the other anthropomorphic vessels also may have had matter attached to them – for example, suspended from pierced ears (2013: 26). If something like feathers were added to the Malia figure's wing-like arms, the effect would certainly further complicate its status (physical, textural, notional) between avian, human and vessel.
54. Simandiraki-Grimshaw 2010b: 101, working with ideas of Counts 2008 (following the work of Bhabha, e.g., 1994) and Meskell and Joyce 2003.
55. Marthari 1987: 375–376 fig. 25 #1837.
56. Notable are engraved seals from LBA Zakros (with motifs often called "monsters"); however, the dynamics of copresence between woman and bird are distinct in these exceptional glyptic embodiments (see Chapter 4).
57. Simandiraki-Grimshaw 2010b: 95.
58. Wolf 2020.
59. McGowan 2011: 67-70, with images, citing Weingarten 1988.
60. Kristeva 1982. See also Phillips' dedicated discussion of abjection in the inaugural issue of *Transgender Studies Quarterly* (2014).
61. For example, Kristeva 1982: 69–79.
62. Butler 1993.
63. Wilson 2001.
64. Simandiraki-Grimshaw 2010b: 101–102, as part of a compelling rethinking of "animal mastery."
65. Especially Gell 1992, 1998.
66. Gell 1998: 71.
67. See also Simandiraki-Grimshaw 2013: 24.
68. Murphy (e.g., 1998, 2011) has discussed this extensively.
69. Whitelaw 2001.
70. Legarra Herrero 2014.
71. Murphy 1998, 2011; Déderix 2015, 2017. See other contributions in Branigan 1998, and Relaki 2004 on "networks of relevance."
72. Driessen 2010b.
73. Driessen 2010b: 109. Driessen also discusses tombs beyond the Prepalatial period.
74. Driessen 2010b: 109–111.
75. Driessen 2010b: 111.
76. Driessen 2010b: 114–115.
77. Warren 1973: 142.
78. A clay head, rather similar in size and form to that of the vessel body, was discovered in the "northern Rubbish Pit" at the settlement (Warren 1972: 70–71, pl. 72e–g). Warren describes this "figurine" fragment (Figurine 70) as solid and made to "fit into a separate body." This might be another peculiar clay object body that was active at Myrtos.
79. Whitelaw 1983, 2007.
80. Warren 1972: 86.
81. Cadogan 2010: 41.
82. See Simandiraki-Grimshaw 2013: 28–29, discussing "tactile feedback" and the "blurred interface" of the vessel and human bodies. While I do not follow this to the point of considering the vessel an extension of the acting human, Simandiraki-Grimshaw's discussion is rich and valuable.
83. Cadogan 2010: 43, also Simandiraki-Grimshaw 2013: 30–31.
84. Simandiraki-Grimshaw 2013: 30–31, 67 fig. 04.
85. For example, at Koumasa; see Xanthoudidēs 1924. Warren (1973) provides basic contextual information for the broader group of body vessels.

86. Concerning the sociocultural affordances of courts in Bronze Age Crete, see Driessen 2007, Todaro 2012; Anderson 2016.
87. Murphy 2009, with references.
88. Murphy (2009) argues in part that the distribution of similar objects suggests that we should rethink the "religious" status of some types.
89. Simandiraki-Grimshaw 2013: 35–36.
90. Chlouveraki, Betancourt, Davaras et al. 2008; Driessen 2010: 111, fn. 30.
91. Letesson and Driessen 2020: 8.
92. Letesson and Driessen 2020: 13.
93. Todaro 2020.
94. Papadatos 2020: 53–54, 58–59; Papadatos 2011.
95. Papadatos 2020: 54–59.
96. Driessen 2010: 46–47, 55–57.
97. See also Papadatos 2020, who considers both the boons and problems of seeing Houses in relation to social units in Bronze Age Crete. Whitelaw (e.g., 2014) offers valuable critical discussion.
98. Hamilakis (2002) discusses the Prepalatial tholoi of the Mesara as "heterotopic" spaces (Foucault 1986).
99. See Simandiraki-Grimshaw's catalog (2013; MAV 008–011) for variable dating of the Koumasa vessels.
100. Whitelaw 2001.
101. Papadatos 2020: 53–54.
102. Papadatos 2020: 54–59.
103. Peatfield's focus (1995) is on "religious" culture. Considering ritual action more broadly, the body vessels may have been key performers within liquid-based rituals – repeated traditional actions – involving the community.
104. Simandiraki-Grimshaw 2013: 35–36.
105. Simandiraki-Grimshaw (2013) emphasizes the comparability of the vessel and biological human bodies.
106. Koehl 2006; Simandiraki-Grimshaw 2013.
107. HM 3489.
108. HM Λ2171; Simandiraki-Grimshaw 2013: 54, MAV 016, with references; Koehl 2006, no. 1092.
109. Koehl describes several rhyta with trapezoidal body forms similar to those of the core group of Prepalatial "anthropomorphic" vessels, as "bird hybrids"; for example, HM 4124, with ram's head from Koumasa.
110. Koehl 2006.
111. Koehl 2006; Whitelaw 2007: 73.
112. Koehl 2006: 308.
113. Koehl 2006: 74 describes that this bull vessel, from a "pillar room" at Phaistos, unusually has its secondary opening positioned in the throat versus the muzzle. The throat is often cut on a biological cow during killing/bleeding out.
114. Koehl 2006: 281.
115. Koehl 2006: 308, with references.
116. See bovine rhyton painted with a net/grid-design (NAM AKR 563): Marinatos 1999: 12 (incl. fig. 1), 59, pls. A.2, 8.2 and 54. 1–2; also Koehl 2006 no. 20, p. 74.
117. Koehl 2006: 32–37, 39–43.
118. Koehl 2006: 32, 39, 126–127, with references.
119. Koeh 2006: 41l, Shapland 2021: 312.
120. Koehl 2006: 127–128, with references.
121. Koehl 2006: 32, 39.
122. Koehl 2006.

123. Koehl (2006: 267–8) offers excellent discussion of the holding, filling and decanting of rhyta in his "Type II Head-Shaped" class. One possibility is that an assistant helped in the performance, as discussed also by Rehak (1995: 443–444, n. 55).

124. Koehl 2006: 267–268.

125. Younger's estimate is given in Rehak 1995b: 444.

126. Koehl 2006: 267–268.

127. Simandiraki-Grimshaw 2010b.

128. Karetsou and Koehl 2013; Shapland 2021: 311.

129. Cf. Rehak 1995: 454.

130. Morgan 1995a.

131. Koehl notes Matz's theory that the bull-head rhyta were linked to sacrifice, which Rehak (1995) and Shapland (2021) also consider; fragments of such rhyta found within an ash layer with oxen bones could support this link (Koehl 2006: 268, after Dawkins 1904–5).

132. For example, possibly the holder's garment, performative behavior and so on.

133. If the flow of liquids through the muzzle of the stone bull head was reminiscent of the flow of blood in the process of a bull's killing; see Rehak 1995.

134. Relaki 2004.

135. Peatfield (1987, 1990) argues that certain peak sanctuaries became associated with palaces during the early Neopalatial.

136. Letesson and Driessen 2020: 16.

137. See discussion of such dynamics in Haggis 2002 and Anderson 2016.

138. HMp no. 4126. Xanthoudidēs 1924: 40, pls. II, XXVIII.

139. For further details, discussion and references see Foster 1982: 81–82, 109 (also for comparable objects); Younger 1995: 525 #9; Koehl 2006: 71.

140. HMp 5052. Xanthoudidēs 1924: 62, pls. VII, XXXVII.

141. Foster 1982: 81–82, 109; Younger 1995: 525 #7; Koehl 2006: 72.

142. Foster 1982: 81–82 109; Younger 1995: 525 #8.

143. Younger 1995.

144. BM 1966,0328.1. See Shapland 2013: 202, 205 on the possible origin in the area of the Preveli Gorge, following Pendlebury 1939: 217.

145. Shapland 2013: 203. Shapland draws attention to the contact made between the human and the bull in this figure, commenting that it was an aspect of the interaction that was lost in a twenty-first-century CE television advertisement that reenacted the scene with a live person and bull (2013: 201).

146. See description of the object at www.britishmuseum.org/collection/object/G_1966-0328-1.

147. Evans 1930: 428–433, color pl. XXI.

148. Evans 1930: 431–432.

149. See Alberti 2001 concerning the formulation of the gendered body at Knossos, with the ivory bull leapers as a focus (esp. 194–298).

150. Evans 1930: 429.

151. Evans 1930: 429. In his consideration of Neopalatial bull imagery, Shapland (2022: 93–94) also remarks on these objects, noting how their "skilled crafting and restricted materials" demonstrate that bull-leaping was linked to the domain of the "palatial collective."

152. Quoted text is from the label for this object in the Chania Museum.

153. Those of Koehl's Type II, with a smaller primary aperture, which was the predominant type in the Neopalatial period (Koehl 2006).

154. Koehl 2006.

155. Rehak 1995; Rehak cites Laffineur 1986. For a different view on the possible ritualized treatment of head rhyta, see Shapland 2021, and discussion below.

156. Especially Shapland 2010b, 2022.

157. Shapland 2010b: 120; 2022.

158. For paintings from the area of the Court of the Stone Spout at Knossos, see Evans 1930: 209–32 figs. 144–6, 148, 164 B, col. pl. XXI opp. 216; IV 892; index 53; Hood 2005: 79–80, pls. 12.1–3, 40.1–2, with discussion and further references. For fragments from the area of the Queen's Megaron, see Evans 1930: 209 fig. 143, and Hood 2005: 70–71 and fig. 2.22 for details, discussion and further references.

159. Shaw (1997: pl. CXCI) offers a reconstruction (referenced in Hood 2005: 70–71, fig. 2.21).

160. Blakolmer (2012, also 2016b) provides excellent discussion of indications of interior architecture in Cretan visual culture.

161. Evans 1930: 167–191; also Davis 1974: 479–480 (citing Woodward's critique [1972]).

162. Davis' (1974) argument, that one of the Vapheio cups was made by a Cretan and the other by a Mycenaean craftsperson, is well known but controversial. See Shapland's discussion of the cups in the context of valuable consideration of bovine imagery at Knossos (2022: 92–95).

163. See Younger 1995, with references.

164. Younger 1995.

165. See account of Lecile Harris (2018), known as the "Dean of Rodeo Clowns/Bullfighters.

166. See, for example, famed Spanish *torero* Eduardo Davila Miura's discussion of his earliest fight with a bull in the countryside, at age seven, in Corbett 2017.

167. See Shapland's valuable comparison of Minoan bull games and rodeo culture (2022: 89–95).

168. Hanes 1977: 23–28. The "bulldogging" technique that Pickett introduced to the rodeo involved biting the lip of a cow while taking it down to the ground.

169. See Molloy 2012: 109–110, who discusses a Neopalatial seal impression (CMS II.8.235) and a fragment of a Neopalatial stone relief vessel from Knossos, the latter also considered by Logue (2004: 167, 168 fig. 13; and Kaiser 1976 fig. 13a).

170. See especially Shapland 2022: 92.

171. For example, Walcot 1979.

172. Herzfeld 1985.

173. Campbell 1974; see also Campbell 1992.

174. See Isaakidou (2005: 238) on this.

175. See, for example, Bennet 1985: 246; Halstead (1995) discusses the costliness of keeping up teams of oxen; his discussion concerns the Mycenaean era and which farms made use of oxen plow teams, but the point is surely relevant more broadly – supporting cattle requires a significant output of resources and would need to be justified by the production possible.

176. See Godart 1971: 420–421, concerning the situation on Crete, especially for breeding animals. Concerning ideal circumstances for raising cattle, see, for example, Wells and Cook 2017. Bennet (1985: 237) discusses grazing land in Bronze Age Crete. On the expense of feeding cattle fodder (to supplement poor grazing land), and whether feasible in the Late Bronze Age Aegean (based on Linear B evidence), see Palaima 1989: 101–102.

177. Isaakidou 2005: 229–30, 238; Reese 2016 for the evidence from Chania. Concerning possible free-range farming and hunting of cattle in Bronze Age Crete, see Shapland 2022: chapters 3 and 5.

178. Isaakidou 2005: 238.

179. Rackham and Moody 1996.

180. See, for example, "Drought and Livestock," "Drought Management Strategies" 2022. Halstead (2012: 24–26) discusses the effects on cattle of reduced and/or altered diet during times of poor harvest.

181. Driessen and MacDonald 1997, 2000; Driessen 2013.

182. Isaakidou 2005: 250, 285.

183. Isaakidou (2005: 250, 285). Isaakidou notes that the Final Palatial evidence from Knossos describes specialized oxen teams being raised by the palace (2005: 69).

184. Scasta, Lalman, and Henderson 2016.

185. Isaakidou 2005: 285.

186. See, for example, Shapland 2013: 202–203; Younger 1995: 93.
187. Isaakidou 2005: 294.
188. Isaakidou 2005: 39, 294.
189. See also Godart 1971.
190. Halstead 1996: 32–33.
191. Palaima 1989: 115–118.
192. Killen 1994.
193. See Shapland 2022 on "palatial collectives" as a potential context for human–animal relations; see especially 2022: 91–93 concerning the "extending" of the Knossos palatial collective to take in cattle and animal practices such as bull leaping.
194. Driessen 2013: 12. See Shapland 2022: 92–93 concerning Ayia Triada's possible link to Knossos concerning cattle.
195. For example, Younger 1995: 521–523; Rehak 1995: esp. 448–450; the term "propaganda" in relation to the "Knossian bull" stems from Hallager and Hallager 1995.
196. Blakolmer 2016a: 111–112; see discussion of the establishment of broader iconographic trends at this time in Blakolmer 2012.
197. Shapland 2022: 90.
198. Peatfield 1990; Devolder 2009.
199. Campbell 1974: 210–212.
200. Shapland 2022: 89–100.
201. Shapland 2022: 93–99, 112–117. Cf. Younger 1995: 520–521 regarding special attention to head of cattle evident in Minoan material culture.
202. On the frontal gaze in Aegean visual culture, see Morgan 1995a; cf. Younger 1995: 520; see also Chapter 4.
203. See Younger 1995: 520 on vessel attachments in the form of bucrania; cf. Rehak 1992 on bosses in the shape of figure-8 oxhide shields on Neopalatial vessels. On the embodiment of animalian entities in repetitive friezes, see Chapters 5 and 6.
204. See Chapter 4.
205. See Banou 2008, with discussion of earlier scholarship.
206. Shapland 2022: 83, 89.
207. See, for example, Marinatos 1986, 2010; Rehak 1992, 1995: 452.
208. Whittaker 2015; also Shapland 117–120; Haysom 2010; Molloy 2012; Rehak 1992: 124.
209. Isaakidou 2005: 295–6.
210. Isaakidou 2005: 213.
211. Isaakidou 2005: 213, n. 6. A specimen of bovine horn core was found in a MM context at Chania (I thank D. Reese for sharing this information with me; Reese saw the specimen in 2013).
212. See Isaakidou 2005: 295.
213. Isaakidou 2005: 295, citing Killen. See also Killen 2000–2001; Killen suggests that the craftwork perhaps is to be carried out at a central location (389). Killen's reading of the crucial first term in this text, *ke-ra-e-we*, as "worker in horn," differs from that preferred by Melena, which is γέραϛ, "portion of honor" (Melena 2000–2001: 380–384).
214. Melena 2000–2001: 382, Killen 2000–2001: 387; both refer to specific descriptions of objects in Linear B tablets.
215. Shapland 2022: 97–98.
216. See, for example, Reese 2016 for Chania.
217. American Veterinary Medical Association. 2014. "Literature review on the welfare implications of the dehorning and disbudding of cattle." https://www.avma.org/sites/default/files/resources/dehorning_cattle_bgnd.pdf.
218. Mack Keller, cattle farmer, pers. comm.
219. Shapland 2021, 2022: 112–121 on "trophies."
220. Younger 1995: 521, 539 nos. 146–148 and pl. LXII e, f.
221. Shapland 2022: 102, 111–117.

222. Younger (1995: 520–521) notes instances of dehorned skulls recovered at Knossos and "immured in the blocking wall of the inner chamber of Tholos A at Archanes-Phourni." Shapland considers various Protopalatial and Noeopalatial instances of skull and horn remains (2022: 102–117).

223. Koehl 2006: 117 nos. 303, 268, citing Dawkins 1904–5: 287 along with further references.

224. Mathioudaki 2018.

225. Evans 1928 (1): 302, fig. 175; Evans' presentation of this space is set in the context of the finds from the Room of the Fallen Blocks and a consideration of seismic impact on this region.

226. See Isaakidou 2005: 24 on this deposit and Evans' interpretation, and discussion in Shapland 2022: 106–108.

227. Simandiraki-Grimshaw 2010b: 101.

228. For example, Younger 1995: 518–521.

229. Palaima 1989: 88–89, with references.

230. Isaakidou (2005: 295–6) discusses Killen's and Halstead's ideas concerning how palaces may have intentionally "fragmented" the production process of certain elite material culture, as a means of controlling its crafting and circulation.

231. The butchering of cattle still typically follows a particular sequence, even if tools and contexts involved naturally can differ; Mack Keller (cattle farmer) pers. comm. See also Younger 1995: 520–521, Shapland 2022: 72.

232. See also Younger 1995, and Rehak 1995: 452–453, who focuses on symbolic and religious actions, especially sacrifice and bull games leading up to it.

233. Shapland 2022: 95–99.

234. Molloy 2012.

235. Peatfield 1990; also Devolder 2009.

236. Following Shapland's (2022) notion of "palactial collectives."

THREE

STONE POETS

Between Lion and Person in Glyptic and Oral Culture of Bronze Age Crete and the Aegean

LIVING WORDS AND DYNAMIC THINGS

In the previous chapter, we examined certain zoomorphic objects from Bronze Age Crete that likely were the focus of community actions and queried how, as participants in such contexts, these things variably brought emphasis to humans and nonhumans. This involved investigating the performative dynamics of these objects, including the impressive animations of living and nonliving bodies that they elicited. Comparing certain zoomorphic vessels from the Prepalatial and palatial eras, remarkable changes in the experiential and social affordances of these animalian things became apparent. A crucial dimension of this examination entailed contextualizing the objects within contemporaneous arenas of social practice. This included consideration of peoples' experiences within venues of collective action as well as their interactions with both other types of animalian object and biological animals. Through this more holistic view on the zoomorphic vessels and their position in sociocultural experience, we could better appreciate how these object-bodies contributed, as enlivened participants, in the changing sociopolitical landscape of Crete, along with living humans.

In the present chapter, we will further consider the relationship of biological and fabricated animalian bodies across the periods of the later third to mid-second millennia BCE, as our attention shifts also to problematizing the interconnections of material and *im*material creative cultures. Here, our focus comes to a particular species, the lion, and to a specific type of material culture, engraved seals and the impressions stamped by them in moist clay. I argue that since populations of living lions were not present on Crete, representational embodiments were the primary basis of people's physical encounters with the species and, with this, that the peculiarities of these object-bodies powerfully contributed to the characterization of the beast on the island. Throughout the Bronze Age, the vast majority of Cretan lion representations occurred in glyptic objects – a position that brought the lion uniquely intimate involvements in people's experiences. Seals, including those engraved with leonine figures, were worn directly on people's bodies. Seals could also actively contribute to the signification of the identities of these persons, through the practice of creating stamped imprints in clay. Such clay imprints novelly reembodied the leonine form as part of an index of the human's action and were engaged with, as such, in contexts of social relation. These distinctive qualities of glyptic objects (their statuses as worn items and things embodying social identity) consistently placed the leonine in direct relation to the human; such juxtaposition had both physical and sociocultural dimensions.

I consider this paralleling of human and lion enacted through glyptic objects within its broader lived context. While the ecology of Crete did not afford direct engagements with living lions, lived social practice on the island very likely did involve other encounters with the beast, beyond the objects – in oral traditions. Early Aegean poetic traditions formulate a paralleling of human and lion through the spoken (and eventually written) form of the simile, creating a comparison that is, in its essence, remarkably similar to that generated through the relationship of a lion seal and a person. In the period from MBA III to LBA II, after centuries of development in Crete, the lion's association with glyptic extended to the early Mycenaean mainland, in part through the sharing of Cretan objects and practices. This was a moment of intense, multidirectional intra-Aegean exchange that had linguistic, practical and material dimensions. Evidence indicates that the Aegean epic tradition was taking form at this time, including the lion similes. Through its different embodiments, both thingly and oral, the lion contributed to this interactive moment as part of various areas of social experience; with this, the beast's juxtaposition with humans fluidly continued and developed. Archaeology provides material vestiges of this, and epic poetry seems to offer another. I consider the poetic juxtapositions realized through material and oral cultures as two interacting aspects of a broader creative articulation of the lion and its relation to persons within the early Aegean.

INHERITED INROADS AND OBSTACLES IN THE STUDY OF AEGEAN LIONS

Reflections of Verse or Primary Embodiments?

The presence of lions in the creative culture of the ancient Aegean has long been celebrated and discussed. Much attention has focused on the Homeric similes and the charged parallels they so vividly formulate between humans and lions. Over generations of scholarship, the origins of this association of humans and nonhuman beasts have been sought both beyond the Aegean and within, including attempts to identify reflections of it in Mycenaean imagery.[1] Such efforts have been fruitful in some respects but also can suffer from a tunnel vision that is skewed by its teleological focus on the later textual material at the cost of a meaty problematization of the Bronze Age evidence. Disciplinary boundaries erected around the idea of Greekness have hampered work that might truly flex the parameters of investigation,[2] as have the limitations emplaced by the lens of traditional iconographic analysis that focuses on imagery more or less in isolation.

My aim is to newly problematize the Bronze Age Aegean material culture embodying lions by taking seriously the fact that it was the principal means through which people actually engaged with the beast as a physical entity. The lineage of Aegean representations of lions begins in Crete and in glyptic objects.[3] From the later EBA (ca. 2300–1900 BCE), the lion was given form in seals, and this would be the beast's primary home on the island for the remainder of the Bronze Age, even as the details of its rendering significantly altered. The lion's position in glyptic objects – seals and stamped impressions – meant that the beast was embedded in sociocultural life. Since seals were worn on a person's body, the leonine was consistently encountered, and understood, immediately alongside the human. I believe we should appreciate this juxtaposition as being deeply poetic in nature and consider how it established a distinctive and long-standing paralleling of lion and human in Cretan culture that inevitably would have developed in tandem with spoken characterizations of the beast, notably in oral traditions.

As the strong association of lion and glyptic objects was shared across the Aegean and with mainland Greece during the late MBA and early LBA, the narrative dimensions of lion imagery were further developed, even as the beast's fundamental position paralleling the human persisted. Contemporaneous developments in Aegean oral poetry, including the tradition of the lion simile, can be considered as parts of the same ecology as the glyptic objects representing lions. In this context, it would make little sense to approach these objects simply as reflections of the content of poetry; instead, the seals and impressions themselves were active generators of poetic dynamics.

These were real, material embodiments of the beast, and their relationship with humans was physical, meaningful and social. Hence, we can better understand the lion simile's presence in Aegean poetry if we consider its mutuality with and perhaps indebtedness to the material culture embodying the lion. More importantly, examining the fuller ecology surrounding embodiments of the beast, oral and material, helps us to appreciate how relationships with a nonhuman animal could become a substantive and persistent element of Aegean culture even if the animal was rarely known in the flesh. To begin, we need to reconsider the matter of the lion's distinctive occurrence in the Aegean, and in Crete specifically, appreciating the particular character of its embodiments and thinking through the ways in which the species was very much present.

The Realities of Aegean Lions

Lions are often assumed to have been a nearly universal symbol of power in the ancient Mediterranean and Near East. Yet how the beast was engaged with by humans, and hence related to and characterized, would have varied dramatically throughout this broad and diverse region. This is not to deny the rich potential for, and no doubt reality of, cultural sharing, occurring by land and sea, voice and thing; clearly, such interaction stimulated both spectacular and subtle creative acts, some involving lions. Nevertheless, the variable contexts in which people experienced lion phenomena would have contributed to distinctive senses of what the beast was and how it was positioned in a particular cultural and social space. Persons dwelling in places where living lions were an encountered reality would have had a fundamentally different ground for their perceptions of and associations with the beast compared to people living where the lion was known only through representations, oral or physical, or rarer traces such as an imported skin, tooth or bones.[4] Even in those areas of Anatolia, southwest Asia, southern Europe and Africa where lions were an indigenous species, there would have been considerable variation within the human population concerning interaction with the beast. For example, Morris notes that in Thailand, although lions live in the jungle, in fact few persons have any sort of direct experience with the living beast and it has an "almost mythical" status, despite being a prominent social symbol.[5]

The lion's presence in the early Aegean is an even more complicated topic.[6] While lions almost certainly roamed highland areas of northern Greece until the first century CE,[7] it is not clear how substantial the population was; people's engagements with the beast may have been quite infrequent. Herodotus' account of lions attacking Xerxes' camel train in Thrace is often cited, but the precise factuality of this report should at least be pondered; the imagery of a fearsome Aegean-born beast ambushing a vulnerable eastern foe may have

3.1. Map of key places mentioned in Chapter 3

proven irresistible to an historian who was a consummate storyteller. He places the animals solely in the area between the rivers Nessos and Achelous in northern Greece (*Histories* 7.125–126) (Figure 3.1). Other ancient authors also refer to lions in the region of Greece. In the fourth century BCE, Aristotle describes them as confined to the same northern interriverine zone as Herodotus but also proclaims them very rare (*Hist. an.* 6.579b).[8] One must also consider the nature of rare encounters with lions when they did happen: were people fending off predators from their flocks or seeking out formidable opponents for extravagant feats?[9] By the end of the LBA, any lion population in the Peloponnese in the southern Greek mainland, the heartland of Mycenaean society, is thought to have fully disappeared.[10] Faunal evidence of lions from this area is extremely limited and could in part represent bones brought in from elsewhere for ritual use.[11] In carefully cataloging the current leonine faunal evidence known from southern Europe and Greece, Thomas notes that there is an apparent shift in the nature of the finds and their depositional contexts between the Chalcolithic and Bronze Age remains;[12] this shift also has geographical dimensions. She notes that in the pre–Bronze Age/Chalcolithic evidence – all of which is from southern Europe and not Greece, save one bone from a Late Neolithic level at the far northern site of Dikili Tash, in Greek Thrace[13] – "the lion bones are larger and less often purely associated with pelts; greater numbers of other wild animal bones are regularly found with the lion bones; and the find spots are more frequently habitation sites than otherwise."[14] In the Bronze Age evidence, with which the emphasis switches to Greece, she notes by contrast, "there are fewer collections of larger bones and more finds of single or small bones related to pelts; the massive numbers of wild game bones decline; when important groups of lion bones are found in association with other game animals, it is likely to be at habitation sites such as Tiryns; and the find spots now include several places that will be sacred in the Iron Age."[15] These observations are important. Looking more closely, we can also note that most substantial Greek finds are unsurprisingly from northern Greece. Meanwhile, we have finds from only five sites in the Bronze Age Peloponnese (if we include the island of Aegina, in the Saronic Gulf). Tiryns stands out for its level of evidence, suggesting a particular interest in the animal over time.[16] Most of the finds from the Peloponnese seem to be smaller portable body fragments that could have been transported over significant distances, such as teeth, pelts or isolated bones.[17]

As Thomas notes, the evidence from Bronze Age Greece appears to be more focused on acquisition of smaller traces;[18] and this is especially marked in southern Greece. Given that these traces easily could be moved or exchanged, we should recognize that the place of their final deposition might be significantly removed from their ultimate point of origin in an encounter such as a hunt. A couple of finds from Iron Age contexts in the Peloponnese (a period in which the lion population in that region would likely have been entirely gone) remind us that moving such body fragments over considerable distances was possible – as it would have been in the Bronze Age; three teeth from Kea, in the northern Cyclades, also demonstrate how such rare small traces could move.[19]

Taken together, although all assertions must remain cautious given the nature of the data, the evidence indicates that an apparent increase (although still modestly evidenced) of interest in and acquisition of lion traces in mainland Greece during the late MBA and LBA, which would have involved procurement through exchange or rare hunts, coincided with the species' diminishment in southern Europe and eventual disappearance from the southern Greek mainland by the end of the LBA.[20] With this, interactions with the living animal in that area would have been exceedingly infrequent during the later Bronze Age. The encounters are more likely to have happened in the highlands of more northern Greece and involved the beast being sought out; the rareness of the lion likely contributed to its social power.[21] Meanwhile, yet farther south in the Aegean, lions were never an indigenous species in the Cyclades nor on the large island of Crete that marks the southern limit of the Aegean Sea.

While living lions never roamed the mountains and fields of Crete, this does not mean that we should reduce the beast's existence in early Cretan culture to something purely symbolic and immaterial. Lions were not known in the flesh, but they were known as concrete physical presences, with their own distinctive bodily forms. Lions are a prominent species in the material culture of Bronze Age Crete. Already in the EBA, their bodies were rendered in the hard, smooth surfaces of engraved stamp seals, and they continued to hold this significant position for almost a millennium, throughout the rest of the Minoan period. Strikingly few examples of lions exist in other object types. This is not to say that there were no representations of lions in other media, but presently they are notably rare. From the Prepalatial period, we have a small gold charm with granulation, probably an import, from Koumasa (EM III–MM IA).[22] Sanavia has recently published a remarkable fragment of a ceramic vessel painted with a lion (likely part of a file of lions) from Protopalatial Phaistos.[23] Meanwhile three (two quite fragmentary) stone lion-head rhyta from Knossos are variably dated to the Neopalatial period or later (LM IIIA),[24] and three from eastern Crete probably postdate the Neopalatial (they have been dated Late Minoan IB–IIIA:1).[25] Among the three LM I or LM IIIA rhyta from Knossos is the masterful limestone lioness. The design of this object is similar to the bovine-head rhyta of the Neopalatial period considered in Chapter 2, and this stone piece clearly seems to be part of the technical tradition of Aegean rhyta, even if its leonine subject was peculiar therein. Its material, craftsmanship and findspot indicate that it was an exclusive palatial object, crafted by someone both skilled in the Aegean tradition and privy to the details of a lion's physical appearance. It is a type of object to which very few persons in Crete would have had access, and the distinctive experience of the lion it afforded would have been highly restricted.[26] It is interesting to note that three lion-head rhyta of definite LB I date (LH IA and LC I) come from elsewhere in the Aegean – Akrotiri and Mycenae[27] – raising the possibility that this rare subject for a head rhyton was brought to Crete from farther north. Meanwhile, the overwhelming majority of Cretan embodiments of lions continued to occur in seals and impressions.

As the primary tangible forms in which people engaged with lions on Crete, the physical and material properties, associations and interactive potentials of seals and stamped impressions should be closely examined. We can consider how these embodiments of the lion contributed to the very existence of the beast in its sociocultural context – to perceptions and conceptions of it, senses of its fundamental nature and its relations within the lived world.

Glyptic and Other Bodies

In the Bronze Age Aegean, seals had a paradoxical spatial existence. Seals were engraved with motifs that could be stamped into moist clay to create an impression. This seal-impressed clay could be attached to an object closure and, once dried, would secure it as a direct sealing. The impressed clay could also function in other ways – for example, as the receipt documenting a transaction. The impressed motif signified the seal user's identity and will (e.g., in sealing or authenticating a sealed object) and thereby served as a proxy means of communication.[28] Hence, glyptic objects were a powerful tool for extending social interaction across time and space and enriching interpersonal connectedness. At the same time, Aegean seals were, almost without exception, pierced so that they could be strung and worn directly on a person's body (Figure 3.2). This corporeal association would have been consequential; it established the physical link between the acting person, the sealing object and the stamped impression that would subtend all sphragistic seal use. While the connection between these three bodies – in seal stone, flesh and clay – was practical, it also carried other experiential weight.[29]

Recognizing the intimate somatic relationship of the seal and person is crucial for our discussion of lions in Bronze Age Crete. Simandiraki-Grimshaw

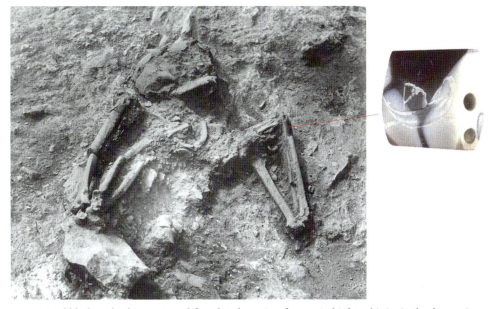

3.2. Veined black-and-white agate seal found at the wrist of a man in his late thirties in the destruction level of MM IIIA Anemospilia, Crete. Herakleion Museum HM-Σ-K 2752. Photographs from Sakellarakis, Yannis and Efi Sapouna-Sakellaraki, *Archanes: Minoan Crete in a New Light* (Athens: Ammos Publications, 1997): 302 fig. 264; 693 fig. 795. Courtesy of Efi Sapouna-Sakellaraki. Objects © Hellenic Ministry of Culture and Sports

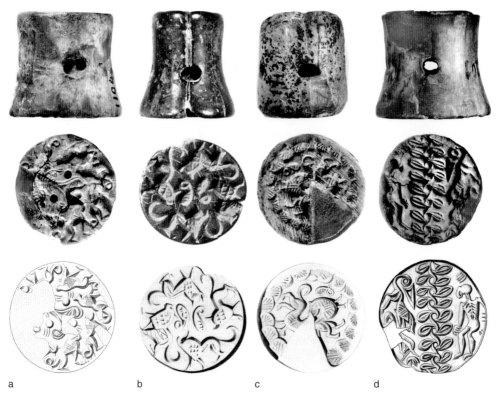

3.3. Examples of the Cretan Prepalatial Parading Lions seal group. a. CMS II.1.312, Platanos. b. CMS II.1.3, Drakones. c. CMS II.1.321, Platanos. d. CMS II.1.222, Marathokephalo. Images courtesy of the CMS, Heidelberg. Objects © Hellenic Ministry of Culture and Sports

and Stevens have astutely recognized the distinct power that comes of animals being worn upon the human body as materially rich items of adornment in the Aegean Bronze Age, creating relationships that were not only symbolically but also physically and sensorially complex.[30] This power was a crucial aspect of the Cretan lion's existence. Lions made their earliest appearance on Crete in Prepalatial glyptic. In the first examples, from the later EBA, we find lions engraved into cylindrical and conical sections of imported hippopotamus teeth that had been cut for use as stamp seals (Figure 3.3).[31] Most of the engraved motifs involved multiple lions progressing head to tail around the circular face of the seal. We currently have about forty examples of glyptic objects engraved or impressed with such imagery from sites across the island, with a concentration in south-central Crete; collectively they are known as the Parading Lions Group.[32] The soft inner ivory of the seal face would have required skill to work but not highly specialized tools, a fact that facilitated dispersed production. Each of these seals was pierced to be suspended by a string, and they were likely hung around their possessors' necks. Here, the weight of the ivory chunk would have been felt by the wearer, while the seal's impressive toothy character would be readily notable.

What we should consider first is the very fact that the earliest lions evidenced in Crete were part of seals and that this remained their principal location throughout the entirety of the Bronze Age. Given that lions were not present as a living species on Crete, the reason for their embodiment in the island's material culture is not self-evident, particularly in objects as central to internal community building and identification as seals.[33] The imported hippopotamus ivory used for the seals underscores our need to look overseas for contextualization. But how would the external origins of lions and ivory – and their combination – have been understood by Cretans? This is of course impossible for us to grasp fully, but we should consider certain factors. Very few Cretans would have been in a position to encounter a living lion overseas, and Crete also was not home to any large nonhuman predators that might have been recognized as posing a similar threat. We can imagine that bounding dogs and stalking cats[34] possibly fed Cretans' vision of a lion's behavior relative to prey, and perhaps the hippopotamus teeth were taken to be lion teeth.[35] At the same time, the physical contours of the lion bodies with which Cretans actually engaged were diminutive in scale, silent, sleek and stone-cold, and their potential for activity was connected to the distinctive dynamism of seal use.

Scholars consistently identify Egypt or the Near East as potential sources for the lion form and ivory, with the Levantine coast being seen as a likely conduit for both.[36] Yet Near Eastern and Egyptian glyptic traditions that might have served as models in fact diverge from the Cretan seals in a number of ways, a point adeptly demonstrated by Aruz.[37] Differences involve the form of the lions, the composition of the designs, the material of the seals and the technique of carving.[38] For example, lions engraved in mid- to late third-millennium BCE Early Dynastic and Akkadian cylinder seals from Mesopotamia are typically engaged in an attack, locked in violent contact with other animals (Figure 3.4a). Meanwhile, the imagery of the Cretan Parading Lions Group, while chronologically aligned with the Mesopotamian evidence, rarely if ever depicts a lion attacking, or even in contact with, another animal – even when other creatures appear in a motif with lions.[39] The roll-cylinder technology most prevalent in Mesopotamian glyptic created potentially repetitive rectilinear seal impressions, while the Cretan stamp seals engraved with self-contained lion motifs were usually round, meaning that the two traditions differed in this physical dimension of their clay impressions as well.

If we turn to Egypt, the outline style evidenced in the rendering of lions in the stamp-seal iconography of the Sixth Dynasty and the First Intermediate Period (FIP) (ca. 2345–1938 BCE; Figure 3.4b) can be compared broadly to the often-unmodeled engraving of the Cretan Prepalatial lion glyptic. Likewise,

3.4. Examples of Near Eastern and Egyptian glyptic involving lion imagery. a. Early Dynastic IIIA (ca. 2500–2375 BCE) shell cylinder seal from Ur and a modern impression; scene of lions attacking horned animals and an approaching nude hero; inscribed, *Lugal-shà-pà-da*. From the body of a groom in the dromos of Queen Puabi's Tomb. Courtesy of the Penn Museum, object no. B16747. b. Egyptian Sixth–Eighth Dynasty (ca. 2345–2160 BCE) stamp seals engraved with pairs of inverted lions (ca. 2345–2160 BCE). Adapted from Wiese 1996: pl. 20 nos. 400–402. Images courtesy of André Wiese

the early Egyptian lions are seldom engaged in contact with other beasts.[40] Beyond these general similarities, however, the Egyptian and Cretan motifs diverge significantly. The circular or rotating compositions so characteristic of the Parading Lions imagery – often carefully elaborated and balanced with additional elements, or through manipulations of the beasts' pose[41] – are remarkably distinct from the counterpoised designs of the Egyptian stamp-seal corpus.[42] In terms of the seals' overall form and material, the relationship to Egyptian glyptic is also complex. Unlike Near Eastern cylinder seals that were engraved around their curved barrel and rolled in order to make impressions, stamp seals have the potential to be rendered in various, sometimes amuletic forms.[43] In the Egyptian FIP stamp-seal corpus, lions are found not only within the intaglio motifs, but sometimes also as the overall form into which the seal has been carved. These lions are typically depicted either sitting full-length, with head raised, or in the form of the lion's head alone. On Crete, already in the mid-third millennium BCE, we have bone seals carved in theriomorphic forms, and, in the late third millennium BCE, some seals are fashioned specifically in a leonine form; several more examples of lion-bodied seals stem from later MBA (Protopalatial, ca. 1900–1700 BCE) contexts on the island

3.5. Lion-form seals, from Prepalatial (a–c) and Protopalatial (d–f) Crete: a. CMS v.SIA.304; b. CMS II.1.17; c. CMS II.1.130; d. CMS IV.7D; e. Petras inv. PTSK 12.1390; f. Petras inv. PTSK 12.1624. Photographs of seal profiles a–d courtesy CMS Heidelberg; e–f courtesy Krzyszkowska 2017: 147. Objects © Hellenic Ministry of Culture and Sports

(Figure 3.5). Some of the sculptural lion seals from Crete resemble Egyptian ones of roughly contemporaneous date, and there may indeed be a link, but the occurrence of comparable lion-form objects in other areas, including Mesopotamia, warns against drawing a firm connection.[44] Moreover, the hippopotamus ivory used for the Parading Lions seals, while stemming from Egypt or the Levant, was not typically used for seals in these areas. Hence, the ingredients of the Cretan lion glyptic may have been of overseas derivation but something markedly distinct was crafted therewith.

Two significant contextual factors further distinguish the Cretan lion imagery already in its first generation. First, in the contemporaneous iconographical repertoires of both the Near Eastern and Egyptian glyptic, lions were embedded within a teeming menagerie of animal species. They were not consistently singled out as the primary subject of glyptic motifs and were not imaged with disproportionate frequency. Other beasts – such as monkeys, hippopotami, dogs, goats, composite figures and insects – are equally at home in these glyptic traditions. On Crete, the situation was different in a key regard. The Parading Lions seals in many respects grew out of a long-standing craft on the island, but they also present some extraordinary innovations. Certainly, the use and working of imported ivory is one of these, but there are other seals fashioned of this restricted material contemporaneously. Most remarkable, instead, is the development of what we can securely identify as a discrete glyptic iconography, something that had not been seen in Crete in earlier phases, when the majority of seals were engraved with crosshatched lines. Indeed, the Parading Lions seals arguably represent Crete's earliest extant figural iconography in any medium, self-consciously reproduced across different communities and regions.[45] Within this common iconography, newly elaborated and individualized seal motifs could signify the identities of particular users. At the center of this crucial innovation, which dramatically extended the interactive potential of seal use and impacted the way in which sociocultural identity was experienced, were lions. Lions were not merely one potential option in the iconography of this seal group, they were strongly preferred, by far the most frequent and prominent subjects of the seals' engraved imagery. Other creatures might accompany or even replace lions, but the lion is the defining subject and holds a striking and unique pride of place within the glyptic corpus of Crete at the turn of the second millennium BCE. This status distinguishes the Cretan lion within the broader field of contemporaneous eastern Mediterranean and Near Eastern glyptic.

The second important distinguishing aspect of the Prepalatial Cretan lion imagery is that, apart from seals, lions are almost nonexistent in Crete during this period. This, by contrast, certainly is not the case in Egypt and the Near East, where lion bodies appear in a host of other object types – such as cosmetic containers, mace-heads, painted pottery, magical devices (Figure 3.6), feeding cups (Figure 3.7), weights,[46] metal tools/weapons,[47] large-scale sculpture (Figure 3.8) and gaming pieces – with which persons in a range of social positions would have interacted. Through these media, people in the Near East and Egypt would have encountered the beast as part of a broader spectrum of sociocultural circumstances and engaged with it through a great variety of materials and forms. This diversity of objects representing lions existed within

3.6. Middle Kingdom Egyptian apotropaic rod with animal forms; glazed steatite. Metropolitan Museum, NY, 26.7.1275a–j; Purchase, Edward S. Harkness Gift, 1926. (CC0 1.0) www.metmuseum.org

3.7. Egyptian late Middle Kingdom faience feeding cup with lion imagery. Metropolitan Museum, NY, 44.4.4; Rogers Fund, 1944. (CC0 1.0) www.metmuseum.org

3.8. Egyptian Old Kingdom (Fourth or Fifth Dynasty, ca. 2575–2450 BCE) granite entrance figure in the form of a lion, from Herakleopolis Magna, southeast of the Fayum oasis. L. 201 cm, h. 87 cm. Metropolitan Museum, NY, 2000.485; (CC0 1.0) www.metmuseum.org

the same broad contexts as living lions present in these regions, a factor that would have brought further dimensions to people's characterization of the beast. Meanwhile, on Crete, the lion was encountered primarily in two related places: as seals tied to their human owners, in direct juxtaposition to the owners' bodies, or manifest in the clay of impressions stamped by the seals, acting in some ways as a legitimated substitute for the human owner.[48] Hence, for Cretans, from this initial moment in the late EBA, the existence of the lion was intimately and directly bound to the existence of a person and was animated by the peculiar movements and mobility inherent in seal use. With this, the acting corporeal human was a fundamental aspect of the early Cretan lion, whether present or presently implied.

The Cretan Lion in Time and Space

Glyptic remained the primary material home of the Cretan lion from the later third millennium BCE through the end of the Bronze Age (ca. 1100 BCE). Through this time, the intimate relationship of seal and human persistently subtended the embodiment of the beast and infused it with particular sociocultural depth and animacy. Within this situation of striking continuity, however, the specifics of the lion's embodiments varied significantly. Changes and divergences in the beast's formal and compositional dynamics warrant closer consideration.

The engraved motifs of the Prepalatial Parading Lions Group all clearly participate in a recognizable macrostyle while also demonstrating finer-scale technical and stylistic variations that sometimes concentrate in specific regions or subregions.[49] Across these distinct subtraditions, however, the motifs typically image more than one lion, and compositions often eschew understanding the beasts as being located in time or place. Instead, we often find the lions endlessly rotating in chains (e.g., Figure 3.3a–b) or situated *tête-bêche*, in inverted pairs (e.g., Figure 3.3c), with no common grounding orientation. Sophisticated renderings of the lion bodies, often stylized, can contribute to and complicate the overall rotational dynamics of the motif, as when the beasts' forms have been manipulated into regardant or contorted poses to establish distinct rotational currents that counter the overall circulation of the image (e.g., Figure 3.3c). The most striking aspect of these motifs, however, is the sheer proliferation of lions and the great prominence that they hold in this pioneering iconographic group. The lion's repeated presence establishes its primary relationship to seals and to what seals were becoming within the increasingly interconnected landscape of transitional second-millennium BCE Crete.[50] Moreover, given that seals and impressions of the Parading Lions Group have been found across much of the island, the particular fashioning of the beast embodied in the iconography reached a widespread audience and likely took root as a foundational rendering of the lion. Sbonias argues that depictions of lions in seals produced in the Protopalatial Malia workshop, in northeastern Crete, were indebted to the Parading Lions imagery.[51] That the distinctive formal dynamics of the Parading Lions motifs were deeply engrained in Cretan cultural traditions is further indicated by multiple examples of heirloom seals and deliberate imitations in the Protopalatial and Neopalatial records (e.g., CMS II.5.281 from the Protopalatial *vano* 25 sealing deposit at Phaistos).[52] This association is also beautifully demonstrated in Sanavia's recent study of a lion motif found painted on the rim of a Middle Minoan (MM) IB bridge-spouted basin at Phaistos, which he compellingly identifies as an instance of "symbolic transference" from the Prepalatial Parading Lions seal types.[53] This is one of few extant examples of lions occurring beyond the glyptic corpus, but the exception clearly underscores the definitional role of glyptic in the beast's early Cretan identity.

The Parading Lions corpus also holds some surprisingly precocious features that should warn against charting simple chronological advancements in the representation of lions on the island. Notable is a small subgroup of motifs in which figures are arranged linearly, forming what seem to be simple narrative scenes that sometimes combine humans and lions.[54] In at least one case, CMS II.1.222 from Marathokephalo (Figure 3.3d), the interaction depicted appears to be a hunt. On one side of the field, a large human figure, with defined rib bones and bent legs, seems to crouch; the right arm ends in what could be a delineated hand or alternatively a barbed object held by the figure. A leafy chain divides the middle of the composition. On the opposite side of this vegetation, two lions are engraved with feet directed toward the same edge of the field, as if running behind one another. Above the rear lion, a large, pointed item hovers, perhaps a spear; in front of the lead lion, a second barbed item floats, very similar to the form appearing at the end of the human's arm.

This scene clearly relates lions and humans in an event while also creating a visual parallel between the two, one species set beside the other on the two halves of the field.

Krzyszkowska's recent publication of two ivory stamp cylinders from House Tomb 5, Room 10, at Petras adds to this small but increasingly well-established Prepalatial scenic repertoire. In the motif engraved on the first seal, PTSK12.950,[55] she tentatively reads a man positioned behind a lion while a (hunting) dog approaches the beast from below. On the second, PTSK12.1051,[56] she describes "hunters," wearing "caps or helmets" and carrying probable weapons, who stand in the midst of hunted quadrupeds. Taking this material together, we have remarkably early evidence of the lion being conceived in a potentially antagonistic relationship with humans (see also the person in an unenviable position below a lion in Figure 3.5c). These vignettes play out within the primary juxtaposition of human and beast that was created as the lion-themed seal was worn by a person; thus, the elaborated seal imagery formulated a nested expression of the relation between the two species.

In the Protopalatial period (ca. 1900–1700 BCE), as Anastasiadou has recently shown, different regional glyptic styles were active in eastern and central Crete. With this, we move from the Parading Lions Group, in which the lion was embodied in a common iconographic tradition distributed across much of the island, to stylistically distinct renderings of the beast. It should be noted that the fundamental characterization of the lion was apparently shared across these regional styles: the lion is consistently depicted with broad frame and fierce demeanor, typically with the mouth open in a roar, and the teeth sometimes bared. In both regions, the lion is most often imaged alone. How this fundamental impression of the solitary fearsome lion is then given form in the notably distinct regional styles is quite remarkable. Lions occur in each of the three primary eastern glyptic subgroups delineated by Anastasiadou but are most frequent in the extensive Malia Steatite Group (Figure 3.9). Like all figures, the lion most often appears here in multisided prisms. It is normally isolated as the sole creature on a surface, often regardant. The engraving is deep, not complicated by modeling, and the bodies can be highly schematized. Anastasiadou describes the style as "pictographic," since, like the signs of Cretan Hieroglyphic, the scale and orientation of each figure can vary independently, and they are "not bound in an image by landscape elements."[57] These unbounded figures could have functioned emblematically, but they also may have acted as iconograms with further narrative implications;[58] these possibilities are not mutually exclusive.

Other recent findings from Petras are relevant for our consideration of the lion in its Protopalatial East Cretan context and its possible narrative dimensions. Among the seals recovered in the cemetery were several representing

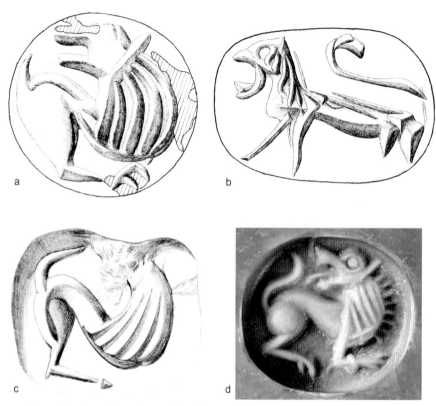

3.9. Examples of East Cretan Protopalatial glyptic imagery of the lion. a. CMS III.42 ("Lassithi"). b. CMS III.203a (findspot unknown). c. CMS II.2.245c (Kato Metochi). d. PTSK12.602 (Petras, East Crete). a–c. Drawings of motifs, courtesy CMS, Heidelberg. d. impression of seal face, photograph courtesy Olga Krzyszkowska

lions, a significant fact that in itself demonstrates the beast's strong association with Protopalatial glyptic in the area (e.g., Figure 3.9d). Two of these seals have been carved in the round, in leonine form (Figure 3.5e and f). We should imagine these sculptural lion bodies visibly suspended on the bodies of seal owners, powerfully emphasizing the juxtaposition the seal formulates between lion and human.[59] The first of these (Figure 3.5e) is formed of black steatite in the shape of two recumbent lions, arranged *tête-bêche*. The seal face has been engraved with another *tête-bêche* animal pair, this time bulls. This compositional echoing suggests an interaction between the sculptural and intaglio beasts, perhaps as hunter and prey. A similar dynamic is apparent in the second sculptural lion seal, where the beast is carved in a recumbent posture (Figure 3.5f). The intaglio imagery seems to depict an attack scene, in which a goat is met by a "stockier animal with a swollen muzzle," which Krzyszkowska reads as potentially being a dog;[60] its proportions suggest it could also be a lion. The relationship between the seal's sculptural form and intaglio imagery could be read in at least two ways, depending on the identity of the second animal in the engraved motif. If the second creature is a dog, the lion is paired not simply with an attack scene, but a hunt. As in PTSK 12.950, a Prepalatial seal also from the Petras cemetery, and in later glyptic compositions, the dog would be a hunting dog attacking from below, therefore implying the role of an unseen human companion. If the second figure of the intaglio is leonine instead of canine, the motif of predatory behavior would offer further characterization of the lion embodied in the seal's overall form. In either case, despite the lack of groundlines or other scenic cues, this seal expands our understanding of the narrative complexity of glyptic in this region during the Protopalatial period and of the lion's role therein. A narrative dynamic extends over the space and time generated by the seal, involving its various dimensions as a sculptural and an engraved thing – as an impression was made, the seal's story and the lion's character were further developed.

In central Crete, attestations of the lion in Protopalatial glyptic arise in large part from deposits of preserved clay sealings that richly augment the evidence available from seals recovered in the region. At the palace of Phaistos, a deposit in *vano* 25 contained more than 300 distinct seal motifs, impressed into over 6,500 sealings, which had been gathered there before the palace's destruction.[61] The Phaistos sealings are especially important for the light they shed on narrative and naturalistic glyptic imagery in central Crete. Here the representational dynamics are quite different from those seen in eastern Crete. In the Phaistos material, the lion is a popular subject in imagery that often includes groundlines and landscape features such as rocks and vegetation (Figure 3.10).[62] This is illustrated by CMS II.5.270 (Figure 3.10b), where a lion stands facing

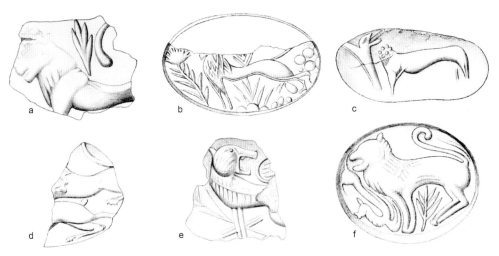

3.10. Lion motifs from the Protopalatial Phaistos *vano* 25 sealing deposit in central Crete. a. CMS II.5.274. b. CMS II.5.270. c. CMS II.5.273. d. CMS II.5.286. e. CMS II.5.271. f. CMS II.5.272. Drawings courtesy CMS, Heidelberg

left, mouth agape,[63] feet positioned in a stony ground with flowers and branches rising up around its body (cf. Figure 3.10a, c–f). Certainly, the presence of landscape elements in such motifs is not a definite indication of developments in narrative traditions involving the lion. Yet such features do place the lion *somewhere*, in a physical context, and thereby clarify its status as an actor, a doer. These features also offer information concerning the beast's physical and social position, given that it is typically shown in a natural (versus built) environment and occasionally interacts aggressively with another nonhuman species. With such contextual details, the particular character of the lion embodied in the seal, and hence juxtaposed to the human wearer, is further articulated.

In the subsequent Neopalatial period (ca. 1700–1450 BCE), glyptic imagery of lions demonstrates notable continuity with Protopalatial image types. Much of the extant Neopalatial glyptic can be seen to participate in broadly represented technical, thematic and compositional trends that make it possible to discuss a Neopalatial glyptic "mainstream," complicated by finer stylistic divergences and certain dramatically distinctive smaller-scale traditions.[64] This being said, significant dating issues plague especially the soft-stone corpus and complicate attempts to detail chronological developments. Studies by Younger and Pini, among others, provide frameworks to navigate the evidence, but differentiating between LM I and II material is often difficult, and this difficulty might reflect real fluidity in glyptic characteristics across these periods.[65]

Single lions, often regardant, continue to be a popular theme in LM I–II, especially in soft stone seals (see Younger's Cretan Popular Group). Beginning in LM I, a plumed feature, presumably vegetation, is often conventionally positioned behind the beast and creates a sense of landscape (see Figure 3.17, p. 148).[66] These simple scenes easily relate to Protopalatial types, especially those from the central Cretan tradition. Motifs involving two lions also become popular in LM I (Figure 3.11), and when the imaged beasts rotate in a whirl-form, they recall the Prepalatial lion imagery.[67] If another species is instead combined with a lion in these arrangements, the result can be a stylized attack (Figure 3.11d); when the second beast is the (now more frequently imaged) griffin,[68] the lion can appear in the unfamiliar position of victim (Figure 3.11e). In Neopalatial glyptic, in fact, the theme of lions attacking other creatures becomes frequent, occurring across stylistic groupings (Figure 3.12).[69] This theme has precedents, in content and composition, in earlier Cretan glyptic (e.g., Figure 3.10d), and it could also have drawn on Near Eastern glyptic imagery, for example, from early second-millennium Syria or even from antique objects, such as a recarved third-millennium Eblaite cylinder found at Neopalatial Knossos (CMS II.2.29).[70] The Cretan lion seems to assault other creatures indiscriminately, with goats, deer, bulls and other animals appearing

INHERITED INROADS AND OBSTACLES 121

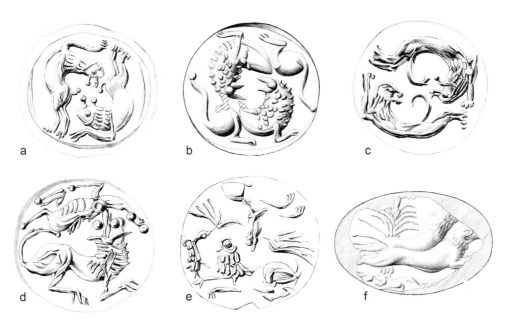

3.11. Examples of recurrent themes in LM I–II glyptic imagery of the lion. Rotating lions (a–c): CMS VII.90, CMS II.3.348, CMS VI.353; lion rotating with another creature (g–h) CMS IV.285, CMS VI.393; two lions: CMS II.8.298. Images courtesy CMS, Heidelberg

3.12. Examples of LB I–II glyptic imagery of lions attacking other nonhuman animals, from Crete (a–f) and the mainland (g–l): a. CMS II.7.101; b. CMS II.3.60; c. CMS II.6.234; d. CMS II.7.100; e. CMS II.6.247; f. CMS II.1.419; g. CMS I.278; h. CMS I.190; i. CMS I.251; j. CMS V.S1B.140; k. CMS V.S1B.93; l. CMS I.204. Images courtesy CMS, Heidelberg

as prey. It attacks from the top, bottom and flank and sometimes seems to wrap around its victim; occasionally, lions hunt in pairs. The lion also encounters the human in Neopalatial glyptic imagery far more often than ever before, a topic considered below.

Broadly defined, each of these motif types persists into subsequent periods, even as their stylistic and technical character can flex; the temporal depth of the lion imagery is impressive.[71] Just as remarkable, however, is the spatial and cultural reach of many lion glyptic types during the LB I and II, when it becomes absolutely necessary to consider Aegean glyptic broadly, embracing Crete, the mainland and the islands. On current evidence, Cretan and mainland glyptic traditions have especially strong links in lion imagery. This cross-Aegean relationship and its implications are discussed in detail in what follows, especially regarding developments in the imaging of human engagements with lions. With these developments, the relationship of lion to person – always central in the lion glyptic because of the seal's relationship to its human owner – gains further narrative and cultural elaboration.

Coming to Crete: Utterances, Both Spoken and Material

The ingredients of the earliest Cretan embodiments of the lion, the EM III–MM IA Parading Lions seals, clearly had origins overseas, yet these elements were rapidly and creatively developed into a distinctly Cretan material tradition. While the language of Bronze Age Crete still confounds us, it is important to consider the complexity of imported notions of the lion on a linguistic front as well. This is because the oral tradition of early Crete, though elusive, stands as the other primary means through which the Aegean island's population was likely to have experienced lions and their attributes, through uttered words that surrounded and interacted with the material forms we have been discussing. Oral forms would have moved from one culture to another, overseas and onto Crete, transforming along the way. Imagining the contexts of these movements that initially brought the lion to Crete forces us to grapple with the complexities of sharing across cultural and geographic distance, something relevant for oral and material phenomena alike.

For evidence of the lion's presence in the textual and oral repertoire of the Aegean Bronze Age, let us begin on later, surer ground, in the Mycenaean period. That the lion was a creature known within Mycenaean culture is richly attested in the visual evidence. We also know more or less how its name was uttered in Mycenaean Greek, since it appears as *re-wo* in the Linear B documents. Masson asserts that this term for the beast (Linear B *re-wo* = λέων) is "common to all the regions around the Mediterranean."[72] Ulanowski points to Egyptian as a likely source of the word λέων, and he suggests Semitic languages as a possible origin for another term for lion found in Homer, λίς.[73]

The term for lion found in other Indo-European languages of the region, such as Luwian *walw(i)*, can also be connected (linked to Indo-European **lew-*).[74] As the wide distribution of common terms for the lion indicates, linguistic transfers and adaptations must have often taken place across languages and sociocultural boundaries within the eastern Mediterranean; such moments of human-to-human reckoning should also be recognized in the wealth of exchanged objects and ideas evidenced archaeologically. Indeed, terminology for lions would not have been reported in isolation; it would have been embedded in meatier oral accounts, sometimes in direct conjunction with things.

While the surviving (and deciphered) Aegean textual evidence for the lion dates to the Late Bronze Age, we can expand our consideration of the beast's position in the region by embracing the significance of the late third to early second-millennium BCE Cretan material that first established the lion's presence in the Aegean. We can now consider other dimensions of these Cretan objects and their broader context. Simultaneously with its presence in material culture, the lion also appeared in the narrative traditions of multiple sociocultural groups across the Near East and eastern Mediterranean, known through corpora of extant written sources. One can conjecture that far more extensive currents of an oral nature were also at play. Of the traditions preserved in writing, most notable perhaps are the Sumerian and Old Babylonian works of the later third and early second millennia BCE. Most renowned is the heroic poetry involving Gilgamesh (Bilgamesh) and Enkidu, which speaks of lions met and fought by a hero, of the beasts' ability to inspire fear even in the brave and of lions killing humans (e.g., the Sumerian "Gilgamesh, Enkidu, and the Netherworld," line 279,[75] or the Old Babylonian "Epic of Gilgamesh," Philadelphia Tablet, lines 110–113: "He put on a garment, becoming like a warrior, he took up his weapon to do battle with the lions").[76]

Of particular relevance within the Mesopotamian texts is the rich use of what we can generally refer to as metaphoric language – that is, nonliteral language that compares or equates one thing to something else. Nonhuman animals are a frequent presence in Sumerian metaphoric language, and the lion in particular is compared to various entities. For example, in the poem "Gilgamesh, Enkidu and the Netherworld," waves battering a boat are powerfully likened to the beast.[77] But the lion has an especial association with kingship, as do bulls. Watanabe sees this connection as arising from the perception of "fierceness" (Sumerian *bàn.da*, Akkadian *ekdu*) in these animals, an exclusive quality also identified with the king (as well as with divine beings and gate figures).[78] The introductory discussion in Heimpel's *Tierbilder in der sumerischen Literatur* provides an initial problematization of the nature of the relations acting in these poetic expressions, including the distinction between metaphor (*Metapher*) and simile (*Vergleich*),[79] a topic subsequently taken up by others.[80] Black, following Heimpel, observes that the division between metaphor and simile in Sumerian literature was seemingly not firm and that the subjects being associated in such expressions, including lion and king, might have been understood not merely as similar but, in some respects, as the same.[81] On this, he observes that in "parallel phrases or even in different manuscripts of the same passage," the suffix *-gim*, translated to "like/as," "is sometimes replaced with, or alternated with" the suffix *-am*, which stems from the verb "to be" and has the "function of expressing the identity of two entities, not their similarity."[82] With this, the embodiment of lions in revered objects of kingship also testifies to the great closeness, or even unity, of these figures.[83]

How much of such cultural association might have been conveyed to persons living in Crete, and how? We should envision paths for the oral traditions that, like those of the material evidence, were mediated and circuitous. The Kaphtorite man,[84] recorded in a text at Mari, who (ca. 1780–1760 BCE) traveled to Ugarit to obtain tin, which had been brought to Mari from a point farther east, is indicative.[85] People exchanging materials undoubtedly would have shared stories and songs. Some may have been recognized as storytellers; but probably most were casually recounting versions of tales gleaned from their memories of listening, while also creating, improvising, tailoring and combining along the way. Broodbank has highlighted the role of Cycladic voyagers in the exchanges that invigorated the eastern Mediterranean in the Early Bronze Age. Integrating anthropological perspectives, he considers the renown that long-distance travelers would have amassed.[86] Certainly, vivid storytelling would have been one of the principal ways in which the impressive identities of such persons (from the Cyclades and elsewhere) were demonstrated and realized, through interactions occurring in different places and along a multitude of paths.

Through the voices of travelers and then of locals, many sorts of accounts of lions might have reached the Aegean and imparted familiarity with the beast's positioning beside a human. Heroic tales, such as those of Gilgamesh, would have paralleled man and lion both in the action of their narrative and in the imagery the stories conjured, as a fierce fighter faced a leonine foe (Figure 3.13). In many instances, however, it was probably the vital sense that a lion was a creature immediately proximate with impressive people that made its way from place to place, through lips and ears and minds. Descriptions of extraordinary, even legendary objects imaging lions (e.g., a king's mace-head)[87] – in addition to some smaller but provocative objects that actually made their way to Crete – would have further emphasized these relationships. Burns' recent study of imported objects in Mycenaean Greece powerfully delves into the complex ways in which things, notably those with distant origins, could contribute to the embedded realization of identities and sociopolitical power

3.13. Akkadian (2400–2200 BCE) chalcedony cylinder seal and area of its impressed motif that images a bearded hero wrestling a lion. British Museum 89147. © Trustees of the British Museum

in the Bronze Age Aegean, in part by connecting their owners to overseas power holders; Colburn has compellingly argued for seeing similar dynamics at play in Prepalatial Cretan material.[88] Names likewise could have strengthened the parallel of lion and human. Watanabe discusses how, during the Early Dynastic and Ur III periods, in Sumerian royal names, the term for lion was set in direct, unbroken juxtaposition with the name of the king. In translating these names to English, we insert a verb, "is": for example, *Šulgi-pirig* becomes "Šulgi [is] a lion."[89] It is not difficult to imagine that, when a long-distance traveler, whether a trader or storyteller or refugee, identified the ruler of a foreign kingdom in his stories, he preserved the dramatic parallel with a lion manifest in such names. The lion lived and traveled through both oral culture and material embodiments. These manifestations would have been mutually informing and sometimes simultaneous. Together, they brought the lion to Crete; from there, it would take on new Aegean life.

CRETAN POETICS

At this point, I would like to consider how the Cretan glyptic lion objects, and their dynamic associations with people, might correspond to contemporary oral traditions on the island that also had the potential to animate the beast and characterize its relations to other entities. That oral traditions were active on Crete in the Bronze Age seems undeniable, as does the involvement of lions therein, given the beast's established and vibrant presence in Bronze Age Cretan material culture. We have seen that, during the period when the lion first became situated in the Cretan glyptic repertoire (late Early to early Middle Bronze Age), the broader region of the eastern Mediterranean and Near East was ripe with such traditions. At this time, the lion was not simply adopted but was actively developed and freshly realized on the Aegean island. Over the course of the Minoan palatial periods, through significant variations in how the lion was represented (as discussed above), the animal's basis in glyptic, and hence its juxtaposition with people, endured. This material home for the lion continued to inform its ongoing position within the Cretan cultural imaginary, but how might the formulations of oral culture also have contributed?

As a means of getting at the Bronze Age Cretan poetic tradition, it can be useful to cautiously assume an intra-Aegean perspective and look backward, with new interest and revised motivations, from the position of the later textual evidence of Greek poetry. Certainly, we now must abandon attempts at establishing simple links between forms of material culture from the Bronze Age and objects mentioned in the *Iliad* and the *Odyssey*. We stand to benefit in at least two ways from fresh analyses of later poetics. First, we gain insight into the temporal depth of the Aegean poetic tradition and its fluid contexts across the region. This involves mining the textual scholarship for subtle indications of how the linguistic and cultural lineage of particular poetic elements extends back into the Bronze Age. Second, by drawing on analyses of certain poetic effects within the Greek epic tradition, we can newly problematize comparable poetic dynamics in Bronze Age forms.

Positioning the Lion in the Cultural and Linguistic Environment of Bronze Age Crete and the Aegean

Nagy asserts that the earliest period of transmission of epic poetry in the Homeric line began in the early second millennium BCE, before the advent of writing in the Aegean, as do Morris[90] and Sherratt, who combine textual and material evidence.[91] Dactylic formulae naming distinctive early Mycenaean weaponry attested archaeologically have been highlighted by Janko as indications that these epic phrases share the antiquity of the objects.[92] Horrocks and West also argue that dactylic verse was in use in the Bronze Age and that it predates the Greek of Linear B.[93] Early Mycenaean origins for the Greek epic tradition are advocated by others such as Ruijgh. Both he and West also consider yet deeper roots.[94] They are interested in tracing out evidence that particular formal qualities were already present in Aegean heroic poetry during the Bronze Age and, when possible, in providing some further delineation of their early character. West considers the simile. That the Homeric simile was a component of oral poetry, involving oral composition and transmission, is at this point well established.[95] Although Shipp demonstrated that the ultimate form of the extended similes contains late elements,[96] West has shown that vestigial features evident in Homeric language clearly indicate that similes were already an element of Greek poetry before the phase of Greek attested in the extant Linear B texts.[97] He emphasizes the Bronze Age origins of the lion simile tradition specifically, arguing that short lion similes of Bronze Age vintage are directly evidenced in the Homeric texts and that, through comparative analysis, we have grounds for assuming extended similes were also present in Bronze Age poetry.[98] With this, the lion similes could be placed in the oral traditions of the Aegean essentially as far back as the extant linguistic evidence can reach, to a phase of Greek that predates the Linear B evidence of Late Helladic (LH) III.

West also looks broadly, seeking connections to traditions beyond the region, primarily in Semitic and Indo-European poetic cultures.[99] This broad view acknowledges the need to consider storytelling as a living practice, embedded in myriad interactive contexts and processes, which unquestionably leaped and tunneled through linguistic boundaries and sometimes, but not always, involved movement across considerable spatial distances. Sorting out Crete's position in all of this is complicated. The perspective offered through the textual evidence is indirect but striking. Ruijgh argues that we should place the origins of the Proto-Achaean epic tradition in mainland Greece ca. 1600 BCE (the early Mycenaean period), yet he sees this tradition as standing on the shoulders of earlier Aegean poetic culture.[100] Following Antoine Meillet, he argues that dactylic hexameter, based in the metrical principle of isochrony, would not have originated in Indo-European verse, which instead is characterized by isosyllabicity.[101] He then asserts that it is "tempting" to see dactylic hexameter as a poetic feature "taken over from" Minoan poetry by Proto-Achaean poets during the early Mycenaean phase (ca. 1600–1400 BCE).[102] Ruijgh's assertion has its basis in the theory that the as yet undetermined linguistic identity of Bronze Age Crete was not Indo-European. Duhoux's work has indicated that the language encoded in Cretan Linear A documents likely was not Indo-European,[103] and Davis' study of objects carrying Linear A inscriptions supports this understanding.[104] It thus looks increasingly possible that Bronze Age Crete was home to a distinct linguistic tradition (or multiple) with its own ancestry, cultural contents and poetic possibilities, on which early Mycenaean Greek speakers – and poem-tellers – could have fruitfully drawn.

A Beast across the Island: The Lion within Crete's Multiple Regions

Duhoux's discussion of the linguistic profile of Bronze Age Crete does not rest at the question of an Indo-European root.[105] Some of his further observations bear on the question of regionalism on Bronze Age Crete, a topic that is also relevant to the matter of leonine glyptic material. Duhoux considers particular "morphological similarities" evident between Cretan Bronze Age script traditions. The strongest of these is a high tendency for "prefixing" apparent in both Linear A and the Phaistos Disc;[106] this link is strengthened by recent studies by Anastasiadou and Davis, which both independently indicate that the languages encoded in the Phaistos Disc and Linear A material are one and the same.[107] Duhoux further notes that Linear A, the Phaistos Disc and Cretan Hieroglyphic all "very frequently use reduplicated signs," which might be further indication of a common linguistic base.[108] Yet he then takes a turn, despite these observations, and strongly argues that we should not become comfortable with the idea of a single linguistic identity for Bronze Age Crete. After outlining eight points in support of his assertion, ranging from the sheer multiplicity of Bronze Age scripts that are in some cases functionally redundant and in simultaneous use at a given site, to detailed considerations of evidence suggesting linguistic divergence between the languages encoded in the scripts, he states of the Cretan Bronze Age textual evidence, "I think it is probable that our five pre-Hellenic corpora might well conceal more than one tongue."[109]

Our earliest extensive evidence of writing in Crete stems from MBA contexts, when the island's multiple scripts seem to have been regionally based.[110] That the Cretan landscape was characterized by multiple distinct regions during the Protopalatial period is at this point widely agreed, although the sociopolitical, administrative, ideological and cultural nature, and interrelation of those regions is still debated. Anastasiadou has recently contributed to this discussion by demonstrating that glyptic traditions were regionally anchored at the time and that they were interacting with particular script practices within their home areas.[111] Aligning her work on the glyptic evidence with the assertions of numerous other studies, she argues for seeing a regional "boundary" distinguishing central and eastern Crete, which extended north–south on an axis running from a point roughly between Knossos and Malia southward into the area west of Myrtos-Pyrgos;[112] she identifies finer subregional distinctions as being active within these zones. According to Anastasiadou, glyptic traditions based in eastern Crete were interacting with Cretan Hieroglyphic script and the textual practices associated with it there, while those in central Crete were interacting with Linear A.[113]

Anastasiadou's observations are significant to our discussion for various reasons. Seals and seal impressions are peculiar objects, with distinctive material attributes, affordances and roles in sociocultural processes. Recognizing that these objects varied in definite ways between different areas of the island brings new dimensions of insight onto the question of what regionalism actually involved in MBA Crete. Among the most significant factors to consider here is how figural representation, including renderings of animals, participated in the realization of cultural aspects of regionalism. In some cases, glyptic imagery provides a unique lens onto how certain forms were developed between regions of the island – these forms include, among others, fantastic and exotic beasts such as the lion. The particulars of how a beast is materialized in a fabricated manifestation (e.g., its substance, scale, style, formal composition, posture, action) naturally hold great importance for its identity. They do not merely echo notions of the foreign or fantastic creature that were active within a culture, they in fact constitute primary instances of it, in embodiments that are as substantively real as they may also be imagined. As such, they inform the identity of the beast as they substantiate it. We have seen how the lion was realized in distinct ways within glyptic objects from areas in central and eastern Crete during the MBA, even as indications of interaction are naturally evident; this aligns with Anastasiadou's argument for glyptic regionalism. Underlying this, however, is the important fact that the lion does occur frequently on both sides of the primary regional divide between Protopalatial glyptic traditions that Anastasiadou outlines and, moreover, that it occurs within each subarea described (eastern and east-central Crete; central Crete and south-central Crete).[114] If glyptic and script traditions shared regional identities in this period as she persuasively argues, and if the multiple scripts of the island might be encoding distinct linguistic traditions as Duhoux suggests, we could conceivably also imagine variation in oral cultures between these regional sociocultural zones. In this case, *seeing* the lion in the imagery of both these regions likely would further indicate its presence in the broader cultural life of both areas, including the *telling* and *hearing* of the beast in their oral traditions. I raise this idea very tentatively, as a correlation between the multiple Cretan scripts and the hypothetically multiple Cretan languages can only be uncertain, and, even if such a correlation did exist, how a language encoded in a given script would relate to the language spoken by the population of the region where that script was used (or even to the language spoken by users of the script) is not necessarily simple.[115] With these cautions in mind, we are nevertheless left with very strong evidence in the glyptic record that the lion passed across apparent regional sociocultural divisions of the Protopalatial period to inhabit the traditions of each.

That the lion was already well at home across Crete in the Protopalatial period should perhaps not be surprising when we recall the distribution of the Parading Lions seal group during the preceding Prepalatial period. The ivory seals of that group, and impressions stamped by them, have been discovered at sites spanning central, eastern and western Crete. By far the greatest concentration is in the central area of the island, where traveling seal carvers may have engraved the eponymous dashing lions into sections of hippopotamus teeth for members of the communities they visited. The tholos tombs of south-central Crete have provided especially robust numbers. Seals of the Parading Lions group found in other areas of the island testify not only to the spread of the lion as a cultural entity but also to its early association with glyptic across Crete, traversing multiple local and regional territories within the Prepalatial landscape.[116]

From this early moment, the Cretan lion was characterized by the sociocultural dynamism and power of seals and impressions, and by their intimate relationship to humans. That this association not only continues on the island, but moreover ripens, is clear in the lions embodied in the fresh glyptic traditions of the Protopalatial period. Sbonias' suggestion, noted above, that the lions of the Parading Lions seals informed the imagery developed in the Protopalatial seal workshop at Malia, in northeastern Crete, underscores how cultural traditions involving the beast could travel over time and region to take on fresh life.[117] As material embodiments of the lion proliferated in the island's multiple glyptic traditions, other dimensions of its cultural identity also must have traveled and fluidly developed *viva voce* across its dispersed Cretan homes, possibly integrating different tongues in the process.

Such intra-Cretan cultural sharing involving the lion is also evident looking forward from the Protopalatial period, into the Neopalatial period of MM III–LM IB. Schoep has hypothesized that something of a cultural and ideological contraction took place during the early Neopalatial period, in which Knossos may have temporarily taken on a more explicit island-wide focal role.[118] In Chapter 2, we saw that this Knossian prominence may have eventually waned in the later Neopalatial period, perhaps in the context of environmental and social stress.[119] While some are hesitant to accept the idea that Knossos held interregional sociopolitical and administrative sway during LM IA based on current evidence, the cultural might of the site in the period is generally agreed upon.[120] A moment of Knossian eminence in the early Neopalatial period, involving processes of cultural coalescing that engaged social spaces in areas throughout the island, could have substantively impacted not only the material and narrative cultures of the time, but also their ongoing formulation, if an integration of cultural forms persisted on some levels even as sociopolitical tides changed. As glyptic remains the primary material home for the lion through this period, with very few exceptions in other media, it is in seals and impressions that we would look both for evidence of the beast's distribution and for indications of possible regional variation in its characterization. As evidence stands now, the lion is widely represented across the island in Neopalatial glyptic, where it is crafted in various different materials and compositional styles. Despite certain highly localized Neopalatial glyptic groups, evidence indicates that several major seal styles were widely occurring across the island, and that specific motif types involving the lion (e.g., animal attacks or a wounded lion) can appear across multiple stylistic groups – in divergent materials, with variable technical attributes and on objects from different areas of the island. In this context, there is nothing to suggest that these characterizations of the beast were not broadly compatible elements of a common cultural corpus surrounding the lion, which took form across a plurality of styles of materialization and verbalization, likely with streams of influence from beyond Crete. We can fold this evidence into the ideas concerning the island's linguistic profile. If distinct sociolinguistic traditions were active on Bronze Age Crete into the Neopalatial period (which remains uncertain), the sharing and development of cultural forms and practices involving the lion seemingly were not hindered by such diversity. In fact, the Cretan lion may have been enriched by such ongoing cultural interplay across Crete, and by the distinct sociocultural interconnections that different regions and communities had, including those that extended overseas.

Across the Sea: Voices and Things Realize an Aegean Lion

That Cretan things were moving across the Aegean during MB III–LB II is amply demonstrated in the archaeological record of the islands and early Mycenaean mainland. But the movement of material and influence across the Aegean, in practice, also would have involved vibrant and varied relations of people – craftspersons sharing techniques, traders reckoning a fair exchange, harbor workers swapping a good joke, curse or gesture. Within these human interactions, very specific contexts of translation were at play, including linguistic ones.

Given the extant textual evidence, it is undeniable that translation between the Minoan language(s) and Mycenaean Greek was occurring at this time in the social spaces of Crete and the Greek mainland. Palaima believes that the development of Linear B, which encoded a Greek language, from Linear A, which encoded a Cretan language, likely occurred "over a period of years, even decades" extending back to LB II. According to his compelling discussion, this process was probably led by Cretans:

> We say that the Mycenaeans adopted writing from the Minoans by adapting Linear A so that the new script, Linear B, could represent Greek efficiently. But that is just a manner of speaking. It is difficult to imagine how recent illiterates in the first generation of the use of script could adjust it to the peculiar features of their language. Much more likely, in my opinion, is that tablet-writers who had used the Linear A script, who were what we conventionally call ethnic Minoans and who spoke the language or languages that were privileged within Minoan palatial culture, adapted the Linear A sign repertories to fit the language that would be thenceforth the main language of written communication in the Mycenaean states.[121]

Palaima's ideas force us to embed this process of script invention within a human context of bilingualism, a context of voices and hands working across language divides. If "ethnic Minoans" were in a position to adapt Linear A to fit (more or less) the peculiarities of Mycenaean Greek, they must have known the language they were adjusting toward. This likely betrays a deeper history of crosslinguistic interaction. Likewise, Palaima points to the legacy of some degree of bilingualism within the Mycenaean scribal practice, suggesting that Minoans may have continued to serve as scribes within Mycenaean administrations, training new generations within their "extended families" to fill what could have been effectively "hereditary" professional roles.[122] Meanwhile the use of Linear B at LM III sites indicates at least some level of bilingualism in Cretan contexts concurrently.[123]

Palaima's discussion underscores the role of scribes in the intense cultural sharing that was occurring across the Aegean in the timeframe corresponding to the Cretan Neopalatial and early Mycenaean periods (and onward).[124] It also offers a more tangible demonstration of the inevitable linguistic dimensions of that sharing, both oral and written. This was not a simple transfer of static content between Crete and the mainland, but an innovative productive process, in which social and cultural forms were fluidly developed. While literacy was likely highly limited at this time, this does not mean that multilingualism was.[125] People's knowledge of a second (or further) language would have involved variable degrees of fluency and would have focused on different subject areas of interest and necessity that facilitated a range of connections. This is as true of interactions running across the Aegean as of those occurring throughout the broader eastern Mediterranean, as discussed previously. Thus, beyond scribes, other persons' voices were also realizing movements of culture in the Aegean, including those of laborers, mercenaries and administrators, as well as musicians and poets, whom Renfrew considers specifically (and of course, as West reminds us, such categories could overlap – indeed a bilingual Minoan sailor, or scribe, may have been in a fine position to sing a Cretan story to Greek-speaking listeners).

Renfrew examines the non-Greek origins of later Greek terms for various musical instruments, including the lyre, phorminx and kithara, which often accompanied a storyteller's song. Given the early occurrences of such instruments in the material and visual cultures of Crete and the Cyclades, he and others identify Crete as the likely place where these instruments of poetic song first reached the Aegean and through which they were shared with the Greek mainland.[126] The discovery of a Linear B tablet at Thebes referring to two lyre players (TH Av 106.7) demonstrates that musicians were offering song to mainland ears with these instruments in LH IIIB, while Younger's stylistic dating of ivory phorminx fragments from Chamber Tomb 81 at Mycenae would push back the lyre's mainland appearance further, to LH I.[127] When we pair this evidence with Ruijgh's proposal that dactylic hexameter may have come to the mainland from Cretan poetic traditions by LH I,[128] we begin to have the strong suggestion that some of the fundamental poetic apparatus of the epic tradition took form in this early moment, in part through cross-Aegean pollination, and building on yet earlier traditions.

Ruijgh considers the presence of Cretan content within the nascent Proto-Achaean epic tradition of the early Mycenaean period, highlighting the figure of Meriones. He argues that this Cretan hero, with a pre-Greek name, was already incorporated into the earliest phase of Greek epic (in LH I), before the phase of Mycenaean Greek captured in the Linear B tablets. He further hypothesizes that, in this early stage, the Cretan hero still played a greater role in the poetic tradition, as his vestigial hexameter-long noun epithet demonstrates – an impressive length, which Ruijgh argues is entirely dispro-portionate with his later secondary status in the Homeric *Iliad* (Μηριόνης ἀτάλαντος Ἐνυαλίῳ ἀνδρειφόντῃ [Meriones, who has the same weight as Enyalius, the killer of men], *Il.* 2.651, 7.166, 8.264, 17.259).[129] Notably, West makes a parallel assertion that the two Iliadic characters who appear to be of greatest (and pre–Linear B) antiquity in the poetic tradition are the Cretan heroes Meriones and Idomeneus. His reasons for identifying them as early poetic personages are multifold, etymological and artifactual. They are, he suggests, "a pair of genuine Minoans from the heyday of Knossos."[130]

Taken together, such evidence points to the period from MB III to LB II as being saturated with the transmission and further development of linguistic culture across the Aegean, including oral poetry. Crete emerges in this context as likely being a rich field for oral traditions in the Bronze Age, one that impacted the region broadly. The amply evidenced material cultures of the island are highly relevant here, not only because representational objects may shed light on the content of oral stories but also, more fundamentally, because poetic culture involved not just the craft of human voices but also that of human hands – in objects that contributed directly to the creative rendering of the lived world. These material things were also poetic fabrications that took form and imparted form within the same cultural imaginary as oral traditions. Embodiments of nonhuman animals figured prominently in this creative cultural space.

We have robust material evidence of links between Crete and the mainland during MB III–LB II, ranging from small objects to architectural forms. In addition to long-standing evidence from the Saronic Gulf and the eastern Peloponnese, from contexts such as the Shaft Graves at Mycenae and the so-called Aegina Treasure,[131] Davis and Stocker have persuasively argued that Messenia had very significant ties to Minoan Crete early on. Their reassessment of Tomb IV at Pylos, which integrates Nelson's architectural studies at the site, recognizes substantive engagements between the region and Crete already during the later Middle Helladic period and extending through the early Mycenaean period.[132] Nelson's work indicates that cut-stone architecture, likely learned from Crete, was integrated into Pylian praxis in MH III or earlier. Their arguments for the region's early links with Crete have since been further substantiated by the exquisite material from the LH II

Grave of the Griffin Warrior at Pylos. Located just southwest of Tomb IV, the grave contained many objects of likely Minoan crafting, especially seals (including some worked with lion imagery) laid to rest with the body of a man.[133] The excavators' study of this material, as well as initial reports of findings from Tholos Tombs VI and VII, discovered in 2018 to the east of Tholos IV, further support a view of areas of the early Mycenaean mainland being deeply engaged with Crete.

Objects embodying lions were a notable element of this sharing between Crete and the mainland. As Thomas notes, after a dearth of lion representations of any kind in the Middle Bronze Age mainland record, the beast emerged quite suddenly as a frequent subject of representational material culture during the Shaft Grave Era (MH III–LH I), "[with] the advent of strong Minoan influence on the mainland."[134] This is vividly demonstrated in Minoan-style seals found in the shaft graves at Mycenae[135] and in many other early Mycenaean burials, for example, the twelve lion seals from the LH IIA context of the Vapheio tholos, Lakonia (CMS 1.243–254). These objects indicate that the long-standing Cretan association of lions and glyptic persisted in this period and extended to the mainland. The lion stands out as the second most frequently depicted subject in Aegean glyptic during LB I and II, second only to the bull.[136] However, we would be foolhardy to see the wealth of lion glyptic from this period as a simple matter of cultural transfer. Whether such seals discovered in mainland contexts were imports, Mycenaean imitations of Minoan craft or the work of traveling Minoan artisans remains unclear and, in fact, somewhat beside the point. These things were Mycenaean in practice, active participants in mainland social spaces. That they embody interaction with Crete underscores the deep sociocultural entanglement of the moment – a situation that continues into LB III.[137] What becomes clear is that the early Mycenaean lion glyptic finds its precedents not in the mainland but in Crete. From here, we will do best to understand further developments in the representation of the beast as arising from MB III to LB II sociomaterial contexts across the Aegean, and from the interaction between these contexts.

Paratopic Bodies

While glyptic objects and oral poetry might involve different ways of engaging people, they were two aspects of the same cultural creation of the lion and would have developed mutually. In this light, scholarly analyses of similes in the Aegean epic tradition could prove enlightening for our investigation of engraved seals, which can be understood as cultural devices that also formulated a comparison between two paralleled entities: the lion engraved on the seal and the human who wore and used it. Thus, here we are interested in the similes not as components of codes, nor as a symbolic means of signifying specific qualities characterizing the lion, but for the very real cultural positioning that they can structure between human and nonhuman subjects.

Juxtaposition is a relational dynamic through which the creative work of material culture and narrative meet. It is characterized by copresence, whether physical or voiced. When this copresence involves animal bodies, it can be keenly affective, something we see through both glyptic and similes. In her discussion of the performance of similes within the Homeric oral tradition, Minchin foregrounds the significance of their imagery and image making:

> If there is any key to the similes it is precisely this, as banal as it may seem, that they are all readily pictureable. It is this quality which unites them in their service to the storyteller, as mind's eye and memory work together to give expression to song. It unites them in their service to the audience, as memory and mind's eye interpret what is heard or read. And it unites them in their service to the song itself . . . whether similes serve to clarify what has been described within the narrative, to enlarge on it, to empha- size it, to evaluate it, or to enhance it; or whether they work to involve the audience's emotions in the action through their play on image and memory.[138]

Minchin sees the visual aspect of the similes as key to their mnemonic effect and hence to their power in the context of storytelling and story hearing. She argues that imagery, both "actual" physical pictures and mental ones, "promote comprehension and recall" by offering the viewer, listener or reader a "conceptual outline" or "schema" with which to better comprehend what is being told.[139] Hence, images both reveal and direct. Swarming around this fundamental assertion is a host of rich poetic potentialities. Minchin explores these, examining how the simile acts to bring emphasis, elaboration, emotion, clarification, intimacy and pleasure to the listener's experience.[140]

Tsagalis builds on Minchin's work concerning the cognitive role of imagery in the similes.[141] It is his emphasis on not just the visual but, further, on the spatial dimension of similes that is especially valuable for our discussion of glyptic and lions. He describes the space of the simile as *paratopic*, "denoting a space that exists 'next to' and 'beyond' story space,"[142] a term that also aptly describes the space of the seal worn against a human. As the imagery of the simile dynamically dwells alongside a subject in the story space, offering a parallel that enhances the status of the compared subject from its juxtaposed position, an engraved seal similarly occupies a space alongside its wearer, enhancing the person's active identity through the comparison the seal articulates.

While the relationship of Homeric similes to the main narrative has been addressed by many scholars, including studies of the simile spaces, or *Gleichnisorte*, Tsagalis wants us to consider how the robust, animate nature of

Homeric similes provides for complexity in this relationship.[143] According to Tsagalis, the juxtaposition of a simile with a unit of the narrative provides for correlations between their two spatially complex spheres of action. In a sense, appreciating the dynamic nature of a simile enhances a person's experience of the juxtaposed narrative scene, as the textured mental experience of one sphere augments one's ability to see such textured dimensions in the other.[144] Hence, it is crucial that we understand the simile not as a static image but as an active context, with its action unfolding through its distinct spatiality, both separate from yet intimately and provocatively related to the primary action. In the case of the lion similes, the beast is vigorous, motivated, and brings with it an emotional charge.[145] We see this, for example, in the simile that describes Menelaus as he closes in for combat with Paris in the *Iliad* (3.21–26):

> Now as soon as Menelaos the warlike caught sight of him
> Making his way with long strides out in front of the army,
> He was glad, like a lion who comes on a mighty carcass,
> In his hunger chancing upon the body of a horned stag
> Or wild goat; who eats it eagerly, although against him
> Are hastening the hounds in their speed and the stalwart young men.[146]

The relationship formulated between an engraved seal and its human wearer can be fruitfully compared to that between the simile and its paralleled subject in the main story. But before exploring how glyptic could constitute a rich, dynamic space for cultural comparison, like that of the simile according to the ideas of Minchin and Tsagalis, let us first consider the implications of their work for the possible interplay of oral poetry and material culture, particularly with regard to the lion's presence in these two cultural forms on Bronze Age Crete. Both scholars stress that one crucial aspect of the simile's efficacy is its making familiar that which otherwise was unfamiliar, unimaginable, difficult to grasp or, more to the point, difficult to picture.[147] Hence, they see the similes as providing approachable content that grounds extraordinary elements of the main narrative in something that is comparable but recognizable. From this perspective, the lion, the single most frequent comparative subject of the Homeric similes, was often in the position of offering the listener a familiar touchpoint. This is a seemingly problematic idea, primarily because the presence of living lions in the Aegean was variable, often very limited and in some cases nonexistent. Indeed, the role of lions in the extended similes of Homer is one factor often pointed to in support of the idea that the versions of the poems that we have today were composed in western Anatolia.[148] Yet even when considering areas where the lion demonstrably once lived,[149] scholars have questioned whether the Homeric verses reflect firsthand observation of the living beast at all, while others debate the contexts in which such observations would have been made – whether in the wild, while defending domesticated beasts in agrarian circumstances, as the similes often describe, or in orchestrated hunts.[150] Meanwhile, for many persons who heard lion similes, the living beasts were entirely unknown. This was true in later periods, but certainly also for essentially all people in Bronze Age Crete and the Cyclades, and most in the southern mainland. How would these listeners have heard a lion simile? What would have filled out their vision of the beast and its vigorous bodily character, and how would that have been somehow familiar and recognizable? We should perhaps wonder this especially when considering simpler similes that liken an exceptional human to a lion (e.g., "he rushed against them like a lion," Hom., *Il.* 11.129), since they provide the vivid comparison to the active beast but lack further scenic cues – but ultimately the similes always leave much of the formal characterization of the lion to the hearer. For many listening to a simile, the mention of a lion likely conjured something formed from a web of different sources, incorporating facets of observed behavior in other species[151] and associations stemming from stories heard previously. But at the core of what the mention of a lion conjured also would have been representations of lions that the person had seen and possibly handled in immediate sociocultural and sensorial experiences. In EBA–MBA Crete, and then in both Crete and the mainland during LB I–II, the majority of these encounters involved engraved seals and their clay impressions. We must recognize that the relationship of lion glyptic to lion similes would not only have been to provide a vision of the beast's bodily character. These glyptic objects, like similes, also established parallels between lion and man. They did this by setting their human wearers in juxtaposition to physical lion bodies that were charged with the vibrant character of seals and seal use. Hence, the lions conjured in similes may indeed have been familiar to these listeners, but that familiarity arose in part from their experiences with another fabricated cultural form, lion seals, and from the comparable relational dynamics lion seals embodied. It may even be that the paralleling articulated in the lion similes had one of its origins in the similar, long-established juxtaposition effected through Cretan lion glyptic.[152]

To consider how glyptic objects could be a source of real animation and enrichment for the lion, we need to appreciate that these things were not static, nor was their imagery abstract and isolated. Simandiraki-Grimshaw and Stevens have beautifully considered how Minoan zoomorphic objects worn on the human body could gain animation from bodily movements and the objects' affordances.[153] Seals, we can see, have their own ranges of movements and potent relationships to the physical and notional person. In the realm of ancient material culture, seals had uniquely dynamic existences. They were highly interactive. As something perched against a human's skin, a seal moved with that body.[154] A seal was held close to a person because it was recognized as a uniquely empowered thing. It was, in a real sense, a legitimate double, another physical entity that could substantively embody aspects of the seal owner's action and social identity.[155] The object, including the motif engraved into it, would have been a known entity with an established link to the person, a link that was recognized and active even in moments when the imagery was not visible. As such, the seal was invested with the sociocultural weight of the person's identity and also contributed to it; this was the real vulnerability inherent in systems of sphragistic seal use, the endowing of a distinct thing with such potential. This vulnerability was most acute in the clay impressions rendered by the seal. These objects *were* separated from the person. As a communication device that was formed when a human stamped their seal, a clay impression subsequently existed as a dynamic document that attested the prior stamping event (and all it implied) within a context where that human was not present (e.g., a clay impression attached to a vessel in a storeroom, or kept as a receipt in an archive or legitimating a shipment). Consequently, the social interactions in which clay impressions engaged, the messages they articulated through their inevitably imperfect stamped forms, often played out at a distance from the seal owner, occurring beyond their immediate control. It was this exceptional dynamism of seals and seal impressions that rendered them so valuable; their great kinetic and potential energy invigorated them with remarkable efficacy as sociocultural bodies. Surely, this is part of why seals so frequently accompanied persons in graves: they were a type of object that had a very close kinship to social personhood. Seals' persistent presence with deceased persons in mainland burials, and their positioning as objects strapped upon people's wrists in Mycenaean visual culture, demonstrate that this intimate relationship continued unabated. Even if sphragistic usage of seals may not have been notably active in the early Mycenaean mainland (where Cretan glyptic culture clearly was highly valued), this distinguishing affordance of seals surely was still recognized (see Chapter 4), and sphragistic seal usage did became prevalent in LH II–III.[156]

With glyptic objects as the substance of their bodies, the lions most familiar in Bronze Age Crete and the Aegean were active in their own way, and their distinctive dynamism would have informed people's sense of the lions encountered in oral traditions. With these juxtapositions, oral and material, the lion was experienced as proximate to humans, even if many persons who listened to a simile or used a seal never encountered a lion in the flesh. The Bronze Age glyptic objects demonstrate that such paratopic closeness between humans and lions was in fact an aspect of cultural life in the Aegean from very early on; this was metaphor as a matter of embodied experience.

TRACES AND ENCOUNTERS

The lion glyptic of the Bronze Age Aegean requires us to think anew about how objects can be involved in the relations of humans and nonhumans, reaching beyond the question of symbolic content and into that of lived action. In this context, Shapland has provided deeply important considerations of animals in Minoan Crete, including the lion.[157] His principal move is away from conventional iconographical readings that see animal images primarily as elements of codes and result in interpretations that often have little to do with the animals themselves; in this, he builds on the valuable work of Bloedow and Thomas.[158] Shapland rethinks the implications of Minoan lion imagery by suggesting that, over time, representations of the beast came to be associated with people's direct encounters with living lions, in hunts undertaken by Cretans overseas. Moreover, he offers an elegant argument that lion pelts, garnered during such hunts as trophies, were being brought to Crete during the late Protopalatial and Neopalatial periods and that these provided the basis for representations of the beast that, in his assessment, demonstrate an increasing awareness of the lion's "affordances" as a dangerous beast.[159] Shapland uses Summers' notion of "traces" to think about these pelts.[160] He thus moves us from symbolic readings of the Cretan lion imagery toward an indexical one, in which the images, as well as the pelts (for which there is as yet no direct evidence in Crete), refer to actual hunting encounters and knowledge of distant places in which they occurred.[161]

We gain much from Shapland's analysis, but, in my opinion, we would be wrong to make the experience of a lion hunt – which precious few Cretans would have undertaken – the primary means for interpreting lion imagery on Crete. With this focus, Shapland ultimately considers most of the variation evident in the representation of lions, both diachronic and synchronic, in terms of greater or lesser acquaintance with lion hunting; thus the "absences" of the rare and hypothetical past events effectively take precedence over the plentiful material presences of Cretan representational embodiments of lions, despite Shapland's clear appreciation of the latter and their performances.[162] Shapland crucially considers that there would be different audiences for the lion imagery, but this needs to be taken further. Addressing the widespread presence of lions in glyptic imagery in Crete, in a variety of materials and rendered in different qualities of engraving, he suggests that some elite seal owners would have had direct knowledge of lions through their own experiences in hunts, while others, of lesser status, were emulating those elite figures and their participation in the restricted activity by also choosing to engrave seals with lion imagery.[163] We risk overlooking much if we problematize the attributes of the lion glyptic primarily in this light. Shapland is right to assert that persons who actually took part in a hunt would have interacted with lion representations differently than those having had no engagement with the living beast. But how many Cretans in fact would have participated in such hunts? It seems far more likely that such an undertaking would be idiosyncratic, the bold overseas undertaking of a few particular personalities over time, instead of a regularly occurring adventure tourism; the fact that no faunal remains of lions have as yet been found in Bronze Age contexts on Crete supports seeing this as an extremely rare activity for Cretans. This is not to say that the likely infrequency renders the activity insignificant; it is very important for us to recognize the range of engagements Cretans may have had with lions. Thomas' discussion of the limited lion remains found at Bronze Age sites elsewhere in the Aegean indicates rare but probable hunting events in areas of the mainland and some collection and circulation of lion remains (teeth, bones, pelts).[164] Hunts, whether the stuff of practice or story, were likely a dimension of other Aegean cultural traditions surrounding the lion that would have been folded into the long-standing Cretan ones. Some of these may have had roots shared with southern European cultures, as Thomas considers. But the apparent infrequency of Aegean-based hunts, and especially ones involving Cretans, should at the same time force us to more deeply problematize the means through which most Cretans would have actually, physically encountered and formed notions of the beast, and that is primarily via the seals themselves. Lions had been represented on Crete for centuries by the time that, in Shapland's hypothesis, Cretans engaged in such hunts – centuries rich in overseas interaction and internal innovation.[165] This long, unbroken presence of the leonine on the island, in glyptic, would have been fundamental to the beast's evolving Cretan identity moving forward.

All this being said, Shapland profoundly shifts our view on the motivations and social performance of Minoan animal imagery to new ground by focusing on the experience of human–animal relations.[166] In so doing, he also looks critically at how and where objects representing lions were embedded in Cretan social spheres.[167] His work, including his discussion of traces as a means of human–animal engagement, should have a fundamental impact on studies of Aegean animal imagery. If various types of traces of lions, such as oral accounts from travelers, teeth and (eventually) pelts, offered experiences of the unknown biological beast to certain persons in Crete, then contemporaneous glyptic embodiments of lions would have had a dynamic relationship with them, as manifestations of the leonine that were different, but just as real. Moreover, if the sections of massive hippopotamus tooth from which the earliest Cretan lion seals were fashioned were understood as lions' teeth by some, the trace and fabricated lion body would have been materially merged.[168]

The underlying point here, well established in the field of animal studies, is that people actually encounter and relate to nonhuman creatures in a rich multiplicity of bodily forms; people's experiences of animals potentially (and often) involve bodies that are not those of living biological beings (see Chapter 1).[169] The distinctive qualities, animacies and interactive potentials of these other embodiments, including representational objects, contribute in their own peculiar ways to humans' experience of nonhuman animals and, in turn, to animals' positions in sociocultural spaces. Hence, binary divisions between real and false embodiments cannot alone capture the multiplicity of ways in which humans experience nonhumans as physical, material, embedded animalian entities.

MB III–LB II AEGEAN BODIES

In the MB III–LB II Aegean, certain changes in the material and formal qualities of fabricated leonine bodies would have contributed to developments in the beast's cultural identities. Among the most notable innovations in the glyptic repertoire of this phase, evidenced across the Aegean, was the frequent formulation of narrative scenes in which the lion is one of multiple figures. These images further articulated the nature of the beast being juxtaposed to the human seal wearer. We have seen that animal attacks, involving the lion and another nonhuman species, gained new popularity (Figure 3.12). In these images, the lion is typically the aggressor, its powerful figure being both narratively and compositionally dominant. It is at this time that we also have a true blossoming of glyptic imagery depicting engagements between lion and human, usually in either hunts or combats (Figure 3.14). The dynamics of these compositions are quite different from the lion attacks on other animals, though both propound the lion's violent nature. In the small engraved fields of seal motifs, the lion tends to meet the man on even ground, both being alike in stature and force (Figure 3.14a–e). The compositions typically offer spatial balance between the two subjects, who appear simultaneously as opponents and equals; one animal, one species, does not dramatically dominate.[170] Thus, in these scenes it is not the lion alone who constitutes the primary figure but both beast and man together; it is the commonality formulated both narratively and compositionally that is the focus. We see a similar dynamic articulated in a contemporaneous group of motifs, evidenced both in Crete and the mainland, in which a lion is imaged peacefully standing alongside a (sometimes-capped) human (e.g., Figure 3.14f, h; cf. Figure 4.12b, p. 205). Clearly, such a scene implies that the beast is subdued, but the formulation of the image itself presents the figures as a harmonious pair brought into an equilibrium that can border, visually, on corporeal unity.[171] Even when a leash is attached to the beast (Figure 3.14h–i), the lion remains proudly upright and foregrounded. In these scenes, the imaged human (or anthropomorphic figure) possesses a distinct rapport with the lion that might stem from divinity or from a backstory involving the taming of the beast.[172] In either case, it is the common ground of the two beings that is articulated.

Most MB III–LB II Aegean glyptic imagery that depicts lions and humans together shows such balance. Exceptions exist, such as two images of men

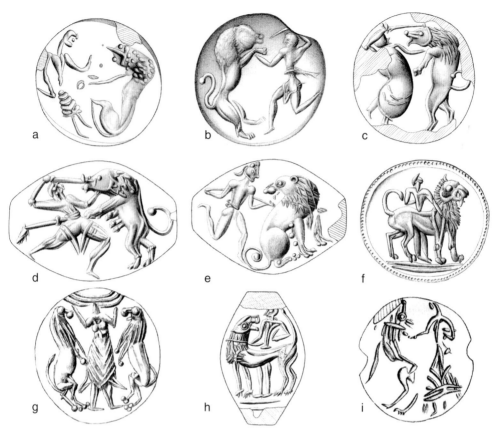

3.14. Encounters of humans and lions in LB I–II Aegean glyptic imagery from Crete (a, b, f, g) and the mainland (c, d, e, h): a. CMS II.3.14; b. CMS V.S1A.135; c. CMS I.228; d. CMS.I.290; e. CMS.I.112; f. CMS II.3.24; g. CMS VI.316; h. CMS V.S1B.77; i. CMS XI.256. Images courtesy CMS, Heidelberg

binding a lion, which might represent an actual hunting practice but could also be transferred from scenes with other species – for example, a motif imaging the binding of a bovine was discovered in the same sealing deposit at Zakros as one of the two lion-binding scenes.[173] The motifs of the master or mistress of lions that appear more frequently in LB I, and later, might also diverge from this even-standing, at least thematically. Yet even this imagery can suggest acquiescence versus violent domination (e.g., CMS II.8.256, CMS VI.312, and Figure 3.14g–h) and might indicate another narrative strain drawn into the paralleling of lion and human in these seals.[174] More fundamentally, as with the other motifs involving lions with humans, the compositional balance in these images is striking. Indeed, it is remarkable that even in scene types such as lion–human combats, which could easily stress a dominant actor (as is the case with lions' attacks on other creatures), an equilibrium is instead effected. The details of these engraved scenes thus provide further elaborations of the aspects of the lion being juxtaposed to the human who is wearing or using the seal. The motifs do this through imagery that gives particular form to interactions involving equally impressive persons and lions.[175]

How might these MB III–LB II scenes relate to the oral traditions of their day? It is highly probable that a person interacting with one of these seals or an impression stamped by it (perhaps the craftsperson who engraved the seal, the seal owner wearing it, a child held close and examining the engraved stone tied against a parent's wrist or an administrator authenticating a clay sealing) would have associated the succinct narrative images with more extensive scenes from contemporary oral poetry and lore. We have seen that this is thought to be the same period when the Greek epic tradition took root, brimming with the deeds of Cretan and Achaean heroes as well as lion imagery, both of which fit comfortably with the contemporary glyptic themes. But it is the poetic structure of these MB III–LB II glyptic objects that is most strikingly akin to what we eventually see in epic. The primary juxtaposition of the seal and its human wearer, with whom the lion had long been associated in Crete, is now often further articulated in a developed scene involving the beast and its relations to other animals, human and nonhuman. It is through such a "pictureable" scene that the seal's lion–human parallel gains further elaboration.[176] This is, in its essence, the same dynamic described by Minchin and Tsagalis concerning the Homeric similes. There, we see the paralleling of the lion and hero given robust form through nested scenes that open within, or beside, the main narrative and describe the lion's feats against other creatures and human foes.[177] We cannot say that earlier generations of glyptic lion imagery, often depicting a single lion, did not have cultural associations that were just as complex as the more detailed lion scenes. However, the visual and material realization of the more elaborate scenes in MB III–LB II, clearly arising from the long tradition of Aegean lion glyptic reaching back to early Crete, patently evidences a poetic structure remarkably similar to that of the epic simile, and these two creative devices (oral and material) might have been part of a common development in poetic formulations during these periods. With this, the lion's identity seems to have been gaining a very particular character through both of these means, as a beast and as a fitting parallel for certain figures, notably heroes or warrior-hunters. These figures are often distinguished by other complex animalian entities – boar's tusk helmets and oxhide shields, which are the focus of Chapter 5. These developments may be part of what Malafouris has described as "the emergence of a new Mycenaean ethos the focus of which is the warrior's body" at this time.[178]

We stand to gain further insight on the narrative position of the lion in the MB III–LB II Aegean if we consider other media. One of the remarkable aspects of the early Mycenaean material is that, from the earliest extant instances in the Shaft Grave Era, the lion's basis in glyptic is perpetuated even as the beast came to be embodied in a variety of other object types. These objects have different affordances[179] arising from their distinct material, formal and relational attributes.[180] Together with the seals, they contribute in their diverse ways to the ongoing cultural identity of the lion and its distinctive animacy and efficacy as an embodied sociocultural animal. We can understand these constellations of interacting elements as "assemblages," which Bennett describes as "ad hoc groupings of diverse elements, of vibrant materials of all sorts. . . . Each member and proto-member of the assemblage has a certain vital force, but there is also an effectivity proper to the grouping as such: an agency of the assemblage."[181] Assemblages can cross the divide between living and nonliving to incorporate the contributions of objects, materials, people and nonhuman animals, and they can take form at different spatial scales, from highly localized to broader sociocultural territories.

The MB III–LB II Aegean lion was involved in various scales of assemblage that further developed its dynamic character. In Grave Circle A at Mycenae, for example, we find twenty objects that embody the lion, interacting spatially, materially, socially, pictorially and in terms of their relations to living and dead human bodies. Thomas persuasively places all of these objects in LH I, rendering their simultaneity even more marked.[182] These lion objects range in size from a pinhead (no. NAM 274) to daggers (nos. NAM 394, 395), from stelae (e.g., no. NAM 1427) to inlays (nos. NAM 119, 120). The lion is shown in a range of moods and postures – recumbent, rampant, running and wounded, both solitary and in groups – and at times it appears in the midst of attack. The majority of these objects (sixteen of twenty) embody the lion in gold, a vibrant characteristic that associates different manifestations of the beast across their scalar, formal and mechanical diversity. On the ceremonial Lion Hunt Dagger from Grave IV, four gold lions populate scenes of chase and attack, devastating a human and a deer (see Figure 5.3, p. 259). On a gold repoussé cup from Grave V (Figure 3.15), three lions run harmlessly around the body in flying gallops, chasing only themselves. A cup introduces sustenance into the social and biological body; a dagger breaks flesh and harms.[183] As different instances of leonine object-bodies, these things gave the beast distinct connotations associated with their imagery, object-types and positions in sociocultural actions. Their coincidence in the same funerary monument contributed to a rich local formulation of the lion, as a beast who could proudly nourish one's social being while threatening the livelihood of others.

We can also see assemblages active at other levels, with concurrent implications. Take, for example, the three gold cushion seals found within Tomb III of Grave Circle A (Figure 3.16). The closely shared form and crafting of these objects indicate that they have an especial association within the grave deposit, as a set or a microassemblage; their intaglio motifs bear this out in a dynamic

MB III–LB II AEGEAN BODIES   145

3.15. LH I (ca. 1600 BCE) gold repoussé cup with lion circling the body. Mycenae, Grave Circle A, Grave V, LH I. National Archaeological Museum, Athens, 656. Photograph by Mary Harrsch (CC BY-SA 4.0). Object © Hellenic Ministry of Culture and Sports

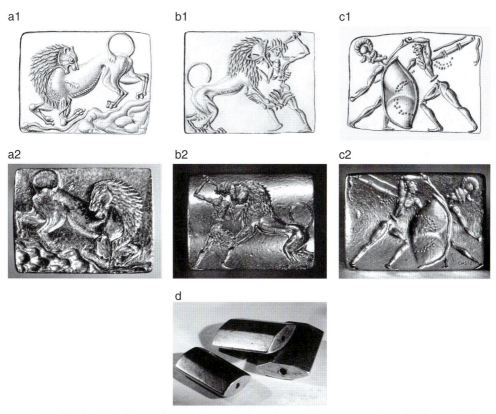

3.16. Set of LB I gold cushion seals from Grave Circle A, Grave III, Mycenae. a, b, c. CMS 1.10; CMS 1.9; CMS 1.11. d. View of the three seals together. Images courtesy CMS, Heidelberg. National Archaeological Museum, Athens. Objects © Hellenic Ministry of Culture and Sports

fashion. These seals depict three distinct scenes: in the first, CMS I.10, a solitary wounded lion turns its head back toward the fletched arrow embedded in its shoulder; in the second, CMS I.9, a lion and a man are in combat, the man, on the right, drives a blade down toward the beast's head as it mauls his shoulder; and, in the third, CMS I.11, two men meet in combat, the man on the right thrusting his sword down into the neck of his helmeted opponent. While narratively separate (these are not scenes from the same sequence of events), these objects imply one another. The composition of CMS I.9 sets the lion and the armed human in a balanced engagement, asking us to liken the two opponents and to focus on their tense equivalence.[184] By drawing together the two animals (lion and man) that we then see separately in the other two seals of this set, this object unambiguously indicates that all three are to be associated. This microassemblage thus makes clear that the lion and the human warrior-hunter, even when separate, were somehow associated; their relation did not depend on their meeting directly within the same storyline or object.

The Grave III gold seals participate in a broader cultural assemblage involving imagery of lions and armed warrior-hunters in the MB III–LB II Aegean. A related instance plays out in a "squarely contemporary" assemblage at LC IA Akrotiri.[185] In the fresco of the south wall of Room 5 in the West House, we find a dashing lion closing in on a group of deer on a hilltop;[186] meanwhile, on the parallel north wall, on a parallel hillside, we find a line of shielded, helmeted warriors closing in on a walled settlement to which they will lay siege.[187] Lions and human warriors are again paralleled in another vignette from the south wall, where their juxtaposition is close: in the flotilla scene, a group of seaborne warriors, helmets close at hand, sits on the deck of a ship while a row of running lions decorates its hull just below; leonine stern figures also mount the backs of two of the ships.[188] As Morgan has keenly recognized, a person standing within Room 5 would have been immersed within a gathering of human and lion bodies that occupied distinct but simultaneous narrative spaces;[189] the resultant dynamic of parallel copresences was surely quite impressive.

The material culture of the MB III–LB II period brought further articulation to the Aegean lion. The larger representational fields offered by objects such as daggers, goblets and murals provided for imagery that involved more protagonists and more detailed settings, while even within the small surfaces of glyptic we see a greater number of elaborate scenes. The materials used are more diverse, including metals, plaster, ceramic and pigments, each bringing new textures, technical demands and colors to the lion's Aegean existence. Novel zoomorphic object types also appear. The rare Aegean lion-head rhyta discussed previously (p. 108) are born in this period, evidenced in a distinctive gold form in Grave Circle A at Mycenae (LH I),[190] in two clay examples at LC IA Akrotiri,[191] and in three objects from Knossos, possibly already in LM I, including the extraordinary limestone head. As Shapland discusses, such things would offer people new material engagements with the lion, undertaken in different social microcontexts and involving distinctive experiential dynamics both for those handling the lion objects and for those watching the performance.[192] These far rarer objects coexisted with lion glyptic, as seals were still the beast's primary Aegean home. Morgan and Morris have both eloquently considered how the Lion Hunt Dagger parallels the deeds of heroic humans, on one side, and of mighty lions, on the other – Morris specifically likens this to the parallels of similes.[193] Their observations beautifully underscore how the juxtaposition of lions and humans, long enacted through seals, began to take on other – but relatable – dynamics during this period, through the voices of other things.

The evidence strongly indicates that these developments in the material culture involving the lion arose not only within the context of intensive interaction in the MB III–LB II Aegean, but arguably as a result of it.[194] Surely, as the long-standing Cretan association of lions and glyptic moved throughout the Aegean in this period, it must have met and interacted with other ideas and practices involving the beast, some perhaps equally old, even if the latter are not as materially evident. It is significant that the association of lions with armed human hunter-warriors gained articulation at this time. We have seen that lion-hunt imagery occurred already in the earliest phase of Cretan lion glyptic, in transitional EM III–MM IA, and that from the subsequent Protopalatial period onward the lion was consistently characterized as a threatening beast. The MB III–LB II record provides a wealth of material elaborating the association of aggressive lion and armed human, both by embodying the hunter and lion as interactors in the same scene and through what appears to become a widespread paralleling of the two throughout the Aegean. It is possible that oral traditions stemming from the mainland or the Cyclades,[195] perhaps with lineages extending beyond the Aegean, involved a figure with conventional martial attributes or a huntsman's identity. Famed accounts of lion hunts, and perhaps firsthand knowledge of the extraordinary practice, may have entered by similar routes and informed the articulation of the Aegean lion that took form during MB III–LB II. Scenes of such interactions in material culture are easily relatable to imagery in the epic similes and might indicate a crystallization within the Aegean poetic tradition in this moment.[196] At the same time, the specific, and fundamentally poetic juxtaposition of lion and human, which was formulated at least in part by the beast's embodiment in glyptic, stemmed from Crete over centuries before and clearly persisted at the core of the lion's developing identity in the Aegean.

As a last component of the MB III–LB II material to consider, we can return to the small surfaces of glyptic. In the midst of the diversification of media in which the lion was embodied, and the increased frequency of imagery depicting the lion with other figures, a striking glyptic motif took hold in the

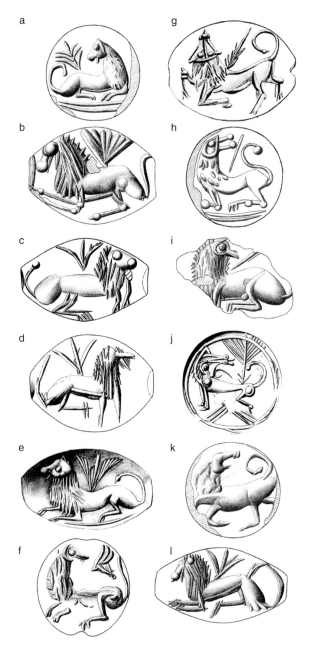

3.17. LB I–II Aegean glyptic imagery of lions with a shaft feature, either a spear in the back or a plume of vegetation. a. CMS II.6.160; b. CMS III.378; c. CMS II.3.192; d. CMS V.S3.165; e. CMS II.3.346; f. CMS III.387; g. CMS I.S.81; h. CMS II.382; i. CMS II.6.89; j. CMS II.3.277; k. CMS II.6.88; l. CMS III.508c. Drawings courtesy CMS, Heidelberg

Aegean: the solitary wounded lion (Figures 3.17, 3.18). This motif became established at the same time as the flourishing of lion-hunt and attack scenes, and it persisted through the remainder of the Late Bronze Age; it is extensively evidenced across the Aegean.[197] Within the motifs, an attack by a human is

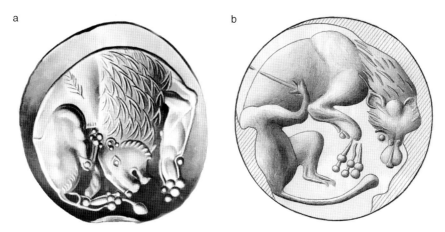

3.18. Examples of LB I–II wounded-lion glyptic motifs. a. CMS I.277; b. CMS II.6.91. Images courtesy CMS, Heidelberg

implied by the presence of a weapon – an arrow or spear – that remains in the injured lion's body. This implication of an immediately past interaction brings the scenes narrative and temporal depth, despite their imaging of the lion alone. Such enhanced dynamism might also be at work through another aspect of these wounded-lion scenes. This arises from the motifs' relationship to another established scene-type from glyptic of the same period: the single lion with a plume of vegetation rising behind it. These two scene-types can be strikingly similar in composition and style (Figure 3.17).[198] In common versions of both, the lion is represented in a reclining posture. It may gaze forward or, as is most often seen in the wounded lion version (but also occurs in scenes with the vegetal plume; e.g., Figure 3.17a, f), can look back in a regardant pose, in the direction of the shaft at its back.[199] In the tiny field of the engraved seal face, it would be extremely difficult to discern between a plumed shaft of vegetation rising from behind the back of the beast and a (potentially also plumed/fletched) shaft of a weapon, rising from its back. Both involve an incision for the shaft rising upward from the depression that constitutes the top of the beast's body and potentially fanning outward above it – in the worked surface of the stone, the spaces of what stands *behind* the lion's back and what sticks *within* it are coterminous.[200] Meanwhile, the lion's centrality as a single subject, the posture it assumes, the styles of working the stone and the materials of which the seals are fashioned, are all shared across these two scene-types, making them readily related – or confused – by someone who has encountered both. The ambivalence between the contents of the highly similar scenes also creates a slippage between the status of the lion, as a beast in a natural setting, void of human presence, or as a beast struck, definitively drawn into the sphere of dominant human action. Hence, the visual closeness of these scene-types lends a biographical and narrative development to the lion, which plays out through people's experiences with its contemporaneous embodiments in glyptic things. And although the role of a human is clearly implied in the wounded-lion motif, the particular narrative effect that takes form between these two types of glyptic scene does so because both image the lion alone. One wonders if this was an intended "double meaning," as Morgan mentions could be evident in ambiguous elements of glyptic imagery. More importantly, as Morgan also discusses (concerning talismanic seals), such double readings would arise from knowledge of multiple seals and thus get at an important midlevel scale of experience, above the individual thing or encounter.[201] McGowan has offered further consideration of this dynamic across seals, in her discussion of "multivalency" in glyptic imagery.[202]

The wounded-lion motif could also take a different shape in Aegean LB I–II glyptic. In these cases, the lion is still a solitary figure, but its body is curved in a dramatic c-form, with head, seen from above, extending down toward the tail; an arrow appears in the beast's torso. Examples come from Crete and the mainland. Compare the exquisite embodiments in a clay impression from LM IB Ayia Triada and a sardonyx lentoid from LH II Pylos, Rutsi Tholos 2 (Figure 3.18). In both, the massive, curved body of the lion fills the entirety of the circular field; the beast is monumental even as it fits on the small surface. A human's role in the scene set before us is clear, and we can easily relate it to the narratives of contemporary lion-hunt imagery.[203] Yet even as the arrow in the abdomen betrays both violent human action and glorious human skill, this weapon is dwarfed by the immense presence of the lion. Here, the lion has been defeated but is also given the field.

The fact that the human is not imaged radically alters the dynamics of the composition compared to scenes of confrontation. As the single focal point of the engraved object, it is the lion's impressive form, not the human's, that is set in juxtaposition to the seal wearer. Here, we could be glimpsing a distinct aspect of the lion active in the cultural traditions of the LBA Aegean, one that saw something remarkable in the dying beast specifically. One is reminded again of the similes of the *Iliad*, in which lions are many times juxtaposed to men in their dominating vitality. But there are also similes that celebrate the wounded or dying lion for its fierceness even in the face of death (e.g., *Il.* 12.40–49, in comparison to Hektor).[204] It seems that a similar dimension of the beast may be embodied in these seals. With the human excluded, it is not victorious action that is actually given form. We do not see a human majestically thrusting a blade into a lion; the beast is on stage alone. This does not preclude other significations being inherent in the image – of domination and appropriation, or even of human success in an actual lion hunt. But it does constitute a notably distinct focus for juxtaposition with the seal wearer, one that could invest social power and magnitude in a dying body by making it the solitary subject of an engraved seal. In this position, the dying lion contributed something unique to the characterization of the person's identity performed by a seal and, in so doing, also novelly contributed to the lion's identity in the region.

STONE POETS

The lion of the EB III–LB II Aegean was anything but static. Through its surviving material manifestations, we can appreciate diachronic and synchronic variation in its form and associations, from Prepalatial Crete to the early Mycenaean mainland. Running through this fluidity, over time and space, is the remarkable fact that the beast's embodiment in glyptic endured as its primary home. The seal, and with it a highly dynamic juxtaposition with people, continued to frame how the lion was experienced. The distinctive animacy of glyptic invigorated the lions and contributed to their characterization along with other sources, including stories shared and created. Various particular lines of evidence – linguistic, material, sociocultural – have been helpful when contemplating the multimedia poetic culture of the early Aegean and possible interconnections realized therein. But it is when put on the table together that discussions surrounding each of these topics contribute to one another and to a common impression of the period from MB III to LB II as a moment of robust cultural sharing, perpetuation and innovation across the Aegean. Poetry and lions were embroiled in this not as travelers on separate paths but as confluent aspects of the same cultural phenomena. Their deepest coincidence may be in the distinctive juxtapositions formulated by both glyptic and the simile. With this, we need to expand our identification of the Aegean poet to embrace the idea that things, seals, with their distinctive animacy, in a very real sense contributed to authoring the dynamic, poetic juxtaposition of lion and human in the region. The lion's existence early and persistently in glyptic not only formulated a basis of this juxtaposition but brought it a distinctive poetic complexity. This is not a question of specific symbolic or narrative content associated with the lion, which was no doubt open-ended, but one of position and nature, which were at the same time physical and poetic – and something between.

NOTES

1. See discussion in Sherratt 1990: 808–809.
2. See Burns 2010: 57–66.
3. Compare observations in Blakolmer 2016a: 62; Shapland 2010a, 2022.
4. Shapland 2010a (esp. 276 for definition of "traces"), 2022; Thomas 2014 expertly discusses and catalogs leonine faunal evidence from the Aegean (none has yet been found in Crete).
5. Morris 1990: 152 n. 23, citing Tambiah 1969.
6. Bloedow 1992; Ballintijn 1995; Thomas 2004; Alden 2005.

7. Bartosiewicz 2009: 2; Schnitzler 2011: 227, following de Planhol 2004.
8. Bartosiewicz 2009: 2–3.
9. Bloedow 1992: 301–304; Alden 2005; Bartosiewicz 2009.
10. Schnitzler 2011: 229–230.
11. Thomas 2004, 2014 (including helpful catalog) and Bartosiewicz 2009 for review of evidence; also Alden 2005; Shapland 2010a. Compare recent discussion of lion's presence in the Aegean in Zimmer 2022; I thank Nancy Thomas for drawing my attention to this fascinating piece.
12. Thomas 2014: 379.
13. Thomas 2014: 382, with bibliography.
14. Thomas 2014: 383.
15. Thomas 2014: 379.
16. Thomas 2014: 384.
17. Catalogs in Bartosiewicz 2009; Thomas 2014. Relatively more substantial finds from Aiegera (including a pelvis fragment) are possibly evidence of a votive deposition.
18. Thomas 2014: 379. Thomas notes that a single large humerus from Kolonna, on Aegina, shows marking that "could indicate that the bone was broken when the corpse was being butchered" (2014: 382). Thomas speculates that this might indicate that a "a captive lion or two" was present there and takes the further step to say, then "why not send one to Crete?" (2014: 389). Without further evidence, I do not follow the suggestion that we move from this bone on Aegina to imported living beasts there or on Crete.
19. Three finds of lion teeth from Ayia Irini on Keos were possibly brought there for amuletic use; see Trantalidou 2000: 716 n. 19; Bartosiewicz 2009: 7, 11; Thomas 2014: 383.
20. Bartosiewicz 2009.
21. Hamilakis (1996, esp. 163–164) discusses the social role of hunting, including rare animals like the lion.
22. Colburn notes this object (2008: 208 n. 51); see Xanthoudidēs 1924: 29, nos. 386, 388.
23. See Sanavia 2018 and discussion below, p. 116. Isolated small objects also exist, some unpublished.
24. Dating of the three lion-head rhyta from Knossos, associated with the Central Treasury, is unclear; HM 44, AE 784 and AE 1181 (with twelve associated fragments); Evans 1928.2: 820–831; Koehl 2006: 36, 122–123 nos. 329–331.
25. Ceramic lion-head rhyta from Palaikastro and Zakros seem to postdate the Neopalatial period (Rhyne 1970: 408, 430; Thomas 2004: 171 n. 51, figs. 9.8, 9.9, citing Vanschoonwinkel's LM IB–IIIA1 dating (1996, nos. 395, 396).
26. See Shapland 2010a for discussion.
27. Akrotiri lion-head rhyta, both clay: NAM AKR 1855, from West House Room 2 (Marinatos 1972: 35, pl. 80); NAM AKR 116, Sector Alpha Room A2 (Marinatos 1969: 19); Koehl 2006: 123, nos. 333 and 334. Mycenae lion-head rhyton, metal: NAM 273, Shaft Grave IV (Schliemann 1878: 211 number 326, 222); Koehl 2006: 121 no. 328.
28. A seal impression inevitably relates to a person's basic bodily identity through the implication, as an index, of a hand's act of stamping/creating it. This corporeal identity also carries sociocultural depth, but the particulars of this could differ (Anderson 2016).
29. Anderson 2019.
30. Simandiraki-Grimshaw and Stevens (2012) problematize the dynamics of interaction between a human body and a worn animal body, including how they "coperform" and transform – as when a hair ornament in the form of a water creature turns human locks into waves. See also Simandiraki-Grimshaw 2010b on "heterosomatic" hybrids in the Aegean.
31. Krzyszkowska (e.g., 1988) identified hippopotamus tooth as the ivory used for many Prepalatial Cretan seals; see also Colburn 2008; Schoep 2006; Anderson 2016.
32. Yule (1981: 208–9) identified this group; see also Sbonias 1995, esp. 89–99; Anderson 2016.

33. See also Colburn 2008.
34. Ballintijn (1995) considers whether other, familiar species served as models for the lion in Crete. Determining the presence of cats in prehistoric Crete is a complicated matter; see Moody 2012: 241, 247.
35. Anderson 2019, and discussion below, p. 149–150.
36. Especially Krzyszkowska 1988: 226–228; 2005: 63–64; Aruz 2008a.
37. Aruz 2008a.
38. Aruz 2008a; Anderson 2016.
39. Compare Shapland 2010a: 279–280; see Anderson 2016: 86–93.
40. Wiese 1996.
41. Anderson 2016, esp. 171–282.
42. Compare Aruz 2008a: 40.
43. Additionally, imported cylinder seals may have been experienced as having extraordinary properties; see relevant discussion in Kopanias 2012; Feldman 2014; Burns 2010: 138.
44. See careful discussion in Aruz 2008a; Pini 1990 on various forms; Shapland 2010a: 279–281.
45. Sbonias 1995 and Anderson 2016.
46. For example, lion-form weights from the LBA shipwreck off the coast of Uluburun, Turkey; see Pulak 1996.
47. For example, a copper-alloy pickaxe reportedly from Mesopotamia or western Iran, EBA, Met 57.13.5.
48. At least in the basic sense of conveying a message or indication through the impression, versus *in person*.
49. Anderson 2016.
50. The frequent practice of repeat stamping in Prepalatial seal use (as discussed by Relaki 2009) would have further engrained the lion's position in the material and social matter of Cretan glyptic.
51. Sbonias 1995, 109–111.
52. Compare CMS II, volume 6: 149 from LM IB sealing deposit at Ayia Triada.
53. Sanavia (2018) analyzes a MM IB pictorial Polychrome Ware bridge-spouted basin sherd (now joined with a second) from an MM IB–IIA dumping ground near the West Court area at Phaistos. The lion motif is painted on the rim's interior.
54. Anderson 2016, esp. 208–233, on "Linear-Zoned Subgroup."
55. Krzyszkowska 2017: 146.
56. Krzyszkowska 2017: 146.
57. Anastasiadou 2016b: 162.
58. Eco 1976: 138–139.
59. Compare Simandiraki-Grimshaw and Stevens' description of small Cretan pendants or beads in the form of lions that (in some cases), because of their perforation, could "rotate or rest" on a person's skin or worn textile (2012: 600). Through their reading, the human support transforms into an "inhabited" land-like surface where the lion exists in closeness to the person.
60. Krzyszkowska 2017: 147.
61. For the glyptic from Phaistos *vano* 25, see CMS II, volume 5 and Levi 1958; also Krzyszkowska 2005: 104–108.
62. See Krzyszkowska 2010 on landscape in Aegean glyptic.
63. The continuation of the upper outline of the lower jaw indicates the mouth is open.
64. Krzyszkowska (2005: 171) describes much of the glyptic evidence from Neopalatial Ayia Triada as "firmly set in the mainstream of neo-palatial glyptic." Even across smaller-scale traditions (e.g., the LM IB–III Cut Style), representation of lions nevertheless participates in broader Cretan themes, including wounded lions or lions paired with vegetal plumes (see below, pp. 149–150).
65. Younger 1983, Pini 1995.

66. Pini 1995: 200.

67. See Pini 1995: 193–199, on "wirbelförmig" compositions and "chimera" types.

68. See extensive discussion of griffins in Chapter 4.

69. Again, the tables can turn when a griffin enters, for example, CMS II, volume 6, Ayia Triada.

70. Aruz 2008a.

71. For LM II–III instances, for example, CMS II, volume 4: 75 CMS II, volume 3: 333; CMS II, volume 4: 202.

72. Masson 2007: 733.

73. Ulanowski 2015: 255 n. 6, with references.

74. See the online *Annotated Corpus of Luwian Texts* at http://web-corpora.net/LuwianCorpus/search/index.php?interface_language=en, with further references to publications of the material.

75. "Did you see the man that was eaten by a lion?" "I saw him." "How does he fare?" Gadotti 2014: 159.

76. George 2003: 177.

77. "Against Enki, the water at the stern of the boat / Was mangling it like a lion" (lines 25–26 in "Gilgamesh, Enkidu, and the Netherworld," trans. Gadotti 2014: 154).

78. Watanabe 2002: 4, 42–68.

79. Heimpel 1968: 11–14, 15–23, 24–42, 50–53. Heimpel uses four categories to structure his examination of Sumerian animal imagery: *Metapher* (metaphor), *Vergleich* (simile), *Parabel* (parable) and *Gleichnis* (comparison); see Heimpel 1968: 11–72 and Black 1998: 14–19.

80. For example, Watanabe 2002; Minchin 2001: 138–139; Black 1998 with further references; see also Kramer 1969.

81. Black 1998: 15–17; see also Heimpel 1968: 34; Watanabe 2002: 21. Black in fact "draws attention" to Heimpel's observation (1968: 34) that the suffixes *-gim* ("like/as") and *-am* (related to verb "to be") are sometimes exchanged; see Black 1998: 16.

82. Black 1998: 15–17; see esp. Heimpel 1968: 34; also Watanabe 2002: 21.

83. For example, Watanabe 2002, esp. 42–56; Gadotti 2014: 20, 29, 38.

84. Kaphtor/Kaptar, a place name that occurs in various Bronze Age Near Eastern texts, likely refers to Crete; see Strange 1980.

85. Strange 1980: 90–91, text no. 33, from an inventory from the palace of Zimrilim.

86. Broodbank 2002: 272–275.

87. For example, Louvre AO133b, mace-head of Gudea of Lagash, from Tello (EBA).

88. Burns (2010) considers access to imports, from various perspectives and regarding both finished and raw materials; Colburn 2008: 212–214, 218–220.

89. Watanabe 2002: 45–46.

90. In her superb analysis of the "flotilla" frieze in Room 5 of the West House, Akrotiri, Morris writes: "I would add that not only the form but the content of these frescoes is difficult to imagine without a contemporary narrative tradition in poetry. Few would deny that the formative period of the Iliad and the Odyssey, as we know them, lies centuries later; but their source in older tales is as least as early as 1500 B.C. Since these frescoes and other early Mycenaean art were unknown to later Greeks, the very survival of Bronze Age history presumes a narrative tradition inherited from Bronze Age poetry (1989: 94).

91. Nagy 1996: 109–112; also Morris 1989; Sherratt 1990; Nagy 1998.

92. Janko 1992: 10–11.

93. Horrocks 1980. See also West 1988: 158.

94. See especially West 1988, Ruijgh 1995. Important to both scholars is the evidence of *tmesis* (separation of preverb and verb) in some Homeric verse. Tmesis had gone out of practice by the phase of Greek documented in Linear B, indicating a pre–Linear B origin for the verse preserving tmesis. Horrocks argued this point already in 1980. For a critical view, see Haug 2011.

95. Notably Scott 1974; Lonsdale 1990: 13–18.

STONE POETS   155

96. Shipp 1972.
97. West 1988: 157–159; also Webster 1964. West provides a lion simile to exemplify an early Mycenaean type. He also notes that "the comparative particle ὥς <*yós is frequently treated as if it had an initial consonant," "a 'phantom consonant' where once there was an initial s- or y- (normally leaving an aspirate in classical Greek)." He takes this phenomenon as a vestige of Mycenaean Greek (1988: 157). Because ὥς often introduces a simile, this observation is significant for considering the antiquity of this poetic element in Aegean poetry.
98. West 1988: 158, 169.
99. West 1988; 1997.
100. Ruijgh 2011: 258.
101. Ruijgh (2011: 257–258, 287) explains that with the principle of isosyllabicity, "a given verse form is characterized by a fixed number of syllables, while, in origin at least, syllabic quantity was for the most part irrelevant." By contrast, dactylic hexameter is based on the "metrical principle" of isochrony; that is, "a sequence of feet with equal duration" (see 257, for both quotes).
102. Ruijgh 2011: 257.
103. Yet Duhoux (1998, with further references) does not entirely exclude the possibility that an Indo-European language was encoded in Linear A. Compare Renfrew's (1998) suggestion that Crete was home to a non-Greek branch of Indo-European (via Anatolia) from which Mycenaean Greek speakers borrowed; Renfrew also considers that a non–Indo-European language could have been active on Crete (hence seeing possible linguistic diversity in Bronze Age Crete and the Aegean, as does Duhoux).
104. Davis 2014.
105. Duhoux 1998: 25–26.
106. Duhoux 1994, esp. 291–294; 1998, 9–10, 13–14, 24–25.
107. See Davis 2018.
108. Duhoux 1998: 10, 14, 24–25.
109. Duhoux 1998: 25–26. The five Pre-Hellenic Cretan linguistic "corpora" that Duhoux mentions here refer to the Bronze Age scripts of Linear A, Cretan Hieroglyphic, the Phaistos Disc, and the Arkalokhori Axe, as well as Eteocretan, which is evidenced in first-millennium BCE material but is also considered Pre-Hellenic.
110. See Duhoux 1998. The status of the "Archanes Script," engraved on seal stones, is debated. The Cretan evidence probably should be dated MM IA–B. Scholars disagree regarding its relationship to Linear A or Cretan Hieroglyphic, and its very status as a true script (see Anastasiadou 2016b; Decorte 2018, with refs.).
111. Anastasiadou (2016b, esp. 159–160, with refs.) cites various studies that support seeing a division between central and east-central zones of the island in the Protopalatial.
112. Anastasiadou 2016b: 169.
113. The so-called Hieroglyphic Deposit at Knossos has a complicated position in this regional picture: see, for example, Weingarten 1995; Krzyszkowska 2005: 112–116; Anastasiadou 2016b, esp. 165–167, 185; and Chapter 4.
114. Anastasiadou 2016b.
115. For example, Palaima explains that the language encoded in Linear B might have been a "fossilized Greek" used for record-making over more than 200 years, which preserved an archaic character as well as apparent elements of the Cretan language encoded in Linear A (Palaima 2011: 123, 124 n. 167). Meanwhile, Michailidou (2001, esp. 18–19) discusses the possibility that the distribution of Linear A texts in the Aegean does not necessarily correspond to the distribution of the language of Crete.
116. On the work and movement of the seal carvers behind the Parading Lions glyptic, see Anderson 2016. Concerning Prepalatial regional and local landscape dynamics, see, for example, Relaki 2004; Legarra Herrero 2014; Déderix 2017 and Chapter 2.
117. Sbonias 1995: 109–111, referred to in Anastasiadou 2016b: 178.

118.	Schoep 1999, esp. 217–221; cf. Krzyszkowska 2005: 191–192. See also Blakolmer 2012 concerning iconographic streamlining during this period.
119.	Driessen and MacDonald 1997; Driessen 2013; Letesson and Driessen 2020.
120.	For example, Krzyszkowska 2005: 191–192.
121.	Palaima 2011: 115.
122.	Palaima 2011: 124.
123.	Naturally, it is possible that Mycenaean Greek was also being spoken in Crete by others, who were not involved in Linear B-based administration, for example, individuals or social groups who had migrated to the island.
124.	Michailidou 2001 (with refs.) concerning scribes' status.
125.	See discussions in Pluta 2011; Michailidou 2001; Zadka 2012; Montecchi 2020.
126.	West 1997: 612; Renfrew 1998: 246–247, with references.
127.	Younger 1998: 18, 22, 61, pls. 3, 4, 7, and generally on lyre 22–27. For Av 106: Aravantinos, Godart and Sacconi 2001: 176–178. See also Palaima 2011: 122–123 with references; Ruijgh 2011: 258.
128.	Ruijgh 2011: 257.
129.	Ruijgh 1995: 85–88; 2011: 287–289, including his translation, which is reproduced here.
130.	West (1988: 159) points to Meriones' and Idomeneus' occurrence in "formulaic verse of Pre-Linear B vintage" (citing Ruijgh); frequent narrative association with other apparently early figures such as Ajax; ownership of an iconic Bronze Age artifact (the boar's tusk helmet); and famed excellence in archery, a skill lauded in the Bronze Age and shared with other early epic figures, notably Odysseus.
131.	Tartaron 2013: 216–235 concerning the Bronze Age Saronic and Aegina. The "Aegina Treasure" indicates significant influence from Crete (Higgins 1979; Fitton 2009).
132.	Davis and Stocker 2015: 175–78, citing Nelson 2001: 49–55, 114–117, 185. For the Grave of the Griffin Warrior: Davis and Stocker 2016; Stocker and Davis 2017.
133.	Marchant 2017.
134.	Thomas 2014: 378 n. 21.
135.	For example, CMS I.9, CMS I.10, both from Grave Circle A, Grave III.
136.	Krzyszkowska 2005; Shapland 2010a: 279.
137.	On entangled evidence in glyptic, see also Younger 1978, 1979, 1984, especially regarding his Mycenae-Vapheio Lion and Line-Jaw Masters; concerning LB II–III, see Krzyszkowska 2005: 193–195.
138.	Minchin 2001: 160.
139.	Minchin 2001: 137 and 132–160.
140.	Minchin 2001: 137–139.
141.	Tsagalis 2012: 261–448.
142.	Tsagalis 2012: 261–269.
143.	Compare Scott 1974: 85–87. Tsagalis' work arises from the context of earlier studies considering the spaces of the Homeric similes (*Gleichnisorte*) from various interpretive perspectives (notably Elliger and Moulton; see Tsagalis 2012: 271–272 for refs.), but his approach is distinguished by a focus on the cognitive aspects of memory and their role in poetic effect, including spatial dynamics.
144.	Tsagalis 2012: 259–372.
145.	See Clarke 1995, esp. 145–153. Cf. Lonsdale 1990: 35–36.
146.	Translation by Lattimore (2011).
147.	Compare Scott 1974: 4–5.
148.	There are reasons to see late versions of the poems as composed in western Anatolia, including details reflecting local topographical knowledge; see West 1988: 165–166; 2011: 20–27; Lonsdale 1990: 28–29; Alden 2005: 335–337, and nn. 9–10 with references. This does not mean that all earlier oral traditions that fed into the Homeric tradition were Anatolian; see West's masterful discussion of Bronze Age Aegean roots (1988). Sources were likely multifold: Aegean, Anatolian and beyond.

149. The presence of lions in Anatolia was definite but variable. They were reportedly hunted in areas of Anatolia into the nineteenth century CE, yet bones from some Bronze Age Anatolian sites were potentially imported trophies from Syria; Schnitzler 2011: 228–229, 236; de Planhol 2004: 67–71.

150. Alden 2005.

151. See Ballintijn 1995.

152. Watrous considers the relationship of glyptic imagery and Homeric imagery (including epithets and similes) in a forthcoming piece, "Male Identity on Bronze Age Aegean Seals."

153. Simandiraki-Grimshaw and Stevens 2012.

154. Reading Simandiraki-Grimshaw's (2010b) study of Minoan hybridity in tandem with her coauthored 2012 piece with Stevens brings another layer of depth to their consideration of animal-form worn objects, including seals, jewelery and garments. Among numerous examples of Minoan renderings of hybrid animals being involved in contexts of change and action, Simandiraki-Grimshaw (2010b: 101) notes that "hybridity enacts private corporal and behavioral fusions on the physical human body (e.g., a moving 'bird lady' seal on a hypothetical wrist)." She considers various ways that "hybrids" can be constituted, both as renderings and between a human and a worn object as "heterosomatic hybrids."

155. Anderson 2016, 2019.

156. See Younger 2010 for discussion, including characterization of palatial Mycenaean seal use.

157. Shapland 2010a, 2010b, 2013, 2022.

158. Bloedow 1992; Thomas 2004, 2014. Hamilakis' work (e.g., 1996) has been crucial to problematizing human relationships to nonhuman animals in the Aegean Bronze Age.

159. Shapland 2010a: 282–283, citing Pini 1985.

160. Shapland quotes Summers' description of *traces*, as indexes, being "an indication of former presence and contact" (Shapland 2010a: 276, following Summers 2003: 687).

161. Shapland 2010a: 277–278, 283.

162. Shapland 2010a: esp. 280–283, following Belting (2005) on "staging an absence."

163. Shapland 2010a: 281.

164. See especially Thomas 2014.

165. Compare Blakolmer 2016a: 62.

166. See Shapland 2013.

167. See rich analyses in Shapland 2022.

168. Anderson 2019: 214–216.

169. See discussion of different modes of engagement with nonhumans in Chapter 1; also Shapland 2022.

170. Compare Thomas 1999.

171. Morgan describes the effective "hybridity" that can occur when forms "meld" in the engraved surface (1989: 151). In this case, the effect of the human and lion bodies being almost merged arises from the engraving of the one "behind" the other in the seal surface and is no less powerful for having resulted from the engravers' negotiations with seals' scale and material.

172. CMS II.6.36, from Ayia Triada, hints at such by showing a lion with a "human" holding a bow or leash. Possibly elements of this backstory compare to ones involving leashed griffins (see Chapter 4).

173. CMS II.7.33 (impressions from Zakros) and CMS I.224 (Vapheio); compare scenes of binding a bovine, for example, CMS II.7.32, from the same deposit at Zakros as CMS II.7.33.

174. Think, for example, of the occurrence of "lion-hearted" Herakles in the *Iliad* (11.266–268), where the lion is primarily met in similes. Such coincidence of lion traditions is also possible in the Bronze Age material.

175. Compare Morgan 1995b, considering symbolic implications.
176. Quoting Minchin's (2001) term.
177. This is not to assert that extended similes of specifically Homeric type were occurring in the LB I–II poetic tradition. They may have been – see West 1988: 158, 169 on the likelihood – but we do not presently have textual evidence to firmly support such a claim.
178. Malafouris 2008: 8, in discussion of Mycenaean swords. Malafouris engages with Voutsaki's discussion of an "agonistic ethos" (Voutsaki 1993).
179. Knappett (2004: 46) engaging with Gibson 1979.
180. Compare Thomas 2004: 172. Shapland (2010a) also discusses different representational media having distinct affordances, especially concerning rhyta versus seals.
181. Bennett 2010: 23–24. Bennett also describes the fluid and historical character of assemblages. She develops the understanding of assemblages in conjunction with the notion of "affective bodies," for which she draws on the work of Spinoza, Deleuze and Lucretius.
182. Thomas 2004: 164. Thomas provides an excellent discussion and catalog of the material (the twenty items from Grave Circle A, Mycenae, are nos. 5–24 [2004: 194–198]).
183. See Morgan 1988: 47–48. Cf. Watanabe 2002: 42–45 on dangerous properties of Mesopotamian royal weapons being like the lion's attributes.
184. Compre Morgan 1988: 46–47, 1995b: 175–176.
185. Thomas 2004: 171.
186. Morris (1989: 516) compellingly compares this scene to epic similes; her broader discussion of the West House's relation to epic is powerful. See also Morgan 1988: 48–49, 155–165; 1995b: 172–180; Doumas 1992: 45–97; and studies in Vlachopoulos 2007 and Watrous 2007.
187. Morgan 1995b: 163–164, on intent versus action in the scenes.
188. Doumas 1992; Thomas 2004: 169–171, figs. 9.6, 9.7; Morgan 1988: pls. 8, 9, 55, C.
189. Morgan 1988, esp. 163–165.
190. NAMA 373.
191. NAMA AKR 116 and 1855.
192. Shapland 2010a: 283–284.
193. Morgan 1988: 47–48; Morris 1989: 516–517. Both of these exceptional studies were deep inspirations for me with this project.
194. Compare Thomas 2004.
195. Both Morgan (1988) and Thomas (2004, esp. 169–171) crucially recognize the role of the Cyclades.
196. Compare Sherratt 1990, esp. 817–818. Sherratt sees similes as susceptible to diachronic change, but her reason for this highlights the cultural specificity of similes, an idea that could support identifying both the Bronze Age and Homeric evidence as part of a fluid but perpetuated Aegean-specific cultural tradition.
197. Discussions in Pini 1995, and Krzyszkowska 2005: 201–203.
198. Pini (1995: 200) notes that in renderings of single lions in glyptic imagery of this period, free space above the beast's back provided room for an additional motif, such as a plant, star or sun, and that these are also found in other contemporary seal images.
199. Both of these poses are also embodied by lions imaged without a shaft (weapon or vegetal plume), suggesting that they were a standard base for renderings of the beast.
200. Morgan (1989: 151) comments on just this effect; see note 171 above, p. 157.
201. Morgan 1989: 148–149, 152–159.
202. McGowan 2018.
203. Shapland (2010a, esp. 280–82) reads this scene as a testament to a human's participation in a hunt.
204. See discussion of the wounded animal simile in Lonsdale 1990: 42. On the complex psychology of the defiant, driven beast in Homeric similes, see Clarke 1995: 148–159.

FOUR

LIKENESS AND INTEGRATION AMONG EXTRAORDINARY CREATURES

Rethinking Minoan "Composite" Beasts

THE FRESCOED GRIFFINS THAT GUARD THE THRONE ROOM AT KNOSSOS are often regarded as quintessential embodiments of the Minoan fantastical creature, their elegant forms testament to the vivid Cretan imaginary and the central place of composite beings therein.[1] As with other extraordinary creatures known from Cretan Bronze Age evidence, such as the Minoan genius, the overseas ancestry of the griffin has been much discussed. This is often framed by the notion that the reworking of such exotic entities to Cretan tastes reflects a broader character of Minoan art and culture, which is posed as simultaneously eclectic and inventive. Griffins, genii, sphinxes and other complex beasts are present in a variety of media from the island and region, from tiny seals to expansive wall paintings, appearing already during the Middle Bronze Age and gaining prominent ground in the Neopalatial period and onward.[2]

We take for granted that beasts like griffins are "composites." As creatures that combine features possessed by multiple animal species within their singular bodily forms, griffins certainly fulfill the standard definition for composite or "hybrid" beings, and, along with numerous other types of fantastical creature represented in the visual/material record of Bronze Age Crete, they have long been established and discussed as such. I do not wish to challenge this identification, but to complicate it. Such beasts do stand as remarkable beings, wonders of creative fabrication, but their status within the cultural context of the Aegean seems more related to strangeness and extraordinariness than compositeness, as such, and their rich complexity as animalian entities arises in part from the specific nature of their embodiment as things. With this recalibration, our problematization of griffins and other strange creatures that have (some) roots in imported objects shares ground with discussions in Chapters 2 and 3, which examined Cretan renderings of lions and category-defying animalian objects.

I certainly do not mean that Cretan renderings of griffins and other fantastical beings are not distinctly Aegean because they are related, in part, to foreign predecessors – far from it. It is not the cultural ascription of the creatures that I wish to rethink so much as the combinatory dynamics that they embody. To explore these ideas, I begin by considering the nature of composite creatures as they have been defined and discussed as a class. On that basis, we can then turn to Crete and the Aegean specifically. Ultimately, I argue that distinctly integrative ways of rendering animalian bodies are apparent in Bronze Age Crete. In some cases, we see these creative dynamics embracing the forms of fantastic hybrid creatures from overseas while also fluidly drawing in the character of other phenomena – both artificial and biological animals, as well as objects. Fluidly emerging from this integration was a host of extraordinary creatures distinguished by a potency that likely arose more from the strangeness of their bodily characters and thingly efficacies, than from marked modularity.

This chapter is organized into three sections. We begin in the first section, "Creatures of Change," by examining current scholarly thinking concerning the occurrence and nature of "composite" beasts in the ancient world, and how, in particular, they were related to foreignness. These ideas are then considered for their applicability and implications in the Aegean Bronze Age specifically, with a focus on MBA Crete. Working in this direction, and as a means of exploring these matters through the particularities of objects themselves, I turn to a close analysis of the earliest extant renderings of the griffin within Cretan material culture, from the Protopalatial period. In the second and third sections, I consider how foreign, strange or unfamiliar animalian forms became entangled in Aegean ecologies of living and nonliving things and, in that context, became part of novel embodiments of creatures that had their own distinct associations and affordances. The griffin provides a base for these considerations. I investigate the dynamic nature of the beast's formal and contextual identity both during the MBA and looking forward into the Neopalatial period. Each of these sections of the chapter is framed by close analysis of one of two distinguishing bodily features common to early renderings of the griffin in Crete: chest elaborations ("Griffins Controlled or Taking Wing") and head appendages ("Crowned Beasts, Potent Gazes and Moving Things").

The earliest extant examples of Cretan griffins, embodied in impressions from a Protopalatial sealing deposit at Phaistos, all have prominently elaborated chests, but each takes a distinct form – from dramatic feathered tufts, to a striated encircling band, to an attached collar and pendant. In addition to close examination of these three griffins and their MBA context, problematizing the presence of these features involves, in part, looking forward, into the later MBA and early LBA, to query how the trope of chest embellishments in Aegean griffins is further realized in the more extensive evidence of these phases. Discussion here concerns how the articulation of bodily features in the chest/neck region of griffins could have given rise to simultaneous yet divergent implications concerning the status of the beast. In numerous cases beginning already in the Protopalatial period, defining basic formal components of a griffin's chest/neck area (e.g., outlines of anatomy) can simultaneously seem to constitute added objects *upon* the beast's body, such as a collar; such uncertainty can also involve the distinction between a feature having an abstract "ornamental" or figural/pictorial character (e.g., a spiral-form ornament or a cord-like leash). Beyond generating complexity around the immediate corporeal status of the individual griffin in question, this uncertainty also lays the groundwork for realizing a tense diversity of relations between the griffins and other creatures and contexts – from establishing similarity with the markings of impressive biological Cretan vultures to echoing imagery of leashed fantastic creatures from overseas.

In the third section, we consider the presence of head appendages on the early Cretan griffins from Phaistos as a jumping-off point for tracing out a web of extraordinary Aegean fabricated creatures and the distinguishing attributes that embody links between them. While these creatures are seen to participate in a broader, peculiarly Aegean way of rendering animals that is integrative but not additive, they are also set apart by the manner in which they draw together foreign and local animalian forms. As modern scholars, we might traditionally identify some of the creatures in this group, such as griffins or sphinxes, as being composites, but other creatures that I draw in, such as owls and humanoid front-facing figures, would not typically be classified as such. Yet by focusing on various features that recur throughout this web of animals, and on the particulars of their existences as material objects, it becomes apparent that their shared status as strange and extraordinary – potent and potentially laced with an aura of the foreign – was likely the most prominent aspect of their unique identities. Indeed, it seems that even those creatures of the group that we label as composites or hybrids likely were experienced more as wonderful wholes than as jarring or counterintuitive combinations.

Part of what arises through the course of these discussions is that these creatures, remarkable as they are, would have been experienced as being *similar to* a rich host of other animals and phenomena, and not simply as fixed pairings of specific parts. Realizing this helps us to place these Aegean beasts within the particular ecologies where they were crafted and creatively engaged with by people – ecologies that involved other animals as well as further components of lived worlds. It was within and between these contexts that the extraordinary creatures actually acquired their characters as distinctive material and sociocultural beings. Hence, it is especially important to consider how these fabricated animals superseded single spheres of interaction. They were experienced as elements of *simultaneous* scales and varieties of interconnected phenomena, ranging from the highly local context of a single community and its social forms and practices, to regional-scale spheres characterized by shared traditions and particular zoological and environmental circumstances, to the more idiosyncratic contexts of long-distance exchanges – some extending overseas. Case studies, always based in particular things, allow us to explore the complexity of these simultaneous fields of experience and comparison as they pertain to renderings of the creatures.

CREATURES OF CHANGE

Recent years have seen various significant discussions concerning how to define and problematize composite figures in the ancient world, and specifically those from the Aegean Bronze Age. Simandiraki-Grimshaw has offered a sophisticated schema for considering Minoan "hybrids" that concerns the nature of the relationship they embody between joined creatures in its physical/material and temporal dimensions.[3] "Heterosomatic hybrids" are entities in which one creature (typically a human) temporarily takes on a bodily component of another, for example, by wearing an object of adornment (this dynamic situation will be considered in Chapter 5). Meanwhile "homosomatic hybrids" are permanent mergings of parts from different species as a single body (griffins and sphinxes are traditionally identified as such mergings). It is this latter type of being that is most often discussed and problematized as a "composite" or "hybrid," in Aegean and other contexts.

Wengrow has provided an extensive examination in which he considers the relationship between, on the one hand, the rise and spread of urbanism in western Asia, Egypt and the Aegean and, on the other, representations of figures that combine elements of different species.[4] This study is powerful for various reasons, especially for its equal focus on social context and material culture. Central to Wengrow's discussion is the phenomenon of "modularity," in both its cognitive and technical dimensions. In developing this topic, he draws together two forms of "intuitive knowledge" that he sees as especially relevant to the consideration of composites – one is "presumably universal," and the other is "historical." The first, "intuitive biology," describes a capacity of the human mind that "allows properties of vitality and movement to be attributed unreflectively to artificial composites, based on the mind's innate tendency to compensate for gaps and absences in the visible world, conjuring organic-seeming wholes out of ill-fitting parts."[5] This notion, that human cognition, inherently, can accord fundamental properties of living, complete creatures to fabrications consisting of multiple, potentially mismatched, body elements joined together, has various implications for our discussion of Minoan composites and will be returned to below. The second type of "intuitive knowledge" discussed by Wengrow emerges within the context of certain historical social environments. Concerning the ancient world, he explains that the activation of this particular knowledge depended on the appearance and interaction of specific types of technological and institutional phenomena in early urban spaces, and on the experiences they generated. These developments impacted the nature of production and processing, as well as people's basic intuitions of segmentation and integration. Wengrow examines the case of southern Mesopotamia during the Late Uruk period and the simultaneous development of modular technologies, such as protocuneiform writing and mudbrick architecture, and the production of standardized material culture.[6] He argues that in the context of such developments, emergent urban environments "fostered the cultivation of an otherwise latent mode of perception that confronts the world, not as we usually encounter it – composed of unique and sentient totalities – but as a realm of divisible subjects, each comprising a multitude of fissionable and recombinable parts."[7] In the realm of material culture, Wengrow highlights seals and figurines. He argues that during the Bronze Age, the logic and form of these types of object were increasingly characterized by standardization and the relationship of part-to-whole, and, in this light, draws attention to how both seals and figurines sometimes embodied newly popular composite creatures.

Through his discussion, Wengrow identifies a generative context in which composite creatures were cultivated as a markedly more prevalent subject in representational material culture, locating this development within the human dimensions of early urban spaces and their cognitive, sociocultural and technological aspects. After examining the environments in which such composite figures originated, Wengrow moves on to consider the apparent spread of such subjects to other protourban contexts. With this, he argues that composites not only emerged, but also appealed and thrived, within societies that were dealing with distinctive circumstances associated with increased complexity and interaction, and that this accounts for the adoption and success of composites within certain spaces. Wengrow ultimately argues that composites embodied something of a novel sense of the foreign in these newly urban contexts and were an effective means of dealing with the risks implied by new types and levels of interconnection in a manipulable form; in his words, composites "'provided the locus for a heightened cultural interplay between 'self' and 'nonself,' condensing some anticipated danger into an image that could be fixed and managed within existing structures of meaning."[8] Two aspects of the resultant composite figures become especially relevant in this light: their modularity (combining a novel diversity of parts in a new shared context) and their strangeness (embodying the unfamiliar).

Becoming Anew: Creativity in Contexts of Cultural Sharing

Since Wengrow is associating the increased development and appearance of certain material forms (renderings of composite creatures) with a particular constellation of societal characteristics ("early urbanism") that is evidenced within different locations across southwest Asia, northern Africa and the Aegean at somewhat-different times, his study raises the sticky matter of identifying primary and secondary manifestations of the forms. This distinction is at work as he uses specific case studies to explore the concomitant sociopolitical and representational components of this "dissemination" and "migration" of forms between contexts.[9] His discussion rests on the Aegean at times, as a locus of such "influx" and "adoption."[10] As these case studies are examined, the initial question of *transfer* in turn begins to feel insufficient, while the need to consider the occurrence of *transformation* and *innovation* between contexts instead becomes apparent. Indeed, closer inspection of what actually occurs as composite creatures travel between social spaces brings with it the realization that not only do changes take root in the formal and notional contours of the creatures, but also that distinct creative processes are at work behind their materializations within novel contexts.

In his recent study of Aegean Bronze Age art, Knappett has picked up on just these aspects of "ontogeny" and "mobility" in the realm of material culture in the region, including the case of composites specifically.[11] He makes a critical contribution here, by emphasizing that something's meaning and identity, in the broad sense of these terms, arise in large part from the embedded experiences through which that thing is created and engaged with. He explores a variety of analytical approaches to this matter, in particular developing ideas that arise from cognitive and praxeological theories (see Chapter 1). Considering both imported finished objects and situations in which the techniques of making a type of thing are apparently shared between areas, Knappett stresses that we must look at each instance of transfer in its various specific dimensions, as matters of mobility and immobility cannot easily be predicted or categorized.[12] As an example, he refers to the situation of seals and seal use moving between Crete and the Greek mainland in the LBA. Wengrow also discusses seals as crucial movers of (fantastic) animalian imagery, as have we. Our consideration of lion glyptic has shown that within streams of intense intra-Aegean interaction during the MB II–LB II period, the sociocultural dimensions of glyptic objects were complex and involved more than their utility as sealing devices alone. Moreover, while the practice of sphragistic seal use may not at first have been incorporated into burgeoning Mycenaean social processes, an appreciation of this affordance of seals (perhaps even within the biography of particular antique objects) likely remained an active part of seals' identity in this new context, and it was eventually incorporated in palatial Mycenaean administrative practice. Mainland funerary deposits and visual culture demonstrate that, as in Crete, seals were intimately associated with persons' bodies – worn in life and kept close in death. Such deep bodily and hence experiential associations with an object type naturally would impact its cultural standing, and if these associations were retained between cultural spheres, they could constitute a powerful current of shared experience (including experience of animalian forms), even as other aspects of usage and meaning varied. Hence, as Knappett astutely recognizes, the question of mobility is indeed complex and cannot be simply assessed along separate lines concerning matters of form, meaning or practice.[13] Certain aspects of people's engagements with and understanding of things might powerfully persist across distances, even as others notably diverge, being complicated by factors such as interest and memory, at personal and cultural levels. And the matter of whether a particular aspect of practice and experience would transfer does not map easily onto the question of geographical distance: the case of certain Old Assyrian sealing procedures, based on sphragistic usage, being reproduced within the administrative systems of Protopalatial Crete during the MBA, indicates that, in other situations, such practices *could* move overseas quite effectively.[14] Thus, we should not deny the potential for such continuities – but should complicate or approach it through careful parsing. In this light, we are unlikely to have simple instances of relocation and adoption. Instead, cases of apparently perpetuated formal, material and cultural elements can be understood to embody rich but knotty situations of generative reengagement.

An appreciation of the particular complexity that belongs to cultural forms that move across social and geographic distances is important to have in hand as we consider the matter of composite creatures. Such animalian forms, which travel as material things or through shared word and practice, never fully persist with such movement. The nature of their alteration is situationally specific. In our case, we need to examine how renderings of certain extraordinary creatures from distant places were drawn into distinctly Aegean creative ecologies. As aspects of these foreign creatures were engaged with in the Aegean, the particular dynamics of combinability and relationality surrounding them may have diverged or developed in novel manners. Hence, our focus must take in not only what seems to have transferred, but also the diverse experiential factors through which reembodiments – or new embodiments – took form. In such situations, both elements of apparent innovation *and continuity* should be recognized as culturally creative.[15] Moreover, the fruits of this creativity, what are effectively novel cultural forms, can wash back upon and contribute to changes within the very traditions that had been drawn upon earlier, in ongoing processes of intercultural sharing.

Being Strange: Dynamics of Unfamiliarity, Novelty and Foreignness

Creatures we identify as composites or hybrids often seem strange. Their strangeness is not of a single origin or nature. It can arise from various distinctive aspects of their constitution and can carry diverse implications for their identities. I would like to think through several of them. There is the facet of strangeness that arises from something being *unfamiliar*. In part, this could relate to a composite creature being understood to have distant origins – as arriving from beyond the familiar sociocultural and/or geospatial present. Because composites are fabrications, they all have origins that, in one sense or another, ultimately lie "elsewhere." These external origins may be understood to be located in a faraway, hidden, divine or fantastic realm or may remain undefined. In some cases, certain composites beings, whether a singular beast or a full species, can come to be understood as having a specific distant homeland. For example, in the *Iliad* (6.170–185) and later accounts, we hear that the Chimaera's homeland was in Anatolia (Lycia). Meanwhile, an Athenian visitor to the fifth-century BCE Acropolis would have been stirred by the presence of centaurs (a race of "composite" creatures) in the stone metopes of the Parthenon in part because of their identity as alien beings. In myth, centaurs were associated with Thessaly – an estranged area during the Persian Wars – and then sent yet farther afield by Theseus.[16] The embodiment of centaurs within the scenes of the Parthenon not only harnessed the species' antagonistic outsider status; the sculptures actively contributed to the creatures' identity within Athenian culture. Although we do not have textual accounts from the Aegean Bronze Age with which to probe historical attitudes toward such fantastic beasts with the same resolution, we can appreciate that equally rich associations were potentially at play concerning their identities and backgrounds and that objects surely contributed in the realization of such notions.

In cases where materialized renderings of a composite creature, and ideas surrounding it, moved between regions, notions of distant origins associated with the beast could have developed with the passage of the material culture embodying it, according to the changing perspectives with which it was encountered. It is difficult, and beside the point, to track a sequence for such developments. They arise from the tangled realities of moving things and people, their relationships, experiences and interests – as well as generative instances of translation and misunderstanding. Likewise, in the course of such movements, the things that embodied a creature could become isolated, damaged, repaired and altered, leading to new trajectories in how they were experienced.[17] In this light, we can imagine that certain creatures depicted in

Aegean Bronze Age material, such as the sphinx, griffin or genius, may have had evolving associations with various distant places – places that were, themselves, active subjects of imagination and memory. Such associations would have depended, in part, on the specific means through which representations of a creature reached people in the region, be it in the stuff of voice or in physical matter. For example, a small object, such as a scarab, engraved in Egypt with the form of a fantastic creature, which made its way to Crete via the Levant, may have inspired gnarled and divergent ideas concerning where the animal's overseas homeland lay. Colburn has considered how such small imported things would have taken on distinctly potent social power when worn on the bodies of persons in Crete.[18] Meanwhile, Feldman has examined how foreignness and placelessness could powerfully coincide in certain objects, during certain moments.[19]

This dimension of composites' strangeness, arising from their associations with unfamiliar and distant origins, would evolve yet further if a particular type of creature became an established entity within a local cultural sphere. As the creature became recontextualized in new, but still fluid, iconographical and/or narrative repertoires, its novelty would lessen as its local identity grew, even if it was still understood to have origins in a distant place. Hence, strangeness connected to the unfamiliar can relate to inherent geospatial distance but does not always follow it.[20] The same is true concerning the relationship of unfamiliarity and the fantastic. As discussed in Chapter 2, a creature might still be wondrous and awesome to people who nevertheless are familiar with it.[21] Not only can the wondrous become familiar, and continue to amaze, it can also alter in the process, potentially changing in aspects of its biography, associations, name, demeanor, form and materializations (and hence affordances). In Bronze Age Crete, the iconographical evolution of the Egyptian demon Taweret into the "Minoan genius" is indicative of this (a case discussed by Wengrow, following Weingarten's dedicated study).[22] Even after the Egyptian demon "transformed" into the Minoan genius, the latter further developed within the Aegean, between its already fluid earlier Cretan embodiments and later Mycenaean ones.[23] In these respects, the strangeness of a composite or fantastic creature is largely shared with that surrounding an exotic beast, unknown in living flesh but engaged with through material reembodiments or oral representations that can perpetuate a sense of foreignness even as they (sometimes) also become altered and established within local cultural ecologies.[24]

Strangeness as a matter *novelty* certainly has the potential to coincide with notions of something's distant and unfamiliar origins, but it also has other implications for the study of fantastic combinatory creatures. Whereas the unfamiliar may be understood to belong elsewhere, the novel can be strange because it is experienced as belonging nowhere.[25] Novelty can arise from unprecedentedness in the makeup of composites. Here, the quantitative or mechanical dimensions of forming combinations out of variable individual components is relevant. The formulation of composites could give rise to a vast multiplicity of distinct permutations of combined features, the novelty of each producing a sense of the unexpected and surprising. Aspects of this are fundamental to Wengrow's discussion of modularity and its relationship with the innovations of early urbanism. In particular, he suggests that the potential to generate a diversity of distinct yet comparable graphic composite forms would be very useful in systems of seal use, which typically rely on the existence of multiple differentiable engraved motifs in order to function (different identities being signified by distinct motifs, engraved on different seals).[26] In other words, by treating animal species as sources of divisible formal attributes that could be variably combined with one another, a vast array of distinct subjects for engraved motifs could be generated. Hogarth proffered a similar argument to explain the profusion of composite entities represented within a deposit of impressed seal motifs from Neopalatial Kato Zakros, in east Crete.[27] Discussing the same group, Evans asserted that the proliferation of composite forms, differentiated through variations in the specific body parts combined in each, may have been developed to "baffle forgers."[28] Recently, Anastasiadou has offered an excellent reading of the composite entities in the Zakros corpus, where she focuses on their status as combinations of interchangeable parts (see "Crowned Beasts, Potent Gazes and Moving Things").[29] These discussions importantly ground the rich creativity of composites within real social things, acts and processes.

It is also possible that what we describe as composite creatures were encountered as strange not because they were identified as *combinations*, but, instead, as distinctive overall animalian forms in their own right – in other words, as *remarkable wholes*; I will return to this idea below. But first, I would like to further walk through the idea of composites as embodiments of novel combination in the Aegean.

Seeing Power in Novelty Many scholars identify the distinct power of composite creatures as arising, in part, from their being jarring combinations.[30] This power can be considered a matter of graphic impact, perceived magical efficacy or something else. Put simply, this idea works on the assumption that composites' mismatch of bodily elements is experienced by humans as alarming, attention-grabbing or disconcerting. Yet working below this assertion is the matter of how or why we accept the composite as a single entity, and not simply as a cluster of parts. This is a knotty issue because, on the one hand, such basic formal cohesion would seemingly be at odds with the creature's simultaneous potential to upset as an incongruity; on the other, the basic coalescence of the composite figure's parts is arguably prerequisite to its being understood as a creature at all, and, without this identity, the combination would lack the (potentially impactful) quality of agentive animation.[31] We have seen that Wengrow addresses this very question of cohesion through the notion of "intuitive biology."[32] His discussion explores theories that the human brain will accept an artificial merging of diverse parts, borrowed from different species, as something endowed with the basic nature of a unified being. But this is only because the successful composite creature also plays along with convention, to a certain extent: crucial to Wengrow's discussion is the idea that the potency of composite creatures arises equally from both their "counterintuitive" combinations of elements and an underlying anatomical conventionality. This conventionality anchors a person's recognition of the composite entity as a creature while simultaneously being in tension with its supernatural combinatory qualities.[33] Simandiraki-Grimshaw's distinction between heterosomatic and homosomatic Minoan hybrids also provides a crucial alternative perspective to incorporate here. By comparing the fleetingness of heterosomatic hybridity – in which the joining occurs only temporarily and is then shed – to the permanence of the homosomatic hybrid, which persists in its form, we can see how the latter would also have a degree of familiar constancy.[34]

In discussion of composites being both prominently counterintuitive and basically coherent, Wengrow engages with Boyer's argument that religious imagery is minimally but powerfully extraordinary.[35] Boyer's work helps to move consideration of fantastic visual/material forms into the context of particular sociocultural arenas and institutions – a move that is also central to Wengrow's study of composites.[36] For Boyer, renderings of "supernatural beings" embody a dissonance, couched in sufficient familiarity, that can be acutely productive and motivating in religious cultures. Such representations of supernatural beings, and other instances of religious symbolism, can be digested, manipulated and transferred precisely because they largely flow within established cognitive streams yet simultaneously disturb the current enough to be keenly notable. Boyer argues that these potent creatures draw and potentially focus people's attention. With this idea, he sets the stage for considering the success of religious imageries within particular systems of sociocultural experience (e.g., historical systems of cult and ritual).

We have seen that, like Boyer, Wengrow directs his analysis of composite imagery toward questions of social life and experience. Wengrow, however, is more focused on the historical conditions that gave rise to the formulation and spread of composite creatures, which he associates with emergent urbanism. Through his discussion, these instances of early urbanism are problematized as innovative social moments, in which novel forms and practices kindle within familiar ways of life, such as technologies of communication, tabulation and administration; heterarchies and hierarchies of specialization that relate a person to a complex collective whole; and structural endeavors that afford novel scales and types of built space. These changes are situated within constellations of specific local circumstances, but they also are a means of interconnection between different and sometimes distant social spaces that are experiencing comparable developments; this commonality arises, in part, from the movement of things, people and ideas between such spaces.[37]

Hence, the familiar and local are stimulated and stirred through changes, often catalyzed by increased contact, that do not necessarily overthrow what is already in play but complicate it in very particular and distinctly combinatory ways. In this area, Wengrow's discussion provides for seeing structural similarities between early urbanism and the position that composites hold within human cognition, as both involve remarkable departures that "violate" established norms while, at the same time, "typically affirm[ing]" a host of the "underlying structural principles." Within this, he poses composite creatures both as agreeing, in their underlying logic, with the technical and social modularity characteristic of developing urban contexts and, in many cases, as embodying the disturbing alienness that such social changes, and especially an increase in foreign contacts, brought to these contexts.[38]

Combinatory Creatures? The idea that what we describe as "composite creatures" are in some ways inherently relatable to foreignness deserves examination. We have been exploring how there can be a potentially signficant distinction between experiences of the unfamiliar and the novel. Working further along these lines provides a useful means for building toward a new understanding of the unique dynamics of Aegean embodiments of so-called composite creatures and how they may have been connected to distant spaces. In the case of such animalian entities, the distinction between unfamiliarity and novelty could involve that between a beast being experienced as having a backstory versus being the immediate outcome of unprecedented combination. Naturally, these distinctions are fluid and can encompass a great deal of diversity. Moreover, the experience of novelty and unfamiliarity concerning a composite creature could potentially coincide or shift into one another. We can see this if we imagine a person's initial moment of encountering a rendering of a beast. It may at first be perceived as an unprecedented creation but subsequently be recognized as a member of an established fantastic species if/when further manifestations are met. It is the bodily persistence of the combination manifest in a "homosomatic hybrid," as identified by Simandiraki-Grimshaw, that would provide the basis for such establishment to occur.[39] This could also play out on a broader cultural level, if a given combination became frequently rendered and encountered. Knappett suggests that this could lead, with time, to a composite beast becoming effectively "naturalized" as a "blend,"[40] an idea which still preserves an element of combination, as such, in its identity. In the case of many Aegean "hybrids," however, I think that there are reasons to suspect that the creatures were not primarily viewed as combinations, and that assuming they were is, in fact, a more problematic reading. Instead, many of the Aegean composite beasts may better be understood as creatures experienced as extraordinary species, likely related to foreignness, and that, with time, aspects of their unfamiliarity may have given way to familiarity. Whether they were viewed as an exotic biological or fantastical species can be harder to ascertain and likely was variable – and need not have been a hard and fast distinction – but their developing identities would have been based in their thingly embodiments and the relations these afforded.

Among extraordinary creatures in Bronze Age Crete, the ones we identify as composites or hybrids would have been distinguished by the fact that they could never be met as living beasts. Such creatures would have been experienced as being from beyond the present context, from a realm real or imagined, even if the boundaries were considered breachable (e.g., through glimpses, traces, intrusions or epiphanies). With such inevitably extrinsic roots, an association with foreign places may indeed have been a core factor in how some creatures we define as composites were experienced in Crete and the Aegean, but not necessarily all of them. Moreover, emphasis on and elaboration of origins would have varied. Some composite beings may have had particular ethnic identities or origin stories; but others may not have been characterized by such notions. How a given composite creature was experienced would have depended on the particularities of its contextualizations and materializations in the Aegean, as well as the matter of how, and whether, its biography was actively developed. We will see that, in many cases, Aegean renderings of animals traditionally described as hybrids, as well as a host of related ones, do exhibit prominent indications of connections to foreign renderings of such creatures. But what I would like to draw out now is how this possibility – that distant origins were a principal feature of some of these creatures' complex identities – calls into question the notion that the primary identifying element of what we describe as composite beings was, consistently, a status as *combinations*. This is how *we* have identified these complex fantastic creatures who draw together features seen in multiple species, but can we generically project this back onto the people in the past whom we study? Doing so is especially problematic concerning composite figures that were, in one way or another, shared between social spaces. In Chapter 3, we saw that the boundary between "real" and "imaginary" would have been far from clear for nonnative species, such as the lion, which people encountered in Crete through material culture, stories or even traces, but not in living flesh – at least for almost all Cretans. The stuff of Cretan people's engagements with such exotic foreign species was effectively the same as their engagements with species that we, today, describe as imaginary or fantastic. In neither case did interactions with living biological animals form the basis of the species' Cretan identities; instead, representational material culture and voice gave the beasts their interactive forms and presence, in distinctive Cretan embodiments. Hence, the line between real and imaginary was not relevant in these cases or at least was quite differently demarcated than it is in our modern world.

This would also be true of interactions with "traces" of foreign animals that may have made their way to Crete, such as a tooth or pelt, since, as isolated fragments of a beast, these may have been unpacked in a person's mind into wholes that diverged quite dramatically from the corporeal or behavioral identities we ascribe to complete biological specimens of the source species. In other words, a section of hippopotamus tooth, an ostrich feather or a panther claw, passed between hands, could have become something remarkably different from a zoologically "correct" hippopotamus, ostrich or panther in the mind's eye of one who had never engaged with these living creatures. Moreover, in these persons' minds and subsequent representations of an animal, such fragments could have been "completed" with parts *familiar to their Cretan beholder* that stemmed from other types of beast. The resultant entity might appear like a "composite" to our modern eye, but that does not necessarily align with how it was understood in the past. From that perspective out, these beasts, experienced "at home" through material culture, traces and stories, may have been thought of as exotic creatures with distant homelands that were in some ways (and attributes) related to species one knew – but this does *not* mean that the animals were viewed, *in essence*, as mergings of distinct species parts. With time, such creatures could become further entangled in Cretan and Aegean ecologies of animals (biological and fabricated), taking on fresh associations, formal and material dimensions and identities.

Creatures Like Many

We turn now to a close consideration of Aegean renderings of creatures that possess bodily features shared with multiple species. I focus first on early embodiments of the griffin from Crete. My aim is to work below traditional assumptions that take for granted that a primary combinatory identity defined Aegean animals that we today categorize as composite beings. Stepping back, I reexamine how Cretan embodiments of these remarkable creatures relate to contemporaneous renderings of other species on the island. I consider whether these relationships seem to indeed arise from division and recombination of parts or are better understood as evidence that the creatures would have been experienced as sharing corporeal *comparability* with various species. On the basis of my initial exploration of early griffins, discussion turns to examination of bodily features and qualities that seem to connect a host of animalian entities in the region, and to indicate that the category of "composites" is insufficient, and in some ways inappropriate, for describing the nature of these creatures' interspecific relations.

I recognize griffins as both a focus and a guide in this context. While we launch our discussion with the immediate aim of placing early renderings of griffins within the ecology of animalian phenomena in which they would have been known in the Aegean, understanding the nature of that ecology is the broader objective. The extant evidence of griffins from the Aegean MBA is limited, but by drawing out their distinguishing bodily attributes, and tracing the relationships that those attributes find in renderings of other animals, we gain a view of larger contexts of remarkable creaturely forms. We will consider a cluster of apparently interconnected features that link these distinctive creatures. The point here is not to propose a hard and fast grouping, in which possession of a given attribute indicates membership in a class of creature. Instead, we are using a close consideration of the fabricated animalian bodies themselves to identify their fluid relationships to other animals and phenomena. This forces us to take into account a broader range of possible relationships, instead of simply prescribing links that we assume should be present (e.g., between particular sets of species thought to constitute a given composite animal) and then trying to establish their occurrence or absence. Moreover, we approach observable connections between renderings of different animals not merely as *reflections* of conceived interspecific links in the minds of the objects' makers, but, more fundamentally, as materialized bases for people's *perceptions of similarities* between embodiments of species. It is evident that renderings of animalian bodies from overseas are crucially at play in the network of extraordinary Aegean creatures that comes to light here (and foreignness, in some sense, was likely part of their identities), but the connections are far more complex than straightforward instances of adoption.

The Extraordinarily Relatable Bodies of the Early Aegean Griffin Aegean embodiments of the griffin are one of the most widely recognized "composite" creatures from the region during the Bronze Age and have been a traditional element of art historical discussions concerning iconographic sharing across the broader eastern Mediterranean.[41] While the vast majority of extant embodiments of Aegean griffins stem from the LBA, here I will focus first and foremost on the very limited but fascinating evidence we have for griffins rendered in Crete during the MBA. Focusing early allows us to consider a moment before the form and perhaps the identity of the griffin had become more consistent in the Aegean, when its coming-into-being as part of the region's animalian universe instead appears to have been more open-ended.

The first attestations of the griffin in Crete appear in the Protopalatial period. The deposit of clay seal impressions preserved in *vano* 25 at the first palace of Phaistos gives us a remarkable view on early renderings of the beast. The deposit contained at least three representations of what seem to be griffins, in the impressions of CMS II.5.317, CMS II.5.318 and CMS II.5.319 (Figure 4.1a–c). The deposit also crucially provides a rich context of contemporaneous renderings of other animalian forms within which to consider the griffins. These include readily identifiable species as well as some whose identities are less clear but remain relevant. The three Phaistian griffins display certain shared features between them but also notable formal heterogeneity. Moreover, they have both distinctions from and similarities to renderings of the LBA Aegean griffin, which is more consistent in its forms and more widely manifested throughout the region.

All three of the griffins within the MBA Phaistos corpus are rendered in profile, facing left. Already in this early evidence, each of these three griffins seems to have some sort of appendage or extension on its head, constituting what we might describe as a crest or plume. On CMS II.5.317 (Figure 4.1a), this is comprised of three elongated ovoid forms of approximately equivalent size, which could be schematically rendered feathers. The overall shape of this beast's head is markedly triangular, but it is actually formed in two merged parts: a circular area (likely shaped with a rotating solid drill bit) joined with a more shallowly engraved isosceles triangle that projects forward and appears like a drawn-out beak or nasal ridge. The head appendages emerge from the

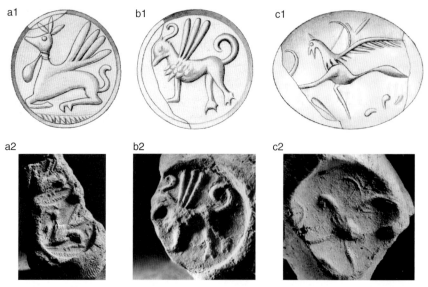

4.1. Three griffins from the Protopalatial sealing deposit at *vano* 25, Phaistos. a. CMS II.5.317; b. CMS II.5.318; c. CMS II.5.319. Images courtesy CMS, Heidelberg. Objects © Hellenic Ministry of Culture and Sports

CREATURES OF CHANGE   175

corner that marks the top of the head; the third and lowest corner of the head extends into the narrowed neck. The three upright head appendages, which together form a sort of crest, echo the shape of the wing, which, viewed in profile, emerges from the back with a thickened base and then fans into four long and erect ovoid segments with curved termini.

Turning to the griffin of CMS II.5.318 (Figure 4.1b), we find another instance of a head appendage or plume, but here it takes the form of a single, slender, forward-curving hook that swings back from the top of a rounded head. While its front portion is partially obscured, the head of the CMS II.5.318 creature appears to be engraved as two merged components: a rounded back area (cranium) and a pointed forward projection (beak). This is generally comparable to what we see on CMS II.5.317, but in CMS II.5.318 the beast seems to have a somewhat shorter and slenderer beak. The wing can also be related to that of the CMS II.5.317 creature. In CMS II.5.318, the griffin's wing consists of three long, straight segments, each of which emerges directly from the back and tapers slightly outward to a rounded end.

In the case of the griffin in CMS II.5.319 (Figure 4.1c), the head (other than the face) is formed as a continuation of the mass of the neck that softly tapers and arcs forward through the crown, ultimately peaking in a small, rounded protrusion at the top of the head. In the clay impressions, a fine linear mark visible above this area of the head may be a simple plume, but this detail remains difficult to decipher, even under the microscope. It is notable, however, that the area of the head from which this possible plume emerges seems to constitute itself a projection of some sort. Its shape is rather unclear, but it could be a horn, an ear or another type of extension or appendage. The animal's face is indicated by an eye, positioned just above two protrusions that emerge from the front of the head/neck mass and suggest a parted beak or mouth opening downward; their angle heightens the impression that the head is lowered.[42]

Compared to the other two griffins from the *vano* 25 deposit, the wing of the beast in CMS II.5.319 is much closer to what we will see in most Cretan renderings of griffins from the LBA: a slightly arcing upper ridge defines the wing's fundamental structure and provides the base from which many small parallel feathers descend. A wispy arced line emerges about halfway up the wing and mirrors its curve; this could suggest a second wing. Alternatively, a fine linear feature that extends outward from the back of the neck and seems to broaden or connect into a wider feature in the area of the wispy arced line could form a second wing. The body of this griffin is also quite distinct. As the shaft of the neck broadens downward, a segmented-band feature that continues into the wing marks the transition between neck and the wide torso. The front section of the body then slims backward into an extraordinarily thin and extended "wasp-like" waist, before opening into a wider hip lobe. Only the two thin front legs are visible. They project from the upper torso, with one extending almost straight in front of the animal and the other pointing downward. Together the legs form an inverted v, suggesting a wide, rapid stride. Since the hind legs of this griffin are not captured in the impressions (despite the area below the body being visible), they may be extended outward behind the beast, as is the case in a flying-gallop posture.

The lower bodies of the other two Phaistian griffins differ considerably from that of CMS II.5.319, both in form and posture. In the case of CMS II.5.317, the beast is recumbent. Its body has bulk throughout. A marked narrowing below the head clearly distinguishes the head from the neck, which in turn opens onto a broad, approximately triangular body. While there is a narrowing that defines the waist, this is subtle, and the hip appears as part of the same general mass as the torso. The one visible lower haunch descends into a hind leg that bends beneath the body; the thinner front leg is also tucked back and extends toward the hind leg. CMS II.5.318 instead stands upright, facing forward. Its stiff body neither bends nor strides. The single front leg is straight, while a small forward projection at its base suggests a foot; the two hind legs are also straight but end in marked segmentations, perhaps indicating claws.

From Lions to Insects There is nothing distinctly leonine shared between the three griffins of the MBA *vano* 25 deposit, but this is not to say that the beasts are unlike lions. The same is true regarding raptors. Yet by referring to the creatures of impressions CMS II.5.317, CMS II.5.318 and CMS II.5.319 as "griffins," we are implicitly asserting that they embody attributes of lions and raptors. In fact, the link we are making to these two species is probably more indirect and compromised: we find the three winged quadrupeds from the Phaistos deposit comparable enough to more established animalian forms that we identify as griffins within visual culture from other contexts and moments to warrant extending the term here. With this, we transfer not only the identification, but also the assumed pairing of species it entails, back upon these three creatures from the basis of other traditions – including later Aegean ones. Not only is this a more honest account of our imprecise grounding, it also is a perspective that opens new analytical vistas. Both in our modern present and likely in the ancient past, ambiguity is at play within the form of these three beasts and in their associations with other species. We will see that there do seem to be real connections between the three MBA Cretan griffins (and others from the Aegean) and later, Neopalatial griffins – enough to support use of the same name. However, along with this, we must grapple with knottier interspecific relationships involving the beasts.

To consider the implications of interspecific similarities, we need to begin by stepping back to assess how the three Phaistian griffins compare not only to contemporaneous renderings of lions and raptors, but also other creatures. We will base this contextualization first within the renderings of animals preserved within the deposit of clay seal impressions found in *vano* 25 at the palace of Phaistos. Doing so provides the unique opportunity to consider these beasts in the context of other animals that coexisted with them, within the same medium and same particular sociocultural space. Within this space, people could have compared the renderings of griffins to those of other animals, thereby forming a sense of their bodily character.[43] Taking this more open view upon the evidence indicates that the three Phaistian beasts may not, in all cases, have shared the same interspecific connections.

Among the motifs impressed in the clay sealings discovered in *vano* 25 at Phaistos, we find that each corporeal attribute of the three griffins is also represented in some other species; some of the attributes are widespread, some quite rare. We focus first on the lower body (below the neck), which is the area of griffins where leonine elements are typically identified. We can examine not only bodily components, but also indications of the animals' movement and attitude. Several features in this area of the three bodies do find parallels with those of lions seen in the impressed motifs of the *vano* 25 deposit. However, in key respects, equally compelling if not stronger parallels can be identified in other species. It is useful to draw out and contextualize certain attributes of the griffins' lower bodies that are especially distinctive, namely the clawed feet and long, upward-curving tails of CMS II.5.317 and CMS II.5.318, and the rapid striding posture and wasp-like body of CMS II.5.319. While segmented/clawed feet appear on lions such as CMS II.5.275 (Figure 4.2a), and CMS II.5.286, they also appear on animals such as goats (e.g., CMS II.5.256; Figure 4.2b), birds (CMS II.5.308; Figure 4.2c) and even a bee/wasp (CMS II.5.314; Figure 4.2d). The tails of the CMS II.5.317 and CMS II.5.318 griffins find their closest parallels among lions within the Phaistos deposit. However, the CMS II.5.319 griffin seemingly does not have a tail at all (this can be asserted because, although the segment of the impressed motif showing the area behind the beast is obscured, the full curve around the hip and down the top of the hind leg is visible, and no tail projection is apparent). Both the standing posture of the CMS II.5.318 griffin and the recumbent posture of the CMS II.5.317 griffin are unremarkable and widely paralleled across species. Meanwhile the distinctive striding posture of the CMS II.5.319 griffin does not have any exact equivalents in the *vano* 25 sealing deposit. That said, several quadrupeds are depicted with extended legs, suggesting brisk motion. These include the animals of CMS II.5.277 and CMS II.5.276 (Figure 4.2e), identified as lions or dogs. But the closest parallel for the CMS II.5.319 griffin's particular striding posture is found in the goat of CMS II.5.259 (Figure 4.2f), whose hind leg extends straight backward (as we assume also in CMS II.5.319) and whose front legs are parted, one extending downward (in this case, the front legs bend at joints).[44] The lithe, slender body form of the CMS II.5.319 griffin is also notable. The animals of both CMS II.5.276 and CMS II.5.277 (lions or dogs) are

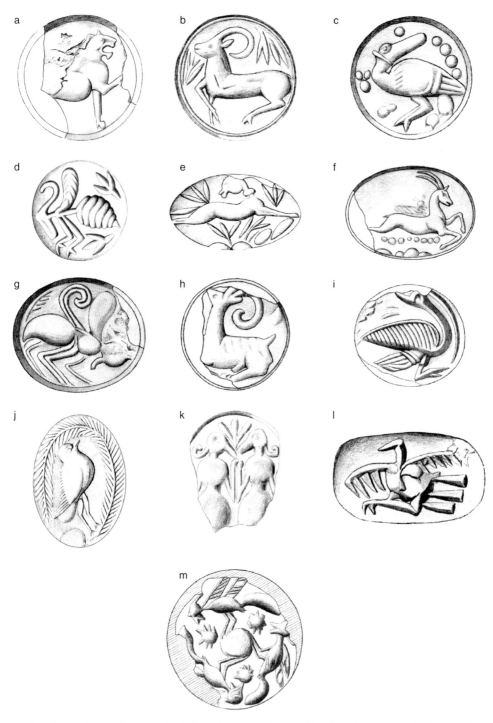

4.2. Motifs imaging nonhuman animals from the Protopalatial sealing deposit at *vano* 25, Phaistos, and two comparative objects. a. (lion) CMS II.5.275; b. (goat) CMS II.5.256; c. (water bird) CMS II.5.308; d. (bee) CMS II.5.314; e. (lion/dog) CMS II.5.276; f. (goat) CMS II.5.259; g. (bee) CMS II.5.315; h. (goat) CMS II.5.257; i. (water bird) CMS II.5.307; j. (bird) CMS II.5.310; k. (beaked humans) CMS II.5.323; l. (raptor) CMS II.2.234b, from MM II Malia; m. (rotating bees/wasps) CMS II.8.149, from LM I Knossos. Images courtesy CMS, Heidelberg

similar to it, as are those of CMS II.5.255 and CMS II.5.270 (goat and lion), but do not have the same degree of attenuation, nor the distinctive lobed body and thin waist juncture of the CMS II.5.319 beast. It is the bee or wasp of CMS II.5.314 that most closely resonates with the overall body formation of the CMS II.5.319 griffin. Interestingly this insect also parallels CMS II.5.319 in the tucked, downward-facing profile and the shape of the head. This insect shares features with the other two Phaistian griffins as well. Its forward-curving antenna is very close in form to the crest of CMS II.5.318, and the position and uprightness of the wings are also comparable to that of this griffin; in both of these respects, the bee/wasp of CMS II.5.315 is also similar (Figure 4.2g). Meanwhile, as noted, the CMS II.5.314 insect also shares the feature of clawed/segmented feet with both CMS II.5.317 and CMS II.5.318, bringing this bee/wasp a dynamic relationship with the trio of early griffins (it is worth noting that in a later impression, CMS II.8.149 (Figure 4.2m), from LM I Knossos, winged insects are rendered with remarkably similar head forms and lobed bodies to the griffin of CMS II.5.319, and with head appendages comparable to that of the CMS II.5.318 griffin). Based on these observations, it becomes apparent that within the *vano* 25 corpus – which provides an opportunity for comparing an array of contemporaneous renderings of animals that also likely were compared to one another during the MBA – the bodies of the three earliest extant Cretan griffins are *similar* in certain ways to those of lions, but that similarity certainly is not exclusive.

An examination of the region of the upper body and neck of the Phaistian griffins likewise results in indications of dispersed links with various species, instead of narrow connections to raptors. The general triangular shape of the CMS II.5.317 griffin's head is comparable to the heads of various goats seen within the deposit (e.g., what we see in CMS II.5.257 [Figure 4.2h)] and CMS II.5.258), yet, unlike the two-part construction of the pointed head of the CMS II.5.317 griffin, these goats' heads are formed as an engraving that tapers but remains relatively broad at its terminus/muzzle. In the realm of beaked animals, the long, broad-based, pointed projection forming the front of the head of the griffin of CMS II.5.317 stands as the strongest parallel we have for the vulture-like profiles of Neopalatial renderings of griffins; it could embody an early connection between Aegean griffins and such raptors (see pp. 185–195). Meanwhile, the rounded shape of the head of the griffin of CMS II.5.318 (before the beak) is more readily relatable to what we see on birds in the *vano* 25 corpus, including both the longer-beaked water birds of CMS II.5.307 (Figure 4.2i) and CMS II.5.309 (upper bird), and the shorter-beaked (song?) bird of CMS II.5.310 (Figure 4.2 j). The form of the beaked head of CMS II.5.318 is, however, equally comparable to what we see on the humanoid figures of CMS II.5.323 (Figure 4.2k; in fact, these figures are identified as "bird-people" because of their beak-like protrusions, but cf. the projection of CMS II.5.314, an insect [Figure 4.2d]).[45] Moreover, these humanoid figures share another notable attribute with the griffin of CMS II.5.318: each has a near-identical single, open-looped head appendage – on the griffin, it rises back from the crown of the head, while on the humanoid figures of CMS II.5.323 it is positioned somewhat lower on the back of the head. The open-beaked profile of the griffin of CMS II.5.319 finds a strong a parallel in the early Minoan genius of CMS II.5.321 and in the lower water bird of CMS II.5.309. Meanwhile, we have seen that in other respects, including its tucked profile, the head/neck of this griffin resonates with representations of insects in the sealing deposit. The formation of the head in two parts – what we can call a base and projecting element – stands as another parallel between the three griffins and two renderings of insects from *vano* 25, CMS II.5.314 and CMS II.5.315; such two-part head formation is also shared with most birds seen in the deposit. Whether intended by the craftsperson or not, such formal similarities may have been grounds for a person interacting with the impressed griffins to understand the beasts as sharing a distinctive feature of the head with another species (e.g., a proboscis or beak), thus informing the griffin's identity.

Regarding the formation of wings, the three griffins do not have close parallels in the deposit. Nevertheless, concerning their position and directionality, the wings of CMS II.5.317 and CMS II.5.318 most closely resonate with those of two insects (CMS II.5.314 and CMS II.5.315). The carefully structured wing of CMS II.5.319 has no compelling parallel in the Phaistos deposit, but it is worthwhile noting that a similar wing appears on a bird with pronounced talons, possibly a raptor, engraved on a three-sided steatite prism at MM II Malia (CMS II.2.234b; Figure 4.2l). Looking forward, the wing of CMS II.5.319 is the closest to what we will see on Neopalatial renderings of the creature (more on this below).

When the embodiments of these early Aegean griffins are considered among the other renderings of animals that surrounded them, they find resonances across various species – from lions to insects, goats to birds. We could assume that craftspersons who engraved the seals were purposefully signaling a connection to particular other species through the details of the griffins' bodies they formed. While this may have been the case on some level, we cannot take such for granted – nor do we have grounds for asserting that particular pairings of species were intended (e.g., lion + raptor). The evident corporeal similarities with other species could also result from unreflexive associations, or from generic carving conventions used for forming certain body components (such might still betray a sense that there were points of comparability recognized between the species). Yet there is also something more fundamental at stake here. This concerns how, once formed, people experienced these creatures as present animalian entities, and how, in these embodiments, they would have been perceived as comparable to material-ized instances of other beasts. Put plainly, beyond the question of intentions involved in their design or making, these thingly animal bodies ultimately shared features with other thingly animal bodies that were also being encountered within this sociocultural space, and these commonalities would have constituted real relationships in people's senses of the different species. This point is undeniable once we recognize that objects were a principal way in which people met and engaged with animals – a fact that is especially true when considering exotic and fantastic beasts not known in the flesh.

Creative Bodies The attributes of the animals embodied in the sealings of the *vano* 25 deposit, which took form in stone and then in clay, contributed to establishing what species *were* – what they were to the hand, eye and mind. This occurred not in a single object or body, but across manifestations that people connected to one another. It was in this way that the three griffins would have found their place in their most immediate universe of animals at the site and in the broader sociocultural space where they were active. The griffins' place therein was not fixed. In essence, as people encountered what they deemed comparable attributes across renderings of multiple animals, those attributes became the stuff of links and associations. These links could connect multiple instances of what was taken as a single species or could draw together different species. Not only could these creatures (griffins and beyond) appear similar to one another, they could *feel* similar, as they were met and engaged with in the same substances, at the same tiny scale and through comparable bodily actions and sociocultural contexts involving seals and seal use. These contexts included the productive work of humans, from the fine-scale tool use that brought analogous bodily features into being in different small stones, to the social events during which people stamped their seals and created the animalian impressions in moist clay. At the same time, and in other senses, these object-bodies were themselves generative. They did not simply reflect ideas about a given creature, about its properties, connec-tions and contexts; they were what actually *gave body to* those properties and, in the process, were participants in the active creation of connections and contexts.

Elements of this creativity may have arisen from human design, but the objects, and the situations they were part of, also contributed to the process. As Simandiraki-Grimshaw and Stevens discuss concerning animal ornaments of the Aegean Bronze Age, the materials that make up these objects impacted the form and substance of the animals' bodies.[46] The smallness and curvature of the surfaces afforded tools certain paths and confounded others. The range of actions through which people handled these thingly animal bodies were contoured by the particular dimensionality of the objects, by the available light, by the decorum and mood of an event. Was the stone that was engraved with an animal's body slick and hard to handle? Was the intaglio incision of a bodily feature deep enough, and the clay of a sealing fine-grained enough, to allow each of the engraved details to be captured in an impression? Was the size of the seal or impression so small that a person needed to clutch it close to their face in order to make out the details of the minuscule body, turning it in the sunlight? Did the fine clay ridges of the dried impression crumble with time, obscuring or altering the form of the creature's body? Did a given person interact with numerous sealings stamped by different seals, engraved with imagery of various types of animal? If so, were the different animals' forms composed of comparable series of rises and falls in the textured surfaces of the impressions, giving the person the sense that different species had similar bodies? All of these matters arise through meshworks of engagements, in momentary stews of interest and intent – but also of accident, environment, incident, energy and matter. I say this not to indicate that we should throw up our hands and abandon attempts to think systematically through the sociocultural processes surrounding such material culture; far from it. My point is that these objects were potentially highly charged and dynamic creative loci and that their creativity was stemming fluidly from different sources and interactions. As Knappett argues in his recent study of Aegean Bronze Age art, we need to broaden our sights to "include ideas, actions and materials in our efforts to locate creativity";[47] in other words, creative work is not the work of human designers alone. Objects that were representational (taken in a broad sense of what it means to re-present phenomena; see Chapter 1) carried particular aspects of such creativity. Moreover, objects that embodied animals were characterized yet further by the particular ways in which they not only drew novel material and physical realities into people's experiences of an animal but also, in this process, could realize dynamic connections between species. This was true of species that were known also in biological embodiments as well as those known only in things. Aegean fabricated animal bodies were remarkably rich in these creative dynamics and in the cross-phenomena connections they cultivated. Representations of what we identify as "hybrid" creatures are splendid parts of this, although they perhaps are not, in their fundamentals, exceptional.

It is in this context that our pioneering band of early griffins (or at least what seem to be pioneering and griffins) existed at Phaistos. Their presence in seals and seal impressions is significant to their identity and to the relationships they had with other species. If these media were the main ones in which griffins were met as material bodies in MBA Crete, the position would have consistently put them in intimate juxtapositions with humans (as seals worn on persons' bodies and as impressions stamped by people's hands and signifying their identities),[48] a location they would have shared with lions at that time. Their rendering in glyptic objects also restricted their scale – an effect that afforded interesting possibilities concerning the identity of the griffins. Naturally, it meant that the griffins were engaged with as very small bodies, which would impact persons' direct interactions with the individual instances of the beast. But the small scale also carried implications for interspecific comparisons. Many of the figural glyptic motifs we have from this period, and from this particular deposit, are characterized by a single engraved subject that occupied the central area of the engraved seal face; often these motifs consisted of a representation of a lone creature. This meant that our early griffins were encountered in a comparable size and position as a wide array of other beasts – bees, lions, owls, goats, genii and so on. If the griffin was not widely embodied in other media and contexts at this time, the consistent tiny size, bounded by the area of the engravable seal face, would have meant that they were met as scalar equals with other beasts – on a level playing field, so to speak. With this, the door would be left open concerning how the dimensions and bodily character of a full-sized living embodiment of the beast were extrapolated and hence would allow for various types of interspecific relation to be formulated, with creatures of dramatically different sizes.[49]

From the very limited evidence we have, certain things are nevertheless apparent concerning the "griffins" of MBA Crete. While we may be interested in the possible symbolic and narrative aspects of the beasts, we will do well to instead focus on tracing their identity as a matter of the nature of their embodiments and relations. People's understandings of the creatures surely were variable, as were their characteristics, but this variability is not simply a hindrance to our examination. We have seen that acknowledging and interrogating the formal variability of the beasts can also help us to better appreciate their complex but particular position within the cultural milieux of early Crete. The material embodiments through which people actually engaged with the griffins as physical realities were rather heterogeneous in their formal details – a fact that rendered them comparable to various species. This would have brought a distinct dynamism to how they were experienced within the realm of animals. With this, we can say that the relationships these early griffins had with other animals appear to have been characterized by eclectic similarities versus strict and specific derivations.

GRIFFINS CONTROLLED OR TAKING WING? THE DYNAMISM OF EMBELLISHED CHESTS

Each of the three early griffins seen in impressed motifs from the *vano* 25 sealing deposit at Phaistos is marked by prominent elaborations in the area of the chest/

neck. Contextualizing this distinctive quality of the beasts necessarily involves looking both broadly in space, at contemporaneous material from across the Aegean and eastern Mediterranean during the MBA, as well as forward into the early LBA, where plentiful renderings of Aegean griffins indicate that the embellishment of the chest/neck region was traditional for the beast, if variable in its particular manifestations. Analysis must be based on close examination of the rendering of the chest features themselves, paying particular attention to how they were formed within different substances, as part of a variety of media. With this, we contemplate how ambiguity in the formation of this area of many Aegean griffins' bodies may have contributed to two distinct but potentially interacting sets of associations – one based on the griffin being fitted with an added device, such as a collar or leash, and the other potentially relating the griffin's body to the markings of a remarkable biological Cretan vulture. Considering this link to the local biological ecology is especially important, given that Aegean griffins seem to introduce specifically vulture-like features to the beast, compared to wider eastern Mediterranean renderings that are more relatable to falcons. Each of these strands of association could have participated in characterizing perceptions of the griffin in Crete and the Aegean, as both a creature of local tradition and one that likely had a potent aura of connection to distant places.

Between Crafted Bodies

Along with the presence of head appendages (considered in the third section, ("Crowned Beasts, Potent Gazes and Moving Things"), additions to the chest/ neck zone stand as a distinctive corporeal feature held in common by the three early griffins of the *vano* 25 deposit. In each case, the chest and upper torso are elaborated in a notable way, although we see variation in the particular form this takes between the beasts.

In CMS II.5.318 (Figure 4.1b), we find the chest and upper torso of the griffin stippled with heavy rises. We can appreciate the substantial nature of these features because several extend beyond the front of the beast's body, as tapering projections. These markings find limited but significant resonances within the corpus of contemporaneous lions represented within the *vano* 25 deposit. On the upper body of multiple lions, we find hatching, a feature that seems to perpetuate a convention for rendering manes in seal carving that is well represented in Prepalatial glyptic from the same region of the island.[50] Among lions, the strongest comparandum for the chest treatment of the griffin of CMS II.5.318 can be found on the beast of CMS II.5.270, who stands facing left with inverted v-markings covering its upper torso and chest. While the hatching on the upper body of another lion from the deposit, CMS II.5.272, is notably different from the heavy stippling seen on the CMS II.5.318 griffin, it can be compared because, in both cases, the features are rendered as pushing beyond and hence complicating the front line of the body; this brings a distinctive texture to this area of the beasts. Despite these basic similarities, the remarkable tuft-like chest elaborations of the CMS II.5.318 griffin appear quite different from what we have seen on both of these contemporaneous lions. Moreover, if we look forward to Neopalatial evidence, we find little in the way of close parallels for the chest treatment of the CMS II.5.318 griffin. Griffins are not depicted with this type of tufted chest in Neopalatial glyptic, nor in other media. And although certain lions with highly textured manes engraved in Neopalatial seals provide the closest comparanda across other species, they, too, are unsatisfying parallels, given that their manes tend to be constituted by more linear, "hairy" striations (e.g., CMS II.3.19, CMS II.8.291, CMS II.3.257, CMS III.387). The tuft-like texture of the chest of the CMS II.5.318 griffin is instead far more suggestive of a heavy coat of feathers.

The characterization of the chest and torso area on the griffin of CMS II.5.319 (Figure 4.1c) differs from that of the CMS II.5.318 beast. Here, we instead see what appears to be a continuous band of striations running across the chest and extending through the length of the wing. The closest parallel for this bodily feature within the *vano* 25 corpus is on the lion of CMS II.5.274, where we also get the sense that a partially striated mass is ringing the neck and upper body of the beast. There is only so far that this parallel can go, however, given the lion's lack of wings, which are an integral element of the striated band on the griffin.

The distinctive banding feature of the griffin may have been more relatable to what people were observing on living birds of prey on Crete. Much has been made of the fact that the LBA Aegean griffin is remarkably similar to embodiments of griffins crafted contemporaneously elsewhere in the eastern Mediterranean, especially in Syria, but that the beaked head of the Aegean griffin is clearly that of a vulture or eagle while those seen elsewhere have the shorter and rounder profiles of a falcon or hawk – likely linked to Egyptian renderings of the sacred bird.[51] This discussion goes back to Evans. He believed that the Aegean eagle-griffin was developed from early Egyptian representations of hybrid creatures with the body of a lion/feline and the head of what he called a "sparrow-hawk" (the *Seref* and *Saha*); on this, he says, "a direct indebtedness to Egyptian suggestion cannot be denied."[52] Evans argues that renderings of the Egyptian creatures incorporated the facial markings of the biological bird, but that, in addition to changing the beak to that of an eagle, the Minoan artist also altered these naturalistic features and in their place fashioned "decorative" elaborations of the chest and wing area, including the addition of a spiral at the neck/shoulder.[53]

In the context of Evans' theories concerning the innovations of the Aegean griffin, it is useful to consider a furniture plaque engraved with a griffin from the Old Assyrian site of Acemhöyük in Anatolia (ca. eighteenth century BCE). On the plaque, the griffin is met fully in profile, upright and facing left, its posture somewhere between crouching and seated, with its front leg extended at an angle that holds the upper body off the ground (Figure 4.3). The elongated torso of the beast narrows back toward the curve of the haunch and tucked hind leg. The clawed feet have heft, especially the back one, comparable to what we would expect of a large feline. A thin tail emerges upward from the hip to first bend forward over the hindquarters and then curve back in a nearly closed loop.[54] The wings are extended and slightly separated and have tapering striations, representing feathers, lining their bottom edges and broadening into the tips; another slender band of these striations extends upward along the inner edge of the upper chest and neck, marking the base of the wing, where it meets the body. A tight pendant spiral descends from the upper line of the neck. An area of fine hatching above this spiral merges into a zone of solid engraving to form a dark chalice-shaped marking that descends alongside the spiral, between it and the face. This darkened zone is wide at the top of the head then narrows as it extends beside the spiral, before widening again below the curve of the cheek, thus framing the tear-drop-shaped face with its large eye. The face ends in a small hooked falcon's beak. In her discussion of the plaque, Aruz describes the markings of this area of the griffin as clearly related to contemporaneous and earlier renderings of the Peregrine Falcon[55] and falcon-headed figures in Egyptian visual culture.[56] She also comments on the addition of the spiral-form bodily embellishments, which, like Evans, she frames as a feature characteristic of Neopalatial Aegean griffins.

4.3. MBA ivory plaque incised with griffin from Acemhöyük, Anatolia. 4.09 × 2.64 cm. Metropolitan Museum, NY, 36.152.7; gift of Mrs George D. Pratt, in memory of George D. Pratt, 1936. (CC0 1.0) www.metmuseum.org

Aruz importantly suggests that the griffin of the MBA Acemhöyük plaque could be intermediary between the Egyptian and Aegean forms, by both embodying the established Egyptian conventions for representing the Peregrine Falcon's head and providing early evidence of changes that would be seen in many Aegean renderings of the griffin moving forward.

As Aruz's discussion recognizes, the formal characteristics associated with the Aegean griffin in fact seem part of a complex creative development that does not easily correspond to a single time or place. Nor should we act as though the griffin's form developed in isolation, relating only to other renderings of griffins. Here I wish to reconsider Evans' notion that the markings we see on griffins within the Bronze Age Aegean represent a further movement away from natural forms and toward a composite creature that is fully concocted and separated from people's engagements with living animals. While discussions of the Aegean griffin's form often focus on what have been identified as stylized ornamentations present upon the neck/chest of some ripe Neopalatial (and later) renderings, taken in a broader light we can see that this zone of the body was being embellished already in the MBA and early LBA evidence, in a variety of forms. Certainly, this is a moment in which the griffin's constitution was not fully standardized, but amid the formal variety of different renderings, we can also trace recurrent characteristics, types of embellishment and even particular repeated tropes in the elaboration of griffins' upper bodies. These bodily features gain more cohesion when we explore evidence across media and take into account the context of living animals encountered in Crete with which the griffin likely would have been compared, thereby informing its identity.

Finding Connections in the Sky

Given that within Crete and the Aegean, griffins began being rendered with beaks like that of a vulture, clearly the griffin was being newly compared to this type of raptor there. While connections between biological Aegean raptors and Aegean renderings of griffins naturally must remain hypothetical, living vultures stand as a highly probable source of inspiration and association to consider as the context of this change in beak form; it also emerges as potentially significant connection concerning other distinctive characteristics of the griffin. Looking at the extant evidence of early renderings of Cretan griffins, there are indications already in the MBA, and especially by the early Neopalatial, that on the island a specific variety of vulture may have been experienced as being relatable to the griffin. This is not to assume that people living in Crete during the Bronze Age isolated and classified a species of living bird as we do today, nor that they tried to replicate its form in renderings. My suggestion is instead that living birds possessing certain prominent physical and behavioral qualities (that distinguish what we identify as a species) were sharing the island with people and, given the nature of Cretan renderings of griffins, it seems that some of these distinctive qualities may have been likened to those of griffins. Underlying this particular proposal concerning a specific type of bird, my point is to take seriously and explore a broader dynamic: that the ecology of animals in which embodiments of "fantastic" creatures like the griffin existed also included living animals with rich and remarkable characters, and that this shared context mutually impacted the identities of both.

There are multiple species of vulture native to Crete. Prominent among these is the Bearded Vulture, *Gypaetus barbatus*, which is now severely endangered but was common on the island until the twentieth century CE (Figure 4.4).[57] The Bearded Vulture is itself an extraordinary creature, a biological reality whose existence is nevertheless the stuff of legend. It is a beast of great elevations who dwells in the rocky landscapes of mountains and nests within their caves and high ledges. The spaces inhabited by this raptor were also sacred to Cretans of the Bronze Age. Deposits of ritual material at Minoan peak sanctuaries and sacred caves, from the late Prepalatial through the Neopalatial periods, record humans' interest in the same areas and phenomena of the islandscape; we may indeed see renderings of vultures in the stone relief Sanctuary Rhyton from Zakros, which likely depicts a mountain shrine.[58] The Bearded Vulture is also a creature of tremendous size, with a wingspan up to 2.8 meters and a weight usually falling between 5 and 7 kilograms.[59] Unlike other species of vulture that typically have bald heads, the Bearded Vulture's head is completely covered in feathers. Likewise on its legs, thick feathers hang down

4.4. The Bearded Vulture (*Gypaetus barbatus*), native to the mountains of Crete and the Aegean. Picture by Tambako the Jaguar/Getty Images

and can give the limbs remarkable heft. Notable black markings elaborate the face and chest and stand out against their lighter background (these will be considered later, pp. 192–194). As an adult, the feathers of its head and body are primarily white, while its wings and tail are a grayish-black. The white feathers of the bird typically appear a rust color, however, because in the wild this species has the highly peculiar habit of bathing within the waters of iron-oxide-rich mountain sulfur streams and mud sources,[60] an action through which the creature effectively paints its own body (Figure 4.5). During these baths, the bird rubs its body and head within the water or mud, turning the white feathers of these areas a vivid orangey hue; this often brings the neck and chest feathers a textured and mottled character (Figures 4.4, 4.5). While the purpose of this self-painting is debated,[61] it is notable that nesting Bearded Vultures will also return to the nest after such baths and rub their newly bronzed feathers upon their eggs, painting them as well.

This gigantic bird is also distinguished by extraordinary behavior that surely would have made a marked impression on people living in Crete during the Bronze Age, as it does on observers today. The Bearded Vulture is a bone eater. Bones constitute the vast majority of its diet, their marrow being its primary source of nutrition. This grim diet sets the bird apart in the animal world.[62] The massive bird's acquisition of bone can involve dramatic scenes. The Bearded Vulture often scavenges from carrion. Since its object is not the soft tissue of the dead body, it will wait for other birds and animals to clean the carcass before making its move. It then descends upon the remains and can lift away whole bodies or individual bones with its strong talons and beak. This is when the show begins. The Bearded Vulture can ingest even larger bones whole (up to 10 cm in diameter) by working them into its open mouth and down its extended throat in a repetitive tossing motion. Its esophagus is exceptionally elastic, allowing for the passage of large and awkwardly shaped bones and, unlike all other known species of vulture, this creature lacks a crop (a "storage region" prior to the stomach), since bones would likely become lodged within such. This allows the bone to move directly into the stomach where an extraordinarily acid (pH <1) gastric environment causes it to dissolve within twenty-four hours.[63] As this ingestion process is underway, bones, sometimes with tissue and fur still attached, can protrude from the Bearded Vulture's gaping mouth; sometimes bones are even visible projecting from the bird's open beak after it has left its feasting spot, as it soars through the sky.

Surely the sight of these bone-guzzling creatures would have been striking, but another aspect of their consumption ritual likely inspired yet further awe and terror. In order to break up larger bones, Bearded Vultures will carry carcasses or sizable bones high into the air, up to circa 150 meters, and then drop them down upon particularly rocky areas below; at times, they will also

4.5. a. Scene of griffin running beside winding waterway from Room 5 (east wall), West House, Akrotiri; courtesy Akrotiri Excavations. b. Stillframe from video of the Bearded Vulture bathing in an iron-rich mountain stream, taken in the Añisclo Valley, within the Ordesa y Monte Perdido National Park, Huesca, Spain, by Javier Barrio de Pedro; courtesy Javier Barrio de Pedro. c. Photograph of Bearded Vulture bathing itself in iron-rich ochre mud, © Klaus Robin; courtesy Klaus Robin

drop live tortoises and small animals in this way.[64] Once it has dropped its boney load, the Bearded Vulture dives into a dramatic "characteristic spiral" to assess its work, repeating this grisly show until the bones are sufficiently broken to allow the marrow to be extracted. One would not soon forget such a scene – Cretan shepherds today refer to the birds as *kokalas* or "bone [eaters]."[65] The accumulations of shattered bones formed through this grim behavior are called "ossuaries" and may have been viewed as points of fascination, and trepidation, for people happening upon them in Crete's mountains. Hence, while the Bearded Vulture only very rarely preys on the live flesh of other animals, one can see why they have inspired fearful awe in humans. Folk traditions have (fallaciously) painted them as predatory creatures that would carry off living children and flocks; this may be connected to their unique practice of sometimes lifting animal corpses high into the air to drop. For example, in the Alps, they are known as the "Devil Bird" or "Lamb Vulture."[66] Meanwhile, the Bearded Vulture also has a penchant for dramatic "aerial shows" connected to mating and defense, and perhaps play,[67] which involve diving plunges, spiraling acrobatics by nests and "dances" in which two of the creatures lock talons in midair. Certainly, this is no typical bird. It is both fearsome and enthralling and its character – real and imagined, formal and behavioral – is truly astonishing.

There are several reasons why, among raptors, Bearded Vultures seem especially likely to have been associated with the griffin by inhabitants of Crete. To begin, this bird's singular and arresting behavior would have provided vivid spectacles that set it apart from other avian species, including other vultures. With this, it is easy to imagine that the Bearded Vulture was readily relatable to the griffin's identity in the Cretan sphere, as another truly extraordinary beaked flying creature capable of gruesome forays upon the world below; likewise, Cretan glyptic motifs sometimes show the griffin descending upon animals as an apparent predator (e.g., Figure 4.6a–b). Other evidence, from surviving wall-painting fragments, suggests particular links that may have been made concerning the habitat and behavior of the Bearded Vulture and Aegean griffins. On the East Frieze of the West House at Akrotiri, a griffin dashes alongside a winding stream, vividly outlined in swathes of reddish-orange, which has colorfully painted ovoid forms strewn about its shores, including directly below the body of the griffin. Within the same room, on the north wall, hilly slopes are depicted as crisscrossed with similar winding streams, and the East Frieze might represent a scene within such an alpine setting. Given the Bearded Vulture's characteristic penchant for baths in iron-rich mountain streams (Figure 4.5), and its painting of both itself and its eggs with the orangey-red color derived from them, we could be seeing in this painted scene of a griffin evidence of an association with

4.6. Neopalatial renderings of the griffin in glyptic possessing elaborations in the area of the neck/chest, and comparanda. a. CMS II.3.334; b. CMS II.3.25a; c. CMS II.3.79; d. CMS II.3.219; e. CMS II.4.116; f. CMS I. S.152; g. CMS v.S3.245a; h. CMS v.S3.403; i. CMS II.8.193. Images courtesy CMS, Heidelberg

a similar species and its habitat observed in nature. The ovoid forms could be related, as well, as "painted" eggs like the Bearded Vulture's.

Considering the distinctive bodily form and character of the Bearded Vulture suggests further particular ways in which this raptor may have been related to the Cretan griffin. The Bearded Vulture takes its name from a prominent marking of the bird's head: a panel of black feathers that extends across each side of the face, originating above the eye, extending in an arc across the eye and beak, and then emerging in a tuft or "beard" below the beak. Because the feathery panel continues off of the head, the sense that it is a distinct entity *upon* the bird's face is quite keen. We have multiple renderings of birds from Neopalatial glyptic that likely can be connected to the Bearded Vulture with its unique facial marking. The birds of CMS II.6.111 and CMS II.6.113 (and cf. CMS II.6.114) (Figure 4.7b, d, e), clay seal impressions from LM I Ayia

GRIFFINS CONTROLLED OR TAKING WING? 193

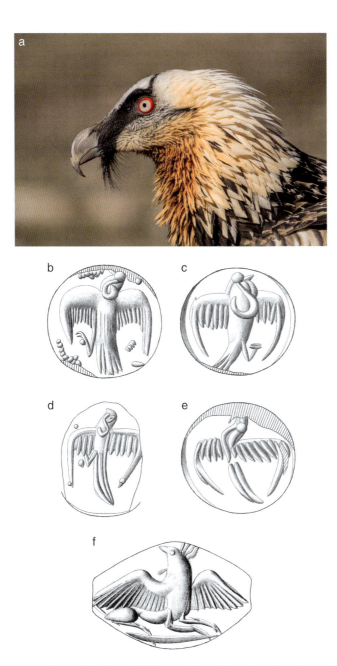

4.7. a. Face of the Bearded Vulture; photo by Jose Luis Ruiz/500px/Getty Images; b. CMS II.6.111; c. CMS II.6.112; d. CMS II.6.113; e. CMS II.6.114; f. CMS III.372. Drawings of glyptic motifs courtesy CMS, Heidelberg

Triada, both have a curved projection extending down from the eye that arcs toward the front of the face and then continues below the area of the head (these birds are rendered with their heads aimed upward and necks elongated, so that the curved projection below the head falls within the outline of the neck). This feature of the birds is highly comparable to the dark panel crossing the Bearded Vulture's face. We see almost identical eye/face markings on the bird of CMS II.6.112 (Figure 4.7c), another preserved impression from LM I Ayia Triada, and in this case the engraved bird also has a protrusion descending from the base of the beak, adding yet more weight to the sense that it is "bearded."

These renderings in seal impressions of birds remarkably like Bearded Vultures allow for interesting comparisons with embodiments of griffins in the same medium. For example, a LM I carnelian amygdaloid seal from the Lasithi in Crete, CMS III.372 (Figure 4.7f), is engraved with a regardant griffin that has a highly similar beard-like projection below its head. This could be a representation of an appendage of the same type as that on the birds of the Ayia Triada impressions. At the same time, we can note that this protrusion, from below the head of the CMS III.372 griffin, also appears much like the lobed pendant worn by one of the MBA Phaistian griffins, that of CMS II.5.317 (Figure 4.1a). The resonance of these beasts is strengthened by the multiple upright appendages that top both creatures' heads, like plumes. These two renderings are not themselves contemporaneous (unless the parent Phaistos seal, or one like it, remained in use into LM I), but their comparability prompts us to recognize another way in which the Bearded Vulture, both as a living creature and one potentially embodied in representational objects, may have been viewed as relatable to renderings of griffins – if its "beard" projection was likened to an item attached to the neck/face (e.g., a pendant, or bridle). Meanwhile, a likely griffin's head from a fragment of a seal impression found in the Domestic Quarter at Knossos (CMS II.8.176) is remarkably akin to the face of the biological Bearded Vulture, with its pronounced eye, tufted beard and long beak with uneven ends; a patch of delineated rises along the neck makes clear that this part of the Knossian creature's body is thickly feathered, as is the Bearded Vulture's (Figure 4.7a). At the same time, beard-like protrusions from the face and neck of griffins and Bearded Vultures may have drawn comparisons to other species as well, for example to bearded male agrimia, themselves beasts of the mountain.[68]

The ground for seeing bodily connections between the Bearded Vulture and Aegean renderings of griffins continues into the zone of the chest and neck. We have seen that one of the earliest renderings of the griffin in the Aegean, that of seal impression CMS II.5.318 from Phaistos, was distinguished by dramatic tufting across the zone of its lower neck/chest (Figure 4.1b). For inhabitants of Crete, this may have been relatable to the upright and mottled appearance typical of feathers along the Bearded Vulture's neck and chest (Figure 4.4). The Bearded Vulture has several other unique markings that should be examined. Among these is a band of black feathers that drapes across the chest and then continues into, and broadens through, the wings. Against the lighter coloring of its body, this continuous pronounced dark band is visible both when the bird is in flight and seated. This characteristic feature of the raptor may have been connected to what we are seeing already on the MBA griffin of CMS II.5.319 (Figure 4.1c), from the *vano* 25 deposit at Phaistos, where a striated band extends across the beast's chest and through the wing. We continue to see a band extending across the chest and into the wing in numerous later, Neopalatial renderings of the griffin (Figures 4.6b–e), and the griffin of CMS II.5.319 seems to possess the earliest extant manifestation of this feature in the creature. While it is possible that the band feature on the biological Bearded Vulture was an inspiration for the griffin's characterization by seal engravers, more basically this feature would have constituted grounds for a link to be made by inhabitants of Crete *between* the two Aegean species – between the griffin, experienced in stone and clay, and a vulture, experienced in feather and flesh.

While it must remain hypothetical, the band encircling the biological Bearded Vulture's chest may in fact stand as another point of common relation between the characterization of the chests/necks of all three early Cretan griffins from the MBA *vano* 25 deposit at Phaistos, including that of seal impressions CMS II.5.317, where we see a pendant hanging at the chest from a ring around the neck (Figure 4.1). Moreover, this topic may shed fresh light on larger trends evident in renderings of Aegean griffins that have not previously been connected to one another. To consider such possibilities, we must first contextualize the treatment of the chest of the griffin of CMS II.5.317. This will involve confronting the potential ambiguity of the engraved details of the tiny seal motifs, including those elements of the engraving that seemingly constitute parts of an animal's corporeal form. It seems that this ambiguity was at times productively developed.

Between Bodies and Things, Forms and Figures

In clay seal impressions of CMS II.5.317, we have a very early and clear instance of a particular trope involving griffins that persists into the Neopalatial period: a griffin fitted with some sort of collar element.[69] In CMS II.5.317, two arcing rises (incisions in the parent seal) that cross the line of the griffin's neck give the impression of an encircling double ring; from these rings, a teardrop-shaped pendant form extends downward by the chest. When we consider this feature in the context of its Neopalatial parallels, we find that similar neck rings are sometimes positioned tightly near the face of griffins (e.g., CMS II.6.101, CMS II.3.219; Figure 4.6d) but can also occur farther down the neck. When high on the neck, the line could be intended to articulate the boundary of the face/head; such is also evident on renderings of other species from the Protopalatial and Neopalatial periods.[70] In this position, the neck line can at times be difficult to distinguish from dramatic outlines of the eye, and indeed it may effectively play both roles (e.g., CMS II.3.334, CMS I.S.152; Figure 4.6a, f). This ambiguity can also engage the wings, since, on some Neopalatial griffins, the line defining the neck boundary is the same as that which extends into the wing (e.g., CMS II.3.79, CMS II.4.116; Figure 4.6c, e). However, it is in numerous other renderings of griffins in Neopalatial glyptic that such ambivalence is enriched with particularly notable effect. In these, the lines appearing to define the anatomy of the neck and chest also play the role of constituting an added object attached to the beast, such as a collar or leash. A comparison between two renderings of griffins illustrates the point. On seal CMS II.3.79 (Figure 4.6c), a simple linear band runs down across the upper wing toward the body then crosses the base of the neck/upper chest; this seems to define elements of the beasts' anatomy. On the beast of CMS I.S.152 (Figure 4.6f), something more is at play. Here, a comparable band extends through the wing then bends to cross the neck/chest; but at this point, it then partially doubles back, giving the dynamic effect of ringing around. A two-stranded short v-projection issues outward from this band, in front of the beast, and appears like the ends of a tied rope. Subtly, the line of neck/chest now seems to be, at the same time, also a cord *put onto* the griffin. Both the bend at the neck and the loop have required careful alignment to give the impression of a continuous band; the result is very effective. In other cases, a similar effect can stem from somewhat different renderings of neckbands. For example, on seal CMS II.3.349 and CMS V.S3.403 (Figure 4.6h), the reduplication of linear bands upon the neck gives the impression of something cord-like being wound repeatedly around it. A recut amethyst scarab seal from Aidonia in the Peloponnese, CMS V.S3.245 (Figure 4.6g), which has been dated stylistically to MB III or LB I–II and may be of Cretan manufacture,[71] provides dramatic narrative development of the linear neckband. Here, the band is rendered as a rope or leash tied onto the neck of a large griffin; this is held by a human standing behind the beast. A similar role is apparent for the neckband seen in CMS II.8.193, an impression of a metal signet ring from Neopalatial Knossos (Figure 4.6i). Here, a pair of griffins are depicted close beside one another, in parallel flying gallops; behind them, a human stands in a chariot, leaning deeply forward with arms outstretched toward the beasts. We have a full view of the upper body of the griffin in the foreground, who has a linear band at the base of its neck. The human's bent posture and reach, together with what seem to be delicate lines extending between its hands and the griffins, indicate that the griffins are connected to reins and pull the chariot forward. With this, the neckband of the griffin also becomes the means by which the reins would be attached to the beast, as the collar of a harness. This scene is reminiscent of the imagery of the incredible Neopalatial gold signet ring excavated in the Phourni cemetery at Archanes, AE 1017, in which a woman with outstretched arms

4.8. Neopalatial gold signet ring engraved with a woman and griffin, from Archanes. Herakleion Museum, HM XA-2017. Photograph from Sakellarakis, Yannis and Efi Sapouna-Sakellaraki, *Archanes: Minoan Crete in a New Light* (Athens: Ammos Publications, 1997): 652 fig. 718. Courtesy Efi Sapouna-Sakellaraki. Object © Hellenic Ministry of Culture and Sports

seems to hover behind and above a griffin who is in the midst of swift movement (Figure 4.8). One of the woman's arms extends over the back of the griffin and toward the upper outline of the beast's wing. This line ultimately bends down to the area behind the griffin's neck, giving the impression that the wing's outline is also a leash attached to the griffin. This impression is strengthened by the fact that the hand of the female figure is positioned directly above a small hash line that intersects the upper outline of the wing, which may indicate that we should understand a second linear feature implied here, such as a leash, sharing the line of the wing's outline. In this case the engraving of this single outline would be doing double duty in the image, both defining the beast's body and constituting an object attached to it – much as the neckbands do in CMS II.8.193. Other examples of related scenes exist in glyptic of various styles in the Aegean, especially from subsequent periods. Within some of these, a comparable formal ambiguity is at play, allowing a feature to be read as either an attached leash or an integral element of the body. For example, in CMS I.98, an impression from Mycenae that stylistically dates to LH II–IIIA1, two griffins are tied to a central column by leashes formed of lines that, as they continue, ultimately become part of the ornate patterning of the beasts' wings.[72] Morgan has problematized ambiguity in Aegean glyptic imagery, questioning whether it arises as accidents of "economy" and "abbreviation" or carries intended "double meaning"[73] by the engraver. Both might be at play, simultaneously, in the imagery of this griffin.

We find important context for the evolving trope of a collared or leashed Aegean griffin, and for related embellishments of the creature's neck/chest region, by looking beyond glyptic. Renderings in other media also shed light on how these facets of the griffin's Aegean identity were simultaneously developing through other material dimensions, including an array of painted colors and the broader scales and distinct affordances of ceramic vessels – and (eventually) frescoed walls. At Akrotiri in the Cyclades, recent construction activities have recovered a wealth of large-scale MBA ceramic vessels, some painted with rich polychrome imagery.[74] These date to Phase C of the Middle Cycladic chronology, which is contemporaneous with MM IIB–IIIA at Knossos in Crete.[75] We find the griffin among these Cycladic vessels. On a large pithos from Pillar Shaft 67 N, a griffin runs in unending chase with a feline through a field of large spirals and fronds that rise from the vessel's base (Figure 4.9).[76] Another vessel, the so-called Griffin Pithos, is painted with a scene of two large griffins who stand within an environment filled with palms issuing from uneven ground, amid spiral-form vegetation (Figure 4.10). Like their smaller Cretan counterparts in glyptic from Phaistos, these large MBA Aegean griffins, which stand ca. 0.70 m tall, possess both head appendages and chest embellishments (given their date range, these griffins could be either roughly contemporary with or somewhat later than the MM IIB griffins from

4.9. Pithos painted with griffin and lion, from Pillar Shaft 67 N, MC (Phase C) Akrotiri, Thera. Photograph (a) and drawing of painted surface (b). Images courtesy Akrotiri Excavations. Object © Hellenic Ministry of Culture and Sports

4.10. The Griffin Pithos from MC (Phase C) Akrotiri, Thera. Photograph (a) and drawing of painted surface (b). Images courtesy Akrotiri Excavations. Object © Hellenic Ministry of Culture and Sports

the *vano* 25 deposit at Phaistos). The crests on the Middle Cycladic griffins from Akrotiri are rendered as a series of backward-sweeping curving strands. On the griffin from the pithos of Pillar Shaft 67 N, the crest's primary element is a substantial projection that curves back into a dramatic spiral loop; small projections branch off from this main strand and two smaller, lighter ones curve back from the head just above it. On the beasts of the Griffin Pithos, the crests are comprised of a series of upward-looping spirals that emerge from a finely striated mass lining the back of the head and neck. The looping crests of all of these beasts have comparanda both within the Aegean and beyond. They are similar to what we see on some griffins in MBA Syro-Palestinian glyptic and also to the single spiral curling back upon the head of the CMS II.5.318 griffin at Phaistos (Figure 4.1b); looking forward slightly, they are also closely relatable to the short appendages that may have lined the back of the head and neck of the tethered griffins in the restored high relief frescoes from fill above the North–South Corridor at Knossos, which Hood believes could date to MM IIIB.[77]

The neck/chest elaborations of the MC Akrotiri griffins also take the form of curvilinear and spiral features. Although the paint is abraded in some places, it is clear that these features are positioned in the same areas of the creatures' upper bodies that we have seen elaborated with added elements on the griffins of Cretan MBA glyptic. On the Pillar Shaft 67 N pithos, the elaboration of the griffin's neck is tiered: below a double band defining the neck and surrounding the eye, four thin, wavy streamers descend vertically to another double band; below this band, five pendant spirals descend. This gives the impression of a feature encircling the neck with components suspended from it. The streamers of the upper register recall the feathery texture in the neck/chest area of the griffins of both CMS II.5.318 and CMS II.5.319 from Phaistos, as well as on the neck/chest of the biological Bearded Vulture; meanwhile the pendant components of the second register resonate with what we see on the griffin of CMS II.5.317.

On the Griffin Pithos, the chest embellishment of each griffin takes the shape of a large, curving motif that forms a ring at the neck and then extends downward into a wide pendant spiral at the chest/shoulder. This motif brings further color and texture to the extraordinary beasts, while also contributing to an internal formal coherence across their bodies, through the repetition of spirals at different scales – as the neck/chest spirals resonate with the series of smaller spirals lining the back of the head and neck. These spiral-form embellishments also integrate the griffins within the formal context of the whole vessel, by echoing both the spirals that constitute vegetation below the beasts and the spiral banding that forms an abstract upper border at the pithos' rim. Similar dynamics of formal assonance are apparent on the pithos from Pillar Shaft 67N, between the spiral and wavy features that comprise the embellishment of the griffin's cheek/nest, the vegetation rising around them and the border set below the vessel's rim. At the same time, the spiral-form chest embellishment of each griffin of the Griffin Pithos is also strongly suggestive of a looping strand encircling and hanging from the neck, like as a rope. This motif, of a rope tied about a griffin's neck, is rendered unambiguously in Akrotiri during the subsequent period, on the LC IA griffin painted in the north wall of Room 3a of Xeste 3,[78] and during the Neopalatial period, it also occurs in various other media and contexts (see pp. 331–344 and below). Through their suggestion of a cord or rope attached to the neck, these spirals thus also enrich the animals' narrative involvement in what becomes a *scene* within a complex setting.

The spiral motifs painted on the Griffin Pithos both create formal assonance across the object and productively hover between abstraction and figural representation. These remarkable dynamics are not without parallels in the MBA Aegean. We have seen that subtle but powerful ambiguities in the formation of griffins' bodies in Aegean glyptic sometimes develop into creative renderings of a device attached to the beast's neck/chest. Meanwhile, remarkably strong parallels for the dynamics of formal assonance evident on these pithoi from Akrotiri occur in contemporaneous vessels from Phylakopi in Melos that are painted with front-facing "gorgon" figures, where elements of the creatures' bodies echo abstract free-floating motifs in the surrounding field.[79] A tension between ornamental and pictorial aspects of imagery has also been discussed concerning the interplay of different representational paradigms between MBA media – namely glyptic, painted ceramics and emergent mural arts. Here, I wish to highlight Immerwahr's discussion of MBA Cretan Kamares ware ceramics, where she has identified forays away from the ornamental motifs most prevalent in the ware's decorative repertoire and toward "pictorialization."[80] Immerwahr argues that this pictorialization was the work of innovative ceramicists who drew from an iconographic repertoire well established in seal engraving of the time; in turn, she contends, the work of these path-breaking ceramicists would influence the development of figural wall painting.[81] Her analysis of a pithoid vessel from Phaistos identifies painted elements poised between figural and non-figural statuses. On it, an abstract paisley design, common in Kamares ware, is transformed into a carefully articulated fish, whose mouth is caught with an abstracted hook/net that echoes the fish's shape, emphasizing the ambiguous status of their shared form. A second Kamares vessel, this from Knossos, also blurs the distinction between the ornamental and pictorial. The pithos is painted with a continuous series of large, rather stylized palms. Immerwahr highlights the undulating painted zone at the base of the vessel, which, instead of being a standard border feature, subtly gives the impression of being an uneven *ground* from which the trees rise, thus moving the "ornamental" composition toward a natural scene. Vlachopoulos has elaborated on Immerwahr's discussion of cross-craft innovations and compellingly argues that key technological connections between the painting of ceramic vessels and the frescoing of walls may have occurred in the Cyclades.[82] He highlights the role of large-scale Middle Cycladic polychrome vessels in this, including the Griffin Pithos. In this light, we can appreciate that the curvilinear motifs that elaborate the neck/chest of the two griffins of the pithos, and also the spirals that rise from the "ground" like plants, embody a liminality between the ornamental and pictorial in the sense discussed by Immerwahr. The connections drawn by Immerwahr and Vlachopoulos between such painted vessels and early scenic wall painting are convincing. Vlachopoulos' consideration of the Griffin Pithos links this directly to our examination of the griffin and its growth in Aegean material culture. The vessel realizes the powerful integrative dynamics that could draw the griffin into its material and narrative environment through productive ambiguities – something that we have also seen at play in glyptic embodiments of the beast, but through the distinct affordances of that engraved medium. That such dynamics are evident in various media that gave body to the griffin indicates that a suggestive ambiguity was part of the fabric of the beast's complex existence in the Aegean during the MBA and earliest LBA.

Feathers and Pendants, Lines and Leashes

We have considered previously that renderings of griffins could have been contextualized in various ways by people in the Aegean, including through experiences of foreignness. The MBA Griffin Pithos from Akrotiri constitutes a rich point from which to again consider the simultaneous contexts that embraced the Aegean griffin, now querying how such dynamism may have contributed to the development of a tension between representational and abstract aspects of the griffin's body. While the spiral motifs upon the upper bodies of the two griffins of the pithos from Akrotiri connect the beasts to the renderings of griffins with chest/neck embellishments from MBA Crete, they can also be compared to the spiral visible upon the neck of the griffin engraved in the MBA furniture plaque from Acemhöyük (see Figure 4.3). This comparison complicates the matter of the emergence of the spiral-form element that is often present on the neck or shoulder of Neopalatial Aegean griffins, which Aruz rightly observes is already evidenced on the MBA Anatolian plaque. With the discovery of the MC pithoi painted with griffins at Akrotiri, we see how the formulation of spiral-form features on griffins' bodies was also taking place within the Aegean. Indeed, one of our best early examples of the spiral-clad Neopalatial Aegean griffin comes not from the palaces of Crete, but from the painted walls of Akrotiri, on the LC IA griffin of Xeste 3. Clearly both intra-Aegean and overseas ancestries were creatively at play together (regardless of which "came first") as griffins such as these were being crafted and encountered.

Looking broadly throughout the eastern Mediterranean also brings further light on the development of representational and possible narrative components of the griffin's identity that involve the recurrent motif of a cord attached at the creature's neck. We have seen ways that this motif subtly emerged in the Aegean from the formation of the griffin's body, and how emphasis was sometimes placed on the neck/chest region through the addition of embellishments, reaching back to the extant MBA Cretan renderings from Phaistos. The griffin of CMS II.5.317 demonstrates that the figure of a griffin clearly fit with a collar was being given form in Crete already during MM IIB. We have seen that this motif finds context within the wider MBA Aegean, through renderings of griffins with suggestive chest/neck embellishments (esp. on the Griffin Pithos). At the same time, the theme of a leashed or tethered griffin (or griffin-like beast) also occurs in material culture from MBA Egypt and the Levant.

4.11. Painting of "Detail of a Griffin, Tomb of Khety" at Beni Hasan, Egypt (Middle Kingdom), tempera on paper by Nina and Norman de Garis Davies. Metropolitan Museum, NY, 33.8.14; Rogers Fund, 1933. (CC0 1.0) www.metmuseum.org

From Egypt, the vivid Middle Kingdom wall paintings from the tomb of Khety at Beni Hasan give form to a striking polychrome beast with a falcon's head and the body of a large feline (the *Saget*; Figure 4.11). The creature's body is rendered in a patchwork of geometric patterns and colors. A series of swollen blue triangular teats descend from its lower body, clearly indicating its maternal status. Around its neck appears a thick checkered collar connected to a cord or leash. Such prominent thick collaring can be broadly compared to the wide neck/chest embellishment of the griffin on the pithos from Pillar Shaft 67 N at Akrotiri. Renderings of similar falcon-headed beasts, wearing collars and sometimes also leashes, appear on (easily transportable) MK magical wands (e.g., BM EA24426). Very similar renderings of collared and leashed griffins occur in MBA Syro-Palestinian glyptic (e.g., Figure 4.15e; cf. Figure 4.6h, from Akrotiri).[83]

To consider how such renderings of leashed creatures from overseas (and perhaps elements of traditions surrounding them) may have been related to comparable griffin-figures in the Aegean, we should again lengthen our temporal view, looking forward into the Neopalatial evidence, as we did regarding the closely connected matter of ambiguous neckbands engraved on griffins in glyptic. It is possible that the trope of a collar/cord at a griffin's neck in the Aegean can, in part, be traced to overseas imagery, even if, simultaneously, there were other contexts for its cultivation within the region. We have seen that there are numerous renderings of collared/leashed griffins in Neopalatial and LB II glyptic. Aegean griffins were also embodied numerous times in the large-scale, colorful medium of wall frescoes during these periods. These frescoes will be a focus of Chapter 6, as will the elaboration of the griffin's identity as part of painted spaces. For now, we can highlight two early Neopalatial-era frescoes, one from Knossos in Crete, and the other from Akrotiri in Thera, that show leashed griffins. These indicate both a perpetuation of this theme in the Aegean as well as its development – materially, contextually and likely conceptually – from the Middle to the Late Bronze Age, including possible evidence of cultural associations shared with similar creatures overseas.

In the palace of Knossos, in fill above the North–South Corridor,[84] Evans' team recovered pieces of painted plaster preserving fragments of multiple griffins. These were formed with an advanced technique, in which the surface of the painting is built up with stucco in certain areas and shaped, in order to give parts of the painting – in this case the bodies of the griffins – dramatic dimensionality (see Figure 6.13, pp. 340–344).[85] On these relief griffins, we find an ornamented band positioned across the base of the face, in the very location where bands appear on many griffins engraved in seal stones; this feature may also be relatable to the facial markings of the Bearded Vulture (Figure 4.7). In the relief fresco, this band forms an intricate bridle that seems to extend into a cord that has been restored as tethering the griffin to a column, also rendered in relief. From a roughly contemporaneous level at Akrotiri,[86] in a nonpalatial building that was extensively painted, Xeste 3, we have the large, frescoed scene involving a griffin that rears up behind a seated female figure (see Figures 6.11 and 6.12, pp. 332–340).[87] Around the neck of this griffin, there is a deep reddish linear band that gathers to form a looped knot on the back of the beast's neck; this tethering cord then extends upward, behind the wing, to emerge above the griffin, where it appears to be tied up by the actual window of the room. Within this space, the tethered griffin is associated with not only the large seated female but also a group of other women of various ages. The clear sexing of the creature painted at Beni Hasan is interesting when compared to this and other Aegean renderings. In the LB I–II Aegean glyptic evidence, we have multiple depictions of female griffins with prominent pendant teats (CMS II.3.129, from Avdou, CMS II.6.99 from Ayia Triada (Figure 4.12a), CMS I.260 from Mycenae).[88] We also have an intriguing rendering of what seems to be a scene of a human carrying (away?) a very small griffin, perhaps a young beast (CMS II.6.029, from Ayia Triada (Figure 4.12b); cf. fresco fragment from the Cult Center at Mycenae depicting a woman holding a small griffin). The brilliant Neopalatial signet ring from Archanes discussed above (Figure 4.8), pairing a woman and an apparently leashed griffin, is another relevant piece. One can only speculate, but these may be glimpses of one or more cultural traditions, perhaps passed through shared narratives, concerning the capture/control of griffins, some of which may have involved mother animals and/or their young; other connections to femaleness may also be in play.[89] These possible associations between griffins and

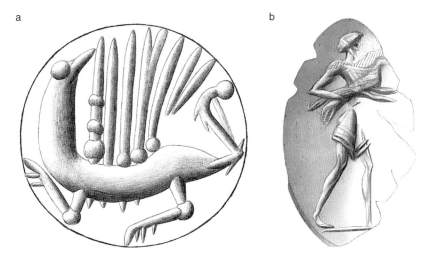

4.12. Female and perhaps young griffins in Neopalatial glyptic. a. CMS II.6.99. b. CMS II.6.29. Images courtesy CMS, Heidelberg

femaleness in the Aegean can be compared to renderings of collared griffin-like creatures in Egyptian visual culture that sometimes have prominent female attributes and/or are involved in material traditions surrounding women (e.g., when incised on ivory birthing wands). It may be that such underlying cultural connections, or related narratives, were moving by voice between these social spaces, along with the animalian things, informing how attributes such as neck/chest embellishments were understood.[90]

Where Local and Distant Meet: Creative Connections to Living and Crafted Beasts

A variety of persons were likely to have interacted with Aegean renderings of griffins during the MBA and early LBA. These include those who interacted with seals or seal impressions (from bureaucrats, to the family members of seal owners, to laborers moving sealed items). These people likely would have compared the griffins embodied in glyptic objects with both living animals and other crafted renderings of creatures, experiencing them all as concurrent instances of comparable beings – that is, as relatable animalian bodies, of stone, feather, clay and plaster. Some of these animalian bodies were of local derivation while others came from overseas, but the creative moments in which they were experienced and actively related to one another occurred within the distinctive ecology of the MBA–LBA Aegean. In this context, it is possible that imagery of griffins wearing collars and leashes recalled the impressive Bearded Vulture with its dark band ringing the chest. Or perhaps local traditions, developed separately, read the chest band of the Bearded Vulture as an object (rope?) attached upon the bird's body, and these later became points of association with the leashed creatures with raptor-like heads imaged in imported objects and stories accompanying them. Such potential associations certainly are not mutually exclusive, nor would they rule out others – this is a fundamental aspect of what is coming into view: such associations do not necessarily occur at the cost of one another; they can coexist and interact, enriching the cultural existence of the animals involved and feeding into the dynamic creation of new animalian forms. Here, we can note that the large feline who runs with the griffin on the MC pithos from Pillar Shaft 67N at Akrotiri has at its chest a feature comprised of pendant spirals that is identical to the lower register of the motif embellishing the griffin's chest. This feature may have emerged in part through a comparison of the griffin with an impressive living species in the Aegean, or with elaborated griffins' bodies seen on imported objects – or through another observation. Yet on this Cycladic pithos, the chest embellishment creatively took on its own distinct character and was shared with a large cat, thereby generating interspecific similarity. The LB IA griffin frescoed in a wall of Xeste 3, in Akrotiri, evidences similar creative dynamics. The vivid black markings on the head of the griffin indicate contrasting dark and light feathers, the presence of which distinguishes the Bearded Vulture among other vulture species (most being bald). The dark-on-light nature of the markings and the focus brought to the eye relate this griffin and the Bearded Vulture. Yet the dark facial markings of the beast could have carried multiple associations simultaneously. They are also relatable to the rendering of Peregrine Falcons' heads in Egyptian and southwest Asian objects, including what we see on the griffin of the Acemhöyük plaque (Figure 4.3). The Peregrine Falcon is also present in the Aegean, as is the comparably marked Eleanora's Falcon, which migrates through the Cyclades and feasts on large insects such as dragonflies (notable in light of the dragonfly necklace worn by the seated woman that the Xeste 3 griffin seemingly protects). Hence, it is possible that the markings of the Xeste 3 griffin, and other similar griffins of the Neopalatial era, were connected (directly or indirectly) to these falcon species as well, even as the shape of the head has been developed as distinctly *vulture-*like. In their finer details, the dark markings of the Xeste 3 griffin in fact match neither the Bearded Vulture nor the Peregrine or Eleanora's Falcons – in this LB IA embodiment, the griffin's particular character is fundamentally its own, inviting various comparisons but no easy matches.

CROWNED BEASTS, POTENT GAZES AND MOVING THINGS

We return now to our three Middle Bronze Age griffins from the *vano* 25 sealing deposit at Phaistos: CMS II.5 317, CMS II.5.318 and CMS II.5.319. In addition to embellishments in the area of the chest/neck, each of these early griffins is distinguished by a head appendage. These appendages invite

CROWNED BEASTS, POTENT GAZES AND MOVING THINGS

comparisons to a restricted array of creatures that share the remarkable attribute. By looking first at other animals embodied in the sealings of the Phaistos deposit, we find an unlikely fellow creature sharing this feature: a tiny owl. Through this small but provocative avian body, we open a wider examination of extraordinary creatures, both in the Aegean and abroad, that are related to one another through comparable head appendages. With this, we consider both connections to biological species that were present in Crete and fabricated creatures embodied in objects. This discussion leads us to explore another distinguishing bodily feature that is often copresent with head appendages in renderings of fantastic creatures, either on the same figures or closely affiliated ones: a potent forward gaze. We consider the types of objects and interactions that may have been involved in the sharing of such creaturely forms, as well as the creative situations in which they became embroiled in distinct ecologies of animals and animalian things within Aegean communities.

Horns, Familiar and Exotic

The head appendages of the three griffins of the *vano* 25 deposit each has distinct character. We can account for this variation in part by assuming that the objects are the work of different craftspersons who were working with their own techniques and ideas concerning what constituted the attribute. Even if such is the case, we should consider how the materialized forms that the head appendages took informed people's impressions of these griffins and, with this, impacted their sense of the beasts' animalian identities. The common presence of a head appendage likely contributed to uniting the group, even as finer differences between the forms that it took on each griffin could have led to the creatures being seen to have distinct links with other species. In the first section, we saw that the head appendages of the three Phaistian griffins could be compared to those of an assortment of familiar animals appearing in the stamped motifs of the *vano* 25 deposit, with varying degrees of similarity. For example, the "feather-like" crest of CMS II.5.317 may have appeared more akin to birds than the looped-crest of CMS II.5.318, with its resemblance to insect antennae, while the griffin of CMS II.5.319 may have been likened more to renderings of beasts with short upright horns and/or a simple plume.

If we broaden our view somewhat to take in other varieties of head appendage evident on animals represented within the *vano* 25 glyptic corpus, we find this attribute on another winged creature stamped in sealings of CMS II.5.311 (Figure 4.13a). This animal, and another very similar one engraved into a *petschaft* seal with unknown provenance now in the Ashmolean, CMS VI.130[91] (Figure 4.13c), have consistently been identified as owls. The owl of CMS II.5.311 sits with its body depicted in profile but its head turned in a frontal view. The attenuated element that descends between the eyes

4.13. Owls rendered in Protopalatial glyptic. a, b. CMS II.5.311, motif of a stamped sealing from the *vano* 25 deposit at Phaistos. Object © Hellenic Ministry of Culture and Sports. c, d. CMS VI.130, a *petschaft* seal in the Ashmolean Museum (AM 1910.282). Images courtesy CMS, Heidelberg

corresponds to the drawn-out outline of an owl's beak when viewed from the front. This owl has two antithetical projections that emerge from the top if its head and curve alongside its face, before then curling away in tight loops; a cluster of three short pointed tufts have been added to the top of the head between the bases of the projections. The intended identity of the projections is not clear, and they may have been interpreted in different ways by persons in Crete who encountered these objects or similar ones. We can consider the appendages first in the context of the local ecology of biological animals in Crete. In this light, the projections could be read as representations of the distinctive breadth of owls' neck/shoulder region and of the dramatic markings that surround the faces of many species of owls, including two found on Crete: the Tawny Owl (*Strix aluco*) and the Scops Owl (*Otus scops*) (Figure 4.14). In this case, the looped ends of the projections may have been taken as a stylized two-dimensional rendering of the notable three-dimensional widening that occurs as some owls' seemingly neckless heads taper outward and back across the shoulders. (It becomes quite clear that the curving head projections seen in CMS II.5.311 and CMS VI.130 contribute to the sense that the birds have an

4.14. Biological owls native to Crete. a. Tawny Owl. Photo by Main Uddin/500px/Getty Images. b. Scops Owl. Photo by sonnyrollins/Imazins/Getty Images

owl's distinctive bulk in the neck/shoulder region if we momentarily imagine the projections extracted – at which point the birds appear more like pigeons). An appreciation of the breadth and curvature across this region of owls' bodies is apparent in another MM rendering of the bird, this one in the round. In this case, a seal (CMS VI.7) takes the overall shape of a sitting owl that faces forward, its large head, dominated by massive eyes, resting upon its two legs. Its body form is broadly consistent with both the Scops and the Tawny Owls; no indication of head appendages are present. We can also consider the head projections visible on the owls of CMS II.5.311 and CMS VI.130 as related to another aspect of living owls. The prominent markings that outline the faces of Tawny and Scops Owls (and other species) can turn down across the shoulders/wings and appear to trace the broad curvatures of this zone of the bird's body. Suggesting this rich dimensionality through the curving lines on the CMS II.5.311 owl would be in keeping with the mixed frontal and profile views that are clearly evident in the rendering of its body. Meanwhile, the central three-part tufted element that appears at the top of the head of the CMS II.5.311 owl would potentially correspond to the distinctive tripartite marking that arises from the central axis of the Tawny Owl's face. With these readings, the protrusions from the head would be taken, in part, as representations of the owl's markings and not (only) the outlines of its bodily mass.

Alternatively, the long projections of the CMS II.5.311 owl may have been intended or read as horns; possession of such could in effect make this an instance of what is typically described as a composite creature. That said, in Cretan glyptic, representations of the horns of biological species known on the island do not typically have this type of upward/forward curvature. Goat horns instead usually swing back and downward, toward the back (e.g., see the goats of MM II CMS II.5.257 from Phaistos (Figure 4.2h), or LM I CMS II.7.95, from Zakros), while cattle's horns tend to be depicted straighter and more upright (e.g., CMS II.5.266, CMS II.5.268, or CMS II.5.269).

Close consideration of the rendering of head projections on the two MBA Cretan owls (CMS II.5.311 and CMS VI.130) allows us to imagine ways that people encountering these clay and stone birds may have related them to familiar biological embodiments of animals. However, we can, at the same time, cautiously step back, maintaining our focus on the dynamics of people's interactions with fabricated creatures in the Aegean, in order to also contextualize the MBA Cretan owls, and griffins that share the feature of head appendages (CMS II.5.317, CMS II.5.318, CMS II.5.319), within broader scales of material from within the contemporaneous eastern Mediterranean. In this context, the head appendages find particular interspecific associations that bring fresh implications for the creatures.

On the owl of seal impressions CMS II.5.311, the combination of two long projections that extend to the sides of the head, which could be described as horn-like, and the three-pointed tuft positioned at their center, finds a strong parallel in the contemporaneous rendering of a griffin in the surface of the tiny ivory furniture plaque from the Old Assyrian site of Acemhöyük, in Anatolia, discussed previously (Figure 4.3). On this plaque we find a griffin fitted with headgear composed of two long, thin horns extending horizontally to opposite sides, and three short, upright spikes situated at the center, directly atop the beast's head. While the horns are essentially symmetrical, the right one has more of an upward curve as it tapers toward its end;[92] meanwhile, the central spike is somewhat larger than the other two. The griffin's head and body are rendered in profile, but we see the headgear in full frontal view, as we do with the CMS II.5.311 owl.

The headgear of the griffin in the Acemhöyük plaque has a rich array of parallels within the wider eastern Mediterranean. In her publication of the plaque, Aruz connects the rendering of the griffin to examples of griffins and sphinxes found in Syro-Palestinian glyptic that wear what she describes as Egyptian "crowns composed of horizontally displayed ram's horns and upright feathers."[93] I would like to focus on this Syro-Palestinian evidence for a moment. In part, this is because here, too, we are dealing with glyptic media and hence with objects that are – in their role, scale, crafting and substances – comparable to those in which we find owls and griffins rendered within the contemporaneous Cretan sphere. Moreover, Syria has been identified by various scholars as a space in fruitful cultural contact with Crete already during the EBA and MBA and as a venue through which materials and cultural content from Egypt were likely to have reached Cretans.[94] Small, movable objects such as seals and impressions are a means through which we can easily imagine representational embodiments of creatures and other phenomena crossing geographic and social distance to reach new hands and eyes – an idea that has been powerfully discussed by Aruz[95] and various other scholars concerning the Aegean and eastern Mediterranean.[96] Hence, such things stand not only as instances of renderings of creatures, but, with this, as movable links between sociocultural spaces and traditions. Aruz draws on Teissier's study of Egyptianizing Syro-Palestinian glyptic in the MBA. Teissier parses the indebtedness of certain iconographic and stylistic elements of MBA Syro-Palestinian glyptic art to Egyptian visual culture. In this context, she describes renderings of griffins and sphinxes in the Syro-Palestinian corpus as incorporating characteristics of both Egyptian and non-Egyptian (e.g., Levantine and Cappadocian) prototypes but asserts that attempts to discern separate strands of influence between these two sources are often "spurious" given how frequently they become "integrated" in the renderings of the beasts.[97] Sphinxes and griffins generally seem closely related to one another in Syro-Palestinian seal imagery, appearing with comparable attributes and in similar contexts and attitudes; at times, they are found paired within the same composition.[98] Among the attributes that they can share are various manifestations of headgear involving two horns and a central upright element. Of the seals discussed by Teissier, the griffin engraved on a hematite cylinder seal from the Seyrig Collection (SC. 15; Figure 4.15g, top right) wears headgear that is the closest parallel to that of the griffin on the Acemhöyük plaque. This seal is engraved with two registers of figures. The griffin occupies one of the registers along with various other creatures, including fantastic beasts; in the lower register we see a human wrestling a lion, creating a juxtaposition of species that was well established in Crete, as well as what appears to be a scene of bull leaping/wrestling, constituting another link to Minoan human–animal relations (see Chapters 2 and 3).[99] The griffin is engaged in a stylized attack, its front legs raised atop the back of a smaller feline animal that turns its head to the griffin in distress. The base of the griffin's neck is elaborated with a jagged line that extends back into a raised feathered wing, much as we see on the Phaistian griffin of CMS II.5.319 and then on later Aegean griffins. The beak on the griffin of the cylinder seal appears long and hooked – longer than the short falcon-type beak of the griffin on the Acemhöyük plaque. On its head, two slender animal horns extend horizontally, one to the left and one to the right, and three upright pointed elements are set between them; as on the Acemhöyük griffin, the central pointed element is somewhat larger than those flanking it. A similar headdress is worn by a pair of heraldic griffins engraved on another hematite Syrian cylinder seal, YBC/Buchanan 1221 (Figure 4.15b, lower right). In this case, each griffin is again crowned with a headdress composed of three spikes positioned directly over the head, but here only a single long appendage curves back and upward over the body. Beyond seals, Teissier relates the griffin of seal SC 15 to what she identifies as an "Asian griffin" engraved on a small box from New Kingdom Egypt (Figure 4.15f, g).[100] This griffin has comparable bodily features and also a three-plume head appendage but lacks the addition of animal horns. Without horns, the headdress of this griffin appears akin to the tripartite plumed head appendage of the griffin of CMS II.5.317 from Phaistos (Figure 4.1a). Meanwhile, both the Phaistian griffin and the griffin engraved on the Egyptian box are depicted with a pendant suspended at their neck/chest. As we have seen (pp. 183–206), the presence of embellishments in the area of the neck/chest is broadly characteristic of the MBA griffins from Phaistos and is also found on some MBA griffins and related creatures from Egyptian and other Syro-Palestinian objects; in each of these regions, this trope is also evidenced in the LBA.

The repeated presence of a central tripartite component in the headgears of each of these creatures is notable and finds parallels within the corpus of Aegean MBA fabricated beasts. If we follow possession of that tripartite element, then headgears such as those seen on the griffins of the Acemhöyük plaque and Syrian seal YBC/Buchanan 1221, which pair the tripartite component with horns, are also comparable to the rendering of the griffin of CMS II.5.317 from Phaistos (Figure 4.1a). Here, we should also draw in CMS II.2.251, a tiny MM II *petschaft* seal from Mochlos (see Figure 4.22, p. 230). Engraved on the seal face, we have what appears to be a humanoid frontally rendered face, bedecked with two antithetic appendages that rise upward from the top of the head before curving outward; set between them is a lower upright projection that rises on a short linear stalk and ends in a slightly bulbous terminus. Along both sides of the face (best preserved on the left) are linear forms that rise up to the level of the top of the head, where they end in a fan of multiple projections (four projections appear on the raised form that is fully preserved); these fanned forms have been read as raised hands. I will return to this object later but here simply wish to note that this rendering of a face with tripartite headgear should potentially be associated with the broader evidence of tripartite head appendages under discussion and can be compared especially to some Egyptian-style solar crowns represented on Syro-Palestinian glyptic, which are composed of two upright outwardly curving horns and a central round disc (e.g., headdresses worn by griffins, Figure 4.15c, d; cf. Mesopotamian-style two-horned headgear such as that worn by front-facing humanoid figures [Figure 4.15a] which also resemble Minoan "horns of consecration"; see Chapter 2).

4.15. Motifs from MBA Syro-Palestinian glyptic. Drawings from Teissier 1996, reproduced courtesy Orbis Biblicus et Orientalis. a. Teissier 1996: 81 no. 137; b. Teissier 1996: 81 no. 139; c. Teissier 1996: 87 no. 162; d. Teissier 1996: 87 no 163; e. Teissier 1996: 87 no. 164; f. Teissier 1996: 89 no 2b; g. Teissier 1996: 89 no. 166

Inventiveness in Sharing and the Unique Situation of Movement over Seas

Between Egyptian and southwest Asian visual cultures, renderings of creatures and attributes can exhibit notable connections with one another. Yet even in situations where it appears that iconographies have been "faithfully adhered to" between these social spaces,[101] often considerable changes have in fact occurred not only in context, but also in the formal and material/physical properties of the *things* of which the creatures are part. Labels such as "Egyptianizing imagery" can sometimes mask the need to remain attentive to such significant divergences. The Syro-Palestinian glyptic discussed by Teissier exemplifies this, especially in relation to depictions of griffins and sphinxes fitted with forms of headgear. Some of these are quite clearly relatable to Egyptian prototypes, but they are reembodied as part of object types (cylinder seals), animalian bodily forms, compositions and lived sociocultural contexts that alter the status of the features to varying extents both materially and notionally. Part of this alteration arises from the pairing of such headgear with fantastic creatures that are embroiled in distinct Near Eastern and Anatolian traditions (this of course is also the case with the crowned Acemhöyük griffin and many other objects that evidence engagements with Egyptian figural forms). Above all, we need to recognize that Syro-Palestinian glyptic objects were elements of a unique sociocultural space with idiomatic if "eclectic" visual and material cultures of its own. We see this idea articulated already in Kantor's description of Canaanite art as emerging in the later MBA as a "separate entity" where "influences from Egypt and Mesopotamia met and mingled,"[102] but the "autonomy" of the Syro-Palestinian tradition has been more strongly asserted by scholars in recent years, including Teissier. Teissier argues that Syro-Palestinian glyptic motifs have often been reductively identified as "confused" adoptions of Egyptian imagery by scholars who view a complex context of intercultural back-and-forth, involving things, people and ideas, through an overly simplistic lens of derivation and transfer.[103] As we turn to considering a situation in which objects, verbal culture and ways-of-making crossed the sea to reach the Aegean, and vice versa, we should realize that the complexities of recontextualization alter and deepen.

Engagements with persons, communities and cultures across the eastern Mediterranean basin are clearly evidenced in elements of Cretan Middle Bronze Age material, such as pottery, metalwork, stones, musical objects, seals and – as we have already seen (p. 165) – sealing practices.[104] Cretan-made things were also making their way overseas. We see this in examples of Minoan ceramics from sites around the eastern Mediterranean, Near East and Egypt (e.g., the brilliant MM Kamares ware),[105] as well as in textual references in the MBA Syrian corpus to Cretan travelers and imported objects, including goods ranging from textiles to finely crafted metal objects such as vessels and weapons.[106] There are indications that Minoan craftwork was highly valued abroad, potentially by various segments of the population.[107]

Despite the clear signs that persons and materials from Protopalatial Crete were participating in overseas exchange, we can imagine that the frequency of interactions would have been considerably lower than what was occurring between regions of Syro-Palestine, the Near East and Egypt. Places such as Byblos and Ugarit were likely key nodes for interactions running in many directions, both by land and over water, but the dynamics of engagement with points across the ocean in the Aegean would have necessarily been distinct. These interactions entailed some qualitatively different experiences that developed over generations of practice. Routes between Levantine places and points in Crete may have already been established by the Protopalatial period – Colburn, for example, has convincingly argued that Byblos was already a crucial point for exporting materials to Crete during the Prepalatial period.[108] If this was the case, relationships between social groups living in communities that were located on the Aegean and Levantine "ends" of such routes, and along the way, may have also been old by the Protopalatial. We can imagine that certain groups may have maintained and developed roles in long-distance journeying, which would certainly have been a powerful component of social identity in the MBA Crete, and increasingly we are recognizing strands of continuity between the later Prepalatial and Protopalatial societies on the island.[109] The term "long-distance sea trade" conceals an incredible amount of highly particular knowledge and experience (bodily, sociocultural, specialized) that would have been necessary for undertaking trips across the eastern Mediterranean basin, which involved movement between islands, communities, ports and linguistic spheres, as well as the need to cope with threats ranging from currents and storms to raiders, bureaucrats and displeased exchange partners. Some of this know-how would have transferred from contexts of land-based travel, but much would be specific to a marine world. Hence, while clearly there were elements of concurrence in the places and people involved in cultural exchanges between areas of the broad eastern Mediterranean, Near East and northern Africa during the MBA, those engaging the Aegean were also unique in various significant and consequential respects.[110]

Comparatively fewer travelers, human and nonhuman, likely crossed the sea between Crete and the coasts of Syro-Palestine or Egypt than would have passed overland and by shore-hugging boats between those adjacent regions where environmental, zoological and sociocultural boundaries were, in most cases, more fluid.[111] Likewise, material culture moving toward Crete would have required precious space on seacraft, an inevitably limiting factor, especially in light of a likely focus on bulky but much-needed metal in Cretan-bound shipments.[112] This not only would have restricted quantities and sizes of imported objects, it also would have affected how people engaged with those objects that did make the passage. Surely the relative scarcity of things with overseas origins would have contributed to the identities construed for such material in the Aegean; it also would have meant fewer means for contextualizing imported objects and forms encountered as part of them. With fewer objects arriving at Cretan communities from overseas (and we still must imagine far more than what we have recovered archaeologically), it may be that even single pieces could be, comparatively speaking, quite potent in their impact. Interpretation and reformation of imagery could have taken place relatively unchecked, given that it was unlikely that many people had encounters with enough embodiments of a given foreign motif to acquire extensive context on its character and potential range of variation. Naturally, perpetuating the "original" or earlier character of a form might not have been of interest to someone engaging with an imported thing, but generally we would expect potential conformity with a motif's form and identity to diminish as it became more isolated within a new distant context where few other manifestations of it were known. This idea could be viewed as both painfully obvious and problematically reductive, but my point goes beyond this observation alone, to underscore the distinct creative possibilities that arise within such circumstances. In other words, we need to take seriously what it would mean for material culture, including objects embodying creatures, to cross the sea in the MBA and become part of new ecologies. This is not simply a scalar matter (e.g., *less* imported material means it is *more* valuable; or *more* distance crossed equates to *less* similar meaning); it is a matter of practice and affordance. The distancing and recontextualization of fewer things would contribute to peculiar generative dynamics in Crete and the Aegean that must be freshly considered.

Horns, Wigs and Headdresses

We can now return to the owls of Cretan seal CMS VI.130 and impressions CMS II.5.311 from Phaistos (Figure 4.13), in order to probe their connections to broader traditions of headgear worn by animalian entities across the wider eastern Mediterranean and Egypt and, with this, to consider the portable things through which such foreign beasts may have come to bear on the outfitting of the peculiar Aegean birds. We have seen that in the fundamentals of their form and composition, the head appendages of these owls correspond remarkably with those of the griffin of the ivory plaque from Acemhöyük: both involve two long horns or projections extending to opposite sides of the head, with three upright pointed spikes positioned in the center. At the same time, they diverge in their particular form. The Acemhöyük griffin has relatively straight and tapering "ram's horns" much like those seen on certain Egyptian crowns, including solar crowns worn by Hathor and other figures. These crowns are frequently reproduced and recontextualized in Syro-Palestinian glyptic, where they can appear on griffins and sphinxes. The head appendages of the two Cretan owls could potentially be described as comparable to ram's horns, but they have a downward directionality and a heavily curvilinear form that is quite distinct.

It seems likely that somewhere in the ancestry of the MBA Cretan owl seals, someone was inspired by an imported rendering of a creature wearing an Egyptian-style headdress like the one we see on the Acemhöyük plaque and Syro-Palestinian seals (or by descriptions of such). Yet with the owls, there seem to be different creative dynamics at play. We saw above that the distinctive form of the owls of CMS II.5.311 (impressions) and CMS VI.130 (seal) likely would have been understood as incorporating features observed in species of biological owl encountered in Crete. Now we can further appreciate that those features of biological owls may have been recognized as resonant with the headgear worn by creatures observed in imported things. Not only do the head appendages of the engraved owls realize an integration of biologically attested features and an Egyptian-style horned crown, I believe they could also indicate creative mergings with other varieties of foreign headdress, which may have been encountered in some of the same or similar imported objects as those bearing the renderings of horned crowns. This could account, in part, for the distinctive formation of the owl's "horns."

Syro-Palestinian cylinder seals such as those discussed by Teissier, small and rich in imagery, are a very likely conduit through which iconographic motifs could reach Crete, including imagery of numerous fantastic creatures and attributes – indeed, Syrian cylinder seals of MBA date have been excavated on Crete (e.g., Siteia Museum 8540, from Protopalatial Tomb Λ at Mochlos). In addition to the types of "crown" discussed above, we also find sphinxes, in particular, wearing another type of headgear in Syro-Palestinian glyptic. This is clearly connected to the *nemes* or Egyptian wig known from Egyptian visual culture. These headdresses frame the face, wrapping around the sides of the cheeks downward to the shoulders. In their form and position, these headdresses are remarkably similar to the masses/appendages framing the faces of the Cretan owls in CMS II.5.311 and CMS VI.130. However, we typically see only a side view of the *nemes* or wig in Syro-Palestinian glyptic, when worn by sphinxes rendered in profile. The two owls of MBA Cretan glyptic, on the other hand, are distinguished by the striking forward gaze of their front-facing heads, even though their bodies are set in profile.

While at first the owl might seem out of place in this discussion, alongside griffins and sphinxes, its characteristic forward gaze brings into view further connections with motifs evidenced in MBA eastern Mediterranean visual culture. This includes a motif of Egyptian origin that frequently occurs in Syro-Palestinian glyptic in the company of sphinxes and griffins: the "Hathor Face."

4.16. Motifs from MBA Syro-Palestinian glyptic. Drawings from Teissier 1996, reproduced courtesy Orbis Biblicus et Orientalis. a. Teissier 1996: 82 no. 147; b. Teissier 1996: 87 no. 160; c. Teissier 1996: 85 no. 149; d. Teissier 1996: 85 no. 151; e. Teissier 1996: 85 no. 150

The Hathor Face is characteristically rendered front-facing in the seals, as it is in Egyptian material culture such as scarabs and sistra handles. The "Hathor wig" frames the Hathor Face (e.g., Figure 4.16c–e). This wig is formed of symmetrical rounded flanks that emerge from a central part at the top of the face, then swell and curve down around the cheeks, before narrowing and returning back, in smaller antithetic upward curves, at the shoulders (visible, e.g., on an Eighteenth Dynasty faience figurine, Figure 4.17). In Egyptian renderings, ears are often visible, either bovine or human, but in Syro-Palestinian manifestations, their presence is variable. The Hathor-style wig is also seen in MBA Anatolia, for example on zoomorphic ivory furniture supports (Figure 4.18) that likely stem from a palace context at Acemhöyük – the same site and period where the ivory box plaque engraved with a horned griffin was found.[113] The gazing eyes, in these instances inlaid, are a prominent feature of Hathor Faces. In their embodiment as furniture supports, these particular faces belong to full

4.17. Fertility figurine, ca. 1938–1630 BCE. Faience, 2 × 5 3/16 in. (5.1 × 13.1 cm). Brooklyn Museum, Charles Edwin Wilbour Fund, 44.226. Figure wears the Hathor wig. Creative Commons-BY (Photo: Brooklyn Museum, 44.226_SL1.jpg)

4.18. Furniture support: female sphinx with Hathor-style curls; MBA Anatolia, probably from Acemhöyük. Metropolitan Museum, NY, 32.161.47; gift of George D. Pratt, 1932. (CC0 1.0) www.metmuseum.org

bodies with leonine character, making them sphinxes. The Hathor wig also appears on certain Egyptian examples of sphinxes associated with royal women. Aruz notes that, moving forward, the Hathor-style wig/curls become integrated into standard Anatolian renderings of sphinxes, crossing gender lines to be part of both bearded and beardless faces.[114] She further highlights the prominent nose of the Acemhöyük furniture-support sphinxes, explaining that this feature becomes typical of Anatolian representations of human faces; we can also note the protruding nose visible on sphinxes engraved in profile in Syro-Palestinian glyptic, which can appear beak-like (e.g., Figure 4.16a–b).

On the Acemhöyük furniture supports, the gilded headdress worn by each sphinx is characterized by a central protrusion, just above the forehead. Its position as a central projection generally recalls what we see on the owls of Cretan glyptic objects CMS II.5.311 and CMS VI.130. Aruz tentatively connects this to the uraeus projection seen on royal Egyptian headdresses, including ones worn by some sphinxes in combination with the *nemes* headcloth or Hathor wig.[115] This feature indicates another way in which the formal identities of sphinxes and griffins were interconnected in the material and visual cultures of MBA Syro-Palestine and Anatolia and, perhaps through these channels, how they became entangled in Aegean animal fabrications. The uraeus appears as a projecting appendage or full-bodied snake atop the heads of numerous figures in MBA Syro-Palestinian glyptic (e.g., Figure 4.16a). Meanwhile, a single curling projection, curving upward or downward, can appear further back on the head of some sphinxes and griffins and perhaps developed from renderings of the uraeus.[116] We have seen similar curling projections in the impressions of the *vano* 25 deposit, at Phaistos, both on the griffin of CMS II.5.318, as well as the beaked humanoid figures of CMS II.5.323 (Figures 4.1b, 4.2k). The sphinx engraved on a green jasper *petschaft* seal, reportedly from Archanes, CMS VI.128 (Figure 4.19a), has a comparable hair formation, pulled into a stiff, low curl that swoops backward behind the head.

The Extraordinary Recontextualized

The Phaistian owl of CMS II.5.311 (impressions), and its counterpart in seal CMS VI.130, seem to draw on various iconographic attributes cultivated in the types of small-scale material culture we have been considering. The owls' distinctive head appendages, in conception remarkably like the Egyptian-type animal-horn crowns seen on sphinxes and griffins in Syro-Palestinian glyptic and the tiny Acemhöyük box plaque, at the same time clearly share the distinctive scrolled form of Hathor wigs seen in some of the same contexts,

4.19. Extraordinary creatures with prominent hair projections and/or a potent forward gaze in Protopalatial glyptic. a. Seal CMS VI.128 (engraved face and view of *petschaft* seal); b. Seal CMS VI.101a (modern impression and view of engraved face); c. Seal CMS III.105 (modern impression and engraved face). Images courtesy CMS, Heidelberg. Objects © Hellenic Ministry of Culture and Sports

as well as in small Egyptian objects such as scarabs and mirror handles.[117] The fact that within the extant Cretan glyptic corpus we have two strikingly similar, and strikingly peculiar, owls fitted with such head appendages suggests that they may belong to what was a larger corpus of similarly rendered figures. How were such features contextualized by Cretans – craftspersons and others – when they encountered them in the small surfaces of seals and impressions on the island? Were connections to foreign figures such as Hathor maintained on any level? There are indications that some elements of overseas cult came to Crete and the Aegean, including Hathor-related material. Sistra, instruments with connections to cultic practices surrounding the worship of Hathor in Egypt, have been recovered from various sites, including MBA Archanes and Hagios Charlambos; exquisite hand-shaped "clappers," another rhythmic instrument associated with Hathoric cult in Egypt, have also been excavated in Xeste 4, at LC I Akrotiri.[118] Meanwhile, the beaded object held by the "Necklace Swinger" in the fresco of Room 3 on the ground floor of Xeste 3 (just down the street from Xeste 4)[119] could be related to the menat, a dynamic object that was both instrument and item of adornment, which shared its name with Hathor and was associated with her cult.[120] Nevertheless, though notable, the evidence of such links remains relatively thin across the MM I–LM I southern Aegean, and, especially in certain cases, Egyptian forms have clearly been quite digested through local materials, practices and interests.[121] The musical implications of this material are enlightening. Mikrakis has discussed how the majority of musical instrument technologies that appear to have been shared from Egypt to the Aegean at this time were rhythmic and not melodic, which he argues supports seeing the "musical systems" of these two regions as having been "incompatible."[122] In terms of sound culture, we thus may also have evidence of both notable sharing and, simultaneously, significant divergence and reinvention between the Aegean and neighboring cultural spaces.

We cannot assume robust and widely held knowledge of foreign religious forms in the Cretan population through the evidence we currently have, as provocative as it may be. Weingarten's discussion of Cretan engagements with the figure of Egyptian Taweret is insightful here.[123] She notes that the evidence we have in Crete of foreign-made objects embodying the Egyptian demon are physically small and could have readily traveled with seafarers. These people may have been familiar with foreign popular religions active in the "liminal zones"[124] of ports and boundary locales of Egypt and the eastern Mediterranean; some Hathoric cults were associated with such spaces during the Middle and Late Bronze Ages.[125] Beyond the hands of such traveling persons, hence for much of the population of Crete and the south Aegean, the figural forms rendered in imported objects during the Middle to Late Bronze Age surely were culturally stimulating but would have been freshly cultivated in novel contexts. The resulting Cretan forms may have preserved some overseas associations, or developed novel ones, but these were part of new dynamic identities that, in turn, could have their own further impacts through intercultural exchange.

Looking Forward: Further Associations Come into View

Tracing particular formal similarities between renderings of creatures with head appendages has drawn the early Cretan griffins, and the owls of seal CMS VI.130 and seal impressions CMS II.5.311, into a field of extraordinary fabricated animals from across the broader eastern Mediterranean. Seals, small and easily transported, are a frequent medium in which such creatures are given form, and imported seals would have been a ready means by which their remarkable animalian bodies became known to Cretan persons across the sea. Moving forward, we can examine how a prominent forward gaze, often embodied in combination with head appendages, was also shared by a highly distinctive array of creatures within Crete and the Aegean and that here, too, seals and seal impressions appear to be primary media. With this, such creatures would have become distinguished by the peculiarities of Aegean glyptic objects.

Locking Eyes with Extraordinary Aegean Creatures Within the biological avian world, the flat-faced owl, known in several species in Crete, has an unusual capacity for a full-frontal gaze. The unique renderings of owls seen in Cretan glyptic objects CMS II.5.311 and CMS VI.130 indicate that these birds were being creatively related to and integrated with animalian forms encountered in material from overseas, including ones characterized by a forward stare, such as renderings of the Hathor Face and apotropaic animals. Such a potent gaze can carry specific cultural implications. As Morgan notes, in Egypt, front-facing figures are associated with music and birth, as is the case with renderings of Hathor or Bes, and in Mesopotamian imagery – especially in glyptic – a frontal gaze is largely reserved for certain extraordinary creatures, such as bull-men and naked heroes, or with phenomena related to birth.[126] Such intercultural associations may have powerfully informed the identities of these creatures in the Aegean, yet their forward gaze likely would have also held specific potency there. Morgan has compellingly associated a forward gaze in Aegean Bronze Age visual culture with a status of death or dying.[127] Aamodt has recently argued that frontal faces engraved in Mycenaean amulets were apotropaic, and it may be that such magical capacities, or others, were also associated with objects manifesting the gaze in earlier periods – an idea that is supported by Morgan's discussion.[128] This matter must remain open-ended but can be cautiously explored.

Within the Aegean, many discussions of the iconography of forward-gazing figures have focused on so-called "gorgons," "gorgoneia" or monsters. Most of these have humanoid facial features. Evans offered early consideration of such figures, and, in more recent years, scholars have updated the topic with fresh material, perspectives and interests.[129] Much newly excavated MBA evidence, the majority glyptic, has been drawn into the corpus, from sites including Malia and Petras. The frontal gaze is crucial to the identification of creatures in this category of beings. The characterization of the mouth is more variable but can take the distinctive form of a toothy grin or, in at least one case, a protruding tongue (in a carnelian four-sided prism seal from Petras, P.TSK05/322c;[130] this is comparable to a creature on a vessel from MBA Phylakopi).[131] In most cases, the MBA front-facing humanoid visages also have notable head appendages.[132] Typically, these emerge outward in opposite directions and then curl upward. Such curving side appendages are often accompanied by short upright projections along the top of the head; in some cases, only one or the other is rendered (e.g., P.TSK05/322c from Petras and CMS III.105, a *petschaft* from Knossos; Figure 4.19c). Taken together, these elements of the humanoid figures are much like the headgear from Egyptian and southwest Asian iconographies that we have been considering, as well as the Aegean comparanda. On a small four-sided prism from "central Crete" discussed by Evans (CMS VI.101a; Figure 4.19b), what appears to be hair, given its multistrand nature, is formed into two impressive symmetrical masses framing the side of the humanoid head. The effect is highly comparable to that of the Hathor wig, which, we have seen, was often rendered as part of a disembodied frontal face (the "Hathor Face"; Evans made precisely this connection).[133] The masses of hair projecting from these faces also resemble what is seen on sphinxes – another fabricated creature typically possessing a humanoid head (CMS VI.128,[134] Figure 4.19a) – although these beasts are usually rendered in profile.[135] In other examples of the humanoid front-facing figures, the head appendages are slenderer undulating projections that can appear similar to the horns of solar crowns, or to the appendages of the owls in CMS II.5.311 and seal CMS VI.130; these comparisons are yet stronger when shorter, centrally positioned spikes are combined with long head appendages on the humanoid faces (e.g., Petras P.TSK05/261a,[136] CMS VI.101a from central Crete and Malia CMS III.237b (Figures 4.19b, 4.20). In some cases, a second set of long side projections issues from lower on the head/neck (cf. the lower curls of a mane or beard on the stone relief inlay in the form of a sphinx, from Malia).[137] Ears are usually present on these humanoid heads and often dramatically protrude, to the extent that they can appear as appendages in their own right; in some cases they are elaborated with earrings. We can compare the presence of ears to Egyptian renderings of Hathor Faces. On CMS III.237b (Figure 4.20), reportedly from Malia, each ear seems to take the form of a figure-8 shield, a distinctly Aegean object type first attested at this time. Figure-8 shields were defensive items that also held symbolic associations. The shield's incorporation into the body of this humanoid figure would

4.20. Humanoid face with prominent head projections, ears and a potent forward gaze, engraved in a MM prism seal reportedly from Malia, CMS III.237b. a. Drawing of motif; b. Engraved seal face; c. Modern impression. Images courtesy CMS, Heidelberg. Object © Hellenic Ministry of Culture and Sports

stand as a realization of formal assonance (between the bilobed shapes of the shield and human ear) and could contribute to the object's potency as an apotropaic device, if indeed the frontward gaze was associated with such properties.

Many of the figures we are dealing with in this front-facing corpus are constituted by heads without bodies, but there are some notable exceptions. At Petras, along with several contemporaneous seals engraved with front-facing (bodiless) heads, there is also a striking full-bodied, front-facing dwarfish figure rendered on P.TSK05/261a, an agate rectangular bar seal.[138] The figure appears comparable to the protective Egyptian household demon Bes, or his female counterpart Beset, both of whom, like Taweret, were associated with the protection of pregnant and birthing women in Egypt (e.g., on a apotropaic wands).[139] As Weingarten discusses, renderings of Taweret were making their way to Crete during the MBA and, already by then, Taweret's form was being cultivated into the figure of the "Minoan genius."[140] In the context of discussing the full-frontal figure of the Petras seal and its possible association with Bes or Beset, both Weingarten and Krzyszkowska (in separate studies) cite several further examples of MM imagery involving full-bodied front-facing humanoid figures.[141] Within this group, a remarkable steatite three-sided prism seal from Malia, published by Anastasiadou and Pomadère,[142] is engraved with a deeply squatting female form distinguished by full breasts, open mouth, and arms that are bent and raised; ears protrude from the sides of the head and spikey projections arise atop it. As Weingarten describes, this figure appears to be in a birthing position, and it could be that this Cretan seal perpetuates aspects of the protective role held by embodiments of Bes and/or Beset.[143]

Many of the provenanced renderings of front-facing humanoid figures from MBA Crete stem from sites in the north and east of the island;[144] most of these are embodied in glyptic objects. As was discussed in Chapter 3, it has been argued that distinct sociocultural regions were active at this time between eastern and central Crete. Anastasiadou compellingly argues that such is observable in the glyptic evidence. Schoep paints a similar picture through an argument based in various forms of material culture, drawing prominently on evidence of scripts and sealing technologies.[145] It has also been suggested that we cannot rule out the possibility that different linguistic cultures were in play, perhaps corresponding to the densities of divergent scripts observable between these regions.[146] The seals engraved with the front-facing heads are caught up in this discussion, because they are elements of the very glyptic and script traditions that have been drawn on as evidence of regionalism and, as such, can hint at further distinctive dimensions of cultural life in northern Crete, including, perhaps, elements of interregional sharing between the eastern and central zones.

Many of the MBA seals engraved with front-facing humanoid heads also carry Cretan Hieroglyphic signs. Cretan Hieroglyphic is a script primarily associated with eastern Crete that, nevertheless, is significantly attested in the so-called Hieroglyphic Deposit at Knossos in north-central Crete, which contained documents and impressed sealings.[147] Anastasiadou suggests this deposit may have resulted from the presence of easterners at Knossos at some point.[148] Cretan Hieroglyphic inscriptions occur in a majority of MBA prismatic seals, most of which stem from eastern Crete. Moreover, among glyptic, most Cretan Hieroglyphic inscriptions are in prisms seals.[149] Anastasiadou notes that, beyond inscriptions, humanoid and hybrid animal figures often occur on these prisms; likewise, Weingarten has observed that the front-facing humanoid heads or gorgons seem to have a strong relationship with prism seals frequently produced in eastern Crete, especially the four-sided type.[150] It may be that the humanoid figures embodied on these prism seals were embedded in traditional beliefs and practices within the region, perhaps as magical figures. The fact that comparable manifestations occur between multiple sites suggests not only that the figures had some cultural consistency throughout this region, but also that this type of hardstone prism seal, and its particular qualities and affordances, was effectively *part of* the identity of the humanoid figures and their involvement in sociocultural activities. The role of Cretan Hieroglyphic script itself is directly relevant here, especially in its presence as a material-visual component of seals.[151] Cretan Hieroglyphic can be copresent with a front-facing humanoid face on a prism seal (e.g., CMS III.237b, reportedly from Malia). Meanwhile, cats with an intense forward gaze appear on numerous MBA prism seals and sometimes appear as a disembodied head that may serve as a sign within Cretan Hieroglyphic inscriptions (e.g., prism seals CMS IV.156b or CMS II.2.316d; Figure 4.21a and c).[152] The interaction between script and animalian body can be complicated in other ways, too. Of note here is a carnelian prism reportedly from the Lasithi (northeast Crete), engraved with a frontward-gazing full-bodied cat as well as Cretan Hieroglyphic signs that surround the cat (CMS VI.93, Figure 4.21b).[153] The cat has the same distinctive twisted posture as the owls of CMS II.5.311 and CMS VI.130. Centered directly above the cat's head, between the ears, is CHIC 031, a sign in the form of a tripartite branch on which each projection ends in a small lobe. Although this sign is part of an inscription, the positioning of the tripartite form simultaneously gives the visual effect that the animal is topped with a three-pronged head appendage – a situation with many contemporaneous iconographic parallels in the Aegean and overseas, as we have seen. The question of whether biological cats were present on Crete in the Bronze Age is still open-ended,[154] but whether it was an exotic or familiar species in the flesh, the cat's embodiment as a forward-gazing creature in the prisms connected it to other distinctive and potent animals. Through such objects, animals with a penetrating gaze set in stone seals likely became a familiar phenomenon in eastern and perhaps northern Crete during the MBA. Their efficacies, as tools and creatures that were perhaps accorded magical potency, would have been experienced in various arenas of social action in the regions.

Scales of Contextualization in a Northeastern Cretan Community

The density of objects from eastern and northern Crete embodying forward-gazing figures with head appendages may indicate that traditions surrounding such creatures had particular character and time-depth in those regions. Local communities may have had their own connections with such phenomena as well, based on distinctive things and practices. Regional and local connections certainly need not have been mutually exclusive with one another – or with more broadly held Cretan and southern Aegean ideas surrounding such figures. Instead, these scales of contextualization could have coexisted (perhaps combining or even contradicting) and brought significant complexity to people's engagements with the penetrating stare of remarkable animalian bodies.

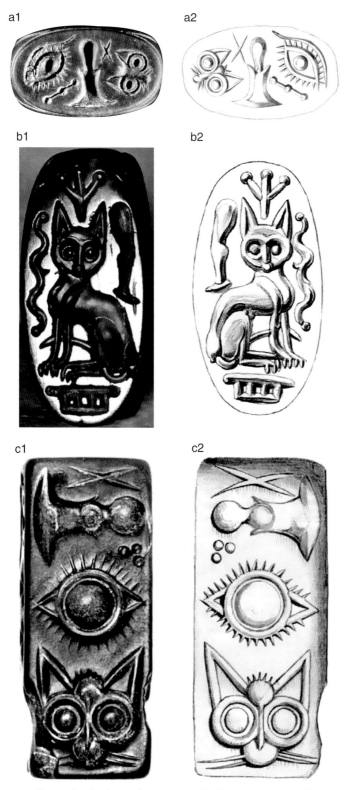

4.21. Protopalatial prism seals engraved with front-facing cats and Cretan Hieroglyphic signs. a. CMS IV.156b; b. CMS VI.93a; c. CMS II.2.316d. Drawings of motifs on right, photographs of engraved seal faces on left. Images courtesy CMS, Heidelberg. Objects © Hellenic Ministry of Culture and Sports

To gain more of a sense of such dynamics, we can now briefly return to the small MM II *petschaft* seal from Mochlos mentioned previously (p. 212), which is engraved with the head of a peculiar front-facing humanoid figure, seemingly with raised arms (CMS II.2.251; Figure 4.22). We have seen that this face has three projections extending from the top of its head: two longer curving appendages that flank a shorter one topped with a slight lobe. Together, these projections constitute a tripartite head feature notably similar to some we have considered on creatures in Egyptian and southwest Asian material culture as well as on relatable Aegean animalian figures. Meanwhile, we can now appreciate that the front-facing directionality of this creature from Mochlos likewise finds strong connections with various remarkable animals embodied contemporaneously in the Aegean, including other humanoid figures in glyptic from eastern Crete. Various authors discussing Aegean front-facedness and gorgoneia have included the figure of the Mochlos *petschaft*.[155] Glyptic objects are primary media for both foreign and intra-Aegean comparanda, along with other types of small movable object, all of which are easy to imagine within scenarios of importation and sharing at different scales.

Mochlos, situated along the northeastern coast of Crete, is a site rich with evidence of cultural interaction during the Bronze Age. Evidence recovered from the site indicates that the town was well established within networks of overseas and domestic exchange. Notable finds from the Neopalatial period include an ivory pyxis carved with detailed imagery of a scene of presentation or epiphany, which contained eighty beads crafted of overseas materials, including lapis lazuli.[156] Also remarkable from Neopalatial levels is a copper-alloy sistrum that constitutes a link (direct or indirect) to Egyptian ritual practices.[157] Among the MBA evidence from the site is a Syrian cylinder seal engraved with a religious presentation scene that was deposited in Tomb Λ not long after its crafting overseas during the later nineteenth to eighteenth century BCE, suggesting that interactions between Mochlos and people or places across the eastern Mediterranean were not infrequent at this time (Siteia Museum 8540).[158] Evidence of overseas connections is especially rich for the EBA, which led Branigan to argue that Mochlos was a "gateway" community during the period.[159] Certain house tombs at the site contained significant numbers of ivory objects, such as plaques and inlays, as well as silverwork and beads. An EBA silver cylinder seal of Syrian manufacture stands as a clear instance of a small finished object that made its way across the sea to Mochlos, in the company of various other types of material.[160] Significant amounts of goldwork, including jewelry, have been recovered from Prepalatial graves at the site.[161] Colburn's examination has indicated that Egypt was the source of much of the gold found in Prepalatial Cretan contexts, including that from Mochlos, although she argues that it likely reached Crete via the Levant, potentially through Byblos.[162] In addition to the raw material itself (which would have traveled as dust, nuggets or sheet), certain techniques evidenced in the Prepalatial goldwork from Mochlos, and some of the objects into which the gold was formed, also have connections overseas.[163]

Prominent within the corpus are a number of diadems – objects of adornment consisting of a band element that would wrap around the wearer's head. Metal diadems are evidenced throughout the eastern Mediterranean in this period, from Anatolia and Syria to Mesopotamia and Egypt, and their use at Mochlos may have had an aura of exoticism or even carried specific overseas associations.[164] Diadems have also been discovered at sites across Prepalatial Crete and the Cyclades. In Crete, extant examples are all rendered in gold, while silver is typical of those of Cycladic manufacture.[165] Despite their presence as a class of object represented across Crete, according to Hickman's study, an exceptional density stems from Mochlos (35 percent of the entire known Cretan corpus), and the examples from the site are unique for the frequency of "pins and accessories" added to the diadems, including upright attachments.[166] Upright attachments of various types are evidenced, including stemmed flowers and leaves rendered in gold, as well as "antennae" crafted of strips of sheet gold attached to the top edge of the band, which are known solely from Mochlos.[167] Some of these antennae were pierced along their tops as well (as on the Dog Diadem), and Hickman has explored the possibility that these were attached – perhaps sewn – to another material, so that the diadem would effectively become part of a larger headgear (also involving a substance such as cloth), serving as its headband and dramatic supports.[168] In other cases, the antennae seem to have been attached at their bases to the band of the diadem and to have risen as freestanding elements.[169] On the Agrimi Diadem, such antennae rise from the front of the diadem at three slotted points, each instance effectively consisting of an overlapping pair of flat strips (Figure 4.23).[170] The end of each antenna is shaped into a pointed terminus, and each is decorated with lines of repoussé dots that coalesce into the shape of a horned animal as they near the tip. The diadem's headband itself, which was intentionally cut before deposition, is also elaborated with the forms of three horned animals rendered in dot repoussé, thus creating thematic and formal cohesion across the composite object.[171]

Hickman's careful analyses have identified considerable evidence of wear on the diadems and other jewelry from the site. Through the reassembled components of the remarkably well-preserved Agrimi Diadem in particular, we get a vivid sense of how a diadem with such impressive appendages would have appeared rising from the top of a person's head during social rituals in the community, perhaps over generations of use. Discovery of numerous other such antennae at Mochlos, now separated from bands, indicates that we are glimpsing only a small fraction of the original corpus of such diadems that were in use in this community; as Hickman states, "so many extant antennae, recovered from several different contexts, would indicate that headdresses decorated with gold bands and upright extensions may have been a tradition at EM Mochlos."[172]

Various scholars have connected the Prepalatial diadems to later evidence of impressive headgear in the Aegean and to representations of Aegean people abroad. Colburn likens the Early Minoan diadems to headgear with upright projections worn by Cretan persons depicted in paintings within the Tomb of Rekhmire in Thebes, Egypt (Eighteenth Dynasty, New Kingdom or LBA). Hickman draws on a wealth of material, from the Prepalatial through the Postpalatial periods, in her contextualization of Early Minoan gold jewelry, including numerous headbands and headdresses that she generally relates to the diadems.[173] In this context, she refers to Davaras' comparison of the Mochlos Agrimi Diadem, with its three antennae, to the headdress seen on the Postpalatial "Poppy Goddess" from Gazi (LM III). The Gazi figure is one of a class of large clay sculptural objects, each rendered in the form of a stylized, almost tectonic woman with arms raised upward, wearing an elaborate headdress and a wheel-made cylindrical skirt. The Poppy Goddess' distinct headgear consists of a band fitted with three upright appendages, the central one lower than the other two, each topped with poppy-shaped finials. Citing the similarities between this headgear and the form of the Agrimi Diadem, Davaras asserted that the Mochlos diadem was a "prototype" for headdresses crafted subsequently in Crete.[174] The similarity of the tripartite designs of the two headgears is indeed notable. I think that the figure engraved in the Mochlos *petschaft* seal (Figure 4.22), from the same site and a more proximate time period, stands as an even-stronger comparandum for the Mochlos diadems. On the *petschaft*, too, we see a figure with prominent forward gaze and three

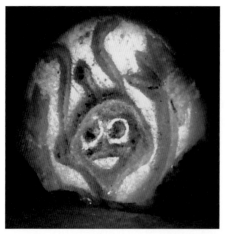

4.22. Forward-facing figure with upraised arms and prominent tripartite head appendages, engraved in a *petschaft* seal from Mochlos (CMS II.2.251). Photograph of seal face. Image courtesy CMS, Heidelberg. Object © Hellenic Ministry of Culture and Sports

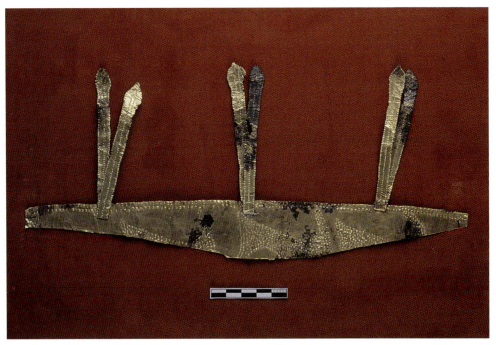

4.23. Gold Agrimi Diadem from Mochlos, Crete, Agios Nikoloas Museum, 4314. Photographed for Jane Hickman by Chronis Papnikolopoulos, INSTAPEC. Courtesy Jane Hickman. Object © Hellenic Ministry of Culture and Sport

head appendages; interestingly, the gesture of upraised arms is also present here, as on the Poppy Goddess.[175]

If indeed there was a tradition of diadems with dramatic upright appendages at Mochlos during the Prepalatial period, such impressive material components of social ritual could have remained "familiar"[176] in the cultural memory of the community into the Protopalatial period (or much longer). Through association with active human bodies, these objects would have been remarkably vibrant and animated elements of cultural life. Simandiraki-Grimshaw and Stevens have powerfully considered how a human's wearing of the Dog Diadem would constitute a type of "hybridity" born of the "*combination of animal ornament and human body*," as the gold dogs are set in motion by the human's movements and the human body becomes "a place where the dogs are animate."[177] The agrimi of the Agrimi Diadem could also be seen in this light. Yet we can also recognize another type of dynamic bringing-together at play in the wearing of a diadem, between human and vibrant thing, which could bring fresh cultural identity to the figure.[178] As the diadems were worn, they would have effectively become combined with the human faces of their wearers, and with the forward gaze of the eyes positioned just below the shimmering gold band. That the human's forward gaze was drawn together with the diadems is made clear in the Eye Diadem, also from Mochlos, on which two large, unblinking eyes have been rendered directly into the diadem's gold band in dot repoussé. The figure of a plumed, gazing head of a diadem wearer, in which aspects of the object and the human were effectively integrated, could have been a lasting cultural form for this community. Some of the diadems themselves, or pieces of them,[179] may have even remained in circulation as heirlooms or have been reintroduced as remarkable finds made in the landscape (e.g., if discovered in an old tomb).

Given this sociocultural background, a figure with head appendages and a forward stare likely would have carried very particular associations within the Mochlos community. These may have been linked to the rituals in which diadem-clad figures were involved (e.g., religious, social, magical, funerary or political actions), or with other aspects of the community's past and present (e.g., if diadems became linked to particular social units, authority figures or historical events). Such highly local possibilities would in no way preclude other associations with front-facing figures and head appendages also being active at Mochlos concurrently. We have seen that creatures possessing front-facedness and head appendages, often together, had rich webs of associations within the broader eastern Mediterranean and also within the MBA southern Aegean;[180] the area of northeast Crete may have had a nested tradition connected to humanoid faces with these attributes, including those embodied in stone seals, including prisms. People at Mochlos likely would have shared in the associations active across these different sociogeographic scales, with varying emphases, even if figures possessing these features also held meanings that arose from community-specific life in the town. Moreover, some of the Mochlos diadems were decorated with the forms of other animals (e.g., agrimia and dogs). These figural elaborations of the diadems realized further animalian associations with head-appendage-bedecked human faces at Mochlos but also afforded further interconnections with other Cretan communities where renderings of the same species were present.[181]

As we query the identity and positioning of fabricated creatures in Cretan culture during the MBA, and especially those creatures that integrate attributes (also) found in multiple other types of animal (what, in some cases, have been called "composites"), the case of the figure engraved on the Mochlos *petschaft* seal is instructive. People's experiences of such creatures took place in the midst of various coexistent meshes of cultural associations. These associations, concurrently active at different scales, drew links to other types of creature that possessed similar attributes. Our discussion has attempted to trace out some of these particular webs of association, including those that extended across the eastern Mediterranean, or throughout the southern Aegean, as well as those that were concentrated within regional and local spheres. These, together, were part of the distinctive ecologies in which these peculiar embodiments of animals gained physical and sociocultural substance.

AEGEAN CREATURELY CONNECTIONS: BEYOND "COMPOSITES" AND TOWARD INTEGRATION AND AFFORDANCE

A particular group of creatures embodied within Cretan and southern Aegean material culture of the MBA has come into focus. These creatures possess and sometimes unite certain distinctive bodily qualities, notably head appendages and a forward gaze. Engagements with iconographic material with overseas heredities constitute a noteworthy element in the background of this web of Aegean fabricated animals. Among them are griffins and other creatures traditionally described as composite beings. Our discussion has demonstrated that we cannot take such figures for granted as mergings of bodily pieces borrowed from other species and that, in Bronze Age Crete and the southern Aegean, they seem to have existed in a much more complicated and creative ecology of animals and things. Some of these remarkable creatures may not have been considered any more or less imaginary than biologically "real" but directly unknown living species like the lion or perhaps the cat; some may have been perceived as dynamic beasts, relatable to various species. There is little to indicate that their integrity as coherent animalian wholes was in question. What instead draws them together formally are distinctive attributes and attitudes and their integrative nature.

While many of the Cretan creatures we have considered have rich connections to renderings of fantastic animals from overseas, few appear as neat adoptions from foreign menageries. These creatures instead were creative realizations of connections – connections that could find similarities between species, between media and across the living/nonliving divide. With this, these animals seem to participate in a distinctly integrative creativity involving animalian forms that is evidenced more broadly in Crete and areas of the southern Aegean during the Bronze Age. This integration characteristically embraces the physical/material dimensions of animalian objects and suggests that they were taken together with the representational aspects of the things to particularize the animals. In other words, it is not enough to say that these objects were "carriers" of imagery or attributes of animals; they were embodiments of animals – animals that took form through the particular nature of the objects, as real material things, with distinguishing affordances. The particular group of extraordinary beasts that we have recognized in this chapter were marked out by certain unique qualities, but they nevertheless exhibit the same intuitively integrative dynamics evidenced more broadly in Aegean animalian material culture. With this, their embodiments realize assonance between different forms, thus giving rise to newness. In this light, we can return to certain ideas with which we opened the chapter.

We have seen that Wengrow's discussion of composite creatures works with the notion that they are keenly impactful in part because they are "minimally counter-intuitive" while still possessing basic attributes that allow them to be considered as coherent animalian entities. He argues that the effect of the counterintuitiveness was to draw and hold attention, to excite and perhaps bewilder a beholder with a sense of the unfamiliar and unprecedented. For Wengrow, this effect is one reason why composite creatures were associated with early urban societies in the Bronze Age Near East and eastern Mediterranean and with the increased foreign contact that they experienced. Wengrow is drawing on an established line of scholarship with his assertion about composites' counterintuitive character. Knappett echoes ideas concerning the counterintuitiveness of composites within his examination of "combination" in the Aegean Bronze Age.[182] In the course of this discussion, Knappett highlights Anastasiadou's recent study of composite creatures from the glyptic material discovered by Hogarth's team at LM I Kato Zakros in eastern Crete.[183] Her work is indeed important to draw into this discussion. As Anastasiadou argues, the Kato Zakros-style creatures are an exceptional corpus of composite entities within the known Cretan material. As such, the logic of combinability that they embody stands as a crucial intra-Aegean counterpoint to the integrative dynamics we see in other renderings of animalian bodies from the island during the Bronze Age, including extraordinary creatures that are typically described as composite creatures, such as the griffin. Considering this exceptional group from Zakros helps us to better grasp how the Aegean material we have been discussing differs from the counterintuitive dynamics that can characterize composite entities.

The 550 stamped-clay nodules recovered from House A at Kato Zakros are exceptionally rich in imagery of composite beings and stand as an important repertoire in the Bronze Age Aegean. The nodules preserve impressions made by 257 different seal faces and, of these, Anastasiadou classifies 96 as composites.[184] She recognizes in the glyptic material from Zakros a class of composite creature that differs from what is seen more broadly in Crete contemporaneously; she calls these "Zakros Type" composites. Anastasiadou handles this complex material with subtlety. In her study, she raises a point very similar to Wengrow's concerning the cohesion of the bodily components of a composite entity, yet also addresses apparent variation in this matter and how such variation impacts the status of a composite in complex ways. Anastasiadou divides the Zakros Type composites into two principal subgroups, which consist of "organic" and "inorganic" combinations. The first group she describes as beings in which the "constituent parts fuse together to a form which has the character of a clear organic unit."[185] While she does not draw on the same cognitive and cultural studies referred to by Wengrow, Anastasiadou's characterization of this subgroup of composites makes a very similar point – that (some) composites can be recognized as coherent wholes, despite their combination of parts stemming from different species, because they adhere to certain fundamental characteristics of living things. While she sees these organic composites as being defined by the combinations they embody, they are nevertheless imaginable as workable wholes. We can tentatively describe this situation in another way as well: that their status as compilations of isolated parts is somewhat complicated or obscured by their practical cohesion, as a single entity. Anastasiadou's study of the Zakros glyptic material also identifies another, "inorganic" status within the corpus. In this second grouping, the distinct bodily elements brought together do not convincingly cohere and their status as a compilation of dissimilar parts is acutely apparent; these are "mainly put together by a combination of limbs and edges of creatures, namely heads, arms, legs, tails, wings, and breasts, unconnected to a body to which they could be attributed and which would bring them together as parts of a unified whole."[186] Anastasiadou in fact asserts that it is possible to see a yet further level of differentiation within this "inorganic" subgroup, "on the grounds of the degree of cohesion" a composite possesses.[187] She sees only some of the composites from this "inorganic" group as possessing the requisite elements and cohesion to be defined as "creatures."[188]

For Anastasiadou, these composite entities from Zakros were studies in "interchangeability." It does indeed seem that the variable permutation of attributes was involved in the production of the motifs (see Figure 4.24). Anastasiadou connects this back to Hogarth's notion that manipulating the combination of parts from one composite to another was utilized as a means for generating differentiable seal motifs (as discussed above, p. 168).[189] This interchangeability also would have impacted how people at Zakros experienced and related the composite entities, potentially increasing the number of links made between rendered composites while also obstructing the settling of a given composite's identity. McGowan contends that some formally ambiguous motifs, including ones that seem to combine disjointed bodily elements, such as these, demand being read not in isolation, but as "multivalent" participants in "networks" of imagery between objects, through formal similarities (her compelling observations are discussed further in Chapter 5, in relation to my notion of "formal assonance").[190] This reading underscores how such composites presented distinctive combinatory dynamics.

What is especially important for our discussion is that Anastasiadou describes the formulation of composite entities evidenced *across* her broad Zakros Type group – thus encompassing both the inorganic and organic subgroupings – as being distinct from other Cretan Bronze Age composite or hybrid beings. This relates directly to their unique combinatory status:

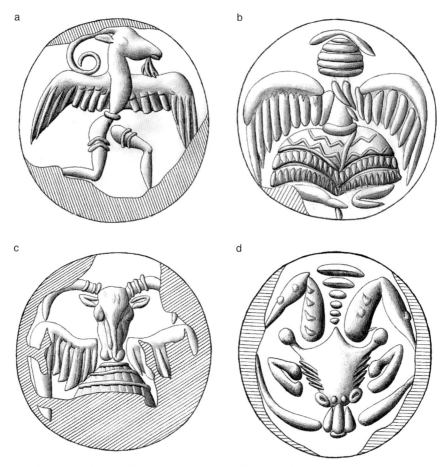

4.24. Examples of remarkable composite creatures from the glyptic of LM I Kato Zakros. a. CMS II.7.140; b. CMS II.7.129; c. CMS II.7.177; d. CMS II.7.194a . Drawings of motifs courtesy CMS, Heidelberg

> The iconographical building blocks [of the Zakros composite entities] could thus be imagined as pieces of a puzzle which can be combined interchangeably and in any combination in order for different images to be created. . . . The Kato Zakros creatures are distinct from other neopalatial composite creatures in that they lack a standard nature.[191]

The main distinction for Anastasiadou revolves around frequency – repetition of particular combinations is very rare in the Zakros material, which she contrasts with other "standard composite creatures" of Crete, whose relative consistency suggests to Anastasiadou that, "their form was impressed in the cognition of society as that of an animal seen in everyday life."[192] Working with Simandiraki-Grimshaw's discussion of hybridity, Wolf makes an observation that can also be drawn in here. She points to the long-standing nature of the conjoinings manifest in creatures like the griffin, versus the "flexibility" inherent in heterosomatic hybrids, and suggests that the former "might have been preferable to communicate qualities such as durability and stability."[193] In this respect, too, we have reason to see some "hybrids" as being met as established presences. Through careful contextualizations undertaken in this chapter, we have examined how, beyond the Zakros "puzzle pieces," it is not only that Cretan creatures commonly identified as "composites" can exhibit standardizing consistency across their embodiments, but also, and more fundamentally, that the nature of their formation indicates a recognition and generation of *likeness* between animalian entities, and an *integration* of animalian forms, versus being a matter of additive combination.

Our discussion has moved beyond the category of composite beasts to recognize a web of remarkable fabricated animals related to one another by distinctive formal and thingly qualities. As we have seen, renderings of these animals, ranging from dashing griffins to staring felines, and from wild-eyed "gorgons" to owls with curving head appendages, are better described as being *similar to* a range of other contemporaneous creatures, both biological and crafted. These remarkable creatures themselves were embodied as things and should also be understood in terms of the unique positions in which they existed as material culture. As Wengrow has noted, seals seem to have been a crucial element of intercultural interaction in the Bronze Age,[194] along with other movable objects that could readily make the passage across the eastern Mediterranean, and between Aegean communities, such as ivory attachments and perhaps textiles. Embodied as seals and impressions, many of the remarkable Cretan and Aegean creatures do indeed have an intimate historical and material association with "technologies of early urbanism" in the region (seals and script), as Wengrow argues. Yet in the Aegean context, it is less convincing to see that relationship in terms of modularity and to understand the distinctive efficacy of the creatures as arising from an existence as jarring combinations. Instead, we have shifted our approach to take seriously how these creatures – sharing not only certain corporeal qualities but also, in many cases, the substances and affordances of glyptic – would have been characterized by a distinctive potency and productiveness that had both physical and socio-cultural dimensions. These distinctive thingly creatures may have shared a status as magical entities and brought this to their common role as active participants in contexts of administration, resource management and communication, as components of sealing systems that were formalizing in their nature during the Protopalatial period; we have seen that script was also part of this. As Simandiraki-Grimshaw eloquently writes, sealings impressed with engraved-seal imagery of composite creatures would have "created 'positive' from 'negative' hybrids"; with this, such creatures became deeply immersed in channels and materials of interaction.[195] Certain aspects of Wengrow's "protective mode" regarding the transfer and function of composite creaturely forms could relate to these practices, even if the ideas concerning the combinatory status of the animalian forms, and the social implications of such, would need to alter for the Aegean situation.

These remarkable creatures were not embodied solely within glyptic objects in the Aegean – our discussion has considered renderings in other MBA media and, during the early Neopalatial period, such creatures become vibrant elements of wall painting in particular. Yet some of the distinctive potency of the creatures, which surely was associated with them even when they were embodied in other media, likely took root in their early associations with MBA glyptic. With this, they existed as integrative beings that could cross boundaries of the local and foreign, of the scriptural and nonscriptural, of the animate and inanimate, and of the old and novel. Yet, even for the so-called composite creatures of the group, there is little to indicate that they would have been experienced as possessing power as combinations of disparate parts. Instead, their animalian figures creatively embodied similarities to other beasts while also establishing their own creaturely identities. Recognizing this opens the door for approaching their participation in the experiences of Cretan persons and communities in a fresh light.

Our work in this chapter has been to substantively rethink the nature of what have traditionally been identified as composite animalian entities in Bronze Age Crete and areas of the southern Aegean, and to draw to the fore a new appreciation of what distinguishes them, instead, as members of a diverse but interconnected host of extraordinary creatures. The aim was not to be exhaustive, but to dig deep for new ground concerning the beasts in question and their relations. This has involved careful explorations of material from beyond the region. In the next chapter, we turn the tables. Here, we will identify a group of three distinctly Aegean animalian things that have *not* commonly been described as composite entities, but which, I argue, were peculiar embodiments of Aegean integrative creativity that likely *were* valued and even celebrated for the syntheses they explicitly manifested. These entities – the boar's tusk helmet, oxhide shield and ikrion – each prominently incorporated an element of a nonhuman animal's body into their defining form, but, therein, they combined it with equally defining human and thingly dimensions.[196] Their identity as charged sociocultural entities arose equally from each of these three components, announcing their combination with one another while denying their distillation. With this, the helmets, shields and ikria did not break from the integrative dynamics that we have identified in other contemporaneous animalian things in the Aegean – we will see at work in these three entities the same fundaments of *fluid incorporation*, *formal comparability* and *creative realization of likeness* that we have also recognized in other crafted animalian entities, and we will again consider how the distinction between objects and animals was blurred or even dissolved. But in this particular group of objects, the dynamics of integration are realized in intense and particular coalescences that appear more self-consciously mediated in their drawing together of phenomena.

NOTES

1. For a brilliant recent study of the frescoes in the Throne Room at Knossos, see Galanakis, Tsitsa, and Günkel-Maschek 2017.
2. For example, Hogarth 1902; Frankfort 1936; Dessenne 1957a, 1957b; Bisi 1965; Crowley 1989, 1995; Poursat 1973, 1976; Gill 1963, 1964; Weingarten 1985, 1991, 2013; Morgan 1988, 2010; Marinatos 1993; Zouzoula 2007; Blakolmer 2015, 2016a; Anastasiadou 2016a; Shank 2018; Knappett 2020; also now contributions to the 2021 volume in the Aegaeum 45, *ZOIA* (Laffineur and Palaima 2021).
3. Simandiraki-Grimshaw 2010b fruitfully develops the ideas of various scholars, including Meskell and Joyce 2003, to consider the distinctive material of Bronze Age Crete.
4. Wengrow 2011, 2013.
5. Wengrow 2013: 110.
6. Wengrow 2013: 68–70.
7. Wengrow 2013: 110.
8. Wengrow 2013: 106–107.
9. See especially Wengrow 2013: 59–67.
10. For example, Wengrow 2013: 92–93.
11. Knappett 2020, esp. 100–117, 186–202.
12. Knappett 2020: 186–203.
13. Knappett 2020: 186–203.
14. For example, Weingarten 1992.
15. See, for example, Hallam and Ingold 2007; also Anderson 2016 concerning Bronze Age Crete.
16. See, for example, Spivey 1997.
17. Such variability has been examined regarding representations of the centaur, despite subsequent tightening up of its identity (Scobie 1978).
18. Colburn 2008.
19. Feldman (2006) problematizes the existence of an "international koine" in elite material/ visual culture of the broader eastern Mediterranean and Near East during the LBA.
20. See, for example, classic work of Helms (1988) and Colburn's (2008) excellent engagement concerning the Aegean.
21. Gell's views on the potentially mystifying effects of objects are relevant here (1998).
22. Wengrow 2013, Weingarten 1991; 2015; also Gill 1964.
23. See Blakolmer 2015.
24. See Morgan 1988: 45.
25. Relevant here is Feldman's incisive consideration (2006) of hybridity, including hybrid beings, as embodied in an elite class of eastern Mediterranean/Near Eastern LBA material culture. Feldman explores the inability to designate specific (cultural, platial) identities for these remarkable things. "Hybrid" beasts often appear in imagery on the objects and they, too, embody a melding that defies simple attribution and classification.
26. Wengrow 2013: 68–73; Anderson 2016 concerning Crete.
27. Hogarth 1902.
28. Evans 1921: 702.
29. Anastasiadou 2016a, with extensive references and discussion.
30. This is important in Wengrow's study; he engages with the ideas of, e.g., Arnheim, Boyer, Descola, Sperber and Hirschfield (Wengrow 2013: esp. ch. 2).
31. Compare Anastasiadou 2016a
32. Wengrow 2013: 27–28, 110.

33. Wengrow 2013: 24.

34. Simandiraki-Grimshaw 2010b.

35. Boyer 1994.

36. See Wengrow's engagement with Boyer's work (2013: 22–23).

37. This is true of Wengrow's different "modes of transmission and reception" (2013: 90–107).

38. For example, Wengrow 2013: 90–94, 106–107.

39. Simandiraki-Grimshaw 2010b.

40. Knappett 2020: 99–100, 128.

41. For example, Evans 1928; Frankfort 1936; Kantor 1947, Dessenne 1957b, Bisi 1965, Morgan 1998, Crowley 1989, Marinatos 1993; Shank 2018.

42. The state of the preserved clay impressions of CMS II.5.319 are somewhat problematic, hindering analysis of details (and making it hard to assess possible divergences apparent between them). Nevertheless, I was able to discern the fundamental formation of the head as described here through microscopic analysis of casts held at the CMS in Heidelberg.

43. The seals that were stamped in the sealings of the *vano* 25 deposit may have been engraved locally or elsewhere. Likewise, we are not certain of where precisely the acts of stamping took place. Their gathering in the same microcontext, however, constitutes a material, social and spatiotemporal simultaneity in which all shared status and location. In this context (and perhaps in prior actions), the motifs could have been compared. For a path-breaking study of the sealing system at Phaistos, see Weingarten 1986. Krzyszkowska (2005) provides an excellent recent discussion and overview.

44. The recumbent posture, while less remarkable, also has numerous parallels within the *vano* 25 corpus.

45. Simandiraki-Grimshaw includes these figures in her discussion of Minoan homosomatic hybrids (2010b: 95, citing Weingarten 1983: 91, 1991: 168).

46. Simandiraki-Grimshaw and Stevens 2012.

47. Knappett 2020: 23, discussing contributions of "developmental approaches" in archaeology.

48. Anderson 2015, 2016, 2019.

49. Neopalatial renderings of griffins in the presence of other figures indicate a wide range of relative sizes for the creature. In the north wall of room 3a, in Xeste 3, for example, the rearing griffin is considerably smaller than the seated woman (perhaps a goddess). Within the same scene, this griffin has height similar to both the blue monkey and the girl pouring crocus flowers. In glyptic, the griffin can appear comparably sized to lions (e.g., CMS II.3.167), boars (e.g., CMS II.3.25a) and humans (CMS II.3.328); or smaller than a goat (CMS II.7.95) and lion (e.g., CMS II.6.103); or larger than a lion (CMS II.4.73). On potential loss of relative scale between subjects *within* MBA seal motifs, see Anastasiadou's insightful observations (2016b: 162).

50. See Chapter 3 and Anderson 2016. The *vano* 25 deposit contained a sealing stamped by a Prepalatial seal engraved with lions, indicating knowledge of earlier forms.

51. See recent biography of the Aegean griffin by Shank (2018). While Shank focuses on the Aegean's iconographical "adoption" of the griffin from the Near East, and also the Aegean griffin's influence back upon the eastern Mediterranean (e.g., in the paintings of Tell el-Dab'a), my primary focus is instead on the life of the Aegean griffin within the Aegean ecology of animals (fabricated and biological). This includes careful consideration of the types of material culture from overseas that likely contributed to how people contextualized the beasts in the Aegean, but my aim is not to examine the full spectrum of foreign renderings (something that Shank does expertly).

52. See Evans 1921: 709, 709–712. See also Knappett's (2020) consideration of griffins; Aruz 2008c.

53. Evans 1921

54. Aruz 2008c: 138.

55. Evans 1921: 710–711, following F. L. Griffith's identification as a "sparrow-hawk."

56. Aruz 2008c: 138.
57. Xirouchakis, Anastasiou and Andreou 2001: 184. Once common in Greece's continental massifs and all mountains of Crete, it is now nearly extinct in the mainland. Crete remains the only area of Greece where the Bearded Vulture population is still active but greatly reduced.
58. Two large birds with features of raptors are present in the worked surface of the Zakros Sanctuary Rhyton (Herakleion Museum AE-2764).
59. Pers. comm., Klaus Robin.
60. Pers. comm., Klaus Robin.
61. Theories range from an antimicrobial function to a mating show. See, for example, Saha 2015.
62. The Bearded Vulture is one of the only (if not the only) animal known to subsist almost entirely on bones.
63. Houston and Copsey 1994: 75.
64. Saha 2015; more information on the species at https://4vultures.org/vultures/bearded-vulture/.
65. Report of the Natural History Museum of Crete, republished at www.explorecrete.com/nature/gypaetus.html.
66. Runwal 2020, Saha 2015.
67. Blumstein 1990.
68. The agrimi is a type of goat "unique" to Crete. Agrimia live in the wild but have been identified as feral descendants of early domesticated goats brought to the island; see Bar-Gal, Smith, Tchernov et al. 2002.
69. Cf. Shank 2018.
70. For example, CMS II.5.283, CMS II.8.319, CMS II.6.106, CMS II.6.20.
71. Younger places its manufacture in MM III Crete (2012: 750).
72. See also, for example, signet ring CMS V.S1B.137, from a LH II context at Kalamata in the Peloponnese, and a "Cypro-Aegean" cylinder seal, CMS II.3.199, from Astritsi on Crete.
73. Morgan 1989: 148–149.
74. See Vlachopoulos' excellent discussions of these objects (2013, 2015).
75. Vlachopoulos 2015: 42.
76. Nikolakopoulou 2018: 202 fig. 6.
77. Hood 2005: 75–76. The head appendages of the griffins of the MC II Griffin Pithos are also relatable to that of the Minoan genius in seal impression CMS II.5.322, also from the MM II *vano* 25 deposit at Phaistos.
78. Doumas 1992: 158–159 fig. 122, 165 fig. 128.
79. Edgar 1904: pl. XIV, fig. 4.35. Interestingly, a vessel painted with small, striding griffins was found within the same House deposit at Phylakopi.
80. Immerwahr 1990: 32–34; Walberg 1987 on Kamares ware.
81. Gates (2004) discusses the development of pictorial wall painting in Bronze Age Crete as an element of political change (focusing on Knossos). Crowley (2020) offers another perspective that also sees glyptic as fundamental to iconographic developments in other media.
82. Vlachopoulos 2015.
83. Teissier 1996: 87 and no. 164. See Teissier's Seal Register and Illustrations List for bibliographic details for all objects in her catalog (1996: 197–208).
84. Evans 1930: 495–518, figs. 342a, 342b, 345, 348a, 348b, 350a, 350b, 351–3, 354a, 354b, 355–359, pls. XL, XLI, as cited in Hood 2005: 75–76 fig. 2.26.
85. On the relief stuccos, see esp. Blakolmer 2018; von Rüden and Skowronek 2018; and Chapter 6.
86. Hood (2005: 76) asserts that the relief fragments from above the North–South Corridor, including the griffins, could date to a predestruction moment in MM IIIB; Immerwahr

dates them broadly to MM IIIB–LM IB, noting they are from the early phase of stucco relief paintings at Knossos (1990: 52–3, 85, 90).

87. On the paintings of Xeste 3, see Doumas 1992: 127–175; for griffin of Room 3a (first floor), north wall: 130–131, figs. 122, 123–128.

88. There are also later examples, for example, CMS I.128 (LH II–IIIA1).

89. The fresco from the Cult Center at Mycenae (Mylonas 1966: 167) has variably been interpreted as depicting a woman holding a living griffin or an effigy of one, or as a sculptural group of human and beast (Morgan 2005: 169–170, with refs.).

90. Underlying specific characterizations/accounts, a broader association may have linked various fantastic creatures and femaleness in the Aegean. Like griffins, Tawaret (connected to maternity in Egypt) and the Minoan genius can also be rendered with pendant breasts/teats (see Weingarten 1991).

91. AM 1910.282

92. This slight asymmetry appears due to the craftsperson having shifted the positioning of the left horn upward, and then running out of space.

93. Aruz 2008c: 138.

94. Colburn (2011) makes the case for much of the gold from Prepalatial Cretan contexts having originated in Egypt but having made its way to the island via Syro-Palestine, likely through Byblos. See also Krzyszkowska's discussion ivory's likely path to Crete (e.g., 1988); also Phillips 2008.

95. Aruz 2008a.

96. Weingarten 1991; Colburn 2008; Feldman 2014, 2018; Wengrow 2013; Anderson forthcoming, among many others who explore such in the context of particular material.

97. Teissier 1996: 80, 88, 90.

98. Teissier 1996: 88, 90. Beyond glyptic, Teissier comments on the pairing of sphinx and griffin in the Investiture wall painting within the eighteenth-century BCE palace of Zimri-Lim in Syria. On this, see also Shank 2018.

99. Although in Crete, the bodily relation of lion and human can be different, often involving less physical contact; see Chapter 3.

100. Teissier 1996: 89–90, figs. 2b, 166.

101. Teissier 1996: 47, in defining her use of the terms "Egyptian" and "Egyptianizing" in discussion of Syro-Palestinian glyptic imagery.

102. Kantor 1956: 153–154. See also Teissier 1996: xii.

103. See Teissier 1996: xii, 39–46, 88–90.

104. As a few examples, see Warren 1969; Foster 1976, 2008; Weingarten 1991, 1992; Bevan 2007; Aruz 2008a, Phillips 2008; Soles 2011; Mikrakis 2011; Watrous 2021.

105. For example, Merrillees 2003; Koehl 2008.

106. For a relevant text from Mari, see Strange 1980, 90–91, text no. 33.

107. Koehl suggests that exported Cretan metalwork and ceramics may have been destined for different social classes abroad – metalwork for elites and ceramics for a "middle class" (2008).

108. Colburn 2011.

109. See Broodbank's pioneering study of Cycladic seafaring (2000).

110. The sea could also *connect*; see Cline 1994, Panagiotopoulos 2011.

111. See Foster 1999 on the case of moving animals.

112. See Wiener 1987.

113. Met Museum nos. 32.161.46, 32.161.47, 36.70.1, 36.70.8.

114. Aruz 2008b: 83–84.

115. Aruz 2008b: 83.

116. For example, Teissier 1996: nos. 152, 153.

117. Teissier 1996: 185 for discussion and references.

118. For discussion and bibliography of these objects, see Mikrakis 2011, Soles 2011.

119. Mikrakis sees possible links between activities in Xeste 3 and Xeste 4 (2011: 59–60).

120. The emphasis on women/girls in the paintings of Xeste 3 (leading some to see it as a venue of female rites of passage) provides an intriguing context in which to see hints of a relationship to Hathoric cult, with its emphasis on female reproductive life. For now, however, the evidence of connections remains speculative.

121. For example, Mikrakis (2011) considers the Akrotiri clappers, especially no. 8585, an Aegean redesign of an object type also known in Egypt.

122. Mikrakis 2011: 6.

123. Weingarten 1991.

124. In discussion of occurrences of hybridity, Simandiraki-Grimshaw (2010b: 102) considers its involvement in "harbors and administrative centers" that "often serve as liminal zones of commerce, culture, society, art and corporeality."

125. Teissier 1996: 182–185.

126. Morgan 1995a: 136–137.

127. Morgan 1995a.

128. Morgan 1995a: 13; Aamodt 2021. But see apt cautions of Krzyszkowska (2016).

129. For example, Morgan 1995a; Weingarten 2013, 2015; Krzyszkowska 2016; Lazarou 2019.

130. Krzyszkowska 2016.

131. See, for example, rich discussions in Weingarten 1985 (e.g., 174–176 re: gorgoneia); Krzyszkowska 2016, esp. 118. For the Petras seal: Krzyszkowska 2012, 2016 (pl. xivd); comparandum from Phylakopi: Edgar 1904: pl. XIV, fig. 4.35, no. 3.

132. Simandiraki-Grimshaw suggests that the head-appendages, or "streamers" that appear from some gorgons' heads "may be interpreted as antennae or snake hair," thus connecting them to her discussion of "homosomatic hybrids." In this context, she refers also to a "goddess" figure rendered in profile on a Protopalatial vessel from Phaistos, which she suggests might also be wearing an oxhide skirt, thereby enriching the figure's multispecies character (Simandiraki-Grimshaw 2010b: 96–97, fig. 34a, referencing Weingarten's treatment of this figure (incl. 1985: 178–9, fig. 34l).

133. Evans 1930: 419–420.

134. AM 1938.93.

135. A large-scale steatite headdress element discovered in the Drain Shaft at Knossos could embody just this component of a sculptural sphinx's body. Knappett incorporates this piece into his discussion of "combining" (2020: 103–104).

136. Krzyszkowska 2016: xlva.

137. Various scholars date the attachment's deposition at Malia to the fifteenth century, in part through other material in the deposit, including LM IB Marine Style pottery. Stylistically, it compares to sphinxes evidenced already in MK Egypt: Michaelidis 1995 with bibliography, Poursat 2022.

138. Krzyszkowska 2012, 2016.

139. For example, Met 30.8.218 (Middle Kingdom wand). Cretan craftspersons were drawing upon front-facing renderings of both Bes and Beset (perhaps without marking a distinction in identity), which changed over time. See Krzyszkowska 2016, esp. 119–120, who cites MBA Anatolian and Levantine material; Weingarten 2013, 2015.

140. See Weingarten 1991, 2013. The Minoan genius is itself a fluid creature in the Aegean. It appears within the MM II *vano* 25 deposit at Phaistos, in impressions of two different seals (CMS ii.5.321 and CMS ii.5.322); see also Blakolmer 2015.

141. See Weingarten 2015, Krzyszkowska 2016. In discussion of Cretan MBA front-facing figures (and other imagery) and the "monsters" embodied in Neopalatial glyptic at Kato Zakros, Weingarten also notes several MBA renderings of figures with front-facing bodies and averted faces (1985: 174–176, e.g., CMS ii.2.127).

142. Anastasiadou and Pomadère 2011: fig. 4.

143. See Weingarten 2015, esp. 190–192, who reads this figure's upraised arms as a "warding-off gesture." Simandiraki-Grimshaw raises important questions about gender and Minoan

"hybrid" creatures, which she takes to include some "gorgons" (Simandiraki-Grimshaw 2010b).

144. Compare observations by Weingarten 1985: 168, 170, 174, and Krzyszkowska 2016: 120.

145. Schoep 1999, also 2002.

146. Duhoux 1998: 25.

147. See Chapter 3.

148. Anastasiadou 2016b: 185.

149. Anastasiadou 2016b: 166 n. 51.

150. Anastasiadou 2016b: 165. Weingarten 1985: 174.

151. This topic is the focus of a longer study by the author, in preparation.

152. Jasink 2009; Krzyszkowska 2015; Ferrara, Weingarten and Cadogan 2016; Shapland 2022: 192–194 with references.

153. See excellent discussion of this seal in Ferrara, Weingarten and Cadogan 2016.

154. Moody 2012: 241, 247; Shapland 2022: 193–4.

155. For example, Weingarten 1985, 2015; Morgan 1995a; Krzyszkowska 2016, Lazarou 2019.

156. See Soles 2016.

157. See Soles 2011 and further references above.

158. Davaras and Soles 1995.

159. Branigan 1991.

160. Hickman (2008: 70–74) provides further discussion and references. On the seal, see Aruz 1984 with bibliography.

161. Davaras 1975 and Hickman's extensive study of Prepalatial gold jewelry with close analysis of material from Mochlos (2008).

162. Colburn 2011; also Hickman 2008: 89–97.

163. Colburn 2008, 2011; Hickman 2008: esp. 103–131, 238–309.

164. See Davaras 1975, Hickman 2008: 238–297, Colburn 2008: 215–217.

165. Hickman 2008: 97–98.

166. Hickman 2008: 139–143 for distribution in Crete and the Aegean.

167. Hickman 2008: 215. For initial description of such attachments as "antenna-like," see Davaras 1975: 104.

168. Hickman 2008: 131, 142, 205–6 and ch. 9.

169. As on the Agrimi Diadem; also seems to be the case for other diadems inferred through extant "antennae"; see Hickman 2008: 204–206 citing Davaras 1975:109–110. On the Agrimi Diadem from Mochlos, see also de Checchi 2006.

170. The Agrimi Diadem (HNM 4313) was discovered in a deconstructed/folded state in a silver cup that also contained other gold material; see Davaras 1975: 102–104; Hickman 2008: 204–205, pl. 24.

171. Hickman 2008: 204–205, Colburn 2008: 215.

172. Hickman 2008: 206.

173. Hickman 2008: 174–179; amongst the Prepalatial objects considered are the "anthropomorphic" vessels from Myrtos, Koumasa and Mochlos (see Chapter 1).

174. See Hickman 2008: 178–179, who engages with Davaras' discussion (Davaras 1975: 112).

175. Weingarten (2015) argues that this gesture is protective, while others have associated it with a divine status (e.g., Anastasiadou and Pomadère 2011).

176. Hickman 2008: 166.

177. Simandiraki-Grimshaw and Stevens 2012: 598–599.

178. Although the Prepalatial diadems and antennae were not rendered of an animal-derived substance, nor were all of them elaborated with animal forms (as were, e.g., the Agrimi Diadem and Dog Diadem), the underlying dynamic of an object and human body being momentarily joined that I discuss here can be compared in some respects to the powerful notion of "homosomatic hybrids" discussed by Simandiraki-Grimshaw (2010b).

179. Some of the Mochlos diadems, including the Agrimi Diadem, show evidence of being intentionally torn or cut; removal of antennae is sometimes apparent (Hickman 2008: 204–205, 212–214 and catalog entries).

180. Hickman (2008: 159) considers the widespread apotropaic role of eyes in discussion of those occurring on the Eye Diadem.

181. For example, the figure of a dog forms a handle on two nearly identical pyxis lids, from Mochlos (HM 1282) and Zakros (HM 2719), as well as on a contemporaneous and very similar marble lid from Aplomata, Naxos (Warren 1969: 82, 182–183; Bevan 2007: 86–87).

182. Knappett 2020, esp. 98–100, 108.

183. Anastasiadou 2016a; Hogarth 1900/1901, 1902.

184. Anastasiadou 2016a: 77–78.

185. Anastasiadou 2016a: 80.

186. Anastasiadou 2016a: 81.

187. Anastasiadou 2016a: 81.

188. Anastasiadou 2016a: esp. 82.

189. Anastasiadou 2016a: 83.

190. McGowan 2011, 2018.

191. Anastasiadou 2016a: 82.

192. Anastasiadou 2016a: 82.

193. Wolf 2020: 59, drawing on ideas of Simandiraki-Grimshaw 2010b.

194. Wengrow 2013: 62.

195. Simandiraki-Grimshaw 2010b: 99.

196. An alternate view, powerfully offered by Simandiraki-Grimshaw (2010b), that objects like boar's tusk helmets and hide garments could form *part of* "heterosomatic composites" when joined with wearers, is engaged with in Chapter 5.

FIVE

SINGULAR, SERIATED, SIMILAR

Helmets, Shields and Ikria as Intuitive Animalian Things

IN WHAT FOLLOWS, I ATTEMPT TO CARVE OUT A SPACE FOR WHAT could be thought of as a uniquely Aegean variety of animalian composite entity, with a focus on evidence from Crete and Thera. With this, I identify three entities that embody a particular coalescent nature: boar's tusk helmets, oxhide shields and ikria.[1] These objects share the more widely evidenced integrative dynamics that characterize many renderings of animalian bodies in the region, but they stand as more explicitly combinatory things, which distinguishes their identities. My discussion involves three fundamental contentions and areas of problematization, considered in tandem as I proceed:

1. The first is to recognize that these combinatory entities are drawing together in their singular figures elements of not only different animalian species, including the human, but also, and with equal significance, particular types of object; this renders them highly dynamic incorporations of human and nonhuman components. Furthermore, their dynamism as boundary-blurring combinatory entities arises both from their status as unique material things and through the prominent human experiences with biological nonhuman animals involved in their coming-into-being.[2]

2. In keeping with the fundamental nature of fabricated animals that we have been exploring more broadly in the Aegean material, I advocate here for embracing renderings in representational media as *equally real* embodiments of these animalian composite entities, with their own physical/material

properties and affordances. Dynamics of isolation and repetition, formal assonance, and spatial complexity are especially rich in their representational embodiments, which are often rendered in series.

3. I argue that these composite entities are highly *intuitive* in the drawing-together that they embody. I consider this on dual levels: in terms of the combined internal components of each composite entity, and concerning the external relationships (formal and cultural) that the entities find with other things, including with each other.

As I discuss these matters in relation to boar's tusk helmets, oxhide figure-8 shields and ikria, I stress how each of their embodiments are themselves creative spaces, in which intuitive links are actively generated through recognition, cultivation and relation of inherent characteristics. A problematization of boar's tusk helmets serves as the initial basis of this discussion, to which the situations of oxhide figure-8 shields and ikria are related.

VIBRANT ROOTS AND WEIGHTY BIOGRAPHIES

The Aegean boar's tusk helmet has been a focus of much strong scholarship (Figure 5.1).[3] Morris has offered an incisive examination of the biographical complexity of the helmet, focusing on the Mycenaean era. By problematizing

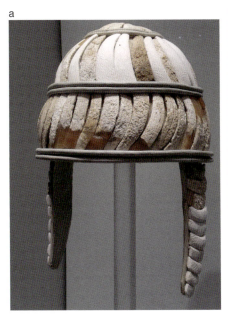

5.1. Aegean Bronze Age boar's tusk helmets, reconstructed from excavated remains. a. Herakleion Museum O-E175, from Knossos, Zafer Papoura, LM II; photograph by Eunostos (CC BY-SA 4.0); b. National Archaeological Museum, Athens 6568, from Mycenae, Chamber Tomb 515; photograph by Jebulon (CC0 1.0). Objects © Hellenic Ministry of Culture and Sports

5.2. Examples of swine in Aegean Bronze Age glyptic. a. CMS v.S1B.60; b. CMS II.294; c. CMS II.2.213. Drawings of motifs courtesy CMS, Heidelberg

a helmet's coming-into-being, she draws attention to the way in which its ongoing object-life integrates not only activities of war but also, and first, of hunting (Figure 5.2).[4] Morris argues that the skills acquired and honed during the pursuit and killing of boars, in which tusks for helmets were obtained, may have been framed as preparatory for combat undertaken with other humans and contends that boar hunting and warring may have been explicitly linked to one another through rites of passage.[5] In this light, the helmet emerges as a weighty testament to the person's process of maturation: the tusks required for the crafting of a complete helmet necessitated some thirty to forty successful kills,[6] and the finished object that emerged from this gradual accumulation of experience and material was a conspicuous, practical and traditional accoutrement of the warrior. Morris also points to images of hunters wearing the helmets, which indicate how the donning of this headgear, and representations of it, may have further blurred the boundary between hunt and battle – and between hunter and warrior – in Aegean Bronze Age society.[7] In Chapter 3, we saw that within LB I–II Aegean visual culture, the helmet became a prominent adornment of persons engaged in combat, with both animals (e.g., a lion or boar) and other humans. The helmet's presence provides a direct link between both scenarios, indicating not only a possible biographical connection between the status of hunter and warrior, but also comparability in the human and nonhuman opponents. We can imagine that this exchangeability (and relatability) between possible opponents may have been active in similar scenes within oral narrative as well, with spoken voices enacting similar indications of the entanglement of hunting and warring, animals and beasts. Traditional activities like those discussed by Morris may have figured in such scenes.

Although she does not draw on the terms of Peircean semiotics, Morris' reading poses the helmet as both an index and a symbol. As an index, the helmet, fashioned of tusks, signifies the boar and the hunt, as a part born directly of them; with this, the helmet is also metonymic. This observation of the helmet's status corresponds with Shapland's rich discussions of "traces" in Aegean imagery of animals.[8] Morris' study ultimately is focused on the boar's tusk helmet as a *symbol*, which she describes as a "multi-referential" signifier that can "condense" complex meaning in its sometimes simple form.[9] In this role, Morris explores how the boar's tusk helmet may have carried specific semantic content. Her discussion here takes a crucial step, which I will return to below, by likening the boar's tusk helmet to the oxhide figure-8 shield. Making this link, she draws on various scholarly discussions of the symbolism of the figure-8 shield, a distinctly Aegean form itself.[10] She refers to Mylonas' notion that the shield was an "emblem"[11] for the Minoan warrior goddess (to whom hunted animals were offered) but turns with more interest to Marinatos' argument that the shield, as an icon, was "the most important of a series of symbols referring to sacrifice."[12] Morris rightfully sees the boar's tusk helmet as sharing much with the shield, from their origins with animals and practical roles as objects of defense to their symbolic meanings. Concerning the last, her discussion draws in the work of Morgan, noting how both she and Marinatos have emphasized the central role of animals in Aegean symbolic systems (Blakolmer's valuable study should now be added here).[13] Morgan's discussion of how Aegean iconography of animals serves both to associate them with humans and, moreover, to ultimately draw their power into that of the human is closely related to Morris' fundamental message concerning the symbolic dimensions at stake with helmets, and at one point Morris refers to "animal dynamism" specifically.[14] Simandiraki-Grimshaw has further developed these ideas in her incisive discussion of Minoan hybridity. Here, she considers the relationship of a human wearing a boar's tusk helmet (and other types of animalian object, including ones made of hide) as being a temporary union – a "heterosomatic hybrid" – in which the body of the human is temporarily joined with the swine-toothed helmet to form an interspecific figure. More generally, Morris aligns with other authors by drawing attention to the rich parallels that are sometimes drawn between humans and animals, as is notably the case in the lion-hunt dagger from Grave IV at Mycenae, which images both lions and humans in comparable roles and, on one side, positions them in the situation of an armored hunt. The dagger becomes a pivot point for Morris as she asserts that the rich symbolism associated with figural imagery – "iconographic images" – should be extended to objects; in her words, "if an image can be used to express parallels or relationships between man and animal, why not an object?"[15]

I certainly agree with Morris that the material dynamics of an object can convey rich meaning (something that Morgan and Marinatos also recognize implicitly in their discussion of the dagger) and would add that objects can actively *create* meaning, associations and vibrant sociocultural experiences, in concert with their environments (which could include other living and nonliving things). But I would also stress that images are never just images, somehow alone; they are always themselves things, with distinct materialities, so this division of image and object should collapse. I wish to explore this further and, ultimately, will turn to examining *representations* of the helmets and shields (as well as ikria) in order to recognize greater depth in the material and spatial character of the representations and to think about them beyond symbolism.

DEFYING BOUNDARIES: THE SLIPPERY REALITIES OF SWINE

Morris' insightful association of the helmet and shield draws attention to the fact that each of these objects has, at its core, elements of the body of an animal and, with that, an event that engaged humans with the animal. For her, these "animal origins" of the substances – tusks from boars and hides from cattle – are the key to the symbolism of the objects: "in both cases the activity which provides the raw material is that most strongly associated with the given animal," which she sees as sacrifice in the case of the hides/shields/cattle and hunting in the case of the tusks/helmets/boars.[16] Her recognition of the dynamic existence of these objects provides for a deeper sense of their socio-cultural identities in the Aegean.

Morris is surely correct in her contention that the helmet was a locus of traditional symbolic signification connected to its ritualized mediation of multiple arenas of meaning and activity. Yet I think on the rich ground of her discussion, we can move beyond the question of what the helmets and shields conventionally signified to instead consider how they were experienced, and the deep dynamism of interconnections that experience afforded. The boar's tusk helmet – as well as oxhide shields and ikria – has complex essences that equally incorporate, and rise above, discrete categories of the nonhuman, human and thing. This complexity involves the simultaneity of their matter and form (the former born of a nonhuman animal, the latter articulated in response to the human figure), as well as the crosstemporal and crossspatial mesh of bodies, environments, actions and associations of which their biographies are elements – as body becomes thing and thing conforms to body. Moreover, it embraces the rich spectrum of their manifestations, not only as practical objects, as Morris emphasizes, but also as representational things, in ways that deserve closer examination.

We need to consider how people would have known the nonhuman animals embodied in the objects. Relations with biological cattle were considered in Chapter 2; here, I will focus on swine as part of a close examination of the boar's tusk helmet.[17] From an archaeozoological perspective, distinguishing between wild and domesticated swine, both of which are identifiable as *Sus scrofa*,[18] is extremely problematic. Consequently, researchers have had to develop classification schemes that recognize a diversity of "intermediary" stages for which the binary of wild-versus-domesticated, often employed in archaeological studies, simply does not provide.[19] Recent genetic studies indicate that movements from wild toward domesticated swine did not occur in a single monumental step but instead played out multiple times, at different scales, over the past several millennia, a situation that underscores the complex fluidity of these animals across classifications. Studies indicate that the pig was first domesticated in the Near East and reached Europe via Anatolia with early agriculturists ca. 8000 BP. There, it met and bred with the larger wild Eurasian boar, and a genetic "turnover" toward the Eurasian profile occurred over the course of the next 3,000 years, with the eventual loss of the Near Eastern ancestry (ca. 5900 BP).[20] Islands in the Mediterranean, including Aegean islands such as Crete, seem to have held onto elements of the Near Eastern domesticate's genetic profile longer than other areas in Europe, beyond the Neolithic (until ca. 3100 BP for Crete).[21] Eventually, the Eurasian profile became dominant in these island locales as well. Despite such genetic distinctions, swine encountered throughout Europe and the Mediterranean during the Bronze Age, including the eastern Mediterranean and Aegean, were characterized by a complex variability in their behavior, phenotypical attributes and environmental circumstances.

Based on her study of faunal evidence from Crete, Isaakidou discusses the difficulties in distinguishing between wild, domesticated and feral populations of swine in the record, given their strong physical similarities;[22] we can assume that some of this ambiguity between populations was experienced by persons interacting with the animals during the Bronze Age as well. For the mainland, populations of swine living in the wild would have been hunted and killed, likely as a prestige sport, a means to protect crops and a source of food.[23] At the same time, there is extensive evidence that pigs, with their highly comparable faunal profile, were kept as domesticated stock. Feral animals exist between these already close categories, as do captured wild animals. On Crete, *Sus scrofa* was introduced by humans.[24] While in some cases wild stock may have been brought to the island in order to be rewilded and hunted, Isaakidou emphasizes that feral populations stemming from domesticated sounders were likely to have occurred on Crete, both initially and over time, and that there may have been considerable interactions between kept and feral populations.[25] As Long notes, swine are distinguished by their apparent readiness to return to the context and behavior of an undomesticated life.[26] The physical profile of those swine that were (at least partially) domesticated may not have differed markedly from those that were not supported by humans, especially given that notable physical variation would be expected in both groups, with possible attributes overlapping with one another.[27] The presence of tusks is sometimes noted as an indication of a swine's wildness. Tusks, or long canine teeth, grow on all *Sus scrofa*, regardless of sex or sexual alteration. The canines of the lower jaw are longer and are continually sharpened and worn by the upper canines. On male swine, these lower canines continue to grow throughout the animal's life, while on female individuals, growth stops after three to four years.[28] The lower tusks can dramatically protrude and curve. Study of modern samples has demonstrated that wild swine tend to have longer and narrower teeth, but that there is considerable overlap in size across populations ranging from wild to domesticated.[29] Generally female individuals will have shorter canines than males within the same population, consistent with marked sexual dimorphism in the species. It is possible that tusks were trimmed or removed from some domesticated stock in order to deter injury from aggression between individuals or toward humans, as is often done today. At the same time, since tusks were a utilized resource, removal, if practiced, may not have occurred until the animals were older and the tusks longer.[30] This means that people likely would have experienced some domesticated swine as tusked, and these animals may have posed a similar threat to humans as tusked wild or feral swine. Moreover, farmed swine may have also included "captive wild" and "crossbred" animals, further confounding firm distinctions between the physical attributes of different populations. In some respects, the distinction between a domesticated and feral/wild swine is effectively a matter of time, with physical and behavioral adaptations occurring rather rapidly in either direction when the beast's living situation alters; this is especially marked in younger animals.[31]

Given the fluidity of swine's characteristics across domesticated and wild statuses, a primary point of variability in humans' appraisals of *Sus scrofa* could have arisen instead from the spaces and specific activities in which the animals were met. Yet even in this respect, we should expect categories to be blurred: contexts of encounter likewise would not have followed neat divisions between wild and domesticated spheres. Throughout the Aegean, feral and effectively wild boars likely were sought out by hunters in areas of relative wilderness, as is suggested by vegetation in some imagery, but the distances between these spaces and settlement zones would have varied. Feral populations recently derived from domesticated stock may have foraged close to agricultural areas[32] and could have been attacked by humans and dogs when they invaded fields;[33] wild swine also may have been met as interlopers in this way. Distinctions concerning the context of *Sus scrofa*'s interactions with humans become yet more complicated when we consider the likelihood of free-range farming. Given the low threat of predation on Crete, as an island with no large predators other than humans, Isaakidou has indicated that free-range keeping of animals was likely practiced there during the Bronze Age–a possibility that Shapland thoughtfully explores. This is especially likely with swine, and the situation could have contributed toward the large body size observed in Prepalatial and Neopalatial populations.[34] Successfully containing swine is notoriously difficult.[35] Meanwhile, the economic benefits of allowing the resourceful animals to forage food from a landscape are great. With this, the highly "opportunistic omnivores" attain sustenance on their own and can survive off of land ill-suited for other animals or agricultural purposes. With the possible benefits of free-range tending of swine, the practice may have also been active in areas of mainland Greece and other Aegean islands, as it was in parts of Europe and North America until the mid-twentieth century CE.[36] This practice will flex with different conditions, traditions, interests and accidents. In some cases, animals could be captured for a brief spate of containment and fattening prior to slaughter. On the other side, free-range animals could easily "go wild," becoming a fully feral population beyond the grasp of the farmer.[37]

CHALLENGING BEASTS, VARIED CONTEXTS, COMPLEX THINGS

The bodily and behavioral characteristics of swine challenge simple classification, as do the contexts of their encounters with humans. In Bronze Age Crete, the evasive identity of the animal may have contributed to its cultural standing. Certainly, it would seem that killing swine was a recognized and significant activity in the Aegean and that the helmet formed from the fruits of such events was rich as a trace of the challenging undertaking. Yet we cannot know if tusks used for helmets were restricted to those obtained during specific types of encounter, with a certain status of beast, within a particular type of location. Moreover, such factors may have varied over time and space. Morris' discussion of the terms for swine found in Linear B documents further highlights this challenge.[38] Considering the term *kapros* (PIG+KA), found in a tablet from Pylos recording offerings,[39] she hypothesizes that "one possibility" is that the affix KA- should not be taken to indicate male sex (hence "boar"), as it had been interpreted, but instead to qualify the animal as wild. She asserts this in part because swine clearly differentiated by the use of sexual determinatives appear in livestock tablets, without the KA affix; Morris takes these to be "domesticated pigs." Given the fluidity we have recognized in the status of swine, complicating binary classifications, the manner in which linguistic signifiers aligned with distinctions in people's assessments of and engagements with the animals is also necessarily complicated (even if such differences may have seemed clear enough in any given moment). Were swine indicated with *kapros* thought to have a distinct identity from other swine, and, if so, did that arise from perceived physical and/or behavioral distinctions, or differences in the contexts in which they were met or utilized? How did such distinctions in LB III potentially differ from earlier considerations of the beasts, in mainland Greece and elsewhere in the Aegean?

These uncertainties concerning terminology are part of a range of important questions that surround the matter of people's challenging encounters with *Sus scrofa* in the Bronze Age Aegean and their procurement of the tusks eventually used for helmets. Was grappling with and killing a swine who was kept free-range considered to be duly impressive to produce material for a helmet? What of spearing a feral animal that was foraging in agricultural fields? Were swine that were kept semiferal rounded up in seasonal events that also served as rites of passage?[40] Might some of the divergences in represented capturing/killing techniques – including use of different weapons and spearing methods, employment of chariots, the involvement of dogs and the use of nets – relate to differing sociocultural circumstances of encounter with swine that could result in acquisition of tusks?[41] In some cases, tusks stemming from encounters undertaken by various people (collectively or independently) may have been combined in a single helmet. Here, we should also consider whether tusks were sometimes retained after routine slaughter of swine kept by humans. Snyder and Andrikou have identified evidence of probable tusk-harvesting for helmet manufacture in a workshop context at LH IIIB Thebes (Room 2 in the northwest area of the Kadmeia), where multiple *Sus scrofa* mandibles were found.[42] Based on analyses of the faunal material, including evidence of modifications, Snyder and Andrikou believe that the mandibles had been stored before the tusks were removed for crafting into helmets and/or other objects, which was presumably carried out in an adjacent ivory-working space; the remaining mandibles were debris of this craftwork.[43] Moreover, given that excavated helmet tusk plaques can vary in size, it could be that sections of tusk removed during periodic trimming were also sometimes utilized, which would not require the beast's death; indeed, even full tusk removal above the gumline does not necessarily involve killing the animal.

These factors should remind us not only that the realities of procurement and processing of swine tusk were important phases in the biographies of the helmets, but also that these undertakings could involve diverse scenarios that would differently complicate the identities of the animals, tusks, helmets and associated actions. Morris, Rehak, Logue, Molloy, Shapland and others have stressed that divisions traditionally made in studies of the Aegean Bronze Age, between arenas of social action connected to hunting, combat and ritual, are often misleading or false; generally speaking, we have come to realize that projecting such partitions onto past societies is problematic.[44] The helmet, as Varvarighos argued long ago,[45] is a powerful practical object in its finished physical state and any attempt to understand its cultural significance must take that into account along with its symbolic dimensions. But we must also step back and consider how the fluid status of swine, and the variable ways in which their bodies afforded materials and experiences, would have brought both complexity and ambiguity to what the helmets were as sociocultural entities. Hence, we can follow Morris' important lead by further complicating the biographies of the helmets, but this should take us beyond the question of

MANY AT ONCE

The fluidity evident in the identity of *Sus scrofa* should be recognized as we turn to more fully consider the helmet fashioned of its teeth. People's experience of living swine as beasts that were somehow both (and neither) wild and domestic, fierce and maternal (CMS V.S1B.60; Figure 5.2a), proximate and from "out there" undoubtedly informed the animal's cultural status. It would have contributed to interest in the beast and fed people's desire to incorporate the animal into an impressive object of hunt and war. This cannot and should not be separated from the functional advantages of utilizing the strong tusks for defensive objects. These diverse dimensions would have been experienced at once.

At the same time, to state the obvious for reconsideration: a tusk is not a boar, and a helmet is not a tusk. Each of these entities, while intimately related to one another in their materiality and sociocultural identity, has its own distinct character and affordances. The tusk and swine are connected indexically and metonymically, and the helmet also has an indexical link first to the tusk and, through this trace, to the once living beast. But the helmet reworks, repositions and reformulates the trace (Figure 5.1). While the smooth plaques crafted of *Sus scrofa* tusk maintain some of the curved profile of the tooth, they change its dimensionality. Their repetitive arrangement, side-by-side in smooth registered series, introduces a new and rhythmic order to the material. With this, the many pieces joined together take on the rounded form of a single head – but not the head of the animal from which they originated; instead, they circumscribe the form of the human head. In this way the *human* animal is embodied in the helmet as well, not only as an actor in its vibrant biography, but in its defining physical essence.

The ontological status of the human component "within" the helmet is complex. In some senses, it is relatable to other discussions familiar to us in Aegean archaeology, such as the "presence" of the seal in a clay impression it has stamped, or the relationship of a plaster cast to its "parent" object in the round. In the way that they more premeditate than remember the form of the human head, the helmets share something with masks that have been formed in order to be able to fit a human face. From another perspective, discussions of the deep relationship connecting the bodies of armor and human warriors in Homeric and Archaic-Classical cultures are also relevant.[46] In each of these situations, we recognize that there is more at stake than signification or a correspondence of physical forms. There is something uncanny in the heavy void of an object that implies another particular entity; the one accounts for or, in a sense, "longs for" the other, while nevertheless being something separate.[47] The space left open in the one is simultaneously populated by the form (but not the substance) of the other – as a premeditation or recollection of it – so that there is a distinct presence in the absence. Foucault's rich but knotty notion of heterotopias is relevant here.[48] He describes these spaces as absolutely real but "absolutely different"; they are defined by their relationship to familiar or normal spaces, so for the heterotopia there is always a dependence on the presence of this other "site." The heterotopia, as a "counter-site," can invert this other real space/entity, but in that intimate relationship it is not a simple opposite or undoing of it. The heterotopic is real and exists alongside that which it can invert; and, as it implies this other, the heterotopia can also "represent" or "reflect" it.[49] We can see this, for example, in the impression that inverts the surface of the seal but in so doing shares form with it, so that it makes sense to us to say that both seal and impression embody the "same" motif or image (e.g., Figure 4.20, p. 224). In a similar way, the helmet implies the human head by displacing the heft from the head to its circumscription, manifest with its own substance; this is an inversion, but also an echo.[50] The void of the helmet, of course, can temporarily be occupied by a living (or dead) human's head, but the helmet itself possesses the greater permanence of its own form, which steadily, and in its very substance, persistently carries with it the implied presence of the human head. The relationship between the helmet and the head is active and tense; in Foucault's words, the one "exerts a sort of counteraction on the position" of the other,[51] and this persists even when no human wearer is present. For this reason, although I believe Simandiraki-Grimshaw is right to recognize the deep and potentially transformative link that would have occurred when a person donned a swine-toothed helmet,[52] I think that the helmet, *independently*, was a dynamic thing that transgressed and merged species and ontological categories – it itself was an Aegean composite entity.

The boar's tusk helmet, in its immediate physical existence, thus *incorporates*, in one, the corpora of two species, *Sus scrofa* and *Homo sapiens*. In this way, it is a dynamic composite entity. Yet the two species are not put at odds, there is no disjuncture being emphasized. Matter and form integrate the nonhuman and human, as the tusks of swine are melded into the shape of the human head. The contours of the hard, curved plaques are realigned, repeated, and in their recalibration take on the rounded form of the head of a person. This coming-together of the two species is formally and materially intuitive – curve becomes new curve as the pride of one animal's head becomes that of another's. It is also richly creative. Both species are visibly present in the object, but the helmet is not simply a means of their combination, nor a straightforward result of it. As a type of object with its own attributes and affordances, the helmet is an equally consequential third party to this composite entity. A helmet is a worn thing and is defensive in its physiognomy. The density of its construction is distinguishing, and, for this type of helmet, its flexibility is also notable. This arises from its distinctive registered construction, in which the plaques are positioned in alternating rising rows set in leather, cloth, or metal, creating a dome. The upwardly tapering form rises to a summit, but, in many cases, the helmets also have extensions from their base – cheek protectors (sometimes plaqued) that descend like muttonchops from the main body of the helmet to cover the sides of the wearer's face (neck protectors also appear, especially in later Mycenaean examples). The boar's tusk helmet regularly appears crowned with a knob, which can be the base for a crest/plume, protruding from its highest point. This knob was likely formed as the leather or fabric lining of the helmet was gathered together at the top of its dome; this feature persists in later bronze conical helmets, recalling the earlier organic helmet type.[53]

As a specific type of object, the helmet brings distinctive characteristics to its composition with human and porcine physical attributes. In addition to these direct contributions, the helmet also draws in its own array of relationships and similarities with other entities. Helmets appear not only in the context of hunt and war, but also sport. Logue, following Lorimer, has argued that this link in the corporeal paraphernalia of athletes and warriors/hunters in the Bronze Age Aegean was part of a complex relationship between these types of action.[54] Other types of Aegean helmet, beyond the boar's tusk variety, seem to have had a similar registered design, consisting of stacked rows. These were likely constructed of leather bands, and, at times, metal attachments seem to have been added.[55] These objects are readily comparable not only in their roles and affordances, but also in their appearance, and, in some cases, it seems that the boar's tusk helmet was imitated in other materials. It is striking that horizontal banding emerged as a key characteristic of the Aegean helmet's identity. It seems that the boar's tusk helmet, with its rich cultural status and elaborated form, was the most celebrated embodiment of such Aegean helmet-making, toward which more schematic renderings of helmets – some simply marked with horizontal bands – ultimately could refer. Such reference could cross media and substances, so that we even see horizontal banding on helmets rendered in metal, where such features were practically unnecessary. This is evident in a bronze Mycenaean helmet in the collection of the Ashmolean Museum.[56] As Knappett discusses, this type of imitation between materials, or skeuomorphism, can be understood as a dimension of compositeness (taken in a broad sense) in material culture and is a phenomenon that is frequently at play in Aegean Bronze Age objects.[57] As with other dynamics of composite creativity that we have been discussing, skeuomorphism manifests likeness between entities, reaching across formal and material boundaries so that the substance or physical character of one thing can be shared with that of another (e.g., the horizontal registering of boar's tusk plaques could be shared with a helmet formed of solid bronze). That this type of dynamism embraced the boar's tusk helmet contributes yet further to the complex boundary-crossing of these fluidly composite things. Similar dynamics were also in play with cattle hides that become part of shields and ikria.

The similarities between boar's tusk helmets and oxhide shields have been discussed by various scholars. Most discussions relate the objects to one another as components of a warrior's panoply or as symbols. Representations in which the two objects occur together, either upon a human body or as objects without a wearer, support this connection. Marinatos contends that the oxhide figure-8 shied was a symbol of sacrifice;[58] Morris, we have seen, builds on this idea and poses that the helmet conventionally referred to hunt and war, as well as to the broader sociocultural significance of the two.[59] We noted that Morris also discusses the common animal origins of the two objects. I would like to step back to this fundamental dimension shared by the helmet and shield, as well as oxhide ikria, in order to draw out some deeper similarities.

SECOND SKINS: CATTLE FLESH FOR A HUMAN BODY

Like the boar's tusk helmet, the oxhide shield is a complex object whose identity seems to derive from its equal and prominent integration of particular human, nonhuman and thingly elements. This draws the shield and helmet together as embodiments of a distinctive Aegean type of composite creativity. The ikrion, a protective structure that was situated on the deck of ships to shelter important human mariners, should be included in this discussion as well. In Aegean Bronze Age visual culture, both ikria and shields are typically represented as being fashioned of oxhide and, when crafted in the round, each would have been constituted by the skins of cattle stretched across frames of wood or perhaps metal.[60] Thus, like boar's tusk helmets, both shields and ikria conspicuously incorporated bodily elements of fierce nonhuman animals into their physical form. Concurrently with this, each of these three objects was defined by its status as a means of corporeal cover for the human. This common protective status made resilience, strength and conformity principal components of their physical and socio-cultural identities. It also meant that the human body, with its specific qualities and demands, was integral to the objects' characters. Put in other words, the helmet, shield and ikrion were all formed around the shape of the human body, *responding* to its needs and vulnerabilities and affording specific behavior and experience – the helmet rematerializes the rounded contours of the human cranium, with the nose and mouth left unblocked and the fragile neck guarded; the shield rises to the long, upright extent of the human torso, convexing like an exoskeleton about its soft underbelly and vital organs

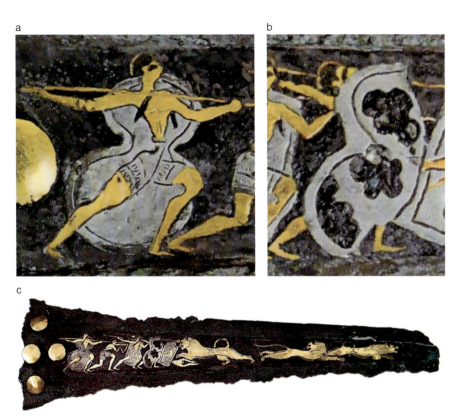

5.3. Figure-8 shields upon human bodies in the Lion Hunt Dagger from Mycenae (National Archaeological Museum, Athens, N394). Excerpted details (above) from photograph by παρακάτω (CC BY-SA 1.0). Photograph of full length (below) by Zde (CC BY-SA 3.0). Object © Hellenic Ministry of Culture and Sports

(Figure 5.3); and the ikrion stretches and bends across the height of a seated sailor who needs both a view upon the distant horizon and protection from crashing waves (Figure 5.4).[61] Being seated was a corporeal quality that held particular significance in the Aegean Bronze Age, both in representations and likely in lived practice; it seems to have imparted distinguished status. Together with the human body, the ikrion was an integral element of a specific manifestation of this culturally construed bodily comportment. In the case of oxhide shields, the figure-8 form in particular seems to respond to the curved human corpus by swelling across its two areas of breadth in the chest and hips; it appears especially resonant with the form of a woman's body – some scholars have even argued that certain renderings of the shield depict it as personified.[62] Meanwhile, like the tusks of swine, the skins of cattle may have been obtained through ritualized and traditionally recognized activities (see Chapter 2). This would have drawn similar biographical complexity into the oxhide shields and ikria, as well as conventionally bringing attention to their formulation.

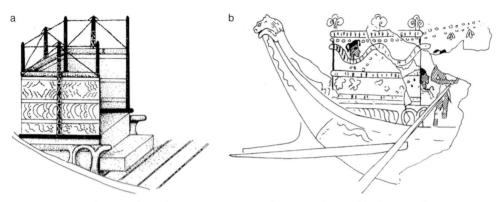

5.4. The Aegean ikrion or ship cabin. a. Reconstruction by Maria Shaw and b. drawing of an excerpt showing an inhabited ikrion from the wall painting of the south wall of Room 5, West House Akrotiri, also by Maria Shaw (as partial copy of Gray 1974 pl. XIII); images courtesy Joseph and Maria Shaw

Each of these objects in the round had remarkable relationships with animals' bodies. While emerging from the substance of nonhuman animals, they incorporated aspects of the human form into their physical being and became integrated into a human's "mode of presence and engagement in the world"[63] in specific ways. These relationships to bodies were readily apparent, likely even ritually celebrated, but the objects were not depictions of bodies, nor did they simply replicate a bodily form – instead they drew from and responded to animals' bodies while also realizing the character and efficacies of particular objects. The independence of each is powerfully generated and emphasized in material and visual culture, underscoring their cultural weight not only as objects of adornment but also as dynamic entities in their own right.[64] As such, they were vibrant with bodily reverberations of both nonhuman and human animals, yet they nevertheless possessed distinct standings in the world.

HELMETS, SHIELDS, IKRIA AND THE CREATIVE MANIPULATIONS OF REPRESENTATIONAL MEDIA

Moving forward, we turn now to examining how similarities between boar's tusk helmets, oxhide shields and ikria were developed yet more deeply through their representational embodiments. We look first at renderings of the entities manifest in engraved seals and painted ceramics. The particular treatment of these distinctive Aegean entities in representational contexts makes clear that they held special status and that they shared some of that status between them; we can recognize this even without venturing deeply into speculations concerning their specific symbolic content. Instead, we will consider how representational embodiments of the helmets, shields and ikria realized further dimensions in their identities as animalian things, in part by enriching their existence across instead of within ontological categories. We have strong indications that these three entities were experienced as comparable or related to one another in Bronze Age Crete and the Aegean, given that they each could be rendered in the same distinctive manners, sometimes within the same contexts. In particular, representations of the helmets, shields and ikria can be characterized by isolation (as discrete units), reduplication (often in seriated friezes) and innovative manipulations of their spatiality. In numerous instances, it is apparent that the creative affordances of representation were being taken advantage of to cultivate similarities in form – what I refer to as "formal assonance" – with other phenomena, further indicating how the identities of these three complex Aegean entities were productively fluid. In Chapter 6, these aspects of the helmets, shields and ikria will be situated within a broader consideration of how renderings of nonhuman animals in Neopalatial wall painting innovatively flexed the boundaries of their representational contexts, complicating the thresholds between representational and lived social space through manipulations of their surface, coloration and indications of relative location.

Alone, and Again: Isolation, Duplication and Juxtaposition in Friezes of Animalian Entities

Given various factors limiting archaeological survival of organic materials, it is through representational media that we today best know Aegean Bronze Age boar's tusk helmets, oxhide shields and ikria. In the Bronze Age as well, people would have engaged with these entities not only through embodiments fashioned of cattle skins and swine teeth, but through ones constituted by other materials, such as engraved stone, painted plaster and clay. Perhaps the most celebrated examples we have come from polychrome wall paintings. Within the corpus of wall paintings, it is striking that the shields, ikria and helmets were each rendered within the distinctive format of vivid horizontal friezes. Here, each appeared as an object shed of any narrative accoutrement, an entity in itself. With this status, the object could be reduplicated in the frieze, forming a string of like entities, or could alternate with other objects. These friezes of seriated items have been commented on by many scholars. The isolation and repetition that they embody, as well as the defensive status of the objects, have often been associated with Mycenaean cultural forms in particular.[65] This association is worth drawing out for consideration, as it carries with it certain cultural stereotypes and assumptions that can stand in the way of appreciating the dynamic performance of such friezes. It also can be an obstacle to recognizing the earlier roots of this manner of rendering Aegean entities in media beyond wall painting.

Mycenaean and Minoan cultures have traditionally been placed in an unlucky opposition with one another. Scholarly discussions throughout the twentieth century have sometimes treated these cultures as monoliths that in essence mutually define one another – where one is aggressive the other is peace-loving, where one is rigid the other is organic, where one is reigned over by the straight line, the other winds with the asymmetrical curve. This reductive and flawed scheme, while disparaged or ignored in recent work, nevertheless has established deep-seated notions concerning the character of Aegean cultural formations and their relation to one another. With this, Mycenaean material and visual cultures can still be treated as derivative, governed by genre and structure over dynamism and symbolic depth. Readings of Minoan artwork, by contrast, can be saturated with speculations of symbolic profundity, often assumed to be religious in nature.[66] In this context, seriated friezes comprised of isolated motifs, which did indeed have a blossoming in wall paintings of the LB II–III, have been stereotypically associated with Mycenaean proclivities for formalism, "arrest" and repetition.[67] Instances of these repetitive forms, especially in wall painting, have often been described as "ornamental" or "decorative," hence denying them situational or symbolic depth. However, the interpretive situation implicitly becomes more complex, even contradictory, when certain objects, including shields and ikria, stand as an element in such friezes, and this disconnect has not often been examined.

Shields and ikria, as well as boar's tusk helmets, have been distinguished by various scholars as having held a special semiotic status in Aegean culture. The occurrence of the objects as isolated and potentially reduplicated elements in representational media is not incidental here – it underlies, in part, these identifications.[68] The fundamental point seems to be that representations of shields and ikria (in particular) in which the objects have been extracted from narrative contexts (as in repetitive friezes) indicate *another* function for the representations, something other than – or more than – denotation of the objects' practical roles in human action. Ornamentation, or aesthetic elaboration, could, of course, be one such further function. Yet given their consequence as celebrated protective objects (and how this would seem to align with the presumed warring interests of Mycenaean society) and their prominence in other representational contexts, including in narrative scenes, some scholars have asserted that, even when shields and ikria occur as isolated units in representational media, they likely stood as more than aesthetic ornaments; instead *their* being singled out and potentially repeated is taken to indicate their reification as a symbol. One semiotic classification that has often been attached to them, as well as to certain other figural motifs seen in such friezes, notably animals (e.g., dogs, dolphins), is that of "emblems." In his careful consideration of the status of different species of animals in Aegean art, Blakolmer indicates that figures represented as isolated subjects, apart from other actors or scenic cues, should be understood as emblematic; others have made similar assertions.[69] The meaning of the term "emblem" is somewhat fluid between scholars' usages. At times it seems to indicate something of "symbolism-lite," that is, to designate a certain level of traditional signification that nevertheless is limited in its notional development and confined in function to a conventionalized identifier, such as a coat of arms or insigne.[70] In other cases, scholars' description of a motif as an emblem identifies it with more complexity as a sign, for example by reading it as a signifier of a particular sociocultural value or ethos (e.g., heroism of warriors, skill as a great hunter or protective power of a particular beast).[71] Renderings of shields, helmets and ikria in other contemporaneous representational contexts, which seem not to concern their established practical roles in bodily protection, could support readings that identify more semiotic depth in the entities' occurrence within friezes. Figure-8 shields in particular have been identified with religious meaning, in part because they can appear in ostensible ritual scenes or settings not immediately associable with combat or hunt (e.g., in the LB I Vapheio Ring, CMS I.219, or in a wall painting in the Cult Center, Mycenae)[72] or be manifested as objects-in-the-round that have distinct affordances associated with ritual (e.g., a metal rhyton in the form of a figure-8 shield from Mycenae).[73] Meanwhile, the idea that the figure-8 shield could be personified as a Mycenaean warrior goddess, first proposed by Mylonas,[74] stands as a counterpoint to readings that see the object in an ornamental role yet upholds traditional associations concerning the aggressive values of the Mycenaeans and their consequent development of the shield as a war-related religious entity.

In some cases, it is clear that ascription of conventional symbolic content to representations of these animalian entities is not considered to be at odds with seeing them also as acting ornamentally when rendered in friezes. Shaw describes figure-8 oxhide shields and ikria as "symbols" of "military power" and "naval power" respectively but then also comments on how both are prominent in "decorative friezes."[75] She specifically draws out a distinction between their occurrence in narrative scenes versus friezes, and points to frieze compositions as possessing a "decorative nature."[76] Immerwahr titles a section in her analysis of Mycenaean painting "Emblematic and Decorative Painting," indicating that these two statuses are basically related, yet goes on to offer some discussion of what distinguishes them in terms of their signification and particular representational signatures.[77] She asserts that motifs that are acting emblematically often appear in repeated "files" or pairs (heraldic or antithetic) and seem disposed to more realism, accomplished through inclusion of variable details between individual units in a series (e.g., color, disposition), a larger scale of rendering (e.g., her discussion of "emblematic" painted series of shields and dogs) and by the presence of borders. She also indicates that wider spacing between units in a series is indicative of an emblematic status, versus the tighter spacing that she, like Shaw, associates with decorative friezes.[78]

Recently the work of Emily Egan has broken new ground in analysis of the rendering of animals within repetitive friezes in Mycenaean wall painting, which she approaches through close study of the painter's craft. In her examination of the argonaut friezes from Pylos, Egan identifies subtle but definite variation between formations of the creatures' bodies seen in repeated series.[79] Egan considers how such variation might indicate ways in which painters were working productively with their knowledge of the living sea creatures, by "reinterpreting" their forms and experiencing "freedom" in their own renderings of them in paint.[80] Egan discusses the rich history of scholarship surrounding Mycenaean argonaut friezes, including apparent "standardization" in painted form, how and why the painted argonauts depart from corporeal details of the biological animals, and the use of "rhythmically" alternating colors when argonauts are repeated in friezes.[81] Yet in her consideration of "variation-amid-repetition" between argonaut friezes at Pylos specifically, Egan turns more fully to examination of divergences in matters of form, drawing out that while some features of the painted argonauts appear to have been "essential" (i.e., are present across known examples), others "were nonessential and therefore 'flexible' in their inclusion and/or appearance. In other words, some aspects of argonaut friezes were negotiable, and some were not." With this carefully drawn out observation, Egan's study incisively cracks open old notions of Mycenaean formalism (which are nowhere stronger than in studies of "repetitive" friezes) with new interest and the perspectives of analysis focused on technique. Her ideas reach into the space of human action to consider questions of the craftsperson's agency, but, at the same time, highlight subtle experiential dynamics of a viewer who would have been in the position to relate different embodiments of the argonaut encountered *between* paintings in multiple Pylian spaces.[82]

Compared to the Mycenaean mainland, our evidence of seriated friezes in the wall paintings of the broad Minoan world – including ones that involve boar's-tusk helmets, oxhide shields and ikria – while definite, is at present far more limited. Egan's work indicates directions in which questions of crafting could fruitfully be brought to bear on that evidence as the corpus grows (and important previous scholarship on related questions in Minoan painting would form a strong basis). The rendering of oxhide shields, boar's tusk helmets and ikria in wall paintings will be discussed extensively in Chapter 6. At this stage, I would like to move away from the idea that these three entities, and their embodiment in friezes in particular, should be connected primarily with mainland palatial culture.[83] My interest is not in dissociating the objects from Mycenaean social formations, nor in denying the robust evidence of their significance therein. Instead, my aim is to examine earlier phases in the formulation of these Aegean animalian entities and to recognize how their embodiment as elements in series contributed to their distinctive dynamism.

With this, we will see that making divisions between symbolic and ornamental statuses, or between realistic and formalized representations, while helpful on some level, must not be an end in itself – the objects' embodiments in friezes have much more experiential and ontological complexity than these divisions alone recognize. Our examination will entail embracing the materialization of shields, helmets and ikria in other representational media, both before and alongside their appearance in wall painting, and recognizing the extensive evidence we have of the objects being manifest as elements of series in the material culture of the southern Aegean in LB I, with some evidence coming already from the MBA.

Rethinking Series: Strength in Isolation and (Then) in Numbers

The vivid files of large polychrome figure-8 shields well known from LB II–III fresco fragments from Knossos, Tiryns and Mycenae boldly announce and reiterate the place of these objects within the monumental halls of the Aegean. Before these grand renderings of shields lined such walls, people engaged with much smaller rows of shields, embodied both in the discreet contours of seals and clay impressions, and around the curved walls of ceramic vessels. In these objects, we find ample evidence that seriation involving shields was well established already in LB I; the same can be observed for boar's tusk helmets and ikria. Seriation has its basis in the singling out of a figure or form. Once isolated from a particular context or association, the entity has the potential to possess commonality alongside others. To understand the embodiment of shields, helmets and ikria in series, we thus need to explore the ways in which they came to be granted independence from other phenomena with which they were associated in contexts of practical usage or narrative representation (such as human bodies, nonhuman animals being hunted or indications of a setting) and how, with that independence, they could newly stand alone, be repeated or set in comparative juxtaposition with other entities. Such handling afforded new ways of experiencing shields, helmets and ikria that reached beyond pictorialism and symbolism.

Groups of shields appear in Cretan glyptic motifs already during the Protopalatial period. In CMS XIII.D1a (Figure 5.5b),[84] a soft-stone seal, we see a crouched human surrounded by a ring of six figure-8 shields.[85] In CMS III.54, also a soft-stone seal, five figure-8 shields fill the roughly triangular seal face in two rows, constituting the motif's only subject (Figure 5.5a). In the Neopalatial corpus, numerous extant glyptic objects image a row of shields as a motif's primary or sole element. In some cases, the shields are held by humans, as in CMS II.8.276, CMS II.8.277 and CMS II.8.278, clay impressions from Knossos (Figure 5.5c–d). In CMS II.8.276, the human holding one of the shields within the row also wears a boar's tusk helmet and clutches a spear.

266 SINGULAR, SERIATED, SIMILAR

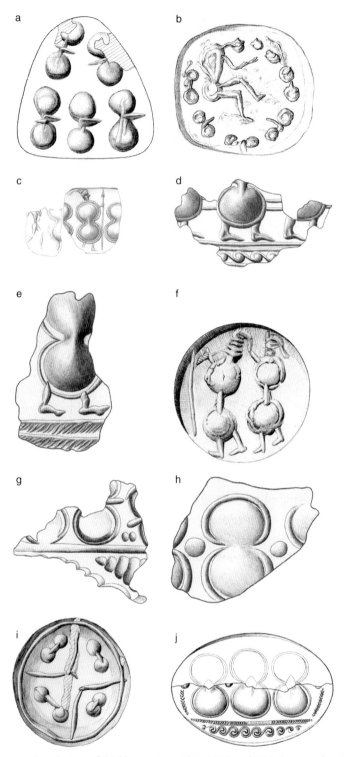

5.5. Renderings of shields in series within MBA and LBA Aegean glyptic. a. CMS III.54b; b. CMS XIII.D1a; c. CMS II.8.276; d. CMS II.8.277; e. CMS II.8.278; f. CMS II.3.32; g. CMS II.8.128; h. CMS II.8.129; i. CMS V.S1B.268; j. CMS II.3.113. Drawings of motifs courtesy CMS, Heidelberg

In an LB I–II seal of the Cretan Popular Group, CMS ɪɪ.3.32 (Figure 5.5f), two large figure-8 shields are set side by side; a boar's tusk helmet positioned at the top of each, and protruding limb lines, indicate that these shields are being worn by humans whose bodies, however, are markedly inconspicuous.[86] We also have seal motifs from this period that image a series of shields alone, entirely without humans. This is the case, for example, on CMS ɪɪ.8.128 and CMS ɪɪ.8.129, also from Knossos (Figure 5.5g–h). The subtle presence of humans in some of these motifs suggests that the imaging of the shield in a series could have had origins, in part, in impressive lived social scenarios in which the shield was met as a repeated element in a collective mass of soldiers or hunters. This need not have been a formally organized alignment, such as the later phalanx. Instead, the impression of an assembly of comparable protective objects, on the bodies of figures with a shared aim, could have arisen more generally from their copresence in a common undertaking, for example while heading off to battle, approaching a target or during fighting. Numerous extant images from Aegean material culture present developed manifestations of just such situations, and we can readily imagine that oral narratives were creating similar scenes for listeners. As discussed in Chapter 3, Aegean material culture imaging armored figures shares not only content but also representational dynamics with storytelling traditions, especially epic. This is certainly the case concerning the miniature wall paintings of Room 5 of the West House at Akrotiri, which include gatherings of figures protected by shields, helmets and ikria – indeed this room seems to swell with poetry concerning exploits of warriors and beasts (we will return to Room 5, below; Figure 6.3–6.4, 6.6–6.7). We see comparable groups of armored persons in other contemporaneous objects, such as the warriors arrayed on the spectacular LH I silver Battle Krater, or the line of hunters inlaid in the niello Lion Hunt Dagger (both from Grave IV, Grave Circle A, at Mycenae; Figure 5.3). As we have seen, the broad fields of such media provided ground for extended scenic development involving hunt and combat, inviting comparisons to epic episodes.[87] Yet returning to the small fields of engraved seals and stamped impressions, we can, at the same time, observe a very distinct dynamism involving shields, helmets and ikria – a dynamism that would also be cultivated in other media. While glyptic could be home to developed scenes focused on the exploits of warriors or hunters, the seals and impressions highlighted here foregrounded, instead, the protective accoutrements themselves, *not* the humans. This is readily apparent concerning shields. With human actors minimized and erased from these renderings of the shields, the gathering together of like things is laid bare. This emphasis on generic commonality removes interest in distinguishing a particular human element – a single person, group or specific undertaking. In this sense, the seriation of the shields does not readily support certain narrative possibilities. Yet the rhythmic parataxis of the series does have poetic potential.[88] The embodiment of repeated forms asserts something strengthened by emphasis and perpetuation. Hence, while a series of entities does not possess the acuteness of an image of a human-centered event, it is also less vulnerable; a series' inherent persistence pushes it above the fray of potential narrative developments, while nevertheless asserting distinctive character and presence. In a sense, repetition creates its own time and space – an effect with rich affordances in oral poetry and visual culture. This is not to say that series of isolated shields, helmets or ikria, met in glyptic or other media, could not have been opened into scenes of narrative stories. Again, we can easily imagine a fleet of ships or line of palace defenders being conceptually "behind" such series – or being drawn forth from them by the tongues of storytellers in particular moments. Yet the emphasis these series enact themselves is distinct and may have been involved in the cultivation of other tense dimensions of social experience and presence, as we will see.

Beyond a Head

Renderings of boar's tusk helmets in Aegean glyptic share comparable dynamics to the handling of shields. We have seen that helmets can be an element of LM I glyptic motifs in which a series of shields form the focus; in CMS II.3.32, the helmet is also repeated, as is the case in some comparable scenes in other media (Figure 5.5f). In these instances, the helmets appear to be worn by a human, but the helmet is also encountered in glyptic motifs from this period as an independent object, apart from human bodies. We see this in numerous LB I–II motifs comprised entirely of a single boar's tusk helmet, where the object's segmented construction and prominent crest are carefully detailed (see examples in Figure 5.6).

In the exceptional group of glyptic objects from House A at Neopalatial Kato Zakros, we also see the boar's tusk helmet as one element combined with others to form composite creatures (e.g., Figure 4.24b). This situation is worth considering further. We have seen that in her study of the material, Anastasiadou highlights how the Zakros-type composites are unique within the broader field of Minoan creatures traditionally identified as hybrids/composites, because of the way in which the Zakros-type composites combine distinct bodily elements from multiple species, as "interchangeable parts," to form distinct permutations that defy standardization and often logic; they are often unconvincing as whole creatures (see discussion in Chapter 4).[89] In this context, she describes that the helmet can sometimes appear in the place of a head. Although at first this situation, where the helmet contributes to the

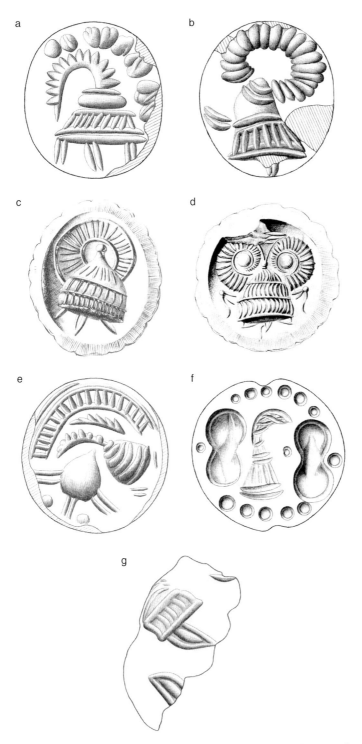

5.6. Renderings of boar's tusk helmets as isolated entities and elements of series in Aegean LB I–II glyptic. a. CMS II.6.136; b. CMS III.499; c. CMS I.153; d. CMS I.260; e. CMS II.8.132; f. CMS V.S3.331; g. CMS II.8.131. Drawings of motifs courtesy CMS, Heidelberg

formulation of a larger entity, might seem markedly different from the isolation it enjoys in other seal motifs (and in some respects it is significantly different), the situation at Zakros powerfully underscores how the helmet could be treated as an object in its own right during this period, apart from and indeed even replacing the human head as an alternate entity. Anastasiadou notes that the helmet is a remarkable component within the corpus of potential parts that were drawn on in the formation of the Zakros composites, being one of just three inanimate objects that can constitute a primary component of a figure (along with snake frames and double axes).[90] Other "elements of attire" do appear in the motifs, but importantly not in the position of a segment of the body in their own right – they instead are worn on or attached to a body part (e.g., the headgear worn on the head of the composite creature in CMS II.7.83). By contrast with these items of adornment, the helmet, at Zakros too, seems to have held a distinct status – physical, material and likely notional – as an entity in its own right, without a reliance on the human head to somehow justify or carry it.[91] Hence, its cultural status and complexity did not depend on its being joined to a human body. In this sense, the helmet appears to have been recognized as an independent whole unit in itself, even if it could also be powerfully combined.

As we have considered, the formal relationship that the Aegean helmet has with the human head is indeed powerful, but it is apparently one of harmony between bodies, instead of unilinear reliance. The helmet's rendering as a subject on its own not only reflects this independent status, it also would have contributed to it, as it afforded experiences of the helmet as a solitary, whole figure. Some of this independence may have also stemmed from people's interactions with boar's tusk helmets in the round, and the identities that they possessed. Boar's tusk helmets had rich biographies in their own right that could have inspired awe and fueled tales. These biographies would have involved the helmet's formation from tusks garnered through numerous challenging encounters with swine, as well as experiences a person had with a helmet as a prized object worn in battle and likely displayed off the battlefield; in some cases, helmets also may have been passed down to other persons, even across generations, gaining yet further depth to their identities. Not all of these moments involved being joined with a human's body, and the possibility that more than one human could be associated with the helmet – from the undertakings involved in acquiring its tusks to the heads who wore it – further underlines the object's distinctive social life and autonomy. The helmet of Achilles, included in the armor he inherited from his father Peleus, provides fodder for imagining how the identity of such an object could take form through unpredictable relationships with multiple persons. The helmet was first a wedding gift from the gods for Peleus. Later he bestows it upon Achilles, while Patroklos wears it and dies in it, as does Hektor; in fact, we never see it upon Achilles' own body in the *Iliad*.[92] Stories describe other such objects being taken as spoils by killers or burnt on pyres upon fallen bodies – an extravagant action that removes the valuable item from circulation and dramatically ends a fate that could otherwise continue to take the object through the hands of others. Such dimensions of boar's tusk helmets surely were at play in the LBA. These were things that possessed their own social depth, with identities that could involve potent relationships with people while also being able to move across and apart from them. Imaging the helmet alone opened a space for recognizing such potentially independent identity, which would have stimulated stories and emotions.

Not only does the helmet appear to have been treated as an entity with an independent status in LB I Aegean material culture, it could also appear as a unit within series. In the realm of glyptic, we have motifs in which the helmet appears as part of a series or cluster with other uncontextualized objects. In CMS II.8.132, a helmet appears alongside a similarly shaped object that has been tentatively identified by some as another type of helmet (Figure 5.6e).[93] In CMS V.S3.331, a helmet occurs as the central element of a three-part series with two figure-8 shields (Figure 5.6f). As we have seen, the helmet and shield are intimately related as objects in the round on various levels. Meanwhile, in representational embodiments, both can be rendered as isolated units. Hence, their juxtaposition in this seal is deeply intuitive, even without speculating on the specific symbolic meaning of each. The helmet's pairing with the second entity imaged in CMS II.8.132 is potentially also based in a perceived similarity, at least in terms of form, an idea I will return to shortly. Fundamentally, we see through both of these extant instances how positioning of the different entities side by side, in roughly equal size with one another, creates a venue for realizing relationships between specific cultural forms; simply put, such juxtaposition affords and even requests consideration of the entities in light of one another. In the Aegean evidence, this simple juxtaposition often seems to carry remarkable complexity; as Knappett astutely notes, "juxtaposition can become a mental operation."[94]

The tight quarters of engraved seal stones were home to some of our earliest representations of Aegean shields and boar's tusk helmets rendered in series; this continued to be a space in which rows of the objects were embodied into LB III (see, e.g., gold signet ring CMS II.3.113 from Kalyvia). In some cases, the groups of represented objects adapt to the shape of the seal face, rendered in curving lines or stacked registers, or spreading about the surface (e.g., Figures 5.5a, b, i; 5.6e, g). Yet often, the engraving of the motifs across the rounded seal faces was handled in such a way that conformed with the inherent horizontality of a linear series extending lengthwise, side by side. The lateral character of such series was augmented in certain instances by the addition of linear bands or subsidiary elements that emphasize the motif's horizontality.[95]

Such additional elements bring a sense of rhythmic structure to the motifs and at times feel architectonic, especially when they subtend the frieze of objects. This structuring effect can be compared to that imparted by the imaged or implied groundline at play within seal motifs that involve a row of shields associated (at least minimally) with humans. In both situations, an orientation is implied that both strengthens the lateral stance of the series and can also give the impression that we are glimpsing the objects occupying a grounded space, for example along a wall.[96] Such effects are apparent, for example, in the motifs of impressions CMS II.8.277, CMS II.8.278 and CMS II.8.127 (Figures 5.5d–e; 5.11 [top]), and a later signet ring, CMS II.3.113 (Figure. 5.5j).[97] These aspects of the glyptic motifs will be returned to later, but here we can note that the horizontality possessed by some of the motifs stands as an area of commonality with friezes of shields, helmets and ikria that were rendered in Aegean painted ceramics and wall paintings. In these other media, we also often see added subsidiary elements structuring and elaborating the friezes of seriated objects.

We have been discussing evidence of series involving shields and boar's tusk helmets in Aegean glyptic but have spoken little of ikria in this context. Representations of ikria in the extant Aegean glyptic corpus are rare. From a Mycenaean context, we have a representation of an ikrion upon a ship that appears on a signet ring from Tiryns, CMS I.180 (Figure 5.7a).[98] An LM I-style carnelian amygdaloid seal of the "talismanic" type in the Herakleion Museum (CMS II.3.361; Figure 5.7b) is engraved with a ship with what appears to be an ikrion positioned at one end of its deck. A contemporaneous clay impression from Knossos, rendered by a metal signet ring (CMS II.8.135; Figure 5.7c), images three nearly identical boats, one stacked atop another; the front of the boats is obscured by a mass of round elements – perhaps representations of rocks or clouds – that seems to be engulfing the vessels. Each boat in this vertical series has the same group of four schematically rendered forms upon its deck (there is slight variation in the second from the left). The last one of these forms, visible just before the edge of the consuming mass, consists of two vertical "beams" with two or three "crossbeams" between them. While the technical style in which these two glyptic images were rendered is quite different, we can tentatively compare the hypothetical ikrion of CMS II.3.361 with the structure depicted on the decks of the vessels in CMS II.8.135. If these are indeed schematic ikria, the seriation of them, as part of the sequence of identical boats, would be an interesting point of comparison for their contemporaneous treatment in the wall paintings of the West House in Akrotiri, where they appear both as elements of a string of ships in the frieze of the south wall (Room 5) and in a large-scale frieze of isolated ikria (Room 4) (see Figures 6.1–6.2, 6.3–6.4). This identification would also support the idea that, as with shields and helmets, seriation of ikria in representational media, including as isolated units repeated in friezes, may

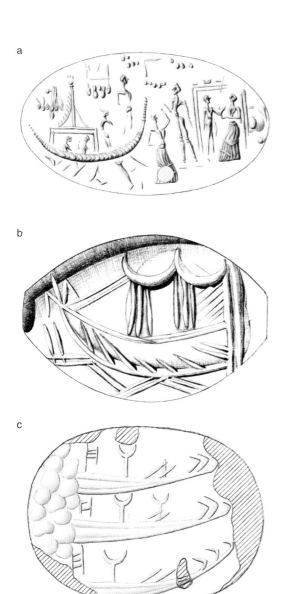

5.7. Possible renderings of ikria in Aegean Bronze Age glyptic. a. CMS I.180; b. CMS II.3.361; c. CMS II.8.135. Drawings of motifs courtesy CMS, Heidelberg

in part have been related to how they were encountered en masse, as practical entities in the round and in oral narratives involving such gatherings – in this case, as elements of a fleet of sea vessels.

The tiny surfaces of Aegean seals and their clay impressions were developed as spaces in which to embody series involving shields, helmets and possibly ikria. These contributed to the rich range of experiences people could have had with these composite animalian entities, across different media and contexts. Glyptic did not merely imitate what was happening in other, more monumental forms of material culture; nor should we treat seals as a proving ground where such motifs were rendered before their full blossoming in wall painting. Glyptic brought distinctive affordances and feelings to people's engagements with these composite entities and with their manifestation in series. The tininess of seals and impressions placed the *multiplicity* that a series always embodies within a person's grasp – at the tips of their fingers. In this way, glyptic embodiments of series afforded some of the dynamics of experiencing power over immensity that Stewart discusses in her consideration of miniaturization.[99] At the same time, underlying the seriation of shields, helmets and ikria, is a *narrowing in* on the particular form and cultural status of each – as each was embodied as an entity in itself. Glyptic objects could help realize the independence of these entities through the concentrated nature of seals' representational space. The rendering of single helmets, alone and free of narrative trappings, keenly illustrates this meditative potential of the medium.

Most fundamentally, seals and impressions brought these entities into an intimate realm of connection with a human, while at the same time providing grounds for dynamic relations to be made with their embodiments in larger and more public media. From the late MBA, these tiny but often spatially complex renderings of the three entities in glyptic could have been experienced in tandem with representations occurring in other media in the Aegean, primarily painted ceramics and murals – as well as with practical objects in the round (helmets, shields and ikria). Blakolmer has explored crosscraft and potential sociosymbolic connections between Aegean seals and wall paintings, especially concerning renderings of processions and indications of architecture.[100] There are certainly ways that the symbolism of helmets, shields and ikria could explicitly act across the different contexts of these media, for example as a repeated emblem. But there are, simultaneously, other dimensions to their crossmedia dynamics. As people experienced embodiments of the three entities in different contemporaneous forms of material culture, each with their own distinctive qualities and affordances, the standing of each entity would have flexed into new dimensions, realizing connections with other media that were physical and sociocultural.[101] As we continue to consider the embodiment of the shields, ikria and helmets within these contemporaneous media, we will problematize both their idiosyncrasies as well as the formal and interactive qualities that they could hold in common. We begin here with the rich dynamics at play between glyptic and painted ceramics.

PRESENCE AND ABSENCE, SCALE AND SPACE

In certain respects, painted ceramics and glyptic objects provided similar circumstances for the rendering of entities. Ceramic vessels, like glyptic objects, are movable things. Both types of thing could be readily recontextualized and involved in dynamic manipulations of space and access. This could happen, for example, if the object was regularly concealed or deliberately *re*vealed in order to change the status of a space or actor therein. We would see this with a painted vessel that was brought out of storage and into a visited space for involvement in a particular ritual action; or in a seal worn on the wrist of a seated authority figure in a reception hall, which was offered to an approaching person for admiration and perhaps ceremonial contact.[102] We find oxhide shields handled in comparable ways between Aegean glyptic and painted ceramics in late MBA–LB I/II. As in glyptic motifs, shields can occur isolated and in series on painted vessels, both as the sole figural subject and in combination with other figures. While more limited, we also have evidence of boar's tusk helmets being rendered on LB I–II pictorial vessels, for example seriated on a painted Palace Style amphora from Katsambas;[103] notable also is a fragment of a stone-relief vessel from Knossos, where a helmet appears to be an entity on its own, not worn by a human.[104] When shields or helmets were juxtaposed with other seriated entities on vessels, it could invite comparison and relation between the gathered elements – as did similar compositions evidenced in contemporaneous glyptic. In both media there was sometimes a particular development of this juxtaposition, in which entities rendered with provocatively comparable forms were set side by side, creating formal assonance that likely was opened into cultural connections.

Even as we see strong similarities between painted vessels and glyptic, there are also important distinctions between the two media and their handling of the seriated entities. Both media typically involve reduction in the size of a represented form, including representations of shields and helmets; this reduction is often dramatic. However, within the corpus of painted ceramics, we have evidence that the representational scale was in certain cases being flexed upward during later MBA and early LBA in the Aegean; with this, the presence of larger painted figures on the vessels afforded new dynamics of engagement for persons interacting with the objects.[105] Interestingly, these experiments also drew the possibilities of painted ceramics toward the craft of figural wall painting, just as it was emerging.

Round and Round We Go

Within the Bronze Age Aegean, where roll-cylinders were not the preferred format for seals, ceramic vessels stood as one of the most fitting venues for rendering a chain of forms in series. Across the continuous surface offered by the curved wall of a vessel, a line of represented forms could maintain their rhythmic succession *ad infinitum*. We see this potential vividly developed in certain early instances of southern Aegean ceramics painted with figures, for example in the Protopalatial Kamares ware pithos from Phaistos, on which a line of rising palms encircles the vessel's belly.[106] We see seriated friezes developed with powerful effect in Cycladic ceramic traditions of the MBA, for example on vibrant MC Black and Red Style vessels, where a row of animals, such as birds or dolphins, were painted in bichrome,[107] or on the stunning polychrome Fishermen Vase from Phylakopi, around which a file of men carrying fish proceed in their endless cycle.[108] A row of figure-8 shields also makes an appearance in Middle Cycladic ceramics, on a large polychrome vessel from Akrotiri (more on this below).[109]

During the Neopalatial period, ceramics painted with a series of figures are seen more frequently. We have numerous examples of pots on which the figure-8 shield is the sole subject of such painted series, repeated around a vessel's body; vessels from Chania, Knossos and Akrotiri, among others, dramatically embody such renderings of shields.[110] Also in the Neopalatial period (but somewhat later therein),[111] ceramics of the LM IB Alternating Style are characterized by a series of painted motifs (usually two) set in alternation, which extends around a vessel's primary decorative zone. Figure-8 shields occur as a seriated element on some Alternating Style vessels.[112] The Alternating Style placed the shield in productive juxtapositions with other entities, by creating contexts for comparison and relation. This effect can be likened to the juxtaposition afforded by contemporaneous seal motifs that image shields in a frieze along with other entities, such as the boar's tusk helmet (e.g., Figure 5.6f). In both media, such juxtapositions could both recognize and generate connections between the entities. These connections could be thematic, formal, cultural or otherwise; such possibilities are far from mutually exclusive.

Rehak has pointed to these Neopalatial vessels as evidence that shield friezes were a motif that first developed in Crete and subsequently spread to the mainland through exports of Alternating Style ceramics; the Neopalatial vessels are significant, he writes, "because they already show the repetitive use of the shield set carefully in a horizontal frieze."[113] Alternating Style ceramics have generally been understood as having had strong influence in the development of early Mycenaean ceramic traditions in the mainland (most directly in the LH IIA–B Ephyraean Style),[114] where repetition of forms became a common syntactic trope in the elaboration of vessels moving forward. By LM II, ceramics decorated with friezes of seriated forms are extensively evidenced in Crete, as well as the mainland.

SERIES AT WORK IN A CONTEXT OF CRETAN RITUAL ACTION

Between Ornament and Picture

A deposit of LM IB material discovered in the Cult Room Basement at Knossos, where it had collapsed from an upper-floor room, contained a host of remarkable vessels, some of which seem to have formed an assemblage.[115] Among these were two vessels that exemplify the distinctive dynamism that could be realized through renderings of series in the Aegean. Both of these vessels are painted with a series that involves figure-8 shields – in one case, shields are the sole subject of the series; in the other, they alternate with other entities. This deposit is extraordinary in its own right. It has been discussed by scholars for the provocative evidence of ritualistic action it contains, including human bones displaying knife marks that were found along with remains of edible snails and shell fragments in the fill associated with a vessel.[116] The apparent ritual nature of this place should be taken into account as we consider the vessels painted with series, not simply because of possible links between the imaged entities and religious content, but because of the ways in which these vessels may have actively contributed to the affordance of extraordinary sociocultural experiences within the North House.

Within the fill of material found collapsed into the Cult Room Basement were three trickle-painted pithoi. The fragments of human bone and edible snails were associated with one of these. In another, twelve smaller vessels had been placed. These vessels were of various shapes and styles. One, a miniature amphora, was painted around its body with a series of four figure-8 shields, each extending in height from the linear banding at the shoulder of the vessel to banding at the base (Figure 5.8). The shields were rendered in black with white dappling added, seemingly to give the impression of oxhide.

The linear banding painted at the base and shoulder of this miniature amphora, and the close-set series of dots encircling its neck, are comparable to the decorative structure of many contemporaneous painted vessels, and, in

5.8. Miniature amphora painted with series of figure-8 shields, from Cult Room Basement, Knossos. Photograph from Warren 1980: 84 fig. 35; courtesy Peter Warren. Object © Hellenic Ministry of Culture and Sports

this light, the frieze of repeated shields positioned around its belly may at first appear consistent with an ornamental character. "Ornamental" elaborations of an entity, be it in the context of a movable object or of architecture, are ones generally taken to be "inessential," subservient to the structure of the ornamented body, drained of signifying heft and, in this respect, approaching abstraction. This vessel is not quite so straightforward, however. A particular detail of the shields in the painted frieze exemplifies one aspect of the complexity at play. Each shield is topped by a tiny arced line that curves upward to meet the painted band lining the vessel's shoulder. Such arcing features depicted on figure-8 shields have been interpreted as representations of hangers for suspension.[117] In light of this reading of the small arcs, the status of the painted content of the vessel's surface quietly, but certainly, shifts. The apparently ornamental nature of the decorative scheme – comprised of linear bands, a row of dots, and a shield frieze, all emphasizing the structure of the vessel's form – suddenly transforms into a pictorial representation of a wall hung with objects. With this, the shields become objects adeptly suspended by mechanical means, the linear bands become floor and ceiling, and the upper row of dots appear like "beam end" features typical of Minoan depictions of architecture (as seen in, e.g., in the Town Mosaic from Knossos, the Archanes Architectural Model or gold "shrine" plaques from Grave Circle A, Mycenae). These two statuses of the vessel's painted forms are simultaneous but in tension – the ornamental emphasizes the vessel's structure *while* the pictorial implies a represented space. They subtly create a powerful dynamism that redesignates the vessel's representational complexity right before a person's eyes. The Knossos miniature shield amphora shares this representational dynamic with other contemporary vessels, including a pair of hydria (likely of Cretan manufacture) from LC IA Akrotiri, painted at the belly with a series of figure-8 shields topped by prominent hangers, with a line of positioned circles above, around the neck zone. These comparable vessels indicate that such dynamism involving shield friezes may have been embodied and experienced with some regularity in social spaces of the southern Aegean already in the early Neopalatial period. Blakolmer proffers a very similar reading of a stately LM II cup from Isopata (Tomb 5), painted with a frieze composed of one figure-8 shield and two large boar's tusk helmets.[118] This later cup and others further demonstrate how the dynamism of such frieze-bearing vessels persisted over time in the region. Of further note for our discussion is the combination of shield and helmet in the frieze of the Isopata cup. As two instances of our Aegean composite animalian entities, their juxtaposition here, as on other vessels and in glyptic, underscores their perceived likeness.

The craftiness of the miniature amphora from Knossos is heightened, and distinguished, by another aspect of its design. This vessel is pierced in its base, allowing it to function as a rhyton. It shares this feature with each of the other eleven small vessels found within the pithos. This secondary opening in the base makes each into a vessel that cannot *hold* a liquid indefinitely but, instead, is characterized by its *mediation* of an active liquid – each vessel slows the flow of fluid and elaborates its passage both physically and most likely socioculturally. Hence, the hole in the base effectively upturns the traditional function associated with a clay container and does so in an inherently performative and uncanny manner.[119] But this particular vessel takes its craftiness dramatically further. The miniature amphora painted with the series of figure-8 shields has been formed with a cone suspended from its rim that descends into the interior of the vessel.[120] This construction creates a cavity between the outer wall of the vessel and the wall of the cone, where liquid could be hidden from the view of a person peering into the mouth. A small airhole into the cavity is positioned at the rim and another discreet opening occurs within the vessel's interior, below the cone, where the cavity communicates with the primary interior space of the rhyton.

Koehl's study of Aegean rhyta considered vessels formed with such internal cones (for the Knossos vessel, see Koehl's no. 1137).[121] He undertook experimental work with replica vessels, each fitted with a cone of this type, in order to ascertain the mechanics of the feature. He discovered that when both the hole at the rhyton's base and the airhole at the rim were covered, liquid could be poured into the vessel, filling the main belly space of the vessel (in the cone) as well as the hidden cavity, the latter filling through the opening low in the cone's interior. Subsequently, the vessel could be tipped and decanted, appearing to completely empty – but as long as the holes at both the rim and base remained covered, the liquid in the concealed cavity would continue to be trapped. After this, the person holding the rhyton could inconspicuously remove their finger from the rim hole, at which point the liquid from the cavity would run, via the interior opening, into the primary internal space of the vessel, causing the belly of the vessel to be suddenly refilled. The person could then remove their finger from the hole pierced in the vessel's base, or tip the vessel, allowing the unexpected liquid to flow. We can imagine that this routine could be put to very dramatic effect. As Koehl writes: "The rhyton would appear to refill itself once the airhole was uncovered, and then could be emptied from either the primary or secondary opening. Because no practical purpose for these rhyta could be ascertained, it seems very possible that those vessels were made for use in ritual, perhaps involving magic."[122]

This miniature amphora is a cunning thing. Through the details of its painted surface and deceptive mechanics, it would have afforded dynamic and unsettling experiences for those interacting with it. We cannot be certain of the particularities of its use or the emotions it inspired (mystification, surprise, amusement?), but it seems clear that its adept overturning of first impressions would have inspired a questioning of status, as people reckoned with a thing that actively defied boundaries and, somehow, was performing in paradoxical ways. More than one person was likely involved in its use. One person would have been needed to hold the vessel, probably placing one hand below it, with a finger covering the opening in the base, while putting the second hand at the rim, where a finger could cover the airhole. A second person would then pour liquid into the mouth of the rhyton. Hence, the trick rhyton demanded specific bodily know-how and coordination between performers. Like the contemporaneous animal-head rhyta considered in Chapter 2, this vessel emphasized the impressive action of human actors within the palatial context.

Given its meditative role as a rhyton, a type of vessel which facilitated and elaborated the passage of liquid, the Knossos shield amphora likely engaged with other objects, and perhaps with bodies beyond those of the people handling it. The rhyton may have been involved in the meaningful movement of a liquid from one place and/or status to another, for example, as liquid was taken from one vessel to pass through the rhyton into another. Or the rhyton may have been involved in changing the status of something else, for example by contributing to an act of libating a liquid atop a body, or of ingesting a liquid into one. The shield vessel was also part of an assemblage with eleven other rhyta, all relatively small shapes (multiple were classed as miniatures), found collected within the same pithos. The twelve small vessels in this grouping each could have afforded similar but distinct actions to a potential user. Their positioning together in the pithos set them in relation to one another, as a gathering of comparable alternatives. This dynamic of multiplicity and juxtaposition would be echoed in the series painted onto the wall of our amphora-shaped trick rhyton: there, embedded in the assemblage of clay vessels, the file of figure-8 shields also embodied an instance of likeness assembled.

Animal, Vegetable, Object: Formal Assonance Realized in a Vessel's Frieze

The amphoroid trick rhyton from the Cult Room Basement had a particular connection with another of the twelve rhyta in the pithos assemblage, a cup rhyton (Figure 5.9). This cup rhyton was also painted around its wall with a series of entities, and one of these, occurring twice in the succession, was a figure-8 shield. The figure-8 shield alternates with two other entities in this frieze. The first, which appears three times in the series, is a large tear-shaped form, its body marked with horizontal bands from which delicate stippling descends, effecting something like denticulation; at its apex, wispy plumes rise and flow to the right. The second element of the series, which appears once, is a frontal bestial face that has been identified as a "primitive gorgoneion."[123] This visage is remarkable in various respects. The head is round and wide, encircled by a spikey ring of hair. At the top center of the head, long thin tufts

5.9. Drawing of LM IB cup rhyton decorated with an alternating series, from the Cult Room Basement, Knossos. Image from Warren 1980: 84 fig. 34, courtesy Peter Warren

of hair waft upward and to the right; at the top left, the dark spikey halo seems to separate into the suggestion of an ear. The face is stippled all over in short dark dashes. Two wide-open eyes, with pinpoint pupils marking their sharp outward gaze, are unevenly ringed in dark paint. The nose/mouth appears muzzle-like and partially obscured. Its upper edge is clearly formed by a semicircular downward-turned arc; while the top edge of this arc is smooth, the bottom edge is markedly uneven. The area where the mouth would appear is obscured by a large, heavy splotch of dark paint. On the center of the forehead, a dark wide ovoid is positioned; another, more uneven in its form, extends downward perpendicularly from the first between the eyes, forming a T-zone of dark paint across the top center of the face.

The frieze of this vessel is marked by what I am describing as formal assonance. This plays out both within the series of gathered elements and through links to other established contemporaneous Aegean forms. To begin, the three elements within this series – the figure-8 shield, the plumed tear-shaped entity and the bestial head – are comparable in their formation. All are basically formed of thick round orbs; their positioning around the widest curve of vessel's body emphasizes this shared character. Each entity is covered by comparable stippling of short dashes; as if to draw out this common feature, clusters of such dashes appear suspended in the spaces between each element in the series. Finally, each entity is topped by a curving linear protrusion (the hanger of the shields, and the nearly identical wispy tufts extending from the head and the tear forms). These shared characteristics generate a strong impression of similarity across the gathered elements as they are apprehended collectively on the vessel. The vessel, which offers a selection of gathered entities and a selective and inventive rendering of them, *creates* this similarity, at least in part. Each element could be imaged in different ways than we see here, but instead they are encountered on the vessel as remarkably akin. This is not identicalness, but likeness. Here, we can draw out the surface of the shield. As Rehak noted, the characterization of the surface of the shields on the Knossos vessel departs from the typical rendering of figure-8 shields, which have large uneven splotches indicative of oxhide.[124] Instead, the shields on this vessel share the stippling of the other two elements collected in this series. Thus, such likeness arises not merely *via* the vessel as a representational object reproducing forms, but *within* the creative space and moment of copresence that this representational thing provides. The links constituted by the formal features held in common between each element of this series dissolve as the elements are instead interpreted individually, each on their own. For example, the protrusions issuing from the tops of each object, which echo one another while encountered in their collective company, each become something quite divergent when the entities are identified and interpreted by themselves – instead of being alike, they become the dissimilar hair of a beast, strap of a shield and plume of some other type of thing, perhaps vegetal.

It is to the identity of this third, tear-shaped form that I turn now. It repeats three times in the frieze of the vessel. Rehak describes these three things as "unidentified ovoid objects (gourds? squills? baskets?) topped by a plumelike tuft."[125] When I first saw them, I took them to be boar's tusk helmets, but, as I looked more closely, the slight curvature along the bottom edges made me question this. I was not alone in my uncertain initial view though. Niemeier identifies them as possible boar's tusk helmets, and Warren, in his publication of the vessel, states that the tear-drop elements, "may be stylized boar's-tusk helmets or, I now think more likely, bulbous plants like the large squill *Urginea maritima*."[126]

The entity's layered formation in serrated horizontal bands, its doming shape and its prominent plume – all the features that suggest an identity as a boar's tusk helmet – fit extremely well with the tunicated squill, as does the gently rounded bottom (Figure 5.10). In this light, we can now revisit seal motif CMS II.8.132, and the identity of the second domed or tear-shaped object embodied there. While this entity remarkably echoes the form of the helmet with which it has been paired, so well that it has been identified as another helmet by some, certain features suggest it might instead be something vegetal. Three sets of strands issue from this entity. Unlike the top plume of the tear-shaped objects on the Knossos vessel, these strands issue from the widening end of the object's body where they appear a great deal like the thin tubular roots of the squill. A squill's roots dramatically flare from its base and are visible once the bulb is taken from the ground. Depending on the conditions of the squill's growth and

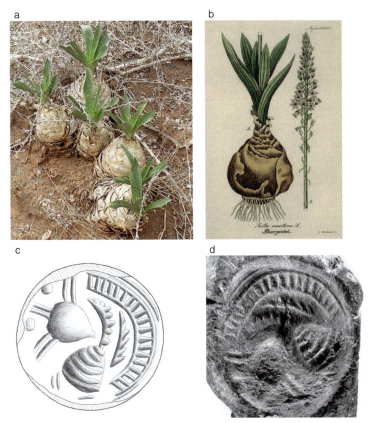

5.10. Views of the squill. a. Leafing bulb emerges from ground; photo courtesy of PassionForPlantation.com. b. *Scilla maritima* L. (*Meerschwiebel*) in W. Artus, *Hand-Atlas sämmtlicher medicinisch-pharmaceutischer Gewächse: oder naturgetreue Abbildungen nebst Beschreibungen in botanischer, pharmacognostischer und pharmacologischer Hinsicht . . .; Zum Gebrauche für Apotheker, Aerzte und Drogisten,* 2, 5th rev. ed. (Jena: Mauke, 1876), facing p. 638. Images of CMS II.8.132: drawing of motif (c.) and seal impression (d.). Images courtesy CMS, Heidelberg. Object © Hellenic Ministry of Culture and Sports.

exposure, the sectioned formation of the bulb can be variably visible on its exterior (and certainly the tunicated nature of the bulb becomes apparent once the squill has been cut open; this distinctive quality of its structure surely would have been associated with the plant). The edges of the rough outer scales typically appear above the surface in jagged rows even as the squill sits in the ground. Sometimes, the body of the squill can appear smoother and less ragged. This is the case especially when the bulb has been removed from the ground, its roots then visible, and its drier, brittle outer layers shed or removed. The object on CMS II.8.132 seems consistent with this latter view of a squill. While the leafy top stem does not appear attached to the bulb, it may still be present in the motif. On the other side of the helmet imaged in CMS II.8.132, we see what appears to be a lone stem, its curvature echoing that of the helmet's arced plume, which it is set alongside. The helmet's plume is remarkably similar to this stem, both being depicted with protrusions lining one edge, extending in the same direction. Indeed, poised between the hypothetical squill and the stem, the helmet, which has both domed body and elongated plume, seems almost to be a compilation of the separate elements of the plant imaged on either side of it (the parts of the plant that would have been positioned above and below the ground; moreover, since the stem's presence varies seasonally, there could be a temporal play here). Botanical drawings of the squill often render the plant with the bulb element separated and set alongside the stem, in just this way (Figure 5.10b).

The positioning of the hypothetical squill in a frieze with figure-8 shields on the Knossos cup rhyton is comparable to the positioning of the boar's tusk helmet in series with figure-8 shields in glyptic, ceramics and other media, as discussed previously (e.g., CMS v.s3.331 (Figure 5.6f), and the Isopata cup discussed by Blakolmer). In essence, we find the squill and helmet occurring in the same company and in the same visual format (series). This connection goes a step further with seal motif CMS II.8.132 (Figures 5.6e, 5.10c–d), where we have what appears to be a direct drawing together of helmet and squill, again within a type of series. This further instance of their pairing, along with the striking similarity of their forms and features in this context, indicate both the perceived closeness of the two entities and their common relationships with the shield.

As we have seen, the link between the boar's tusk helmet and the figure-8 oxhide shield are, in some dimensions, quite clear. The two entities are closely related to one another in their embodiments in the round – both being worn objects of bodily protection, fashioned of parts of nonhuman animal bodies – and also through their copresence in representational media, including in narrative scenes. How exactly the squill finds a seat at the table with these two entities is difficult to know, and consequently our thoughts here are necessarily speculative, but similarity between the formal characters of the squill and the boar's tusk helmet seems crucial. The tunicated nature of the squill bulb is relatable to the segmented design of the helmet, and the squill's composition of numerous individual white scales takes the comparison with the plaqued boar's tusk in the helmet to a yet more specific level. These similarities seem likely to have been observed and remarked on, perhaps traditionally. This may have carried other facets of culturally recognized relationships between boars, squills and helmets. Boars famously eat squills (and are more immune to their toxicity than most other animals). Later Greek accounts indicate that the squill was recognized as a protective device by the Archaic period; if this had earlier roots, such status could parallel the protective – and inherently threatening – roles of shields, helmets and front-facing creatures.[127] At the same time, it seems clear that the relatability between squill and helmet is not only being recognized in the frieze of the Knossos vessel but productively developed through these representational embodiments.

This takes place through the individual rendering of each entity (i.e., which attributes of the entity are depicted, and how) and also through the juxtapositions formulated with other entities – that is, through the pairing, in series, with each other and also with the shield. In other words, the formal assonance of the squill and helmet, richly cultivated in representational spaces, seems to be a leading element in the relationship of the two entities – a relationship that likely also had further cultural dimensions. Their rendering in seriated friezes contributed to the realization of this.

There is another entity that may have been recognized and cultivated for its formal assonance with the boar's tusk helmet. Again, this assonance seems to be, at least in part, generated within the creative space of representations, where similarities in form and composition could be realized. This entity has been identified by scholars as a conventionalized representation of a bundle of cloth, hypothesized to have had a sacred character. The "sacred cloth," "sacral robe" or "sacral knot" are terms used to describe the form when embodied in various LBA Aegean representational media, ranging from faience plaques, to glyptic, to painted ceramics.[128] Here, I would like to highlight the rendering of this bundled textile in LB I–II Aegean glyptic. In CMS II.8.127, an impressed clay sealing from LM I Knossos, we see what have been identified as three such sacral textile bundles positioned in a linear series between two figure-8 shields (Figure 5.11a).[129] This frieze is set above a running-spiral band comparable to horizontal band features present in other renderings of series (some involving figure-8 shields and boar's tusk helmets) in glyptic, as well as in painted ceramics and wall paintings. Each of the textile objects rendered in CMS II.8.127 has a roughly domed shape that leans at its apex toward the left. The object has heavy vertical striations and is crossed by sets of double lines at its base, middle and top. The leaning apex of each bundle appears as a multistrand c-loop, which can be read as folding layers of textile (where the bundle bends over). The general form of this entity is strikingly akin to that of boar's tusk helmets as they are embodied in glyptic objects; we can compare, for example, the helmet of CMS II.6.136, a contemporaneous seal impression from Ayia Triada (Figure 5.6a, cf. 5.6b). In LB I–II Aegean glyptic, both the cloth and the helmet share the common form of a striated, domed shape topped with a multistrand curving element. A lentoid seal from Maroulas, CMS V.S3.331 (Figure 5.11b) vividly demonstrates how likeness between the sacred cloth and boar's tusk helmet was being realized not only formally but also compositionally. Here, three objects appear in a series: two figure-8 shields flanking something that has been described both as a sacral knot and as a boar's tusk helmet. In my view, the leaning apex of this object has an edge of discontinuous lines more consistent with the rendering of a crest/plume than of a folded textile, thus indicating that it is a helmet. That said, the difficulty in assigning one identification versus another is real. I believe that it is also the point – at

286 SINGULAR, SERIATED, SIMILAR

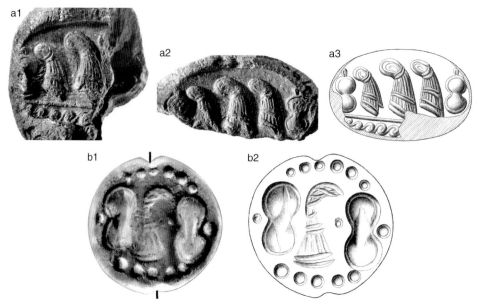

5.11. Renderings of boar's tusk helmets or "sacral cloths" as part of series in Aegean glyptic. a. CMS II.8.127; stamped sealings (left) and drawing of motif (right); b. CMS V.S3.331; modern impression (left) and drawing of motif (right). Images courtesy CMS, Heidelberg. Objects © Hellenic Ministry of Culture and Sports

least in part.[130] We can appreciate how both the form and context of the boar's tusk helmet in CMS V.S3.331 are strikingly close to that of the sacred cloths in CMS II.6.136: their registers of fine lines, rising into curving fibrous crowning elements, appear as variations on the same formal theme, while their shared seriation, set in file with the figure-8 shield, is just as remarkable. A similar connection concerning the form of the helmets rendered in the glyptic from Ayia Triada has been made by McGowan, who relates them to representations of (worn) full skirts seen in contemporary seal imagery – she even briefly notes the similarity to the "sacral knot."[131] These observations are part of a fascinating discussion McGowan offers concerning how such visual connections may have integrated the often ambiguous glyptic motifs into "networks" of images, across objects – thus, crucially, she also recognizes potentially meaningful connections at work between like forms manifest in glyptic imagery. While the renderings of worn skirts do not possess the same representational dynamics that are shared between renderings of helmets and "sacred" cloth bundles – in which they appear as isolated (separate from a wearing body) and potentially seriated entities – the potential link to another textile form is, nevertheless, significant.[132] That formal assonance surrounding renderings of helmets may have also embraced other related embodiments of textiles (beyond the sacred cloth bundles) is remarkable and could indicate that a broader field of comparison was at play between helmets and certain textile entities, potentially embracing aspects of their use, meaning or substance (further links recognized by McGowan within the glyptic corpus, for example, to skirted bird-women and, with them, to, bucrania, are also highly intriguing). Moreover, we should recognize how instances of formal assonance realized between helmets (or textiles) and further entities, through other media (e.g., between helmets and squills, as realized through the painted ceramic vessel from Knossos) may have not only extended but also deepened the nature of such cultural relatability.

While we can only hypothesize, it seems very likely that the remarkable similarity evident across embodiments of these different entities was fostered intentionally, their assonance recognized and actively created through decisions made in the representation of both. McGowan's study establishes further ground for seeing such a connection to textiles across the glyptic repertoire. Rehak has argued that the association of the sacred cloth with the figure-8 shield in Minoan and Mycenaean visual culture, as well as with the bull and sword, indicates that the cloth was connected to ritual actions involving bulls.[133] If so, the boar's tusk helmet and sacred cloth may have been connected as material attestations of impressive and culturally significant encounters with a nonhuman animal; this link would be strengthened if both were worn items.[134] It is possible that the assonance between representational embodiments of the helmet and the cloth was developed in part as a deliberate way of signaling such a specific cultural connection. Certain (potentially intended) connections may have become apparent in different moments, and to different minds; as McGowan eloquently writes, "a change in conceptual context, or in what is expected to be elicted from the material, can catalyze change in the image's perceived associationism."[135] Yet even if we set the question of intent aside, we can still confidently assert that the closeness of these forms would have been experienced by people engaging with the glyptic objects. Glyptic images were encountered in the tiny faces of seal stones and signet rings, and in the equally tiny and also problematically uneven dried clay of stamped impressions. Met in these challenging surfaces, it would have been remarkably difficult to distinguish entities with such similar forms and compositional contexts without close examination. As modern scholars, we work with magnified renderings of these motifs, stabilizing the appearance of the details as much as possible.[136] Still, we have trouble distinguishing the form in CMS V.S3.331 between a helmet or a sacral cloth. This ambivalence belies a broader similarity in their forms that surely would have been real then, as now.

The Fruits of Juxtaposition and Assonance

I would like to turn now to a brief consideration of further links the boar's tusk helmet may have had with the entities we have seen either juxtaposed to it or rendered in a remarkably similar manner. Here, we reach more speculatively into the terrain of possible cultural content connected to the entities. The Knossos cup rhyton provides a base. We have explored the identification of the tear-shaped entity as a squill and its formal assonance with the boar's tusk helmet. Now, we can consider the front-facing head that is also positioned in this frieze, along with the squill and figure-8 shields. This has been interpreted as a gorgoneion and compared broadly to later renderings. As we have seen (in Chapter 4), front-facing gorgoneia and gorgons are attested in the Aegean, and Crete specifically, during the Neopalatial phase and earlier. However, the heads/faces are typically more humanoid in their appearance, especially those from Crete. But front-facedness itself seems to hold particular potency in Cretan Bronze Age visual culture, and the head of the Knossos cup rhyton may have been experienced as sharing such with other creatures, such as gorgons, owls and cats, discussed in the previous chapter. More specific to the figure on the cup rhyton, Morgan has discussed the association of front-facing representations of beasts and their status as dead or dying.[137] The head on the Knossos vessel has various peculiar characteristics that I believe strongly suggest an identification as a dead/dying boar (and there is contemporaneous evidence of representing disembodied swine heads, e.g., on the MM III Anemospilia spearhead (Figure 5.12), in glyptic (Figures 2.14a–b, 5.2c) and boar's head rhyta from Akrotiri). The rhinal area, largely obscured by a painted blotch in the lower zone of the face, is visible along its upper edge in the form of a bold, approximately semicircular downward-turned arc (Figure 5.13b). While this does not fit with the vertical ridge of a humanoid nose, it strongly suggests the curved snout of certain nonhuman animals, and especially the dramatically round and flat rostral plane of swine. The stippling that covers the face suggests a hairy coat, which can be closely compared to the stippling of the front-facing boar's head depicted on the spearhead from Anemospilia.[138] Meanwhile, the bristly ring that encircles the entire head forms a more dramatic feature consistent with the longer mane of male living boars. We can compare this feature on the head of the Knossos vessel to renderings of swine from the Aegean Bronze Age that also show the head/shoulders characterized by a distinct ring of long spikey hair, for example, on a fragment of a stone relief vessel from LM I Palaikastro (Figure 5.14);[139] the frontal boar's head on the Anemospilia spearhead also shows a clear differentiation between the shorter hair covering the face and the ring of longer bristles that surrounds it. Three areas of the face on the Knossos vessel have been covered with distinct zones of solid paint. The two that form a rough T, at the middle of the forehead and descending between the eyes, mark precisely the area of the head that is targeted when killing a boar or pig (see Figure 5.13c). This is the area where the brainstem can be most directly reached, by a spear, bullet, or other weapon, rendering the beast stunned and easier to manipulate for the bleeding process. Depictions of boar hunting from the Aegean

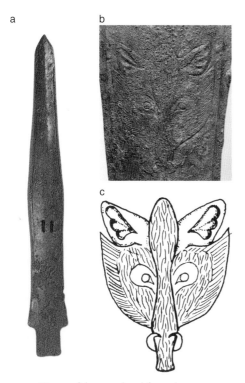

5.12. Views of the spearhead from the west room of the building at Anemospilia. a. Spearhead. b. Detail of image of forward-facing beast (boar). c. Drawing of detail. Images from Sakellarakis, Yannis and Efi Sapouna-Sakellaraki, *Archanes: Minoan Crete in a New Light* (Athens: Ammos Publications, 1997): 597 fig. 621, 598 fig. 622. Courtesy Efi Sapouna-Sakellaraki. Objects © Hellenic Ministry of Culture and Sports

Bronze Age often show a spear directed at this point on the animal's head (e.g., on a seal from Vapheio, CMS I.227, Figure 5.15; cf. Figure 5.2b), and striking swine in this area remains both typical and widespread in the slaughtering practices of the present day. Following the stunning head strike, the animal can be bled out in various ways, depending on the dictates of traditional practices and on the motivations and interests of those undertaking the slaughter. In many cases, the carotid arteries are severed through cuts to the neck tissue. Cutting the throat can also result in severing of the jugular veins, trachea and esophageal passage. Another method of bleeding aims the cut closer to the heart to sever blood vessels issuing from it.[140] As the heart pumps, blood is projected out of the body rapidly. This can cause blood to issue from the mouth and nose of the dying beast. On the Knossos vessel, the two areas with painted blotches are positioned both where the spear would enter the animal's head, causing blood to flow downward from the point of entry, and over the area of the mouth and nose (muzzle). I would add that while we do not see tusks, they would be located in this same darkened area of the muzzle (cf. the location of tusks on, e.g., the Anemospilia spearhead (Figure 5.12), or the LC I boar's head rhyta from Akrotiri.

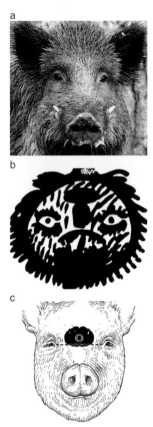

5.13. Comparative frontal views of a swine's head. a. Front view of living swine (Blickwinkel Images). b. Detail of face painted upon cup rhyton from the Cult Basement deposit at Knossos (courtesy Peter Warren; see Figure 5.9). c. Ideal location for stunning strike to a swine's head, which targets the brain. Courtesy J.K. Shearer, Iowa State University.

5.14. Photograph of a fragment of a Minoan stone vessel, carved with figure of a boar. From B. Kaiser, *Untersuchungen zum minoischen Relief* (Bonn: Habelt-Verlag, 1976), fig. 21a. Courtesy Habelt-Verlag.

5.15. Drawing of motif engraved in a seal from Vapheio, CMS I.227. Courtesy CMS, Heidelberg

If this head captures the moment of blood issuing from a bleeding swine's muzzle, it could be compared to the effect of the contemporaneous boar's head rhyta from Akrotiri. As Rehak discusses concerning Cretan bull's head rhyta, liquid, perhaps dark, flowing from the opening in the muzzle of these rhyta could reembody the loss of blood experienced in the dramatic moment of the beast's death at human hands.[141] The head painted on the Knossos vessel seems to be making the same moment manifest.

The plume that tops the head on the Knossos vessel is intriguing. It could be a rendering of a central line of longer bristles positioned along the top of a male boar's body, extending from the head down its back (as seen in glyptic renderings, e.g., Figures 5.2b,[142] 5.15). On biological boars, this ridge of bristles stands erect when the animal is upset or aggressive, thus becoming more visible as a protruding element.[143] On the Knossos vessel, the plume contributes to the formal assonance of the elements of the frieze, by constituting a clear link with the hypothetical squill. If the head is indeed that of a dead or dying swine, then the apparent relationship of the boar's tusk helmet and the squill gains further depth in the context of this frieze, as the absent but alluded to crested helmet is also potentially implied by the swine head. The swine head – if that is indeed what we have – would have both a biographical and indexical link to the boar's tusk helmet. The addition of a dramatic plume to the top of the swine head could also signal the telos of the killing of the animal: the production of a plumed helmet made of the beast's tusks. By already imaging a conventional element of the helmet-to-be on the dying beast, the absent cultural object is again made present, as it is also by the visually assonant squill. Through the frieze, we thus seem to be seeing a dynamic rendering of forms that are each, simultaneously, connected to observed features of entities in the round (vegetable, animal, inanimate object) and creatively linked to one another through their representational embodiments.

Coming Undone and Coming Together: Recomposition as a Means of Relating Animal Entities

Underlying formal assonance is a mental decomposition and recomposition of two specific forms in order to recognize grounds for similarities between them; it could be that one of the forms leads in this process – that assonance is developed after one of the forms has already been reembodied in a certain representational form, by rendering the second entity in a way that appears similar to the representational form of the first.[144] We seem to see such decomposition at play in the assonance cultivated between the helmet and the sacral knot. In essence, the complex constitution of each of these entities is decomposed to a striated rounded triangle with a multistranded crown and reembodied with these as their primary formal attributes. This need not have been an esoteric process; it is simply inherent to recognizing and formulating graphic similarity. Whether the process or the relation of the resultant forms had specific significance is a further matter.

I believe we can see a related dynamic of formal decomposition at work in another seal motif, which also realizes a connection between the sacred cloth and the boar's tusk helmet. In a clay seal impression excavated from the area of the Court of the Stone Spout at Knossos, CMS II.8.126 (Figure 5.16a), we see what seems at first to be a series of objects – and, on one level, it is just such. Two striated triangular objects with curving tops, identified as sacred cloths, flank, in mirror symmetry, a third object. The central object appears as a long, tapering and almost-tubular shaft, which is barbed at its narrower end with short antithetical dashes (three on each side) and topped, at the other end, with a stemmed plume of longer striations. On the outside of each sacred cloth, a small amygdaloid shape is positioned with one tip leaning toward the curving apex of the neighboring cloth. Set side by side, the forms seen in CMS II.8.126 constitute a series, which brings with it the suggestive relational dynamics of juxtaposition between them. While the two triangular entities appear consistent with the conventional form of the sacred cloth and can be accepted as instances of such, the identity of the central object is less clear. It looks somewhat vegetal, but the barbed narrow end is instead more in keeping with renderings of a weapon; likewise, the spray at the opposite end appears like the fletching of a spear (perhaps feathered). The amygdaloid elements are too generic to identify with a specific entity.

Why are these entities set side by side? The sacred cloth motif, we have seen, occurs in other representational material culture with the figure-8 shield, as

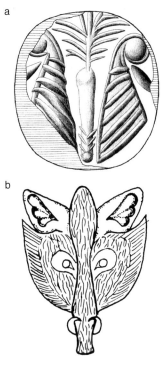

5.16. a. Drawing of motif from sealing CMS II.8.126; courtesy CMS, Heidelberg. b. Detail of swine head from the Anemospilia spearhead; from Sakellarakis, Yannis and Efi Sapouna-Sakellaraki, *Archanes: Minoan Crete in a New Light* (Athens: Ammos Publications, 1997): 598 fig. 622. C ourtesy Efi Sapouna-Sakellaraki

well as with the sword. Thus, its juxtaposition with a spear in this impression would fit with a broader iconographic association with weaponry. The sacred cloth's formal assonance with the boar's tusk helmet is of course also relevant in this connection, providing another link to an item of war and hunt and the sociocultural implications that carries. Hence, the seal image speaks on an immediate level, as a series, and as such is already complicated by assonance and ambivalence within the juxtaposed forms. But, simultaneously, this gathering of seriated entities seems to also be saying something else, in unison, as each form also contributes to the impression of an unfused whole – or an image "disintegrated," as Morgan puts it.[145] On this more inclusive level, I believe we can see emerge in this assemblage of interacting forms an abstracted rendering of a front-facing boar's head. The specific and somewhat peculiar formation of the individual entities provides for this composite view.

The curving apexes of the sacred cloths have been formed here as perfectly circular, the center of each effectively constituted by a solid round mass (cf. other contemporaneous renderings of the cloth, where the apexes instead appear more as multistranded semicircles, e.g., CMS II.8.127 or CMS II.8.398). Taken together, these two circular masses become a pair of unblinking eyes. Widening below these eyes, the striated bulk of the two sacred cloths appear as the buccal regions of the beast; with this, the small amygdaloid forms that angle out from the sacred cloths emerge as ears, taking a pointed shape consistent with contemporaneous renderings of swine ears (cf., e.g., CMS II.2.213a, CMS II.3.196, CMS II.2.220b, CMS I.227, CMS I.276; as well as on the Anemospilia spearhead (Figure 5.16b) and Akrotiri rhyta. The linear striations of the sacred cloths can be compared to linear markings that sometimes appear on the cheeks of swine in Aegean visual culture, for example on the Anemospilia spearhead and seals CMS I.227, CMS II.213a and CMS v. s1B.60 (Figures 5.2c, 5.15).

We have strong precedent for the representation of boar's heads as essentially fused triangular units. The distinctive biplanar facial structure of wild swine, where relatively flat cheek-flanks slope downward from a long central rhinal ridge, is rendered in numerous Aegean zoomorphic objects as two broad, symmetrical and basically triangular segments that come together along their long edge. We can clearly appreciate this triangular facial structure in three-dimensional renderings of the beast, such as swine-head rhyta (e.g., the pair from Akrotiri) as well as in profile renderings of swine heads occurring in Aegean glyptic (e.g., CMS II.2.213a, CMS I.227 or CMS II.220b; Figures 5.2c, 5.15). Seal impression CMS II.8.126 is consistent with this convention, but with a twist. Here, we see the swine's recessing triangular cheek planes as if pivoted upward to be fully visible from a frontal perspective, despite the fact that it is rendered in the single plane provided by an engraved seal face.

The front-facing rendering of a swine's head that we see in impression CMS II.8.126 is paralleled by various contemporaneous renderings of the beast – including that painted on the Knossos cup rhyton from the Cult Room Basement (following the reading of that painting offered here). However, the angle upon the forward-gazing head is somewhat different in the seal impression: instead of looking at the beast straight on, across the barrel of the muzzle, as we do on the cup rhyton, we seem to be looking downward upon the face. Here the long, shaft-like character of the central form of the motif comes into play. This elongated feature, flanked by the wide-set eyes and triangular cheeks, matches top-down renderings of the boar's extended rhinal ridge that we have seen in other representational objects, including the Anemospilia spearhead and an LM I seal impression from Ayia Triada, CMS II.6.92 (Figure 2.14b). In these objects as well, the rhinal ridge has been formed essentially as a distinct long, narrow mass. And as in these representations, here on CMS II.8.126 we also see the points of the tusks rising tightly from the end of the muzzle – the antithetic barbs of the central shaft constitute these in the case of CMS II.8.126. Meanwhile, the rounded form of a swine's rostral plane is suggested here by the central shaft's gently curved terminus.

If, indeed, the rendering of an animal's head with front-facing directionality carried a signification of death in Aegean visual culture, this dimension of loss of life seems powerfully developed in the Knossos seal motif, given that the very form constituting the long central area of the animal's head is, at the same time, the barbed spear that could usher in its death through a head strike. The plume issuing from atop the head, which is also the fletching of the spear, could be a representation of the spikey hair that can be seen rising from this area of the head of swine. But it is also possible, as we considered in the case of the face painted on the Knossos cup rhyton, that this plume alludes to the plume of the boar's tusk helmet that would be understood as the eventual outcome of the beastly death dynamically imaged here.

There is a history of scholarship concerning the topic of abstracted figural motifs in Cretan Bronze Age visual culture. As we discussed in Chapter 4, a wealth of motifs in the corpus of late Protopalatial Kamares ware ceramics have been problematized for their hovering across the figural/nonfigural divide.[146] Meanwhile, in the small fields of glyptic, abstraction and stylization can be especially prevalent and powerful, given the motivation to be efficient in rendering a motif in a tiny surface. In his Talismanic group, Evans identified a group of predominantly hard-stone seals that are characterized by stylization and abstraction. In these objects, drillwork is left "undisguised,"[147] and figural forms are often unencumbered by finer detail. Whether their simplicity of form was intended to carry significance or was fundamentally a matter of economy in the crafting process, the resultant motifs are often visually bold renderings of entities. Evans believed that these objects were not used sphragistically but functioned instead solely as apotropaic amulets; Hussein has recently argued against this.[148] As Morgan has discussed with characteristic incisiveness, certain motifs of the Talismanic group and contemporaneous glyptic flirt with the boundaries of representation, making our categorization of them difficult.[149] More recently, McGowan's studies have valuably addressed the matter of apparent ambiguity in Cretan glyptic imagery, which she addresses through the relevant lens of "multivalency," as elements of a motif might find connections in other images, engraved in other seals.[150] Discerning between the pictorial and nonpictorial can be challenging – as can be determining the subject of pictorial renderings that have been boiled down to basic elements. We see this, for example, in various "ornamental" motifs engraved into MM III–LM I soft-stone seals, or in a subgroup of the Talismanic group that Evans, and Kenna after him, described as "lion's masks" but were subsequently reinterpreted by Onassaglou as "papyrus" motifs.[151] The ambiguity in these motifs stems from an inability to determine their defining identity, or the potential to read multiple identifications into them. Morgan has delved the matter of ambiguity in this group, considering different ways that it could have been experienced, as alternatives or connected possibilities. In CMS II.8.126, we have not so much ambiguity as ambivalence between two simultaneous pictorial statuses that are not mutually exclusive. This motif is two things at once: a series of objects and an abstracted front-facing boar's head; these simultaneous statuses are deeply relevant to one another.

Through consideration of seal impression CMS II.8.126 and the Knossos cup rhyton, we can see distinct but related ways in which seriation and formal assonance contributed to dynamic representations of a boar touched by death. The boar's tusk helmet is not actually present in either representation, but its presence is potentially implied in both. Indeed, experiences of presence/absence are apparent in various other dimensions of these objects and their active contexts as well. As a rhyton, the Knossos vessel, painted with the frontward-gazing beast, squills and figure-8 shields, would have been dramatically marked by the flow of liquids whose presence within the rhyton was always fleeting. The deposition of this vessel with the trick rhyton, also painted with a series, puts further emphasis on the play of presence and absence in their shared context. Glyptic objects are also distinctly energized by matters of presence and absence, visibility and hiddenness, as worn objects and sphragistic devices.[152] Meanwhile, we have seen that the boar's tusk helmet, as a practical thing in the round, itself performs a distinctive presencing of animals – swine and human – through its form and substance, while actually embodying neither beast. Humans engaged with these different objects (rhyton, seal impression, helmet) in contexts ranging from hunt, to war, to ritual action, to administration. Across these, it is not simply a shared icon that connected them, but their rich dynamics of presence, relation and allusion.

APPROACHING AND RETREATING: BETWEEN POTS, PAINTINGS AND PEOPLE

The cup rhyton and miniature amphora-shaped trick rhyton from the Cult Room Basement deposit at Knossos were both relatively small things. While certainly not as tiny as seals, they were also movable and likewise could be recontextualized, hidden and revealed. These objects, ceramic and glyptic, involved looking closely and provided people with representational embodiments of entities that could be taken within the hand – providing both intimacy and control. While seals are more or less always very small, ceramics are a medium with remarkable range. I would like to turn now to some vessels that pushed at scalar and chromatic thresholds of ceramic painting and, with that, engaged humans in novel ways – by meeting them where they were (or at least closer to it).

In a nuanced discussion of the cultural complexity evident in painted material from Akrotiri, Vlachopoulos has discussed a class of larger-scale

5.17. Two views of the Hunter's Asaminthos from Akrotiri, Thera (late MC Phase 3 or LC I). Courtesy Akrotiri Excavations. Object © Hellenic Ministry of Culture and Sports

late MC ceramic vessels as being trailblazing in their character and crosscraft connections.[153] Painted in vivid color, these objects bring pictorial and, in some cases, apparently narrative compositions to the curved surfaces of pots. At the same time, like Kamares ware, the painting of these vessels seems to work across the pictorial–nonpictorial divide, creating dynamism and interest; here, the effect is far more scenic than what we see with Kamares painting, however.[154] In the previous chapter, we considered the bold griffins that stand tall across the walls of the Griffin Pithos, their feet set within a zone of rising spirals that seem, at the same time, to be a terrain teeming with vegetation. Now, I would like to focus on another vessel, the Hunter's Asaminthos (Figure 5.17).[155]

The asaminthos has a straight wall that tapers very slightly outward from its base to reach the simple flanged lip; two uncomplicated lug handles momentarily break the smooth, curved surface on opposite sides of the vessel. The vessel's large painted surface draws together two seemingly distinct scenes, each impacting how the other is experienced. On one side, the vessel rushes with animal life. We see the silhouette of a human (perhaps originally paired with a second), painted in red, standing in a landscape in which, to the human's right, a host of beasts leap and dash. The nonhuman animals are rendered in black, red and stippled red paint. We have at least one goat and several other wide-horned quadrupeds that appear to be cattle, as well as a very large red bird positioned just above the rightmost quadruped. Three equally large swallows

298   SINGULAR, SERIATED, SIMILAR

dart straight outward, forming the forward line of the rush of animals. Below these figures and the human, a bold, dark, rocky ground undulates; it extends to the flat base of the vessel. In the field above this stony base, around the bodies of the animals, we see red crocus blossoms and petaloid forms scattered.

As the vessel wall continues to the right of the rushing animals, we walk into a different type of representational space – or so it seems at first. Here, three large figure-8 shields appear, painted red, black and red. Their forms occupy the entire height of the vessel's central zone, extending from the horizontal banding below the rim to the painted base. We have here a strikingly early instance of a painted shield frieze, a motif that, we have seen, is often treated by scholars as being ornamental, or as operating as a conventionalized signifying device, such as an insigne. In this light, the shield frieze of the Hunter's Asaminthos can be compared to series that were painted on later vessels; on these, including the cup rhyton from the Cult Room Basement and the pair of hydria imported to Akrotiri, among others, shields extend around the entire vessel wall. Yet the Hunter's Asaminthos has strongly distinguishing attributes that would impact how it was experienced. To begin, the shield frieze here is not continuous. On both ends, it meets the vivid, motion-filled scene of human and animals. As different as these two elements of the vessel's painted content may at first seem, they are in fact powerfully drawn together. The coloration of the animals and shields is shared. This not only indicates that the shields could be understood as being fashioned of animal hides, but also, and more immediately, it visually integrates the different entities imaged across the vessel – the animals and the shields. The dark and rocky terrain that provides the ground for the vibrant outdoor animal scene continues with the same swelling determination around the entire vessel, rising up around the bases of the figure-8 shields just as it rises below the feet of dashing animals. Likewise, the field of crocus blossoms surrounds both the shields and animals.

What occurs at the top of the painted scene, above the heads of the animals and shields, is especially remarkable. Just below the vessel's rim, we have three alternating painted bands, in black, red and black. The first two are straight horizontal linear features, comparable to the simple banding that demarcates such junctures on the bodies of many painted ceramic vessels of this era and later periods. But the lowest black band is different. While its top edge, where it confronts the red band, is straight, its lower edge undulates irregularly, echoing the color and character of the dark terrain below as it, too, encroaches on the space of the painted entities. Positioned above the landscape of running beasts, this encroaching upper ground is comparable to what we see in many wall paintings and scenic painted vessels (as well as in other representational media) of the Neopalatial period, including in wall paintings from Akrotiri. Such "hanging ground" becomes a convention in southern Aegean visual culture, used to indicate figures' embeddedness within a depicted land or seascape.[156]

There is a complex representation of spatial depth at play in scenes where hanging ground is indicated. This takes form through a combination of bird's-eye and side perspectives, constituting what has been described as a "cavalier perspective."[157] With this, the foreground of a scene appears in profile, with a section of the ground, such as the rocky terrain of the Hunter Asaminthos, imaged rising from the lower boundary of the painting. All figures are also rendered in profile. At the same time, as the painting rises upward on the wall, we are to understand the space occupied by the painted figures as receding backward, away from the viewer, as we look down upon it. We see this arrangement clearly, for example, on the MM II–III Sacred Grove fresco from Knossos, where paved pathways extending across the ground appear as if viewed from above, while human figures and trees are rendered in profile but are set at different levels, indicating that some are farther back in space, at a greater distance from the viewer. One of the two LB I–II gold cups from Vapheio also richly illustrates the creation of depth through this means (Figure 5.18).[158] Here, in a scene playing out between a lower and upper (hanging) ground, a bull is captured in a net tied between two trees. One of the trees is set above the other in the field, indicating its position farther back in the landscape. The c-form of the net appears essentially as a vertically oriented element on the surface of the cup, but its tension between the two trees makes clear that it extends across a planar distance in the depicted landscape – a distance that the captured bull, in its contorted struggle, vividly occupies. We seem to be seeing an early instance of this representational dynamic at work on the Hunter's Asaminthos, as the dashing animals range across the crocus field

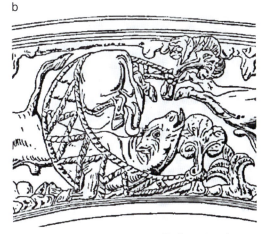

5.18. Gold repoussé cup from Vapheio, fifteenth century BCE, showing capture of bull; National Archaeological Museum, Athens, 1758. Photograph: Bridgeman Images. Drawing: Kaiserlich Deutsches Archäologisches Institut (public domain). Object © Hellenic Ministry of Culture and Sports

set at different heights upon the vessel's surface. With this, the figures are made wholly and equally available to the human viewer.

This way of representing spatial depth leaves the upper border of a painting in a challenging spot: since the field is pivoted upward, and we look *down* upon a ground that recedes from the lower boundary of the field, the upper border is not the sky, nor is it the horizon; it is instead the ground of some place "back there." This back-ground is indicated by another sliver of terrain rendered in section, now extending downward from the painting's upper boundary – this is the "hanging ground." Hence the imaged space is in essence bounded – above and below – by the underlying ground. Where does this leave the shields of the Hunter's Asaminthos? Just as the rocky terrain set below the animals continues underneath the shields, so, too, does the hanging ground extending from the upper border. These encroaching grounds announce that the shields are somewhere, in space, and are not simply an abstract frieze. But where are they? This is left in limbo. While both their coloration and the rocky, crocus-filled ground they are embedded in are shared with the animals that bound in an outdoor setting, are the shields supposed to be understood as being within this landscape? Marthari has discussed the continuation of these landscape features across the vessel, and the positioning of the three swallows between the animals and the shields, as "unifying" the decoration as a continuous narrative, that should be read from left to right, embracing the shields.[159] Papagiannopoulou has also argued for the narrative structure of the scenes, specifically suggesting that a hunt-based rite of passage is depicted.[160] For these scholars, the shared terrain underlines a continuity in storyline, and this certainly seems possible.

On a formal level, several factors complicate the shields' relationship with the animals and their context. First is their scale. The shields occupy the full height of the field opened between the upper and lower borders. Their size sets them apart from the quadrupeds on the vessel, which all are notably smaller, but it seems to connect the shields to the human. The upper half of the human's body is lost to damage, but the waistline corresponds with the level at which the narrow middle of the shields is positioned. Yet, even as the human shares its size, waistline and ground with the shields, it still seems to be separated from them. This is because the setting of the shields is complicated by an additional attribute. Extending between the shields, but not into the area of the vessel painted with the human and nonhuman animals, are three even linear bands, in red, black and red. The bands run between the midsections of the figure-8 shields. We can compare this linear feature to what appears on numerous renderings of friezes of figure-8 shields dating to the Neopalatial period. We have seen that in Cretan glyptic, multiple instances of friezes in preserved clay impressions from LM I Knossos associate figure-8 shields with a band/line feature. This feature can be set below the shields, appearing as a ground (e.g., Figures 5.5d, 5.11a), or (and) can align with the middle area of the shields, as we see on the Hunter Asaminthos (e.g., Figure 5.5d, h; 5.6f). In the latter position, the linear feature seems to run behind the shields, as if it were banding painted on a wall in front of which the shields are set. Blakolmer has discussed the possible link between renderings of these horizontal features in glyptic (when positioned in the lower and/or mid-zones of a figural motif) and elements of architectural wall painting, such as painted dadoes and friezes.[161] Marthari connects this aspect of the Hunter's Asaminthos to a LC I "Minoanizing" piriform jug from Pillar Shaft 77N-78A at Akrotiri, on which a series of figure-8 shields is depicted with striated linear bands running between them, giving the sense that the bands extend behind the shields.[162] In this case, similar striated bands also occur on the shields themselves, complicating our sense of their status. Such banded features, of course, also occur in friezes of objects painted in wall frescoes dating from LB I to LB III. Of these, the LB II and III shield frescoes from Crete and the mainland are especially well known (from Knossos, Tiryns, Mycenae, Pylos; see Figure 6.8), but an LM IA fresco with a series of large boar's tusk helmets set "upon" such linear banding is now also known from Room 2 in Xeste 4 at Akrotiri (see Figure 6.5).[163] Considered in these muralistic contexts, the linear bands have been a key element in interpretations that read the frescoed shield friezes as illusionistic, because the bands are seen to contribute to the sense that the shields are hung *atop* a painted wall. We will return to this topic below, but first, as we consider the Hunter's Asaminthos, we should appreciate that the linear banding complicates our sense of the shields' presence in a space. The rocky and flower-strewn terrain, which the shields share with the running animals, pulls the shields outside, into an expansive imaged space, while the linear bands seem to suggest an interior setting, against or upon a painted wall. The dimensionality of the representation seems to widen and contract between these different elements of the vessel's painting and their spatial implications.

Walls and Open Spaces

To our modern eyes, which observe with the aid (and burden) of hindsight, two attributes of the Hunter's Asaminthos from Akrotiri seem to indicate a relationship with wall painting. First is the presence "behind" the shields of what appear like painted linear banding features seen in wall frescoes; the later murals that pair such banding with shield friezes underscore this crosscraft link.[164] Second is the asaminthos' apparent utilization of the convention for rendering spatial depth through the depiction of hanging ground extending from the upper border of the figural field – a convention that becomes a frequent feature in Neopalatial figural wall painting. The dating of the Hunter's Asaminthos is complicated. Its context seems to be LC I, but the vessel has been dated to the later Middle Cycladic Phase 3 at Akrotiri (Phase 3 corresponds approximately to MM IIB–IIIA in the Cretan chronology). Papagiannopoulou has suggested it is an heirloom, while Marthari suggests it may be LC I, in part because of its remarkable "indication of natural setting," which becomes common in mature LC I.[165] The Hunter's Asaminthos does indeed seem ahead of its time. If the MC dating holds, it predates the earliest evidence we currently have for wall painting of any kind in Akrotiri[166] and is likely contemporaneous with the earliest extant evidence in Cretan wall painting for the convention of hanging ground (see the MM IIIA–B Saffron Gatherer fresco, from Knossos).[167] In terms of parallel features in other ceramics, we find an undulating terrain painted below the series of figure-8 shields and bands on the LC I jug from Pillar Shaft 77N-78A at Akrotiri; meanwhile, curving pendant masses, painted around the small handles set below the vessel's dark shoulder banding, may be renderings of rocky hanging ground. The use of hanging ground becomes very popular in later Neopalatial painted ceramics, such as the LM IB Marine Style, where the depth of seascapes is rendered through it. Remarkably, figure-8 shields can appear in the watery environs painted on those vessels, set within or even suspended from the rocky border.[168] Yet even in the context of its own medium, the MC asaminthos from Akrotiri appears to be at the leading edge in its manifestation of this feature.

On the Hunter's Asaminthos, the representation of bodies in space is enriched by both the presence of hanging ground and the pairing of background banding with the shield frieze; the spatial effect is especially complex, and powerful, because these features occur in combination. In the linear banding associated with the shields, we may be seeing a depiction of objects in a painted room.[169] While fragmentary, we do have evidence of band features frescoed on the walls of Protopalatial structures at Phaistos and Knossos, indicating that such wall painting may have already been associated with rooms in important built spaces in Crete during the time that the asaminthos was crafted. If so, renderings of a line of shields upon bands may have been developing as a means of signaling the sociocultural weight of these places. With this, we could understand the bands on the asaminthos as contributing to a representation of shields suspended upon or placed against such painted walls (an idea that Evans suggested long ago concerning later renderings of shield friezes in wall frescoes). The asaminthos, however, is from Thera, not Crete. Perhaps the shields-on-bands composition traveled from Crete to Akrotiri, and/or knowledge of the practice of hanging shields on the walls of important buildings did – or perhaps it was already familiar in the Cycladic town. We could be missing part of the picture. While we do not have any pure MBA evidence of wall painting from Akrotiri, the transitional MC III–LC I Seismic Destruction Phase at the site has produced plaster wall fragments that already display sophisticated nonfigural polychrome designs.[170] Perhaps simpler polychrome banding was present in the earlier painted walls of Phase 3 buildings in the town, as it was contemporaneously in Crete, even if evidence of it presently eludes us; this would impact how the spatiality of the shields on the asaminthos was experienced by people engaging with the vessel in Akrotiri. On these points concerning the motif's background in Akrotiri we can, at present, only speculate. However, across such variable possibilities, we can see that if the banding in this area of the Hunter Asaminthos does indeed represent a wall painting feature, then the shields painted on the vessel are caught in an especially tense place – between a rocky field and a wall. Even if we assume that the banding that appears with the shields was intended to be nonrepresentational, the fact remains that it serves to separate the shields from the animals even as the shared terrain encompasses both; the relationship of these two simultaneous effects produces an unsettled spatial complexity.

The Hunter's Asaminthos is one of a group of large-scale Middle Cycladic or LC I painted vessels from Akrotiri that also includes other extraordinary pictorial objects such as the Griffin Pithos and the Ganymede Jug. Nikolakopoulou, Papageorgiou, Marthari, Papagiannopoulou and Vlachopoulos[171] are correct to point to these vessels as crucial contributors to the development of painting in the region, potentially being ancestral to practices realized *across* painted media – a matter that we also touched upon in the previous chapter, in discussion of the Griffin Pithos. In this light, I would like to return to the matter of scale. These vessels are, simply put, big. The Hunter's Asaminthos stands over a third of a meter high, as does the Ganymede Jug; the asaminthos also extends to a half-meter diameter at its rim; meanwhile, both the Griffin Pithos and the Lillies Jug tower at over a meter in height. The enlarged surfaces of these vessels are richly cultivated as representational fields that bring new, impressive dimensions to renderings of figures in paint. We are not seeing figures represented at fixed ratios relative to represented subjects, nor is there a consistent sizing of represented entities between the vessels. Yet each of these vessels is participating in something common, and innovative, as they reach beyond the traditional boundaries of their object type to represent entities in sizes that would have been unexpected and novelly engaging.[172] They brought humans, nonhuman animals and complex animalian entities such as shields to the edge of what was familiar in the painted walls of a ceramic vessel and, with this, subtly but provocatively challenged how the vessels, and the bodies manifested in their painted walls, were present in the lived world. They did this also in an extended range of color, stepping into polychromy, in a move that built upon a tradition of brilliant Middle Cycladic bichrome painted vessels, especially the Black and Red ware.

In these ways, these large-scale MC vessels from Akrotiri move beyond the established parameters of their medium. In so doing, they seem to premeditate some of the representational dynamics of wall painting – especially in their expanded scale and coloration, as well as their zoning and pictorial subjects. Egan has insightfully drawn out how large painted ceramics could share spatial and experiential effects with murals, even while also having distinct properties, like portability and hence more mutable and potentially "immersive" presence.[173] Likewise, the Cycladic vessels were movable (if heavy) things, with contours that are connected to a range of affordances that do not pertain to the walls of rooms. The vessels can hold substances,[174] some have spouts to pour, their walls curve around in an interminable circle, and handles remind a person that one can reach out and hold them. These qualities were retained as the large MC vessels provocatively stepped beyond the normal character of ceramics, and into areas that would come to overlap with that of wall paintings. Hence, these vessels offer something of a glimpse between the possibilities of different media, both chronologically and in terms of particular attributes that they realize.

NOTES

1. See Blakolmer 2016a for a rich discussion of Aegean "composite" creatures, including a meaty overview of types and consideration of their occurrences; he does not include these three entities in the category.
2. Knappett (2020) offers an astute examination of "combining" in Aegean Bronze Age art, which takes in both acts of making and the topic of "composite" entities. I believe many dimensions of my approach concur with Knappett's, especially in expanding consideration of composites and the deeply creative potential of objects. He does preserve the idea that (Aegean) composites are "counter-intuitive," marking a key point where our views diverge Knappett (e.g., 2020: 98). See Chapter 4.
3. For example, Xenaki-Sakellariou 1953; Varvarighos 1981; Morris 1990; Krzyszkowska 1991; Rehak 1999; Molloy 2012; see Anderson 2021 for further bibliography.
4. Shapland asserts that imagery of hunting in BA Crete has been underrecognized (2022: 127).
5. Morris 1990: 152, 155.
6. Morris provides this estimate (1990: 155).
7. Morris 1990: 150–151.
8. See Shapland 2010a (esp. 276), 2022: 146, and the work of Summers (e.g., 2003), on which Shapland draws. See Chapter 3 here for engagement with these ideas.
9. Morris (1990: 155).
10. Morris (1990) focuses on the work of Mylonas (1983), Rehak (1984) and especially Marinatos (1986).
11. Morris 1990: 154–155.
12. Morris 1990: 155.
13. Blakolmer 2016a.
14. Morris 1990: 155.
15. Morris 1990: 155.
16. Morris 1990: 155.
17. I am using the term "swine" to refer to the full spectrum of *Sus scrofa*, including individuals that are identified as wild, domesticated, feral or somewhere between such categorizations, as described here: swine (noun) "any of various stout-bodied short-legged omnivorous artiodactyl mammals (family Suidae) with a thick bristly skin and a long flexible snout," Merriam-Webster.com Dictionary, s.v. "swine," www.merriam-webster.com/dictionary/swine.

18. With which, the "domesticated pig" could be identified as the subspecies *Sus scrofa domesticus*.
19. Evin, Dobney, Schafberg et al. 2015.
20. Frantz, Haile, Lin et al. 2019: 17232.
21. Frantz, Haile, Lin et al. 2019: 17232.
22. Isaakidou 2005: 229–231, 251–259; also Halstead 1987.
23. Morris 1990.
24. Isaakidou 1990: 229–230.
25. Isaakidou 2005: 229–230, 251–259; also Long 1978: 39–40.
26. Long 1978: 39–40.
27. Isaakidou 2005: 229–230.
28. Elmore 2019.
29. Evin, Dobney, Schafberg et al. 2015 esp. 5, 7, 8, 10, who also note variation in size ranges for the teeth of *Sus scrofa* between geographic locations; also Isaakidou 2005: 233.
30. Approximately two-thirds of the tusk's full length is accounted for in the (unerupted) socket area of the jaw; Elmore 2019.
31. Comer and Mayer 2009: 51, with references; Evin, Dobney, Schafberg et al. 2015; Lega, Raia, Rook and Fulgione 2015.
32. Range extension for feral pigs is slow, recorded at circa four miles annually; Bennett 2014.
33. Compare Morris 1990: 150.
34. Isaakidou 2005: 259, 285. See Shapland 2022 for valuable considerations of human-animal engagements in the context of possible free-range farming in BA Crete.
35. Mayer 2009: 10–13.
36. See, for example, Mayer on free-range "woods hogs" (2009: 10).
37. Mayer 2009: 10.
38. Morris 1990: 150 n. 7.
39. *Un 6*; Ventris and Chadwick 1973: 484.
40. Compare Morris 1990: 150–151 on whether boar hunts were rites of passage; also Rehak's suggestion (1999: 229) concerning one's first kill, in particular (referring to *Od.* 19: 428–477).
41. See Morris' discussion of the Mycenaean evidence: 1990: 150, 152–3.
42. Snyder and Andrikou 2001.
43. Snyder and Andrikou 2001. Dakouri-Hild (2005) discusses the palatial context of this craftwork at Thebes and the possible relationship with "traditional" nonpalatial practices. Morris (1990: 150) explores references within the Pylian Linear B archive to hunting personnel titled *ku-na-ge-tai*, also indicating that this activity could sometimes come under Mycenaean palatial purview – another sociocontextual variable surrounding swine.
44. Morris 1990; Rehak 1999; Logue 2004; Molloy 2012.
45. Varvarighos 1981, esp. 39 and discussion in Morris 1990: 154.
46. Zeitlin 2018.
47. With "longing," I point toward the rich ideas of Stewart (1993).
48. Foucault 1986.
49. Foucault 1986: 24.
50. In the same sense that an echo has its own temporal and sound quality.
51. Foucault 1986: 24.
52. Simandiraki-Grimshaw 2010b. While my understanding of the hybridity of a boar's tusk helmet (as well as oxhide shields and ikria) diverges from Simandiraki-Grimshaw's reading, which sees a hybridity involving such objects realized instead through their momentary contact with a human body (hence the hybrid arises as the merging between the two), her alternative perspective is fascinating and an extremely valuable contemplation of Aegean animal–human relations.
53. Mödlinger 2013: 403, who is citing Buchholz, Matthäus and Wiener 2010: 158, figs. 74–5.

54. Logue 2004: 160–161, 167–171, citing Lorimer's work (1950: 220).
55. See Salimbetti's webpage devoted to Aegean Bronze Age helmets: www.salimbeti.com/micenei/helmets2.htm.
56. Buchholz, Matthäus and Wiener 2010; Mödlinger 2013 esp. 401–403, and *Ashmolean Review* (2014/15) 10.
57. Knappett 2020: 98–129, esp. 108–110.
58. Marinatos 1986.
59. Morris 1990.
60. Shaw 1980, 1982. Some representations of shields and ikria diverge from tradition and indicate a substance other than oxhide. Shaw, for example, reconstructs painted wall fragments from Mycenae as a frieze of ikria, including some that appear to depict panels fashioned of woven fabric and others of stone veneer (1980: 177–179 and 1982: 54–55).
61. Shaw 1982: 56–57, figs. 5 and 6.
62. See especially Rehak 1984, 1999; Warren 2001.
63. Csordas 1993.
64. This is why they clearly stand as composite entities in their own right, and not merely when worn by a human – on this, my thinking fundamentally differs from that of Simandiraki-Grimshaw's (2010b), but I feel that our readings form a productive dialogue.
65. For example, Immerwahr 1990: 139.
66. See Chapin 2004; Shapland 2022, for excellent discussions.
67. Understandings of Mycenaean iconography as being based in imitation of Minoan symbols is another manifestation of these same underlying stereotypes, since imitation is a form of repetition.
68. For example, Betancourt 2004: 295, concerning the effect of repetition.
69. Blakolmer 2016a: 61.
70. For example, Blakolmer's description of the sphinx (2016a: 64) and Immerwahr on painted lions as a "heraldic device of the kings of Mycenae" (1990: 137).
71. For example, Shaw 1980; Rehak 1992, 1999; Molloy 2012; Warren 2001.
72. Immerwahr 1990: 140.
73. National Archaeological Museum, Athens, 608.
74. Mylonas 1983.
75. Shaw 1980.
76. Shaw 1980: 177, 178.
77. Immerwahr 1990: 133–142 (with discussion of Lang's idea that some friezes acted like "wallpaper").
78. Immerwahr 1990 esp. 139–140; Shaw 1980: 177–178.
79. Egan 2020. This study builds on the study of Egan and Brecoulaki 2015.
80. Egan 2020: 383, with references.
81. Egan 2020: 383–384, with further references.
82. Egan 2020: 384–385.
83. As does Rehak (1992).
84. Noted as dubious by the CMS.
85. The peculiar, double-lobed formation of the human's body may in fact itself be a rendering of a figure-8 shield.
86. CMS II.3.32 was found in a LM II–III context (Mavro Spelio Grave VII, Chamber B) but is dated stylistically to LM I–II.
87. On the interaction of oral and visual/material narratives in the Bronze Age Aegean, see, for example, Morris 1989; Vlachopoulos 2007; Watrous 2007; and Anderson 2020.
88. While discussing distinct dynamics, Watrous (2007) and Vlachopoulos (2007) both offer powerful considerations of the cyclical nature that can drive both oral poetry and visual narrative in the Aegean.
89. Anastasiadou 2016a.
90. Anastasiadou 2016a: 79–80.

91. Here, we can contrast the rich views of Simandiraki-Grimshaw (2010b).

92. A point noted by Wilson (1974), who discusses the complex life of the armor and horses that Peleus received from the gods at his wedding, including their passage through different persons' lives.

93. Both the CMS record and Crowley's IconAegean database suggest the reading of the second element as a helmet (in the CMS database, a question mark accompanies this identification).

94. Knappett 2020: 99.

95. For example, in CMS II.8.127, CMS II.8.128, CMS II.8.129, CMS II.8.278, CMS V. S3.331.

96. This connects to a long-standing discussion of shield friezes in the Aegean. Evans (1930) proposed that friezes of figure-8 shields in LB III frescoes imitated shields in the round hung along a wall; see discussion in Chapter 6.

97. Blakolmer 2016b problematizes this extensively in his fascinating discussion of how built space may be indicated in glyptic and related imagery.

98. See Shaw 1980: 177.

99. Stewart 1993.

100. For example, Blakolmer 1995, 2016b.

101. See, e.g., Palyvou 2012, and Chapter 6 for discussion.

102. Anderson 2019.

103. Sapouna-Sakellaraki 1994: 155 fig. 20.

104. Kaiser 1976: pl. 13a; see Logue 2004.

105. See discussion in Egan 2018.

106. HM 5691.

107. See, for example, Doumas 1994: 57, fig. 18.

108. NAMA 5782.

109. Vlachopoulos 2015.

110. For examples, see Rehak 1999; Marthari 2018: 208–209; Warren 1980: 83–84 fig. 35; Shaw and Laxton 2002: 98.

111. Betancourt 2004: 295.

112. Mountjoy 1984: 187 fig. 15, also 166–167 figs. 8, 19 for related occurrences of shields.

113. Rehak 1995: 118, 123. Although not discussed as such, some of the yet-earlier material in Rehak's study in fact also embodies the figure-8 shield in repetitive series, for example, MM IIIB faience plaques from the South Propylon at Knossos (1995: 116–117 fig. 4), in which female figures wear necklaces formed of a line of figure-8-shield pendants strung alongside one another; hypothetical actual necklaces of this type would also manifest such series, in the round.

114. Mountjoy (1983) describes the Mycenaean Ephyraean style as then being picked up in LB II Crete.

115. Warren 1980.

116. See Warren 1980 (esp. 81–83); Wall, Musgrave and Warren 1986; and Rehak 1995. The finds of human bones from the Cult Room Basement have been associated with more extensive finds of children's bones from the "Room of the Children's Bones," also in the basement of the North House; Warren has argued that the remains may indicate cannibalistic behavior of a ritual variety.

117. Shaw and Laxton 2002.

118. See Blakolmer (2012), who notes that Evans saw similar dynamics of "architectonic suggestion" at play; Rehak (1995: 122) also discusses this vessel and engages with Evans' treatment.

119. Anderson 2011.

120. Warren 1980: 83–84.

121. Koehl 2006: esp. 273, 275–276.

122. Koehl 2006: 213, no. 1137; 273, 275–276.

123. Warren describes this as a "gorgoneion" similar in form to later renderings; Rehak and others preserve this identification (Warren 1980: 83, 1984; Rehak 1995: 117–118).

124. Rehak 1995: 118 n. 23.

125. Rehak 1995: 117–118.

126. Warren 1980: 83–84, figs. 33 and 34; Warren 1984 for meatier consideration; Niemeier 1985: 125.

127. Al-Tardeh 2008, with further references. Some folk names for squills directly relate it to swine, for example, "hog's garlic," "wild boar's squill" and "Grice's onion." Meanwhile, Pythagoras and Dioscorides were said to hang squills as defensive devices. See Warren 1984 for discussion of protective role of squills in the Aegean, continuing to the modern age.

128. See Rehak 1999 esp. 231.

129. Compare motif of gold signet ring HM X-A-990 from Archanes; Sakellarakis and Sapouna-Sakelleraki see it as Mycenaean-era, along with other rings with shield friezes (1997: 659–662, figs. 725–728).

130. See Morgan 1989 for excellent discussion of ambiguity in Aegean glyptic engraving, and discussion in Chapter 4.

131. McGowan 2011: 67–74; sacral knot mentioned on 71. McGowan's identification of this similarity between renderings of helmets and skirts is exciting and, I believe, strengthens the case for seeing complex dynamics of connection in play within Minoan imagery, through such "ambiguity." McGowan's study (2010) is also valuable for providing a rich discussion of the history of scholarly attitudes toward this apparent ambiguity.

132. See how McGowan also draws in an extraordinary motif from the Kato Zakros glyptic corpus, CMS II.7.177, which involves a skirt, wings and bucranium, which do not seem to add up to a body – this is what Anastasiadou describes as an "inorganic" composite in her discussion of the Zakros material (2016a).

133. Rehak suggests that the sacred cloth or "robe," along with the sword, were prizes awarded to successful participants in bull-leaping sports (1999: 233–234) and identified objects in which shield and cloth are imaged together. This pairing also occurs in LB II–III glyptic, e.g., CMS XIII.32 and CMS XIII.33.

134. Compare Shapland 2022: 146–147.

135. McGowan 2011: 67.

136. See Pini 1992 concerning how the complications or our means of analysis are relevant to this discussion of glyptic imagery.

137. Morgan 1995a.

138. The boar's head appears on both sides of the spearhead. Sakellerakis and Sapouna-Sakellaraki 1997, esp. v. 2: 596–598, figs. 621–622.

139. Kaiser 1976: pl. 21a.

140. For description of slaughtering techniques, see, for example, Anil and von Holleben 2014: 561–563; also www.hsa.org.uk/bleeding-and-pithing/bleeding, or https://the grownetwork.com/preparing-pig-slaughter-2/

141. Rehak 1995.

142. Compare female Fig. 5.2a.

143. Allwin, Gokarn, Vedamanickam et al. 2016.

144. Compare Morgan 1989, especially 148 and 158–159.

145. Morgan 1989: 148.

146. See, for example, Walberg 1987; Immerwahr 1990; Betancourt 2001.

147. Krzyszkowska 2005: 133.

148. See Evans 1921; Hussein 2018. For an overview of discussions of the Talismanic group and new means of technical analysis, see Stram 2017.

149. Morgan 1989.

150. McGowan 2011, 2018. See McGowan 2011 for a strong historical overview of scholarly views on the topic of ambiguity, paired with theoretical problematization.

APPROACHING AND RETREATING   309

151. Onassaglou 1985.
152. See Anderson forthcoming.
153. Vlachopoulos 2015: esp. 42–46, 53–54.
154. For comparison of Kamares ware and the Akrotiri "pictorial style" vessels, see Vlachopoulos 2015: 39–43.
155. Vlachopoulos 2015: 55 fig. 13; Marthari 2018: 208–209.
156. See, for example, Walter 1950.
157. Walberg 1986 for extended discussion; see also Blakolmer 2012: 18.
158. In consideration of the two Vapheio cups, Davis (1974) discusses the appearance of hanging ground in their imagery – she in fact argues that on the other, "quiet" cup, the hanging ground is a representation of clouds (1974: 480, with references concerning the convention).
159. Marthari 2018: 209.
160. Papagiannopoulou 2018.
161. Blakolmer 2010: esp. 92–94, 2012, 2016b.
162. Marthari 2018: 208; Pillar Shaft 77N-78A was located north of Sector Alpha.
163. See Akrivaki 2003; also Vlachopoulos 2015: 50–55 fig. 12; Marthari 2018: 210 figs. 12a and 12b.
164. See also sophisticated discussion in Marthari 2018: 208–209 figs. 9–11.
165. Marthari 2018: 208–209 figs. 9–11.
166. See Marthari 1987; Nikolakopoulou, Georma, Moschou and Sofianou 2008; Nikolakopoulou 2010; Vlachopoulos 2015: 43–46, with refs.
167. Hood 2005: 62; Vlachopoulos 2015; Marthari (2018: 209) points to the use of this type of border as a possible indication that the asaminthos is LC I in date.
168. See Mountjoy 1984, for example, figs. 15 (fragments of vessels from Knossos, Malia) and 19 (Zakros).
169. See Blakolmer 2012 for sophisticated consideration of how such features imaged in Neopalatial and later Aegean portable media (e.g., seals, painted ceramics) would relate to wall paintings and reliefs.
170. Marthari 1987, Vlachopoulos 2015: 46.
171. Nikolakopoulou 2008; Papagiannopoulou 2008, 2018; Vlachopoulos 2015; Papageorgiou 2018; Marthari 2018.
172. For excellent discussions of scale in Aegean Bronze Age figural art, see MacGillivray, Driessen and Sackett 2000; Knappett 2020.
173. Egan (2018) brilliantly examines Final Palatial Palace Style vessels and murals.
174. On containing, see Simandiraki-Grimshaw 2013; Knappett 2020.

SIX

MOVING TOWARD LIFE

Painted Walls and Novel Animalian Presences
in Aegean Spaces

W ALL PAINTINGS PRESERVED AT AKROTIRI IN THE FALLOUT OF THE
Theran LC I/ LM IA volcanic eruption provide us with an extraordinary and at times breathtaking impression of the cultivation of painted spaces in
the Cycladic town during the early Neopalatial era. Within two buildings
positioned at opposite ends of the excavated area of the town, Xeste 4 and
the West House, we have vivid evidence demonstrating that, already during
this phase, entities were being painted in large, bold series across the walls of
rooms. This evidence occupies the temporal and creative space between, on
the one hand, renderings of shield series among earlier painted ceramics from
Akrotiri (see Chapter 5), and, on the other, the large-scale shield series known
from multiple later Aegean wall paintings. Strikingly, it is the two other entities
we have identified as distinctive Aegean animalian composite phenomena –
ikria and boar's tusk helmets – that appear embodied in series within the LC I
wall paintings of Akrotiri. In the West House, a series of large ikria encompasses
the walls of Room 4/4b. The evidence from Xeste 4 is more fragmentary, but
there we have fragments of painted plaster from a frieze of large boar's tusk
helmets. Both of these wall paintings are deeply significant to our discussion in
various respects.

The series of ikria painted in Room 4/4b of the West House extends
determinedly across the walls, spanning breaks for doorways and a window.
The ikria are positioned atop a dado zone, shared between Rooms 4 and 5. The
dado is painted as if constituted by juxtaposed panels, each characterized by

6.1. Large-scale ikria from painted frieze, Room 4, south wall, West House, Akrotiri. From Doumas 1992: 86 fig. 50. Courtesy Akrotiri Excavations. Object © Hellenic Ministry of Culture and Sports

vibrantly colored patterns of wavy channels thought to be imitating variegated stone; orange-yellow vertical strips positioned in the interstices likely depict wood frames (Figures 6.1, 6.2). Set atop the dado, each ikrion rises some one-and-a-half meters above the floor and is embodied in vivid color and fine detail. The bottom portion of each ikrion, its main body or cabin, consists of a rectangular form that is scalloped along its top edge and covered in brightly colored, uneven splotches upon a contrasting white or red ground. This pattern appears on numerous Aegean representations of shields and is a bold rendering of the piebald flesh of domesticated cattle. Horizontal bands, some finely patterned, cross the body of each ikrion at its base, midsection and along the scalloped upper edge. These occur in different colors between the ikria, including orange-yellow, blue and white, and have been read as a framework of wood or metal. Three evenly spaced vertical elements, colored orange-yellow, rise from the top edge of each ikrion's main body and are presumably support beams. A small nodule marks the attachment point of an elaborate bicurved and ornamented finial topping each vertical beam. Crossing just below the nodules is a horizontal strip that defines the top of the cabin. This cross-strip is decorated in patterns and colors that differ across the ikria, including delicate curvilinear designs in white, blue and yellow. Just below the top strip, garlands, strung with intricate beads in a variety of forms and

6.2. Large-scale ikrion from painted frieze, beside window, Room 4, west wall, West House, Akrotiri. From Doumas 1992: 87 fig. 51. Courtesy Akrotiri Excavations. Object © Hellenic Ministry of Culture and Sports

colors, swoop between the three vertical beams of each ikrion. Above the series of ikria, around the top of the walls, extends a border comprised of multiple linear bands.

SIZE AS A BASIS FOR LIKENESS BETWEEN ENTITIES IN THE WALL AND IN THE ROUND

If the walls of the Hunter's Asaminthos from Akrotiri, painted with a large shield frieze, pushed beyond the familiar representational boundaries of ceramics, then the walls of rooms painted with early friezes in the same town pushed *into* the dimensions of lived experience. Set upon the dado, each ikrion in Room 4 of the West House reaches up to a height of about 1.6 m., where its embellished finials address the upper border of the frescoed wall. With this, the ikria occupy the entirety of the middle zone of the wall, a zone that Palyvou connects to "the boundaries of the human body, adhering to its scale and verticality and defining the area of action."[1] Immerwahr has described the ikria here as "lifesize."[2] Do the ikria painted on the walls of Room 4 in fact have the same dimensions as ikria in the round, utilized on ships of the day? Without any

6.3. Segment of wall painting showing ships; Room 5, south wall, West House, Akrotiri. From Doumas 1992: 68–70 fig. 35. Courtesy Akrotiri Excavations. Object © Hellenic Ministry of Culture and Sports

surviving remains of such to compare, we cannot decisively answer this. However, in the room next door within the West House, we have a contemporaneous painting through which to assess people's sense of the relative proportion of human bodies and ikria that were in use aboard ships. Here, in Room 5, painted on the other side of a partition wall that also holds some of the frescoed ikria of the Room 4 series, the miniature flotilla frieze images at least six instances of humans standing and sitting with ikria (Room 5, south wall; Figures 6.3, 6.4).[3] Through these, generally speaking we can say that the ikria in use shared their height with that of an adult man. The height from the base of an ikrion to its topmost crossbeam typically is somewhat less than the height of a person standing beside it, while the height to the top of its finials (if depicted) is somewhat greater than that of the same person. Meanwhile, the height of an ikrion's uppermost crossbeam corresponds to the seated height of the person within. There are variations across the multiple ikria and humans painted in the flotilla, which affect their relative heights as we see them. In some cases, the head of an oarsman standing beside an ikrion reaches the level of the top crossbeam and is essentially at or just above the eye level of the person seated within (Figures 6.4a, b).[4] In other cases, the platform upon which the ikrion sits (a feature that Shaw's study has elucidated;[5] Figure 5.4) is taller, raising the ikrion higher, so that the oarsman's head instead is on the level of the oxhide body of the ikrion.[6] At the same time, while the head of the person seated within an ikrion usually reaches just to the upper beam, in one instance it extends above it and is partially obscured by the painted line of the beam, indicating an open top of the ikrion.[7] These variations are notable – they might indicate diversity in the stature of the depicted people, in the size of ikria and related structural elements and, probably, some fluidity in representation. What they give us, however, is ground on which to consider how ikria were experienced as relating to the human body in this period. We can take this back to our consideration of the larger ikria depicted in the room next door.

Many adult persons standing within Room 4 would have, more or less, shared their height with that of the host of ikria positioned atop the painted dado around them.[8] The ikria have some variation in their sizes, but each rises between 1.55 m and 1.67 m (approx. 5'1"–5'6") above the floor. This puts them within the range of heights that we can figure for ikria, on their own,

6.4. Details showing people sitting in ikria, from wall painting of Room 5, south wall, West House, Akrotiri. From Doumas 1992: 80–81, figs. 39, 40. Courtesy Akrotiri Excavations. Objects © Hellenic Ministry of Culture and Sports

based on what we see in Room 5, and indeed would have set them at a comparable level alongside a standing human to that which we see between people and ikria aboard some of the ships of the flotilla (see, e.g., on the third ship from the left). Heights of people range, of course, but fundamentally, within Room 4, ikria would have been experienced as entities that were comparable in stature to that of an adult human, and this also seems to have been the case for ikria used on ships.[9]

Attempts to deduce a specific scale of representation at play in the renderings of ikria in the West House are foiled by variations in the heights at which humans and ikria themselves are represented. But I do not believe that a specific scalar proportion relative to ikria in the round was being sought or achieved here. Instead, the crucial point seems to be that the ikria embodied in Room 4 were brought up into the dimensional range within which the entities were experienced as objects in use in the world beyond the room. In this respect, people met these frescoed ikria as they would have met ikria known from ships. With this, size newly emerged as an aspect of the entities that representations could share with embodiments in the round – in other words, size became a means of enacting commonality between the experiences of the entities that one had on a ship and in the walls of a building. The novel affordances of painted walls were being recognized here. Walls offered a larger representational space in which size could be cultivated as a means of attaining likeness between an entity known in the round and its reenactment in a very different medium and context. Across earlier case studies, we have seen that the distinct qualities of other media had been recognized for their potential to possess something similar to a represented animalian entity known in the round (e.g., when EM piriform jugs were recognized and cultivated as having a curved form comparable to that of a woman, both entities also being able to hold something in their belly; see Chapter 2). Not only did the ikria frescoed in the LM IA walls of Room 4 share their height with ikria in the round and the living people who used them, they were also rendered in a rich palette of colors that likely suggested specific links to materials used in the ikria known from ships (e.g., the orange-yellow of the frame of the frescoed ikria being relatable to wood, while bluish-gray perhaps referred to metal). Hence, size would have acted with color to bring new affinities between representational and familiar in-the-round embodiments.

Down the road from the West House, the wall of Xeste 4 featured a series of boar's tusk helmets during the same phase that the ikria frieze was created (Figure 6.5).[10] One nearly complete helmet and fragments of another were discovered in 2000. The white tusk plaques of the helmets are formed through reserve areas of the lime-plaster background, with delicate black outlines elaborating their shape. Blue and black linear features articulate the helmets' structure, along with a dramatic blue-and-black plume. As in the shield friezes of the Hunter's Asaminthos and the later shield frescoes, a bold linear band feature runs between the helmets in the Xeste 4 fresco, appearing to extend behind them; this creates the impression that the helmets themselves are positioned farther forward than the band, toward the viewer. These helmets in fresco are described as being "larger than life-size."[11] Indeed, their height, at about 23 cm for the main body or "cap" of the helmet, not including the cheek/neck guards or the top knob, somewhat exceeds what we might expect from a worn helmet, which, based on extant examples of comparably shaped metal helmets from the Aegean Bronze Age, would be closer to 17–18 cm.[12]

6.5. Fragment of large-scale frieze of boars tusk helmets, from wall painting in Xeste 4, Akrotiri (a.); reconstruction of the frieze (b.). Courtesy Akrotiri Excavations. Object © Hellenic Ministry of Culture and Sports

But again, I think we need to step back and understand these reembodiments of helmets in their context. In a moment during which the walls of Akrotiri – and of the southern Aegean – were newly being explored as venues for painted figural forms, the helmets of this frieze manifest a *pulling up* of representation into a scale range shared with living humans' bodies. These helmets burst into lived space as entities met in detail and proportions that had a new type of presence. The fact that they are yet somewhat-larger in height and width than helmets that were actually donned only emphasizes the boldness of their entrance into a novel representational range – they are an exaggerated embodiments of helmets as-in-life.

OTHER EXPERIENCES OF THE EXPANSIVE: SERIES IN ACTION WITHIN THE WEST HOUSE

We have seen that helmets, shields and ikria, each a complex animalian entity, are embodied in series early on within Aegean Bronze Age representational material culture, and that the association with this format persists within the region. The ceramic and fresco evidence from Akrotiri indicates that during the later MBA and early LBA, each of these entities was involved in innovative pressure asserted on familiar representational parameters, pushing into new ground with sizes that approached the dimensions that the entities possessed when met as three-dimensional objects used in the world, beyond the painted room. The novel affordances of large painted walls were part of this development. Yet these explorations in scale also took craftspersons, and viewers, into terrain located in the *other* scalar direction. Simultaneous with their large-scale renderings in series, wall frescoes painted on a highly reduced scale were also an important venue for the reembodiment of these entities. In Room 5 of the West House, we see shields, ikria and helmets in action as tiny forms, embedded within narrative scenes. The miniature nature of these pictorial friezes provides for an expansive view, through which other aspects of vastness are novelly put into reach.

In the foregoing, we have considered various vivid examples of ikria, shields and helmets embodied as repeated elements within series, occurring across media. In some cases, we have seen them alternating with other figures in series, for example, on the cup rhyton from the Cult Room Basement at Knossos. Such juxtaposition with other entities provides an immediate context with which to approach the embodiment of an entity at hand. In Room 5 of the West House, ikria, shields and helmets also would have been understood within the context of other phenomena represented within the frescoes, but here the compositional dynamics are distinct. In this situation, the entities are embroiled within highly developed visual narrative structures with other figures and settings. What is remarkable, however, is how their embodiment in series is maintained even in this changed context.

Boar's tusk helmets appear twice in this room, as part of the frescoed miniature scenic friezes positioned high up, around the upper zone of the walls.[13] In the frieze of the south wall, a series of ships carries men across the sea. A couple of the men stand, including steersmen, but most are seated either as passengers or paddlers. Poised above many of the passengers on the deck are carefully rendered boar's tusk helmets, apparently the personal accoutrements of these travelers (Figure 6.6). The helmets are not actually worn. Instead, they hang from the beams of shelters and, with this, appear suspended directly above the human heads, where they form their own elevated series.[14] In multiple cases, a helmet tops the vertical beam of an ikrion positioned at the stern of a ship, sheltering a single person of distinction. These ikria themselves are recurrent elements of the fleet and, taken together, constitute another series of remarkable entities.

The material culture that accompanies the travelers on their sea journey in the scene of the south wall indicates a militaristic identity, if not a militaristic intent;[15] the presence of boar's tusk helmets enriches this narrative framework.

6.6. Detail of wall painting showing people sitting in ship under suspended helmets; Room 5, south wall, West House, Akrotiri. From Doumas 1992: 75–77 fig. 37. Courtesy Akrotiri Excavations. Object © Hellenic Ministry of Culture and Sports

6.7. Detail of wall painting showing shielded persons progressing in a line; Room 5, north wall, West House, Akrotiri. From Doumas 1992: 58 fig. 26. Courtesy Akrotiri Excavations. Objects © Hellenic Ministry of Culture and Sports

On the north wall, a more fragmentary frieze images an assault on a settlement undertaken by forces arriving by sea.[16] Rising up an incline from the coast is a line of armed warriors (Figure 6.7). Their bodies are covered from shoulders to knees by rectangular "tower" shields.[17] These shields have a light ground and are dramatically dappled in uneven splotches of color, vividly representing piebald oxhide (the connection to cattle skin is especially clear here, as the shields share their piebald appearance with cows depicted just above them in the painting). There are no indications of clothing worn by these figures, leaving the outlines of the shields uncomplicated. With this, the shields appear as bold units in an uninterrupted series. While we see no garments on these men, they wear delicately painted boar's tusk helmets on their heads. On the extant examples, a slender strap wraps below the wearer's chin, and a wispy plumed crest emerges from its apex; small dash marks loosely surround the helmet.[18] Each of the warriors holds a long naval spear extending from one hand, while a tasseled scabbard is visible at the hip.

As in the frieze of the south wall, the boar's tusk helmets in the north frieze exist as a series of repeated items set within a complex narrative vignette, now plainly involving martial activity. The helmets' presence in this context is clear and logical. But there are other aspects to consider as the boar's tusk helmet is reembodied here in the medium of fresco. The scale of the painted helmet relative to a biological human encountering it has altered incredibly. The north and south miniature friezes of West House Room 5 both have heights of circa 0.45 m. Each helmet is but a minuscule element of this, occupying a square centimeter or less. This is a far cry from their size as worn defensive items, which we have seen would be closer to 17–18 cm in height; it is also markedly smaller than the helmets embodied in fresco in Xeste 4. People within Room 5 would crane their heads upward and narrow their eyes in order to discern the helmets within the friezes. While the helmets' proportionality with humans is more or less maintained *within* the fresco, the fine scale of the friezes necessitated that the painters formed the helmets with incredibly delicate brushstrokes – fine black outlines upon the bare white of the lime plaster. Given that their whiteness is simply borrowed from the background of the fresco, the helmets have a lightness within the smooth surface of the paintings that is quite distinct from the tough, solid make of the leather-and-tusk helmet a living human would don.

WITHIN AND BEYOND THE WALL: SPATIAL COMPLEXITY THROUGH BANDS AND SERIES

In the miniature frescoes of Room 5 in the West House, despite being met just through the doorway from the large-scale series of ikria painted in Room 4, the muralist took advantage of the extensive surface of the wall in another way. The narrow but long space afforded by the top portion of the wall in Room 5 was cultivated as a venue for expansive, unfolding land-scapes, both natural and social. In the walls of this room, series of tiny embodiments of ikria, shields and helmets were visible, contributing to narratives that would have surrounded the viewer. These paintings remind us that series were seemingly integral to the identity of these three entities in the Aegean, characterizing their embodiments in a variety of contexts, from the eventful stories of Room 5 to the repetitive friezes found in Room 4, as well as in Xeste 4. Realizing this not only helps us to better appreciate the standing of ikria, shields and helmets in Aegean culture, it also forces us to recognize the real dynamism of series, which surpasses the categories of ornament, abstraction, narrative and iconicity with which we tend to approach them.

The miniature friezes of Room 5 in the West House can help us to draw out another characteristic aspect of seriated entities manifest in wall paintings of this era. This concerns the integration of the represented bodies within the structure and materiality of the wall in which they are rendered. Let us turn first to the depiction of the boar's tusk helmet. As in the West House, the white tusk plaques of the Xeste 4 helmets are rendered simply as black outlines upon the base lime plaster (Figure 6.5).[19] Yet in these helmets, substantial horizontal blue and black strips alternate with the rows of white plaques, likely relatable to the leather substructure of worn helmets. These strips strongly echo the black and red banding that forms the background of this area of the fresco and runs parallel to the horizontal registers of the helmets. By drawing out and emphasizing the intervening strips of the helmets, the painters thus have powerfully reinforced the horizontality of the overall painting and have dynamically integrated the helmets into the structure of their frescoed ground. At the same time, the positioning of the banding just here, "behind" the helmets, also has another, very different yet equally powerful effect. A sense of depth is simultaneously created as the helmets emerge outward *in front of* the wall, whose positive presence behind them is marked by the banding, a typical motif in wall decoration; with this, the helmets are made to come out into the room, approaching the human standing therein. Hence, the banding, in its relationship with the helmets, generates a complex spatial tension and poises these renderings of helmets – themselves rich composite entities – in a further ontological limbo. While narrative is not actively at play here, as it is in Room 5 of the West House, there is much taking place with these helmets. In this room, we see a complex rendering of forms in space, at once giving the impression of figural elements being both layered atop and collapsed into the background of the painted wall.

We have seen the type of banding that runs between or behind the helmets of Xeste 4 in other contexts. Earlier, we considered the presence of such banding in combination with figure-8 shields in the surface of the Hunter's Asaminthos and the spatial implications it has for the representation (Figure 5.17). Marthari has also connected the occurrence of the banding in these two instances of painting at Akrotiri, along with the LC I piriform jug painted with a shield frieze from the site.[20] We have seen that such banding also occurs in renderings of seriated objects in Neopalatial and later Aegean glyptic, as well as in friezes of shields embodied in wall paintings, of which we have several examples from LB II–III, including those at Knossos and mainland palatial sites (and perhaps, following Blakolmer, already in a fragment of an LC I shield frieze from the walls of the House of the Ladies).[21] These objects help us to query the association between the banding and series of entities, and the possibility that the former indicated the presence of a painted wall behind the latter. With the helmet frieze of Xeste 4, and the later frescoes, this signification becomes quite complex. Is the banding part of a frieze motif, embodied in different media, or is it part of the underlying painted wall, *upon which* a frieze of helmets has been added? Is it a painting of a painting – a painted wall depicted upon a painted wall? Put another way, if a wall is signified by the banding when we see this pairing rendered in a seal stone or on a painted vessel, as Blakolmer argues,[22] is a painted wall also signified when the banding is rendered in a wall painting? The recurrence of the motif of seriated objects together with such banding in various media suggests that their pairing had become traditional. Certainly, the frieze of Xeste 4 does not dispel the sense that the banding is in a sense glued to the series of entities, and vice versa. Yet at the same time, the impression of layers – of variable depth between the banding "back there" and the helmets lined up in front of it, in a "shallow" but real depth[23] – is very much active.

The large dimensions of the helmets within the Xeste 4 frieze contribute to the impression of depth. Since they are rendered in a size similar to that of helmets known in the round, the sense of their being things somehow pushed outward into the lived world in front of the wall is heightened – in a way, they fit there. The same can be said of the large-scale shield friezes with such banding known from LB wall paintings (in examples from LB II and III, and possibly LB I) wall paintings.[24] In this respect, the large ikria painted in Room 4 of the West House have a related effect. While no banding is present behind the ikria, the size of each ikrion makes it somehow more approachable, as a thing that shares its stature with the human who stands in front of it, as would have been the case with an ikrion met on a boat. Shaw's careful analysis of the representation of ikria in the West House and in a later frieze from Mycenae indicates that they were structures that sat upon a raised platform.[25] On the ships of the Room 5 flotilla, one can see that a person appears to sit on the step leading up to this platform, directly in front of each ikrion. It is striking that the frieze in Room 4 seems to maintain this sense that the ikria are raised upon something, by positioning them atop the painted dado. The height of the dado is circa 0.45 m, comparable to what we would expect the height of the platforms subtending the ikria on ships to have been, if we follow the renderings of such in Room 5. These cases illustrate a powerful spatial dynamism at play with the seriated entities, in which their location either as part of the wall, or somehow in front of it – moved toward the viewer in the room – was being problematized.

Flirting with Illusion

In various ways, the seriated ikria, helmets and shields embodied in various Aegean wall paintings offered people something akin to the experience of engaging with the entities as objects in the round. Most notably, the size of the representational embodiments, their enriched coloration, the implication of a built context relative to which they were situated in a space (a banded painted wall, a platform) and their occurrence as gatherings of like things (as they were also met, in the round, in fleets, files of armed figures and perhaps hung on walls) all seem to make these frescoed entities dynamically present, in familiar ways, within the world that the viewer inhabits. Given this, should we consider these to be illusionistic representations?

Evans certainly thought so, at least in regard to the later shield fresco associated with the Loggia of the Grand Staircase at Knossos: "the[se] shields are real Minoan shields," he asserts (Figure 6. 8a).[26] Evans describes the shields of the Loggia frieze as appearing to "stand apart" "as if suspended in the field."[27] In his discussion, he draws out some of the same qualities that we have highlighted regarding seriated entities rendered in frescoes. He comments on the shields' vivid color, which gave a sense of oxhide, as well as their hatching and contouring; he even goes so far as to suggest that something like an early chiaroscuro has been used to bring the shields an illusion of depth.[28] In contrasting the Knossos shield frieze to the smaller, later and what he sees as derivative and "purely ornamental" shield frieze at Tiryns,[29] he remarks on the impressive height of the painted shields at Knossos, each of which is reconstructed at some 1.63 meters.[30] This is about the same height as the seriated oxhide ikria of Room 4 in the West House in Akrotiri (ca. 1.55–1.67 m), likely indicating that, in both cases, the representational embodiments were meant to capture the sense that these animalian things, shields and ikria alike, occupied the space of the human body.[31] As we discussed in the previous chapter, ikria and shields in the round were both objects rendered of animal skin that conformed with the stature of a human, a quality that these reenactments of the entities in fresco maintain. Ultimately, Evans reads the fragments of the Loggia shield frieze in tandem with remains of a spiral frieze fresco from a space downstairs, which he describes as the audience area of the Hall of the Double Axes.[32] In this space, the remnants of a frescoed spiral frieze appear to have been positioned just above the gypsum dado slabs of a wall, running across the location of an original horizontal wooden beam set at an elevation of some 90 cm from the floor.[33] Given that a similar band of spirals appears within multiple renderings of shield friezes, both in the Knossos shield fresco and in wall painting and other media from different sites (e.g., glyptic and painted ceramics), Evans believed that shields belonging to Knossian warriors were actually hung upon the wall in the area of the spiral frieze in the audience

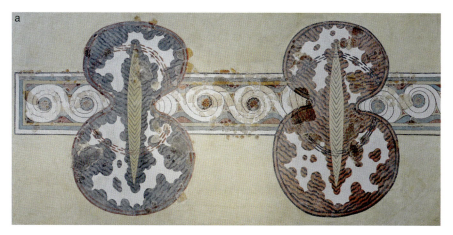

6.8. Reconstructed fragments from large-scale shield friezes in LBA Aegean wall painting. a. Knossos. Herakleion Museum; photograph by Olaf Tausch (CC BY 3.0). b. Mycenae; photograph by George E. Koronaios (CC BY-SA 4.0). Objects © Hellenic Ministry of Culture and Sports

section of the Hall of Double Axes. Hence, he proposes an interaction between the painted shields of the Loggia, lifelike and large, that one would have met while descending upon the Grand Staircase, and the oxhide shields in the round that one would then encounter hanging on the walls of the audience hall below:

> Nor was it for nothing that these great shields were here [in the Loggia frieze] depicted as suspended across the purely decorative spiral band. The complement, as we shall see, is to be found in the Great Hall below, where remains of the spiral band existed immediately above the upper borders of the gypsum dadoes, but without any indication of the shields themselves.

> Nothing here can be more eloquent than this omission, which clearly points to the actual suspension of the originals across the band, in conformity with the Homeric usage of hanging up the shields in the warriors' hall.[34]

Shaw and Laxton have offered an extensive discussion of the shield frescoes, also arguing that the bands that appear with the shields therein clearly indicate painted walls upon which shields were hung.[35] Their discussion updates and enlarges upon Evans treatment of the subject and considers what appear to be depictions of hangers above the shields (see Chapter 5). These consisted of a peg (sometimes capped by a decorative rosette) and two hooks that curved outward below it, as preserved in multiple renderings in Mycenaean frescoes (and in earlier Minoan painted ceramics) (Figure 6.8).[36] They argue that this detail of the fresco represents a real device used in Aegean built spaces for suspending shields. The inclusion of this device in the wall paintings would underline the realism of the shields painted in such friezes, providing a justification, of sorts, for their presence upon the wall. Shaw and Laxton propose, on the basis of these representations, that there would have been places for "more permanent displays" of shields suspended from walls.[37] The frescoed shield friezes, with their as-in-life details, would attest to this practice in the very type of place that the real shields would have hung, namely on frescoed walls – so we seem to have reality and representation circling into one another. Shaw and Laxton also move beyond the assertion that the shield friezes indicate the practice of hanging shields on walls. For example, in their consideration of the shields fresco from Tiryns, they argue that arced, wavey "streamers" rendered between the shields evidence a "dissolution of form" as the suspension devices represented in other shield friezes were abstracted. They suggest that this abstraction occurred as artists "became more removed from the actual model and turned to copying other representations,"[38] an assertion that, again, is based on the idea that the shield friezes are fundamentally imitating realities, and that both actual shield and representation occupied the same spaces – the painted rooms of important buildings. This coincidence of locale would embolden an illusionistic experience of the frescoed shield friezes, since one would expect to find a gathering of shields in just such a spot. As we have seen (Chapter 5), the shield frieze with "background" banding on the Hunter's Asaminthos might be an indication that the practice of suspending shields on a painted wall was already quite old by the time that the later, large-scale frescoes brought new representational complexity to the motif by seemingly rendering a painted wall within the medium of wall painting.

What of the series of ikria and helmets that were depicted in large-scale frescoes already in LB I – should we view these representations as having been intended as illusions of objects in the round gathered together within the interior built spaces? It is hard to fully accept this notion, for a couple of reasons. First, in the case of ikria, a small room of a building feels an unfitting place to gather a host of ship cabins – a point that would seem to undermine the acceptance of the illusion. Meanwhile, there is no indication that another setting is being recreated here, such as a harbor, where we might expect to find ikria. Of course, we might be missing cues from movable furniture in the room, but painted details of Room 4, such as the flower pots frescoed in the window jambs and the dado rendered with stone-like designs that lines both Rooms 4 and 5, indicate, in harmony with the architectural reality, that we are indeed within an interior room. The situation is somewhat different in Xeste 4, where we find a collection of frescoed helmets. While helmets certainly could be gathered in a room, would they have been suspended in a line along the wall in this way? The helmets of the Xeste 4 frieze are rendered in profile (a strange angle for suspension), without any form of suspension device apparent, and do not seem to hang.

Yet looking at the ikria and helmets in the large-scale friezes of West House Room 4 and Xeste 4 Room 2, one cannot help but feel that they, like the shields discussed by Evans, "betray the painter's endeavor to break through the trammels of purely decorative Art."[39] We have seen that the size of the entities as they were rendered in the friezes provocatively stepped into the same range as that of ikria and helmets embodied as practical objects in the round. Along with this, their close representation of details and materials, such as fittings, straps and fine toolwork, as well as their positioning as if in front of or atop a structural element of the room, brought a palpable depth and texture of realism to these embodiments of the entities in fresco, which tugged them away from a status as flat pictures. So how do we reconcile this with the attributes that would seem to keep them in the wall? We do not – or, far more importantly, the paintings do not.

One with the Wall: In the Rhythmic Grip of Structure

The large-scale Aegean friezes of shields, ikria, and helmets innovatively effected similitude with objects in the three-dimensional world beyond their walls, and, at the same time, participated, with splendid regularity, in the structural order of their architectural context. As Palyvou has eloquently elucidated, "the Minoan world is a horizontal world."[40] Its built spaces extended alongside lived action. The frieze is a form that echoes and contributes to this horizontality; this is especially powerful when the subject is a series of entities. Set one beside another, the paratactic string of bodies announces the elongation of space, enumerating its length. The interior walls of Aegean buildings had the structure of long, stacked zones – usually three. While naturally there were variations, this organization was remarkably consistent. The large-scale seriated friezes we are discussing occupied the middle zone of the wall, as did essentially all large-scale Aegean wall paintings of the era. When elaborated, the narrow lower zone could be painted with a colorful dado or simply with a solid color, while the upper zone often contained a border of bands or running spirals. Vertical elements could break the dominant horizontal zones, in some cases creating panels. This zoned organization of Aegean wall painting was in large part determined by the underlying structure of the wall – and had been, it seems, since the earliest instances of elaborated plastered walls in the region.[41] In some cases, painted elements in the plaster surface directly correspond to beams embedded within the wall.[42] The relationship to the wall's underlying construction is especially apparent in the case of the West House wall paintings, where Palyvou has described what is essentially a "grid iron" structure working through the three zones of the frescoed walls. She argues that the architect's and painter's work intentionally operate in tandem, with "common goals."[43] For all of their novel steps toward illusion, the ikria of Room 4, like the later shield friezes located in other Aegean buildings, did nothing to disturb this established order – indeed they participate in it with vibrancy and boldness. In Room 4, we see the dado and border zones preserved with colorful bands and painted panels, thus framing the ikria with motifs that belong in a painted wall – but not in a ship or harbor. These features keep the ikria in limbo, on the one hand working in the service of the wall's structure and, on the other, standing as if objects in space. In the case of the shield frescoes, we see how these two aspects – a dynamic lifelikeness of figures and their enlistment in the wall's architectural order – need not be viewed as fully at odds, but nevertheless as emphasizing different simultaneous aspects of the painted entities. The vivid rendering of bands and spiral friezes between (and/or above, and/or below) the shields situates them as part of a highly structured painted wall, while these same linear elements also provide for experiencing the shields illusionistically, as being hung atop such a wall. Evans, followed by Shaw and Laxton, even suggests that the spiral friezes depicted behind/between the shields in wall paintings indicate the location of a wooden beam that could readily receive nails for hanging.[44] This understanding would fold yet further complexity into the relationship between the generic, structurally based conventions of painting a wall, and the representation of a specific and in this case practically significant reality (a beam that could accept nails for suspension). Scale is part of this. Palyvou uses the terms "x-ray" or "simulation" to describe such situations, in which architectural components of a room – such as a dado, cornice or beam – appear as painted elements within a fresco.[45] In those contexts where we see, within a painting, an object of lifelike size set upon an architectural feature (e.g., as we have seen with the ikria set upon a dado/platform) or located in the same place that the entity would have also been encountered in the room as an object in the round (e.g., the shields set upon the painted horizontal beam), she offers the further term "projection."[46] In the case of these large-scale friezes, the size of the represented entities maintains a lifelike proportion with the painted architectural components. This contributes to the tension of the friezes, as the effect is twofold and somewhat paradoxical: the seriated entities appear more integrated *into* the wall, as the substance of pictorial components and architectural structure is shared; and, at the same time, the illusion of the entities being objects in the round present *upon* the wall is enhanced, since, through the medium of painting, it is possible to create visual cues that indicate relations between the entities and the wall's structure – such as superposition and attachment – and these bring a sense of depth and realism.

Aegean Rococo?

We can describe the tension at play in the large-scale friezes of helmets, ikria and shields as being between ornament and verisimilitude, as the conventional structure of the painted wall and the affordance of elements of lifelike experiences of the entities are *both* active. As we discussed in Chapter 5, identifying an "ornamental" status for a given form implies that its presence is in some sense secondary to, or determined by, the structure that it is part of. This typically limits the semiotic or representational complexity of the form along with its agency in the space. Meanwhile, for a robust lifelike experience to be offered through a wall painting, the demands of an illusionistic effect would have to take precedence over or *overtake* the structural character of the architecture. Hence, there is a struggle for dominance characterizing the spaces of the friezes – but it is a quiet one, in which neither side proffers a full claim. Another historical context in which a tension has been identified between ornament and verisimilitude of representation is the Rococo church architecture of Bavaria (Figure 6.9). Philosopher Karsten Harries has examined this situation extensively.[47] He draws out a situation there in which illusion is both fruitfully developed and also undermined in the wall painting and stucco work

6.9. View of interior ceiling of Wieskirche, Steingaden, Germany. Frans Sellies/ Getty Images

of the church. Harries distinguishes these dynamics in the Bavarian churches from the handling of sacred architecture in the Italian Baroque, which, in some instances, very effectively forged a sublime illusion of uninterrupted space that embraces both the human standing within a church and the heavens depicted on its walls, as if the continuous space reaches far beyond (see, e.g., Pozzo's Sant'Ignazio, Rome). In contrast, the Bavarian Rococo church never fully released its groundedness in a reality that was no illusion. Through means such as the manipulation but preservation of framing devices,[48] or the depiction of painted figures in receding landscapes that nevertheless excluded the viewer by rising from groundlines originating far above the church's floor[49] or realistic asymmetrical sculptural features that ultimately were reclaimed by the order of the church's structure by being answered across the space of the church,[50] the Bavarian church, according to Harries, kept the viewer's experience caught in a beautifully unresolved space that did not aim to dissolve the boundary of architectural and represented space through unbridled illusion. Harries explores the possible ethical implications and effects of this. Ultimately, the Bavarian Rococo church did not make the heavenly world available to earthly humans as did the High Baroque Italian church. The Bavarian Rococo church kept the two spaces distinct even as it made the unfathomable seem closer – possibly glimpsed before the impressive earthly structure reasserted itself around the viewer.

While both Harries' discussion and our consideration of the large-scale friezes of the Aegean Bronze Age deal heavily with the medium of wall painting, allowing for certain productive comparisons, the ways in which a tension between the agencies of architectural structure and painted representation plays out in the two historical contexts are significantly distinct. The Rococo space is predominantly vertical, while we have seen that Aegean architecture and wall painting were essentially horizontal; this distinction, along with highly divergent architectural forms, carries real differences for how a painting could approach a viewer and how relationships between painting and built space could be formulated. Meanwhile, the technical means through which architectural and painted spaces could be articulated were in some key respects also different. For example, in the Bavarian Rococo church, stucco ornament could be crucial as both a softening mediator and a boundary maker between architecture and painting; while stucco is innovatively utilized in Minoan wall painting, it does not serve the same role. Moreover, the play with full illusion in the Rococo church involved formal and perspectival manipulations that were not active in Aegean Bronze Age art and, more basically, entailed a very different problematization of the representation of distance. And while the Bavarian Rococo paintings were primarily scenic, with substantial extents of space represented, the Aegean friezes we are considering were suggesting shallower spatial depths. Despite these significant divergences, there is a very particular irresolution held in common between these historically distant spaces. What we can see in both contexts is an artful combination of features that prioritized both structural order and the affordance of experiences of represented bodies as-in-life. This simultaneity effected an uncertainty that brought the contents of paintings toward the space of the viewer while also keeping them within the structure of the room's wall. These crafted spaces thus realized a distinct if subtle pressure on the viewer – not a simple pull between two separate spaces (present and illusory), but a constant vibrating pressure between different ways of experiencing the painting's status in relation to one's own standing within the room.

Frames as Complicated Borders

Harries discusses the significance of the frame across various examples of Bavarian Rococo church design and the effect of framing more broadly. A frame, he describes, "creates first of all a barrier separating the picture from what supports it. The reality in which the observer stands, and beyond this the familiar world with its cares and concerns, are bracketed out."[51] In some cases, when the framing follows the architectural junctures of the building, it can emphasize and integrate the painting *into* the building's structure (e.g., in the case of the Bavarian church, when a frame limits a painting to an apse, dome or vault), thereby constricting the potential for illusionism (as at Wieskirche, Figure 6.9). We have seen that in the case of the ikria frieze in Room 4 of the West House, and in the various Aegean shield frescoes, the persistence of conventional painted borders at the top and base of the friezes maintains the framing structure of the wall and counters the realism of the painted entities' form and scale. Yet since these framing elements are also painted elements, their delimiting contrasts with the figural elements of the painting are somewhat relaxed. Harries also considers situations in which the frame has been manipulated in order to "weaken the usual function of the frame without surrendering it altogether."[52] This can occur if the frame is created as a less rigid and unambiguous boundary between architectural space and the space created by the painting. One way in which this is effected in the Bavarian Rococo church is the "pictorialization" of the frame, through which the frame is rendered in a form that can participate in the painted scene it delimits, for example if the frame at the base of a painted ceiling dome is crafted as a three-dimensional stucco balustrade, creating a miniature inhabitable space (Figure 6.9).[53] Such elaborate artistry might seem entirely unlike what we are seeing in the Aegean Bronze Age paintings, and in some ways of course it is. But underlying such features is a problematization of the frame's liminal status between architectural space and represented space, and how its form can be made to participate in both simultaneously, and this is inherently shared with the Aegean bordering devices. We can appreciate this more fully in the case of Room 4 of the West House, where we have much of a room's painting preserved and can observe how the ikria frieze is incorporated into its broader context. Here, we see that the painted dado affirms the generic structure of the flat, zoned wall, which is shared across rooms in the building. But it also doubles as an element with implied depth upon which the ikria sit as if on a platform, as they are wont to do in the wide world beyond. And this dado itself has a complex status between vibrant wall painting and the illusion of three-dimensional substance: as a skeuomorph of panels of variegated stone, the dado is a form that is at once a representation and a creative original.

Looking more widely, we see that Aegean wall paintings involving animalian entities are rife with innovative manipulations of framing elements that both manifest and challenge the boundary-making effects of such borders. This can be realized in various ways. In some cases, framing bands that assert the wall's zoned structure are rendered as a positive presence, traditional and expected, that is then transgressed. We see this in the House of the Frescoes at Knossos, where the painting of an expansive rocky landscape, teeming with plants, waterways, foraging monkeys and flying birds, has been reconstructed across multiple walls in the Main Hall.[54] The striped bands defining the upper border of this painting are breached by irregular rockwork that climbs upward from the landscape and seems to be too much for the painted linear border to contain (Figure 6.10);[55] we see similar situations in various other Aegean Bronze Age frescoes.[56]

6.10. Reconstruction of area of Neopalatial wall painting from House of the Frescoes, Knossos. Photograph by ArchaiOptix (CC BY-SA 4.0). Objects © Hellenic Ministry of Culture and Sports

Such transgression of the border complicates the status of the painting in subtle but powerful ways, by giving body to simultaneous counterforces that each impact how the represented entities are experienced – we have both the structuring of the bandwork, which would keep the landscape and its lively contents as part of the ordered wall, and the transgressive rockwork that seems to betray the landscape as a distinct phenomenon that momentarily overcomes and reaches beyond the confines of the wall. In this light, we can also recognize how, in the friezes that image bandwork between/behind seriated entities – including the large-scale helmets frieze from Xeste 4, and the friezes of shields from various Aegean sites – the representation of this traditional structuring feature of wall painting (the bandwork) becomes a means through which the limits of the wall are challenged and partially overrun. This effect does not extinguish the structuring effect of the paintings' banding, which still appears in place. Instead, both effects coexist, as two simultaneous layers that create a sense of physical and ontological depth in their copresence. This keeps the standing of the distinctive animalian entities embodied in the paintings vibrantly open-ended.

THE TETHERED GRIFFIN

We have seen that the painted friezes embodying our three animalian composite entities – the boar's tusk helmet, the oxhide shield and ikrion – were highly dynamic in their generation and complication of space. This was especially pronounced when the entities were rendered in wall paintings, where their scale, color and positioning alongside living human action within a room afforded new types of engagement. In this context, the entities had a bold presence that in some ways approached how they were experienced as objects in the round. In subtle tension with this was their enmeshment in the structured wall, and the concomitant expectations of what a wall painting was and entailed as part of the building. These renderings of the Aegean animalian entities dynamically existed in and *generated* this tense space, standing between the confines of the flat wall and the depth of three-dimensional bodies.

I would like to step back now and revisit some Aegean beasts that we examined in Chapter 4 in the fresh light of the spatial dynamics currently under discussion. Griffins were rendered in Aegean wall paintings of the LB I and II, where they embodied a tension strikingly similar to what we have seen in the large-scale friezes of helmets, shields and ikria, although it was effected in distinct ways. The griffin may, in fact, have shared a path to Aegean frescoed walls with the seriated entities. We have seen that the griffin was vividly embodied in the large-scale Middle Cycladic ceramic vessels, most notably in the Griffin Pithos discussed in Chapter 4. On this vessel, two griffins stand, one behind the other, within a landscape of stylized plants. The composition clearly sets a scene, even as it plays with abstracted forms and repetition. While the base of the field appears as a vegetated terrain, the upper border, at the neck of the vessel, is defined by a band of running spirals. The presence of this border feature, combined with the vessel's strikingly large scale and polychrome figural painting, remind one of the qualities of murals that would develop subsequently in the town – and, like the Hunter's Asaminthos, suggest that this object may offer a glimpse of innovative developments in the craft of painting.

As we examined in Chapter 4, renderings of griffins in Aegean MBA–LBA material culture, including on the Griffin Pithos (Figure 4.10), often involve the presence of some sort of embellishment or added feature at the beast's neck. In glyptic, as on the Pithos, there can be ambiguity in the identity of the feature, and it can appear as both an element of the creature's body (e.g., pronounced chest feathers, a curved body marking, the boundary of the neck and chest) and a worn object, such as a collar, pendant or leash. On the griffins of the Griffin Pithos, a feature in the shape of an s-spiral, situated with a curve at the neck and with a pendant loop extending downward across the shoulder/chest, could be an elaboration of the extraordinary animal's bodily character but is also strongly suggestive of a leash. This latter identity for the curvilinear neck/chest feature is further hinted at by the positioning of each griffin directly in front of and facing an upright tree. Intuitively, the trees seem to stand as supports to which the griffins could be tied – that this connection is not actually articulated keeps the reading of the cluster of features ambivalent.

The Griffin Pithos belongs to Phase 3 at Akrotiri, the later segment of the Middle Cycladic period at the site. As we step into the early LC I, we find another large-scale painted griffin in Akrotiri, here within the walls of Xeste 3 – and this one is certainly leashed. As on the Pithos, the griffin of Xeste 3 is represented in an outdoor landscape, but here it is part of an elaborate scene with clear narrative dimensions. In a frequently discussed series of paintings extending across the east and north walls of Room 3a on the first floor of the building, we find a scene of young women gathering crocuses from a rocky landscape and, on the north wall, a vignette in which part of this flower harvest is presented to a seated woman (Figure 6.11).[57] The rendering of the landscape generally seems to fit with the conventions for creating spatial depth that we have discussed – the rocky landscape of the east wall is shown in a profile section along the base of the wall and the human crocus gathers, also rendered in profile, stand upon it; as the wall extends vertically, we find a field of crocuses running behind and around the figures, reaching all the way to the multicolor banded border at the top of the wall. With this, the sense that the girls are working within an expansive flowered landscape is conveyed. While no hanging ground is depicted here, such does appear in a thematically related painting within the corresponding room below. This would seem to confirm

6.11. Views of wall painting showing the "Potnia" scene; north wall of Room 3a, first floor, Xeste 3, Akrotiri. a. Drawing of the Potnia wall painting from Xeste 3, Akrotiri Thera, LC I. Drawing: Maria Krigka; courtesy Andreas Vlachopoulos; b. Photograph from Doumas 1992: 159 fig. 122. Courtesy Akrotiri Excavations. Object © Hellenic Ministry of Culture and Sports

the dynamics of spatial depth at play in the wall paintings of the building, with receding depth created in the painted scene as the wall extends from floor to ceiling.

As Palyvou describes, a young woman painted in the corner of Room 3a on the first floor, upon the edge of the north wall, indicates that the setting and action of the east wall continues across the juncture. This woman, with remarkable red hair and a pot of freshly picked crocuses perched upon her shoulder, walks across the same rocky terrain as the figures in the east wall; the profile of this colorful ground continues its unbroken undulation across the corner. The young woman moves westward, but here the structure of the wall does interrupt her course – as we see it. A couple steps ahead of her, the wall breaks into a window. Palyvou has described how this break in the wall is incorporated into the painted scene, writing that "the gap acts as an intermediary, as a passage or a link between the events taking place in the mountain and those below in the valley, as if time and space have been condensed in this gap or as if the window acts as a change of paragraph in the text of narration."[58]

It is what takes form on the other side of this window that is of particular interest to us. Beginning in the west of the painted scene and moving toward the window, we see a presentation playing out across an elaborate structure of stepped risers, consisting of platforms set at increasing heights, all within a landscape of crocus plants that extends across the frescoed field. Farthest to the west, a young woman bends slightly as she pours her basket of gathered crocus flowers into a larger, brimming container, which sits upon the next step up from her (Figure 6.11). In front of the container, upon the same step as it, rests one foot of a tall, upright blue monkey. The monkey's second foot is placed upon the next step, beside a smaller container of crocuses. The monkey raises its paw, holding flowers up toward the outstretched hand of the large seated female in front of him. One foot of this figure rests in front of the monkey's basket of flowers, continuing the rhythm of figures and containers upward across the stepped platforms. She herself sits at the apex of the risers, upon the top platform, her seat formed of three stacked cushions. There is much about this female figure that is remarkable, and she has been the subject of considerable scholarly attention. Her elaborate adornments, both textiles and jewelry, enrich her identity, which is clearly important – whether she is a mortal or a divinity. The young woman and monkey fix their gazes upon the woman from below, indicating, along with her seated position and the apparent offerings being made, that she is the object of their adoration. It is, however, a fourth figure in this vignette to which I would like to turn.

Behind the seated female, the stepped risers descend back downward from their summit. Here, one level removed from the seated woman, we find a griffin (Figures 6.11, 6.12). The griffin's body fills the narrow space between the woman and the window. One hind foot rests behind the seated woman's stacked cushions while the other, which determines the beast's relative height, is set below, on the second step. The griffin's neck and head, characterized by elegantly curving black markings,[59] are held almost vertically so that its bright orangey-yellow beak bows slightly toward the woman's shoulder. The body of the beast has been left white, but the extended wings are an intricate tapestry of color and design. For the most part, we are seeing the beast's left wing in profile, since it is positioned in front, with the edges of the right wing appearing in glimpses from behind. The leading edges of the wings rise up from the beast's back where the neck meets the shoulder. Here, we catch sight of the bottom zone of the right/back wing's upper edge, in the area of the propatagium.

6.12. Detail view of griffin in wall painting of north wall of Room 3a, first floor, Xeste 3, Akrotiri. From Doumas 1992: 165 fig. 128. Courtesy Akrotiri Excavations. Object © Hellenic Ministry of Culture and Sports

Because the griffin is holding its wings erect, it is the outer side of the right wing that is peeking out here, and it is painted in a vibrant blue. Upon this blue ground, the delicate outlines of feathers have been rendered in black, each rising up and back in unison. Set beside this blue area of the right wing, the underside of the griffin's left wing is in full view. At the base of the left wing, a dark round feature and possibly red striations occupy the area of the chest, and an inverted heart-shaped form is set at the shoulder; the centers of the heart-form's incurving lobes are punctuated by deep red dots. A bright blue diamond-shaped element, outlined in black, is positioned toward this heart-form's narrowing end. Where the left wing lifts from the body, a wide ribbon of spirals rises as a continuation of the curvilinear elaboration of the chest and shoulder area and constitutes the beast's powerful wingpit. There are seven bold spirals in all, decreasing in size as they rise through the tapering zone. Each spiral is constituted by a thick, black, tightly curving line with a large red dot set at its center. This section of spirals is bordered, on the right, by a narrow band of blue, beyond which the splendid sweep of secondary and primary wing feathers crescendos through to the wingtip. Each of these feathers is essentially rectilinear and has a white ground that is elaborated with pendant black triangles alternating with deep red dots; each feather is capped by a band of blue outlined in black, which, taken together, define the trailing edge of the wing. From behind the upper edge of the left wing, we can see the corresponding area of the right wing rising in a second spray of identical feathers.

We considered this griffin briefly in Chapter 4. In the present context, I would like to turn more closely to the beast's relationship with the north wall of Room 3b. While the frescoed wall plaster in this area is fragmented, obscuring some details of the griffin's body, we can very clearly appreciate a red painted band that appears tied around the animal's neck, forming a simple loop knot. Just below the loop, we see the red band, a leash, continue upward from the back of the griffin's neck, until it meets the blue zone of the leading edge of the beast's right wing. Here, it appears to run behind the wing, momentarily obscured, before reappearing above the upper primary feathers, where it rises yet farther above the griffin. At this point, something remarkable occurs. The red leash seems to form a loop in midair; from this loop, the rope's flanged end hangs limply down. This is the view we have if we follow the band through the space represented within the painting, for this loop at the end of the leash is set within the open landscape of the crocus field. The rope could in theory be understood as extending behind the griffin, running toward a fixed point in the ground below the beast that appears higher on the wall (because of the convention for depicting receding planes), but such a view is contradicted by several details. First, the rope departs the beast's neck angled upward, which implies that the cord is lifted. There are no distinct objects apparent in the crocus-filled background toward which the rope might have been specifically heading for anchorage. If the intention had been to convey that the beast was tethered down upon the ground, the painter likely would have represented the rope angling downward from the griffin's neck, to a lower point behind or below the beast – there is space available on the wall to do so. Instead, the upward angle from the knot at the neck signals the rope's rise, and its upward slope on the wall parallels the dramatic and definite upward sweep of the griffin's extended wing. Finally, we see the limp far end of the rope dangling straight down from the loop it forms, as if it is hanging; this disposition would not make sense if the rope was lying upon the ground. And so the leash rises, but where to? Upon which point, hovering in the air of the crocus field, does it loop?

The position of the leash only makes sense if, as we follow the rope upward from the griffin's neck, we abandon the represented space of the vignette and instead see the rope within the built structure of Room 3a. From this perspective, the red leash finds a secure fixed point within the firm white wall of the room. This tethering point is intuitively positioned at an edge of the wall where a wooden beam forming the jamb would easily receive a peg; as Palyvou asserts, "the leash is tied to the real post of the nearby window."[60] Hence, with this simple strand of crimson paint, the space of the painting is deeply complicated, and with it, our space, as viewers confronting it. The otherworldly griffin, who seemed to be *there*, perched on risers in a crocus field with an extraordinary figure, is suddenly bound right *here*, in this upstairs room, with us, the living humans gazing upon it.

In her sophisticated study of Xeste 3, Palyvou has described this tethered griffin as contributing to a "merging" of the space of the room and the "illusionary space" of the painting.[61] She rightfully points to the fact that the groundline of the scene painted on the north wall is essentially even with the floor of Room 3a itself and identifies this as another factor supporting the elision of spaces. Here, Palyvou closely considers the details of the painted risers. She notes that no landscape features appear in the foreground of the painting, which instead is occupied entirely by the "mobile" risers. With this, she describes the risers as appearing "almost as if coming out from the wall to the room, linking real space to the illusionary beyond."[62] Palyvou's balanced engagement with the painting and architecture of the room, and her consideration of the experiential dimensions of being within the space, are exceptional. She ultimately sees the tethering of the griffin and the depiction of the risers as part of evidence that "the illusionary space of the wall is meant to be read in absolute connection with the real space of Xeste 3."[63] Her reading eventually takes a turn toward the symbolic, in which she envisions the drawing-together of the room's built space and the represented outdoor setting as signifying the cultural connection of Akrotiri and its mountainous landscape; as she states, "I would suggest therefore that we are witnessing the merging of pictorial and the real, as a symbolic statement of the strong and inextricable relationship between the countryside and the town."[64] Hence, Palyvou sees the painting of Room 3a, and especially of the north wall, as breaking down the divisions of representation and creating a continuity between the two spaces. Here, my understanding of what the painting of the room affords departs somewhat from Palyvou's reading, although not by disagreeing with her analysis of the complexity of the particular features. I think that there is in fact yet more complexity – and more tension – at play in how this space would be experienced.

A Beast That Is Distant, Near and Here

Palyvou states from the outset of her examination of Xeste 3 that she is interested in getting at the "intentions" of the painter and architect.[65] She does so through careful consideration of formal and experiential dimensions created, but her symbolic reading ultimately draws these toward a particular objective in the design of the space. As with other material culture we have considered, I believe we benefit here, too, from shifting away from the matter of intentions, instead placing our focus more fully on experiences afforded by the painted space. Of course, people's experiences of a crafted thing can follow the intentions of its makers in some respects, so it certainly is not that a focus on experience abandons questions of intent. Yet by changing the emphasis of our discussion, I believe other aspects of these paintings – ones that are perhaps messier, more obstinate or nonconforming – come into view and also demand to be problematized. We then can consider how they, and their likely effects, may or may not have been intended.

If we return to the griffin of Xeste 3, I believe we can see that the leash extending from its neck to the wall does not create a merging of spaces between the painting and the room but in fact forces one to grapple with their distinction. There is an unsettling that occurs as one's gaze reaches the end of the leash and with it the end of the painted scene taking place upon the risers. What is *unsettled* is one's comfortable perspective upon the open space represented in the painting: at the end of the leash, one confronts the fact that this space is in fact closed – the viewer suddenly runs into a wall, so to speak. This effect would only be intensified by the copresence within the north-wall painting of attributes that could draw the viewer into the painted space, such as the foregrounding of the risers and the nearly floor-level groundline, both highlighted by Palyvou. With the pull enacted by these attributes in play, a viewer would have been yet more disturbed by the abrupt undermining of the scene's depth that was effected by the tethered leash. It is not only that with these simultaneous dynamics at work the whole painted presentation scene seems to oscillate across space, but also that the oscillation involves the space in which the living human is present. The leash tacks the presentation scene to the flat wall, while also dragging the wall into the outdoor space of the landscape. At the same time, the risers sitting on the shared ground/floor of the room seem to pull the scene outward, into the space of the living viewer.

Closer consideration reveals that there is in fact yet more complexity at work here, and that in certain respects this painting shares attributes and spatial dynamics with the large-scale helmet, shield and ikria friezes we have been discussing. If we return to the foreground of the north wall of Room 3a, we find a familiar feature of wall frescoes lurking behind the risers. Between the supports of the platforms we have clear glimpses of three thick, deep-red linear bands that conventionally announce the boundary of the painted wall (Figure 6.11). The copresence of these border bands and the painted risers is unreasonable. While the foregrounded risers seem to create an illusion of the presentation scene having an extensive depth that spills out into the space of the room, the bands clearly assert the presence of the wall, painted with traditional borders. This wall should not be there, behind the risers – according to the details of the scene read illusionistically, this should be an open field.[66]

The paradoxical relationship of the border bands with the risers echoes that of the griffin and its tethered leash – both complicate the painting's spatial assertions by belying the presence of the wall. Yet even as the bands and the leash similarly complicate the painting, on another level they also counter one another, creating further tension: as the leash seems to deny the depth of the represented bodies, by putting them *on* the wall, the red band feature, appearing as if *behind* the risers, seems to push them outward from the wall, toward the space of the room. In this respect, the painted bands behind the risers in Room 3a act like the banded features that are painted behind shields and helmets in the large-scale frieze frescoes. As we have seen, this way of presencing the painted wall to then transgress it implies depth between elements within the painting (the band and the entities that are painted atop it, thus being pushed outward), while nevertheless insistently reminding the viewer that this all is indeed a painted wall that ultimately answers to the rhythmic, ordered structure of the room's zoned architecture. Interestingly, although the upper border bands run across both the north and east walls, the lower red bands are not continued in the area of the north wall that is positioned east of the window (where the red-haired woman carries a container of crocuses across the rocky landscape), nor do they appear on the east wall, with its hilly scene. Whether by design or accident, this lower red border asserts itself only in the company of the risers, where its spatial implications are most problematic – and rich.

Color subtly contributes to the spatial tension of the north wall painting, as it does in the large-scale friezes of seriated entities. The simple red line of the griffin's leash embodies the tension that tugs between spaces in the north wall. The griffin's body also contributes to this tension. While the wing opens out in intricate polychromy, the beast's white body itself is barely differentiated from the wall, being simply a reserve area of the unpainted lime plaster, only indicated by fine outlines. The outward thrust of the open wing, asserting itself in space, countered by the body, withdrawn in the flat white background of the wall, imparts a tension across the griffin's form that reasserts the limbo effected by the leash.

In the north wall of Xeste 3, as well as the large-scale frieze frescoes, we see a complex rendering of forms in space, where figural elements seem, at once, to be both drawn outward from and collapsed back into the painted wall. This occurs through various means, such as size, coloration and the impression of dimensionality and spatial relationships (such as superposition) that imply physical depth. We have seen that our three Aegean animalian composite entities – boar's tusk helmets, oxhide shields and ikria – are all prominently engaged in the embodiment of this distinctive representational dynamism. The griffin, an extraordinary animalian being in its own right, is also drawn into this, as is dramatically apparent in the painting of Xeste 3. There, the impressive exotic beast is tethered between the flatness of a wall, the openness of a landscape and the present of the room in which the living human stands. In this position, the griffin embodies a distinctive spatial back and forth not only through the manner in which it is rendered, but also in its identity as a winged exotic beast that is leashed to a built space – indeed, the griffin tied to the wall of Room 3a seems an icon of the taut spatial dynamism that it manifests.

As was discussed in Chapter 4, the constrained griffin acquires the status of an iconographic trope during the Neopalatial period and LB II–III in the Aegean. Subdued, leashed and collared griffins, sometimes tied to a column or hitched to a chariot, occur in glyptic and painted ceramics, as well as in wall painting. Vivid embodiments were present in the core of Crete's monumental social space, in the walls of the palace at Knossos. However rich, the Knossian evidence is highly fragmentary and its reconstructions are problematic; consequently, we must take variables into account.

Remains of wall frescoes apparently involving griffins were discovered in fill from the area of the North–South Corridor at the palace, likely having been deposited there (from elsewhere in the building) after a moment of damage during the Neopalatial period (Figure 6.13).[67] While out of context and fragmentary, we can nevertheless appreciate that this painting would have realized a remarkably dynamic relationship between the winged beasts and the impressive confines of a monumental built space. These particular beasts were rendered through an innovative craft technique, in which their bodies are raised outward with stucco, thereby gaining notable three-dimensional heft and contour above the flatter surface of the wall.[68] With this, their bodies effectively reached out into the space of the room occupied by the living human engaging with them. At the same time, they are both substantively and thematically caught in the space of the painted wall. In order to form the raised zones constituting the bodies, stucco was carefully built up in layers from the still-moist underlying wall plaster, thus anchoring the relief areas into the fabric of the wall's plane.[69] Evans' reconstruction of the painting involves multiple griffins arranged in pairs on either side of columns, to which the beasts are tethered by ornate leashes. These leashes, constituted by rows of dots, rise

6.13. Reconstructed stucco-relief wall painting involving tethered griffins, from Knossos. Photograph by ArchaiOptix (CC BY-SA 4.0). Herakleion Museum. Object © Hellenic Ministry of Culture and Sports

along the neck shaft and then extend into the line of a simple red bridle with white dots that crosses the neck.[70] Fragments of the area where the hypothetical leash and bridle meet are preserved, as are portions of the body, including what appear to be areas of a wing, legs, torso and two tails, as well as a possible segment of a column's capital. Evans' reconstruction was based in scenes known from glyptic imagery, such as that of CMS I.98 (to which he explicitly compares the wall painting).[71] Hägg and Lindau reconstructed the wall painting scene differently, with the griffins arranged heraldically not about a column, but instead on either side of a goddess with snake frame.[72] I would like to draw out that underlying the variation in these readings (and further possible ones), we can see that the basic situation attested here, of apparently bridled griffins innovatively rendered as bodies in sculpted relief, generates an acute tension. This tension is between the beasts being controlled *within* the space of the wall and their simultaneous pushing powerfully beyond the wall, into the flux of lived social space. As we saw in Chapter 3, the antithetic disposition of beasts is one that implies control and a level of what we can describe as subduing. If such is indeed embodied in this painting, along with the beasts' bridled nature, the domesticating effect would be even more notable. At the same time, the griffins' extraordinary and (here seemingly) winged character, and their bodies rising from the wall's surface, pull against this constrained status with remarkable dynamism.

The frescoes of griffins in the Throne Room at Knossos seem to embody a similar tension between painted and lived space, yet this arises from distinct qualities (Figure 6.14).[73] The dating and preservation of these paintings are fraught. They likely date to LM II but seem strongly informed by Neopalatial

6.14. Photomontage reconstruction of the wall painting of the north wall of the Throne Room at Knossos. Courtesy of Ute Günkel-Maschek and Yannis Hamilakis

phenomena.[74] Fragments of three frescoed griffins were preserved; a fourth is conjectured. Along the north wall of the room, two antithetically arranged griffins flanked the doorway opening into another chamber (the so-called Inner Sanctuary). On the west wall, a vivid red palm plant was painted just to the east of the stone throne, as if issuing from it; just beside this palm, the foot of another griffin was preserved, seemingly facing the throne. No painting was preserved on the north wall to the west of the throne, yet, in an extensive recent study, Galanakis, Tsitsa and Günkel-Maschek very tentatively suggest that another palm and griffin likely would have been present there, mirroring those painted on the other side, given that other aspects of symmetrical design characterize the space (including the antithetically arranged griffins of the north wall).[75]

In some ways, the painted griffins of the Throne Room exhibit a markedly situated character, their rendering being closely bound to the fixed elements of the charged interior space. As with the large ikria in the frieze of Room 4 in the West House, Akrotiri, these Knossian griffins sit atop a skeuomorphic dado imitating variegated stone, as if it were a supporting entity. Upon the west wall of the Throne Room, the antithetic pairing of griffins embraces the architectural unit of the doorway, whether or not this passage was involved in a rite of revelation, as has been proposed.[76] Meanwhile, the (purely hypothetical) heraldry of two griffins poised on either side of the fixed stone throne along the north wall has been discussed by various scholars.[77] Rehak, in particular, has argued that when taken together, the painting and the occupied seat would have effectively created a familiar scene involving animals and a central anthropomorphic figure, which was deeply established in the visual culture of the broader eastern Mediterranean and Near East by the LBA; as Hitchcock puts it, "the resulting arrangement, in this interpretation, is a multimedia blending of human actors, architecture, and iconography working together to create a Master or Mistress of Animals motif."[78] Even if only one griffin was present beside the throne, Rehak's problematization of the composition created by the immovable seat, the frescoed beast(s) beside it and a living person who could temporarily "complete" it is compelling. We can see that different components of this crafted space would have involved multiple substances and temporalities that could fluidly give rise to powerful moments of social experience. Egan has remarked on how the painting's scale and ground-level positioning contribute to a "sense of immersion."[79] Tully and Crooks have recently built on Shaw's observation that the back of the Knossos throne is shaped in a waved "rocklike" manner.[80] They consider the performative dimensions of such an object and context, connecting them to ideologically charged mountainous landscapes.[81] Meanwhile, taking a fresh view on the Knossian space, Hitchcock has argued that the throne may never have been occupied by a human and, instead, could have manifested "sacred emptiness" in a manner well attested elsewhere in the eastern Mediterranean and Near East, including in instances of intentionally empty thrones.[82] Across these diverse readings, we are confronted with the rich possibility that other varieties of space – such as rocky landscapes or framed voids – were being made present in the room along with human and nonhuman animals. This complicates, instead of denying, the situatedness of the griffins.

The coming together of furniture, frescoed bodies, and fleshy living ones within the Knossian Throne Room would have both firmly engaged the wall and, simultaneously, reached beyond it, into the vital space of the chamber. In this, it is comparable to other Neopalatial griffin frescoes we have considered. Blakolmer's astute observation that hatching observable on the undersides of the griffins of the Throne Room may have been a means of creating depth in their bodily forms, perhaps in imitation of relief stucco, suggests another manner in which the beasts inherently pulled against their embeddedness in the wall[83] – in so doing, they may have recalled the effect of other griffins, embodied in true relief, that had occupied earlier walls at the palace.[84] The dynamic relationship of painted space and lived space in the throne room, connected through a bridging seat, is, in essence, what Palyvou sees in the north wall of Xeste 3. Yet unlike the frescoed risers of that space, the single stone seat, along with the stone benches that run outward from it along the wall, *did* project outward upon the stone floor of the chamber. In moments where the central seat at Knossos was occupied, a human would have sat prominently amongst the furniture of the room, with an impressive griffin (or two) immediately beside her, and other griffins not far away. Rows of seated humans potentially also flanked the enthroned person – but they did so from within the living din of the room. The beasts uniquely contributed here by both being positioned beyond the lived flux of this socioculturally charged room and, at the same time, remaining inescapably bound to it. We can further note that the acute spatial tension created across the frescoed griffins and the protruding stone seat certainly still would have been active if the seat remained empty. That pregnant emptiness, a heterotopia of sorts, would only have enhanced the complexity of presence and absence created in the company of these griffins – the antithetic griffins flanking the open space of the doorway in the west wall in fact participate in the articulation of such.

Palyvou sees the icon of a griffin attached to a column as a means of drawing the beast's strengths into a symbolized sociocultural body: "the attributes of the griffin are transferred to the royal/religious power that this architectural element represents while at the same time the griffin is secured against flying away."[85] This reading shares the logic of Morgan's and Morris' arguments that oxhide shields and boar's tusk helmets served to bestow their wearers/users with the power of the beasts from which the bodily substances were taken; these ideas also connect to Simandiraki-Grimshaw's notion of heterosomatic hybrids. I feel that these authors are probably correct, on one level, to see such animalian things as effecting a conferral of character from beasts to other phenomena – such as buildings, institutions or humans. My primary interest, however, is in stepping back to consider how their embodiments in wall paintings would have afforded keen types of spatial engagement between the animalian entities and living humans, thereby contributing to dynamics of sociocultural experience. This pertains to paintings of griffins, but also of series of shields, helmets and ikria.

THE SOCIAL CONTEXTS OF UNCERTAIN WALLS

Never is the spatial complexity of the tethered griffin more intense than when embodied in a large-scale wall painting, where represented architecture and actual built architecture coincide. We have discussed the effect of such coincidence between represented wall and actual wall in conjunction with the large-scale friezes (e.g., concerning scenes of suspended shields), and it marks another way in which embodiments of painted griffins and the animalian composite entities relate. The tension between represented space and architectural space was given body in these wall paintings. This afforded the human viewer simultaneous counterindications that would have charged their experience of being within these painted rooms with a productive unsettledness. This effect is in some ways relatable to what Harries discusses in the Bavarian Rococo church, where illusion and the ornamentation of built structure both laid strong claims, resulting in a splendid spatial irresolution. Of course, the ways in which illusion and structure were rendered, experienced and brought to interact could not be the same between the Rococo in Bavaria and the Aegean Bronze Age – naturally not; as obvious as this may be, it is important to reiterate. The comparison is nevertheless helpful in part because it invites us, like Harries does in his analysis of the Bavarian churches, to consider these Aegean spaces in part by recognizing what is *not* taking place therein. With this we can appreciate how the experience afforded in a space where illusionistic verisimilitude was the wholehearted, unchecked aim would have been remarkably distinct from what we are seeing. Equally different would be a space whose painted elaborations were fully determined as responses to its structural order. It is the simultaneity of both (ultimately unfulfilled) effects that generates the particular dynamism of these tense Aegean spaces – in which illusion is sensed, but one is also able to see around its edges to the surface where structure persists. This tension reveals the power and complexity of artifice to a person, by allowing its work to be appreciated as such. Here, that artifice is distinctly spatial. The wall emerges in these contexts as a tortured but wondrous thing.

Why was the tension surrounding the large-scale friezes and griffin frescoes being manifested in such distinctly spatial terms? Palyvou provides a lens for thinking through this with her ideas concerning how the Xeste 3 paintings may have symbolized crucial cultural links between the spaces of the town and countryside. If the marriage of these dissimilar spaces was being grappled with culturally, wherewith the possibility of their union held specific significances, it may be that visual culture was a venue through which communities tried to articulate this disjuncture – and perhaps to enact their coming together. This would pose the wall paintings as a response to a cultural phenomenon, as a symbolic means that served community members as they sought to express and harness religious power. This may indeed have been a role played by the paintings, both in Xeste 3 and elsewhere contemporaneously in the Aegean, as relationships between urban spaces and hinterlands underwent social recalibrations. As we have discussed across the previous chapters, the Neopalatial era in Crete saw profound changes in the landscape of outdoor sacred spaces, including rural peak and cave sanctuaries. The number of these sanctuaries diminished during this period, and it seems that those that continued in use had strong relationships with specific palaces. Palatial economic interests in agriculture would have also altered how rural areas were incorporated into formative urban social spaces, working in part through developments in writing technologies. Meanwhile, impacting all of this would have been the matter of climate changes connected to the eruption of the Theran volcano, which, as Driessen and MacDonald,[86] Bicknell[87] and others have compellingly argued, would have significantly impacted Aegean communities' connections to the natural worlds of which they were part. How space was dealt with in painted culture very likely reflected these dramatic changes in how people dwelt within the lived spaces of the Aegean. Yet to take a different but not mutually exclusive approach and again step away from the matter of intent, we can see that these wall paintings may have also *created* spatial dimensions of power in this period and characterized it, in part, with the energy of uncertainty.

Throughout the foregoing chapters, we have seen that crafted animalian bodies long held distinctive power in the Aegean. This power was fluid and highly particular in its realizations across different contexts and media, but it seems that in many cases Aegean animalian things were invigorated by their combination of lifelikeness and artifice. To put this another way, these objects seem to possess a high level of dynamism connected to their identity as embodiments of animals, but this dynamism arises through engagement with and cultivation of the affordances of the object's particular thingly nature. This means that both similarities to biological animals and the limitations on recreating the qualities of the biological are explored, even celebrated. Instead of being inferior imitations of biological originals, these things developed the qualities and relations of the animalian in novel ways, realizing new experiential dimensions. We have examined the powerful spatial dynamics of Aegean objects representing animals – from anthro-/zoomorphic Early Minoan vessels that could be moved between tombs and domestic spaces as bodily members of communities, to leonine glyptic objects that gained distinctive social and spatial vigor through their movements with and away from human bodies. The Aegean LB I–II wall paintings brought the unique dynamism of crafted animalian bodies into built spaces, not as movable things but as part of the very substance of the walls themselves. As with the materializations in other media, the dynamics of the animalian were developed anew in this context.

With wall paintings, the crafted animal became a fixed element of a place. While immovability brought security to these impressive manifestations of the animalian, it also carried its own vulnerabilities. A mural cannot be hoarded away, selectively handed down, protected or newly contextualized as can smaller movable representations of animals. The dynamics of access, visibility and bodily relation are dramatically altered. With wall paintings, embodiments of animalian entities became first and foremost a property of a place. Even if that place was strongly associated with an individual, walls can be breached, thrones can be abdicated, generations can pass, but a painting that is part of a wall does not so easily follow the individual person who is relocated through such events, unless it is destroyed. The fixedness of a wall painting and the lack of secure physical intimacy with a human body also rendered the forms embodied therein more vulnerable to defacement or removal. With murals, the fate and weight of the crafted animalian body were taken out of particular human hands and placed, instead, in the grip of a built space.

The animalian body acted differently in this context. In increased color and size, it could become part of spatial "surrounds" as never before.[88] But more fundamentally, the dynamism of the animalian, as we have seen, could be novelly characterized by a spatial tension that arose within the context of the wall – this tension could not take full form in other settings. The distinctive spatial irresolution that was generated by the large-scale friezes and griffin frescoes seems to have drawn from the unique vigor associated with renderings of animalian entities in other Aegean media but newly cultivated it within the ground of a painted wall, with its unique potentials. This invested painted spaces with something unprecedented and distinctive. The reasons behind the choice of an animalian subject could be multifold, and I do not think that we can easily identify them. The individual animalian entities selected likely held particular meanings for communities, and engagement with animals more broadly may have carried metaphoric value that played a role in sociopolitical processes associated with certain painted locales. Meanwhile, the specific sociocultural experiences that took form within painted contexts naturally would have varied between locations across Crete and the southern Aegean. In light of such inevitable variation, it is especially remarkable that in numerous distant but culturally interconnected places, a similar fundamental association *was* realized between particular built spaces and a distinctive dynamism arising from crafted animals.

THE VARIABLE DIMENSIONS AND DYNAMISMS OF ANIMALIAN ENTITIES

Crossing Space: Feeling Connections between Different Kinds of Animalian Bodies

The association of "lifesize" animal bodies and Aegean built places certainly was not new in the Neopalatial period. Thinking about this will help us to appreciate, in this respect, too, what the wall paintings were not doing, and how they were innovative. Care of living animals, acts of sport, slaughter and sacrifice, as well as preparation and consumption of substances from animal bodies, sometimes surely took place in built locales prior to the era of the animalian wall paintings, and then contemporaneously with them. Such engagements with biological animals involved their own robust experiential dimensions, marked by a different temporality and presence than the paintings. The sounds, smells, tastes, sights and emotions of sharing space with biological animals – ones that are living, birthing, dying, dead, fragmented or processed – are deeply unique and affecting. Wall paintings and other representational objects did not replicate these experiences, even if in some cases they represented them, or their results. These engagements with biological animals in built spaces, from ritual arenas to workshops, had distinctive implications for sociocultural experience; we considered some of these in Chapter 2, concerning cattle, and in the previous chapter, concerning the formulation and use of boar's tusk helmets, oxhide shields and ikria. We can imagine other types of interaction that do not leave ready material traces, such as interactions of sound between a dying animal and a musical instrument being played, as Younger discusses with reference to the scene frescoed on the Ayia Triada sarcophagus.[89]

Certain engagements between people and living animals may have taken place within rooms charged with the presence of animalian wall paintings; we can imagine instances of gift-giving, sacrifice or athletic performance – or simply scraps of food being tossed beneath the table. Likewise, movable embodiments of animals in other media – for example, animal-head rhyta or figural painted vases – may have interacted with the animalian wall paintings. While we must tread carefully in recreating hypothetical room assemblages, we need to recognize, as Egan has compelling argued regarding the enormous Palace Style vessels of LM II–III Knossos,[90] that movable objects played a crucial role in creating spaces. Objects such as decorated vessels, furniture, textiles, food and trash would have been present in spaces along with the bodies of humans and nonhuman animals. In the case of the painted rooms, these objects would have been in dialogues with murals – whether those interactions were choreographed or not. Scholars have considered how objects likely obstructed views upon wall paintings and how this interaction may have been managed or manipulated (e.g., by raising the ground level of a fresco to avoid being blocked by furniture, or hanging textiles in order to frame or conceal a mural).[91] Meanwhile Egan sees the Final Palatial Palace Style vessels, painted with dramatic vegetation, as assuming some of the role of earlier landscape murals in creating space. Crossmedia interactions also may have involved lifelike "projections" of objects/bodies known in the round, as they became appropriately positioned entities within wall paintings. Doumas and others have discussed this concerning, for example, the vases painted in the window jambs of the east wall of the West House.[92] Similar thinking subtends Evans' argument that the shield frieze at Knossos was located in the loggia of the Grand Staircase and that in an audience area of the Hall downstairs, where a spiral frieze may have run across the wall, the warriors' shields were actually suspended.[93] Even if Evans' reconstruction is flawed, it helps us to consider the interaction of the painted entities and ones present in the round. Between the relative fixedness of the painted shields and the movability of the actual ones, a spatial dynamism would have flexed temporally, physically and emotionally. We can see through Evans' discussion how the displayed storage of shields within a room in the palace – wherever that may have been – would have created a cross-spatial connection between the lifelike shields of the frieze and the shields suspended elsewhere: for anyone who knew of both, the one would be experienced in part as a recollection of the other, generating an extended copresence.[94] Thus, the frescoed shields not only would have seemed to approach a person directly in their midst, through realism and implications of depth but, through the lens of a person's memory, also would have reached out toward a corresponding file of oxhide shields present out *there*, in the lived space of the palace. Such correspondence between fixed, painted entities and movable manifestations could have elicited a host of emotional responses, depending on the particular person and sociocultural context. Seeing the paintings and knowing of the objects they echoed may have inspired a certain gravity, in which a sense of social conformity and expectation was satisfied; but one equally may have been amused at the sight of the objects artfully reembodied. While the actual oxhide shields could presumably be removed, possibly to be used in combat, the frieze would remain. This absence of the corresponding entities in the round could have inspired feelings such as longing or stress, as both the painted and emptied walls were seen. Beyond their potential relationship with shields in the round, the spatial tension of the frescoed shields may have been further enhanced and characterized by other emotional interactions with bodies in the room. In quieter moments, younger persons may have feigned authoritative stances alongside the lifelike shields; or persons discontent with the martial interests of the elite may have scowled at the colorful announcements of its traditional grip on the palace.

Before and beside the Wall: Animals in the Hand

Animals and animalian entities painted into Neopalatial walls would have coexisted with those rendered in a host of other media. Such fabricated animalian things would have made their own dynamic claims on people's experiences, along with those made by the animals in the walls – and in some cases, the dynamisms of the frescoes and movable objects may have poignantly coincided. In the corpus of Protopalatial vessels from Crete, we have evidence that certain innovative approaches to the rendering of animalian entities known from Neopalatial murals were already being fruitfully explored in the preceding period and that related traditions continued to flourish alongside the later wall paintings. On a number of remarkable Protopalatial vessels, animals' bodies were rendered as modeled and molded appliqués, introducing high relief to the surfaces.[95] We find a three-dimensional dolphin diving around the curvature of a MM II cylindrical stand from Phaistos, its body moving amid a host of full-bodied clams that rise and nearly free themselves from the wall (Figure 6.15). A ceramic vessel from Protopalatial Malia, and fragments from Knossos, similarly carry high-relief embodiments of sea creatures. The remarkable faience sphinx appliqué from Malia likewise complicated the curves of a vessel with the contours

6.15. Protopalatial cylindrical stand with plastic forms of dolphin and marine creatures, from Phaistos. Herakleion Museum. Photograph by Zde (CC BY-SA 4.0). Object © Hellenic Ministry of Culture and Sports

6.16. Vessel with relief bull, from Anemospilia. Photograph from Sakellarakis, Yannis and Efi Sapouna-Sakellaraki, *Archanes: Minoan Crete in a New Light* (Athens: Ammos Publications, 1997): 549 fig. 543. Courtesy of Efi Sapouna-Sakellaraki. Herakleion Museum. Object © Hellenic Ministry of Culture and Sports

of its distinctive animalian body. Meanwhile, a libation vessel shattered into 105 fragments, discovered in the corridor of the late Protopalatial cult building at Anemospilia, had a colorful piebald bull rendered in relief rising from its surface (Figure 6.16). Numerous other examples of such relief vessels exist.[96] The Protopalatial vessels put animalian forms into people's hands, as haptic elements of movable things. In this way, they afforded unexpected experiences, by drawing animals' forms off of the familiar, smooth surface of vases; this is what the Neopalatial relief wall frescoes would also do – a connection explored in multiple recent studies.[97] A tradition of Neopalatial relief vessels perpetuated this affordance in ceramics, and shelled sea creatures also figure prominently within the repertoire of sculpted subjects of those later vessels (Figure 6.17). The two exquisite faience relief plaques from the Temple Repositories at Knossos, which embody a cow and goat suckling their young, indicate that other media – such as the wooden piece of furniture in which the plaques were likely inlaid – were also creatively bringing the contours of animals' bodies to people's fingers within Neopalatial built spaces. These objects demonstrate that the cultivation of such spatial and dimensional complexity in renderings of animals, which challenged the limits of their media, had significant time depth in the Aegean; this parallels the boundary-defying scale of MC painted vessels, such as the Griffin Pithos. In the case of the Neopalatial relief vessels and plaques, people may have associated them with the peculiar qualities of relief frescoes, which were their contemporaries.[98]

The coexistence of animals embodied in figural wall paintings and other media would have opened new edges in people's polygonal experiences of creatures, as engagements with painted walls and movable things were drawn together with

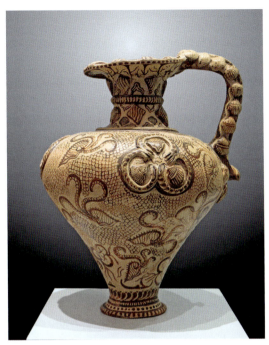

6.17. Neopalatial Marine Style ewer with relief shells, from Poros. Herakleion Museum. Photograph by Jebulon (CC0 1.0). Object © Hellenic Ministry of Culture and Sports

experiences with biological beasts. For example, a given person could know marine creatures as beings swimming in the sea, across a frescoed wall and around the curves of a painted vessel – or as the flowing body of a zoomorphic rhyton. We see early evidence of such crossmedia and intraspatial dynamics in the Protopalatial period, through exquisite animalian things such as the high-relief ceramic vessels, or a stone triton-form rhyton inscribed with images of genii from Malia. Protopalatial wall-painting fragments from Knossos, made by dipping sea sponges in orange paint and pushing them against a dark wall, hint at early interest in capturing the colorful bodily presence of sea creatures and bringing them into palace interiors.[99] Certainly, such crossmedia dynamism was wondrously at play in the Neopalatial period, through objects such as Marine Style vessels, the flying-fish fresco from Phylakopi and marine creatures in a miniature wall fresco from Archanes,[100] but also in later periods, for example in the LM II argonaut frieze fresco from Knossos, which was likely contemporary with the Throne Room griffins and shield frieze, or in the marinescape floor of the east wing. Egan keenly observes how this floor, painted with dolphins, afforded a beholder the novel experience of "walking through (over)" the sea while within the palace.[101] Rich crossmedia dynamics also would have embraced LB I–II painted ceramics imaging friezes of shields and helmets. Experiences with such objects brought yet further depth to the spatial tensions created by the animalian wall paintings, as their reach was drawn outward across greater and changeable distances, via connections made with similar but mobile things, crafted and biological.

Stories Find Fertile Ground

In Chapter 3, we considered how the fact that lions were embodied primarily in glyptic objects in Bronze Age Crete would have established a dynamic and distinctly poetic relationship between the beasts and humans. As we have seen, griffins were also frequently rendered in glyptic (but also in other media). Seals and seal impressions provide our earliest extant evidence of the griffin in Crete, and we have examined how, over time, the species' embodiment in glyptic objects would have informed its relationships with other animalian entities, including humans. As seals and signets worn on persons' bodies, and as stamped clay impressions that signified persons' identities, griffins rendered in glyptic objects could accompany the movements of a living human and enjoy mobile social lives between contexts of social activity. But when embodied in a wall painting, a griffin's connection to a room became more fundamental than any relationship it had to an individual person, even if we can imagine that the beast may have symbolized or momentarily been joined by a prominent human, for example someone sitting in Room 3a of Xeste 3 or the Throne Room at Knossos. The rendering of a griffin as constrained or tethered intensified the effect of its location within a built interior. It also carried with it the implication of a backstory – a *how* and *why* the mighty beast was caught *here*. We have previously considered the implicit narrative aspect of the tethered griffin trope, in relation to its manifestations in other media (pp. 202–206). Now we can appreciate how the platial complexity born of the trope's inherently scenic nature would have gained new depth when the constraining of the griffin occurred in a real wall. As Palyvou observes, meeting a griffin in a wall painting is a unique "corporeal and emotional" experience and, "It may be that once you have experienced a large griffin on a wall this recollection will always affect the way you see its small image on a movable object."[102] It is very likely that renderings of tethered griffins were related to or became the basis of traditional narratives concerning the beast. These might have been lengthy tales of capture or simpler vignettes. Such stories could have been conjured when a griffin was met in a painted vessel, a textile or a seal. But when it was met in a wall, the storytelling performed by the constrained griffin's body became situated as part of a living place. Whether that locale was itself an element of the content of the story (e.g., an oral narrative concerning the capture of the beast by a founding figure of a particular palace), we cannot know, and it surely varied. We can imagine that people's voices may have referred to some version of a griffin's backstory in the presence of the frescoed beast, be it through an epithet or a full-blown legend. Running beneath such possibilities is the more fundamental *placedness* of the silent storytelling that the controlled beast inherently and persistently enacted, which the painting's dynamic spatiality made distinctively engaging. Hence, these controlled griffins also infused the vitality of *telling* into the fabric of the built spaces they inhabited.

We have stepped away from treating the animalian subjects of the LB I–II frescoes primarily as symbolic expressions of authority and the murals that involve them as means of adorning great places. In so doing, the wall paintings, rich and irresolute in their representational dynamics, have emerged as significant creative forces in their own right. These crafted things contributed to how certain built spaces were imagined and experienced and, in a basic but crucial way, contributed to the articulation of what spatial power was and was becoming during this period in the Aegean. Thus, we can see that it is not simply that shields, griffins and other animalian forms were powerful as symbols; it is that the particular spatial tension generated by their embodiment in wall paintings afforded experiences of power. The vibrant nature of their embodiment in these contexts called the status of the walls into question, not through transporting illusion, but by asserting different types of presence simultaneously – the walls were rendered both flat and deep and were characterized by both lifelike entities and generic order. These counterqualities were not reconciled; they quietly excited the space with their copresence. The animalian paintings may at times have been the focus of attention in their rooms, or, surely more often, they may have contributed to momentary contexts of action along with a host of other gathered bodies; connections made to movable animalian things would have further complicated the spatial engagements of the paintings. Fundamentally, what we should recognize is that, within rooms where both illusion and structure laid claim to the walls themselves, the ground for social experiences was novelly charged – and this distinctive character became a defining quality of the crafted spaces themselves. Such innovative spatial energy took form in part through the artful rendering of animalian bodies.

VENUES OF SPECIATION

Aegean Blue

Through close consideration, we have recognized the griffin and frieze frescoes as embodiments of animalian entities with keen spatial complexity. With this, their status as representations has been complicated, as the paintings' generative work within sociocultural contexts comes to the fore. Simply put, these wall paintings do particular things that other embodiments of the entities cannot, and the status of the animalian body develops in the process. Although the effects of these wall paintings are particular and have necessitated their own problematization, in its fundaments our approach to them has been consistent with that taken throughout the foregoing chapters, being based on an examination of what crafted animalian entities uniquely afforded and how this substantively contributed to people's experiences of nonhuman creatures in the Aegean. At this point, I would like to close our discussion of wall paintings by considering how, with their realization in this medium, certain animals and elements of animals' bodies took on new characterizations that pushed their very identities as species and substances into new ground. Here, the artifice of the representations established a traditional newness.

On the east side of the seated woman painted on the north wall of Room 3a in Xeste 3, across her body from the rearing griffin, a blue monkey intently stands (Figure 6.11). Its gaze, and its toils, are firmly focused on the seated figure, as are those of the young woman positioned behind it. This monkey shares its size with that of the human girl and the griffin. Its posture and actions are essentially the same as those of the girl – both stand upright but inclined slightly forward; both are in the midst of making an offering of fresh-picked crocuses to the seated figure; both appear moving to the right, their bodies echoing one another across the rise of the platforms. This impressive blue monkey is but one of numerous known from the wall paintings of the Bronze Age Aegean, where they draw our attention with their fascinating and, in some senses, familiar, human-like bodies (Figures 6.18–6.20).

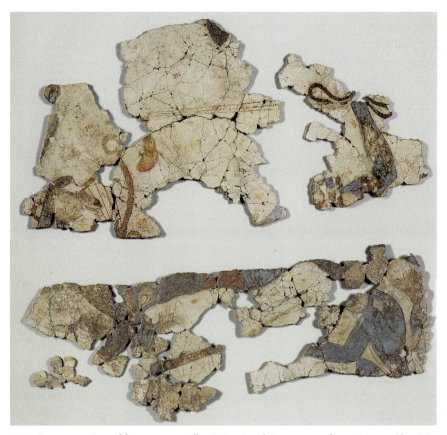

6.18. Reconstruction of fragmentary wall painting involving moneys from Xeste 3, Akrotiri. Courtesy Akrotiri Excavations. Objects © Hellenic Ministry of Culture and Sports

6.19. Reconstruction of Saffron Gatherers fresco from Knossos. Herakleion Museum. Photograph by ArchaiOptix (CC BY-SA 4.0). Herakleion Museum. Objects © Hellenic Ministry of Culture and Sports

6.20. Fragment of scene of blue monkeys from wall painting of west wall, Beta 6, Akrotiri. From Doumas 1992: 122 fig. 87. Courtesy Akrotiri Excavations. Objects © Hellenic Ministry of Culture and Sports

Most scholarship concerning representations of simians in Aegean art have focused on African species.[103] In addition to formal features that connect the Aegean representations to species that occur there, exchange with Africa during the Bronze Age is well evidenced (and, in the case of Egypt, has been extensively studied). Moreover, Africa stands as the closest location to the Aegean with an indigenous monkey population. The two species most frequently associated with the Aegean renderings of blue simians are baboons and monkeys of the *Chlorocebus* genus (vervet, green monkey, grivet). Given the wealth of depictions of these simians within Egyptian material and visual culture, it seems likely that representations in the Aegean could ultimately be traced back to these two species.[104] If Aegean craftspersons were working, at least in part, on the basis of Egyptian representational culture, they could have drawn formal characteristics from renderings of baboons and monkeys, as well as color associations – numerous representations of simians in Egyptian art embody the animals in blue and green, for example in glazed steatite or faience objects, but also in paintings (other animals also appear in blue). Blue was a color that could indicate a sacred status in Egyptian culture, and baboons had sacred standing, especially in association with Thoth. Monkeys also appear to have been linked to ritual action.[105] Certainly, there is a rich ground for understanding Aegean representations of simians through this Egyptian lens. However, a recent study by an interdisciplinary team, which was led by Pareja and also included primatologists and a taxonomic illustrator, has argued that in one case, monkeys of a Colobinae species from the Indian subcontinent, of the genus *Semnopithecus*, are depicted in Aegean art.[106] In particular, they identify a host of formal and behavioral attributes seen in the monkeys painted on the walls of Room 6 in the Beta Complex in Akrotiri with the biological Gray Langur species (Figure 6.20).

While species identifications have varied,[107] numerous scholars have asserted that the blue monkeys and apes of Aegean wall painting are in fact representations of gray simians, arguing that the blue of the frescoes was the closet approximation of the biological animals' gray coloration that was possible, given the painter's resources.[108] This suggests a way in which painters worked from the complexity of color observed in the living animal world to a different scope of chromatic potential in the representational realm. Here, we are, of course, speaking of a matter of design – a craftsperson's conscious approximation or substitution of one color value for another. It is likely that such substitutions were conventionally recognized not only by craftspersons but also by others who engaged with the paintings, such that the blue of the painted monkeys was widely understood as standing in for the gray of biological simians, just as it has also been hypothesized that blue was a stand-in for silver and stone in Aegean painting.[109] Yet this substitution of colors, even if conventionalized, would have been experienced variably. Those who had interacted with living gray monkeys and apes abroad could have compared the paintings with their memories of the biological animals. Given the animals' small and transportable size, it is possible that some captive monkeys may have even been brought to the Aegean (the delicate faunal remains would have poor archaeological survival). Foster sees the blue coloration as indication that Aegean artists were familiar with the living beast.[110] We can assume, though, that in many cases, representational material culture would have been the sole basis of a person's knowledge of monkeys in the Aegean, and wall paintings, to which access was also relatively limited, would have been the primary physical embodiment in which the monkey's color was experienced there. This may have been the case for some of the painters who crafted the Aegean blue simians, as well as other people who subsequently saw them. With this, it becomes especially important to recognize that, in the Aegean, the painted monkey had a distinct chromatic existence compared to living ones – a vivid, unambiguously blue existence. This blueness was part of a host of characteristic attributes that distinguished this animal's substantive existence and its cultural connections in the Aegean.

The blueness of the Aegean painted monkey had a basis in specific pigments. Various studies have clarified the identity of colorants used by Aegean painters, including those used for blues. During the second millennium BCE, a synthetic colorant, Egyptian Blue, was used in some renderings of monkeys in wall frescoes. It had been thought that Egyptian Blue, a copper calcium silicate, was imported to the Aegean, but Brysbaert's work has shown that it was likely (also) locally produced.[111] Depending on the preparation of the colorant, especially granule size, the blue produced can be of varying vividness. Another colorant, a raw substance of wide occurrence in the Aegean, was also used for blues in Aegean frescoes: magnesio-riebeckite.[112] The pioneering study by Cameron, Jones and Philippakis established the presence of riebeckite in blue samples from frescoes at Knossos, including its occurrence in combination with Egyptian Blue, and more recent studies have refined and updated this impression.[113] Vlachopoulous and Sotiropoulou have shown that in Akrotiri, as well, Egyptian Blue and riebeckite could be layered, creating more variation in the color and potentially reflecting the particular statuses of the pigments. It has been suggested, based both on comparison of samples' chemistry and the chronological range of its use, that the riebeckite used for blue coloration in Cretan painting likely came from Thera.[114]

Egyptian Blue can be used to produce a vivid color. We see such, for example, in the monkey who approaches the seated figure on the north wall of Room 3a, on the first floor of Xeste 3. According to infrared photoluminescence analyses, this beast is painted in "bright Egyptian Blue."[115] We find this vividness also in the blue monkeys painted in the Porter's Lodge in Akrotiri, who, like the Xeste 3 offering-bearer, also seem to be engaged in a presentation scene.[116] In this composition, Egyptian Blue was variably combined with riebeckite: Egyptian Blue was detected in the monkeys but not in blue doves, suggesting to Vlachopoulos and Sotiropoulou that choices in colorants were at the painter's discretion and might have been iconographically based.[117] These authors and others have noted that it can be impossible to discern with the naked eye between blues in frescoes that were produced with Egyptian Blue versus riebeckite (or a mixture of the two), given the dramatic color variability that can occur between applications of either as a result of the pigment's preparation and combination.[118]

The simians that appear in Aegean frescoes, as well as in glyptic arts, often exhibit extraordinarily human-like behavior and contextualizations. We have seen that in Room 3a of Xeste 3, the monkey's body and actions are closely echoed by the girl standing directly behind it; the monkeys painted in the Porter's Lodge share this human-like status as adorants.[119] Also on the first floor of Xeste 3, the fragmentary wall frescoes of Room 2 depict a group of blue simians engaged in a range of distinctly human activities.[120] They carry on with accoutrement connected to the social realm of a human community, strumming lyres and wielding swords (Figure 6.18).[121] At Knossos, we see blue monkeys in a clearly domestic setting within the MM IIIA Saffron Gatherers fresco, where they wear armlets and waistbands and pick or place flowers in vessels (Figure 6.19).[122] Doumas saw the representation of monkeys engaged in "human tasks" as something adopted in the Aegean from traditions in "the Orient," an idea that other scholars have also explored, from various angles.[123] Opinions vary concerning the possibility that some Aegean renderings of simians are depicting them "in the wild." Shaw discusses the Knossos Saffron Gatherers scene in her study of representations of Aegean gardens. She leaves the identification of this scene's setting open-ended but notes the blue simian's harness and implied control in the harvesting action and compares the practice to ones involving monkeys in Egypt and Asia.[124] Morgan sees the settings in which monkeys are depicted in Aegean paintings as potentially all being "controlled environments"; she describes the lush setting of the foraging blue monkeys in the House of the Frescoes at Knossos as a garden or park, following Platon (Figure 6.10).[125] Shaw does not see this setting as a garden but does discuss the possibility that it is a maintained context or even a sanctuary or zoo, of sorts; Chapin has further elucidated the artificial nature of this setting.[126] Morgan sees the fresco of blue monkeys in Room 6 of the Beta Complex in Akrotiri as a "direct" "abstraction" of the scene in the House of Frescoes at Knossos (Figure 6.20).[127] Generally, she makes the case that the saffron crocus was a cultivated crop, and its appearance in Aegean frescoes indicates controlled settings; this is significant here because simians are frequently associated with the saffron crocus in Aegean visual culture.[128] Masseti refers to Morgan's discussion in his work and connects the "raiding" behavior of the blue monkeys in the House of the Frescoes with that observed in living populations of green monkeys within agricultural and domestic contexts in Africa and the Near East; Morgan also notes that scavenging eggs, as witnessed with the monkeys in the fresco, "is not characteristic of the animal in its natural surroundings but only in captivity."[129] Urbani and Youlatos argue that we are in fact seeing two types of African simian in Aegean art, smaller vervets and terrestrial baboons.[130] They describe Aegean renderings of baboons as anthropomorphizing and set in ritualized contexts, while vervets – which they consider to be in a "landscape context" in the painting of Room 6 of the Beta Complex in Akrotiri – are linked to nonreligious "leisure activities."[131] Meanwhile Pareja et al., who argue that the Beta 6 simians are langurs, discuss a Minoan carnelian amygdaloid seal from Prassa, in Crete, where a monkey is imaged in a leashed halter held by a man (CMS II.357). They connect this scene to representations of leashed monkeys from southwest Asia and cite Mendleson, who traces the motif to Elamite prototypes.[132] Shaw considers similar scenes in Egyptian material culture.[133]

From the extant evidence, we can clearly appreciate that Aegean wall paintings created a strong association between simians and humans. Saffron crocuses do seem to be part of this connection. On the first floor of Xeste 3, the blue monkey of Room 3a is prominently involved in the presentation of picked crocuses to the seated figure (Figure 6.11). A couple of rooms over, the pack of blue monkeys engaged in sword and musical play in the frescoes of Room 2 are carrying on among blooming crocus plants.[134] The blue monkeys gathering crocuses in the Saffron Gatherers painting from Knossos have a direct and human-like link to the plant, and Morgan highlights the fact that in the House of the Frescoes at Knossos, as in Beta 6 in Akrotiri, the paintings involving blue monkeys shared a space (a building, set of rooms or single room) with other compositions involving crocuses.[135] It has been highlighted that women in particular are the human associates of Aegean blue monkeys. Shaw explores the possibility that living monkeys accompanied or perhaps assisted women in gathering flower crops, stating that "the Aegean women harvesters may have had monkeys as pets and as work companions who could prove useful as help."[136] Foster has considered this relationship, and asserts that there appears to have been an, "emblematic triad of simians, saffron crocuses, and women" in the Aegean.[137] Meanwhile Morgan sees the association more in the light of mythical or religious tradition:

> If the Minoan world had left behind a literary legacy I would not have been surprised to have found the crocus and the monkey involved in some mythic episode, nor to have found that both bore a relation to a female deity. As it is, we can only glimpse the implications of such repeated associations in the visual arts.[138]

The blueness of the painted Aegean simians may have brought further character to their relationship with humans. Certainly, an association between women and the nonhuman animals is evident in the wall paintings from Akrotiri, especially in Room 3a on the first floor of Xeste 3, and a connection involving crocus collection and saffron-dyed textiles, worn and likely made by women, is possibly a significant part of a larger link. Foster has discussed this connection with women and insightfully draws out how blue – what she calls a "vervet blue" – occurs frequently across the renderings of them in the paintings of Xeste 3, from their jewelry to eyes to clothing."[139] I believe the blue bodies of the animals also, and more fundamentally, embodied a direct and conspicuous corporeal link to young humans, whose shaved heads were traditionally rendered in blue in the Theran frescoes. That shaved heads and other types of hairstyling were elements of the cultural construction of age in the Bronze Age Aegean is indicated by a wealth of material culture that has been analyzed by numerous scholars.[140] The frescoes of Akrotiri form a crucial part of this material corpus, but material from elsewhere in the Aegean attests to the wider nature of the tradition. Evidence ranging in media from paintings and stone vessels to ivory sculpture, indicate that children's heads were shaved and, as they matured, hair growth was manipulated. Over time, specific areas were allowed to grow in, thus allowing for certain styled features to be articulated, such as fore- and backlocks and topknots. While representations indicate that there were different trajectories and versions that these sequences of hairstyles could take, likely indicating distinct sociocultural statuses, evidence for the practice of head-shaving in childhood clearly extends across genders, emphasizing its fundamental association with youth.

The Theran frescoes bring vibrant blue color to representations of shaved heads, through a rare wealth of depictions of young humans (Figures 6.21–6.23). Olsen has explored the infrequency of clear representations of children in Minoan and Mycenaean visual and material culture.[141] While the corpus is slowly growing, there is reason to suspect that cultural perspectives on young people, or on representing them, may have in some way limited the frequency of their rendering in material culture. If Aegean girls were typically rendered in the same types of clothing as women, we could be overlooking representations of them – or they may not have been consistently differentiated from older individuals; distinguishing age can be quite difficult in media where the treatment of hair is not clearly differentiated, especially through color.[142] For example, stone and ivory figures typically did not feature added color detailing such bodily features, or it is not extant.[143] However, the use of gray-green serpentine for the apparently shaved scalp (save for a "mohawk" lock down the back) of the Palaikastro Kouros[144] – which otherwise is chryselephantine – likely corresponds to the use of blue pigment for renderings of the shaved heads of youth in frescoes (Figure 6.24). Shaved heads and stippled regrowth are clearly indicated on two other ivory figures of young boys from Palaikastro and in other figures in stone relief, ivory and glyptic from Cretan sites;[145] but color is not apparent. Sakellarakis and Sapouna-Sakellaraki suggest that ivory figures from Archanes (Area 17, Tourkoyeitonia), including a youth with a stippled scalp, may have originally been painted, although no color remains, and that a hair attachment may have originally topped a figure of an older male.[146] Taken in this light, the paintings of Akrotiri provide a relative abundance of representations of young people in color and, with this, a variety of heads depicted in vivid swaths and glimpses of blue.[147]

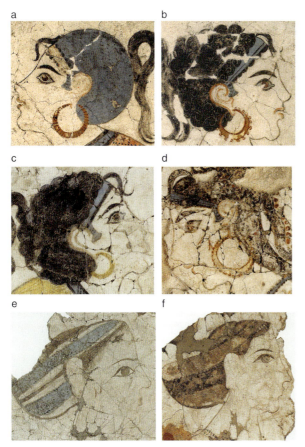

6.21. Views of persons' heads from the wall paintings of Xeste 3, Akrotiri, first floor. a–d from Room 3a. a. Girl, right, east wall; b. Girl, left, east wall; c. Girl, left, north wall; d. Potnia, center, north wall. e–f from Room 3b. e. Woman, left; f. Woman, center; from Doumas 1992: 155 fig. 119; 156 fig. 121; 161 fig. 124; 163 fig. 126; 169 fig. 132; 170 fig. 134. Courtesy Akrotiri Excavations. Objects © Hellenic Ministry of Culture and Sports

In the frescoes of Akrotiri, blueness as a defining aspect of the youthful human body coexists with blueness as a defining aspect of the simian body. Nowhere is this juxtaposition more clearly appreciable than in the rooms of Xeste 3 (Figures 6.21, 6.22). In Room 3a on the first floor, the girls who participate in the same crocus gathering event as the blue monkey embody different phases of hair manipulation, including shaving.[148] The girl farthest to the right in the scene, along the east wall, has a nearly fully shaven head, indicated by a vibrant blue scalp (Figure 6.21a). This fills the area across the curve of the head to the hairline, which extends from the base of the head at the neck, up behind the ear, through the fanned peninsula of the sideburn, and along the forehead. The initial emergence of fine hairs on the shaved surface of the head has been subtly indicated with rows of black stippling that cross the blue scalp as well as the sideburn area.[149] Only a forelock at the forehead and a longer backlock, set at the crown, have been

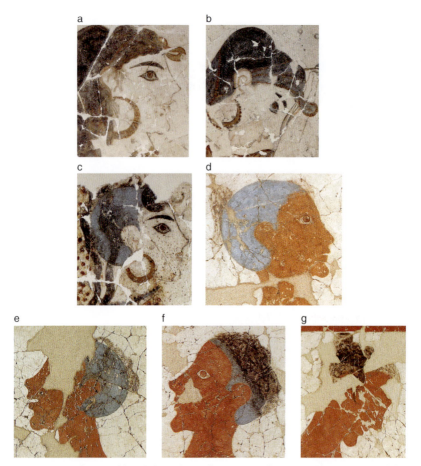

6.22. Views of persons' heads from the wall paintings of Xeste 3, Akrotiri, ground floor. a–c from Room 3a. a. Necklace Swinger, north wall; b. Wounded Girl, north wall; c. Veiled Girl, north wall. d–g from area 3b. d. Ochre Boy; e. Cloth holder; f. Basin holder; g. Seated Man. From Doumas 1992: 139 fig 102; 143 fig. 106; 145 fig. 108; 148 fig. 112; 149 fig. 113; 151 fig. 115; 150 fig. 114. Courtesy Akrotiri Excavations. Objects © Hellenic Ministry of Culture and Sports

allowed to grow in. The three other girls in the scene exhibit what must be a next phase of growth and maturity (Figure 6.21b,c).[150] On the girl positioned on the left side of the east wall, as well as the one who bends at the base of the risers on the north wall, the scalp is now brimming with short black curls; the fore- and backlock are clearly preserved, evidently attributes of youth. On each figure, as if another badge of youth, we still see the bright blue and stippled area of the shaved sideburn set along the side of the face, just beside the ear. The blue sideburn is also visible on the young red-haired woman who is located in the corner of the room, upon the north wall. Remarkably, we also see the bright blue sideburn on the seated figure, the "potnia," indicating her connection to the young persons gathered about her in the room (Figure 6.21d).

The distinctive characterization of the young women on the north and east walls of Room 3a can be further appreciated if we step back and compare them to the splendidly rendered older women painted in the walls of the hall (3b)

6.23. Views of persons' heads from the wall paintings of Akrotiri. a. Woman in threshold between Rooms 4 and 5, West House; b. Fisher from the north wall of Room 5, West House; c. Left Boxer from Beta 1, south wall. From Doumas 1992: 57 fig. 25; 55 fig. 23; 114 fig. 81. Courtesy Akrotiri Excavations. Objects © Hellenic Ministry of Culture and Sports

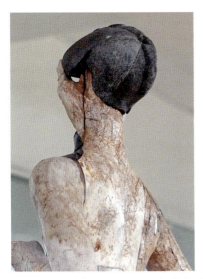

6.24. View of the serpentine scalp/hair of the Palaikastro Kouros. Archaeological Museum of Sitia. Detail from photograph by Olaf Tausch (CC BY 3.0). Object © Hellenic Ministry of Culture and Sports

leading into the room (Figure 6.21e, f).[151] On the two women painted in the north wall of 3b, the hair is fully grown in and worn up in a snood; there is no evidence of a fore- or backlock. One figure wears a crocus flower tucked behind her ear. Of particular interest for us is the careful rendering of fine hair growth along the edges of these women's faces, specifically along the forehead, at the neck and in the area of the sideburn. This area of fine detail clearly differs from the prominent blue, shaved sideburn of the younger women seen in 3a. On the more fragmentary woman painted on the south wall of the corridor between Room 3 and the secondary stairway, a black sideburn is clearly visible, again contrasting with the shaven blue of the younger persons in 3a.

The ground-floor rooms of Xeste 3 provide more painted human bodies to consider. In Room 3a, situated directly below the room of the crocus gatherers, we find another painting that represents young women (Figure 6.22a–c). Here, three female figures line the north wall and are associated with a building façade painted around the corner of the room, to the east; these paintings are positioned directly above a lustral basin. The ages of these young women are typically placed around late pubescence or early postpubescence. The central figure (Figure 6.22b) is depicted in a peculiar condition, sitting on a rock with one hand to her forehead and another reaching to a bleeding foot. The imaging of blood flow from the figure's foot has been linked to bloodshed during the reproductive life of women (menstruation, hymenal rupture) and taken as an indication that the painting was related to a female rite of passage, potentially performed in the space.[152] The age of the figures is read in this light but is based on the characterization of their bodies and hair. Compared to the girls upstairs, the westernmost and central young women of the ground-floor painting have fuller breasts, revealed through the loose and diaphanous bodices of their garments. Their hair is long and lush, with no evidence of shaving. As on the older women painted in Hall 3b upstairs, fine dark hair growth in the area of the sideburn is visible on these two young women; it is especially pronounced on the woman farthest to the west. The inclusion of this subtle detail in both of these paintings, thought to be painted by different hands,[153] underscores the significance of the bodily feature. In the ground-floor painting, only the third figure, farthest to the east (Figure 6.22c), differs in her hairstyling. This young woman holds a large veil around her body. Her head is characterized by the bright blue of a shaved scalp, including the area of the sideburn. Unlike the younger girls upstairs, however, she has a series of dramatically long locks descending from her blue scalp. The length of these locks, and her presence downstairs with the young women, likely indicates that the veiled girl is also at an advanced age, around late puberty, but her distinctive hairstyling, including the largely shaved scalp, has indicated to some that she is on an alternate life path.[154] Her potentially exceptional status, as indicated by her hairstyling, can be compared to that of the figure painted in the door jamb between Rooms 4 and 5 in the West House; the boxing boys painted in Room 1 of the Beta Complex also have relatable hairstyling.[155]

To the west of Room 3a on the ground floor of Xeste 3, in the wall paintings of the north, south and west walls of the corridor area in Room 3b, we have four depictions of male humans (Figure 6.22d–g). These figures seem to span ages from the very young to full adulthood, and the treatment of their hair offers a rich glimpse of the styling associated with male bodies at different ages.[156] Three of the figures – thought to be a young, fully prepubescent boy, and two older, likely pubescent boys – exhibit blue shaved scalps (Figure 6.22d–f). Despite differences in the details of their hairstyling, which involves preserved locks in two cases and something of a bowl haircut in the third, each of these figures exhibits a cap-like blue scalp that reaches down into a notable shaven sideburn zone. The figure located on the southern half of the west wall of Room 3b appears to be an adult man. His age is indicated by his full body, including a slight stomach pouch held in by a cream-colored kilt, and a full head of hair, which is worn in a topknot; no shaved area is apparent (Figure 6.22g).

Figures in other painted spaces of Akrotiri also exhibit the blue shaved scalp associated with youth. In the West House, in addition to the "priestess" painted in the doorway between Rooms 4 and 5 (Figure 6.23a), we also have the two large-scale male youths or "fisherboys" painted in Room 5 (Figure 6.23b). Both of these figures have prominent locks preserved at the front and crown of the head, with the rest of the scalp fully shaven and blue. On both of these male figures, as well as the female figure in the doorway, the area of the sideburn is clearly articulated in blue. Stippling that marks the hairline along the face and neck on these figures is also apparent at the bottom edge of the sideburn, further indicating its identity as part of the shaved head. While rendered in a different style, this stippling corresponds to that seen on the sideburns of the figures in the crocus-gathering scene in the first floor of Xeste 3; the flanged form of the West House female figure's sideburn is also highly comparable to that on the Xeste 3 gatherers. In the painted space of Room 1 in the Beta Complex, two boxing boys, with physiological characteristics of youth,[157] sport a host of dramatic long locks issuing from shaven blue scalps (Figure 6.23c).[158] Here, too, the blue sideburn zones are prominent.

With the rendering of these human forms in the wall paintings of Akrotiri, a negligible area of the body – a small stretch of flesh in front of the ear – gains prominence as it is marked out by blueness. In other words, the embodiment of youthful persons in painting brings the shaved sideburn a novel substance, making the absence of hair the presence of a vivid feature defined by the color of youth. This substantive quality assumed by the shaved sideburn is surely what led Davis to interpret it as a "sideburn-shaped ornament," for it exists, like the preserved locks, as a present attribute of these painted persons. This is significant because it indicates another traditional cultural association held by blueness alongside its association with the simian body.

Given the consistent relationship that both the youthful human body and the simian body had with blueness – something realized, in both cases, through paintings – it is extremely likely that the two animals (human and nonhuman) were associated with one another by people who interacted with both species in this medium. The rooms of Xeste 3 afforded numerous juxtapositions of blue simians and young persons who had blue shaven features. Likewise in the Beta Complex, a person could experience both the blue heads of lively young people (in Room 1) and the blue bodies of equally rambunctious monkeys (in Room 6). The clear articulation of the blue shaven sideburn on each of the figures in Room 3a in the first floor of Xeste 3 indicates the significance of marking this blueness as part of a youthful corporeal identity; this occurs in the company of a large blue monkey. Interestingly, another hint of blue seems to also indicate youth in these paintings. Streaks of blue occur in the eyes of all the youthful female figures in the area of Room 3 of Xeste 3, across the ground and first floors, as well as in the eye of the young boy in corridor 3b on the ground floor. Meanwhile these blue streaks are absent from the eyes of all of the other male figures in the ground-floor area of 3b and all of the older women of the first-floor hall. Davis, who noticed this feature decades ago, took the blue eye streaks to be a "physical characteristic of youth."[159] Since then, others have discussed the attribute and suggested that it indicates a particular cultural association, and perhaps elements of shared gender, between young, prepubescent boys and youthful females.[160] Whether or not this is the case, the blueness of the eyes does suggest another way in which this color was part of the embodiment of human youth in Aegean painting.

Living monkeys are uncanny in their similarities to humans and can seem like small people. It is not only the form of their bodies but their active presence and nature that reminds us of ourselves, inspiring both affection and uneasiness. Photographer Jill Greenberg, who photographed a series of monkeys for her book, *Monkey Portraits*, writes: "the subjects appeared almost human, expressing emotions and using gestures I thought were reserved only for people."[161] Such familiarity has driven people's fascination with these barely nonhuman nonhuman animals in many cultures, and the evidence we have been considering indicates that such fascination was also the case in the Bronze Age Aegean, where some imported biological monkeys may have been known. What I wish to draw out here is how the relationship that simians had to humans within the Aegean took on further dimensions and novel characteristics through the embodiments of both types of primate within wall paintings. This occurred as simians and young humans were represented in similar contexts, with comparable behavior and roles. But it also involved their sharing of the corporeal quality of blueness – something that their living counterparts did not possess.

NOTES

1. Palyvou 1990: 419.
2. Immerwahr 1990.
3. The frescoes between Rooms 4 and 5 in the West House powerfully embody ikria at different scales. While this changes to dynamics of their comparison, these two juxtaposed spaces could be fruitfully considered through the lens that Egan brings to renderings of argonauts in friezes between spaces at Pylos (Egan 2020), with a focus on matters of a craftsperson's "freedom" in rendering the forms and the viewer's experience between multiple spaces.
4. For example, figure visible in Doumas 1992: 77.
5. Shaw 1982.
6. Doumas 1992: 75.
7. Doumas 1992: 68 fig. 35, and 73.
8. See Palyvou's work concerning the dynamics of viewing the Theran paintings (esp. 2012, problematizing the West House).
9. I am working with an adult height range of ca. 1.5 to 1.75 m.
10. Doumas 2008; Vlachopoulos 2015; Marthari 2018: 210 fig. 12, with further references.
11. Vlachopoulos 2015: 50.
12. See study by Mödlinger (2013 esp. 395 fig. 5, 401–404).
13. See Palyvou 2012.
14. This is clearest on the fifth vessel from the left; see Doumas 1992: esp. 68, 74, 75–76.
15. Prytulak 1982.
16. Doumas 1992; Televantou 1990, 1994, 2000.
17. Televantou's reconstructions hypothesize twelve figures with shields in this line (1990: 309–324, esp. 316 fig. 9; see also 1994 for later reconstructions of painting).
18. See Doumas 1992: 60–61 fig. 28. The dash marks around the helmets painted in the north wall are loosely comparable to those occurring between the seriated entities painted on the Knossos cup rhyton, including a hypothetical boar's head and squills that are formally assonant with boar's tusk helmets; the wispy plumes atop the West House helmets are also comparable to what is seen on the entities of the Knossos rhyton; see Chapter 5.
19. Confirmed through personal communication with A. Vlachopoulos.
20. Marthari 2018: 208–210.
21. Blakolmer 2018: 149) astutely identifies certain stucco relief fragments as part of a painted shield frieze.
22. Blakolmer (2012) argues that some architectonic features that appear in imagery on seals and other portable media indicate representation painted walls, a fascinating idea that would add a layer of signification (a seal's image *of* a mural's image *of* a scene). I am posing the further question: was the fusing of *banding*+series, on one level, acting as a conventional visual unit that could occur also on walls?
23. Here I refer to Betancourt's notion (cited in Blakolmer 2012: 16) of a "shallow stage" effected through the spatial dynamics of some Aegean wall paitnings.
24. See Hood 2005: 74–75 and Blakolmer 2018 (with further references).
25. Shaw 1980, 1982.
26. Evans 1930: 301–308; quote from 307.
27. Evans 1930: 305.
28. Evans 1930: 306.
29. Evans 1930: 304–306; in a marginal summation on p. 306, Evans simply states, "Tiryns shields copied from Knossian fresco."
30. Evans 1930: 307.
31. Evans discusses this shared stature (1930: 307).
32. Evans 1930; Hood 2005. Rehak (1995) discusses Evans' reconstruction.
33. Evans 1930: 333–338.

34. Evans 1930: 307.
35. Shaw and Laxton 2002: 99.
36. Shaw and Laxton 2002: 98–99, figs. 4 and 5.
37. Shaw and Laxton 2002: 99.
38. Shaw and Laxton 2002: 99–100.
39. Evans 1930: 307. This also recalls the interplay of observation, convention and technical creativity that Egan (2020) considers in the Mycenaean argonaut friezes.
40. Palyvou 2000: 422.
41. Palyvou 2000: 414, also Immerwahr 1990.
42. Immerwahr (1990) and Palyvou (2000) offer valuable discussions.
43. Palyvou 2012. She suggests the architect and artist may have shared in planning.
44. Evans 1930: 301–303; Shaw and Laxton 2002.
45. Palyvou 2000: 425–431.
46. Palyvou 2000:425–431; Palyvou discusses the Knossos shield fresco in this light.
47. Harries 1983.
48. Harries 1983: 64–66.
49. Harries 1983: 53–54.
50. Harries 1983: 33.
51. Harries 1983: 64.
52. Harries 1983: 64–66.
53. Harries 1983, esp. 18–21, 33.
54. Cameron 1968; Chapin and Shaw 2006.
55. Feature captured in painted fragments described by Cameron (1968: 23, 25, 28 no. 15; in reconstruction, fig. 13; 1976 vol. 2: pl. 68A); also in Evans 1928: pl. x.
56. Palyvou's (2012) remarks on the "pierced borders" of Aegean frescoes that run across wall breaks, including windows where sunlight enters, indicate a related phenomemnon.
57. See Doumas 1992: 130–131, figs. 116–130; Vlachopoulos 2008 figs. 41.19–21; Palyvou's sophisticated reading of the room (2012), which I follow, indicates how the painted figures guide the viewer through "illusionary" and "real" space.
58. Palyvou 2012: 18.
59. See Chapter 4 for discussion of these markings.
60. Palyvou 2012.
61. Palyvou 2012: 9.
62. Palyvou 2012: 22.
63. Palyvou 2012: 22–24.
64. Palyvou 2012: 22.
65. Palyvou 2012: 9.
66. Whether the border is there as a matter of design or as a miscalculation in painting is beside the point; it *is* there and consequently was part of the spatial complexity a viewer experienced when encountering the north wall.
67. These relief fragments were found out of context in a stratigraphically complex situation (see Hood 2005). Evans dated them variably to MM IIIB or LM IA; Kaiser saw them as likely LM IB; Immerwahr places them squarely in the Neopalatial period (MM IIIB–LM IB) and Hood leans earlier, perhaps MM IIIB. Haysom (2018) argues for pushing the date of the Knossian reliefs, including these, later, likely to late Neopalatial.
68. On the Aegean stucco relief paintings, see the foundational study by Kaiser (1976) and excellent recent work of Blakolmer 2018.
69. See careful description of the technique in von Rüden and Skowronek 2018, esp. 217–221.
70. Evans 1930: 511 fig. 355. Cameron 1976, vol. 1: 108–109, 119–120, 156, 316; vol. 2: pls. 132, 136a; vol. 3: 114–115.
71. Evans 1930, in figs. 355 and 361.
72. Hägg and Lindau 1984.

73. See exquisite photomontage by Ute Günkel-Maschek (Galanakis, Tsitsa and Günkel-Maschek 2017: 72 fig. 27).

74. An LM II date for the paintings is very likely; see Hood 2005: 65 and Galanakis, Tsitsa and Günkel-Maschek 2017, who discuss extensively how the Throne Room griffins (and larger decorative scheme) engaged with Neopalatial phenomena while also integrating innovations (e.g., 2017: 80, 83, 84, 88). See Egan (2018) on comparable experiential and temporal dynamics of landscape-painted Palace Style vessels.

75. Galanakis, Tsitsa and Günkel-Maschek 2017: 84.

76. Niemeier 1987, building on ideas of Reusch, esp. 1958. See Galanakis, Tsitsa and Günkel-Maschek 2017: esp. 85–91 for problematization and extensive references.

77. For example, Marinatos 1993; Niemeier 1987; Hitchcock 2010; Shank 2007; Galanakis, Tsitsa and Günkel-Maschek 2017; Blakolmer 2018; Tully and Crooks 2020. The extensive restudy of this painted space by Galanakis, Tsitsa and Günkel-Maschek should be highlighted as a deeply valuable analysis of the complex and challenging material.

78. Rehak 1995. Within his discussion, Rehak argues that since griffins occur far more often with female figures in Aegean visual art, it is likely that a woman would have sat on the elaborated seat in the throne room. Quote from Hitchcock 2010: 207.

79. Egan 2018: 337, with refs.; she connects this to readings concerning the fresco's engagement with the occupied throne.

80. Shaw 1978: 437. This observation is also crucial to Hitchcock (2010).

81. Tully and Crooks 2020.

82. Hitchcock 2010.

83. Blakolmer 2018: 145 n. 22 (with further references); Cameron sees this as hair (1976 vol. 1: 108–109). Shank has argued that a fragment may preserve a wingtip, or alternatively a crest (2007: 162–164). If the griffins here were in fact winged, then the paradox of their boundedness in the wall would be yet further emphasized, but the refutation of this idea provided by Galanakis, Tsitsa and Günkel-Maschek is persuasive (2017).

84. The early Neopalatial relief griffins, in particular. See Blakolmer 2012 concerning the role of Knossian stucco reliefs in establishing long-perpetuated Aegean iconographic "topoi."

85. Palyvou 2012: 22.

86. Driessen and MacDonald 1997.

87. Bicknell 2000 (following on from observations by Mountjoy 1985).

88. For example, Palyvou 2012, Immerwahr 1990, Blakolmer 2016.

89. See Younger 1998.

90. Egan 2018.

91. Immerwahr 1990; Palyvou 2000; Shaw and Laxton 2002.

92. Doumas 1992: 56–57, figs. 24 and 25.

93. Evans 1930: 301–308.

94. This dynamic is comparable to the relationship of the helmet and the human head as discussed in Chapter 4, where the form of the helmet in a sense recalls or longs for the shape of the head it circumscribes – whether the head is currently present or absent.

95. See Evans on "nature moulding," discussed in Shapland 2022 (ch. 6).

96. Sakellarakis and Sapouna-Sakellaraki 1981: 212–213 incl. image 222.

97. Various important studies of the appliquéd vessels and relief frescoes are gathered in Vlachopoulous 2018, each working from a distinct angle: see Militello 2018, Tzachili 2018, Kriga 2018, and Blakolmer 2018.

98. Kriga 2018.

99. These objects embodying marine beings, and others, form the focus of a dedicated study in preparation by the author.

100. Sakellarakis and Sapouna-Sakellakis 1997: 498 fig. 485.

101. Egan 2018: 336–337. She relates this to the effects of the Palace Style vessels.

102. Palyvou 2012: 1, discussing experiences of griffins across media.

103. See, for example, Masseti 1980, 2003; Immerwahr 1990: 41; Urbani and Youlatos 2012, 2022; Foster 2020; Shapland 2022.

104. For example, Marinatos 1984; Immerwahr 1990: 41–42; Shaw 1993: 671–672.

105. Phillips 2008; Greenlaw 2011. On the baboon's sacred status in Egypt, see Binnberg, Urbani and Youlatos 2021. Marinatos (1984) develops the idea of the monkey's sacredness in the Aegean.

106. Pareja, McKinney, Mayhew et al. 2020.

107. See Cline 1991, and recent debate involving Pareja et al., Urbani and Youlatos, and Masseti (Pareja, McKinney, Mayhew et al. 2020, Pareja, McKinney and Setchell; Urbani and Youlatos 2020, Binnberg, Urbani and Youlatos 2021; Masseti 2021).

108. For example, Phillips 2008; Greenlaw 2011; Pareja 2017; Urbani and Youlatos 2020: 3. Concerning the Theran paintings, Vlachopoulos and Sotiropoulou (2013: 254–255 incl. n. 17) state that, as in Crete, the blue simians and blue birds are probably renderings of gray baboons and rock doves; they follow the identifications of Cameron (1968), Doumas (1992) and Georoma (2010).

109. For example, Peters 2008.

110. Foster 2020. What was at once thought to be a skull of the Colobinae subfamily preserved in excavated material from Akrotiri (Poulianos 1972) is now discredited (Greenlaw 2006).

111. Brysbaert 2008; also Aloupi, Karydas and Paradellis 2000: 18–20, citing key earlier studies.

112. Brecoulaki 2014: 8 with bibliography; Aloupi, Karydas and Paradellis 2000, who cite the findings of Chryssikopoulou, Kilikoglou, Perdikatsis et al. 2000, which refined the identification of glaucophane to riebeckite in blue samples from Theran fresco material; Brysbaert, Melessanaki and Anglos 2006: 1099 (for a wider identification concerning Cretan material); Vlachopoulous and Sotiropoulou 2013 (with bibliography).

113. Cameron, Jones, and Philippakis 1977.

114. Aloupi, Karydas and Paradellis 2000: 18–20, with bibliography.

115. Vlachopoulos and Sotiropoulou 2013: 255.

116. Vlachopoulos and Sotiropoulou 2013 on the colorants and scene; also Doumas 1992.

117. Vlachopoulos and Sotiropoulou 2013: 254–255, 259.

118. For example, Brysbaert 2008: 1098–1099, Vlachopoulos and Sotiropoulou 2013: 256, 258.

119. Vlachopoulos 2007. The monkeys' possible scenic relationship with a griffin in the Porter's Lodge paintings is another aspect to compare to Xeste 3.

120. Doumas 1992; Rehak 1999. The blue monkeys have now been associated with the north wall of Room 2 on the first floor; see Vlachopoulos 2008: 493, 497, 505 pls. 41.15–18, 41.51.

121. Doumas 1992: 128, 134 figs 95, 96; Rehak's reconstruction: 1999: pl. 149.

122. Hood 2005: 49, 62. See also Morgan 1988: 29–32; Shaw 1993: 670–671.

123. For example, Masseti 2003; Phillips 2008, Pareja, McKinney, Mayhew et al. 2020: 164–165.

124. Shaw 1993.

125. Morgan 1988: 39–40, after Platon 1947: 515 and 1957, 130.

126. Shaw 1993: 668–669; Chapin 2004.

127. Morgan 1988: 38, 1990: 258–259.

128. Morgan 1988: 29–32.

129. Masseti 2003; Morgan 1988: 39 and n. 202, citing Cameron 1968: 19 n. 50.

130. Urbani and Youlatos 2022.

131. Urbani and Youlatos 2022.

132. Pareja, McKinney, Mayhew et al. 2020: 164–165, with references; they assert that the Elamite prototypes themselves were likely drawn from areas yet farther east, where there were native monkey populations; see also Urbani and Youlatos (2022).

133. Shaw 1993: 670–672.

134. Doumas 1992: 128, 134–135 figs. 95 and 96; Vlachopoulos 2008: 493, 497, 505 pls. 41.15–18, 41.51.

135. For the House of the Frescoes, Knossos, see Chapin and Shaw 2006, esp. 67. In Beta Complex (Akrotiri), fragments of a scene involving quadrupeds (probably bovines or goats) in a setting with crocus plants were also discovered in Room 6 (see Morgan 1988: 29–30).

136. Shaw 1993: 675, as part of larger discussion in 670–675.

137. Foster 2020.

138. Morgan 1988: 29.

139. Foster 2020, who associates the renderings of the blue monkeys with women's sensuality. She also notes a connection to the "lavendar-blue" saffron crocuses.

140. For example, Davis 1986; Koehl 1986, 2000, 2016; Doumas 1992; Rehak 2002; Chapin 2007.

141. Olsen 1998. For excellent recent discussions of youth and childhood in the Aegean Bronze Age, see Rutter 2003 and Günkel-Maschek 2020.

142. For example, the small, skirted figure engraved in a Neopalatial gold signet ring from Isopata, CMS II.3, has been interpreted as a girl, but also as a hovering divine figure or a woman set farther back in space; the detailing of her head/hair is limited.

143. For example, see the ivory figures of a boy and young child from Palaikastro (Bosanquet and Dawkins 1923: pl. XXVII); see also Koehl 2000: 136 fig. 11.1.ia.

144. Moak 2000.

145. Koehl 1986, 2016. For the two figures of younger children from Palaikastro, see n. 132.

146. Sakellarakis and Sapouna-Sakellaraki 1997: 707–719.

147. Perhaps the association of figures with a "blue of youth" could also be effected through other means, for example, manipulation of background color in a fresco.

148. In 1986, Davis provided a careful study of the hairstylings in this scene as indicators of age. Others have added to this discussion, for example, Rehak 1999, 2002; Chapin 1997–2000.

149. Davis (1986: 401) described the blue feature in front of the ears as a "sideburn-shaped ornament," but this is an unnecessarily indirect interpretation. The rendering of the girl positioned on the right of the east wall (3a, first floor) certainly clarifies that the flange-shaped protrusion in front of the ear of each female figure here is simply a sideburn, not an ornament of the hairband. Unlike the others, this girl wears a hairband that now appears as a whitish strip lined on both sides by black circles. The stippled blue flange that emerges below the band, at the ear, is clearly distinct. It is, however, identical in its treatment (blue ground with black stippled rows) to the girl's shaved scalp and should be seen as an extension of it. The blue sideburns on the other figures are the same. Foster (2020) reads this girl's scalp as in fact being a "simian cap."

150. Davis 1986; Chapin 1997–2000.

151. Doumas 1992: esp. 169, 171, figs. 132, 134.

152. For example, Marinatos 1984, 1993; Davis 1986; Rehak 2002.

153. Vlachopoulos 2008: 494.

154. E.g., Rehak suggests she may be destined for a virginal status (2002: 42, 48). Chapin 1997–2000.

155. Compare Davis 1986: 401; Chapin 2007: 247 n. 63.

156. Chapin 2007; Koehl 1986, 2016.

157. Chapin 2007: 241 for discussion.

158. See Doumas 1992: 112–115 figs. 79–81.

159. Davis 1986: 402.

160. For example, Rehak (2002: 48–51) argues the streaks are related to the ingestion of saffron, which he posits was restricted by age and gender.

161. Greenberg 2007; quote from 2004: www.jillgreenberg.com/monkey-portraits.

CONCLUDING THOUGHTS

Restless Bodies in the Minoan World

THE DIVERSITY AND POTENTIAL IMMENSITY OF MATERIAL CULTURE'S contributions to human experience have been richly recognized and explored in recent years, as has the keen and often ineffable involvement of nonhuman animals in people's social and emotional lives. When material culture and animals are one, their potency is something infused with the dynamism of both and yet quite distinct from either or their sum. This dynamism was realized in very particular ways in Crete and the southern Aegean between the late third and mid-second millennia BCE. Through close analyses of a wide range of Aegean animalian things, we have explored the specificity of their involvements in the experiences of people, and how those engagements were part of the unique character of sociocultural life in the region on various levels. In each case, we have considered the distinguishing affordances of the fabricated Aegean embodiments of the animalian. We have paid special attention to the objects' intercorporeal relationships with living humans and the connections that would have been realized through their particular qualities – with other animals, objects and spaces. We have seen such relations afforded through different dynamics, including bodily juxtaposition, cultivation of formal assonance, the sharing of specific features (e.g., a forward gaze), embodiment with the same substances and through connections in size, composition (e.g., in friezes) and contextualization. Such links surely could have carried further cultural dimensions that we cannot grasp, including signified semantic content; we have limited our ventures into such territory. Instead, recognizing how distinctive *congregations of relations* would have been experienced in these embodiments of animals – experienced not just cerebrally, but through acts of "skillful exploration of the world" entailing unified "sensoriomotor and conceptual" means[1] – has cast revelatory light on the fabricated creatures' dynamic presences in Aegean social spaces. Moreover, by working beyond an implicit focus on the design of the objects to instead emphasize people's experiences with them, we have opened the space for appreciating how both intended and unintended associations involving these complex things were in play together. We should view these not as alternative lenses on the objects, but instead as forces working concurrently, and upon one another, in the creative realizations that the animalian objects were.

ARTFUL BODIES

Assuming an analytical perspective that is concerned with experience over intentional design does not mean that the *fabricated* status of these embodiments of animals would not have been fundamental to how people understood them – it surely was. We have seen that the creativity inherent in these renderings of animals brought them very specific character and that, in certain cases, this likely involved affordances of what could be described as artifice or craftiness. In Chapter 2, we saw how such was apparent, in highly distinctive ways, in both zoomorphic vessels and renderings in the round of bovine–human interaction. In each instance, the dynamics of bodily engagement were remarkable. In the case of clay Prepalatial Cretan vessels with intensely ambivalent animalian forms, certain unique physical features would have allowed the strange bodies to be experienced as notably autonomous producers of fluids. Meanwhile, later, sometimes exquisitely fashioned Neopalatial rhyta in the shape of animal heads would have placed great emphasis on the manipulative performances of living humans who adeptly handled and worked the partial bodily things. Craftiness would have further been experienced in other ways in three-dimensional figures embodying "bull sports." In these we see the quick-witted maneuvers of human bodies engaging with massive bovines materialized in impressive objects that likely would have confounded beholders with their striking ability to set interacting bodies in suspended relation to one another.

The potential artifice of Aegean animalian material culture was also explored in Chapter 5. Here, we saw how certain innovative qualities of Neopalatial wall paintings made novel approaches on the dimensionality in which humans experienced animalian bodies as entities in the round. These qualities of the frescoes included inventive creations of spatial depth as well as renderings of animals' bodies that actually emerged from the wall's flat surface in built-up stucco relief – the effect was literally ground-breaking. Even as these frescoes reached toward illusionistic dimensions, they were kept tensely countered by certain prominent features that announced the paintings to be part of the structured order of the flat wall, for example by preserving the repetitive grid-like frame of the wall through the painted elements. That tethered griffins – powerful, otherworldly beasts grounded by leashes – were embodied through both of these innovative means underscores the acute tension that could be at stake in the wall paintings.

Close analysis has helped us to draw out how, in various cases, Aegean animalian things were characterized by inherent formal or physical ambiguities that could fruitfully give rise to divergent perceptions. This was apparent, for example, in multiple renderings of griffins within glyptic and ceramic objects, where engraved lines constituting the beast's body could also be read as objects attached to it, such as leashes or collars. In certain instances, this ambivalence could carry very different implications for the species, such as likeness with a wild winged raptor (if the lines were read as markings comparable to those of biological vultures) or capture by human hands (if read as a tether attached by a dominating person). Such implications could have been restlessly copresent in the griffin's body, invigorating its status with complexity. We have also seen how ambivalence in representations of an entity's physical character could be cultivated in realizations of formal assonance in different media. With this, for example, the layered construction of the plaqued boar's tusk helmet could be likened to the tunicated squill or to a woven bundle of cloth; each could carry distinct cultural implications. Through such divergent and simultaneous implications, people's experiences of animalian entities, and their presences in the lived world, could be charged with productive irresolution.

MAKING SPACE

In each case study, we have placed our consideration of the particular relational dynamics of the Aegean animalian things within their immediate and broader sociocultural contexts. Such contextualization, moving outward from close study of the objects, has brought into view the extraordinary spatial complexity evident in these diverse embodiments of animals. The movable objects actively participated in creating space, but each in unique ways. For example, the fact that, in Crete, lions were embodied primarily in seals and seal impressions would have invigorated the beasts with the distinctive movements and spatial implications of seal wearing and seal use, with concentrated intensity. At the same time, given seals' integral position within the actions of sociocultural life, the lions, and the cultural relations they realized, brought particular, dynamic character to the social space being generated in part through the travels of such objects – including through trans-Aegean exchanges of creative culture. Meanwhile, Prepalatial body vessels may have made less frequent movements, transferring occasionally between tomb and settlement, but their emplacement across such locales could have been part of the essential life and maintenance of Cretan communities. In other cases, we have seen a variety of animalian entities – including griffins, boar's tusk helmets and oxhide shields – embodied in media both tiny and large, movable and fixed. Each of these media realized something distinct in the animalian subjects, but as people experienced the beings *across* these different embodiments, connections were made between the substances, contexts, affordances and relations of each, developing their dynamic identities. We have seen that manifestations of these animalian entities in the large, colorful fields of LB I–II wall paintings were charged with innovations in rendering both distance and immediacy. The simultaneity of these forces would have brought a distinctly unsettling effect to the built spaces of which the paintings were part – contributing as tense animalian presences that were thing, beast and place at once.

NOVELTY AND RELATION

The artfully fabricated embodiments of animals that we have considered each made nonhuman creatures novelly *present* in the Aegean. This involved not simply replicating or imitating forms in new media, but, inherently, *creating* the animalian with new character. The newness of these embodiments of animals can be appreciated in various respects. We can see inventive qualities being drawn into how animals were experienced and hence understood, from establishing distinguishing bodily colors, mechanical abilities and physical dimensions in the beasts, to introducing animals into different contexts of sociocultural activity and thereby setting them in fresh relations. These developments would have enriched and fluidly expanded current identities of animals, in material and notional respects, and, in some cases, the animalian things can be understood as instances of novel speciation. We see such newness in the bright blue Aegean monkey, who could collect crocuses or stand at the knee of power, echoing the stature and action of humans – and who, through the generative efficacy of painting, prominently shared its distinctive hue with the youthful bodies of Aegean children with shaven heads. But it is also evident in the owls with curved head appendages, collared griffins with vulture-like formidability, nippled birds whose swollen clay bellies could fill with wine and shields suspended in teeming seascapes.

Aegean animalian things nourished new connections between human and nonhuman beasts. In some cases, novel relations to people were realized directly within the thing, as elements of the human form were integrated into the embodiment of a creature (e.g., in the nippled ewers). Meanwhile, we can see how some of the objects possessed features that afforded remarkably new repertoires of interaction between nonhuman animals and acting biological human bodies – from being able to tie a lion upon one's wrist or a griffin to the wall at one's side, to hoisting a stony bull's head in one's hands and taking control of the flow of liquid through its rigid mouth. We have further seen that the treatment of certain distinctly Aegean animalian things – including the boar's tusk helmet, oxhide shield and ikrion – indicates that these objects had a peculiar corporeal status – being prominently formed from the very substance of particular biological nonhuman animals and shaped in imme-diate correspondence to the human body and its practical needs, while not actually assuming bodily forms themselves. In other words, these things arose from bodies, and accounted for bodies, but their deeply integrative forms brought something fundamentally new into being. These three animalian entities were also manifest in other media, which realized further character in their identities. Close analysis of renderings of the shields, helmets and ikria in representational material culture has allowed us to appreciate how they would have been experienced as possessing a dynamism that subtly agitated their status as inanimate things. We saw this take form in various ways, especially through their embodiment in seriated friezes, which productively complicated the entities' presence in and relation to spaces of action and, in some cases, also cultivated specific associations with animals and elements of the natural world (e.g., squills, stone and sea creatures; see Chapter 5).[2] By taking in the diversity of their materializations, and considering them in light of one another, we have been able to recognize how this distinct dynamism both arose from and contributed to the peculiar animalian and bodily statuses of the three entities. Hence, while not animals, we can see that boar's tusk helmets, oxhide shields and ikria participated powerfully in what the rich field of Aegean animalian things brought to sociocultural experience.

COMMON DYNAMICS IN HIGHLY PARTICULAR THINGS

In our discussion of Cretan and wider Aegean animalian things, we have examined material from across the centuries between the late third and the mid-second millennia BCE. This has involved, in each case, considering changes and persistences in the ways that these things contributed to lived experiences of humans, and the implications these had for the position and identity of nonhu-man animals in Aegean culture. We have followed both certain types of thing (e.g., zoomorphic vessels) and species (e.g., griffins), querying the evidence for indications of the particular affordances that would have distinguished engage-ments with these fabricated animalian embodiments within different moments and contexts. This has necessitated both close consideration of the material culture and scrutiny of the relations that the animals embodied in the objects would have found and realized within their physical, sociocultural, zoological and environmental surroundings.

As each step in the discussion has progressed, I have tried to make clear how new observations being made connected to what had emerged from the foregoing analyses, while also allowing the material at hand to be problematized in its own right. Through this, despite the keen particularity of these animalian things, several qualities have emerged as held in common across their diversity. These qualities are entangled with one another in the objects.

1. These Aegean animalian things each had highly characteristic spatial dynamics, which complicated their presence within or between contexts of activity in specific ways.

2. Given the bodily nature of many of these things, their presence carried a distinct weight that both drew from and contributed to their creaturely status and afforded engagements with humans that were charged with interanimalian potency.

3. Many of the objects in question cultivated powerful relations and integrations, especially between species and between animals and objects. We have seen that in various instances these relations would have contributed to generating associations that may have carried (or have come to carry) conventional cultural value as well. In some instances, the fluid integrations realized in the animalian things eschewed easy identification of a feature with a single phenomenon, and instead created productive irresolution between statuses (e.g., between the divergent spatial implications of a frieze rendered in wall painting, or, in the case of certain renderings of griffins, between the rendering of a bodily component or an attached object).

4. Each of these fabricated embodiments of animals is fundamentally creative in its material/formal realization and in the relations that it afforded. Hence, while each can and should be contextualized by other embodiments of animals (both biological and crafted) that people would have been experiencing contemporaneously, notions of replication and imitative representation are insufficient for approaching the relationships between these embodiments. Instead, these animalian things should be recognized as having actively cultivated new kinds of relation and presence.

Because the different objects considered here are each highly particular in their character and affordances, there can be no blanket interpretation of their contribution to Aegean sociocultural life; to proffer such would be to disregard both the distinctiveness of their presences and the very nature of how their efficacies and identities were realized, through specific interactions and relations. At the same time, the four core qualities laid out above can be observed throughout the Aegean animalian things and periods analyzed. These matters are not only shared between these embodiments of the animalian but, moreover, are remarkably robust and emphasized in them, distinguishing each as a material reality, and enriching the dynamic experiences of nonhumans that they afforded.

SATURATED AND UNSETTLED DISPOSITIONS

Following the analyses in Chapters 2 to 6, we emerge in a position to say that, in Crete and other areas of the southern Aegean during the late third to mid-second millennium BCE, people would have experienced many animalian things as being distinctively *unsettled*, with peculiar implications for the socio-cultural spaces of which the things were part. In the case studies, we have explored how such characteristically unsettled dynamics, realized in specific ways in each of the animalian objects, may have contributed within contexts of particular human and environmental activity – from incorporating a Prepalatial community's movements between places, to embodying palatial claims on potentially transgressive culture in the face of climatic and social unrest; from activities of rural agricultural communities, to situations of long-distance sea travel and storytelling. These arguments have emerged, first and foremost, on the basis of close considerations of how people would have engaged with the animalian things, rather than arising from theories concerning the nature of sociopolitical organization in a given period and then being led by attempts to read the intentional design of the objects in that light.

This study has not aimed to be a comprehensive account of the myriad Aegean Bronze Age renderings of animals – instead, we have focused primarily on Crete and Thera from the later Prepalatial through Neopalatial periods and closely examined specific varieties of crafted animalian things. The diversity of material culture considered supports a deep new understanding of the peculiar disposition of fabricated animals within this Aegean social space. Given the extraordinary dynamism that these objects could actualize, it is possible that the act of crafting and hence embodying animals held a specific cultural weight, perhaps being recognized as a generative practice in some sense akin to life-giving. That instances of craft production may have been experienced as wondrous in such ways has been compellingly explored regarding later periods and other regions,[3] and Herva's discussion of Minoan attitudes toward repre-sentation of the natural world provocatively indicates paths we might take to consider the possibilities of a fundamentally different and unmodern concep-tion of animacy at play in the Aegean Bronze Age itself. It is, moreover, possible that certain Aegean objects themselves were thought to possess a vibrancy that was, in its essence, not just lifelike but actually alive in a way shared with biological or divine beings.[4] It is fascinating to consider such possibilities, but the current Aegean Bronze Age evidence requires us to venture only tentatively into such interpretive territory. By placing focus directly on the Aegean material culture – on its creative embodiment of animals and the rich and fluid relations it would have realized within the lived world – a sense of things saturated in their own distinctive animalian character has come into view. These things can lead us toward forming a fuller appreciation of the diversity and complexity that the nonhuman animal held within human experience in the Aegean, by integrating a host of embodiments that were at the same time relatable and highly distinct in their presences.

NOTES

1. Noë 2004: 193–194.
2. For example, through relationships of juxtaposition and formal assonance with vegetables (as on the LM I vessel from the Cult Room Basement at Knossos, where the squill is imaged); or through contextualization with elements of the marine worlds (figure-8 shields in particular are imaged on multiple Neopalatial Marine Style Vessels).
3. See, for example, the excellent studies of Morris 1995 and Winter 2003, both of which engage with textual evidence.
4. As with Mesopotamian effigies, which were fed and cared for; see discussion in Chapter 2.

REFERENCES

Aamodt, C. 2021. Personal adornment for ritual protection in Mycenaean Greece. *Journal of Prehistoric Religion*, 27, 46–63.

Abramiuk, M. 2012. *The Foundations of Cognitive Archaeology*. Cambridge, MA: MIT Press.

Akrivaki, N. 2003. τοιχογραφία με Παράσταση Οδοντόφρακτου Κράνους από την Ξεστή 4 του Ακρωτηρίου Θήρας. In A. Vlachopoulos and K. Birtacha (eds.), *Αργοναύτης: Τιμητικός τόμος για τον καθηγητή Χρίστο Γ. Ντούμα από τους μαθητές του στο Πανεπιστήμιο Αθηνών (1980–2000)*, 527–541. Athens: Kathemerine.

Alberti, B. 2001. Faience goddesses and ivory bull-leapers: The aesthetics of sexual difference at Late Bronze Age Knossos. *World Archaeology*, 33.2, 189–205.

———. 2002. Gender and the figurative art of Late Bronze Age Knossos. In Y. Hamilakis (ed.), *Labyrinth Revisited: Rethinking "Minoan" Archaeology*, 98–117. Oxford: Oxbow.

Alden, M. 2005. Lions in paradise. *Classical Quarterly*, 5.2, 335–42.

Alexiou, S. 1969. Μικραί ανασκαφαί και περισυλλογή αρκαίων εις Κρήτην. *Praktika tes en Athenais Archaiologikes Etaireias*, 210–215.

Allwin B., Gokarn, N. S., Vedamanickam, S. et al. 2016. The wild pig (*Sus scrofa*) behavior: A retrospective study. *Journal of Dairy, Veterinary & Animal Research*, 3.3, 115–125.

Aloupi, E., Karydas, A. G. and Paradellis, T. 2000. Pigment analysis of wall paintings and ceramics from Greece and Cyprus: The optimum use of X-ray spectrometry on specific archaeological issues. *X-Ray Spectrometry: An International Journal*, 29.1, 18–24.

Alram-Stern, E., Blakolmer, F., Deger-Jalkotzy, S., Laffineur, R. and Weilhartner, J. (eds.). 2016. *Metaphysis, Ritual, Myth and Symbolism in the Aegean Bronze Age*. Leuven: Peeters.

Al-Tardeh, S. 2008. Morphological and anatomical adaptations of the perennial geophyte *Urginea maritima* (L.) *baker* (liliaceae) to the Mediterranean climate. Master's thesis, Aristotle University of Thessaloniki.

Anastasiadou, M. 2013. *The Middle Minoan Three-Sided Soft Stone Prism: A Study of Style and Iconography*. CMS Beiheft, 9. Mainz: Philipp von Zabern.

———. 2016a. Wings, heads, tails: Small puzzles at LM I Zakros. In E. Alram-Stern, F. Blakolmer, S. Deger-Jalkotzy, R. Laffineur and J. Weilhartner (eds.), *Metaphysis, Ritual, Myth and Symbolism in the Aegean Bronze Age*, 77–85. Aegaeum, 39. Leuven: Peeters.

———. 2016b. Drawing the line: Seals, script, and regionalism in Protopalatial Crete. *American Journal of Archaeology*, 120.2, 159–193.

Anastasiadou, M. and Pomadère, M. 2011. Le sceau à "la figure féminine aux bras levés" du secteur Pi de Malia. *Bulletin de Correspondance Héllenique*, 135.1, 63–71.

Anderson, E. 2011. Through vessels of embodied action: Approaching ritual experience and cultural interaction through late Mycenaean rhyta. In G. Harrison and J. Francis (eds.), *Life and Death in Ancient Egypt: The Diniacopoulos Collection*, 73–88. Montreal: Concordia University.

———. 2015. Connecting with selves and others: Varieties of community-making across Late Prepalatial Crete. In S. Cappel, U. Günkel-Maschek and D. Panagiotopoulos (eds.), *Minoan Archaeology: Perspectives for the 21st Century*, 199–211. Aegis, 8. Louvain-la-Neuve: Presses universitaires de Louvain.

2016. *Seals, Craft, and Community in Bronze Age Crete*. Cambridge: Cambridge University Press.

2019. A sense of stone and clay: The inter-corporeal disposition of Minoan glyptic. In M. Cifarelli (ed.), *Fashioned Selves: Dress and Identity in Antiquity*, 203–18. Oxford: Oxbow.

2020. The poetics of the Cretan lion: Glyptic and oral culture in the Bronze Age Aegean. *American Journal of Archaeology*, 124.3, 345–379.

2021. Intuitive things: Helmets, shields, ikria and the uniqueness of Aegean composites. In T. Palaima and R. Laffineur (eds.), *ZOIA: Animal Connections in the Aegean Middle and Late Bronze Age*, 149–160. Leuven: Peeters.

in press, 2024. The reinvented social somatics of ritual performance on early Crete: Engagements of humans with zoomorphic vessels. In K. Morgan (ed.), *Pomp, Circumstance, and the Performance of Politics: Acting Politically Correct in the Ancient World*, 97–124. Chicago: Oriental Institute of the University of Chicago.

Anil, M. H. and von Holleben, K. 2014. Exsanguination. In M. Dikeman and C. Devine (eds.), *Encyclopedia of Meat Sciences*, 561–563. London: Academic Press.

Aravantinos, V., Godart, L. and Sacconi, A. 2001. *Thèbes: Fouilles de la Cadmée. Vol. 1, Les tablettes en linéaire B de la Odos Pelopidou: Édition et commentaire*. Pisa: Instituti Editoriali e Poligrafici Internazionali.

Arnold, D. 2002. Recumbent lion. *Bulletin of the Metropolitan Museum of Art, New York*, 40.2, 5–6.

Aruz, J., 1984. The silver cylinder seal from Mochlos. *Kadmos*, 23.1–2, 186–188.

2008a. *Marks of Distinction: Seals and Cultural Exchange between the Aegean and the Orient (ca. 2600–1360 BC)*. Mainz: Philipp von Zabern.

2008b. Central Anatolian ivories/46ab furniture support and plaque. In J. Aruz, K. Benzel and J. M. Evans (eds.), *Beyond Babylon: Art, Trade, and Diplomacy in the Second Millennium* BC, 82–84. New York: Metropolitan Museum of Art.

2008c. Ritual and royal imagery; 76, Furniture plaque with griffin; Furniture support and plaque. In J. Aruz, K. Benzel and J. M. Evans (eds.), *Beyond Babylon: Art, Trade, and Diplomacy in the Second Millennium* BC, 136–138. New York: Metropolitan Museum of Art.

Auerbach, E. 1953. *Mimesis: The Representation of Reality in Western Literature*. Princeton, NJ: Princeton University Press.

Ballintijn, M. 1995. Lions depicted on Aegean seals – how realistic are they? In W. Müller (ed.), *Sceaux minoens et mycéniens*, 23–27. Berlin: Mann.

Banou, E. 2008. Minoan {\hbox)}horns of consecration" revisited: A symbol of sun worship in palatial and post-palatial Crete. *Mediterranean Archaeology and Archaeometry*, 8.1, 27–47.

Bar-Gal, G. K., Smith, P., Tchernov, E. et al. 2002. Genetic evidence for the origin of the agrimi goat (*Capra aegagrus cretica*). *Journal of Zoology*, 256.3, 369–377.

Barona, A. 2021. The archaeology of the social brain revisited: Rethinking mind and material culture from a material engagement perspective. *Adaptive Behavior*, 29.2, 137–152.

Bartosiewicz, L. 2009. A lion's share of attention: Archaeozoology and the historical record. *Acta Archaeologica*, 60.1, 275–289.

Baudrillard, J. 1981. *Simulacres et simulation*. Paris: Galilée.

Beardsworth, A., and Bryman, A. 2001. The wild animal in late modernity: The case of the Disneyization of zoos. *Tourist Studies*, 1.1, 83–104.

Beef Cattle Research Council. 2022. Drought management strategies [online] www.beefresearch.ca/research-topic.cfm/drought-management-strategies-96.

Belting, H. 2005. Image, medium, body: A new approach to iconology. *Critical Inquiry*, 31, 302–319.

Bennet, J. 1985. The structure of the Linear B administration at Knossos. *American Journal of Archaeology*, 89.2, 231–249.

Bennett, D. 2014. The collision between wild pigs, agriculture and hunting; an interview with Dr. John Mayer. *Farm Progress*, online 11.10.2014, www.farmprogress.com/man

agement/collision-between-wild-pigs-agri
culture-and-hunting.

Bennett, J. 2010. *Vibrant Matter: A Political Ecology of Things*. Durham, NC: Duke University Press.

Berger, J. 1980. Why look at animals? In J. Berger, *About Looking* 1–22. London: Writers and Readers.

Betancourt, P. P. 2001. Introduction to the Special Issue on Kamares Ware. *Aegean Archaeology*, 5, 7–26.

2004. Knossian expansion in Late Minoan IB: The evidence of the Spirals and Arcading Group. *BSA Studies*, 12, 295–298.

Betancourt, P. P. and Davaras, K. (eds.). 2003. *Pseira VII: The Pseira Cemetery 2: Excavation of the Tombs*. Philadelphia: INSTAP Academic Press.

Bevan, A. 2007. *Stone Vessels and Values in the Bronze Age Mediterranean*. Cambridge: Cambridge University Press.

Bhabha, H. 1994. *The Location of Culture*. London: Routledge.

Bicknell, P. 2000. Late Minoan IB marine ware, the marine environment of the Aegean, and the Bronze Age eruption of the Thera volcano. *Geological Society, London, Special Publications*, 171.1, 95–103.

Binnberg, J., Urbani, B. and Youlatos, D. 2021. Langurs in the Aegean Bronze Age? A review of a recent debate on archaeoprimatology and animal identification in ancient iconography. *Journal of Greek Archaeology*, 6, 100–128.

Bisi, A. M. 1965. *Il Grifone: Storia di un motivo iconographico nell' antico Oriente mediterraneo*. Rome: Centro di studi semitici Istituto di studi del Vicino Oriente Università.

Black, J. 1998. *Reading Sumerian Poetry*. Ithaca, NY: Cornell University Press.

Blakolmer, F. 1995. Komparative Funktionsanalyse des malerischen Raumdekors in minoischen Palasten und Villen. In R. Laffineur and W.-D. Niemeier (eds.), *Politeia: Society and State in the Aegean Bronze Age*, 463–474. Liège: Université de Liège.

2010. Small is beautiful: The significance of Aegean glyptic for the study of wall paintings, relief frescoes and minor relief arts. In W. Müller (ed.), *Die Bedeutung der minoischen und mykenischen Glyptik. VI. Internationales Siegel-Symposium, Marburg, 9.–12. Oktober 2008*, 91–108. Mainz am Rhein: Philipp von Zabern.

2012. Image and architecture: Reflections of mural iconography in seal images and other art forms of Minoan Crete. In D. Panagiotopoulos and U. Günkel-Maschek (eds.), *Minoan Realities: Approaches to Images, Architecture, and Society in the Aegean Bronze Age*, 83–114. Louvain-la-Neuve: Presses Universitaires de Louvain.

2015. The many-faced "Minoan genius" and his iconographical prototype Taweret: On the character of Near Eastern religious motifs in Neopalatial Crete. In J. Mynářová, P. Onderka and P. Pavúk (eds.), *There and Back Again: The Crossroads* II, 199–222. Prague: Charles University.

2016a. Hierarchy and symbolism of animals and mythical creatures in the Aegean Bronze Age: A statistical and contextual approach. In E. Alram-Stern, F. Blakolmer, S. Deger-Jalkotzy, R. Laffineur, and J. Weilhartner (eds.), *Metaphysis, Ritual, Myth and Symbolism in the Aegean Bronze Age*, 61–68. Leuven: Peeters.

2016b. Interacting Minoan arts: Seal images and mural iconography in Minoan Crete, *Bulletin of the Institute of Classical Studies*, 59, 139–140.

2018. "Sculpted with the paintbrush"? On the interrelation of relief art and painting in Minoan Crete and Thera. In A. Vlachopoulos (ed.), *Paintbrushes (Χρωστήρες): Wall-Painting and Vase-Painting of the Second Millenium B.C. in Dialogue*, 143–151. Athens: University of Ioannina/ Hellenic Ministry of Culture and Sports Archaeological Receipts Fund.

Blegen, C. 1954. Excavations at Pylos, 1953. *American Journal of Archaeology*, 58.1, 27–32.

Bloedow, E. 1992. On lions in Minoan and Mycenaean culture. In R. Laffineur and J. Crowley (eds.), *EIKON: Aegean Bronze*

Age Iconography. Shaping a Methodology. 4th International Aegean Conference, University of Tasmania, Hobart, 6–9 April 1992, 295–305. Liège: Université de Liège.

Bloor, D. 1976. *Knowledge and Social Imagery.* London: Routledge.

Blumstein, D. T. 1990. An observation of social play in bearded vultures. *Condor,* 92: 779–781.

Boness, D. and Goren, Y. 2017. Early Minoan mortuary practices as evident by microarchaeological studies at Koumasa, Crete, applying new sampling procedures. *Journal of Archaeological Science: Reports,* 507–522.

Borchhardt, J. 1972. *Homerische Helme: Helmformen der Aegais in ihren Beziehungen zu orientalischen und europäischen Helmen inder Bronze-und fruchen Eisenzeit.* Mainz: P. von Zabern.

Bosanquet, R. C. and Dawkins, R. M. 1923. The Unpublished Objects from the Palaikastro Excavations, 1902–1906. Part I. British School at Athens Supplementary Papers I. United Kingdom: subscribers and sold on their behalf.

Bourdieu, P. 1977. *Outline of a Theory of Practice.* Cambridge: Cambridge University Press.

Boyer, P., 1994. *The Naturalness of Religious Ideas: A Cognitive Theory of Religion.* Berkeley: University of California Press.

Branigan, K. 1991. Mochlos: An early Aegean gateway community? *Aegaeum,* 7, 97–105.

1993. *Dancing with Death: Life and Death in Southern Crete, c. 3000–2000* BC. Amsterdam: Hakkert.

Branigan, K. (ed.). 1998. *Cemetery and Society in the Aegean Bronze Age.* Sheffield: Sheffield Academic Press.

Brecoulaki, H. 2014. "Precious colours" in Ancient Greek polychromy and painting: Material aspects and symbolic values. *Revue archéologique,* 1, 3–35.

Broodbank, C. 2000. *An Island Archaeology of the Early Cyclades.* Cambridge: Cambridge University Press.

Broodbank, C. 2002. *An Island Archaeology of the Early Cyclades.* Pbk. ed. Cambridge: Cambridge University Press.

Brown, B. 2001. Thing theory. *Critical Inquiry,* 28.1, 1–22.

Brysbaert, A. 2008. *The Power of Technology in the Bronze Age Eastern Mediterranean: The Case of the Painted Plaster.* London: Equinox.

Brysbaert, A., Melessanaki, K. and Anglos, D. 2006. Pigment analysis in Bronze Age Aegean and Eastern Mediterranean painted plaster by laser-induced breakdown spectroscopy (LIBS). *Journal of Archaeological Science,* 33.8, 1095–1104.

Buchholz, H.-G., Matthäus, H. and Wiener, M. 2010. Helmentwicklung und ein unbekannter altägäischer Bronzehelm. In H.-G. Buchholz (ed.), *Archaeologia Homerica 1, E (3). Kriegswesen: Ergänzungen und Zusammenfassung,* 135–208. Göttingen: Vandenhoeck & Ruprecht, 2010.

Burns, B. 2010. *Mycenaean Greece, Mediterranean Commerce, and the Formation of Identity.* Cambridge: Cambridge University Press.

Butler, J. 1993. *Bodies That Matter: On the Discursive Limits of "Sex."* New York: Routledge.

Cadogan, G. 2010. Goddess, nymph or housewife; and water worries at Myrtos? *BSA Studies,* 18, 41–47.

Cameron, M. A. S. 1968. Unpublished paintings from the "House of the Frescoes" at Knossos. *British School at Athens,* 63, 1–31.

1976. A general study of Minoan frescoes with particular reference to unpublished wall painting from Knossos. Thesis, University of Newcastle on Tyne.

Cameron, M. A. S., Jones, R. E. and Philippakis, S. E. 1977. Scientific analyses of Minoan fresco samples from Knossos. *British School at Athens,* 72, 121–184.

Campbell, J. K. 1974. *Honour, Family and Patronage: A Study of Institutions and Moral Values in a Greek Mountain Community.* Oxford: Oxford University Press.

1992. Fieldwork among the Sarakatsani, 1954–55. In J. Pina-Cabral and J. K. Campbell (eds.), *Europe Observed,* 148–166. London: Palgrave Macmillan.

Cappel, S., Günkel-Maschek, U. and Panagiotopoulos, D. (eds.). 2015. *Minoan Archaeology: Perspectives for the 21st Century.* Aegis, 8. Louvain-la-Neuve: Presses universitaires de Louvain.

Carter, J. and Morris, S. (eds.). 1998. *The Ages of Homer: A Tribute to Emily Townsend Vermeule*. Austin: University of Texas Press.

Castritsi-Catharios, J., Miliou, H., Kapiris, K. and Kefalas, E. 2011. Recovery of the commercial sponges in the central and southeastern Aegean Sea (NE Mediterranean) after an outbreak of sponge disease. *Mediterranean Marine Science*, 12.1, 5–20.

Chapin, A. 1997–2000. Maidenhood and marriage: The reproductive lives of the girls and women from Xeste 3, Thera. *Aegean Archaeology*, 4, 7–25.

2004. Power, privilege, and landscape in Minoan art. *Hesperia Supplements*, 33, 47–64.

2007. Boys will be boys: Youth and gender identity in the Theran frescoes. *Hesperia Supplements*, 41, 229–255.

2021. What is a child in Aegean prehistory? In L. Beaumont, M. Dillon, and N. Harrington (eds.), *Children in Antiquity*, 26–41. Oxford: Routledge.

Chapin, A. P. and Shaw, M. C. 2006. The frescoes from the House of the Frescoes at Knossos: A reconsideration of their architectural context and a new reconstruction of the Crocus Panel. *Annual of the British School at Athens*, 101, 57–88.

Chlouveraki, S., Betancourt, C. D., Davaras, C. et al. 2008. Excavations in the Hagios Charalambos cave: A preliminary report. *Hesperia*, 77.4, 539–605.

Chryssikopoulou, E., Kilikoglou, V., Perdikatsis, V. et al. 2000. Making wall paintings: An attempt to reproduce the painting techniques of Bronze Age Thera. In S. Sherratt (ed.), *The Wall Paintings of Thera*, vol. 1, 119–129. Piraeus: Petros M. Nomikos and the Thera Foundation.

Clarke, M. 1995. Between lions and men: images of the hero in the Iliad. *Greek, Roman, and Byzantine Studies*, 36.2, 137–159.

Cline, E. 1991. Monkey business in the Bronze Age Aegean: The Amenhotep II faience figurines at Mycenae and Tiryns. *British School at Athens*, 86, 29–42.

1994. *Sailing the Wine-Dark Sea: International Trade and the Late Bronze Age Aegean*. Oxford: Tempus reparatum.

Colburn, C. 2008. Exotica and the Early Minoan elite: Eastern imports in Prepalatial Crete. *American Journal of Archaeology*, 112.2, 203–224.

2011. Egyptian gold in prepalatial Crete? A consideration of the evidence. *Journal of Ancient Egyptian Interconnections*, 3.3, 1–13.

Comer, C. and Mayer, J. 2009. Wild pig reproductive biology. In J. Beasley, S. Ditchkoff, J. Mayer, M. Smith and K. Vercauteren (eds.), *Wild Pigs: Biology, Damage, Control Techniques and Management*, SRNL-RP-2009-00869, 51–75. Washington, DC: Department of Defense.

Corbett, G. 2017. "Interview with a bullfighter (Eduardo Davila Miura)." In Pure Tales, *Pure Andalusia* (online). https://pureandalusia.com/interview-with-a-bullfighter/.

Corbett, J. 2006. *Communicating Nature: How We Create and Understand Environmental Messages*. Washington, DC: Island Press.

Counts, D. B. 2008. Master of the lion: Representation and hybridity in Cypriote sanctuaries. *American Journal of Archaeology*, 112.1, 3–27.

Crowley, J. 1989. *The Aegean and the East: An Investigation into the Transference of Artistic Motifs between the Aegean, Egypt, and the Near East in the Bronze Age*. Jonsered: Paul Åströms Förlag.

1995. Images of power in the Bronze Age Aegean. In R. Laffineur and W.-D. Niemeier (eds.), *Politeia: Society and State in the Aegean Bronze Age*, 475–491. Liège: Université de Liège.

1998. Iconography and interconnections. In *The Aegean and the Orient in the Second Millennium*, 171–182. Aegaeum, 18. Liège: Peeters.

2012. Prestige clothing in the Bronze Age Aegean. In M-L. Nosch and R. Laffineur (eds.), *KOSMOS Jewellery, Adornment and Textiles in the Aegean Bronze Age*, 231–239. Aegaeum, 33. Liège: Peeters.

2020. Reading the Phaistos sealings: Taking the textbook approach of iconographic analysis. *Current Approaches and New Perspectives in Aegean Iconography*, 18, 19–46.

Crown, P. 2007. Life histories of pots and potters: Situating the individual in archaeology. *American Antiquity*, 72.4, 677–690.

Csordas, T. 1993. Somatic modes of attention. *Cultural Anthropology* 8.2, 135–156.

Currie, A., and Killin, A. 2019. From things to thinking: Cognitive archaeology. *Mind & Language*, 34.2, 263–279.

Dakouri-Hild, A. 2005. Breaking the mould? Production and economy in the Theban state. In A. Dakouri-Hild and S. Sherratt (eds.), *Autochthon: Papers Presented to O.T.P. K. Dickinson on the Occasion of His Retirement*, 207–224. Oxford: Archaeopress.

Davaras, C. 1975. Early Minoan jewelry from Mochlos. *British School at Athens*, 70, 40–45

Davaras, C., and Soles, J. 1995. A new oriental cylinder seal from Mochlos. Appendix: Catalogue of the cylinder seals found in the Aegean, *Archaiologike Ephemeris*, 134, 29–66.

Davis, B. 2014. *Minoan Stone Vessels with Linear A Inscriptions*. Liège and Austin: Université de Liège and University of Texas.

2018. The Phaistos disk: A new way of viewing the language behind the script. *Oxford Journal of Archaeology*, 37.4, 373–410.

Davis, E. 1974. The Vapheio cups: One Minoan and one Mycenean? *The Art Bulletin*, 56.4, 472–487.

1986. Youth and age in the Thera frescoes. *American Journal of Archaeology*, 90.4, 399–406.

Davis, J., and Stocker, R. 2015. Crete, Messenia, and the date of Tholos IV at Pylos. In C. Macdonald, E. Hatzaki and S. Andreou (eds.), *The Great Islands: Studies of Crete and Cyprus Presented to Gerald Cadogan*, 175–178. Athens: Kapon Editions.

2016. The lord of the gold rings: The Griffin Warrior of Pylos. *Hesperia*, 85.4, 627–55.

Dawkins, R. M. 1904–5. Excavations at Palaikastro IV. *British School at Athens*, 11, 258–308.

De Checchi C. 2006. Les techniques d'orfèvrerie minoenne: L'apport des objets de Mochlos. In G. Nicolini (ed.), *Les ors des mondes grec et "barbare,"* *Actes du colloque de la Société d'Archéologie Classique du 18 novembre 2000*, 17–33. Paris: Picard.

De Planhol, X. 2004. *Le paysage animal: L'homme et la grande faune. Une zoogéographie historique*. Paris: Fayard.

Decorte, R. P. J. 2018. The first 'European' writing: Redefining the Archanes Script. *Oxford Journal of Archaeology*, 37.4, 341–372.

Déderix, S. 2015. A matter of scale: Assessing the visibility of circular tombs in the landscape of Bronze Age Crete. *Journal of Archaeological Science: Reports*, 4, 525–534.

2017. Communication networks, interactions, and social negotiation in Prepalatial south-central Crete. *American Journal of Archaeology*, 121.1, 5–37.

Déderix, S. and Sarris, A. 2019. Μετακίνηση και αλληλεπιδράσεις στην Προανακτορική νότια κεντρική Κρήτη. In C. Mitsotaki, L. Tzedaki-Apostolaki and S. Giannadaki (eds.), *Proceedings of the 12th International Congress of Cretan Studies: Heraklion*. Herakleion: Society of Cretan Historical Studies. https://12iccs.proceedings.gr/en/proceedings/category/38/32/195.

Demargne P. 1930. Bijoux minoens de Mallia. *Bulletin de Correspondance Héllenique*, 54, 404–421.

1945. *Fouilles exécutées à Mallia: Exploration des Nécropoles (1921–1933); premier fascicule*. Paris: P. Geuthner.

DeMarrais, E., Gosden, C. and Renfrew, C. (eds.). 2004. *Rethinking Materiality: The Engagements of Mind with the Material World*. Cambridge: McDonald Institute Monographs.

Derrida, J. and Wills, D. 2002. The animal that therefore I am (more to follow). *Critical Inquiry*, 28.2, 369–418.

Derrida, J., Mallet, M.-L. and Wills, D. 2008. *The Animal That Therefore I Am*. New York: Fordham University Press.

Descola, P. 2013. *Beyond Nature and Culture*, trans. J. Lloyd. Chicago: University of Chicago Press.

Dessenne, A. 1957a. *Le Sphinx: Étude iconographique*. Paris: E. de Boccard.

1957b. Le Griffon créto-mycénien: Inventaire et remarques. *Bulletin de Correspondance Héllenique*, 81, 203–215.

Devolder, M., 2009. Composantes et interactions sociales en Crète néopalatiale: Investigation des données archéologiques. PhD diss., UCL–Université Catholique de Louvain.

Doumas, C. 1992. *The Wall-Paintings of Thera*. Athens: Thera Foundation.

1994. Cycladic art. In Y. Sakellarakis (ed.), *The Dawn of Greek Art*, 31–129. Athens: Ekdotike Athenon.

2008. The wall paintings of Thera and the eastern Mediterranean, and Wall painting fragment. In J. Aruz, K. Benzel and J. M. Evans (eds.), *Beyond Babylon: Art, Trade and Diplomacy in the Second Millennium B.C.*, 124–125, 441–442. New York: Metropolitan Museum of Art.

Drazin, A. and Küchler, S. (eds.) 2015. *The Social Life of Materials: Studies in Materials and Society*. London: Bloomsbury Publishing.

Driessen, J. 2007. IIB or not IIB: On the beginnings of Minoan monument building. In J. Bretschneider, J. Driessen and K. Van Lerberghe (eds.), *Power and Architecture: Monumental Public Architecture in the Bronze Age Near East and Aegean*, vol. 156, 73–92. Leuven: Peeters.

2010a. Spirit of place: Minoan houses as major actors. In D. Pullen (ed.), *Political Economies of the Aegean Bronze Age*, 35–65. Oxford: Oxbow.

2010b. The goddess and the skull: Some observations on group identity in Prepalatial Crete. *British School at Athens*, 18, 107–117.

2013. The Troubled Island, 15 years later. Heidelberg Conference on Crete and Santorini, 26 (January).

Driessen, J. and Macdonald, C. 1997. *The Troubled Island. Minoan Crete before and after the Santorini Eruption*, Aegaeum, 17. Liège: Université de Liège and University of Texas at Austin.

2000. The eruption of the Santorini volcano and its effects on Minoan Crete. *Geological Society, London, Special Publications*, 171.1, 81–93.

Driessen, J., and Relaki, M. (eds.). 2020. *OIKOS: Archaeological Approaches to House Societies in the Bronze Age Aegean*, Aegis, 19.

Louvain-la-Neuve: Presses universitaires de Louvain.

Duhoux, Y. 1994. LA > B da-ma-te = Demeter? Sur la langue du linéaire A. *Minos*, 29/30: 289–294.

1998. Pre-Hellenic language(s) of Crete. *Journal of Indo-European Studies*, 26, 1–39.

Eco, U. 1976. *A Theory of Semiotics*. Bloomington: Indiana University Press.

Edgar, C. C. 1904. The pottery. In T. D. Atkinson, *Excavations at Phylakopi in Melos*. London: Macmillan.

Egan, E. C. 2018. From permanent to portable: The ceramic perpetuation of painted landscapes at Knossos in the Final Palatial Period. In A. Vlachopoulos (ed.), *Paintbrushes (Χρωστήρες): Wall-Painting and Vase-Painting of the Second Millenium B.C. in Dialogue*, 329–337. Athens: University of Ioannina/Hellenic Ministry of Culture and Sports Archaeological Receipts Fund.

2020. Standardization vs. individualization in the Pylian Painted Argonaut. *Journal of Eastern Mediterranean Archaeology & Heritage Studies*, 8.3–4, 379–388.

Egan, E. C. and Brecoulaki, H. 2015. Marine iconography at the Palace of Nestor and the emblematic use of the argonaut. In H. Brecoulaki, J. L. Davis, and S. R. Stocker (eds.), *Mycenaean Wall Paintings in Context: New Discoveries, Old Finds Reconsidered*, 292–313. Μελετήματα, 72. Athens: National Hellenic Research Foundation, Institute of Historical Research.

Eller, C. 2012. Two knights and a goddess: Sir Arthur Evans, Sir James George Frazer, and the invention of Minoan religion. *Journal of Mediterranean Archaeology*, 25.1, 75–98.

Elmore, D. 2019. Feral hog tusk characteristics. USDA National Institute of Food and Agriculture, Extension Foundation; https://feralhogs.extension.org/feral-hog-tusk-characteristics/.

Evans, A. 1921. *The Palace of Minos*, vol. 1. London: Macmillan.

1928. *The Palace of Minos*, vol. 2. London: Macmillan.

1930. *The Palace of Minos*, vol. 3. London: Macmillan.

Evin, A., Dobney, K., Schafberg, R. et al. 2015. Phenotype and animal domestication: A study of dental variation between domestic, wild, captive, hybrid and insular *Sus scrofa. BMC Evolutionary Biology*, 15.1, 1–6.

Feldman, M. 2006. *Diplomacy by Design: Luxury Arts And an "International Style" in the Ancient Near East, 1400–1200* BCE. Chicago: University of Chicago Press.

2014. Beyond iconography: Meaning-making in Late Bronze Age eastern Mediterranean visual and material culture. In B. Knapp and P. van Dommelen (eds.), *The Cambridge Prehistory of the Bronze and Iron Age Mediterranean*, 337–351. Cambridge: Cambridge University Press.

2018. Interaction with neighboring regions and artistic traditions: Ancient Near East and Bronze Age Aegean. In A. Gunter (ed.), *A Companion to the Art of the Ancient Near East*, 565–584. Oxford: Wiley-Blackwell.

Ferrara, S., Weingarten, J. and Cadogan, G. 2016. Cretan Hieroglyphic at Myrtos-Pyrgos. *Studi Micenei ed Egeo-Anatolici New Series*, 2, 81–99.

Finlayson, S., Bogacz, B., Mara, H. and Panagiotopoulos, D. 2021. Searching for ancient Aegean administrators: Computational experiments on identical seal impressions. *Journal of Archaeological Science*, 136, 105490.

Fitton, J. (ed.). 2009. *The Aigina Treasure: Aegean Bronze Age Jewellery and a Mystery Revisited*. London: British Museum Press.

Flouda, G. 2013. Materiality of Minoan writing: Modes of display and perception. In K. Piquette and R. Whitehouse (eds.), *Writing as Material Practice*. London: Ubiquity Press.

Foster, K. P. 1976. *Aegean Faience of the Bronze Age*. New Haven, CT: Yale University Press.

1982. *Minoan Ceramic Relief*. Studies in Mediterranean Archaeology, 64. Göteborg: Åström.

1999. The earliest zoos and gardens. *Scientific American*, 281.1, 64–71.

2008. Minoan faience revisited: Vitreous materials in the Late Bronze Age Aegean. *Sheffield Studies in Aegean Archaeology*, 9, 173–186.

2020. *Strange and Wonderful: Exotic Flora and Fauna in Image and Imagination*. New York, NY: Oxford University Press.

Foucault, M. 1975. *Surveiller et punir: Naissance de la prison*. Paris: Gallimard.

1986. Of other spaces, trans. J. Miskowiec. *Diacritics*, 16.1, 22–27.

Frankfort, H. 1936. Notes on the Cretan griffin. *British School at Athens*, 37, 106–122.

Frantz, L. A. F., Haile, J., Lin, A. T. et al. 2019. Ancient pigs reveal a near-complete genomic turnover following their introduction to Europe. *Proceedings of the National Academy of Sciences U S A*, 116.35, 17231–17238.

Gadotti, A. 2014. *"Gilgamesh, Enkidu, and the Netherworld" and the Sumerian Gilgamesh Cycle*. Boston: Walter de Gruyter.

Galanakis, Y., Tsitsa, E. and Günkel-Maschek, U. 2017. The power of images: Re-examining the wall paintings from the throne room at Knossos. *British School at Athens*, 112, 47–98.

Galli, E. 2014. Where the past lies: The Prepalatial tholos tomb at Krasi and its stratigraphic sequence. *Cretica Chronica*, 34, 231–248.

Gansell, A. 2018. Dressing the Neo-Assyrian queen in identity and ideology: Elements and ensembles from the royal tombs at Nimrud. *American Journal of Archaeology*, 122.1, 65–100.

Gates, C. 2004. The adoption of pictorial imagery in Minoan wall painting: A comparativist perspective. *Hesperia Supplements*, 33, 27–46.

Gell, A. 1992. The technology of enchantment and the enchantment of technology. In J. Coote and A. Shelton (eds.), *Anthropology, Art and Aesthetics*, 40–63. Oxford: Clarendon Press.

1998. *Art and Agency: An Anthropological Theory*. Oxford: Clarendon Press.

George, A. R. 2003. *The Babylonian Gilgamesh Epic: Introduction, Critical Edition and Cuneiform Texts*. Oxford: Oxford University Press.

Georma, F. 2010. Οι τοιχογραφίες από το Κτήριο Β του προϊστορικού οικισμού Ακρωτηρίου

Θήρας (The Wall-paintings of Building B of the Prehistoric settlement of Akrotiri, Thera). PhD diss., University of Ioannina, Ioannina.

Gibson, J. J. 1979. *The Ecological Approach to Visual Perception*. New York: Psychology Press.

1986. *The Ecological Approach to Visual Perception*. Hillsdale, NJ: Lawrence Erlbaum Associates.

Gill, M. A. V. 1963. The Minoan dragon. *Bulletin of the Institute of Classical Studies*, 10.1, 1–12.

1964. The Minoan genius. *Athenische Mitteilungen*, 79, 1–21.

Girella, L. 2018. Variables and diachronic diversities in the funerary remains of the Kamilari tholos tombs. In Y. Papadatos and M. Relaki (eds), *From the Foundations to the Legacy of Minoan Society: Studies in Honour of Professor Keith Branigan*, 115–140. Sheffield Studies in Aegean Archaeology, 12. Oxford: Oxbow.

Girella, L. and Todaro, S. 2016. Secondary burials and the construction of group identities in Crete between the second half of the 4th and 2nd millennia BC. In M. Mina, S. Triantaphyllou and Y. Papadatos (eds.), *An Archaeology of Prehistoric Bodies and Embodied Identities in the Eastern Mediterranean*, 171–179. Oxford: Oxbow.

Godart, L. 1971. Les tablettes de la serie Co de Cnossos. *Minos*, 12, 418–424.

Gombrich, E. H. 1960. *Art and Illusion: A Study in the Psychology of Pictorial Representation*. London: Phaidon.

Goodison, L. 2009. Gender, body and the Minoans: Contemporary and prehistoric perceptions. In K. Kopaka (ed.), *Fylo: Engendering Prehistoric "Stratigraphies" in the Aegean and the Mediterranean*, 233–242. Aegaeum, 30. Liège: Université de Liège and University of Texas at Austin.

Gosden, C. 2005. What do objects want? *Journal of Archaeological Method and Theory* 12.3, 193–211.

Gosden, C. and Larson, F. 2007. *Knowing Things: Exploring the Collections at the Pitt Rivers Museum, 1884–1945*. Oxford: Oxford University Press.

Gray, D. 1974. *Seewesen: Archaeologia Homerica I–G*. Göttingen: Vandenhoeck & Ruprecht.

Greenberg, J. 2007. *Monkey Portraits*. New York: Little, Brown and Company.

Greenlaw, C. 2006. Monkeying around the Mediterranean: A fresh perspective on ancient primates. In J. Day, C. Greenlaw, H. Hall et al. (eds.), *Symposium on Mediterranean Archaeology 2004*, 63–67. British Archaeological Reports International Series, 1514. Oxford: Archaeopress.

2011. *The Representation of Monkeys in the Art and Thought of Mediterranean Cultures: A New Perspective on Ancient Primates*. British Archaeological Reports International Series, 2192. Oxford. Archaeopress.

Groenewegen-Frankfort, H. A. 1951. *Arrest and Movement: An Essay on Space and Time in the Representational Art of the Ancient Near East*. Chicago: University of Chicago Press.

Günkel-Maschek, U. 2020. Children and Aegean Bronze Age religion. In L. A. Beaumont, M. Dillon and N. Harrington (eds.), *Children in Antiquity*, 299–319. Abingdon: Routledge.

Hägg, R. and Lindau, Y. 1984. The Minoan "snake frame" reconsidered. *Opuscula Atheniensia*, 15, 67–77.

Haggis, D. C. 2002. Integration and complexity in the late Prepalatial period: A view from the countryside in eastern Crete. In Y. Hamilakis (ed.), *Labyrinth Revisited: Rethinking "Minoan" Archaeology*, 120–142. Oxford: Oxbow.

Hale, D. G. 1971. *The Body Politic: A Political Metaphor in Renaissance English*. The Hague: Mouton.

Hallager, B. and Hallager, E. 1995. The Knossian bull: Political propaganda in Neo-Palatial Crete. *Politeia: Society and State in the Aegean Bronze Age*, 2, 547–556.

Hallam, E. and Ingold, T. 2007. Creativity and cultural improvisation: An introduction. In E. Hallam and T. Ingold (eds.), *Creativity and Cultural Improvisation*, 1–24. Oxford: Berg.

Halstead, P. 1987. Man and other animals in later Greek prehistory. *British School at Athens*, 82, 71–83.

1995. Plough and power: The economic and social significance of cultivation with the ox-drawn ard in the Mediterranean. *Bulletin on Sumerian Agriculture*, 8, 11–22.

1996. Pastoralism or household herding? Problems of scale and specialisation in early Greek animal husbandry. *World Archaeology*, 28, 20–42.

2012. Feast, food and fodder in Neolithic-Bronze Age Greece: Commensality and the construction of value. In S. Pollock (ed.), *Between Feasts and Daily Meals: Towards an Archaeology of Commensal Places*, 21–51. Berlin: Edition Topoi, Excellenzcluster Topoi der Freien Universität Berlin und der Humboldt-Universität zu Berlin.

Hamilakis, Y. 1996. A footnote on the archaeology of power: Animal bones from a Mycenaean chamber tomb at Galatas, NE Peloponnese. *Annual of the British School at Athens*, 91, 153–166.

2002. The past as oral history. In Y. Hamilakis, M. Pluciennik and S. Tarlow, (eds.), *Thinking through the Body: Archaeologies of Corporeality*, 121–136. Boston: Springer.

2008. Time, performance, and the production of a mnemonic record: From feasting to an archaeology of eating and drinking." In L. Hitchcock, R. Laffineur and J. Crowley (eds.), *Dais: The Aegean Feast*, Aegaeum, 29, 3–20. Liège: Université de Liège and University of Texas at Austin.

2014. *Archaeology and the Senses: Human Experience, Memory, and Affect*. Cambridge: Cambridge University Press.

Hamilakis, Y. and Momigliano, N. (eds.). 2006. Archaeology and European modernity: Producing and consuming the "Minoans." *Creta Antica*, 7, special issue.

Hamilakis, Y. and Sherratt, S. 2012. Feasting and the consuming body in Bronze Age Crete and Early Iron Age Cyprus. *British School at Athens Studies*, 20, 187–207.

Hamilakis, Y., Pluciennik, M. and Tarlow, S. (eds.). 2002. *Thinking through the Body: Archaeologies of Corporeality*. Boston: Springer.

Hanes, B. 1977. *Bill Pickett, Bulldogger: The Biography of a Black Cowboy*. Norman: University of Oklahoma Press.

Haraway, D., 1978. Animal sociology and a natural economy of the body politic, part I: A political physiology of dominance. *Signs: Journal of Women in Culture and Society*, 4.1, 21–36.

Harman, G. 2018. *Object-Oriented Ontology: A New Theory of Everything*. London: Penguin.

Harries, K. 1983. *The Bavarian Rococo Church: Between Faith and Aestheticism*. New Haven, CT: Yale University Press.

Harris, L. 2018. An interview with rodeo clown Lecile Harris. *Tour Collierville Magazine*, www.tourcollierville.com/lecile-harris-rodeo-interview/.

Haug, D. T. T. 2011. Tmesis in the epic tradition. In Ø. Andersen and D. T. T. Haug (eds.), *Relative Chronology in Early Greek Epic Poetry*, 96–105. Cambridge: Cambridge University Press.

Hayes, A. and Ross, J. 1995. Lines of sight. In R. L. Gregory, J. Harris, P. Heard, and D. Rose (eds.), *The Artful Eye*, 339–352. Oxford: Oxford University Press.

Haysom, M. 2010. The double-axe: A contextual approach to the understanding of a Cretan symbol in the Neopalatial period. *Oxford Journal of Archaeology*, 29.1, 35–55.

2018. The find contexts of Knossian relief wall paintings: Some ramifications. In J. Becker, J. Jungfleisch and C. von Rüden (eds.), *Tracing Technoscapes: The Production of Bronze Age Wall Paintings in the Eastern Mediterranean*, 253–278. Leiden: Sidestone Press.

Heidegger, M. 2006. *Being and Time*. Oxford: Blackwell.

1967. *What Is a Thing? Translated by W.B. Barton, Jr., and Vera Deutsch, With an Analysis by Eugene T. Gendlin*. Chicago: H. Regnery Co.

Heimpel, W. 1968. *Tierbilder in der sumerischen Literatur*. Rome: Pontificium Institutum Biblicum.

Heise, U. K. 2003. From extinction to electronics: Dead frogs, live dinosaurs, and electric sheep. In C. Wolfe (ed.), *Zoontologies: The Question of the Animal*, 59–81. Minneapolis: University of Minnesota Press.

2009. The android and the animal. *PMLA*, 124.2, 503–510.

Helms, M. W. 1988. *Ulysses' Sail : An Ethnographic Odyssey of Power Knowledge and Geographical Distance*. Princeton, NJ: Princeton University Press.

Henare, A., Holbraad, M. and Wastell, S. (eds.). 2007. *Thinking through Things: Theorising Artefacts Ethnographically*. London: Routledge.

Henley, T., Rossano, M. and Kardas, E. (eds.). 2019. *Handbook of Cognitive Archaeology: Psychology in Prehistory*. New York: Routledge.

Herva, V.-P. 2006. Marvels of the system: Art, perception and engagement with the environment in Minoan Crete. *Archaeological Dialogues*, 13.2, 221–240.

Herzfeld, M 1985. *The Poetics of Manhood: Contest and Identity in a Cretan Mountain Village*. Princeton, NJ: Princeton University Press.

Hickman, J. 2008. Gold before the palaces: Crafting jewelry and social identity in Minoan Crete. *Publicly Accessible PennDissertations*. Paper 1540.

Higgins, R. A. 1979. *The Aegina Treasure: An Archaeological Mystery*. London: British Museum Publications.

Hitchcock, L. 2010. The big nowhere: A master of animals in the throne room at Knossos. In D. B. Counts and B. Arnold (eds.), *The Master of Animals in Old World Iconography*, 107–118. Budapest: Archaeolingua.

Hitchcock, L., and Koudounaris, P. 2002. Virtual discourse: Arthur Evans and the reconstructions of the Minoan palace at Knossos. In Y. Hamilakis (ed.), *Labyrinth Revisited: Rethinking "Minoan" Archaeology*, 40–58. Oxford: Oxbow.

Hodder, I. 2012. *Archaeological Theory Today*. Cambridge: Polity Press.

Hogarth, D. 1900/1901. Excavations at Zakro, Crete. *Annual of the British School at Athens*, 7, 121–149.

Hogarth, D. 1902. The Zakro sealings. *Journal of Hellenic Studies*, 22, 76–93.

Hood, S., 2005. Dating the Knossos frescoes. *BSA Studies*, 13, 45–81.

Hopwood, N. 2018. The keywords "generation" and "reproduction." In N. Hopwood, R. Flemming and L. Kassell (eds.), *Reproduction: Antiquity to the Present Day*, 287–304. Cambridge: Cambridge University Press.

Horrocks, G. C. 1980. The antiquity of the Greek epic tradition: Some new evidence. *Proceedings of the Cambridge Philological Society*, 26.206, 1–11.

Houston, D. C., and Copsey, J. A. 1994. Bone digestion and intestinal morphology of the Bearded Vulture. *Journal of Raptor Research*, 28.2, 73–78.

Hurowitz, V. A. 2003. The Mesopotamian god image, from womb to tomb. *Journal of the American Oriental Society*, 123.1, 147–157.

Hussein, A. 2018. The magic and the mundane: The function of "talismanic-class" stones in Minoan Crete. In M. Ameri, S. Costello, G. Jamison and S. Scott (eds.),*Seals and Sealing in the Ancient World: Case Studies from the Near East, Egypt, the Aegean, and South Asia*, 387–400. Cambridge: Cambridge University Press.

Hutchins, E. 2005. Material anchors for conceptual blends. *Journal of Pragmatics*, 37.10, 1555–1577.

Ihde, D. and Malafouris, L. 2019. Homo faber revisited: Postphenomenology and material engagement theory. *Philosophy & Technology*, 32.2, 195–214.

Immerwahr, S. 1990. *Aegean Painting in the Bronze Age*. University Park: Pennsylvania State University Press.

Ingold, T. 2000. *The Perception of the Environment: Essays on Livelihood, Dwelling and Skill*. London: Routledge.

2004. Culture on the ground: The world perceived through the feet. *Journal of Material Culture*, 9.3, 315–40.

Isaakidou, V. 2005. Bones from the labyrinth: Faunal evidence for management and consumption of animals at Neolithic and

Bronze Age Knossos, Crete. Doctoral thesis, University of London.

Janko, R. 1992. *The Iliad: A Commentary*. Vol. 4. Cambridge: Cambridge University Press.

Jasink, A. 2009. *Cretan Hieroglyphic Seals: A New Classification of Symbols and Ornamental/Filling Motifs*. Pisa: Fabrizio Serra.

Joy, J. 2009. Reinvigorating object biography: Reproducing the drama of object lives. *World Archaeology* 41.4, 540–556.

Kaiser, B. 1976. *Untersuchungen zum minoischen Relief*. Bonn: Rudolf Habelt Verlag.

Kantor, H. J. 1947. The Aegean and the Orient in the second millennium BC. *American Journal of Archaeology*, 51.1, 1–103.

1956. Syro-Palestinian ivories. *Journal of Near Eastern Studies*, 15.3, 153–174.

Karetsou, A. and Koehl, R. 2013. Cult object–image–emblem: A life-sized bull's head from the Juktas peak sanctuary. In R. Koehl (ed.), *Amilla: The Quest for Excellence. Studies Presented to Guenter Kopcke in Celebration of His 75th Birthday*, 135–143. Philadelphia: INSTAP Academic Press.

Keuls, E. C. 1978. *Plato and Greek Painting*, vol. 5. Leiden: Brill.

Killen, J. T. 1994. Thebes sealings, Knossos tablets and Mycenaean state banquets. *Bulletin of the Institute of Classical Studies*, 39, 67–84.

2000–2001. A note on Pylos Tablet Un 1482. *Minos*, 35–36, 385–389.

Knapp, A. B. and Van Dommelen, P. 2008. Past practices: Rethinking individuals and agents in archaeology. *Cambridge Archaeological Journal*, 18.1, 15–34.

Knappett, C. 2002. Photographs, skeuomorphs and marionettes: Some thoughts on mind, agency and object. *Journal of Material Culture* 7.1, 97–117.

2004. The affordances of things: A post-Gibsonian perspective on the relationality of mind and matter. In E. DeMarrais, C. Gosden and C. Renfrew (eds.), *Rethinking Materiality: The Engagement of Mind with the Material World*, 43–51. Cambridge: McDonald Institute for Archaeological Research.

2010. *Thinking through Material Culture: An Interdisciplinary Perspective*. Philadelphia: University of Pennsylvania Press.

2011. *An Archaeology of Interaction: Network Perspectives on Material Culture and Society*. Oxford: Oxford University Press.

2020. *Aegean Bronze Age Art: Meaning in the Making*. Cambridge: Cambridge University Press.

Knappett, C. and Malafouris, L. (eds.). 2008. *Material Agency: Towards a Non-Anthropocentric Approach*. New York: Springer.

Knappett, C., Malafouris, L. and Tomkins, P. 2010. Ceramics as containers. In D. Hicks and M. Beaudry (eds.), *The Oxford Handbook of Material Culture Studies*, 588–612. Oxford: Oxford University Press.

Koehl, R. 1986. The Chieftain Cup and a Minoan rite of passage. *Journal of Hellenic Studies*, 106, 99–110.

2000. Ritual context. In *The Palaikastro Kouros: A Minoan Chryselephantine Statuette and Its Aegean Bronze Age Context*, BSA Studies 6, 131–143. London: British School at Athens.

2006. *Aegean Bronze Age Rhyta*. Philadelphia: Institute for Aegean Prehistory Press.

2008. Minoan Kamares Ware in the Levant. In J. Aruz, K. Benzel and J. Evans (eds.), *Beyond Babylon: Art, Trade, and Diplomacy in the Second Millennium BC*, 59–60. New York: Metropolitan Museum of Art.

2016. The Chieftain Cup and beyond: More images relating to Minoan male "rites of passage." In R. Koehl (ed.), *Studies in Aegean Art and Culture: A New York Aegean Bronze Age Colloquium in Memory of Ellen N. Davis*, 113–131. Philadelphia: INSTAP Academic Press.

Kopanias, K. 2012. Exotic jewellery or magic objects? The use of imported Near Eastern seals in the Aegean. In M. L. Nosch and R. Laffineur (eds.), *Kosmos: Jewellery, Adornment and Textiles in the Aegean Bronze Age*, Aegaeum 33, 397–406. Liège: Université de Liège and University of Texas at Austin.

Kopytoff, I. 1986. The cultural biography of things: Commoditization as process. In A. Appadurai (ed.), *The Social Life of Things: Commodities in Cultural Perspective*, 64–91. Philadelphia: University of Pennsylvania Press.

Korzybski, A. 1958. *Science and Sanity: An Introduction to Non-Aristotelian Systems and General Semantics*, 4th ed. Lakeville, CT: Institute of General Semantics.

Kramer, S. N. 1969. Sumerian similes: A panoramic view of some of man's oldest literary images. *Journal of the American Oriental Society*, 89, 1–10.

Kriga, D. 2018. Appliquéd pottery decoration and stucco relief wall-paintings in Crete and Thera in the second millennium BC. In A. Vlachopoulos (ed.),*Paintbrushes (Χρωστήρες). Wall-Painting and Vase-Painting of the Second Millenium B.C. in Dialogue,*129–141. Athens : University of Ioannina/Hellenic Ministry of Culture and Sports Archaeological Receipts Fund.

Kristeva, J. 1982. *Powers of Horror: An Essay on Abjection*, trans. L. S. Roudiez. New York: Columbia University Press.

Krzyszkowska, O. 1988. Ivory in the Aegean Bronze Age: Elephant tusk or hippopotamus ivory? *British School at Athens*, 83, 209–234.

1991. The Enkomi warrior head reconsidered. *The Annual of the British School at Athens*, 86, 107–120.

2005. *Aegean Seals: An Introduction*. London: Institute of Classical Studies, University of London.

2010. Impressions of the natural world: Landscape in Aegean Glyptic. In P. Warren and O. Krzyszkowska (eds.), *Cretan Offerings: Studies in Honour of Peter Warren*, 169–187. London: British School at Athens.

2012. Seals from the Petras cemetery: A preliminary overview. In M. Tsipopoulou (ed.), *Petras, Siteia: 25 Years of Excavations and Studies*, 145–160. [Athens]: Monographs of the Danish Institute at Athens.

2015. Why were cats different? Script and imagery in Middle Minoan II glyptic. In C. F. Macdonald, E. Hatzaki and S. Andreou (eds.), *The Great Islands: Studies of Crete and Cyprus Presented to Gerald Cadogan*, 100–106. Athens: Kapon Editions.

2016. Warding off evil: Apotropaic practice and imagery in the Bronze Age Aegean. In E. Alram-Stern, F. Blakolmer, S. Deger-Jalkotzy, R. Laffineur and J. Weilhartner (eds.), *Metaphysis, Ritual, Myth and Symbolism in the Aegean Bronze Age*, 115–122. Aegaeum, 39. Leuven: Peeters.

2017. Further seals from the cemetery at Petras. In M. Tsipopoúlou (ed.). *Petras, Siteia: The Pre-and Proto-Palatial Cemetery in Context*, 143–157. Athens: Danish Institute at Athens.

Küchler, S. and Carroll, T. 2020. *A Return to the Object: Alfred Gell, Art, and Social Theory*. Oxford: Routledge.

Laffineur, R. 1986. Fécondité et pratiques funéraires en Égée à l'âge du Bronze. In A. Bonanno (ed.), *Archaeology and Fertility Cult in the Ancient Mediterranean: Papers Presented at the First International Conference on Archaeology of the Ancient Mediterranean, University of Malta, 2–5 September 1985*, 79–86. Amsterdam: John Benjamins Publishing.

Laffineur, R. and Palaima, T. (eds.). 2021. *Zoia: Animal–Human Interactions in the Aegean Middle and Late Bronze Age: Proceedings of the 18th International Aegean Conference Originally to Be Held at the Program in Aegean Scripts and Prehistory in the Department of Classics the University of Texas at Austin May 28–31 2020*. Leuven: Peeters.

Latour, B. 1990. On actor-network theory. A few clarifications, plus more than a few complications. *Philosophia*, 25.3, 47–64.

1993. *We Have Never Been Modern*. Cambridge, MA: Harvard University Press.

2007. *Reassembling the Aocial: An Introduction to Actor-Network-Theory*. Oxford: Oxford University Press.

2013. *An Inquiry into Modes of Existence. An Anthropology of the Moderns*. Cambridge, MA: Harvard University Press.

Lattimore, R. 2011. *The Iliad of Homer*. Chicago: University of Chicago Press.

Lazarou, A. 2019. Prehistoric gorgoneia: A critical reassessment. *Studia Antiqua et Archaeologica*, 25.2, 353–385.

Lefebvre, H. 1991. *The Production of Space*. Oxford: Blackwell.

Lega, C., Raia, P., Rook, L. and Fulgione, D. 2016. Size matters: A comparative analysis of pig domestication. *The Holocene*, 26.2, 327–332.

Legarra Herrero, B. 2014. *Mortuary Behavior and Social Trajectories in Pre- and Protopalatial Crete*. Philadelphia: INSTAP Academic Press.

Lemonnier, P. 2016. *Mundane Objects: Materiality and Non-Verbal Communication*. London: Routledge.

Letesson, Q. and Driessen, J. 2020. "On the house": A diachronic look on the configuration of Minoan social relationships. In M. Relaki and J. Driessen (eds.), *OIKOS: Archaeological Approaches to House Societies in the Bronze Age Aegean*, 7–24. Louvain-la-Neuve: Presses Universitaires de Louvain.

Levi, D. 1958. L'archivio di cretule a Festòs. *ASAtene*, 35–36, 7–92.

Logue, W. 2004. Set in stone: The role of relief-carved stone vessels in Neopalatial Minoan elite propaganda. *Annual of the British School at Athens*, 99, 149–172.

Long, C. 1978. The Lasithi dagger. *American Journal of Archaeology*, 82.1, 35–46.

Lonsdale, S. 1990. *Creatures of Speech: Lion, Herding, and Hunting Similes in the Iliad*. Stuttgart: Teubner.

Lorimer, H. 1950. *Homer and the Monuments*. London: Macmillan & Co.

MacGillivray, J. A., Driessen, J. M. and Sackett, L. H. 2000. *The Palaikastro Kouros: A Minoan Chryselephantine Statuette and Its Aegean Bronze Age Context*. Athens: British School at Athens.

Malafouris, L. 2008. Is it 'me' or is it 'mine'? The Mycenaean sword as a body-part. In J. Robb and D. Boric (eds.), *Past Bodies*, 115–123. Oxford: Oxbow.

2010. Metaplasticity and the human becoming: Principles of neuroarchaeology. *Journal of Anthropological Sciences*, 88.4, 49–72.

2013. *How Things Shape the Mind: A Theory of Material Engagement*. Cambridge, MA: MIT Press.

2020. Thinking as "thinging": Psychology with things. *Current Directions in Psychological Science*, 29.1, 3–8.

Marchant, J. 2017. This 3,500-Year-Old Greek tomb upended what we thought we knew about the roots of Western civilization. *Smithsonian Magazine* (January), 3–8.

Marinatos, N. 1984. *Art and Religion in Thera: Reconstructing a Bronze Age Society*. Athens: D. & I. Mathioulakis.

1986. *Minoan Sacrificial Ritual: Cult Practice and Symbolism*. Göteborg: Distributor P. Åström.

1993. *Minoan Religion: Ritual, Image, and Symbol*. Columbia: University of South Carolina Press.

Marinatos, S. 1933–1935. Ένκαι Δέκατη Αρχαιολογική Περιφέρεια (Κρήτη), *ArchDelt* 15, 49–51.

1969. *Excavations at Thera II (1968 Season)*. Athens: Hē en Athēnais Archaiologikē Hetaireia.

1972. *Excavations at Thera V (1971 Season)*. Athens: Hē en Athēnais Archaiologikē Hetaireia.

1999. Excavations at Thera III. In *Excavations at Thera I–III, 1967–1969 Seasons*. Athens: The Archaeological Society at Athens Library, 1–68.

Marthari, M. 1987. The local pottery wares with painted decoration from the volcanic destruction level of Akrotiri, Thera: A preliminary report. *American Archaeology*, 3, 359–379.

2018. "The attraction of the pictorial" reconsidered: Pottery and wall-paintings in LC I Thera in the light of the latest research. In A. Vlachopoulos (ed.), *Paintbrushes (Χρωστήρες). Wall-Painting and Vase-Painting of the Second Millenium* B.C. *in Dialogue*, 205–221. Athens : University of Ioannina/Hellenic Ministry of Culture and Sports Archaeological Receipts Fund.

Masseti M. 1980. Le scimmie azzurre: A fauna etiopica degli affreschi minoici di Santorino (Thera). *Mondo archeologico*, 51, 32–37.

2003. Taxonomic and behavioural aspects of the representation of mammals in Aegean Bronze Age art. In E. Kotjabopoulou, Y. Hamilakis, P. Halstead, C. Gamble and P. Elefanti (eds.), *Zooarchaeology in Greece. Recent Advances, BSA*

Studies, 273–281. London: British School at Athens.

2021. An analysis of recent literature regarding the Minoan "blue monkeys" represented in Aegean Bronze Age art. *Journal of Anthropological Sciences*, 99, 1–4.

Masson, E. 2007. Greek and Semitic languages: Early contacts. In A.-F. Christidis (ed.), *A History of Ancient Greek: From the Beginnings to Late Antiquity*, 733–737. Cambridge: Cambridge University Press.

Mathioudaki, I. 2018. The pottery deposit from the Houses of the Fallen Blocks and the Sacrificed Oxen at the south-eastern corner of the palace of Knossos. *British School at Athens*, 113, 19–73.

Mauss, M. 1979. Body techniques. In *Sociology and Psychology: Essays*, trans. Ben Brewster, 95–123. London: Routledge.

Mayer, J. 2009. Taxonomy and history of wild pigs in the United States. In J. Beasley, S. Ditchkoff, J. Mayer, M. Smith and K. Vercauteren (eds.), *Wild Pigs: Biology, Damage, Control Techniques and Management*, SRNL-RP-2009-00869, 5–23. Washington, DC: Department of Defense.

McEnroe, J. 1995. Sir Arthur Evans and Edwardian archaeology. *Classical Bulletin*, 71.1, 3–18.

2002. Cretan questions: Politics and archaeology 1898–1913. In Y. Hamilakis (ed.), *Labyrinth Revisited: Rethinking "Minoan" Archaeology*, 59–72. Oxford: Oxbow.

McGowan, E. 2011. *Ambiguity and Minoan Neopalatial Seal Imagery*. Uppsala: Åströms Förlag.

2018. Cryptic glyptic: Multivalency in Minoan glyptic imagery. In G. Jamison, M. Ameri, S. Scott and S. Kielt Costello (eds.), *Seals and Sealing in the Ancient World: Case Studies from the Near East, Egypt, the Aegean, and South Asia*, 368–386. Cambridge: Cambridge University Press.

Melena, J. L. 2000–2001. Joins and quasi-joins of fragments in the Linear B tablets from Pylos. *Minos*, 35–36, 371–384.

Merrillees, R. 2003. The first appearances of Kamares ware in the Levant. *Ägypten und Levante/Egypt and the Levant*, 13, 127–142.

Meskell, L. 2000. Writing the body in archaeology. In A. Rautman (ed.), *Reading the Body: Representations and Remains in the Archaeological Record*, 13–21. Philadelphia: University of Pennsylvania Press.

Meskell, L. and Joyce, R. A. 2003. *Embodied Lives: Figuring Ancient Maya and Egyptian Experience*. London: Routledge.

Michaelidis P. 1995. Ägyptische Sphinx aus Malia. *Prähistorische Zeitschrift*, 70.1, 90–95

Michailidou, A 2001. The indications of literacy in Bronze Age Thera. *Minos*, 35, 7–30.

Mikrakis, M. 2011. Technologies of sound across Aegean crafts and Mediterranean cultures. In A. Brysbaert (ed.), *Tracing Prehistoric Social Networks through Technology: A Diachronic Perspective on the Aegean*, 48–71. London: Routledge.

Militello, P. 2018. Wall-painting and vase-painting: The case of Middle Minoan III Phaistos. A. Vlachopoulos (ed.), *Paintbrushes (Χρωστήρες). Wall-Painting and Vase-Painting of the Second Millenium B.C. in Dialogue*, 119–127. Athens : University of Ioannina/Hellenic Ministry of Culture and Sports Archaeological Receipts Fund.

Miller, D. 2008. *The Comfort of Things*. Cambridge: Polity Press.

2010. *Stuff*. Cambridge: Polity Press.

Miller, E. B. 1984. Zoomorphic Vases in the Bronze Age Aegean. New York University.

Mina, M. 2008. Carving out gender in the prehistoric Aegean: Anthropomorphic figurines of the Neolithic and Early Bronze Age. *Journal of Mediterranean Archaeology*, 21.2, 213–239.

Mina, M., Triantaphyllou, S. and Papadatos, Y. (eds.). 2016. *An Archaeology of Prehistoric Bodies and Embodied Identities in the Eastern Mediterranean*. Oxford: Oxbow.

Minchin, E. 2001. *Homer and the Resources of Memory: Some Applications of Cognitive Theory to the Iliad and the Odyssey*. Oxford: Oxford University Press.

Moak, M. 2000. The Palaikastro Kouros. In *The Palaikastro Kouros: A Minoan Chryselephantine Statuette and Its Aegean Bronze Age Context*, 65–83. BSA Studies, 6. London: British School at Athens.

Mödlinger, M. 2013. From Greek boar's-tusk helmets to the first European metal helmets: New approaches on development and chronology. *Oxford Journal of Archaeology*, 32.4, 391–412.

Molloy, B. P. C. 2012. Martial Minoans? War as social process, practice and event in Bronze Age Crete. *Annual of the British School at Athens*, 107, 87–142.

Momigliano, N. and Farnoux, A. (eds.). 2017. *Cretomania: Modern Desires for the Minoan Past*. London: Routledge.

Montecchi, B. 2020. Distribution and functions of Minoan inscribed clay vessels and the consequences for the question of literacy in the Bronze Age Aegean. *Studi Micenei ed Egeo-Anatolici*, 6, 49–65.

Moody, J. 2012. Hinterlands and hinterseas: resources and production zones in Bronze Age and Iron Age Crete. In G. Cadogan, M. Iacovou, K. Kopaka and J. Whitley (eds.), *Parallel Lives: Ancient Island Societies in Crete and Cyprus*, 233–271. BSA Studies. London: British School at Athens.

Morgan, L. 1988. *The Miniature Wall Paintings of Thera: A Study in Aegean Culture and Iconography*. Cambridge: Cambridge University Press.

1989. Ambiguity and interpretation. In I. Pini (ed.), *Fragen und Probleme der bronzezeitlichen ägäischen Glyptik*, CMS Beiheft, 3, 145–161. Berlin: Mann.

1990. Island iconography: Thera, Kea, Milos. In D. A. Hardy (ed.), *Thera and the Aegean World III.1*, 252–266. London: Thera and the Aegean World.

1995a. Frontal face and the symbolism of death in Aegean Glyptic. In W. Müller (ed.), *Sceaux minoens et mycéniens*, 135–149. Berlin: Mann.

1995b. Of animals and men: The symbolic parallel. *Bulletin of the Institute of Classical Studies*, 40, 171–184.

1998. Power of the beast: Human–animal symbolism in Egyptian and Aegean art. *Ägypten und Levante/Egypt and the Levant*, 7, 17–31.

2005. The cult centre at Mycenae and the duality of life and death. *British School at Athens Studies*, 13, 159–171.

2010. An Aegean griffin in Egypt: The hunt frieze at Tell el-Dabca. *Ägypten und Levante/Egypt and the Levant*, 20: 303–323.

Morris, C. 1990. In pursuit of the white tusked boar: Aspects of hunting in Mycenaean society. In R. Hägg, G. Nordquist and A. Persson (eds.), *Celebrations of Death and Divinity in the Bronze Age Argolid: Proceedings of the Sixth International Symposium at the Swedish Institute at Athens*, 149–156. Stockholm: Svenska institutet i Athen.

Morris, C. and Peatfield, A. 2002. Feeling through the body: Gesture in Cretan Bronze Age religion. In Y. Hamilakis, M. Pluciennik and S. Tarlow (eds.), *Thinking through the Body: Archaeologies of Corporeality*, 105–120. New York: Kluwer Academic/Plenum.

2013. Cretan peak sanctuary figurines: 3D scanning project. *Les Carnets de l'ACoSt* [online], 10.

Morris, S. P. 1989. A tale of two cities: The miniature frescoes from Thera and the origins of Greek poetry. *American Journal of Archaeology*, 93.4, 511–535.

1995. *Daidalos and the Origins of Greek Art*. Princeton, NJ: Princeton University Press.

Mountjoy, P. A. 1983. The Ephyraean goblet reviewed. *British School at Athens*, 78, 265–271.

1984. The Marine Style pottery of LMIB/LHIIA: Towards a corpus. *British School at Athens*, 79, 161–219.

1985. Ritual associations for LM I B marine style vases. *Bulletin de Correspondance Héllenique Supplément* 11, 231–242.

Müller, W. (ed.). 1995. *Sceaux minoens et mycéniens*. Berlin: Mann.

Murphy, J. 1998. Ideology, rites, and rituals: A view of Prepalatial Minoan tholoi. In K. Branigan (ed.), *Cemetery and Society in the Aegean Bronze Age*, 27–40. Sheffield: Sheffield Academic Press.

2001. Private life, public death: Contrasts in Minoan Prepalatial society. In A. Karetsou (ed.), *Pepragmena tou H' Diethnous*

Kretologikou Synedriou, A2, 405–411. Herakleion: Εταιρία Κρητικών Ιστορικών Μελετών.

2009. Gods in the house? Religious rituals in the settlements of south central Crete. *Hesperia Supplements* 42, 11–17.

Murphy, J. (ed.). 2011. *Prehistoric Crete: Regional and Diachronic Studies on Mortuary Systems*. Philadephia: INSTAP Academic Press.

Murphy, J. (ed.). 2020. *Death in Late Bronze Age Greece: Variations on a Theme*. Oxford: Oxford University Press.

Mylonas, G. 1966. *Mycenae and the Mycenaean Age*. Princeton, NJ: Princeton University Press.

1983. *Mycenae, Rich in Gold*. Athens: Ekdotike Athenon.

Nafplioti, A. 2018. Isotope analysis as a tool for reconstructing past life histories. In L. Niesiołowski-Spanò, M. Węcowski and L. Niesiolowski-Spano (eds.), *North-eastern Mediterranean in the End of the Late Bronze and Beginning of Iron Age*, 451–465. Wiesbaden: Harrassowitz.

Nafplioti, A., Driessen, J., Schmitt, A. and Crevecoeur, I. 2021. Mobile (after-)lifeways: People at Pre- and Protopalatial Sissi (Crete). *Journal of Archaeological Science: Reports*, 35, 102718.

Nagy, G. 1996. *Poetry as Performance: Homer and Beyond*. Cambridge: Cambridge University Press.

1998. An evolutionary model for the making of Homeric poetry: Comparative perspectives. In J. Carter and S. Morris (eds.), *The Ages of Homer: A Tribute to Emily Townsend Vermeule*, 163–179. Austin: University of Texas Press.

National Centers for Environmental Information, National Oceanic and Atmospheric Administration. n.d. Drought and livestock [online] https://tinyurl.com/34rwd2hu.

Nelson, M. 2001. The architecture of Epano Englianos, Greece. PhD diss., University of Toronto.

Niemeier, W. D. 1985. *Die Palaststilkeramik von Knossos: Stil, Chronologie und historischer Kontext*. Archäologische Forschungen, 13. Berlin: Mann.

1987. On the function of the "throne room" in the palace at Knossos. In R. Hägg and N. Marinatos (eds.), *The Function of the Minoan Palaces*, 163–168. Stockholm: Åströms/Svenska institutet i Athen.

Nikolaidou, M. 2002. Palaces with faces in Protopalatial Crete: Looking for the people in the first Minoan states. In Y. Hamilakis (ed.), *Labyrinth Revisited: Rethinking "Minoan" Archaeology*, 74–97. Oxford: Oxbow.

Nikolakopoulou, I. 2010. Middle Cycladic iconography: A social context for "a new chapter in Aegean art." In O. Krzyszkowska (ed.), *Cretan Offerings: Studies in Honour of Peter Warren*, 213–222. London: British School at Athens.

2018. The painter's brush and how to use it: Elementary and advanced lessons from Akrotiri iconography. In A. Vlachopoulos (ed.), *Paintbrushes (Χρωστήρες): Wall-Painting and Vase-Painting of the Second Millenium* B.C. *in Dialogue*, 195–204. Athens: University of Ioannina/Hellenic Ministry of Culture and Sports Archaeological Receipts Fund.

Nikolakopoulou, I., Georma, F., Moschou, A. and Sofianou, P. 2008. Trapped in the middle: New stratigraphic and ceramic evidence from Middle Cycladic Akrotiri. In N. J. Brodie, J. Doole, G. Gavalas and C. Renfrew (eds.), *Horizon. Ορίζων: A Colloquium on the Prehistory of the Cyclades, University of Cambridge 25–28 March 2004*, 311–324. Cambridge: McDonald Institute for Archaeological Research.

Noë, A. 2004. *Action in Perception*. Cambridge, MA: MIT Press.

Nowicki, K. 1996. Lasithi (Crete): One hundred years of archaeological research. *Aegean Archaeology*, 3, 27–47.

Olsen, B. 1998. Women, children and the family in the Late Aegean Bronze Age: Differences in Minoan and Mycenaean constructions of gender. *World Archaeology*, 29.3, 380–392.

Onassoglou, A. 1985. *Die "Talismanischen" Siegel*. Corpus der minoischen und mykenischen Siegel Beiheft, 2. Berlin: Mann.

Palaima, T. G. 1989. Perspectives on the Pylos oxen tablets: Textual (and archaeological) evidence for the use and management of oxen in Late Bronze Age Messenia (and Crete). In T. Palaima, C. W. Shelmerdine and P. H. Ilievski (eds.), *Studia Mycenaea (1988)*, 85–124. Skopje: Ziva Antika.

2011. Scribes, scribal hands and palaeography. In Y. Duhoux and A. Morpurgo Davies (eds.), *A Companion to Linear B: Mycenaean Greek Texts and Their World*, vol. 2, 33–136. Leuven: Peeters.

Paliou, E. and Bevan, A., 2016. Evolving settlement patterns, spatial interaction and the socio-political organisation of late Prepalatial south-central Crete. *Journal of Anthropological Archaeology*, 42, 184–197.

Palyvou, C. 1990. Architectural design at Late Cycladic Akrotiri. In D. Hardy, C. Doumas, Y. Sakellarakis and P. Warren (eds.), *Thera and the Aegean World III (1)*, 44–56. London: Thera Foundation.

2000. Concepts of space in Aegean Bronze Age art and architecture. In S. Sherratt (ed.), *The Wall Paintings of Thera: Proceedings of the First International Symposium, Thera, 30 August–4 September 1997*, vol. 1, 413–435. Piraeus: Petros M. Nomikos and the Thera Foundation.

2012. Wall painting and architecture in the Aegean Bronze Age. In D. Panagiotopoulos and U. Günkel-Maschek (eds.), *Minoan Realities: Approaches to Images, Architecture, and Society in the Aegean Bronze Age*, 9–26. Aegis, 5. Louvain-la-Neuve: Presses universitaires de Louvain.

Panagiotopoulos, D. 2011. The stirring sea: Conceptualising transculturality in the Late Bronze Age eastern Mediterranean. In K. Duistermaat, I. Regulski, G. Jennes and L. Weiss (eds.), *Intercultural Contacts in the Ancient Mediterranean: Proceedings of the International Conference at the Netherlands-Flemish Institute in Cairo, 25th to 29th October 2008*, 31–51. Leuven: Peeters.

2020. Ανασκαφή Κουμάσας. *Prakt*, 175, 295–311.

Papadatos, Y. 2005. *Tholos Tomb Gamma: A Prepalatial Tholos Tomb at Phourni,* *Archanes*. Philadelphia: INSTAP Academic Press.

2011. Οικιακή οργάνωση και χρήσεις χώρων στο Νεολιθικό-Πρωτομινωικό οικισμό στην Κεφάλα Πετρά, Σητείας. In *Proceedings of the 10th International Cretological Congress*, vol. A., 365–378. Chania: φιλολογικός Σύλλογος Χανίων "ο Χρυσόστομος".

2020. The identification of houses in Prepalatial Crete. In J. Driessen and M. Relaki (eds.), *OIKOS: Archaeological Approaches to House Societies in the Bronze Age Aegean*, 51–62. Aegis, 19. Louvain-la-Neuve: Presses universitaires de Louvain.

Papadatos, Y. and Sofianou, C. 2012. Πολιτισμική ομοιογένεια και διαφοροποίηση στην Προανακτορική Κρήτη: νέα δεδομένα από τις ανασκαφές πρωτομινωικών νεκροταφείων στην επαρχία Σητείας, in M. Andrianakis, P. Varthalitou and I. Tzachili (eds.), *Αρχαιολογικό έργο Κρήτης 2: πρακτικά της 2ης συνάντησης, Ρέθυμνο, 26–28 Νοεμβρίου 2010*, 48–59. Rethymno: Επιλέξτε τιμή Αρχαιολογικό Ινστιτούτο Κρητολογικών Σπουδών.

Papadopoulos, A. 2008. The distribution of the Late Helladic IIIA–B ivory helmeted heads. *Talanta*, 40, 7–24.

Papadopoulos, J. K. 2005. Inventing the Minoans: Archaeology, modernity and the quest for European identity. *Journal of Mediterranean Archaeology*, 18.1, 87–149.

Papageorgiou, I., 2018. The iconographic subject of the hunt in the Cyclades and Crete in the second millennium BC: Sounds and echoes in the art of wall-painting and vase-painting. In A. Vlachopoulos (ed.), *Paintbrushes (Χρωστήρες): Wall-Painting and Vase-Painting of the Second Millenium B. C. in Dialogue*, 301–313. Athens: University of Ioannina/Hellenic Ministry of Culture and Sports Archaeological Receipts Fund.

Papagiannopoulou, A. 2008. From pots to pictures: Middle Cycladic figurative art from Akrotiri, Thera. In N. J. Brodie, J. Doole, G. Gavalas and C. Renfrew (eds.), *Horizon. Ορίζων: A Colloquium on the Prehistory of the*

Cyclades, University of Cambridge 25–28 March 2004, 433–449. Cambridge: McDonald Institute for Archaeological Research.

2018. The beginnings of an island narration. Pictorial pottery and wall-paintings of the second millennium BC. In A. Vlachopoulos (ed.), *Paintbrushes (Χρωστήρες): Wall-Painting and Vase-Painting of the Second Millenium B.C. in Dialogue*, 163–181. Athens: University of Ioannina/ Hellenic Ministry of Culture and Sports Archaeological Receipts Fund.

Pareja M. N. 2017 *Monkey and Ape Iconography in Aegean Art*. Uppsala: Astrom.

Pareja M. N., McKinney T., Mayhew J. A. et al. 2020. A new identification of the monkeys depicted in a Bronze Age wall painting from Akrotiri, Thera. *Primates*, 61, 159–168.

Pareja, M. N., McKinney, T. and Setchell, J. M. 2020. Aegean monkeys and the importance of crossdisciplinary collaboration in archae-oprimatology: A reply to Urbani and Youlatos. *Primates*, 61, 767–774.

Payne, M. 2010. *The Animal Part: Human and Other Animals in the Poetic Imagination*. Chicago: University of Chicago Press.

Peatfield, A. 1987. Palace and peak: The political and religious relationship between palaces and peak sanctuaries. In R. Hägg and N. Marinatos (eds.), *The Function of the Minoan Palaces: Proceedings of the Fourth International Symposium at the Swedish Institute in Athens, 10–16 June, 1984*. Sweden: Svenska institutet i Athen.

1990. Minoan peak sanctuaries: History and society. *Opuscula Atheniensa*, 17, 117–131.

1995. Water, fertility, and purification in Minoan religion. *Bulletin of the Institute for Classical Studies Supplement*, 63, 217–227.

Pendlebury, J. 1939. *The Archaeology of Crete*. London: Methuen.

Pendlebury, H. W., Pendlebury, J. D. S. and Money-Coutts, M. B. 1935. Excavations in the plain of Lasithi: I. The cave of Trapeza. *British School at Athens*, 36, 5–131.

Peters, M. 2008. Colour use and symbolism in Bronze Age Crete: Exploring social and technological relationships. In C. Jackson and E.C. Wager (eds.), *Vitreous Materials in the Late Bronze Age Aegean: A Window to the East Mediterranean World*, 187–208. Oxford: Oxbow.

Phillips, R. 2014. Abjection. *Transgender Studies Quarterly*, 1.1–2, 19–21.

Phillips, J. 2008. *Aegyptiaca on the Island of Crete in Their Chronological Context: A Critical Review*. Vienna: Verlag der Österreichischen Akademie der Wissenschaften.

Pini, I. 1985. Das Motiv des Löwenüberfalls in der spätminoischen und mykenischen Glyptik. In P. Darcque and J.-C. Poursat (eds.), *L'iconographie Minoenne: Actes de la Table Ronde d'Athènes (21–22 avril 1983)*, 153–66. Paris: École française d'Athènes.

1990. Eine frühkretische Siegelwerkstatt? In *Πεπραγμένα του ΣΤ´ Διεθνούς Κρητολογικού Συνεδρίου Α2*, 115–127. Chania: φιλολογικός Σύλλογος Χανίων "ο Χρυσόστομος".

1992. Towards a standardization of termin-ology: Problems of description and identifi-cation. In R. Laffineur and J. Crowley (eds.), *EIKON. Aegean Bronze Age Iconography: Shaping a Methodology. Proceedings of the 4th International Aegean Conference*, 11–19. Aegaeum, 8. Liège: Université de Liège.

1995. Bemerkungen zur Datierung von Löwendarstellungen der spätminoischen Weichsteinglyptik. In W. Müller (ed.), *Sceaux minoens et mycéniens*, 193–207. Berlin: Mann.

1999. Minoische "Porträts"? In P. Betancourt, V. Karageorghis, R. Laffineur and W.-D. Niemeier (eds.), *Meletemata: Studies in Aegean Archaeology Presented to Malcolm H. Wiener as He Enters His 65th Year*, vol. 3. Aegaeum, 20. Liège: Université de Liège and University of Texas at Austin.

Pinker, S. 1997. *How the Mind Works*. New York: Norton & Company.

Platon, N. 1947. Ὁ κροκοσυλλέκτης πίθηκος: Συμβολή εἰς τὴν σπουδὴν της Μινωϊκῆς τοιχογραφίας. *Kretika chronika: Keimena kai meletai tes kretikes istorias*, 1, 505–524.

1957. Ἡ ἀρχαιολογικὴ κίνησις ἐν Κρήτῃ κατὰ τὸ ἔτος 1954. *Kretika chronika: Keimena kai meletai tes kretikes istorias*, 11, 339–340.

Pluta, K. 2011. Aegean Bronze Age literacy and its consequences. PhD diss., University of Texas at Austin.

Poulianos, A. N. 1972. The discovery of the first known victim of Thera's Bronze Age eruption. *Archaeology*, 25.3, 229–230.

Poursat, J.C. 1973. Le Sphinx minoen: Un nouveau document. In G. Rizza (ed.), *Antichità Cretesi: Studi in Onore di Doro Levi*, 111–114. Catania: Università di Catania, Istituto di archeologia.

1976. Notes d'iconographie préhellénique: Dragons et crocodiles. *Bulletin de Correspondance Héllenique*, 100.1, 461–474.

2008. *L'art égéen, vol. 1: Grèce, Cyclades, Crète jusqu'au milieu du IIe millénaire av. J.-C.* Paris: Picard.

2014. *L'art égéen, vol. 2: Mycènes et le monde mycénien.* Paris: Picard.

2022. *The Art and Archaeology of the Aegean Bronze Age: A History*, trans. C. Knappett. Cambridge: Cambridge University Press.

Prytulak, M. 1982. Weapons on the Thera ships? *International Journal of Nautical Archaeology*, 11.1, 3–6.

Pulak, C. 1996. Analysis of the weight assemblages from the Late Bronze Age shipwrecks at Uluburun and Cape Gelidonya, Turkey. PhD diss., Texas A&M University.

Rackham, O. and Moody, J. 1996. *The Making of the Cretan Landscape.* Manchester: Manchester University Press.

Raymond, A. 2001. Kamares ware (and Minoans?) at Miletus. *Aegean Archaeology*, 5, 19–26.

Reese, D. 2016. Wild cattle at Khania. In E. Hallager and B. P. Hallager (eds.), *The Greek–Swedish Excavations at the Agia Aikaterini Square, Kastelli, Khania, 1970–1987, 2001, 2005, and 2008 V, The Late Minoan IIIA:1 and II Settlements*, 393–395. Stockholm: Åströms.

Rehak, P. 1984. New observations on the Mycenaean "warrior goddess." *Archäologischer Anzeiger*, 4, 535–545.

1992. Minoan vessels with figure-eight shields: Antecedents to the Knossos throneroom alabastra. *Opuscula Atheniensa*, 19, 115–124.

1995. The use and destruction of Minoan stone bull's head rhyta. In R. Laffineur and W.-D. Niemeier (eds.), *Politeia: Society and State in the Aegean Bronze Age*, 435–460. Liège: Université de Liège.

1999. The monkey frieze from Xeste 3, room 4: Reconstruction and interpretation. In P. Betancourt, V. Karageorghis, R. Laffienur, and W.-D. Niemeier (eds.), *Meletemata: Studies in Aegean Archaeology Presented to Malcolm H. Wiener as He Enters His 65th Year*, 705–709. Aegaeum, 20. Liège: Université de Liège and University of Texas at Austin.

2002. Imag(in)ing a women's world in Bronze Age Greece: The frescoes from Xeste 3 at Akrotiri, Thera. In N. Rabinowitz and L. Auanger (eds.), *Among Women: From the Homosocial to the Homoerotic in the Ancient World*, 34–59. Austin: University of Texas Press.

Relaki, M. 2004. Constructing a region: The contested landscapes of Prepalatial Mesara. In J. Barrett and P. Halstead (eds.), *The Emergence of Civilisation Revisited*, 170–188. Sheffield Studies in Aegean Archaeology, 6. Oxford: Oxbow.

2009. Rethinking administration and seal use in third millennium Crete. *Cretica Antica*, 10.2, 353–372.

Renfrew, C. 1998. Word of Minos: The Minoan contribution to Mycenaean Greek and the linguistic geography of the Bronze Age Aegean. *Cambridge Archaeological Journal*, 8.2, 239–264.

Renfrew, C. and Zubrow, E. B. (eds.). 1994. *The Ancient Mind: Elements of Cognitive Archaeology.* Cambridge: Cambridge University Press.

Renfrew, C., Frith, C. D. and Malafouris, L. 2009. *The Sapient Mind: Archaeology Meets Neuroscience.* Oxford: Oxford University Press.

Reusch, H. 1958. Zum Wandschmuck des Thronsaales in Knossos. In E. Grumach (ed.), *Minoica: Festschrift zum 80. Geburtstag von Johannes Sundwall*, 334–56. Berlin: Akademie-Verlag.

Rhyne, N. A. 1970. The Aegean animal style: A study of the lion, griffin, and sphinx. PhD diss., University of North Carolina at Chapel Hill.

Ruijgh, C. J. 1995. D'Homère aux origines proto-mycéniennes de la tradition épique. In J. P. Crielaard (ed.), *Homeric Questions*, 1–96. Leiden: Brill.

2011. Mycenaean and Homeric language. In Y. Duhoux and A. Morpurgo Davies (eds.), *A Companion to Linear B: Mycenaean Greek Texts and Their World*, vol. 2, 253–98. Leuven: Peeters.

Runwal, P. 2020. Gravity gives these birds the drop on tough-to-crack foods. Audubon.org (February 12). www.audubon.org/news/gravity-gives-these-birds-drop-tough-crack-foods.

Ruskin, J. 1971 [1857]. *The Elements of Drawing*. New York: Dover Art Instruction.

Rutter, J. 1969. Horned objects in Anatolia and the Near East and possible connexions with the Minoan "horns of consecration." *Anatolian Studies*, 19, 147–177.

2003. Children in Aegean prehistory. In J. Neils and J. H. Oakley (eds.), *Coming of Age in Ancient Greece: Images of Childhood from the Classical Past*, 30–57. New Haven, CT: Yale University Press.

Saha, P. 2015. Sketch: The Lammergeier. National Audubon Society, October 23; www.audubon.org/news/the-lammergeier-0.

Sakellarakis, G. and Sapouna-Sakellaraki, E. 1997. *Archanes: Minoan Crete in a New Light*. 2 vols. Athens: Ammos.

Sakellarakis, Y. and Sapouna-Sakellaraki, E. 1981. Drama of death in a Minoan temple. *National Geographic*, 159.2, 205–222.

Sanavia, A. 2018. Painted parading lions on a MMIB ceremonial basin: A case of symbolic transference and memory of an emblem in early Protopalatial Phaistos. Poster at the 17th International Aegean Conference "Μνήμη/Mneme Past and Memory in the Aegean Bronze Age." Udine-Venice.

Sapouna-Sakellaraki, E. 1994. Minoan art. In Y. Sakellarakis (ed.), *The Dawn of Greek Art*, 131–217. Athens: Ekdotike Athenon.

Sbonias, K. 1995. *Frühkretische Siegel: Ansätze für eine Interpretation der sozial-politischen Entwicklung auf Kreta während der Frühbronzezeit*. Oxford: Tempus Reparatum.

Scasta, J., Lalman, D. and Henderson, L. 2016. Drought mitigation for grazing operations: Matching the animal to the environment. *Rangelands*, 38.4, 204–210.

Schliemann, H. 1878. *Mycenae: A Narrative of Researches and Discoveries of Mycenae and Tiryns*. London: Murray.

Schnitzler, A. 2011. Past and present distribution of the North African–Asian Lion subgroup: A review. *Mammal Review*, 41.3, 220–243.

Scobie, A. 1978. The origins of "centaurs." *Folklore*, 89.2, 142–147.

Schoep, I. 1999. The origins of writing and administration on Crete. *Oxford Journal of Archaeology*, 18.3, 265–276.

2002. Social and political organization on Crete in the Proto-Palatial period: The case of Middle Minoan II Malia. *Journal of Mediterranean Archaeology*, 15.1, 101–132.

2006. Looking beyond the first palaces: Elites and the agency of power in EM III–MM II Crete. *American Journal of Archaeology*, 110.1, 37–64.

2018. The house tomb in context: Assessing mortuary behavior. In Y. Papadatos and M. Relaki (eds.), *From the Foundations to the Legacy of Minoan Society: Studies in Honour of Professor Keith Branigan*, 167–189. Sheffield Studies in Aegean Archaeology, 12. Oxford: Oxbow.

Schoep, I., Crevecoeur, I., Schmitt, A. and Tomkins, P. 2017. Funerary practices at Sissi: The treatment of the body in the house tombs. In M. Tsipopoulou (ed.), *Petras, Siteia: The Pre- and Proto-Palatial Cemetery in Context: Acts of a Two-Day Conference held at the Danish Institute at Athens, 14–15 February 2015*, 369–84. Aarhus: Aarhus University Press.

Scott, W. C. 1974. *The Oral Nature of Homeric Simile*. Leiden: Brill.

Seager, R. B. 1912. *Explorations in the Island of Mochlos*. Boston, MA: American School of Classical Studies at Athens.

Sennett, R. 2008. *The Craftsman*. New Haven, CT: Yale University Press.

Shank, E. B. 2007. Throne room griffins from Pylos and Knossos. In P. Betancourt, M. C. Nelson and H. Williams (eds.), *Krinoi kai Limenes: Studies in Honor of Joseph and Maria Shaw*, 159–165. Philadelphia: INSTAP Academic Press.

Shapland, A. 2010a. The Minoan lion: presence and absence on Bronze Age Crete. *World Archaeology*, 42.2, 273–289.

2010b. Wild nature? Human–animal relations on Neopalatial Crete. *Cambridge Archaeological Journal*, 20.1, 109–127.

2013. Jumping to conclusions: Bull-leaping in Minoan Crete. *Society and Animals*, 21.2, 194–207.

2021. Sacrificial relics or trophies? Animal heads in Bronze Age Crete. In R. Laffineur and T. Palaima (eds.), *ZOIA: Animal Connections in the Aegean Middle and Late Bronze Age*, 307–316. Leuven: Peeters.

2022. *Human–Animal Relations in Bronze Age Crete: A History through Objects*. Cambridge: Cambridge University Press.

Shank, E. 2018. The griffin motif: An evolutionary tale. In A. Vlachopoulos (ed.), *Paintbrushes (Χρωστήρες): Wall-Painting and Vase-Painting of the Second Millenium B. C. in Dialogue*, 235–241. Athens: University of Ioannina/Hellenic Ministry of Culture and Sports Archaeological Receipts Fund.

Shaw, J. W. 1978. Evidence for the Minoan tripartite shrine. *American Journal of Archaeology*, 82.4, 429–448.

Shaw, J. 1998. Kommos in southern Crete: An Aegean barometer for east–west interconnections. In V. Karageorghis and N. Stampolidis (eds.), *Eastern Mediterranean: Cyprus–Dodecanese–Crete, 16th–6th cent. B.C.*, 13–27. Athens: University of Crete/A. G. Leventis Foundation.

Shaw, M., 1980. Painted "ikria" at Mycenae? *American Journal of Archaeology*, 84.2, 167–179.

1982. Ship cabins of the Bronze Age Aegean. *International Journal of Nautical Archaeology*, 11.1, 53–58.

1993. The Aegean garden. *American Journal of Archaeology*, 97.4, 661–685.

Shaw, M. and Laxton, K. 2002. Minoan and Mycenaean wall hangings: New light from a wall painting at Hagia Triadha. *Creta Antica*, 3, 93–104.

Shaw, M. C. 1997. Aegean sponsors and artists: reflections of their roles in the patterns of distribution of themes and representational conventions in the murals. In R. Laffineur and P. Betancourt (eds.), *TEXNH: Craftsmen, Craftswomen and Craftsmanship in the Aegean Bronze Age*, 481–504. Liège: Université de Liège.

Shelmerdine, C. (ed.). (2008). *The Cambridge Companion to the Aegean Bronze Age*. Cambridge: Cambridge University Press.

Sherman, C. R. 1995. *Imagining Aristotle: Verbal and Visual Representation in Fourteenth-Century France*. Berkeley: University of California Press.

Sherratt, ES. 1990. "Reading the texts": Archaeology and the Homeric question. *Antiquity*, 64.245, 807–824.

Shipp, G. P. 1972. *Studies in the Language of Homer*. Cambridge: Cambridge University Press.

Simandiraki-Grimshaw, A. 2010a. The human body in Minoan religious iconography. In P. Warren and O. Krzyszkowska (eds.), *Cretan Offerings: Studies in Honour of Peter Warren*, 321–329. London: British School at Athens.

2010b. Minoan animal–human hybridity. In D. B. Counts (ed.), *The Master of Animals in Old World Iconography*, 93–106. Budapest: Archaeolingua.

2013. Anthropomorphic vessels as re-imagined corporealities in Bronze Age Crete. *Creta Antica*, 14, 17–68.

Simandiraki-Grimshaw, A. and Stevens, F. 2012. Adorning the body. Animals as ornaments in Bronze Age Crete. In M.-L. Nosch and R. Laffineur (eds.). *KOSMOS: Jewellery, Adornment and Textiles in the Aegean Bronze Age*. Leuven: Peeters.

Snyder, L. and Andrikou, E. 2001. Raw material for a helmet? Evidence for boar's tusk harvesting in a Late Helladic context, Thebes;

102nd AIA Annual Meeting, abstract. *American Journal of Archaeology*, 205, 304.

Soar, K. 2014. Sects and the city: Factional ideologies in representations of performance from Bronze Age Crete. *World Archaeology*, 46.2, 224–241.

2015. Cultural performances at the beginning of the Bronze Age: Early Minoan I and II cemeteries as stages for performance. In S. Cappel, U. Günkel-Maschek and D. Panagiotopoulos (eds.), *Minoan Archaeology: Perspectives for the 21st Century*, 283–297. Aegis, 8. Louvain-la-Neuve: Presses universitaires de Louvain.

Soja, E. 1996. *Thirdspace: Journeys to Los Angeles and Other Real-and-Imagined Places*. Oxford: Blackwell.

2008. Thirdspace: Toward a new consciousness of space and spatiality. In *Communicating in the Third Space*, 63–75. London: Routledge.

Soles, J. 1992. *The Prepalatial Tombs at Mochlos and Gournia and the House Tombs of Bronze Age Crete*. Athens: American School of Classical Studies.

2011. The Mochlos sistrum and its origins. In S. Ferrence and P. Betancourt (eds.), *Metallurgy: Understanding How, Learning Why: Studies in Honor of James D. Muhly*, 133–146. Philadelphia: INSTAP Academic Press.

2016. Hero, goddess, priestess: New evidence for Minoan religion and social organization. In E. Alram-Stern, F. Blakolmer, S. Deger-Jalkotzy, R. Laffineur and J. Weilhartner (eds.), *Metaphysis, Ritual, Myth and Symbolism in the Aegean Bronze Age*, 247–254. Aegaeum, 39. Leuven: Peeters.

Spivey, N. J. 1997. *Greek Art*. London: Phaidon Press.

Starke, F. 1985. *Die keilschrift-luwischen Texte in Umschrift*. Wiesbaden: Otto Harrassowitz.

Stewart, S. 1993. *On Longing: Narratives of the Miniature, the Gigantic, the Souvenir, the Collection*. Durham, NC: Duke University Press.

Stocker, S. and Davis. J. 2017. The Combat Agate from the Grave of the Griffin Warrior at Pylos. *Hesperia*, 86.4, 583–605.

Stram, C. 2017. The talismanic seal stone of Crete: A re-evaluation. Master's thesis. University of Nebraska–Lincoln.

Strange, J. 1980. *Caphtor/Keftiu: A New Investigation*. Leiden: Brill.

Summers, D. 2003. *Real Spaces: World Art History and the Rise of Western Modernism*. London: Phaidon.

Tambiah, S. 1969. Animals are good to think and good to prohibit. *Ethnology*, 8.4, 423–459.

Tartaron, T. 2013. *Maritime Networks in the Mycenaean World*. Cambridge: Cambridge University Press.

Teissier, B. 1987. Glyptic evidence for a connection between Iran, Syro-Palestine and Egypt in the fourth and third millennia. *Iran*, 25.1, 27–53.

1996. *Egyptian Iconography on Syro-Palestinian Cylinder Seals of the Middle Bronze Age*. Göttingen: Vandenhoeck & Ruprecht.

Televantou, C. 1990. New light on the West House wall paintings. In D. Hardy, C. Doumas, Y. Sakellarakis and P. Warren (eds.), *Thera and the Aegean World III (1)*, 309–326. London: Thera Foundation.

1994. *Ακρωτήρι Θήρας: Οι Τοιχογραφίες της Δυτικής Οικίας*. Athens: Η εν Αθήναις Αρχαιολογική Εταιρεία.

2000. Aegean Bronze Age wall painting: The Theran workshop. In S. Sherratt (ed.), *The Wall Paintings of Thera: Proceedings of the First International Symposium, Thera, 30 August–4 September 1997*, vol. 2, 831–843. Piraeus: Petros M. Nomikos and the Thera Foundation.

Thomas, J. 2006. Phenomenology and material culture. In C. Tilley, S. Kuechler-Fogden and W. Keane (eds.), *Handbook of Material Culture*, 43–59. London: Sage.

Thomas, N. 1999. The war animal: Three days in the life of the Mycenaean lion. In R. Laffineur (ed.), *Polemos: Le contexte guerrier en Égée à l'âge du bronze*, 297–313. Aegaeum, 20. Liège: Université de Liège and University of Texas at Austin

2004. The Early Mycenaean lion up to date. *Hesperia Suppl.*, 33, 161–206.

2014. A lion's eye view of the Greek Bronze Age. In G. Touchais (ed.), *Physis: L'environnement naturel et la relation homme-milieu dans le monde égéen protohistorique.* Aegaeum, 37. Leuven: Peeters.

Tilley, C. 2004. *The Materiality of Stone: Explorations in Landscape Phenomenology.* Oxford: Berg.

Tilley, C., Hamilton, S. and Bender, B. 2000. Art and the re-presentation of the past. *The Journal of the Royal Anthropological Institute,* 6.1, 35–62.

Tilley, C., Kuechler-Fogden, S. and Keane, W. (eds.). 2006. *Handbook of Material Culture.* London: Sage.

Todaro, S. 2012. Craft production and social practices at prepalatial Phaistos: the background to the first "Palace." In I. Schoep, J. Driessen and P. Tomkins (eds.), *Back to the Beginning: Reassessing Social and Political Complexity on Crete during the Early and Middle Bronze Age,* 195–235. Oxford: Oxbow.

2020. Residential mobility and ritual stability in the Early Bronze Age Mesara: Re-building "Houses" at Phaistos. In M. Relaki and J. Driessen (eds.), *OIKOS: Archaeological Approaches to House Societies in the Bronze Age Aegean,* 25–49. Louvain-la-Neuve: Presses Universitaires de Louvain.

Trantalidou, K. 2000. Animal bones and animal representations at Late Bronze Age Akrotiri. In S. Sherratt (ed.) *The Wall Paintings of Thera: Proceedings of the First International Symposium,* 709–735. Piraeus: Petros M. Nomikos and the Thera Foundation.

Triantaphyllou, S., 2016. Staging the manipulation of the dead in Pre-and Protopalatial Crete, Greece (3rd–early 2nd mill. BCE): From body wholes to fragmented body parts. *Journal of Archaeological Science: Reports,* 10, 769–779.

Tsagalis, C. 2012. *From Listeners to Viewers: Space in the Iliad.* Washington, DC: Center for Hellenic Studies.

Tsipopoúlou M. and Rupp., D. 2019. The Pre-and Proto-Palatial cemetery at Petras-Kephala : A persistent locale as an arena for competing cultural memories. In E. Borgna, I. Caloi, F. M. Carinci and R. Laffineur (eds.), *Mneme, Past and Memory in the Aegean Bronze Age,* 81–94, Aegaeum, 43. Leuven: Peeters.

Tsipopoúlou, M. (ed.). 2017. *Petras, Siteia: The Pre-and Proto-Palatial Cemetery in Context.* Athens: Danish Institute at Athens.

Tully, C. and Crooks, S. 2020. Enthroned upon mountains: Constructions of power in the Aegean Bronze Age. In L. Naeh and D. Brostowsky Gilboa (eds.), *The Ancient Throne: The Mediterranean, Near East, and Beyond, from the 3rd Millennium BCE to the 14th Century CE,* 37–59. Vienna: Austrian Academy of Sciences.

Tyler, A. 2012. Cycladic nippled ewers of the Middle and Early Late Bronze Age: Their symbolism and function. Diss. University of Oslo.

Tzachili, I. 2018. Vases with plastic decoration depicting landscapes from the Vrysinas peak sanctuary. In A. Vlachopoulos (ed.), *Paintbrushes (Χρωστήρες): Wall-Painting and Vase-Painting of the Second Millennium B.C. in Dialogue,*119–127. Athens : University of Ioannina/Hellenic Ministry of Culture and Sports Archaeological Receipts Fund.

Ulanowski, K. 2015. The metaphor of the lion in Mesopotamian and Greek civilization. In R. Rollinger and E. van Dongen (eds.), *Mesopotamia in the Ancient World: Impact, Continuities, Parallels. Proceedings of the Seventh Symposium of the Melammu Project,* 255–284. Munster: Ugarit-Verlag.

Urbani, B. and Youlatos, D. 2012. Aegean monkeys: From a comprehensive view to a reinterpretation, in A. Legakis, C. Georgiadis and P. Pafilis (eds.), *Proceedings of the 12th International Congress on the Zoogeography and Ecology of Greece and Adjacent Regions.* Athens: Hellenic Zoological Society.

2020. Occam's razor, archeoprimatology, and the "blue" monkeys of Thera: A reply to Pareja et al. *Primates,* 61, 757–765.

2022. Minoan monkeys: Re-examining the archaeoprimatological evidence. In B. Urbani, D. Youlatos and A. T. Antczak (eds.), *World Archaeoprimatology:*

Interconnections of Humans and Nonhuman Primates in the Past, 225–280. Cambridge: Cambridge University Press.

Vanschoonwinkel, J. 1996. Les animaux dans l'art minoen. In D. Reese (ed.), *Pleistocene and Holocene Fauna of Crete and Its First Settlers*, 351–412. Madison, WI: Prehistory Press.

Varvarighos, A. 1981. Τό ὀδοντόφρακτον μυκηναϊκό κράνος. PhD diss. University of Athens.

Vasilakis, A., Branigan, K., Campbell-Green, T. et al. 2010. *Moni Odigitria: A Prepalatial Cemetery and Its Environs in the Asterousia, Southern Crete*. Philadelphia: INSTAP Academic Press.

Vavouranakis, G., 2014. Funerary pithoi in Bronze Age Crete: Their introduction and significance at the threshold of Minoan palatial society. *American Journal of Archaeology*, 118.2, 197–222.

Ventris, M. and Chadwick, J. 1973. *Documents in Mycenaean Greek: Three Hundred Selected Tablets from Knossos, Pylos, and Mycenae, with Commentary and Vocabulary*. London: Cambridge University Press.

Vlachopoulos, A. 2007. Mythos, logos and eikon: Motifs of early Greek poetry and the wall paintings of Xeste 3, Akrotiri. In S. Morris and R. Laffineur (eds.), *EPOS: Reconsidering Greek Epic and Aegean Bronze Age Archaeology*, 107–118. Aegaeum, 28. Liège: Université de Liège and University of Texas at Austin.

2008. The wall paintings from the Xeste 3 building at Akrotiri: towards an interpretation of the iconographic programme. In N. Brodie, J. Doole, G. Gavalas and C. Renfrew (eds.), *ΟΡΙΖΩΝ: A Colloquium on the Prehistory of the Cyclades*, 451–465. Cambridge: McDonald Institute for Archaeological Research.

2013. From vase painting to wall painting: The Lilies Jug from Akrotiri, Thera. In R. Koehl (ed.), *ΑΜΙΛΛΑ: The Quest for Excellence. Studies Presented to Guenter Kopcke in Celebration of His 75th Birthday*, 55–75. Philadelphia: INSTAP Academic Press.

2015. Detecting "Mycenaean" elements in the "Minoan" wall paintings of a "Cycladic" settlement: The wall paintings at Akrotiri, Thera within their iconographic *koine*. In H. Brecoulaki, J. Davis and S. Stocker (eds.), *Mycenaean Wall Paintings in Context: New Discoveries and Old Finds Reconsidered*, 37–65. Athens: National Hellenic Research Foundation/ Institute of Historical Research.

Vlachopoulos, A. (ed.). 2018. *Paintbrushes (Χρωστήρες). Wall-Painting and Vase-Painting of the Second Millenium B.C. in Dialogue*. Athens: University of Ioannina/ Hellenic Ministry of Culture and Sports Archaeological Receipts Fund.

Vlachopoulos, A. and Sotiropoulou, S. 2013. The blue colour on the Akrotiri wall-paintings: From the palette of the Theran painter to the laboratory analysis. *Talanta*, 44, 245–272.

Vlasaki, M. and Hallager, E. 1995. Evidence for seal use in Prepalatial western Crete. In W. Müller (ed.), *Sceaux minoens et mycéniens*, 251–270. Berlin: Mann.

von Rüden, C. and Skowronek, T. 2018. Between common craft tradition and deviation. The making of stucco reliefs in the eastern Mediterranean. In J. Becker, J. Jungfleisch and C. von Rüden (eds.). *Tracing Technoscapes: The Production of Bronze Age Wall Paintings in the Eastern Mediterranean*, 213–232. Leiden: Sidestone Press.

Walberg, G. 1986. *Tradition and Innovation: Essays in Minoan Art*. Mainz: Philipp Von Zabern.

1987. *Kamares: A Study of the Character of Palatial Middle Minoan Pottery*. Göteburg: Åstroms.

Walcot, P. 1979. Cattle raiding, heroic tradition, and ritual: The Greek evidence. *History of Religions*, 18.4, 326–351.

Wall, S., Musgrave, J. and Warren, P. 1986. Human bones from a Late Minoan IB house at Knossos. *British School at Athens*, 81, 333–388.

Walter, O. 1950. Studie ein Blumen Motiv als Beitrag zur Frage der kretisch-mykenischen Perspektive. *Jahreshefte des Österreichischen archäologischen Instituts in Wien*, 38, 17–41.

Warnier, J.-P. 2006. Inside and outside: Surfaces and containers. In C. Tilley, S. Kuechler-

Fogden and W. Keane (eds.), *Handbook of Material Culture*, 186–95. London: Sage.

Warren, P. M. 1969. *Minoan Stone Vases*. Cambridge: Cambridge University Press.

1973. The beginnings of Minoan religion. In G. Rizza (ed.), *Antichita Cretesi: Studi in Onore di Doro Levi* 1, 137–147. Catania: Università di Catania, Istituto di archeologia.

1972. *Myrtos: An Early Bronze Age Settlement in Crete.* London: British School of Archaeology at Athens.

1980. Knossos: Stratigraphical museum excavations, 1978–1980. Part I. *Archaeological Reports*, 27, 73–92.

1984. Of squills. In *Aux origines de l'hellénisme: La Crète et la Grèce: Hommage à Henri Van Effenterre*, 17–24. Paris: Université de Paris-I/Panthéon-Sorbonne.

2001. Shield and goddess in Minoan Crete and the Aegean. *Proceedings of the 9th International Cretological Conference*, 457–470. Herakleion: Εταιρία Κρητικών Ιστορικών Μελετών.

Watanabe, C. E. 2002. *Animal Symbolism in Mesopotamia: A Contextual Approach*. Vienna: Institut für Orientalistik, Universität Wien.

Watrous, L. V. 2007. The fleet fresco, the Odyssey and Greek epic narrative. In S. Morris and R. Laffineur (eds.), *EPOS: Reconsidering Greek Epic and Aegean Bronze Age Archaeology*, 97–106, Aegaeum, 28. Liège: Université de Liège and University of Texas at Austin.

2021. *Minoan Crete: An Introduction*. Cambridge: Cambridge University Press.

Webmoor, T. and Witmore, C. 2008. Things are us! A commentary on human/things relations under the banner of a "social" archaeology. *Norwegian Archaeological Review*, 41.1, 53–70.

Webster, T. B. L. 1964. *From Mycenae to Homer*. London: Methuen.

Weingarten, J. 1983. *The Zakro Master and His Place in Prehistory*. Göteborg: Paul Åströms Förlag.

1985. Aspects of tradition and innovation in the work of the Zakro Master. *Bulletin de Correspondance Héllenique*, 11.1, 167–180.

1986. The sealing structures of Minoan Crete: MM II Phaistos to the destruction of the palace of Knossos, Part 1. *Oxford Journal of Archaeology*, 5.3, 279–298.

1988. Seal-use at LM IB Agia Triada: A Minoan elite in action II – aesthetic considerations. *Kadmos*, 27, 89–114.

1991. *The Transformation of Egyptian Taweret into the Minoan Genius: A Study in Cultural Transmission in the Middle Bronze Age*. Jonsered: Paul Åströms Förlag.

1992. The multiple sealing system of Minoan Crete and its possible antecedents in Anatolia. *Oxford Journal of Archaeology*, 11.1, 25–37.

1995. Sealing studies in the Middle Bronze Age III: The Minoan hieroglyphic deposits at Mallia and Knossos. In W. Müller (ed.), *Sceaux minoens et mycéniens*, 285–311. Berlin: Mann.

2013. The arrival of Egyptian Taweret and Bes[et] on Minoan Crete: Contact and choice. In L. Bombardieri, A. D'Agostino, G. Guarducci, V. Orsi and S. Valentini (eds.), *Symposium on Mediterranean Archaeology, 2012*, 371–378. British Archaeological Reports International Series 2581. Oxford: Archaeopress.

2015. The arrival of Bes[et] on Middle-Minoan Crete. In J. Jana Mynářová, P. Onderka and P. Pavúk (eds.), *There and Back Again: The Crossroads II*, 181–198. Prague: Charles University.

Wells, R. and Cook, R. 2017. How to evaluate property for raising cattle. *AG News and Views* 35: 11.

Wengrow, D. 2011. Cognition, materiality and monsters: The cultural transmission of counter-intuitive forms in Bronze Age societies. *Journal of Material Culture*, 16.2, 131–149.

2013. *The Origins of Monsters*. Princeton, NJ: Princeton University Press.

West, M. L. 1988. The rise of the Greek epic. *Journal of Hellenic Studies*, 108, 151–172.

1997. *The East Face of Helicon: West Asiatic Elements in Greek Poetry and Myth*. Oxford: Clarendon Press.

2011. *The Making of the Iliad: Disquisition and Analytical Commentary*. Oxford: Oxford University Press.

Whittaker, H. 2016. Horns and axes. In E. Alram-Stern, F. Blakolmer, S. Deger-Jalkotzy,

R. Laffineur and J. Weilhartner (eds.), *Metaphysis, Ritual, Myth and Symbolism in the Aegean Bronze Age*, 109–114. Leuven: Peeters.

Whitelaw, T. 1983. The settlement at Fournou Korifi Myrtos and aspects of Early Minoan social organization. In O. Krzyszkowska and L. Nixon (eds.), *Minoan Society*, 323–345. Bristol: Bristol Classical Press.

2001. From sites to communities: Defining the human dimensions of Minoan urbanism. In K. Branigan (ed.), *Urbanism in the Aegean Bronze Age*, 15–37. London: Sheffield Academic Press.

2007. House, households and community at Early Minoan Fournou Korifi: Methods and models for interpretation. In R. Westgate, N. Fisher and J. Whitley (eds.), *Building Communities. House, Settlement, and Society in the Aegean and Beyond*, 65–76. BSA Studies, 15. London: British School at Athens.

2014. Feasts of clay? Ceramics and feasting at Early Minoan Myrtos: Fournou Korifi. In Y. Galankis, T. Wikinson and J. Bennet (eds.), *ΑΘΥΡΜΑΤΑ: Critical Essays on the Archaeology of the Eastern Mediterranean in Honour of E. Susan Sherratt*, 247–259. Oxford: Archaeopress.

2017. The development and character of urban communities in prehistoric Crete in their regional context. In Q. Letesson, and C. Knappett (eds.),*Minoan Architecture and Urbanism: New Perspectives on an Ancient Built Environment*, 114–180. Oxford: Oxford University Press.

Wiener, M. 1987. Trade and rule in palatial Crete. In R. Hägg and N. Marinatos (eds), *The Function of the Minoan Palaces: Proceedings of the Fourth International Symposium at the Swedish Institute in Athens, 10–16 June, 1984*. Stockholm: Åströms/ Svenska institutet i Athen.

Wiese, A. 1996. *Die Anfänge der ägyptischen Stempelsiegel-Amulette: Eine typologische und religionsgeschichtliche Untersuchung zu den "Knopfsiegeln" und verwandten Objekten der 6. bis frühen 12. Dynastie*. Fribourg: Universitätsverlag.

Wilson, J. 1974. The wedding gifts of Peleus. *Phoenix*, 28.4, 385–389.

Wilson, N. 2001. Butler's corporeal politics: matters of politicized abjection. *International Journal of Sexuality and Gender Studies*, 6, 109–121.

Winter, I. 2003. Surpassing work: Mastery of materials and the value of skilled production in ancient Sumer. In *Culture through Objects: Ancient Near Eastern Studies in Honour of PRS Moorey*, 403–421. Oxford: Griffith Institute.

Witmore, C. 2012. The realities of the past. In B. Fortenberry and L. McAtackney (eds.), *Modern Materials: Proceedings from the Contemporary and Historical Archaeology in Theory Conference 2009*, 25–36. Oxford: British Archaeological Reports.

Wolf, D. 2020. Embodying change? Homosomatic hybridity as transformational response in LM II/III Crete. *Fontes Archaeologici Posnanienses*, 56, 57–66.

Woodward, W. 1972. The north entrance at Knossos. *American Journal of Archaeology*, 76.2, 113–125.

Wylie, A. 2002. *Thinking from Things: Essays in the Philosophy of Archaeology*. Berkeley: University of California Press.

Xanthoudidēs, S. 1924. *The Vaulted Tombs of Mesará: An Account of Some Early Cemeteries of Southern Crete*. London: Hodder & Stoughton.

Xenaki-Sakellariou, A. 1953. La représentation du casque en dents de sanglier. *Bulletin de Correspondance Héllenique*, 77, 46–58.

Xirouchakis, S., Anastasios, A. and Andreou, G. 2001. The decline of the Bearded Vuture *Gypaetus Barbatus* in Greece. *Ardeola*, 48.2, 183–190.

Younger, J. 1978. The Mycenae-Vapheio lion group. *American Journal of Archaeology*, 82.3, 285–99.

1979. Origins of the Mycenae-Vapheio lion master. *Bulletin of the Institute of Classical Studies*, 26, 119–21.

1983. Aegean seals of the Late Bronze Age: Masters and workshops. Vol. 2, The First-Generation Minoan Masters. *Kadmos*, 22, 109–134.

1984. Aegean seals of the Late Bronze Age: Masters and workshops. Vol. 3, The First-Generation Mycenaean Masters. *Kadmos*, 23, 38–64.

1995. Bronze Age representations of Aegean bull-games, III. In R. Laffineur and W.-D. Niemeier (eds.), *Politeia: Society and State in the Aegean Bronze Age*, 507–545. Liège: Université de Liège.

1998. *Music in the Aegean Bronze Age*. Jonsered: Åströms.

2010. Mycenaean seals and sealings. In E. Cline (ed.), *The Oxford Handbook of the Bronze Age Aegean*, 329–339. Oxford: Oxford University Press.

2012. Mycenaean collections of seals: The role of blue. In M.-L. Nosch and R. Laffineur (eds.), *KOSMOS: Jewellery, Adornment and Textiles in the Aegean Bronze Age. 13th International Aegean Conference, 19–23 April 2010, University of Copenhagen, 749–753.* Liège: Université de Liège.

Yule, P. 1981. *Early Cretan Seals: A Study of Chronology*. Mainz: Philipp von Zabern.

Zadka, M. 2012. Differences in the level of literacy between Minoan and Mycenaean societies in the light of the analysis of types and probable use of inscribed objects. *Lingua Posnaniensis*, 54.1, 133–138.

Zeitlin, F. 2018. Constructing the aesthetic body in Homer and beyond. In B. M. King and L. Doherty (eds.), *Thinking the Greeks: A Volume in Honour of James M. Redfield*, 53–69. London: Routledge.

Zeman-Wisniewska, K. 2015. On performative and experiential aspects of figures and figurines. In S. Cappel, U. Günkel-Maschek and D. Panagiotopoulos (eds.), *Minoan Archaeology: Perspectives for the 21st Century*, 319–326. Aegis, 8. Louvain-la-Neuve: Presses universitaires de Louvain.

Zimmer, K. 2022. The last wild lions of Europe. *Sapiens*, January 4; online www.sapiens.org/archaeology/lions-europe/.

Zouzoula, E. 2007. The fantastic creatures of Bronze Age Crete. PhD diss., University of Nottingham.

INDEX

abjection, 58, 59
abstraction, 200–201, 202
Acemhöyük plaque, 186–187, 206, 210, 211, 212, 214, 216
Achilles, 270–271
actor–network theory, 24
affordances, 25–26, 33, 52
  of vessels, 53, 54, 67
agency, 33
  captivation and, 58
  of vessels, 55, 58, 62
agency, object, 24
Akrotiri, 3, 4
analogism, 30–31
Anastasiadou, M., 57, 117, 128, 129
  on boar's tusk helmets, 268–270
  on composite beasts, 234–236
  glyptic subgroups delineated by, 117
  on Hieroglyphic Deposit, 225
  on prism seals, 225
  on regionalism, 225
Andrikou, E., 254
animal dynamism, 249
animalian forms, new, 206
animalian things, 23. *See also* representations of animals
  connections afforded by, 28
  as embodiments of relation and coalescence, 28
  relational complexity of, 6
  size of, 6
  social life and, 2, 18
  as true embodiments of animals, 28–34
animal practices, 15
animals
  creative relating of, 12–14
  meaning associated with, 32
animals, artificial, 30. *See also* animals, fabricated
animals, biological, 28–30
  interactions with, 15
  as real animalian presences, 31–32
  as real embodiments, 1
animals, fabricated
  dynamism of, 32
  human–animal relations and, 31

  impression of species and, 31
  interactions with. *See* engagement
  relationships to living beings, 1
  relationships with other phenomena, 34
  as representations. See representations
  status of, 31–32
  vs. biological, 34
animal studies, 30
animal thing, vs. animalian thing, 23
animate/inanimate binary, 33
animation, 3
archaeology
  data from Prepalatial period, 38–39
  excavations in Crete, 40–41
  things' engagement with culture and, 24
  use of "thing" in, 22
archaeology, Minoan, 2
archaeology, symmetrical, 22
architecture, 278
Aristotle, 106
armor, human's connection to, 255
Aruz, J., 111, 186–187, 202, 210, 219
assemblages, 144–146
associations, created by objects, 249
autonomy
  of representation, 27
  of vessels, 8, 48
axe, double, 89

Bearded Vulture, 14, 200, 204, 205, 206
Beardsworth, A., 28–29
beastliness, thingliness realized as, 21
beasts. *See* animals
beasts, composite. *See* composite beasts
bees, 21
Bennett, J., 25, 144
Berger, J., 29, 33
Bes/Beset, 222, 224
bilingualism, 132
binaries, 33
biography, object, 24
biology, intuitive, 162–163
Black, J., 124

Blakolmer, F., 86, 249, 262, 274, 278
Bloedow, E., 139
boar. *See also* swine
  dead/dying, 288
boar's head rhyta, 288, 289
boar hunting, 248
boar's tusk helmets, 15–16, 143. *See also* swine
  acquisition of tusks for, 253, 254
  animal origins of, 250
  biographies of, 270–271
  blurring of hunt and war by, 248, 258
  composite beasts with, 268–270
  described, 257
  as dynamic thing, 256
  formal assonance with sacral cloth, 285–287
  formal assonance with squill, 282–285
  form of, 258
  in glyptic, 265–267, 268–270, 271–272
  head and, 256, 270
  human's interactions with, 270
  human animal embodied in, 255
  hybridity and, 249
  identities of, 270–271
  as index, 248
  isolation/independence of, 270–271, 274, 275
  Knossos cup-rhyton and, 282
  link to once-living beast, 255
  Morris on, 247–249
  protective role of, 284
  as reference for design, 257–258
  repetition of, 268
  representational scale of, 275
  representations of. *See* representational embodiments of composite animalian entities
  on seals, 271–272
  in series, 271–272, 275
  shield and, 249, 258, 271, 284
  status of, 257
  status of human within, 255–256
  as symbol, 249
  symbolism of, 250
  on vessels, 275
bodies, abject, 58, 59
bodies, as political entities, 38–40
body techniques, 51–52
  iterative nature of, 53
Bourdieu, P., 52
bovine imagery. *See* cattle; vessels, bovine
Branigan, K., 43, 228
British Museum, 79
Broodbank, C., 124
Brown, B., 22
Bryman, A., 28–29
bull's head rhyta, 291
bulls, 287. *See also* cattle
bull sports, 87, 91
Burns, B., 124

Butler, J., 58
Byblos, 215

Cadogan, G., 43, 61
Campbell, J. K., 82, 86
captivation, 58
case studies, 5
  approach to, 7–8
  contexts of interaction, 8
  key topics in, 18
  time period, 7
cats, 226, 233
cattle, 9–10, 40. *See also* ikria; shields
  agricultural practices with, 82
  bovine imagery from Neopalatial period, 92
  bovine vessels. *See* vessels, bovine
  bull sports, 87, 91
  engagements with, 92
  extraction of resources from, 92
  human engagement with, 76–80, 81–87
  in Neopalatial period, 10
  rhyta, 71–75, 80–81, 87–91
  size of, 85
  theft of, 82–83, 86, 87
  zoomorphic vessels and, 70–71
cattle culture, 9–10
  Knossos and, 85–86
  recontextualization of, 91–93
  social and environmental stress and, 92
caves, 63
cemeteries, Prepalatial, 65
ceramics. *See also* representational embodiments of composite animalian entities; vessels
  glyptic objects' relationship with, 274–275
character, 32
Charalambos Cave, 63
chest/neck embellishments, of griffins, 12, 160–161, 183–206, 212
  ambiguity in, 184, 195, 197
  Bearded Vulture's compared to, 194–195
  collar/leash elements, 195–197, 200, 202–205. *See also* griffins, leashed/tethered
  described, 184–185
  on vessels, 200–202, 206
Colburn, C., 215, 228, 230
communities, multifunctional places in, 63
community action, 75
composite beasts, 11–14, 159, 233
  with boar's tusk helmets, 268–270
  as coherent wholes, 235
  combinability and, 234
  counter-intuitiveness of, 234, 234
  as creative realizations of connections, 233
  described, 159
  durability/stability and, 236
  as established presences, 237
  experience of, 161–162
  foreignness and, 160, 161, 165

INDEX

composite beasts (cont.)
  horns and, 210
  inorganic, 235
  integrative nature of, 233
  interchangeability and, 235, 268–270
  in material culture, 163
  modularity and, 162
  potency of, 238
  roots of, 160
  sealing systems and, 237
  similarities to other beasts, 238
  status of, 14, 159
  urbanism and, 162–163, 164, 234
  in wall paintings, 238
  from Zakros site, 234–236
  Zakros type, 234, 268–270
connections, 32. *See also* sharing, cultural
Corbett, J., 29
court spaces, 62
creativity, 7, 17, 165
creativity, composite, 258
crests. *See* head appendages, of griffins
Cretan Hieroglyphic, 225
Crete
  cultural connections with other societies, 3. *See also* sharing, cultural
  investigation of prehistoric past. *See* archaeology

dactylic verse, 126, 127, 132
Davaras, C., 230
Davis, B., 128
Davis, J., 133–134
death/dying, forward-facing gaze associated with, 222
Déderix, S., 59
depth, 17. *See also* space; spatial complexity
Derrida, J., 33
Descola, P., 30, 31
Devolder, M., 86
diadems, 229–232
difference, 29
Driessen, J., 59–60, 63, 74, 84, 86
Duhoux, Y., 127–128, 129
duplication. *See also* series/seriation
dynamism, 3, 7
  of fabricated embodiments of animals, 32
  of objects, 50
  of vessels, 62
dynamism, formal, 32

ears, 223
efficacy, 33
Egypt
  Bes/Beset, 224
  cultural content from, 211
  cultural sharing with, 11, 211. *See also* lions
  falcons in, 206
  forward-facing gaze in, 222

gold and, 228
  griffins and, 185, 186, 202–203, 205, 212
  Hathor, 221
  Hathor Face, 217–219, 222
  headgear from, 216–220
  influence of on Crete, 2
  lions and, 111–113, 122
  Taweret, 221, 224
  travel to, 215
Egyptianizing imagery, 214
emblems, 263, 274
embodiments, 21. *See also* representations
  distance between, 19
  engagement with. *See* engagement
  as real, 19
  as true, 19, 28–34
encounter. *See* interactions; engagement
engagement
  with embodiments, 2, 19–21, 23
  with nonhuman entities, 25
engagement, overseas. *See* sharing, cultural
entities, composite animalian, 15. *See also* boar's tusk helmets; ikria; representational embodiments of composite animalian entities; shields
  animal origins of, 250
  as combinatory things, 246
  composite creativity and, 258
  cross-media dynamics, 274
  as dynamic entities, 260
  dynamism of, 264, 267
  as emblems, 262–263
  formal assonance and, 247
  in friezes, 263, 272
  identities of, 258, 261
  identities of as animalian things, 260
  incorporations of human and nonhuman components, 246
  integrative dynamics of, 238, 246
  intuitiveness of, 247
  isolation/independence of, 265–268, 274
  juxtaposition with other entities, 275
  part of animal's body in, 23
  protective status of, 258
  as re-presentational things, 250
  relationships of to bodies, 258–260
  relationships with each other, 261
  representations of. *See* representational embodiments of composite animalian entities
  in seals, 15, 16, 274
  in series, 264. *See also* series/seriation
  series and, 265–268, 274, 275
  spatial complexity of. *See* depth; spatial complexity
  status of, 262
  as symbols, 262
  on vessels, 15, 16, 274
  in wall paintings, 17, 274
environmental stress, 92, 130

epic poetry. *See* poetry/poetic tradition; similes
epic tradition, 11, 103, 132–133, 147
  armored figures in, 267
  Early Mycenaean origins for, 126
Evans, A., 2–3, 79
  on bull leapers, 80
  on deposit at House of the Sacrificed Oxen, 91
  on forward-facing gaze, 223
  on griffins, 185
  wall paintings and, 204
ewers, nippled, 56–57
exchange, cultural, 105. *See also* sharing, cultural
  evidence of, 2
  lions and, 103, 111–113, 122, 124–125
  oral tradition and, 122
experience, Noë on, 26–27
experiences, created by objects, 249

fabrication, 30
falcons, 186, 206
fantastical creatures. *See* composite beasts
felines, 206
figurines, 47, 68
  composite beasts and, 163
  studies of, 39
foreignness, 165
formal assonance, 6, 16, 32, 57, 374
  of boar's tusk helmets with sacral cloth,
    285–287
  of boar's tusk helmets and squills, 284–285
  composite animalian entities and, 247, 261
  glyptic objects and, 287
  griffins and, 200, 201
  of Knossos cup-rhyton, 281–282
  of vessels and glyptic, 275
Foster, K. P., 76
Foucault, M., 256
frescoes. *See* wall paintings
friezes. *See also* series/seriation
  composite animalian entities in, 272
  emblems in, 262–263
  ikria in, 272
  interpretation of, 262
  in Mycenaean culture, 261–262
  shields in, 278
funerary contexts, 38–39. *See also* tombs

gaze, wild animal's, 29
gaze/figure, forward-facing, 13, 16, 207, 233
  creatures with, 222–226
  cultural associations and, 222, 224
  death/dying associated with, 74, 222, 288
  diadems and, 231
  gorgons/gorgoneia and, 222, 288
  Hathor Face, 217–219
  head appendages and, 226, 232
  heads without bodies, 224
  on Knossos cup-rhyton, 280–281, 288–291

owls and, 207, 217, 222
petschaft seal from Mochlos and, 228
potency of, 288
protective role of, 284
on seals, 225–226
Gell, A., 21–22, 58
Gibson, J. J., 24, 25, 52
Gilgamesh (Bilgamesh), 123, 124
Gleichnisorte, 135
glyptic. *See also* seals
  affordances of, 274
  ambiguity in, 197
  boar in, 291
  boar's tusk helmets in, 265–267, 268–270, 271–272
  formal assonance and, 287
  griffins in, 191
  ikria in, 272–273
  lions and, 103, 104, 137, 151
  regionalism and, 128–131
  series in, 274
  shields in, 265–267
  vessels' relationship with, 274–275
  woman-bird creatures in, 57
glyptic, Syro-Palestinian, 210–212, 217–219
glyptic subgroups, 117
gold, 228
gorgons/gorgoneia, 222, 225, 288
Gosden, C., 24
graves. *See* tombs
griffins, 4, 11–12, 14, 159, 233. *See also* composite
    beasts
  on Acemhöyük plaque, 202, 206, 210, 211, 212,
    214, 216
  ambiguity and, 200, 202
  associations with other animalian bodies,
    205–206
  bodily features of, 12. *See also* chest/neck embel-
    lishments, of griffins; head appendages, of
    griffins
  creative development of, 187
  cultural sharing and, 219
  on Egyptian box, 212
  Egyptian influence on, 185, 186
  falcons and, 186, 206
  femaleness associated with, 204–205
  in glyptic, 191
  as homosomatic hybrids, 162
  interactions with, 205
  lion seals compared to, 184–185
  renderings of in material culture, 160
  sphinxes and, 211
  tension between representational and abstract
    and, 202
  on vessels, 198–202
  vultures and, 185, 206
  in wall paintings, 191–192, 200, 206
griffins, leashed/tethered, 17, 202–205
  in Egypt, 205

INDEX

griffins, leashed/tethered (cont.)
  in overseas imagery, 202–203
  in wall paintings, 203–204

Halstead, P., 85
Hamilakis, Y., 39
Harman, G., 25
Hathor, 221, 222
Hathor Face, 217–219, 222, 223
Hathor wig, 218–219, 223
head appendages, 233. *See also* headgear
  creatures with, 206–207
  forward-facing gaze and, 222, 226, 232
  horns, 209–210, 211, 212, 223
  of humanoid front-facing figures, 223
  interspecific associations, 210–212
  of owls, 207–210, 216–217, 219, 223
  on *petschaft* seal from Mochlos, 212
  tripartite, 212, 226, 228
  uraeus projection, 219
head appendages, of griffins, 12, 161, 194, 198–200, 207–212, 214
  on Acemhöyük plaque, 210, 211, 212, 214, 216
  on Egyptian box, 212
  identities and, 207
headgear, 216–220. *See also* boar's tusk helmets; head appendages
  diadems, 229–232
  Egyptian, 217, 219
  Poppy Goddess, 230, 231
  of sphinxes, 214, 217
  tripartite, 230
heads, bovine, 87
  activities focused on, 91
  affordances of, 90
  human interactions with biological cattle and, 89–91
  representation of, 87–88, 89
  skulls, 90–91
Heidegger, M., 22, 24, 52
Heimpel, W., 123, 124
Heise, U. K., 30
helmets, 250
Herodotus, 105
Herva, V.-P., 30
Herzfeld, M., 82, 86
heterotopias, 256
Hickman, J., 229,
hides, cattle. *See also* ikria; shields
  acquisition of, 259
  human interactions with biological cattle and, 89–91
  representation of, 87–89
Hogarth, D., 234, 235
Homer. See *Iliad*
Hood, S., 200
horns, 209–210, 211, 212, 223
horns, bovine, 87

activities focused on, 91
craft activity with, 89
human interactions with biological cattle and, 89–91
increased representation of, 87–89
removal of, 90
horns of consecration, 88
Horrocks, G. C., 126
House groups, 74–75
house societies, 8–9, 63–64, 67
human–animal relations, 140
Husserl, E., 24
hybrids. *See* composite beasts
hybrids, animal–human, 55–57
hybrids, heterosomatic, 73, 162, 237, 249
hybrids, homosomatic, 57, 91, 162

identity, social, 215
ikria, 15–16
  described, 258
  form of, 259
  in friezes, 272
  in glyptic, 272–273
  isolated, 272
  representations of. *See* representational embodiments of composite animalian entities
  in series, 272
  in wall paintings, 272
Iliad (Homer), 33, 133, 136, 150, 271
image making, 135
imagery, 135
  abstraction vs. figural representation in, 202
  ornamental vs. pictorial aspects of, 201
  similes and, 135
images, 135
  as things, 250
imagination, 33, 34
imitation between materials. *See* skeuomorphism
Immerwahr, S., 201, 263
imports. *See also* sharing, cultural
  recontextualization of, 216, 221–222
impressions. *See* seals
incongruity, 33, 34
Ingold, T., 24, 52
innovation, 3, 151
innovation, cross-craft, 201
intention, 6
interactions, 25. *See also* engagement
  with biological animals, 15
  with embodiments of animals, 7
  of humans and nonhumans, 30
interactions, overseas. *See* exchange; lions; seals; sharing, cultural
interculturalism. *See also* sharing, cultural
  composite animals and, 14
Isaakidou, V., 85, 89, 251, 252
ivory, 110, 111–113, 140, 265–268

Janko, R., 126
Jediesheit, 22

Kamares Ware, 214, 275. *See also* vessels
Kant, Immanuel, 27
Kantor, H. J., 214
Kaphtorite man, 124
Killen, J. T., 85
    on horn, 89
Knappett, C., 24–25, 32–33, 52, 164, 165, 234, 257
    on juxtaposition, 271
Knossos, 17
    cattle culture and, 85–86
    prominence of, 130
    wall paintings from. *See also* wall paintings
Knossos cup-rhyton, 280–284
    described, 288–291
    formal assonance of frieze elements, 281–282, 291–292
    forward-facing figure on, 280–281, 288–291
    tear-shaped entity on, 280, 282–284, 288
Knossos Shield Amphora, 277–280
knowledge, intuitive, 162–163
Koehl, R., 55, 71, 73, 76, 279
Kristeva, J., 58
Krzyszkowska, O., 117, 118, 225
Küchler, S., 24

Lacan, J., 22
language
    on Crete, 127–128, 129, 131–132, 159
    cultural sharing and, 132
    multilingualism, 132
Latour, B., 52
Legarra Herrero, B., 59
Letesson, Q., 63, 74
Lévi-Strauss, C., 63
likeness, 29, 32, 33, 34. *See also* formal assonance
Linear A, 127, 131–132
Linear B, 131, 132
lion glyptic, 164
Lion Hunt Dagger, 144, 147, 249, 267
lion hunts, 139–140, 141, 147, 148, 150
lion imagery, 150
    animal attacks and, 141
    audiences for, 139
    changes in, 141
    Cretan distinctions in, 113–115
    cultural exchange and, 122
    depicting lions and humans together, 141–143
    double meaning in, 150
    dynamism in, 138, 149
    indexical reading of, 139
    object types found in, 144–147
    oral tradition and, 143
    with plume of vegetation, 149–150
    regionalism and, 129–131

Shapland on, 139
    variation in, 151
lion motifs, 110, 111, 112, 113–114, 115–117, 129–130
    plume of vegetation, 149–150
    solitary wounded lions, 148–151
lion pelts, 139, 140
lion rhyta, 108, 146
lions, 10–11, 103, 233. *See also* seals
    affordances of as dangerous beasts, 139
    in antagonistic relationship with humans, 117
    basis for interpreting, 138–141
    changes in form, 115–122
    characterization of, 103, 117, 147
    cultural identity of, 144
    cultural sharing and, 103, 124–125, 151
    dynamic identity of, 11
    dynamism of, 144
    encounters/engagement with, 104, 105, 114–115, 139, 147
    experience of, 151
    in glyptic, 103, 104, 151
    hero's parallels with, 143
    in Homeric similes, 136–137
    humans' parallels with, 103, 104–105, 115, 117, 137, 147
    humans' relationships with, 130
    identity of, 143, 151
    in *Iliad*, 150
    juxtaposition with humans, 10–11, 118, 120, 126, 134, 141, 146, 147, 150, 151
    kingship and, 123
    likelihood of observing, 136
    lived social practice and, 103
    in material culture, 111. *See also* seals
    in metaphoric language, 123–124
    in Mycenaean culture, 122
    narrative position of, 143
    oral tradition and, 123–125, 138. *See also* oral traditions
    Parading Lions Group, 110, 111, 112, 113–114, 115–117, 129–130
    paratopic closeness between humans and, 138
    poetry and, 151
    presence in early Aegean, 105–108
    rareness of, 107
    regional styles and, 117
    relationship to person, 122
    representations on mainland, 134
    scholarship on, 104
    seals and, 104, 111–113, 116, 184–185. *See also* seals
    as symbol of power, 105
    terms for, 122–123
lion similes, 103, 105, 126–127, 136, 137, 150
liquid, 8, 9, 47–48, 50. *See also* rhyta; vessels
LM II period. *See* wall paintings
Logue, W., 257
    on divisions made in Bronze Age studies, 254
Lorimer, H., 257

414 INDEX

MacDonald, C., 84
magic, 279
Malafouris, L., 24, 52
Malia Steatite Group, 117
Marinatos, N., 4, 249
  on dagger, 249
  on shields, 258
Masson, E., 122
material culture
  archaeological approaches to, 24
  composite beasts in, 163
  griffins in, 160
  with overseas origins. *See* sharing, cultural
  as part of human experience, 21–23
  poetry and, 133, 136
  representation in, 18–19
Mathoudaki, I., 91
Mauss, M., 22, 51–52
McGowan, E., 57, 150, 235, 286–287, 295
meaning, 249
media, 1. *See also* seals; vessels; wall paintings
media, movable. *See* seals; vessels
Meillet, Antoine, 127
Menelaus, 136
Meriones, 133
Merleau-Ponty, M., 24
Mesopotamia, lion form and, 111, 113
metaphor, 123, 124
Mikrakis, M., 221
Miller, D., 24
mimesis, 20–21
Minchin, E., 135, 136, 143
miniaturization. *See* seals
Minoan
  expanding notion of, 3
  use of term, 3
Minoan culture, 2, 261–262
Minoan House, 63, 64
mobility, 164–165
Mochlos *petschaft* seal, 212, 228, 228, 232
model, 19
modularity, 162, 163
Molloy, B., 254
monkeys, 4, 17–18
Morgan, L., 32, 146, 147, 150
  on ambiguity in glyptic imagery, 197
  on dagger, 249
  on forward-facing figures, 74, 288
  on forward-facing gaze, 222
  on symbols, 249
Morris, C., 250, 254, 258
  on boar's tusk helmet, 247–249
  on divisions made in Bronze Age studies, 254
  on terms for swine, 253
Morris, S. P., 126, 147
multilingualism, 132
Murphy, J., 59, 62–63

musical instruments, 132
Mycenaean culture, 261–262
Mylonas, G., 249, 263

Nagy, G., 126
naturalism, 2, 3
natural world, renderings of, 2, 3
Nelson, M., 133
nemes, 217, 219
Neopalatial period, 9, 16. *See also* vessels; wall paintings
  changes in interregional dynamics during, 9
  social organization during, 74–75
Niemeier, W. D., 282
Noë, A., 26–27
nonhuman, use of term, 39

objects, animalian, 25. *See also* animalian things; thing(s)
objects, movable. *See* mobility; seals
Olsen, B., 24
ontologies, object-oriented, 25
oral culture, 11
oral traditions, 122, 124, 125–126, 147. *See also* poetry/poetic tradition; similes
  Crete and, 133
  lions and, 123–126, 138, 143
ornament, 278
  representational embodiments of composite animalian entities as, 263
  transformed into pictorial representation, 278
owls, 13, 207
  forward-facing gaze of, 207, 217, 222
  head appendages of, 207–210, 216–217, 219, 223
oxhide, 87–89. *See also* hides, cattle; ikria; shields

Palaima, T. G., 85, 131–132
Papadatos, Y., 64, 65
Payne, M., 33
Peatfield, A., 67, 86
pendant, bee, 21
perceptual experience, 26–27
perpetuation, 151
petschaft seal from Mochlos, 212, 228, 230, 232
Phaistos, 69
Pickett, Bill, 82
pictorialization, 201
pigs. *See* swine
Pini, I., 120
Plato, 20
poetry/poetic tradition, 104–105, 143. *See also* epic tradition; oral traditions; similes
  fresh analysis of, 126–127
  lions and, 104–105, 151
  sharing and, 151
posthumanism, 30

pouring. *See* vessels
Poursat, J. C., 25
Prepalatial period, 10. *See also* seals; vessels
    data from, 38–39
    social organization in, 8, 59–60
presentation, defined, 28
Protopalatial period, 9, 69. *See also* vessels

quasification, 28

raptors. *See* vultures
realization, 34
recognition, 33
regionalism, 127, 128–131, 225
    forward-facing gaze and, 226
Rehak, P., 4, 276, 282, 287
    on divisions made in Bronze Age studies, 254
    on use of animal-head rhyta, 80
religion. *See also* ritual
    cultural sharing and, 221
religious meaning, shields and, 263
renderings, 2, 3, 19. *See also* embodiments; representations; rhyta; seals; vessels; wall paintings
    as referents to past encounters, 23
    symbolic roles of, 4
Renfrew, C., 132
repetition, 268. *See also* series/seriation
    composite animalian entities and, 247
    in friezes, 262
replication, 53
representational embodiments of composite animalian entities, 250, 260–261, 263. *See also* friezes; series/seriation; vessels; wall paintings
    entities' identities as animalian things and, 260
    functions of, 262
    in isolation, 261
    as ornament, 263
representational things, generative dynamism of, 19
representations, 1, 2–5, 19, 21, 81. *See also* animalian things; embodiments
    autonomy of, 27
    classifications, 6
    defined, 28
    embodiments of relations by, 6–7
    identity of animals in Aegean culture and, 7
    as real embodiments, 246
    sociopolitical experience and, 9
    status as objects, 5
    tension inherent in, 34
    as true embodiments, 5, 7
    use of term, 19–20
reproduction, as part of lived experience, 20–21
rhyta, 9, 71
    with internal cones, 279–280
    Knossos Shield Amphora, 279–280
    vessels from Cult Room as, 279
rhyta, animal-form, 47
rhyta, animal-head, 71–75, 80–81, 288, 289

rhyta, bovine, 71, 87–91, 291
rhyta, lion, 108, 146
ritual, 74, 93, 277. *See also* religion
    vessels for, 279
Ruijgh, C. J., 126, 127, 132, 133

sacral cloth, 16, 285–287
sacrifice, 89
sameness, 29. *See also* formal assonance
Sanavia, A., 108, 116
Sbonias, K., 116, 130
Schoep, I., 130, 225
scribes, 132
scripts, 237
    Cretan Hieroglyphic, 225
seals, 10–11, 12, 103, 115, 141, 237. *See also* glyptic; griffins; lion imagery; lions; representational embodiments of composite animalian entities; *petschaft* seal from Mochlos
    boar's tusk helmets on, 271–272
    composite animalian entities and, 15, 16, 267, 274
    composite beasts and, 163
    described, 109
    dynamism of, 137–138
    fabricated animals on, 222
    forward-facing figures on, 225–226
    from Syria, 13
    in graves, 138
    human and, 109–110, 115, 122, 136, 143
    identity and, 103, 109, 114, 138, 151
    interactions with, 205
    intercultural interaction and, 237
    lions and, 104, 108, 111, 116, 134, 151. *See also* lions
    mobility and, 164–165
    on mainland, 134
    poetic dynamics and, 104
    prism seals, 225
    regionalism and, 128
    sharing and, 211
    shields and, 265–267, 271–272
    sphragistic usage of, 138
    styles of, 130
    tear-shaped object on, 271, 282–284
    vulnerability and, 138
    wall paintings and, 274
    wearing of, 10, 103, 110
seals, Egyptian, 111–113
seatedness, 259
Sennett, R., 52
series/seriation, 15–16. *See also* friezes
    boar's tusk helmets in, 271–272, 275
    composite animalian entities and, 264, 265–268, 274, 275
    dynamism realized through, 277
    glyptic in, 274
    ikria in, 272

series/seriation (cont.)
   shields in, 271–272, 275
   vessels and, 275–276, 277
Shank, E. B., 24
Shapland, A., 9, 29, 30–31, 71, 78, 87, 91, 146, 249
   on animal imagery, 140
   on animal practices, 15
   on bovine-head rhyta, 90
   on bull sports, 86, 87
   on divisions made in Bronze Age studies, 254
   on engagements of humans with biological non-humans, 81
   on horn, 89
   on lion imagery, 139
   on representations of animal heads, 89, 90
   on representations of cattle, 81, 87
   on traces, 92
   use of, 23
sharing, cultural, 3, 105, 151. *See also* exchange
   between Crete and mainland, 133–134
   creativity and, 166
   Egypt and, 11. *See also* Egypt; lions
   evidence of, 2
   intra-Aegean interaction and, 11
   intra-Cretan, 130
   language and, 132
   lions and, 147, 151
   Mochlos and, 228
   poetry and, 151
   recontextualization and, 214, 221
   regionalism and, 225
   religion and, 221
   seals and, 211
   southwest Asia and, 11. *See also* lions
Shaw, M., 263
Sherratt, ES., 126
shields, 15–16, 143, 223, 249. *See also* Knossos cup-rhyton
   animal origins of, 250
   boar's tusk helmets and, 249, 258, 271, 284
   in friezes, 278
   form of, 258, 259
   in glyptic, 265–267
   helmet and, 250
   identity of, 258
   isolated, 275
   on Knossos cup-rhyton, 282
   meaning of in friezes, 263
   protective role of, 284
   representational scale of, 275
   representations of. *See* representational embodiments of composite animalian entities
   sacral cloth and, 287
   on seals, 271–272
   in series, 267, 271–272, 275
   as symbol of sacrifice, 258
   symbolism of, 250
   vessels and, 275, 276

signification, 6
Simandiraki-Grimshaw, A., 47, 50, 54, 55, 61, 67
   on animal–human hybrids, 58
   on hybridity/hybrids, 57, 73, 162, 231, 236, 249
   on location of vessels, 63
   on Neopalatial vessels, 69
   on power of animals worn on human body, 109
   on renderings of animal parts, 91
   on sealings, 237
   on vessels, 69
   on wearing of zoomorphic objects, 137
similarity. *See* formal assonance
similes, 104, 124, 126–127, 134–137, 143, 147, 151
   dynamic nature of, 136
   efficacy of, 136
   juxtaposition with unit of narrative, 136
   lions and. *See* lion similes
   parallels of, 147
   as paratopic, 135
   visual aspect of, 135
skeuomorphism, 32, 33, 257–258
skulls, bovine, 90–91
Snyder, L., 254
social actions, divisions of, 254
social groups. *See* house societies
social organization
   changes in, 75
   house societies, 63–64
   in Prepalatial period, 59–60
social space, 54
social stress, 92, 130
space, 6. *See also* depth
spatial complexity, 247. *See also* depth
spearhead, Anemospilia, 288, 289
sphinxes, 13, 159, 219, 223. *See also* composite beasts
   cultural sharing and, 219
   griffins and, 211
   headgear of, 214, 217
   as homosomatic hybrids, 162
squills, 16, 282–285, 291
statues, cult, 49
Stevens, F., 110, 231
Stewart, S., 274
Stocker, R., 133–134
storytelling, 267. *See also* oral traditions
stucco, 17
Sumerian literature, 123–124
Summers, D., 139
swine, 250–253. *See also* boar's tusk helmets
   classification of, 251–253
   experience of, 255
   fluid status of, 254
   glyptic and, 291
   human interactions with, 252–255, 270
   hunting, 251, 252, 288
   slaughtering practices, 289

squills and, 284
terms for, 253
tusks of, 251–252
swine head, disembodied, 288
symmetry, archaeological, 24
Syro-Palestine, 215
Syro-Palestinian glyptic, 210–212, 214, 217
    griffins in, 203

Taweret, 221, 224
technology, human–animal relations and, 30
Teissier, B., 211–212, 214
Temple of Zeus Diktaios, 91
Thera, 3. *See also* Akrotiri; volcano, Theran; wall
    paintings
thing(s). *See also* entities, composite animalian
    approaching something as, 22
    engagement with people, 23–24
    images as, 250
    perception of, 27
    use of term, 22–23
thingliness, realized as beastliness, 21
Thomas, N., 106–107, 134, 139, 144
Tierbilder in der sumerischen Literatur
    (Heimpel), 123
Tilley, C., 24
Todaro, S., 63–64
tombs, 41, 59–60, 62, 64, 65
traces, 23, 92, 139, 140, 249
    boar's tusk helmet and, 255
Trapeza Cave, 63
travel. *See* mobility; sharing, cultural
Tsagalis, C., 135–137, 143

Ulanowski, K., 122
uncanniness, 33
uraeus projection, 219
urbanism, 162–163, 164, 234, 237

Varvarighos, A., 254
vase, 48. *See also* vessels
vessels, 8–9, 71. *See also* Knossos cup-rhyton
    affordances of, 53, 54
    agency of, 49
    Alternating Style, 276
    autonomy/independence of, 8, 48, 49
    boar's tusk helmets on, 275
    body techniques of, 52–54
    composite animalian entities on, 15, 16, 274. *See
        also* representational embodiments of compos-
        ite animalian entities
    cross-craft innovations and, 201
    decanting of, 49, 61
    experienced as dynamic bodies, 53
    from Cult Room Basement, 276–279
    from Neopalatial period, 69
    griffins on, 198–202
    handles of, 49, 62

human engagements with, 50
human-like attributes of, 50
identity of, 54
Knossos Shield Amphora, 277–280
with miniature jug, 48–49
with pierced breasts, 49
ritual and, 277, 279
series and, 275–276, 277
shields and, 275, 276
in social contexts, 54–59
vessels, anthropomorphic. *See also* vessels,
    zoomorphic
    affordances of, 67
    agency of, 55, 58, 62
    appreciating as bodies, 58
    bird-like character of, 55–57
    body shapes of, 54–58
    changes over time, 68
    community actions and, 59, 66–67
    contexts of, 64
    decanting of, 48, 61
    de-emphasis of living human actor, 68
    described, 41–47
    dynamism of, 47, 62
    experienced as bodies, 39
    findspots of, 62, 66
    from Koumasa, 65–66
    from Myrtos, 60–62
    from Neopalatial period, 69
    from Protopalatial period, 69
    handles of, 62
    identity of, 54, 55, 58, 67
    investigation of, 39
    as metaphors for biological body, 47
    movement of, 65
    nonhuman context of, 69
    as physical social presences, 58
    relationship to social group, 65–66
    social context and, 48
    social efficacy of, 59
    as tangible symbols of social groups, 67
    as zoomorphic, 40
vessels, avian, 56
vessels, bovine, 68
    depicting beast engaging with humans, 75–87
    described, 75–76
    as thingly realization of intercorporealengage-
        ment, 76–78
vessels, zoomorphic
    bird form, 69–70
    bovine form, 70–71
    community action and, 75
    described, 69–71
    performances with, 74
    shift in participation in social contexts, 71–73
Vibrant Matter (Bennett), 25
visual assonance, 89
Vlachopoulos, A., 201

volcano, Theran, 84, 86, 87
vultures, 14
    griffins and, 185, 206. *See also* Bearded Vulture

wall paintings, 16–18
    armored figures in, 267
    composite animalian entities in, 17, 261–265, 274
    composite beasts in, 238
    cross-craft innovations and, 201
    discovery of, 3
    griffins in, 191–192, 203–204, 206
    ikria in, 272
    monkeys in. *See* monkeys
    oxhide represented in, 87
    seals and, 274
    Taureador fresco, 77, 81
    tension between representational and lived space in, 17, 261
Warren, P., 43, 44, 55, 60, 61, 282
water, Minoan ritual culture and, 67
Webmoor, T., 24

Weingarten, J., 221, 224
    on prism seals, 225
Wengrow, D., 24, 162–164, 234, 234, 237, 237
West, M. L., 126, 127, 132, 133
Whitelaw, T., 59, 61, 65, 70
Whittaker, H., 89
Wilson, N., 58
Witmore, C., 24
Wolf, D., 57, 236
wonder, 50
writing, 128

Xanthoudidēs, Stephanos, 40–41, 43
Xerxes, 105

Younger, J., 73, 77, 90, 120, 132, 291

Zakros deposit, 268–270
zoomorphic objects. *See* vessels, zoomorphic
zoomorphism, 19